Dynamic Programming:

Deterministic and Stochastic Models

DIMITRI P. BERTSEKAS
Department of Electrical Engineering
and Computer Science
Massachusetts Institute of Technology

PRENTICE-HALL, INC., Englewood Cliffs, N.J. 07632

Library of Congress Cataloging-in-Publication Data

Bertsekas, Dimitri P.
Dynamic programming.

Bibliography: p.
Includes index.
1. Dynamic programming. I. Title.
T57.83.B484 1987 519.7′03 86-30285
ISBN 0-13-221581-0

Editorial/production supervision: *Raeia Maes*
Cover design: *Ben Santora*
Manufacturing buyer: *Rhett Conklin*

Printed in the United States of America

10 9 8 7 6 5 4 3 2 1

ISBN 0-13-221581-0 025

Prentice-Hall International (UK) Limited, *London*
Prentice-Hall of Australia Pty. Limited, *Sydney*
Prentice-Hall Canada Inc., *Toronto*
Prentice-Hall Hispanoamericana, S.A., *Mexico*
Prentice-Hall of India Private Limited, *New Delhi*
Prentice-Hall of Japan, Inc., *Tokyo*
Prentice-Hall of Southeast Asia Pte. Ltd., *Singapore*
Editora Prentice-Hall do Brasil, Ltda., *Rio de Janeiro*

Contents

Preface

This book evolved from teaching a course on Dynamic Programming and Stochastic Control over a fourteen-year period at Stanford University, the University of Illinois, and the Massachusetts Institute of Technology. The purpose of the book is to provide a unified treatment of the subject suitable for a broad audience from engineering, operations research, and, to some extent, economics and applied mathematics. Thus, for example, we treat simultaneously stochastic control problems popular in modern control theory, Markovian decision problems popular in operations research, and a number of combinatorial problems usually addressed in computer science courses. The theory is illustrated through a large variety of examples, many of them involving applications that are important in their own right. These examples can be covered in class independently of one another, so an instructor can tailor a course to his/her audience by emphasizing the appropriate set of applications.

The mathematical prerequisite for the text is a good knowledge of introductory probability and undergraduate mathematics. This includes the equivalent of a one-semester first course in probability theory together with the usual calculus, real analysis, vector-matrix algebra, and elementary optimization theory almost all undergraduates are exposed to by their fourth year of studies. A summary of this material is provided in the appendixes. While prior courses or background on dynamic system theory, optimization, or control will undoubtedly be helpful to the reader, it is felt that the material in the text is reasonably self-contained.

Dynamic programming is a conceptually simple technique that can be adequately explained using elementary analysis. Yet a mathematically rigorous treatment of general, stochastic dynamic programming requires the complicated machinery of measure-theoretic probability. My choice has been to bypass the complicated mathematics by carrying out the analysis in a general setting while claiming rigor only when the underlying probability spaces are countable. A mathematically rigorous treatment of the subject is carried out in my monograph "Stochastic Optimal Control: The Discrete Time Case," Academic Press, 1978, coauthored with Steven Shreve. This monograph complements the present text and provides a solid foundation for the subjects developed somewhat informally here.

I am thankful to a number of individuals and institutions for their contributions to the book. My understanding of the subject was sharpened while I worked with Steven Shreve on our 1978 monograph. Several proofs and results dealing with infinite horizon problems were improved during that time, and they are now part of the present text. Michael Caramanis, Lennart Ljung, and John Tsitsiklis taught from versions of the book and contributed several substantive comments and homework problems. I had the benefit of interaction with several able teaching assistants over the years and in this connection I would like to mention Paris Canellakis, Panos Constantopoulos, and John Tsitsiklis. A number of colleagues contributed valuable insights and information, particularly David Castanon and Krishna Pattipati. NSF supported the research on infinite horizon problems reported in Chapter 5. MIT, with its stimulating teaching and research environment, was an ideal setting for carrying out this project.

Dimitri P. Bertsekas

Life can only be understood going backwards,
but it must be lived going forwards.

Kierkegaard

CHAPTER ONE

The Dynamic Programming Algorithm

1.1 THE BASIC PROBLEM

This text looks at situations where decisions are made in stages. The outcome of each decision is not fully predictable but can be observed before the next decision is made. The objective is to minimize a certain cost—a mathematical expression of what is considered desirable outcome.

A key aspect of such problems is that decisions cannot be viewed in isolation since one must balance the desire for low present cost with the possibility of high future costs being inevitable. This idea is captured in the dynamic programming technique whereby at each stage one selects a decision that minimizes the sum of the current stage cost, and the best cost that can be expected from future stages.

A very wide class of problems can be treated in this way and in this text we make an effort to keep the main ideas uncluttered by irrelevant assumptions on problem structure. To this end we formulate in this section a broadly applicable model of optimal control of a dynamic system over a finite number of stages (a finite horizon). This model will occupy us for the first four chapters; its infinite horizon version will be the subject of the last three chapters.

Two main features of the basic problem determine its structure: (1) an underlying *discrete-time dynamic system,* and (2) a *cost functional that is additive over time.* The dynamic system is of the form

$$x_{k+1} = f_k(x_k, u_k, w_k), \qquad k = 0, 1, \ldots, N - 1,$$

where

- k indexes discrete time,
- x_k is the state of the system and summarizes past information that is relevant for future optimization,
- u_k is the control or decision variable to be selected at time k with knowledge of the state x_k,
- w_k is a random parameter (also called disturbance or noise),
- N is the horizon or number of times control is applied.

The cost functional is additive in the sense that a cost $g_k(x_k, u_k, w_k)$ is incurred at each time k, and the total cost along any system sample trajectory is

$$g_N(x_N) + \sum_{k=0}^{N-1} g_k(x_k, u_k, w_k),$$

where $g_N(x_N)$ is a terminal cost incurred at the end of the process. However, because of the presence of w_k, cost is generally a random variable and cannot be meaningfully optimized. We therefore formulate the problem as one whereby we wish to select controls $u_0, u_1, \ldots, u_{N-1}$ so as to minimize the *expected* cost

$$E\{g_N(x_N) + \sum_{k=0}^{N-1} g_k(x_k, u_k, w_k)\},$$

where the expectation is taken with respect to the joint distribution of the random variables involved.

A more precise definition of the terminology just used will be given shortly. We first provide some orientation by means of examples.

Inventory Control Example

Consider a problem of ordering a quantity of a certain item at the beginning of each of N time periods so as to meet a stochastic demand. Let us denote

- x_k stock available at the beginning of the kth period,
- u_k stock ordered (and immediately delivered) at the beginning of the kth period,
- w_k demand during the kth period with given probability distribution.

We assume that $w_0, \ldots, w_{N-1}$ are independent random variables and that excess demand is backlogged and filled as soon as additional inventory becomes available. Thus stock evolves according to the discrete-time (or difference) equation

$$x_{k+1} = x_k + u_k - w_k,$$

where negative stock corresponds to backlogged demand (see Figure 1.1).

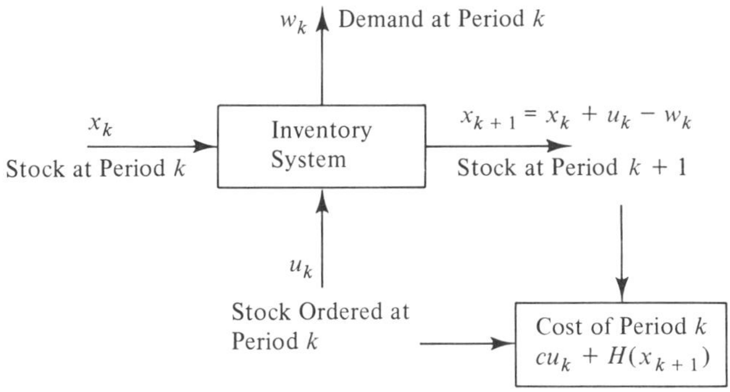

Figure 1.1 Inventory control example. The stock (state) x_k at period k, the stock ordered (control) u_k at period k, and the demand (random disturbance) w_k at period k determine the stock at the next period $k + 1$ and the cost of the kth period using the difference equation $x_{k+1} = x_k + u_k - w_k$.

The cost incurred at each period k consists of two components: (1) the purchasing cost cu_k, where c is cost per unit ordered, and (2) a cost $H(x_{k+1})$ representing a penalty for either positive stock $x_{k+1} > 0$ at the end of the period (holding cost for excess inventory) or negative stock $x_{k+1} < 0$ (shortage cost for unfilled demand). Using the equation $x_{k+1} = x_k + u_k - w_k$, we can write the cost for period k as

$$cu_k + H(x_k + u_k - w_k)$$

and the total expected cost over N periods as

$$E\left\{\sum_{k=0}^{N-1} cu_k + H(x_k + u_k - w_k)\right\}.$$

Our objective is to minimize this cost by proper choice of the orders $u_0, \ldots, u_{N-1}$ subject to the natural constraint $u_k \geq 0$, $k = 0, \ldots, N - 1$. One possibility would be to choose at time 0 all the orders $u_0, \ldots, u_{N-1}$ without waiting to see subsequent levels of demand. However, a clearly better choice would be to postpone ordering of u_k until time k when the current stock level x_k will be known. This mode of operation involves information gathering and sequential decision making based on information as it becomes available and is of central importance in dynamic programming. It implies that we are not really interested in selecting optimal numerical values for inventory orders, but rather we are interested in finding *an optimal rule for choosing at each period k an order u_k for each possible value of stock x_k that can occur.* This is an "action versus strategy" distinction. Mathematically, the problem is one of finding a sequence of *functions* μ_k, $k = 0, \ldots, N - 1$, mapping stock x_k into order u_k so as to minimize the total expected cost. The meaning of μ_k is that, for each k and each possible value of x_k,

$\mu_k(x_k)$ = amount that should be ordered at time k if stock is x_k.

The sequence $\pi = \{\mu_0, \mu_1, \ldots, \mu_{N-1}\}$ will also be referred to as a *control law* or a *policy*. For each such π, the corresponding cost for a fixed initial stock x_0 is

$$J_\pi(x_0) = E\left\{\sum_{k=0}^{N-1} c\mu_k(x_k) + H[x_k + \mu_k(x_k) - w_k]\right\},$$

and our objective will be to minimize $J_\pi(x_0)$ for fixed x_0 over all admissible π. This is a typical dynamic programming problem. We will show in Section 2.2 that, for a reasonable choice of the cost function H, the optimal ordering rule is of the form

$$\mu_k(x_k) = \begin{cases} S_k - x_k, & \text{if } x_k < S_k, \\ 0, & \text{if } x_k \geq S_k, \end{cases}$$

where S_k is a suitable threshold level determined by the data of the problem. In other words, when stock falls below the threshold S_k, order just enough to bring stock up to S_k.

The preceding example illustrates the main ingredients of the basic problem formulation:

1. *A discrete-time system* of the form
$$x_{k+1} = f_k(x_k, u_k, w_k),$$
where f_k is some function; in this example $f_k(x_k, u_k, w_k) = x_k + u_k - w_k$.
2. *Independent random parameters* w_k. This will be generalized by allowing the probability distribution of w_k to depend on x_k and u_k; in the context of the example we can think of a situation where the level of demand w_k is influenced by the current stock level.
3. *A control constraint;* in the example $u_k \geq 0$. In general, the constraint set will depend on x_k and the time index k, that is, $u_k \in U_k(x_k)$. To see how constraints dependent on x_k can arise in the inventory context, think of a situation where there is an upper bound B on the level of stock that can be accommodated, so $u_k \leq B - x_k$.
4. *An additive cost* of the form
$$E\left\{g_N(x_N) + \sum_{k=0}^{N-1} g_k(x_k, u_k, w_k)\right\},$$
where g_k, $k = 0, \ldots, N$, are some functions; in the preceding example $g_N(x_N) = 0$, and $g_k(x_k, u_k, w_k) = cu_k + H(x_k + u_k - w_k)$.
5. *Optimization over control laws,* that is, rules for choosing u_k for each k and possible value of x_k.

In the preceding example, the state x_k was a real number. In other cases the state is an n-dimensional vector. It is also possible, however, that the state takes values from a discrete set, such as the integers, or even a finite set.

A version of the inventory problem where a discrete viewpoint is more natural arises when stock is measured in whole units (such as cars), each of which is a significant fraction of x_k, u_k, or w_k. It is more appropriate then to take as state space the set of all integers, rather than the set of real numbers. The form of the system equation and the cost per period will, of course, stay the same.

In other systems the state is naturally discrete and there is no continuous counterpart of the problem. Such systems are often conveniently specified in terms of the probabilities of transition between the states. What we need to know is $p_{ij}(u, k)$ defined as the probability at time k that the next state x_{k+1} will be j, given that the current state x_k is i, and the control u_k selected is u; that is,

$$p_{ij}(u, k) = P\{x_{k+1} = j \mid x_k = i, u_k = u\}.$$

[If the system is stationary, i.e. the previous probabilities do not depend on k, we will suppress the argument k and write $p_{ij}(u)$ in place of $p_{ij}(u, k)$.] Such a system can be described alternatively in terms of a discrete-time system equation of the form

$$x_{k+1} = w_k,$$

where the probability distribution of the random parameter w_k is

$$P\{w_k = j \mid x_k = i, u_k = u\} = p_{ij}(u, k).$$

Depending on the situation at hand, it may be preferable to use a system description in terms of a difference equation or in terms of transition probabilities. We illustrate these ideas with an example.

Queueing Example

Consider a queueing system with room for n customers operating over N time periods (see Figure 1.2). We assume that service of a customer can start (end) only at the beginning (end) of a period. The probability p_m of m customers arriving during a time period is given, and the numbers of arrivals in two different periods are independent. Customers finding the system full depart without attempting to enter later. The system offers two kinds of service, *fast* and *slow*, with cost per period c_f and c_s, respectively. Service can be switched between fast and slow at the beginning of each period. If fast (slow) service is provided during a certain period, a customer in service at the beginning of the period will terminate service at the end of the period with probability q_f (respectively, q_s) independently of the number of periods the customer has been in service and the number of customers in the system ($q_f > q_s$). There is a cost $c(i)$ for each period for which there are i customers in the system. There is also a terminal cost $C(i)$ for i customers left in the system at the end of the last period. The

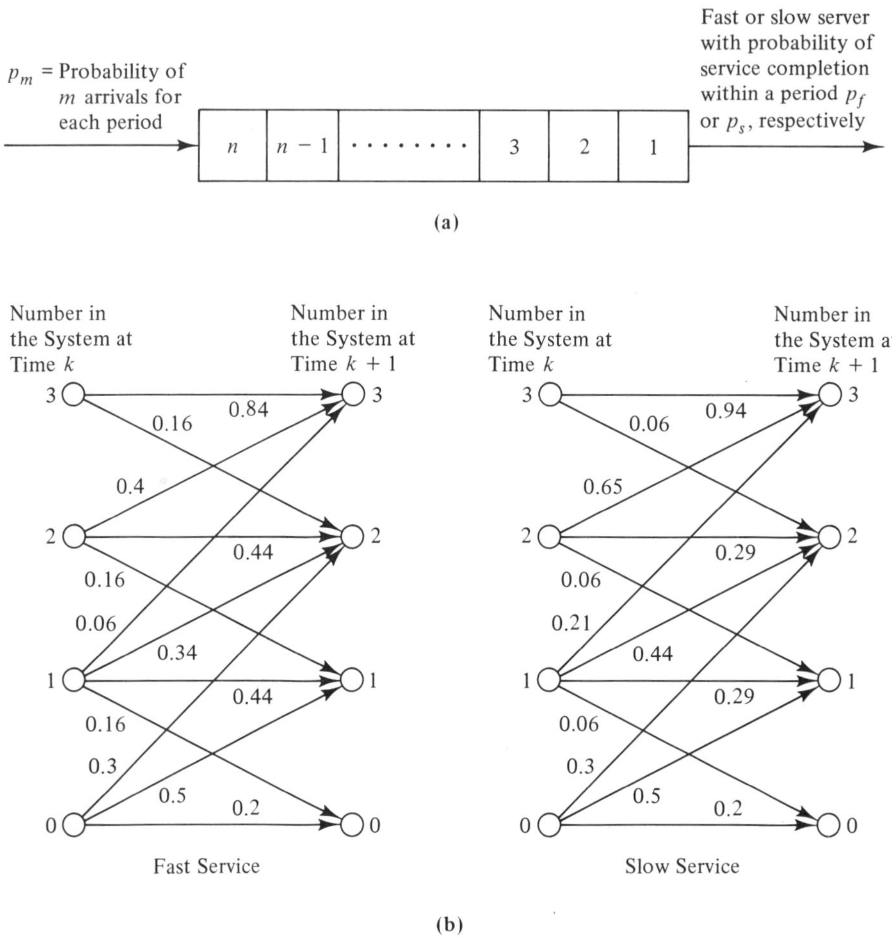

Figure 1.2 Queueing system with room for n customers. The service can be switched between fast and slow at any time period so as to minimize the sum of customer waiting and service costs: (a) Queueing system with room for n customers and two kinds of service. (b) Transition probability graphs for fast and slow service. The data assumed are $n = 3$, $p_0 = 0.2$, $p_1 = 0.5$, $p_2 = 0.3$, $p_m = 0$ for $m > 2$, and $q_f = 0.8$, $q_s = 0.3$.

problem is to choose the kind of service provided at each time period as a function of the number of customers in the system at the start of the period so as to minimize the expected total cost over N periods.

It is appropriate to take as state here the number i of customers in the system at the start of a period and as decision variable (control) the kind of service provided. The cost per period then is $c(i)$ plus c_f or c_s depending on whether fast or slow service is provided. We derive the transition probabilities of the system. When the system is empty at the start of a period, the probability that the next state is j is independent of the kind of service provided. It equals the given probability of j customer arrivals when $j < n$

$$p_{0j}(u_f) = p_{0j}(u_s) = p_j, \qquad j = 0, 1, \ldots, n-1,$$

and it equals the probability of n or more customer arrivals when $j = n$:

$$p_{0n}(u_f) = p_{0n}(u_s) = \sum_{m=n}^{\infty} p_m.$$

When there is at least one customer in the system ($i > 0$), we have

$$p_{ij}(u_f) = 0, \qquad \text{if } j < i-1,$$

$$p_{i(i-1)}(u_f) = q_f p_0,$$

$$\begin{aligned} p_{ij}(u_f) &= P\{j - i + 1 \text{ arrivals, service completed}\} \\ &\quad + P\{j - i \text{ arrivals, service not completed}\} \\ &= q_f p_{j-i+1} + (1 - q_f) p_{j-i}, \qquad \text{if } \ i - 1 < j < n - 1, \end{aligned}$$

$$p_{i(n-1)}(u_f) = q_f \sum_{m=n-i}^{\infty} p_m + (1 - q_f) p_{n-1-i},$$

$$p_{in}(u_f) = (1 - q_f) \sum_{m=n-i}^{\infty} p_m.$$

The transition probabilities when slow service is provided are also given by these formulas with u_f and q_f replaced by u_s and q_s, respectively.

Transition probabilities are sometimes shown on a graph whose arcs represent transitions between various states. This is known as the *transition probability graph,* or simply *transition graph,* and is illustrated in Figure 1.2 for the special case where $n = 3$, $p_0 = 0.2$, $p_1 = 0.5$, $p_2 = 0.3$, $p_m = 0$ for $m > 2$, and $q_f = 0.8$, $q_s = 0.3$.

In our subsequent formulation we will assume that the state x_k takes values from some set S_k called the *state space.* We will not require that S_k be a finite set or a space of n-dimensional vectors. A surprising aspect of dynamic programming is that its applicability depends very little on the nature of the state space S_k (although its effectiveness certainly does depend on S_k). For this reason we find it convenient to proceed without imposing any assumptions on S_k; indeed, such assumptions would become a serious impediment later. We similarly allow u_k and w_k to take values from some unspecified spaces C_k and D_k, respectively.

Basic Problem

We are given the discrete-time dynamic system

$$x_{k+1} = f_k(x_k, u_k, w_k), \qquad k = 0, 1, \ldots, N-1, \tag{1.1}$$

where the state x_k is an element of a space S_k, the control u_k is an element of a space C_k, and the random "disturbance" w_k is an element of a space D_k. The control u_k is constrained to take values from a given nonempty subset $U_k(x_k)$ of C_k, which depends on the current state x_k [$u_k \in U_k(x_k)$ for all $x_k \in S_k$ and k]. The random disturbance w_k is characterized by a probability measure $P_k(\cdot|x_k, u_k)$ that may depend explicitly on x_k and u_k but not on values of prior disturbances $w_{k-1}, \ldots, w_0$. We consider the class of control laws (also called policies) that consist of a sequence of functions $\pi = \{\mu_0, \mu_1, \ldots, \mu_{N-1}\}$, where μ_k maps states x_k into controls $u_k = \mu_k(x_k)$, and is such that $\mu_k(x_k) \in U_k(x_k)$ for all $x_k \in S_k$. Such control laws will be termed *admissible*.

Given an initial state x_0, the problem is to find an admissible control law $\pi = \{\mu_0, \mu_1, \ldots, \mu_{N-1}\}$ that minimizes the cost functional

$$J_\pi(x_0) = \underset{\substack{w_k \\ k=0,\ldots,N-1}}{E} \left\{ g_N(x_N) + \sum_{k=0}^{N-1} g_k[x_k, \mu_k(x_k), w_k] \right\} \tag{1.2}$$

subject to the system equation constraint

$$x_{k+1} = f_k[x_k, \mu_k(x_k), w_k], \qquad k = 0, 1, \ldots, N-1. \tag{1.3}$$

The cost functions g_k, $k = 0, 1, \ldots, N$, are given.

For a given initial state x_0, an optimal control law π^* is one that minimizes the corresponding cost

$$J_{\pi^*}(x_0) = \min_{\pi \in \Pi} J_\pi(x_0),$$

where Π is the set of all admissible control laws. The optimal cost corresponding to x_0 will be denoted $J^*(x_0)$; that is,

$$J^*(x_0) = \min_{\pi \in \Pi} J_\pi(x_0).$$

We view J^* as a function that assigns to each initial state x_0 the optimal cost $J^*(x_0)$ and call it the *optimal cost function* or *optimal value function*.

[For the benefit of the mathematically oriented reader we note that in the preceding equation min denotes the greatest lower bound (or infimum) of the set of numbers $\{J_\pi(x_0) \mid \pi \in \Pi\}$. A notation more in line with normal mathematical usage would be to write $J^*(x_0) = \inf_{\pi \in \Pi} J_\pi(x_0)$. However (as discussed in Appendix B), we find it convenient to use *min* in place of *inf* even when the infimum is not attained. It is less distracting and will not lead to any confusion.]

Role of Information in the Basic Problem

We mentioned earlier that a policy $\{\mu_0, \mu_1, \ldots, \mu_{N-1}\}$ may be viewed as a plan that specifies the control to be applied at each time for every state that may occur at that time. It is important to realize that this mode of operation implies *information gathering*. The information received by the controller is the value of the current state at each time and is utilized directly during the control process, since the control at time k depends on the current state x_k via the function μ_k (cf. Figure 1.3). The effects of the availability of this information may be significant indeed. If this information is not available, the controller cannot adapt appropriately to unexpected values of the state, and as a result the cost can be adversely affected. For example, in the inventory control problem considered earlier, the information that becomes available at the beginning of each period k is the inventory stock x_k. Clearly, this information is very important to the inventory manager, who will want to adjust the amount u_k to be purchased depending on whether the current stock x_k is running high or low.

Note, however, that whereas availability of the state information cannot hurt, it may not result in an advantage either. For instance, in deterministic control problems, where no random disturbances are present, one can predict the future states given the initial state and the sequence of controls. Therefore, optimization over all sequences $\{u_0, u_1, \ldots, u_{N-1}\}$ of controls leads to the same optimal cost as optimization over all admissible policies. The same fact may be true even in some stochastic control problems (see Problem 13). This brings up a related issue. Assuming no information is forgotten, the controller actually knows the prior states and controls $x_0, u_0, \ldots, x_{k-1}, u_{k-1}$, as well as the current state x_k. Therefore, the question arises whether policies that use the entire system history can be superior to policies that use just the current state. The answer turns out to be negative (see [B23]). The intuitive reason is that, for a given problem, time k and state x_k, all future expected costs depend explicitly just on x_k and not on prior history.

Theoretical Limitations of the Formulation of the Basic Problem

Before proceeding with the development of the dynamic programming algorithm, we try to clarify certain aspects of our problem that do not lie on firm mathematical ground. The issue here is one of mathematical rigor and is highly technical in nature. The reader who is not mathematically

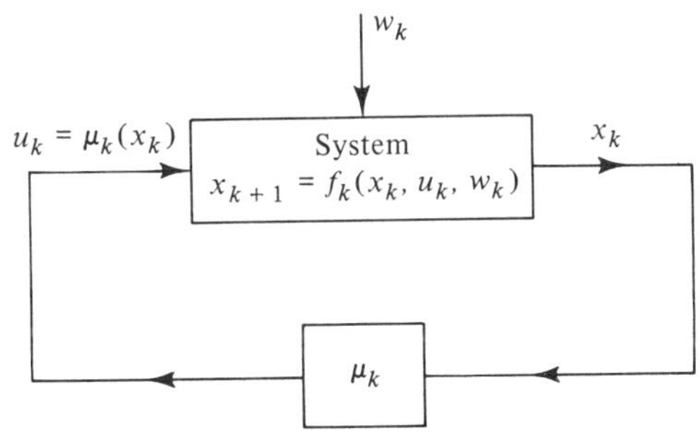

Figure 1.3 Information gathering in the basic problem. At each time k the controller observes the current state x_k and applies control $u_k = \mu_k(x_k)$ that depends on that state.

inclined need not be concerned about it and can skip the rest of this section without loss of continuity.

First, once an admissible control law $\{\mu_0, \mu_1, \ldots, \mu_{N-1}\}$ is adopted, the following sequence of events is envisioned for each stage $k = 0, 1, \ldots, N - 1$:

1. The controller observes x_k and applies $u_k = \mu_k(x_k)$.
2. The disturbance w_k is generated according to the given probability measure $P_k(\cdot|x_k, \mu_k(x_k))$.
3. The cost $g_k[x_k, \mu_k(x_k), w_k]$ is incurred and added to previous costs.
4. The next state x_{k+1} is generated according to the system equation
$$x_{k+1} = f_k[x_k, \mu_k(x_k), w_k].$$
If this is the last stage ($k = N - 1$), the terminal cost $g_N(x_N)$ is added to previous costs and the process terminates. Otherwise, k is incremented, and the same sequence of events is repeated for the next stage.

This process is well defined and couched in precise probabilistic terms. Things are complicated, however, by the need to view the cost

$$g_N(x_N) + \sum_{k=0}^{N-1} g_k[x_k, \mu_k(x_k), w_k]$$

as a *well-defined random variable* with well-defined expected value. The framework of probability theory requires that for each $\{\mu_0, \mu_1, \ldots, \mu_{N-1}\}$ we define an underlying probability space, that is, a set Ω, a collection of events in Ω, and a probability measure on these events. Furthermore, the cost must be a well-defined random variable on this space in the sense of Appendix C (a measurable function from the probability space into the real line in the terminology of measure-theoretic probability theory). For this to be true, additional (measurability) assumptions on the functions f_k, g_k, and μ_k may be required, and it may be necessary to introduce additional structure on the spaces S_k, C_k, and D_k. Furthermore, these assumptions may restrict the class of admissible control laws since the functions μ_k may be constrained to satisfy additional (measurability) requirements.

Thus, unless these additional assumptions and structure are specified, the problem is formulated inadequately. On the other hand, a rigorous formulation of the basic problem for general state, control, and disturbance spaces is well beyond the mathematical framework of this introductory text and will not be undertaken here (see [B23]). Nonetheless, these difficulties are mainly technical and do not substantially affect the basic results to be obtained. For this reason we find it convenient to proceed with informal derivations and arguments in much the same way as in all introductory texts and most journal literature on the subject.

We would like to stress, however, that under the assumption that *the disturbance spaces* D_k, $k = 0, 1, \ldots, N-1$, *are countable sets* all the mathematical difficulties mentioned disappear since, for this case, *with the only additional assumption that the expected values of all terms in the cost* (1.2) *exist and are finite for every admissible policy* π, one can provide a sound framework for the problem.

One easy way to do this when D_k are countable is to rewrite all expected values in the cost as infinite sums in terms of the probabilities of the elements of D_k. Another way is to write the cost $J_\pi(x_0)$ as

$$J_\pi(x_0) = \underset{x_1,\ldots,x_N}{E}\left\{g_N(x_N) + \sum_{k=0}^{N-1} \tilde{g}_k[x_k, \mu_k(x_k)]\right\}, \tag{1.4}$$

where

$$\tilde{g}_k[x_k, \mu_k(x_k)] = \underset{w_k}{E}\{g_k[x_k, \mu_k(x_k), w_k] \mid x_k, \mu_k(x_k)\},$$

with the preceding expectation taken with respect to the probability distribution $P_k(\cdot|x_k, \mu_k(x_k))$ defined on the countable set D_k. Then one may take as the basic probability space the Cartesian product of $\tilde{S}_1, \tilde{S}_2, \ldots, \tilde{S}_N$, where

$$\tilde{S}_1 = \{x_1 \in S_1 \mid x_1 = f_0[x_0, \mu_0(x_0), w_0], w_0 \in D_0\},$$
$$\tilde{S}_{k+1} = \{x_{k+1} \in S_{k+1} \mid x_{k+1} = f_k[x_k, \mu_k(x_k), w_k],$$
$$x_k \in \tilde{S}_k, w_k \in D_k\}, \qquad k = 1, 2, \ldots, N-1.$$

The set $\tilde{S}_k$ is the subset of S_k of all states that can be reached at time k when the control law $\{\mu_0, \mu_1, \ldots, \mu_{N-1}\}$ is employed. The fact that D_0, $D_1, \ldots, D_{N-1}$ are countable sets ensures that the sets $\tilde{S}_1, \ldots, \tilde{S}_N$ are also countable (this is true since the union of any countable collection of countable sets is a countable set). Now the system equation (1.3), the probability distributions $P_k(\cdot|x_k, \mu_k(x_k))$, the initial state x_0, and the control law $\{\mu_0, \mu_1, \ldots, \mu_{N-1}\}$ define a probability distribution on the countable set $\tilde{S}_1 \times \tilde{S}_2 \times \cdots \times \tilde{S}_N$, and the expectation in (1.4) is defined with respect to this latter distribution.

In conclusion, the basic problem has been formulated rigorously only when the disturbance spaces $D_0, \ldots, D_{N-1}$ are countable sets. In the absence of countability of D_k, the reader should interpret subsequent results and conclusions as essentially correct but mathematically imprecise statements. In fact, when discussing infinite horizon problems (where the need for precision is greater), we will make the countability assumption explicit. We note, however, that the advanced reader will have little difficulty in establishing rigorously most of our subsequent results concerning specific applications in Chapters 2 and 3. This can be done as explained in the Notes to this chapter and in Problem 12.

1.2 THE DYNAMIC PROGRAMMING ALGORITHM

The dynamic programming (DP) technique rests on a very simple idea, the *principle of optimality*. The name is due to Bellman, who contributed a great deal to the popularization of DP and to its transformation into a systematic tool. Roughly, the principle of optimality states the following rather obvious fact.

Let $\pi^* = \{\mu_0^*, \mu_1^*, \ldots, \mu_{N-1}^*\}$ be an optimal control law for the basic problem. Consider the subproblem whereby we are at state x_i at time i and wish to minimize the "cost-to-go" from time i to time N;

$$E\{g_N(x_N) + \sum_{k=i}^{N-1} g_k[x_k, \mu_k(x_k), w_k]\},$$

and assume that when using π^* the state x_i occurs with positive probability. Then the truncated control law $\{\mu_i^*, \mu_{i+1}^*, \ldots, \mu_{N-1}^*\}$ is optimal for this subproblem.

The intuitive justification of the principle of optimality is very simple. If the truncated control law $\{\mu_i^*, \mu_{i+1}^*, \ldots, \mu_{N-1}^*\}$ were not optimal as stated, we would be able to reduce the cost further by switching to an optimal policy for the subproblem once we reach x_i. For an auto travel analogy, suppose we have found the fastest route from Los Angeles to Boston and this route passes through Chicago. The principle of optimality translates to the obvious fact that the Chicago to Boston portion of the route is also a fastest route for a trip that starts from Chicago and ends in Boston.

It is perhaps best to introduce the DP algorithm by means of an example.

Inventory Control Example (continued)

Consider the inventory control example of the previous section and the following procedure for determining the optimal inventory ordering policy starting with the last time period and proceeding backward in time.

N − 1 Period Assume that at the beginning of period $N - 1$ the stock available is x_{N-1}. Clearly, no matter what happened in the past, the inventory manager should order inventory $u_{N-1}^* = \mu_{N-1}^*(x_{N-1})$, which minimizes over u_{N-1} the sum of the ordering, holding, and shortage costs for the last time period, which is equal to

$$\underset{w_{N-1}}{E}\{cu_{N-1} + H(x_{N-1} + u_{N-1} - w_{N-1})\}.$$

Let us denote the optimal cost for the last period by $J_{N-1}(x_{N-1})$:

$$J_{N-1}(x_{N-1}) = \min_{u_{N-1}\geq 0} \underset{w_{N-1}}{E}\{cu_{N-1} + H(x_{N-1} + u_{N-1} - w_{N-1})\}.$$

Naturally, J_{N-1} is a function of the stock x_{N-1}. It is calculated for each x_{N-1} either analytically or numerically (in which case a table is used for computer storage of the function J_{N-1}). In the process of calculating J_{N-1} we obtain the optimal inventory ordering policy $\mu^*_{N-1}(x_{N-1})$ for the last period, where $\mu^*_{N-1}(x_{N-1}) \geq 0$ minimizes the right side of the preceding equation for each value of x_{N-1}.

N − 2 Period Assume that at the beginning of period $N - 2$ the inventory is x_{N-2}. Now it is clear that the inventory manager should order inventory $u_{N-2} = \mu^*_{N-2}(x_{N-2})$, which minimizes not just the expected cost of period $N - 2$ but rather the

(expected cost of period $N - 2$) + (expected cost of period $N - 1$, given that an optimal policy will be used at period $N - 1$).

This, however, is equal to

$$\underset{w_{N-2}}{E}\{cu_{N-2} + H(x_{N-2} + u_{N-2} - w_{N-2})\} + \underset{w_{N-2}}{E}\{J_{N-1}(x_{N-1})\}.$$

Using the system equation $x_{N-1} = x_{N-2} + u_{N-2} - w_{N-2}$, the last term is also written $E_{w_{N-2}}\{J_{N-1}(x_{N-2} + u_{N-2} - w_{N-2})\}$.

Thus the optimal cost $J_{N-2}(x_{N-2})$ for the last two periods, given that we are at state x_{N-2}, is given by

$$\begin{aligned} J_{N-2}(x_{N-2}) = \min_{u_{N-2}\geq 0}\ \underset{w_{N-2}}{E}\{&cu_{N-2} + H(x_{N-2} + u_{N-2} - w_{N-2}) \\ &+ J_{N-1}(x_{N-2} + u_{N-2} - w_{N-2})\}. \end{aligned}$$

Again $J_{N-2}(x_{N-2})$ is calculated for every x_{N-2}. At the same time the optimal ordering policy $\mu^*_{N-2}(x_{N-2})$ is also computed.

k Period Similarly, we have that at period k and for initial inventory x_k the inventory manager should order u_k to minimize

(expected cost of period k) + (expected cost of periods $k + 1, \ldots, N - 1$, given that an optimal policy will be used for these periods).

By denoting by $J_k(x_k)$ the optimal cost, we have

$$\begin{aligned} J_k(x_k) = \min_{u_k\geq 0}\ \underset{w_k}{E}\{&cu_k + H(x_k + u_k - w_k) \\ &+ J_{k+1}(x_k + u_k - w_k)\}, \end{aligned} \tag{1.5}$$

which is actually the dynamic programming equation for this problem.

The functions $J_k(x_k)$ denote the optimal expected cost for the remaining periods when starting at period k and with initial inventory x_k. These functions are computed recursively backward in time, starting at period $N - 1$ and ending at period 0. The value $J_0(x_0)$ is the optimal expected cost for the process when the initial inventory at time 0 is x_0. During the calculations the optimal inventory policy, $\{\mu^*_0(x_0), \mu^*_1(x_1), \ldots, \mu^*_{N-1}(x_{N-1})\}$

is simultaneously computed from minimization of the right side of (1.5) for every x_k and k.

The example illustrates the main advantage offered by DP. Our original inventory problem requires an optimization over the set of policies, that is, the set of sequences of functions of the current stock (more generally the current state). The DP algorithm of (1.5) decomposes this problem into a sequence of minimization problems that is carried out over the set of orders (more generally the space of controls). Each of these problems is far simpler than the original.

We now state the DP algorithm for the basic problem and show its optimality.

Proposition. Let $J^*(x_0)$ be the optimal cost. Then

$$J^*(x_0) = J_0(x_0),$$

where the function J_0 is given by the last step of the following algorithm, which proceeds backward in time from period $N - 1$ to period 0:

$$J_N(x_N) = g_N(x_N) \tag{1.6}$$

$$J_k(x_k) = \min_{u_k \in U_k(x_k)} \underset{w_k}{E} \{g_k(x_k, u_k, w_k) + J_{k+1}[f_k(x_k, u_k, w_k)]\}, \quad (1.7)\dagger$$

$$k = 0, 1, \ldots, N - 1.$$

Furthermore, if $u_k^* = \mu_k^*(x_k)$ minimizes the right side of (1.7) for each x_k and k, the control law $\pi^* = \{\mu_0^*, \ldots, \mu_{N-1}^*\}$ is optimal.

Proof. The fact that the probability measure characterizing w_k depends only on x_k and u_k and not on prior values of disturbances $w_0, \ldots, w_{k-1}$ allows us to write $J^*(x_0)$ in the form

$$J^*(x_0) = \min_{\mu_0, \ldots, \mu_{N-1}} \left[\underset{w_0}{E} \left\{ g_0[x_0, \mu_0(x_0), w_0] + \underset{w_1}{E} \left\{ g_1[x_1, \mu_1(x_1), w_1] + \cdots \right.\right.\right.$$

$$\left.\left.\left. + \underset{w_{N-1}}{E} \{g_{N-1}[x_{N-1}, \mu_{N-1}(x_{N-1}), w_{N-1}] + g_N(x_N)\} \cdots \right\}\right\}\right],$$

where the expectation over w_k, $k = 0, 1, \ldots, N - 1$, is conditional on x_k and $\mu_k(x_k)$. This expression may also be written

† Both the DP algorithm and its proof are, of course, rigorous only if the basic problem is rigorously formulated. As explained in the previous section, this is the case when the disturbance spaces D_k, $k = 0, 1, \ldots, N - 1$, are countable sets and the expected values of all terms in the expression of the cost functional (1.2) are well defined and finite for every admissible policy π. In addition, it is assumed that the expected value in (1.7) exists and is finite for all $u_k \in U_k(x_k)$ and all $x_k \in S_k$. We further note that, although not explicitly denoted, the expectation in (1.7) is taken with respect to the probability measure characterizing w_k, which depends on both x_k and u_k.

$$J^*(x_0) = \min_{\mu_0}\left[\underset{w_0}{E}\left\{g_0[x_0, \mu_0(x_0), w_0] + \min_{\mu_1}\left[\underset{w_1}{E}\left\{g_1[x_1, \mu_1(x_1), w_1] + \cdots \right.\right.\right.\right.$$

$$\left.\left.\left.\left. + \min_{\mu_{N-1}}\left[\underset{w_{N-1}}{E}\{g_{N-1}[x_{N-1}, \mu_{N-1}(x_{N-1}), w_{N-1}] + g_N(x_N)\}\right]\cdots\right\}\right]\right\}\right].$$

In this equation the minimizations are over all functions μ_k such that $\mu_k(x_k) \in U_k(x_k)$ for all x_k and k. In addition, the minimization is subject to the system equation constraint

$$x_{k+1} = f_k[x_k, \mu_k(x_k), w_k].$$

Now we use the fact that for any function F of x, u, we have

$$\min_{\mu \in M} F[x, \mu(x)] = \min_{u \in U(x)} F(x, u),$$

where M is the set of all functions $\mu(x)$ such that $\mu(x) \in U(x)$ for all x.

By applying this fact in the equation for $J^*(x_0)$, using the substitution $x_{k+1} = f_k(x_k, u_k, w_k)$, and introducing the functions J_k of (1.7), we obtain the desired result:

$$J^*(x_0) = J_0(x_0).$$

It is also clear that $\{\mu_0^*, \ldots, \mu_{N-1}^*\}$ is an optimal control law if $\mu_k^*(x_k)$ minimizes the right side of (1.7) for each x_k and k, since such a control law attains the optimal cost. Q.E.D.

The argument of the preceding proof can also be used to establish an interpretation of $J_k(x_k)$. It is the optimal cost for an $(N - k)$-stage problem starting at state x_k and time k and ending at time N. We consequently call $J_k(x_k)$ the *cost-to-go* at state x_k and time k, and refer to J_k as the *cost-to-go function* at time k. Ideally, we would like to use the DP algorithm to determine closed-form expressions for J_k. Otherwise, one hopes to obtain useful characterizations of J_k or μ_k^*. In many cases one has to resort to numerical solution of the DP equations. This may be quite time consuming since the minimization in (1.7) must be carried out for each value of x_k. Typically, the state space is discretized and the minimization is carried out for a finite number of states x_k. The computational requirements are proportional to the number of discretization points. Thus for complex multidimensional problems the computational burden may be prohibitive. Nonetheless, DP is the only general approach for sequential optimization under uncertainty.

We now provide examples illustrating the analytical and computational aspects of the DP algorithm.

Example 1

A certain material is passed through a sequence of two ovens (see Figure 1.4). Denote

x_0: initial temperature of the material,

x_k, $k = 1, 2$: temperature of the material at the exit of oven k,

u_{k-1}, $k = 1, 2$: prevailing temperature in oven k.

We assume a model of the form

$$x_{k+1} = (1 - a)x_k + au_k, \qquad k = 0, 1,$$

where a is some scalar from the interval (0, 1). The objective is to get the final temperature x_2 close to a given target T, while expending relatively little energy. This is expressed by a cost function of the form

$$r(x_2 - T)^2 + u_0^2 + u_1^2,$$

where $r > 0$ is a given scalar. We assume no constraints on u_k. (In reality, there are constraints, but if we can solve the unconstrained problem and verify that the solution satisfies the constraints, everything will be fine.)

We see that this is a deterministic problem that fits the basic framework. We have $N = 2$ and a terminal cost $g_2(x_2) = r(x_2 - T)^2$, so the initial condition for the DP algorithm is [cf. (1.6)]

$$J_2(x_2) = r(x_2 - T)^2.$$

For the next-to-last stage, we have [cf. (1.7)]

$$J_1(x_1) = \min_{u_1}[u_1^2 + J_2(x_2)]$$

$$= \min_{u_1}[u_1^2 + J_2[(1 - a)x_1 + au_1]].$$

Substituting the previous form of J_2, we obtain

$$J_1(x_1) = \min_{u_1}[u_1^2 + r[(1 - a)x_1 + au_1 - T]^2]. \tag{1.8}$$

This minimization will be done by setting to zero the derivative with respect to u_1. We thus have

$$0 = 2u_1 + 2ra[(1 - a)x_1 + au_1 - T],$$

and by collecting terms we obtain the optimal temperature for the last oven:

$$u_1 = \mu_1^*(x_1) = \frac{ra[T - (1 - a)x_1]}{1 + ra^2}$$

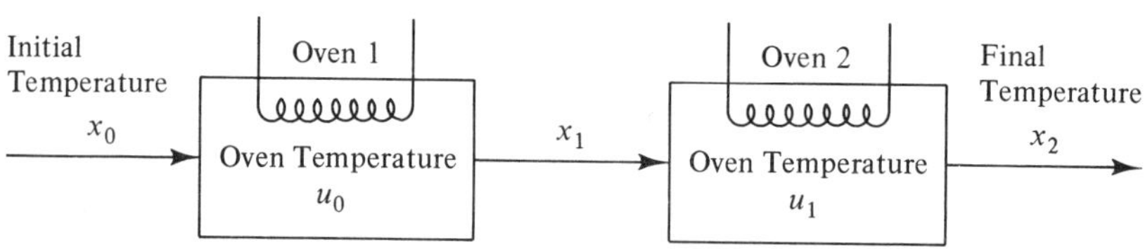

Figure 1.4 Problem of Example 1. The temperature of the material evolves according to $x_{k+1} = (1 - a)x_k + au_k$, where a is some scalar with $0 < a < 1$.

Note that this is not a single control but rather a control function, a rule that tells us the optimal oven temperature u_1 for each possible state x_1.

By substituting the optimal u_1 in the expression (1.8) for J_1, we obtain

$$J_1(x_1) = \frac{r^2a^2[(1-a)x_1 - T]^2}{(1+ra^2)^2} + r\left[(1-a)x_1 + \frac{ra^2[T-(1-a)x_1]}{1+ra^2} - T\right]^2$$
$$= \frac{r^2a^2[(1-a)x_1 - T]^2}{(1+ra^2)^2} + r\left(\frac{ra^2}{1+ra^2} - 1\right)^2[(1-a)x_1 - T]^2,$$

and finally

$$J_1(x_1) = \frac{r[(1-a)x_1 - T]^2}{1+ra^2}.$$

We now go one stage back to stage 0. We have [cf. (1.7)]

$$J_0(x_0) = \min_{u_0}[u_0^2 + J_1(x_1)]$$
$$= \min_{u_0}[u_0^2 + J_1[(1-a)x_0 + au_0]],$$

and by substituting the expression already obtained for J_1, we have

$$J_0(x_0) = \min_{u_0}\left[u_0^2 + \frac{r[(1-a)^2x_0 + (1-a)au_0 - T]^2}{1+ra^2}\right].$$

We minimize with respect to u_0 by setting the corresponding derivative to zero. We obtain

$$0 = 2u_0 + \frac{2r(1-a)a[(1-a)^2x_0 + (1-a)au_0 - T]}{1+ra^2}.$$

This yields, after some calculation, the optimal temperature of the first oven:

$$u_0 = \mu_0^*(x_0) = \frac{r(1-a)a[T-(1-a)^2x_0]}{1+ra^2[1+(1-a)^2]}.$$

The optimal cost is obtained by substituting this expression in the formula for J_0. This leads to a straightforward but lengthy calculation, which in the end yields the rather simple formula

$$J_0(x_0) = \frac{r[(1-a)^2x_0 - T]^2}{1+ra^2[1+(1-a)^2]}.$$

This completes the solution of the problem.

Several noteworthy features in this example, as we will see later, admit broad generalizations. The first is the facility with which we obtained an analytical solution. A little thought while tracing the steps of the algorithm will convince the reader that what makes the easy solution possible is the quadratic nature of the cost and the linearity of the system equation. Indeed, in Section 2.1 we will see that, generally, when the system is linear and the cost is quadratic then, regardless of the number of stages N, the optimal policy admits an analytical expression.

Another noteworthy feature of this example is that the optimal policy remains unaffected when a zero-mean stochastic disturbance is added in the system equation. To see this, assume that the material's temperature evolves according to

$$x_{k+1} = (1 - a)x_k + au_k + w_k, \qquad k = 0, 1,$$

where w_0, w_1 are independent random variables with given distribution, zero mean

$$E\{w_0\} = E\{w_1\} = 0,$$

and finite variance. Then the equation for J_1 [cf. (1.7)] becomes

$$\begin{aligned} J_1(x_1) &= \min_{u_1} E_{w_1}\{u_1^2 + r[(1 - a)x_1 + au_1 + w_1 - T]^2\} \\ &= \min_{u_1}[u_1^2 + r[(1 - a)x_1 + au_1 - T]^2 \\ &\quad + 2rE\{w_1\}[(1 - a)x_1 + au_1 - T] + rE\{w_1^2\}]. \end{aligned}$$

Therefore, using the fact that $E\{w_1\} = 0$, we obtain

$$J_1(x_1) = \min_{u_1}[u_1^2 + r[(1 - a)x_1 + au_1 - T]^2] + rE\{w_1^2\}.$$

Comparing this equation with (1.8), we see that the presence of w_1 has resulted in an additional inconsequential term, $rE\{w_1^2\}$. Therefore, the optimal policy for the last stage remains unaffected by the presence of w_1, while $J_1(x_1)$ is increased by the constant term $rE\{w_1^2\}$. It is easily seen that a similar situation also holds for the first stage. In particular, the optimal cost is given by the same expression as before except for the additional term $r(E\{w_0^2\} + E\{w_1^2\})$.

The property whereby the optimal policy is unaffected by the presence of zero-mean disturbances is a manifestation of the *certainty equivalence principle,* which holds for several types of problems involving a linear system and a quadratic cost (see Sections 2.1, 3.2, 3.3, and 6.1).

Example 2

Consider an inventory control problem similar to the one of Section 2.1 but different in that *inventory and demand are nonnegative integer variables.* Furthermore, assume that *there is an upper bound on the stock* $(x_k + u_k)$ that can be stored and also assume *that the excess demand* $(w_k - x_k - u_k)$ *is lost.* As a result, the stock equation takes the form

$$x_{k+1} = \max(0, x_k + u_k - w_k).$$

Assume that the maximum capacity $(x_k + u_k)$ for stock is 2 units, that the planning horizon N is 3 periods, and that the ordering cost c is 1 unit. The holding/shortage cost per stage is given by

$$H(x_k + u_k - w_k) = \max(0, x_k + u_k - w_k) + 3\max(0, w_k - x_k - u_k).$$

The terminal state cost is zero. The initial stock x_0 is given, and the demand w_k has the same probability distribution for all periods, given by

$$p(w_k = 0) = 0.1, \qquad p(w_k = 1) = 0.7, \qquad p(w_k = 2) = 0.2.$$

The system can also be represented in terms of the probabilities of transition between the three possible states 0, 1, 2 for the different values of control (see Figure 1.5a).

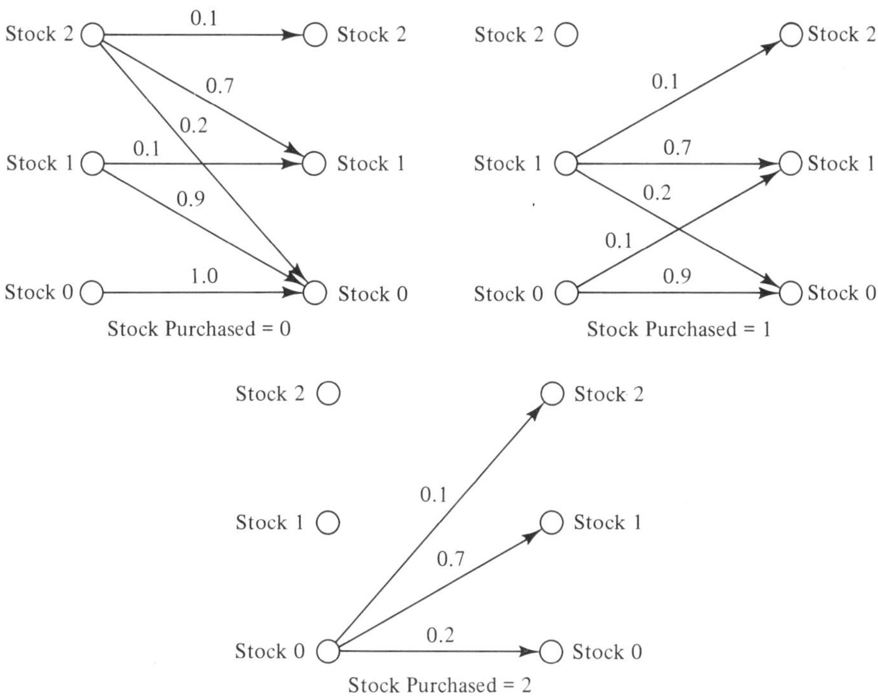

(a)

	Stage 0		Stage 1		Stage 2	
Stock	Cost-to-go	Opt. Stock to Purchase	Cost-to-go	Opt. Stock to Purchase	Cost-to-go	Opt. Stock to Purchase
0	4.9	1	3.3	1	1.7	1
1	3.9	0	2.3	0	0.7	0
2	3.35	0	1.82	0	0.9	0

(b)

Figure 1.5 System and DP results for Example 2: (a) Transition probability diagrams for the different values of stock purchased (control). The numbers next to the arcs are the transition probabilities. The control $u = 1$ is not available at state 2 because of the limitation $x_k + u_k \leq 2$. Similarly, the control $u = 2$ is available only at state 0. (b) Results of the DP algorithm for Example 2.

The starting equation for the DP algorithm is

$$J_3(x_3) = 0,$$

since the terminal state cost is zero [cf. (1.6)]. The algorithm takes the form [cf. (1.7)]

$$J_k(x_k) = \min_{\substack{0 \le u_k \le 2 - x_k \\ u_k = 0,1,2}} \mathop{E}_{w_k} \{u_k + \max(0, x_k + u_k - w_k) + 3\max(0, w_k - x_k - u_k)$$

$$+ J_{k+1}[\max(0, x_k + u_k - w_k)]\}, \qquad k = 0, 1, 2,$$

where x_k, u_k, w_k can take the values 0, 1, and 2.

Stage 2 We compute $J_2(x_2)$ for each of the three possible states:

$$J_2(0) = \min_{u_2=0,1,2} \mathop{E}_{w_2} \{u_2 + \max(0, u_2 - w_2) + 3\max(0, w_2 - u_2)\}$$

$$= \min_{u_2=0,1,2} \{u_2 + 0.1[\max(0, u_2) + 3\max(0, -u_2)]$$

$$+ 0.7[\max(0, u_2 - 1) + 3\max(0, 1 - u_2)] + 0.2[\max(0, u_2 - 2)$$

$$+ 3\max(0, 2 - u_2)]\}.$$

We calculate the expectation of the right side for each of the three possible values of u_2:

$$u_2 = 0: \quad E\{\cdot\} = 0.7 \times 3 \times 1 + 0.2 \times 3 \times 2 = 3.3,$$

$$u_2 = 1: \quad E\{\cdot\} = 1 + 0.1 \times 1 + 0.2 \times 3 \times 1 = 1.7,$$

$$u_2 = 2: \quad E\{\cdot\} = 2 + 0.1 \times 2 + 0.7 \times 1 = 2.9.$$

Hence we have, by selecting the minimizing u_2,

▷ $$J_2(0) = 1.7, \qquad \mu_2^*(0) = 1.$$ ◁

For $x_2 = 1$, we have

$$J_2(1) = \min_{u_2=0,1} \mathop{E}_{w_2} \{u_2 + \max(0, 1 + u_2 - w_2) + 3\max(0, w_2 - 1 - u_2)\}$$

$$= \min_{u_2=0,1} \{u_2 + 0.1[\max(0, 1 + u_2) + 3\max(0, -1 - u_2)]$$

$$+ 0.7[\max(0, u_2) + 3\max(0, -u_2)]$$

$$+ 0.2[\max(0, u_2 - 1) + 3\max(0, 1 - u_2)]\},$$

$$u_2 = 0: \quad E\{\cdot\} = 0.1 \times 1 + 0.2 \times 3 \times 1 = 0.7,$$

$$u_2 = 1: \quad E\{\cdot\} = 1 + 0.1 \times 2 + 0.7 \times 1 = 1.9.$$

Hence

▷ $$J_2(1) = 0.7, \qquad \mu_2^*(1) = 0.$$ ◁

For $x_2 = 2$, the only admissible control is $u_2 = 0$, so we have

$$J_2(2) = \mathop{E}_{w_2} \{\max(0, 2 - w_2) + 3\max(0, w_2 - 2)\}$$

$$= 0.1 \times 2 + 0.7 \times 1 = 0.9,$$

▷ $$J_2(2) = 0.9, \qquad \mu_2^*(2) = 0.$$ ◁

Stage 1 Again we compute $J_1(x_1)$ for each of the three possible states $x_2 = 0, 1, 2$ using the values $J_2(0)$, $J_2(1)$, $J_2(2)$ obtained in the previous stage:

$$J_1(0) = \min_{u_1=0,1,2} \underset{w_1}{E}\{u_1 + \max(0, u_1 - w_1) + 3\max(0, w_1 - u_1) + J_2[\max(0, u_1 - w_1)]\},$$

$$u_1 = 0: \quad E\{\cdot\} = 0.1 \times J_2(0) + 0.7[3 \times 1 + J_2(0)] + 0.2[3 \times 2 + J_2(0)] = 5.0,$$

$$u_1 = 1: \quad E\{\cdot\} = 1 + 0.1[1 + J_2(1)] + 0.7 \times J_2(0) + 0.2[3 \times 1 + J_2(0)] = 3.3,$$

$$u_1 = 2: \quad E\{\cdot\} = 2 + 0.1[2 + J_2(2)] + 0.7[1 + J_2(1)] + 0.2 \times J_2(0) = 3.82,$$

$$\triangleright \qquad J_1(0) = 3.3, \qquad \mu_1^*(0) = 1, \qquad \triangleleft$$

$$J_1(1) = \min_{u_1=0,1} \underset{w_1}{E}\{u_1 + \max(0, 1 + u_1 - w_1) + 3\max(0, w_1 - 1 - u_1) + J_2[\max(0, 1 + u_1 - w_1)]\}$$

$$u_1 = 0: \quad E\{\cdot\} = 0.1[1 + J_2(1)] + 0.7 \times J_2(0) + 0.2[3 \times 1 + J_2(0)] = 2.3,$$

$$u_1 = 1: \quad E\{\cdot\} = 1 + 0.1[2 + J_2(2)] + 0.7[1 + J_2(1)] + 0.2 \times J_2(0) = 2.82,$$

$$\triangleright \qquad J_1(1) = 2.3, \qquad \mu_1^*(1) = 0, \qquad \triangleleft$$

$$J_1(2) = E\{\max(0, 2 - w_1) + 3\max(0, w_1 - 2) + J_2[\max(0, 2 - w_1)]\}$$
$$= 0.1[2 + J_2(2)] + 0.7[1 + J_2(1)] + 0.2 \times J_2(0) = 1.82,$$

$$\triangleright \qquad J_1(2) = 1.82, \qquad \mu_1^*(2) = 0. \qquad \triangleleft$$

Stage 0 Here we need only compute $J_0(0)$ since the initial state is known to be zero. We have

$$J_0(0) = \min_{u_0=0,1,2} \underset{w_0}{E}\{u_0 + \max(0, u_0 - w_0) + 3\max(0, w_0 - u_0) + J_1[\max(0, u_0 - w_0)]\},$$

$$u_0 = 0: \quad E\{\cdot\} = 0.1 \times J_1(0) + 0.7[3 \times 1 + J_1(0)] + 0.2[3 \times 2 + J_1(0)] = 6.6,$$

$$u_0 = 1: \quad E\{\cdot\} = 1 + 0.1[1 + J_1(1)] + 0.7 \times J_1(0) + 0.2[3 \times 1 + J_1(0)] = 4.9,$$

$$u_0 = 2: \quad E\{\cdot\} = 2 + 0.1[2 + J_1(2)] + 0.7[1 + J_1(1)] + 0.2 \times J_1(0) = 5.352,$$

$$\triangleright \qquad J_0(0) = 4.9, \qquad \mu_0^*(0) = 1. \qquad \triangleleft$$

If the initial state were not known a priori, we would have to compute in a similar manner $J_0(1)$ and $J_0(2)$ as well as the minimizing u_0. These calculations yield

$$\triangleright \qquad J_0(1) = 3.9, \qquad \mu_0^*(1) = 0, \qquad \triangleleft$$

$$\triangleright \qquad J_0(2) = 3.352, \qquad \mu_0^*(2) = 0. \qquad \triangleleft$$

Thus the optimal ordering policy for each period is to order one unit if the current stock is zero, and order nothing otherwise. The results of the DP algorithm are given in tabular form in Figure 1.5b.

Example 3

Finite State Systems. We mentioned earlier (cf. the queueing example in the previous section) that systems with a finite number of states can be represented either by a discrete-time system equation or in terms of the probabilities of transition between the states (cf. Figures 1.2 and 1.5). Let us work out the corresponding DP algorithm. We will assume for the sake of the following discussion that the problem is stationary (i.e. the transition probabilities, the cost per stage, and the control constraint set do not change from one stage to the next). Then, if

$$p_{ij}(u) = P\{x_{k+1} = j \mid x_k = i, u_k = u\}$$

are the transition probabilities, we can alternatively represent the system by the system equation (cf. the discussion of the previous section)

$$x_{k+1} = w_k,$$

where the probability distribution of the disturbance w_k is

$$P\{w_k = j \mid x_k = i, u_k = u\} = p_{ij}(u).$$

Using this system equation and denoting by $g(i, u)$ the expected cost per stage at state i when control u is applied, the DP algorithm can be rewritten as

$$J_k(i) = \min_{u \in U(i)} [g(i, u) + E\{J_{k+1}(w_k)\}]$$

or equivalently (in view of the distribution of w_k given previously)

$$J_k(i) = \min_{u \in U(i)} [g(i, u) + \sum_j p_{ij}(u) J_{k+1}(j)], \qquad k = 0, 1, \dots, N-1.$$

As an illustration, in the queueing problem of the previous section this algorithm takes the form

$$J_N(i) = C(i), \qquad i = 0, 1, \dots, n,$$

$$J_k(i) = \min[c(i) + c_f + \sum_{j=0}^{n} p_{ij}(u_f) J_{k+1}(j), c(i) + c_s + \sum_{j=0}^{n} p_{ij}(u_s) J_{k+1}(j)],$$

$$k = 0, 1, \dots, N-1.$$

The two expressions in the minimization correspond to the two available decisions (fast and slow service).

1.3 DETERMINISTIC SYSTEMS AND THE SHORTEST PATH PROBLEM

The main objective of this text is the analysis of stochastic optimization problems and the ramifications of the presence of uncertainty. However, deterministic problems arise in many important contexts, and the present and the next sections are devoted to explaining some of their distinguishing features.

We first note that deterministic problems can certainly be embedded within the framework of the basic problem simply by considering disturbance spaces D_k having a single element. However, in contrast with stochastic problems, *using feedback in deterministic problems results in no advantage in terms of cost reduction.* In other words, minimizing the cost functional over the class of admissible control laws $\{\mu_0, \ldots, \mu_{N-1}\}$ results in the same optimal cost as minimizing over the class of *sequences of control vectors* $\{u_0, \ldots, u_{N-1}\}$ with $u_k \in U_k(x_k)$ for all k. This is true simply because the cost achieved by an optimal control law $\{\mu_0^*, \ldots, \mu_{N-1}^*\}$ for a deterministic problem is also achieved by the control sequence

$$u_k^* = \mu_k^*(x_k^*), \qquad k = 0, \ldots, N-1,$$

where the states $x_0^*, \ldots, x_{N-1}^*$ are defined by

$$x_{k+1}^* = f_k(x_k^*, u_k^*), \qquad x_0^* = x_0, \qquad k = 0, 1, \ldots, N-1.$$

For this reason we may minimize the cost functional over sequences of controls, a task that may be achieved by variational deterministic optimal control algorithms such as steepest descent, conjugate gradient, and Newton's method. These algorithms, when applicable, are usually more efficient than DP. On the other hand, *DP has a wider scope of applicability since it can handle difficult constraint sets such as integer or discrete sets.* Furthermore, *DP leads to a globally optimal solution* as opposed to variational techniques, for which this cannot be guaranteed in general.

Consider now a deterministic problem where the state space S_k is a finite set for each k. Then at any state x_k a control u_k can be associated with a transition from the state x_k to the state $f_k(x_k, u_k)$. Thus a finite state deterministic problem can be equivalently represented by a graph such as the one of Figure 1.6, where the arcs correspond to transitions between states at successive stages and each arc has a cost associated with it. We have also added an artificial terminal node t. Each arc connecting a state x_N at stage N to the terminal node has cost $g_N(x_N)$. Control sequences correspond to paths originating at the initial state (node s at stage 0) and terminating at one of the nodes corresponding to the final stage N. If we view the cost of an arc as its length, we see that a *deterministic problem is equivalent to finding a shortest path from the initial node s of the graph to the terminal node t.* [A path is a sequence of arcs of the form (j_1, j_2), $(j_2, j_3), \ldots, (j_{k-1}, j_k)$; its length is the sum of the length of its arcs.]

If we denote

$$\begin{aligned} c_{ij}^k &= \text{cost of transition from state } i \in S_k \\ &\quad\ \text{to state } j \in S_{k+1},\ k = 0, 1, \ldots, N-1, \\ c_{it}^N &= \text{terminal cost of state } i \in S_N, \end{aligned}$$

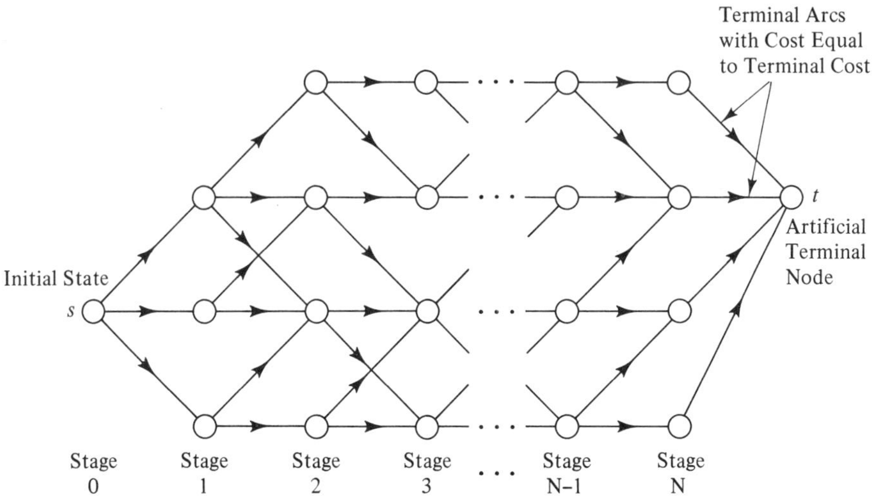

Figure 1.6 Transition graph for a deterministic finite state system. Nodes correspond to states. An arc with start and end nodes x_k and x_{k+1}, respectively, corresponds to a transition of the form $x_{k+1} = f_k(x_k, u_k)$. The length of this arc is equal to the cost of the corresponding transition $g_k(x_k, u_k)$. The problem is equivalent to finding a shortest path from the initial node s to the terminal node t.

the DP algorithm takes the form

$$J_N(i) = c_{it}^N, \qquad i \in S_N, \tag{1.9}$$

$$J_k(i) = \min_{j \in S_{k+1}} \{c_{ij}^k + J_{k+1}(j)\}, \qquad i \in S_k, \quad k = 0, 1, \ldots, N-1. \tag{1.10}$$

The optimal cost is $J_0(s)$ and equals the length of the shortest path from s to t.

The preceding algorithm proceeds *backward* in time. It is possible to derive an equivalent algorithm that proceeds *forward* in time by means of the following simple observation. An optimal path from s to t is also an optimal path from t to s in a "reverse" shortest path problem whereby the direction of each arc is reversed and its length is left unchanged. The DP algorithm corresponding to this "reverse" problem is

$$\tilde{J}_N(j) = c_{sj}^0, \qquad j \in S_1, \tag{1.11}$$

$$\tilde{J}_k(j) = \min_{i \in S_{N-k}} \{c_{ij}^{N-k} + \tilde{J}_{k+1}(i)\}, \qquad j \in S_{N-k+1},$$

$$k = 1, 2, \ldots, N-1, \tag{1.12}$$

and the optimal cost is

$$\tilde{J}_0(t) = \min_{i \in S_N} \{c_{it}^N + \tilde{J}_1(i)\}. \tag{1.13}$$

The backward and forward DP algorithms (1.9), (1.10) and (1.11) to (1.13), respectively, are equivalent in the sense that $J_0(s) = \tilde{J}_0(t)$, and an optimal control sequence (or shortest path) obtained from any one of the two is optimal for the original problem. We may view $\tilde{J}_k(j)$ in (1.12) as an *optimal cost-to-arrive* to state j from the initial state s. This should be contrasted with $J_k(i)$ in (1.10), which represents the optimal cost-to-go from state i to the terminal state t.

In conclusion, *a deterministic finite state problem is equivalent to a special type of shortest path problem and can be solved by either the ordinary (backward) DP algorithm or by an alternative forward DP algorithm.* It is also interesting to note that *any shortest path problem can be posed as a deterministic finite state DP problem,* as we now show.

Let $\{1, 2, \ldots, N, t\}$ be the set of nodes of a graph, and let c_{ij} be the cost of moving from node i to node j (or length of the arc joining i and j). Node t is a special node, which we call the *destination.* We allow the possibility $c_{ij} = \infty$ to account for the case where there is no arc joining nodes i and j. We want to find a shortest path from each node i to node t, that is, a sequence of moves that minimizes total cost to get to t from each of the nodes $1, 2, \ldots, N$. For the problem to have a solution, it is necessary to exclude the possibility that a sequence of moves that starts and ends at the same node (a cycle) has negative total length. Otherwise, it would be possible to decrease the length of some paths to arbitrarily small values simply by adding more and more negative-length cycles.

Since negative-length cycles have been excluded by assumption, it is clear that an optimal path need not take more than N moves, so we may limit the number of moves to N. We formulate the problem as one where *we require exactly N moves but allow degenerate moves from a node i to itself with cost $c_{ii} = 0$.* We denote for $i = 1, \ldots, N$, $k = 0, 1, \ldots, N - 1$,

$$J_{N-1}(i) = \text{optimal cost for getting from } i \text{ to } t \text{ in one move},$$

$$J_k(i) = \text{optimal cost for getting from } i \text{ to } t \text{ in } (N - k) \text{ moves}.$$

Then the cost of the optimal path from i to t is $J_0(i)$. It is possible to formulate this problem within the framework of the basic problem and subsequently apply the DP algorithm. For simplicity, however, we write directly the DP equation, which takes the intuitively clear form

$$\begin{aligned}&\text{optimal cost from } i \text{ to } t \text{ in } (N - k) \text{ moves}\\ &\quad = \min_{j=1,\ldots,N} \{c_{ij} + \text{optimal cost from } j \text{ to } t \text{ in } (N - k - 1) \text{ moves}\},\end{aligned}$$

or

$$J_k(i) = \min_{j=1,\ldots,N} \{c_{ij} + J_{k+1}(j)\}, \qquad k = 0, 1, \ldots, N - 2,$$

with

$$J_{N-1}(i) = c_{it}, \qquad i = 1, 2, \ldots, N.$$

The optimal policy when at node i after k moves is to move to node j^*, where j^* minimizes over all $j = 1, \ldots, N$ the expression in braces. Note that a degenerate move from i to i is not excluded. If the optimal path obtained from the algorithm contains such degenerate moves, this simply means that its duration is less than N moves.

To demonstrate the algorithm, consider the problem shown in Figure 1.7a, where the costs c_{ij}, $i \neq j$ (we assume $c_{ij} = c_{ji}$), are shown along the connecting line segments. Figure 1.7b shows the cost-to-go $J_k(i)$ at each node i and index k together with the optimal path. The optimal paths are

$$1 \to 5, \quad 2 \to 3 \to 4 \to 5, \quad 3 \to 4 \to 5, \quad 4 \to 5.$$

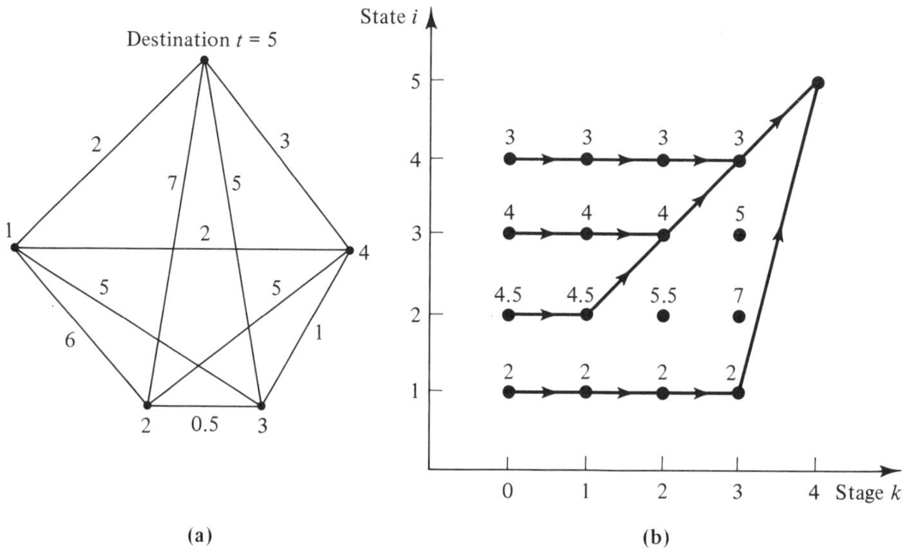

Figure 1.7 (a) Shortest path problem data. The destination is 5. Arc lengths are equal in both directions and are shown along the line segments connecting nodes. (b) Costs-to-go generated by the DP algorithm. The number along stage k and state i is $J_k(i)$. Arrows indicate the optimal moves at each stage and node.

1.4 SHORTEST PATH APPLICATIONS IN CRITICAL PATH ANALYSIS, CODING THEORY, AND FORWARD SEARCH

The shortest path problem appears in many diverse contexts. We provide some examples.

Critical Path Analysis

Consider the planning of a project involving several activities, some of which must be completed before others can begin. The duration of each activity is known in advance. We want to find the time required to complete the project, as well as the *critical* activities, those that even if slightly delayed will result in a corresponding delay of completion of the overall project.

The problem can be represented by a directed graph with nodes 1, . . ., N such as the one shown in Figure 1.8 (also called an *activity network*). Here nodes represent completion of some phase of the project. An arc (i, j) represents an activity that starts once phase i is completed and has known duration t_{ij}. A phase (node) j is completed when all activities or arcs (i, j) that are incoming to j are completed. The special nodes 1 and N represent the start and end of the project. Naturally, node 1 (N) has no incoming (outgoing) arcs.

An important characteristic of an activity network is that it is *acyclic;* that is, it has no directed cycles [sequences of directed arcs of the form $(i, j_1), (j_1, j_2), \ldots, (j_k, i)$]. This is inherent in the problem formulation and the interpretation of nodes as phase completions.

Consider now the time T required to complete all phases of the project and hence the project itself. For any directed path $p = \{(1, j_1), (j_1, j_2), \ldots, (j_{k-1}, j_k)\}$ from node 1 to node j_k, let D_p be the duration of the path defined as the sum of durations of its activities; that is,

$$D_p = t_{ij_1} + t_{j_1j_2} + \cdots + t_{j_{k-1}j_k}.$$

So D_p is the total duration of the sequence of activities $(1, j_1), \ldots, (j_{k-1}, j_k)$ if each could be started immediately after the previous ended. Clearly, D_p cannot exceed the total project duration time; that is,

$$D_p \leq T, \qquad \text{all paths } p.$$

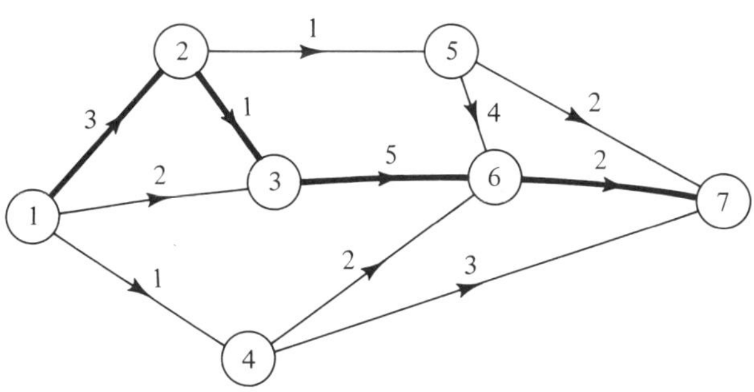

Figure 1.8 Graph of an activity network. Nodes represent completion of some phase of the project. Arcs represent activities and are labeled by the duration. A phase is completed if all activities associated with incoming arcs at the corresponding node are completed. The project is completed when all phases are completed. The project duration time is the length of the longest path from node 1 to node 7.

We claim that

$$T = \max_p D_p,$$

and therefore finding T may be viewed as a problem of finding the *longest* path from node 1 to node N when the length of each arc (i, j) is t_{ij}. Because the graph is acyclic, this problem may also be viewed as a shortest path problem with the length of each arc (i, j) being $-t_{ij}$.

The easiest way to show this is by deriving the corresponding DP algorithm. Let N_k, $k = 1, 2, \ldots$, be the set of phases

$$N_k = \{i \mid \text{the maximum number of arcs contained in paths from 1 to } i \text{ is exactly } k\}$$

with $N_0 = \{1\}$. For each phase i, let

$$T_i: \quad \text{required time to complete } i.$$

Then we have

$$T_i = \max_{(j,i)} \{t_{ji} + T_j \mid j \in N_0 \cup \cdots \cup N_{k-1}\}, \qquad i \in N_k,$$

and a little thought reveals that T_i equals the maximum D_p over all paths p from 1 to i. For $i = N$, we obtain $T = \max_p D_p$.

For the activity network of Figure 1.8, we have

$$N_0 = \{1\}, \quad N_1 = \{2, 4\}, \quad N_2 = \{3, 5\}, \quad N_3 = \{6\}, \quad N_4 = \{7\}.$$

A calculation using the preceding formula yields

$$T_1 = 0, \quad T_2 = 3, \quad T_4 = 1, \quad T_3 = 4, \quad T_5 = 4, \quad T_6 = 9, \quad T_7 = 11,$$

and the critical (i.e., longest) path is $1 \to 2 \to 3 \to 6 \to 7$. Any delay in the completion of the critical activities (1, 2), (2, 3), (3, 6), (6, 7) will proportionately delay the completion of the overall project.

Convolutional Coding and the Viterbi Decoder

When binary data are transmitted over a noisy communication channel, it is often essential to use coding as a means of enhancing reliability of communication. A very common type of coding method, called *convolutional coding,* converts a source-generated binary data sequence

$$\{w_1, w_2, \ldots\}, \qquad w_k \in \{0, 1\}, \quad k = 1, 2, \ldots,$$

into a coded sequence

$$\{y_1, y_2, \ldots\},$$

where each y_k, $k = 1, 2, \ldots$, is an n-dimensional vector with binary coordinates (called codeword)

$$y_k = \begin{bmatrix} y_k^1 \\ \cdots \\ y_k^n \end{bmatrix}, \qquad y_k^i \in \{0, 1\}, \quad i = 1, \ldots, n.$$

The vectors y_k are related to w_k via equations of the form

$$y_k = Cx_{k-1} + dw_k, \qquad k = 1, 2, \dots, \tag{1.14}$$

$$x_k = Ax_{k-1} + bw_k, \qquad k = 1, 2, \dots, \tag{1.15}$$

$$x_0: \quad \text{given},$$

where x_k is an m-dimensional vector with binary coordinates (called state) and C, d, A, and b are $n \times m$, $n \times 1$, $m \times m$, and $m \times 1$ matrices, respectively, with binary coordinates. The products and the sums involved in the expressions $Cx_{k-1} + dw_k$ and $Ax_{k-1} + bd_k$ are calculated using modulo 2 arithmetic.

As an example, let $m = 2$, $n = 3$, and

$$C = \begin{bmatrix} 1 & 0 \\ 0 & 1 \\ 0 & 1 \end{bmatrix}, \qquad A = \begin{bmatrix} 0 & 1 \\ 1 & 1 \end{bmatrix},$$

$$d = \begin{bmatrix} 1 \\ 1 \\ 1 \end{bmatrix}, \qquad b = \begin{bmatrix} 0 \\ 1 \end{bmatrix}.$$

Then the evolution of the system (1.14) to (1.15) can be represented by the transition diagram (called a *trellis*) shown in Figure 1.9. From this diagram and the initial x_0, it is possible to generate the codeword sequence $\{y_1, y_2, \dots\}$ corresponding to a data sequence $\{w_1, w_2, \dots\}$. For example, when the

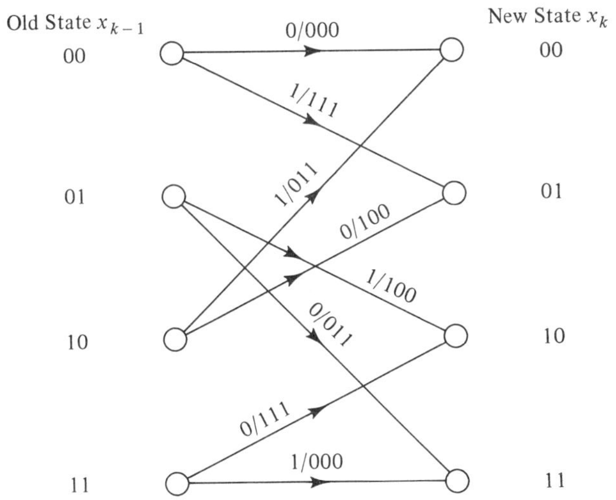

Figure 1.9 State transition diagram from x_{k-1} to x_k. The binary number pair on each arc is the data/codeword pair w_k/y_k for the corresponding transition. So, for example, when $x_{k-1} = 01$, a zero data bit ($w_k = 0$) effects a transition to $x_k = 11$ and generates the codeword 011.

initial state is $x_0 = 00$, the data sequence

$$\{w_1, w_2, w_3, w_4\} = \{1, 0, 0, 1\}$$

generates the state sequence

$$\{x_0, x_1, x_2, x_3, x_4\} = \{00, 01, 11, 10, 00\},$$

and the codeword sequence

$$\{y_1, y_2, y_3, y_4\} = \{111, 011, 111, 011\}.$$

Assume now that the characteristics of the noisy transmission channel are such that a codeword y is actually received as z with known probability $p(z \mid y)$, where z is any n-bit binary number. We denote

$$Z_N = \{z_1, z_2, \ldots, z_N\}$$

the sequence received when the transmitted sequence is

$$Y_N = \{y_1, y_2, \ldots, y_N\}.$$

We assume independent errors so that

$$p(Z_N \mid Y_N) = \prod_{k=1}^{N} p(z_k \mid y_k). \tag{1.16}$$

A *maximum likelihood decoder* converts a received sequence Z_N into a sequence

$$\hat{Y}_N = \{\hat{y}_1, \hat{y}_2, \ldots, \hat{y}_N\}$$

such that

$$p(Z_N \mid \hat{Y}_N) = \max_{Y_N} p(Z_N \mid Y_N).$$

The constraint on Y_N is that it must be a feasible codeword sequence (i.e., it must correspond to some initial state and data sequence). Given $\hat{Y}_N$, one can then construct a corresponding data sequence $\{\hat{w}_1, \ldots, \hat{w}_N\}$ that is accepted as the decoded data.

Viterbi developed a shortest path scheme that implements the maximum likelihood decoder. Using (1.16), we see that the problem of maximizing $p(Z_N \mid Y_N)$ is equivalent to the problem

$$\begin{gathered} \text{minimize} \sum_{k=1}^{N} - \ln[p(z_k \mid y_k)] \\ \text{over all binary sequences } \{y_1, y_2, \ldots, y_N\} \end{gathered} \tag{1.17}$$

for a known received sequence $\{z_1, z_2, \ldots, z_N\}$. To see that this is a shortest path problem, note that, given z_k, *we can assign to each arc on the state transition diagram the length* $-\ln[p(z_k \mid y_k)]$, *where* y_k *is the codeword associated with the arc*. Next we construct a graph by concatenating N state transition diagrams and appending dummy nodes s and t on the left and right side of the graph connected with zero-length arcs to the states x_0 and x_{N-1}, respectively (see Figure 1.10). The solution to problem (1.17)

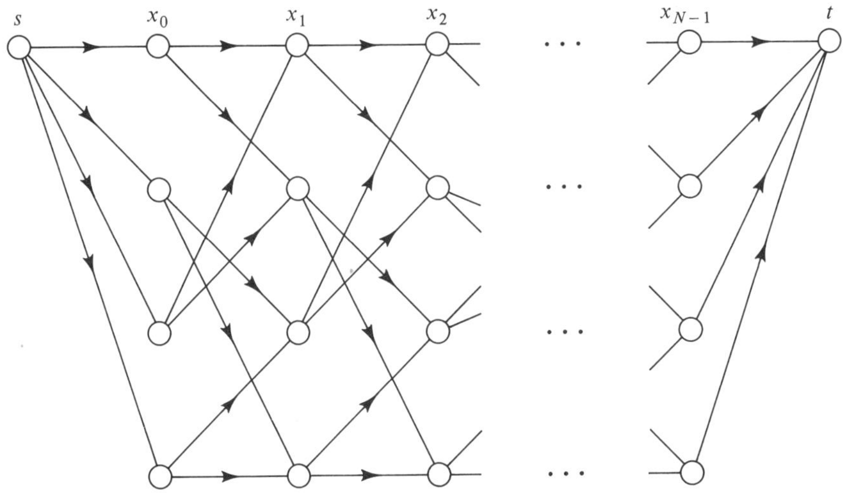

Figure 1.10 Maximum likelihood decoding viewed as a problem of finding a shortest path from s to t. Length of arcs from s to states x_0 and from states x_{N-1} to t is zero. Length of an arc from a state x_{k-1} to x_k is $-\ln p(z_k \mid y_k)$, where z_k is the received codeword and y_k is the codeword associated with the arc.

is obtained by constructing a shortest path from s to t and finding the associated sequence $\{\hat{y}_1, \ldots, \hat{y}_N\}$. From the shortest path and the trellis diagram, we can then obtain the decoded data sequence $\{\hat{w}_1, \hat{w}_2, \ldots, \hat{w}_N\}$.

In practice, the shortest path is most conveniently constructed by calculating the shortest distance from s to each node on-line as soon as the corresponding codeword is received. There are a number of practical schemes for decoding a portion of the data sequence prior to receiving the entire codeword sequence Z_N. (This is useful if Z_N is a long sequence.) For example, one can check rather easily whether for some k all shortest paths from s to states x_k pass through a single node in the subgraph of states $x_0, \ldots, x_{k-1}$. If so, it can be seen that the shortest path from s to that node will not be affected by reception of additional codewords (the principle of optimality), and therefore the corresponding data subsequence can be safely decoded and delivered to its destination.

Forward Search

In some shortest path problems the number of nodes is extremely large. As a result, storing these nodes in a computer's memory can be very difficult. Indeed, the nature of some shortest path problems is such that the solution becomes very simple once the nodes of the underlying graph are enumerated, and the real issue is how to solve the problem while avoiding a complete enumeration of all nodes. In such cases it is frequently possible to save both in memory and in computation by means of a forward search for a shortest path from an origin node toward a destination node. The techniques for doing this have partly originated in artificial intelligence and are typically used in computer progams that solve puzzles or play games such as chess (see Section 4.3). Let us provide some examples.

Example 1

The Four Queens Problem. Four queens must be placed on a 4×4 portion of a chessboard so that no queen can attack another. In other words, the placement must be such that every row, column, or diagonal of the 4×4 board contains at most one queen. Equivalently, we can view the problem as a sequence of problems; first, placing a queen in one of the first two squares in the top row, then placing another queen in the second row so that it is not attacked by the first, and similarly placing the third and fourth queens. (It is sufficient to consider only the first two squares of the top row since the other two squares lead to symmetric positions.) We can associate positions with nodes of an acyclic graph where the root node s corresponds to the position with no queens and the terminal nodes correspond to the dead-end positions where no additional queens can be placed without some queen attacking another. Let us connect each terminal position with an artificial node t by means of an arc. Let us also assign to all arcs length zero except for the artificial arcs connecting terminal positions with less than four queens with the artificial node t. These latter arcs are assigned the length $+\infty$ (see Figure 1.11) to express the fact that they correspond to dead-end positions that cannot lead to a solution. Then the four queens problem reduces to finding a shortest path from node s to node t. Note that once the nodes of the graph are enumerated the problem is essentially solved. Here the number of nodes is small. However, we can think of similar problems with much larger memory requirements. For example, there is an eight queens problem where the board is 8×8 instead of 4×4.

Example 2

The Traveling Salesman Problem. An important model for scheduling a sequence of operations is the classical traveling salesman problem. Here we are given N cities and the mileage between each pair of cities, and we wish to find a minimum-mileage trip that visits each of the cities exactly once. To convert this problem to a shortest path problem, we associate a node with every sequence of n distinct cities, where $n = 1, 2, \ldots, N$. The construction and arc lengths of the corresponding graph are explained by means of an example in Figure 1.12. The origin node s consists of city A, taken as the start. A sequence of n cities ($n < N$) yields a sequence of $(n + 1)$ cities by adding a new city. Two such sequences are connected by an arc with length equal to the mileage between the last two of the $n + 1$ cities. Each sequence of N cities is connected to an artificial terminal node t with an arc having length equal to the distance from the last city of the sequence to the starting city A. Note that the number of nodes grows exponentially with the number of cities, so we would like to have algorithms that do not require the enumeration and/or storage of these nodes.

In the shortest path problem that we will consider there is a single node s with no incoming arcs, called the *origin*, and a single node t with no outgoing arcs, called the *destination*. We assume that every arc (i, j)

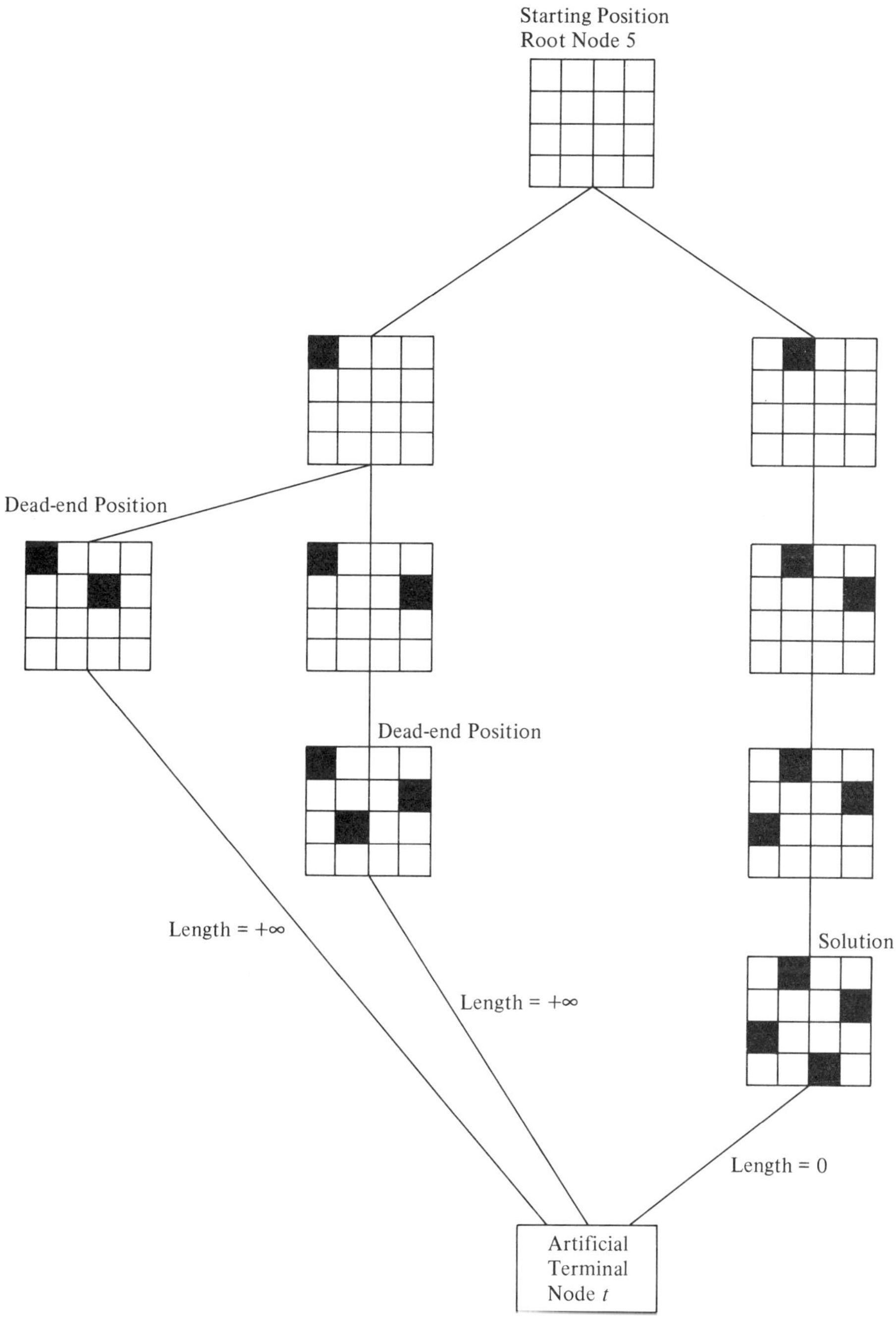

Figure 1.11 Shortest path formulation of the four queens problem. Symmetric positions resulting from placing a queen in one of the rightmost squares in the top row have been ignored. Squares containing a queen have been darkened. All arcs have length zero except for those connecting dead-end positions to the artificial terminal node.

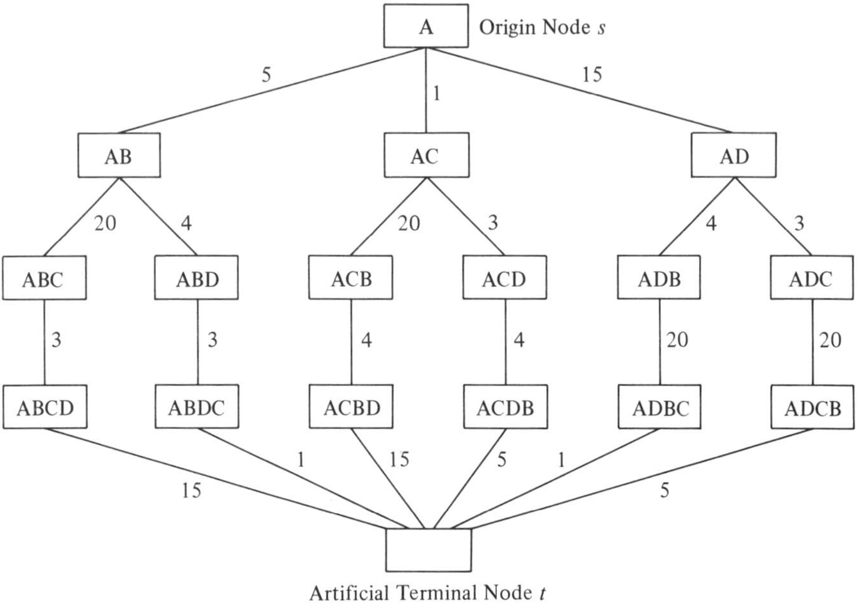

	A	B	C	D
A		5	1	15
B	5		20	4
C	1	20		3
D	15	4	3	

Table of Mileage between Cities

Figure 1.12 Example of shortest path formulation of the traveling salesman problem. The distance between the four cities A, B, C, and D are shown in the table. The arc lengths are shown next to the arcs.

has a length a_{ij} which is nonnegative or $+\infty$, and we wish to find a shortest path from origin to destination. Note that both examples given earlier satisfy these conditions (cf. Figures 1.11 and 1.12). The following algorithm is a general method for solving the problem. In it we make use of two lists of nodes called OPEN and CLOSED. The list OPEN contains nodes that are currently active in the sense that they are candidates for further examination by the algorithm. The list CLOSED contains nodes that were active earlier but have already been examined by the algorithm and are not currently candidates for further consideration. Initially, OPEN contains just the origin node s and CLOSED is empty. The algorithm maintains an upper bound of the shortest distance from origin to destination called UPPER and initially equal to $+\infty$. The algorithm also maintains for each node i an upper bound d_i of its shortest distance from the origin. Initially, $d_s = 0$ and $d_i = +\infty$ for all other nodes i. A node j is called a *son* of node i if there is an arc (i, j) connecting i with j. The steps of the algorithm are as follows:

Step 1 Remove a node i from the top of OPEN and place it in CLOSED. For each son j of i, go to step 1a if $j \neq t$, and go to step 1b if $j = t$.

Step 1a $(j \neq t)$ If $d_i + a_{ij} < \min\{d_j, \text{UPPER}\}$, set $d_j = d_i + a_{ij}$, give j the label i, place j at the top of OPEN, and remove j from CLOSED if it belongs there. (*Note:* The label is needed in order to trace the shortest path to the origin after the algorithm terminates.)

Step 1b $(j = t)$: If $d_i + a_{it} < \text{UPPER}$, set UPPER $= d_i + a_{it}$, and mark node i as lying on the best path found so far from s to t.

Step 2 If OPEN is empty, terminate; else go to step 1.

It can be seen that, throughout the algorithm, d_j is either $+\infty$ (if node j has not yet entered the OPEN list), or else it is the length of a path from s to j consisting of nodes that have entered the OPEN list at least once. Furthermore, UPPER is either $+\infty$, or else it is the length of a path from s to t, and consequently it is an overestimate of the shortest distance from s to t. The idea in the algorithm is that when a shorter path from s to j is discovered than those considered earlier ($d_i + a_{ij} < d_j$ in step 1a), the value of d_j is accordingly reduced, and node j enters the OPEN list so that paths passing through j and reaching the sons of j can be taken into account. It makes sense to do so, however, only when the path considered has a chance of leading to a path from s to t with length smaller than the overestimate UPPER of the shortest distance from s to t. In view of the nonnegativity of the arc lengths, this is not possible if the path length $d_i + a_{ij}$ is not smaller than UPPER. This provides the rationale for entering j into OPEN in step 1a only if $d_i + a_{ij}$ is less than UPPER.

Tracing the algorithm, we see that it will first examine node s (the only node initially in OPEN), place s (permanently) in CLOSED, and assuming t is not a son of s, it will place all the sons j of s in OPEN after setting $d_j = a_{sj}$. If t is a son of s, then UPPER will be set to a_{st} in step 1b, and the sons of s examined after t will be placed in OPEN only if $a_{sj} < a_{st}$; indeed, this should be so since if $a_{sj} \geq a_{st}$ node j cannot lie on a shorter path from s to t than the direct path consisting of arc (s, t). The algorithm will subsequently take the last son $j \neq t$ of s from the top of OPEN, place it in CLOSED, and place those of its sons $j \neq t$ that satisfy the criterion of step 1a in OPEN, etc. When the algorithm terminates, we claim that a shortest path can be obtained by using the node last marked in step 1b as lying on the best path. By tracing labels starting from that node we can proceed backward and construct a shortest path to the origin node. Fig. 1.13 illustrates the use of the algorithm to solve the traveling salesman problem of Fig. 1.12.

To verify that a path obtained as just described is shortest, we reason as follows. We first argue by contradiction that the algorithm will terminate. Indeed, if this is not so, some node j will enter the OPEN list infinitely often, which means that d_j will be decreased infinitely often, each time obtaining a corresponding shorter path from s to j. This is not possible since, in view of the nonnegative arc assumption, the number of distinct lengths of paths from s to j is finite. Therefore, the algorithm will terminate. We next show that the value of UPPER upon termination must equal the shortest distance d^* from s to t. Indeed, let $(s, j_1, j_2, \ldots, j_k, t)$ be a shortest path from s to t. Then each path $(s, j_1, \ldots, j_m)$, $m = 1, \ldots, k$, is a shortest path from s to j_m, respectively. If the value of UPPER is larger than d^* at termination, the same must be true throughout the algorithm, and therefore UPPER will also be larger than the length of all the paths $(s, j_1, \ldots, j_m)$, $m = 1, \ldots, k$, throughout the algorithm. It follows that node j_k will never enter the OPEN list with d_{j_k} equal to the shortest distance from s to j_k, since in this case UPPER would be set to d^* in step 1b immediately following the next time node j_k is examined by the algorithm in step 1. Similarly, this means that node j_{k-1} will never enter the OPEN list with $d_{j_{(k-1)}}$ equal to the shortest distance from s to j_{k-1}. Proceeding backward, we conclude that j_1 never enters the OPEN list with d_{j_1} equal to the shortest distance from s to j_1 (which is equal to the length of the arc (s, j_1)). This happens, however, at the first iteration of the algorithm as discussed earlier, so we have reached a contradiction. It follows that UPPER will equal at termination the shortest distance from s to t. It is seen that the path constructed by tracing labels backward from t to s has length equal to UPPER, so it is a shortest path from s to t.

There are two attractive aspects to this algorithm. The first is a potential saving in computation in that nodes j for which $d_i + a_{ij} \geq$ UPPER in step 1a need not enter OPEN and be examined later. Furthermore, if we know a lower bound to the shortest distance, we can terminate the computation once UPPER reaches that bound either exactly or within an acceptable tolerance $\varepsilon > 0$. (This feature is useful, for example, in the four queens problem, where the shortest distance is known to be zero or infinity. Then the algorithm will terminate once a solution is found.)

The second attractive aspect of the algorithm is a potential saving in memory storage requirements. This is most evident in graphs such as those in Figures 1.11 and 1.12 for which there is a unique directed path from the

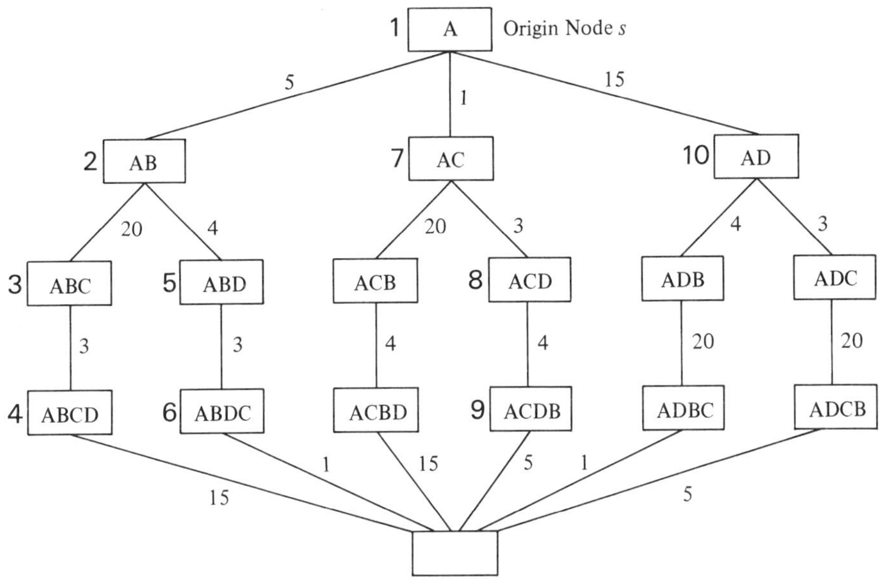

(a)

Iteration No.	List OPEN	Node Entering CLOSED	UPPER
0	1	–	$+\infty$
1	2, 7, 10	1	$+\infty$
2	3, 5, 7, 10	2	$+\infty$
3	4, 5, 7, 10	3	$+\infty$
4	5, 7, 10	4	43
5	6, 7, 10	5	43
6	7, 10	6	13
7	8, 10	7	13
8	9, 10	8	13
9	10	9	13
10	Empty	10	13

(b)

Figure 1.13 The algorithm applied to the traveling salesman problem of Figure 1.12. The optimal solution ABDC is found after examining nodes 1 through 10 in that order. The table shows the successive contents of the OPEN list.

origin node to every other node. Then, in view of our convention of placing nodes at and removing nodes from the top of OPEN, the search proceeds in depth-first fashion, as shown in Figure 1.14. As a result, large portions of CLOSED can be purged from memory, as shown in Figure 1.15. The basis for this is that once all sons of a node enter the CLOSED list then all paths passing through that node have been generated and evaluated. Therefore, it is sufficient to store only the best path found so far and purge all other information relating to such a node.

There are a number of variations of the algorithm just given. The preceding proof of validity of the algorithm does not depend on removing a node from the top of OPEN in step 1 or placing a node at the top of OPEN in step 1a. This allows a great deal of freedom on how the algorithm is operated. An important case is when the node i selected in step 1 is not the node that happens to be at the top of OPEN, but rather the one in OPEN for which d_i is *minimum*. This is accordingly known as *best-first search* and is equivalent for the problem considered here to Dijkstra's

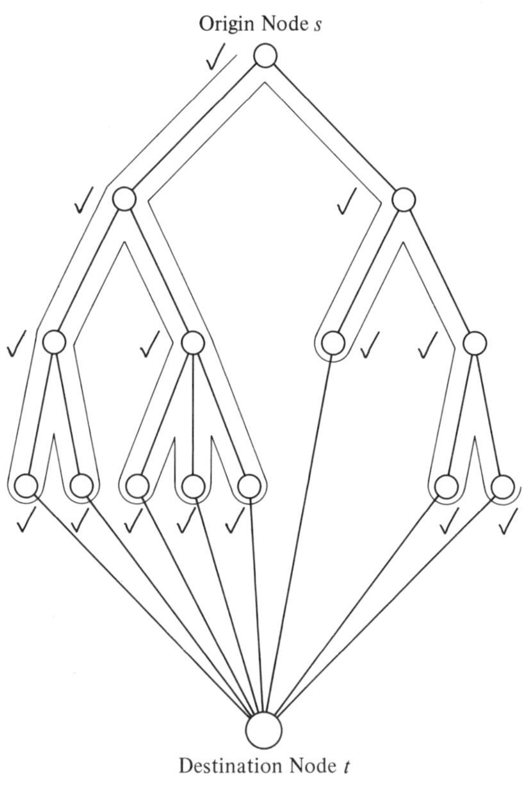

Figure 1.14 Searching a tree in depth-first fashion. The checkmarks show the order in which nodes enter the CLOSED list.

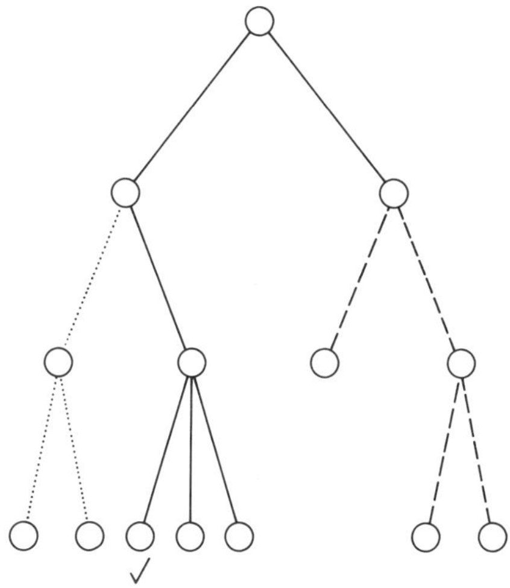

Figure 1.15 Memory requirements of depth-first search for the graph of Figure 1.14. At the time the node marked by the checkmark enters the CLOSED list, only the solid-line portion of the tree is needed in memory. The dotted-line portion has been generated and purged from memory based on the rule that it is unnecessary to store a node with all successors in CLOSED. The broken-line portion of the tree has not yet been generated.

algorithm (see [P2] and Problem 27). Another possibility is *to place in step 1a the node j at the top of OPEN if j currently belongs to CLOSED, to the bottom of OPEN if j does not belong to CLOSED or OPEN, and to leave j in its current position in OPEN if it belongs to OPEN*. This algorithm was suggested by Pape [P4] and turns out to be very effective for important classes of problems [D6].

We mentioned earlier that the key idea of the algorithm is to save computation by foregoing the examination of nodes j that cannot lie on a shortest path. This is based on the test $d_i + a_{ij} <$ UPPER that node j must pass before it can be placed in the OPEN list in step 1a. We can strengthen this test if we can find a *positive underestimate* h_j of the shortest distance of node j to the destination. Such an estimate can be obtained from special knowledge about the problem at hand. We may speed up the computation substantially by placing a node j in OPEN in step 1a when $d_i + a_{ij} + h_j <$ UPPER (instead of $d_i + a_{ij} <$ UPPER). In this way, fewer nodes will potentially be placed in OPEN before termination. Using the fact that h_j is an underestimate of the true shortest distance from j to the destination, the argument given earlier shows that the algorithm will terminate with a correct shortest path.

The idea just described is one way to sharpen the test $d_i + a_{ij} <$ UPPER for admission of node j into the OPEN list. An alternative idea is to try to reduce the value of UPPER by obtaining for the node j in step 1a an *overestimate* h_j of the shortest distance from j to the destination. Then if $d_j + h_j <$ UPPER after step 1a, we can reduce UPPER to $d_j + h_j$, thereby making the test for future admissibility into OPEN more stringent. This idea is used in some versions of the branch-and-bound algorithm, one of which we now briefly describe (see also [P2] and [P9] for further discussion).

Example 3

Branch-and-Bound Algorithm. Consider a problem of minimizing a cost function $f(x)$ over a *finite* set of feasible solutions X. The branch-and-bound algorithm uses an acyclic graph with nodes that correspond on a one-to-one basis with a collection $\mathcal{N}$ of subsets of X. We require the following:

1. $X \in \mathcal{N}$ (i.e., the set of all solutions is a node).
2. If x is a solution, then $\{x\} \in \mathcal{N}$ (i.e., all solutions viewed as singleton sets are nodes).
3. If $Y \in \mathcal{N}$ contains more than one solution $x \in X$, then there exist $Y_1, \ldots, Y_n \in \mathcal{N}$ such that $Y_i \neq Y$ for all i and
$$\bigcup_{i=1}^{n} Y_i = Y.$$
Y is called the *parent* of $Y_1, \ldots, Y_n$, and $Y_1, \ldots, Y_n$ are called the *sons* of Y.
4. Each node other than X has at least one parent.

It is clear that $\mathcal{N}$ defines an acyclic graph with root node X and terminal nodes $\{x\}$, $x \in X$ (see Figure 1.16). If Y_i is a son of Y, we assume that there is an arc connecting Y and Y_i. Suppose that for every nonterminal node Y there is an algorithm that calculates upper and lower bounds $\underline{f}_Y$ and $\overline{f}_Y$ for the minimum cost over Y:

$$\underline{f}_Y \leq \min_{x \in Y} f(x) \leq \overline{f}_Y.$$

Assume further that the upper and lower bounds are exact for a singleton solution node,

$$\underline{f}_{\{x\}} = f(x) = \overline{f}_{\{x\}}, \qquad \text{for all } x \in X.$$

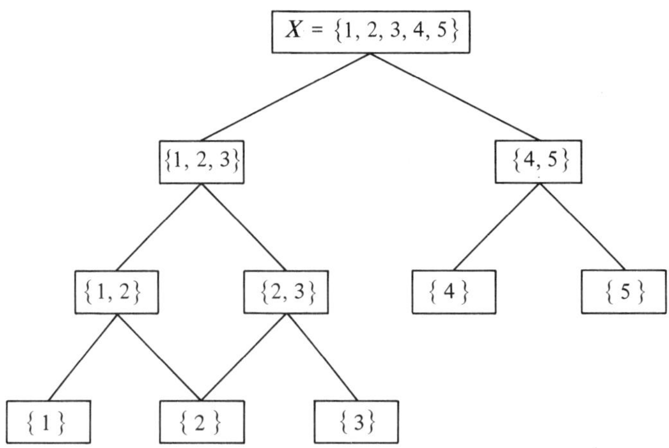

Figure 1.16 A tree corresponding to a branch-and-bound algorithm. Each node (subset) except those consisting of a single solution is partitioned into several other nodes (subsets).

Define now the length of an arc involving a parent Y and a son Y_i to be the lower bound difference

$$\underline{f}_{Y_i} - \underline{f}_Y.$$

Then evidently for every node Y the lower bound $\underline{f}_Y$ is the length of any path from the origin node X to Y. Because of our assumption $\underline{f}_{\{x\}} = f(x)$ for all feasible solutions $x \in X$, it is clear that finding a shortest path from the origin node to one of the singleton nodes is equivalent to minimizing $f(x)$ over $x \in X$.

Consider now a variation of the shortest path algorithm discussed earlier where in addition we use our knowledge of the upper bounds $\overline{f}_Y$ to reduce the value of UPPER. Initially, OPEN contains just X, CLOSED is empty, and UPPER equals $\overline{f}_X$.

Step 1 Remove a node Y from OPEN and place it in CLOSED. For each son Y_j of Y, go to Step 2.

Step 2 If $\underline{f}_{Y_j} < \text{UPPER}$, then place Y_j in OPEN. If in addition $\overline{f}_{Y_j} < \text{UPPER}$, then set UPPER $= \overline{f}_{Y_j}$, and if Y_j consists of a single solution, mark that solution as being the best solution found so far.

Step 3 If OPEN is nonempty, go to step 1. Otherwise, terminate; the best solution found so far is optimal.

An alternative termination step 3 for the preceding algorithm is to set a tolerance $\epsilon > 0$ and check whether UPPER and the minimum lower bound $\underline{f}_Y$ over all sets Y in the OPEN list differ by less than ϵ. If so, the algorithm is terminated, and some set in OPEN must contain a solution within ϵ of being optimal. There are a number of other variations of the algorithm. For example, if the upper bound $\overline{f}_Y$ at a node is actually the cost $f(x)$ of some element $x \in Y$, then this element can be taken as the best solution found so far whenever $\overline{f}_Y < \text{UPPER}$ in step 2. Other variations relate to the method of selecting a node from OPEN in step 1. For example, two strategies of the best-first type are to select the node with minimal lower or upper bound. In closing, we note that applying branch and bound effectively requires the creative use of knowledge of the particular problem at hand. In particular, it is important to have algorithms for generating as sharp as practically possible upper and lower bounds at each node, since then fewer nodes will be admitted into OPEN, with attendant computational savings.

1.5 TIME LAGS, CORRELATED DISTURBANCES, AND FORECASTS

This section deals with situations where some of the assumptions in the basic problem formulation are not satisfied. We shall consider the case where there are time lags in the system equation, the case where the disturbances w_k are correlated, and the case where at time k a forecast on the future uncertainties $w_k, w_{k+1}, \ldots$ becomes available, thus updating the corresponding probability distributions. The situation where the system evolution may terminate prior to the final time either due to a random event or due to an action of the decision maker is covered in the problems. Generally, in all these cases it is possible to reformulate the problem into the framework of the basic problem by using the device of *state augmentation*. The (unavoidable) price paid, however, is an increase in complexity of the reformulated problem.

Time Lags

For simplicity, assume that there is at most a single period time lag in the state and control, that is, assume a system equation of the form

$$\begin{aligned} x_{k+1} &= f_k(x_k, x_{k-1}, u_k, u_{k-1}, w_k), \qquad k = 1, 2, \dots, N-1, \\ x_1 &= f_0(x_0, u_0, w_0). \end{aligned} \tag{1.18}$$

Time lags of more than one period can be handled by a straightforward extension.

Now if we introduce additional state variables y_k and s_k and make the identifications $y_k = x_{k-1}$, $s_k = u_{k-1}$, the system equation (1.18) yields, for $k = 1, 2, \dots, N-1$,

$$\begin{bmatrix} x_{k+1} \\ y_{k+1} \\ s_{k+1} \end{bmatrix} = \begin{bmatrix} f_k(x_k, y_k, u_k, s_k, w_k) \\ x_k \\ u_k \end{bmatrix}. \tag{1.19}$$

By defining $\tilde{x}_k = (x_k, y_k, s_k)$ as the new state, we have

$$\tilde{x}_{k+1} = \tilde{f}_k(\tilde{x}_k, u_k, w_k), \tag{1.20}$$

where the system function $\tilde{f}_k$ is defined in an obvious manner from (1.19). By using (1.20) as the system equation and by making a suitable reformulation of the cost functional, the problem is reduced to the basic problem without time lags. Naturally, the control law $\{\mu_0, \dots, \mu_{N-1}\}$ that is sought will consist of functions μ_k of the new state $\tilde{x}_k$, or equivalently μ_k *will be a function of the present state* x_k *as well as past state* x_{k-1} *and control* u_{k-1}. The DP algorithm (in terms of the variables of the original problem) is

$$J_N(x_N) = g_N(x_N),$$

$$\begin{aligned} J_{N-1}(x_{N-1}, x_{N-2}, u_{N-2}) = \min_{u_{N-1} \in U_{N-1}(x_{N-1})} \ \underset{w_{N-1}}{E} \{ & g_{N-1}(x_{N-1}, u_{N-1}, w_{N-1}) \\ & + J_N[f_{N-1}(x_{N-1}, x_{N-2}, u_{N-1}, u_{N-2}, w_{N-1})]\}, \end{aligned}$$

$$\begin{aligned} J_k(x_k, x_{k-1}, u_{k-1}) = \min_{u_k \in U_k(x_k)} \ \underset{w_k}{E} \{ & g_k(x_k, u_k, w_k) \\ & + J_{k+1}[f_k(x_k, x_{k-1}, u_k, u_{k-1}, w_k), x_k, u_k]\}, \\ & \qquad k = 1, \dots, N-2, \end{aligned}$$

$$\begin{aligned} J_0(x_0) = \min_{u_0 \in U_0(x_0)} \ \underset{w_0}{E} \{ & g_0(x_0, u_0, w_0) \\ & + J_1[f_0(x_0, u_0, w_0), x_0, u_0]\}. \end{aligned}$$

We note that similar reformulations are possible when time lags appear in the cost functional, for example, in the case where the expression to be minimized is of the form

$$E\left\{g_N(x_N, x_{N-1}) + \sum_{k=0}^{N-1} g_k(x_k, x_{k-1}, u_k, w_k)\right\}.$$

The extreme case of time lags in the cost functional is when it has the nonadditive form

$$E\{g_N(x_N, x_{N-1}, \ldots, x_0, u_{N-1}, \ldots, u_0, w_{N-1}, \ldots, w_0)\}.$$

Then, to reduce the problem to the form of the basic problem, the augmented state $\tilde{x}_k$ at time k must include

$$(x_k, x_{k-1}, \ldots, x_0, u_{k-1}, \ldots, u_0, w_{k-1}, \ldots, w_0)$$

and the reformulated cost functional takes the form

$$E\{g_N(\tilde{x}_N)\}, \qquad \text{where} \qquad \tilde{x}_N = (x_0, \ldots, x_N, u_0, \ldots, u_{N-1}, w_0, \ldots, w_{N-1}).$$

The control law sought consists of functions μ_k of the present and past states $x_k, \ldots, x_0$, the past controls $u_{k-1}, \ldots, u_0$, and the past disturbances $w_{k-1}, \ldots, w_0$. Naturally, we must assume that past disturbances are known to the controller for otherwise we are faced with a problem with imperfect state information. The DP algorithm takes the form

$$\begin{aligned} &J_{N-1}(x_0, \ldots, x_{N-1}, u_0, \ldots, u_{N-2}, w_0, \ldots, w_{N-2}) \\ &\quad = \min_{u_{N-1}\in U_{N-1}(x_{N-1})} \ \mathop{E}_{w_{N-1}} \{g_N(x_0, \ldots, x_{N-1}, f_{N-1}(x_{N-1}, u_{N-1}, w_{N-1}), \\ &\qquad\qquad u_0, \ldots, u_{N-1}, w_0, \ldots, w_{N-1})\}. \end{aligned}$$

$$\begin{aligned} &J_k(x_0, \ldots, x_k, u_0, \ldots, u_{k-1}, w_0, \ldots, w_{k-1}) \\ &\quad = \min_{u_k\in U_k(x_k)} \ \mathop{E}_{w_k}\{J_{k+1}(x_0, \ldots, x_k, f_k(x_k, u_k, w_k), \\ &\qquad\qquad u_0, \ldots, u_k, w_0, \ldots, w_k)\}, \qquad k = 0, \ldots, N-2. \end{aligned}$$

Similar algorithms may be written for the case where the control constraint set depends on past states or controls, and so on.

Correlated Disturbances

We turn now to the case where the disturbances w_k are correlated. Here we shall assume that the w_k are elements of a Euclidean space and that the probability distribution of w_k does not depend explicitly on the current state x_k and control u_k, but rather it depends explicitly on the prior values of the disturbances $w_0, \ldots, w_{k-1}$. By using statistical methods (see, e.g., [A1]) it is often possible to represent the process $w_0, w_1, \ldots, w_{N-1}$ by means of a linear system

$$\begin{aligned} y_{k+1} &= A_k y_k + \xi_k, \qquad k = 0, 1, \ldots, N-1, \quad y_0 = 0, \\ w_k &= C_k y_{k+1}, \end{aligned}$$

where A_k, C_k are matrices of appropriate dimension and ξ_k are independent random vectors with given distribution. In other words, the correlated process $w_0, \ldots, w_{N-1}$ is represented as the output of a linear system perturbed by a white process, that is, a process consisting of independent random vectors as shown in Figure 1.17. By considering now y_k as additional state variables, we have a new system equation:

$$\begin{bmatrix} x_{k+1} \\ y_{k+1} \end{bmatrix} = \begin{bmatrix} f_k[x_k, u_k, C_k(A_k y_k + \xi_k)] \\ A_k y_k + \xi_k \end{bmatrix}. \tag{1.21}$$

By taking as the new state the pair $\tilde{x}_k = (x_k, y_k)$ and as new disturbance the vector ξ_k, we can write (1.21) as

$$\tilde{x}_{k+1} = \tilde{f}_k(\tilde{x}_k, u_k, \xi_k).$$

By suitable reformulation of the cost functional, the problem is reduced to the form of the basic problem. Note that it is necessary that y_k, $k = 1, \ldots, N-1$, can be observed by the controller in order for the problem to be one of perfect state information. This is true when the matrix C_{k-1} is the identity matrix and w_{k-1} is observable. The DP algorithm takes the form

$$J_N(x_N, y_N) = g_N(x_N),$$

$$J_k(x_k, y_k) = \min_{u_k \in U_k(x_k)} \underset{\xi_k}{E}\{g_k[x_k, u_k, C_k(A_k y_k + \xi_k)] + J_{k+1}[f_k[x_k, u_k, C_k(A_k y_k + \xi_k)], A_k y_k + \xi_k]\}.$$

When C_k is the identity matrix, the optimal controller is of the form

$$\{\mu_0^*(x_0), \mu_1^*(x_1, w_0), \ldots, \mu_{N-1}^*(x_{N-1}, w_{N-2})\}.$$

Forecasts

Finally, consider the case where at time k the decision maker has access to a forecast y_k that results in a reassessment of the probability distribution of w_k and possibly of future disturbances. For example, y_k may be an exact prediction of w_k or an exact prediction that the probability distribution of w_k is a specific one out of a finite collection of distributions. Forecasts that can be of interest in practice are, for example, probabilistic predictions on the state of the weather, the interest rate for money, and demand for inventory.

Generally, forecasts can be handled by state augmentation although

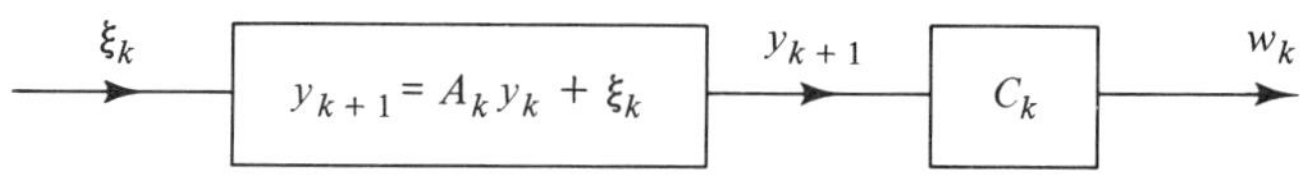

Figure 1.17 Representation of a correlated process $\{w_k\}$ as the output of a linear system driven by a white noise sequence $\{\xi_k\}$.

the reformulation into the form of the basic problem may be quite complex. We will treat here only a simple situation.

Consider the case where the probability distribution of w_k does not depend on x_k, u_k, $w_{k-1}, \ldots, w_0$. Assume that at the beginning of each period k the decision maker receives an accurate prediction that the next disturbance w_k will be selected in accordance with a particular probability distribution out of a finite collection of given distributions $\{P_{k|1}, \ldots, P_{k|n}\}$; that is, if the forecast is i, then w_k is selected according to $P_{k|i}$. The a priori probability that the forecast at time k will be i is p_i^k and is given. Thus the forecasting process can be represented by means of the equation

$$y_{k+1} = \xi_k, \tag{1.22}$$

where y_{k+1} can take the values $1, 2, \ldots, n$ and ξ_k is a random variable taking the values $1, 2, \ldots, n$ with probabilities $p_1^{k+1}, \ldots, p_n^{k+1}$. The interpretation here is that when ξ_k takes the value i, then w_{k+1} will occur in accordance with the probability distribution $P_{k+1|i}$.

By combining the system equation and (1.22), we obtain an augmented system given by

$$\begin{bmatrix} x_{k+1} \\ y_{k+1} \end{bmatrix} = \begin{bmatrix} f_k(x_k, u_k, w_k) \\ \xi_k \end{bmatrix} = \tilde{f}_k(\tilde{x}_k, u_k, \tilde{w}_k).$$

The new state is $\tilde{x}_k = (x_k, y_k)$ and the new disturbance is $\tilde{w}_k = (w_k, \xi_k)$. The probability distribution of $\tilde{w}_k$ is given in terms of the distributions $P_{k|i}$ and the probabilities p_i^k, and depends explicitly on $\tilde{x}_k$ (via y_k) but not on the prior disturbances $\tilde{w}_{k-1}, \ldots, \tilde{w}_0$. Thus by suitable reformulation of the cost functional, the problem can be cast into the framework of the basic problem. It is to be noted that the *control applied at each time is a function of both the current state and the current forecast.* The DP algorithm takes the form

$$J_N(x_N, y_N) = g_N(x_N),$$

$$J_k(x_k, y_k) = \min_{u_k \in U_k(x_k)} \mathop{E}_{w_k}\left\{ g_k(x_k, u_k, w_k) + \sum_{i=1}^{n} p_i^{k+1} J_{k+1}[f_k(x_k, u_k, w_k), i] | y_k \right\},$$

$$k = 0, 1, \ldots, N-1,$$

where the expectation over w_k is taken with respect to the probability distribution $P_{k|y_k}$, where y_k may take the values $1, 2, \ldots, n$. Extension to forecasts covering several periods can be handled similarly, albeit at the expense of increased complexity. Problems where forecasts can be affected by the control action also admit a similar treatment.

It should be clear from the preceding discussion that state augmentation is a very general and potent device for reformulating problems of decision under uncertainty into the basic problem form. One should also realize that there are many ways to reformulate a problem by augmenting the state in different ways. The basic guideline is to *select as the augmented state at time k only those variables the knowledge of which can be of benefit to the decision maker when making the kth decision.* For example, in the case of single period time lags it is intuitively obvious that the controller can benefit from knowing at time k the values of x_k, x_{k-1}, u_{k-1}, since these variables affect the value of the next state x_{k+1} through the system equation. The controller, however, has nothing to gain from knowing at time k the values of $x_{k-2}, x_{k-3}, \ldots, u_{k-2}, \ldots$, and for this reason these past states and controls need not be included in the augmented state, although their inclusion is technically possible. The theme of considering as state variables in the reformulated problem only those variables the knowledge of which would be beneficial to the decision making process will be predominant in the discussion of problems with imperfect state information (Chapter 3).

Finally, we note that whereas state augmentation is a convenient device, it tends to introduce both analytical and computational complexities, which in many cases are insurmountable.

1.6 NOTES

Dynamic programming is a simple mathematical technique that has been used for many years by engineers, mathematicians, and social scientists in a variety of contexts. It was Bellman, however, who realized in the early 1950s that DP could be developed (in conjunction with the then appearing digital computer) into a systematic tool for optimization. Bellman demonstrated the broad scope of DP and helped streamline its theory. His early books [B5, B6] are still popular reading. Other books related to DP are [H8], [H16], [K5], [K14], [N2], [R2], [W7], and [W11]. For a rigorous treatment of DP in general spaces that resolves the associated measurability issues and supplements the present text, see [B23]. For continuous-time formulations, see [B7] and [F3].

The connection of the Viterbi algorithm with the shortest path problem has been clarified in [O2] and [F4]. For further material on search methods and their use in game programs, see [P9]. For background on shortest paths, branch-and-bound, and combinatorial optimization see [P2].

As discussed in Section 1.1, the basic problem was formulated rigorously only for the case where the disturbance spaces are countable sets. *Nonetheless, the DP algorithm can often be utilized in a simple way when the countability assumption is not satisfied and there are further restrictions (such as measurability) on the class of admissible control laws.* The advanced reader will understand how this can be done by solving Problem 12, which shows that if one can find within a subset of control laws (such as those satisfying certain measurability restrictions) a control law that attains the minimum in the DP algorithm, then this control law is optimal. This fact may be used to establish rigorously many of our subsequent results concerning specific applications in Chapters 2 and 3. For example, in linear quadratic problems (Section 2.1) one determines from the DP equations a control law that is a linear function of the current state. When w_k can take uncountably many values, it is necessary that admissible control laws consist only of functions μ_k which are Borel measurable. Since the linear control law belongs to this class, the result of Problem 12 guarantees that this control law is optimal.

PROBLEMS

1. Use the DP algorithm to solve the following two problems:
   (a) minimize $\sum_{i=0}^{3} x_i^2 + u_i^2$
   subject to $x_0 = 0,\ x_4 = 8,\ u_i =$ nonnegative integer,
   $x_{i+1} = x_i + u_i,\ i = 0, 1, 2, 3;$
   (b) minimize $\sum_{i=0}^{3} x_i^2 + 2u_i^2$
   subject to $x_0 = 5,\ u_i \in \{0, 1, 2\},$
   $x_{i+1} = x_i - u_i,\ i = 0, 1, 2, 3.$
2. Air transportation is available between n cities, in some cases directly and in others through intermediate stops and change of carrier. The air fare between cities i and j is denoted $C_{ij}(C_{ij} = C_{ji})$, and for notational convenience we write $C_{ij} = \infty$ if there is no direct flight between i and j. The problem is to find the cheapest possible air fare for going from any city i to any other city j perhaps through intermediate stops. Formulate a DP algorithm for solving this problem. Solve the problem for $n = 6$ and $C_{12} = 30$, $C_{13} = 60$, $C_{14} = 25$, $C_{15} = C_{16} = \infty$, $C_{23} = C_{24} = C_{25} = \infty$, $C_{26} = 50$, $C_{34} = 35$, $C_{35} = C_{36} = \infty$, $C_{45} = 15$, $C_{46} = \infty$, $C_{56} = 15$.
3. Suppose we have a machine that is either running or broken down. If it runs throughout one week, it makes a gross profit of \$100. If it fails during the week, gross profit is zero. If it is running at the start of the week and we perform preventive maintenance, the probability that it will fail during the week is 0.4. If we do not perform such maintenance, the probability of failure is 0.7. However, maintenance will cost \$20. When the machine is broken down at the start of the week, it may either be repaired at a cost of \$40, in which case it will fail during the week with a probability of 0.4, or it may be replaced at a cost of \$150 by a new machine that is guaranteed to run through its first week of operation. Find the optimal repair, replacement, and maintenance policy that maximizes total profit over four weeks, assuming a new machine at the start of the first week.
4. A game of the blackjack variety is played by two players as follows: Both players throw a die. The first player, knowing his opponent's result, may stop or may throw the die again and add the result to the result of his previous throw. He then may stop or throw again and add the result of the new throw to the sum of his previous throws. He may repeat this process as many times as he wishes. If his sum exceeds seven (i.e., he busts), he loses the game. If he stops before exceeding seven, the second player takes over and throws the die successively until the sum of his throws is four or higher. If the sum of the second player is over seven, he loses the game. Otherwise the player with

the larger sum wins, and in case of a tie the second player wins. The problem is to determine a stopping strategy for the first player that maximizes his probability of winning for each possible initial throw of the second player. Formulate the problem in terms of DP and find an optimal stopping strategy for the case where the second player's initial throw is three. *Hint:* Take $N = 6$ and a state space consisting of the following 15 states:

x^1: busted,

x^{1+i}: already stopped at sum i $(1 \leq i \leq 7)$,

x^{8+i}: current sum is i but the player has not yet stopped $(1 \leq i \leq 7)$.

The optimal strategy is to throw until the sum is four or higher.

5. *Min–Max Problems.* In the framework of the basic problem, consider the case where the disturbances $w_0, w_1, \ldots, w_{N-1}$ do not have a probabilistic description but rather are known to belong to corresponding given sets $W_k(x_k, u_k) \subset D_k$, $k = 0, 1, \ldots, N-1$, which may depend on the current state x_k and control u_k. Consider the problem of finding a control law $\pi = \{\mu_0, \ldots, \mu_{N-1}\}$ with $\mu_k(x_k) \in U_k(x_k)$ for all x_k, k, which minimizes the cost functional

$$J_\pi(x_0) = \max_{\substack{w_k \in W_k[x_k, \mu_k(x_k)] \\ k=0,1,\ldots,N-1}} \left\{ g_N(x_N) + \sum_{k=0}^{N-1} g_k[x_k, \mu_k(x_k), w_k] \right\}.$$

The DP algorithm for this problem takes the form

$$J_N(x_N) = g_N(x_N),$$

$$J_k(x_k) = \min_{u_k \in U(x_k)} \max_{w_k \in W_k(x_k, u_k)} \{g_k(x_k, u_k, w_k) + J_{k+1}[f_k(x_k, u_k, w_k)]\}.$$

Assuming that $J_k(x_k) > -\infty$ for all x_k and k, show that the optimal cost equals $J_0(x_0)$. *Hint:* Imitate the proof for the stochastic case; prove and use the following fact: If U, W, X are three sets, $f : W \to X$ is a function, and M is the set of all functions $\mu : X \to U$, then for any functions $G_0 : W \to (-\infty, \infty]$, $G_1 : X \times U \to (-\infty, \infty]$ such that

$$\min_{u \in U} G_1[f(w), u] > -\infty, \qquad \text{for all } w \in W$$

we have

$$\min_{\mu \in M} \max_{w \in W} \{G_0(w) + G_1[f(w), \mu(f(w))]\} = \max_{w \in W} \{G_0(w) + \min_{u \in U} G_1[f(w), u]\}.$$

6. *Discounted Cost per Stage.* In the framework of the basic problem, consider the case where the cost functional is of the form

$$E\left\{ \alpha^N g_N(x_N) + \sum_{k=0}^{N-1} \alpha^k g_k(x_k, u_k, w_k) \right\},$$

where α is a discount factor with $0 < \alpha < 1$. Show that an alternate form of the DP algorithm is given by

$$V_N(x_N) = g_N(x_N),$$

$$V_k(x_k) = \min_{u_k \in U_k(x_k)} E\{g_k(x_k, u_k, w_k) + \alpha V_{k+1}[f_k(x_k, u_k, w_k)]\}.$$

7. *Exponential Cost Functional.* In the framework of the basic problem, consider

the case where the cost functional is of the form

$$\underset{\substack{w_k \\ k=0,1,\ldots,N-1}}{E}\left\{\exp\left[g_N(x_N) + \sum_{k=0}^{N-1} g_k(x_k, u_k, w_k)\right]\right\}.$$

(a) Show that the optimal cost and an optimal policy can be obtained from the last step of the DP algorithm

$$J_N(x_N) = \exp[g_N(x_N)],$$

$$J_k(x_k) = \min_{u_k \in U_k(x_k)} \underset{w_k}{E}\{J_{k+1}[f_k(x_k, u_k, w_k)] \exp[g_k(x_k, u_k, w_k)]\}.$$

Show that the algorithm yields an optimal control law if one exists.

(b) Define the functions $V_k(x_k) = \ln J_k(x_k)$. Assume also that g_k is a function of x_k and u_k only (and not of w_k). Show that the above DP algorithm can be rewritten

$$V_N(x_N) = g_N(x_N),$$

$$V_k(x_k) = \min_{u_k \in U_k(x_k)}\left[g_k(x_k, u_k) + \ln \underset{w_k}{E}\{\exp V_{k+1}[f_k(x_k, u_k, w_k)]\}\right].$$

8. *Terminating Process.* Consider the case in the basic problem where the system evolution terminates at time i when a given value $\overline{w}_i$ of the disturbance at time i occurs, or when a termination decision u_i is made by the controller. If termination occurs at time i, the resulting cost is

$$T + \sum_{k=0}^{i} g_k(x_k, u_k, w_k),$$

where T is a termination cost. If the process has not terminated up to the final time N, the resulting cost is $g_N(x_N) + \sum_{k=0}^{N-1} g_k(x_k, u_k, w_k)$. Reformulate the problem into the framework of the basic problem. *Hint:* Augment the state space with a special termination state.

9. *Multiplicative Cost.* In the framework of the basic problem, consider the case where the cost functional has the multiplicative form

$$\underset{\substack{w_k \\ k=0,\ldots,N-1}}{E}\{g_N(x_N) \cdot g_{N-1}(x_{N-1}, u_{N-1}, w_{N-1}) \cdots g_0(x_0, u_0, w_0)\}.$$

Devise an algorithm of the DP type for this problem under the assumption $g_k(x_k, u_k, w_k) \geqslant 0$ for all x_k, u_k, w_k, and k.

10. Assume that we have a vessel whose maximum weight capacity is z and whose cargo is to consist of different quantities of N different items. Let v_i denote the value of the ith type of item, w_i the weight of ith type of item, and x_i the number of items of type i that are loaded in the vessel. The problem of determining the most valuable cargo is that of maximizing $\sum_{i=1}^{N} x_i v_i$ subject to the constraints $\sum_{i=1}^{N} x_i w_i \leqslant z$ and $x_i = 0, 1, 2, \ldots$. Formulate this problem in terms of DP.

11. Consider a device consisting of N stages connected in series, where each stage consists of a particular component. The components are subject to failure, and to increase the reliability of the device duplicate components are provided. For $j = 1, 2, \ldots, N$, let $(1 + m_j)$ be the number of components for the jth stage, let $p_j(m_j)$ be the probability of successful operation of the jth stage when

$(1 + m_j)$ components are used, and let c_j denote the cost of a single component at the jth stage. Consider the problem of finding the number of components at each stage that maximize the reliability of the device expressed by

$$p_1(m_1) \cdot p_2(m_2) \cdots p_N(m_N)$$

subject to the cost constraint $\Sigma_{j=1}^{N} c_j m_j \leq A$, where $A > 0$ is given. Formulate the problem in terms of DP.

12. *Minimization over a Subset of Policies.* This problem is primarily of theoretical interest (see the end of the Notes to this chapter). Consider a variation of the basic problem whereby we seek

$$\min_{\pi \in \tilde{\Pi}} J_\pi(x_0),$$

where $\tilde{\Pi}$ is some given *subset* of the set of sequences $\{\mu_0, \mu_1, \ldots, \mu_{N-1}\}$ of functions $\mu_k : S_k \to C_k$ with $\mu_k(x_k) \in U_k(x_k)$ for all $x_k \in S_k$. Assume that

$$\pi^* = \{\mu_0^*, \mu_1^*, \ldots, \mu_{N-1}^*\}$$

belongs to $\tilde{\Pi}$ and attains the minimum in the DP algorithm; that is, for all $k = 0, 1, \ldots, N-1$ and $x_k \in S_k$

$$\begin{aligned} J_k(x_k) &= \mathop{E}_{w_k}\{g_k[x_k, \mu_k^*(x_k), w_k] + J_{k+1}[f_k(x_k, \mu_k^*(x_k), w_k)]\} \\ &= \min_{u_k \in U_k(x_k)} \mathop{E}_{w_k}\{g_k(x_k, u_k, w_k) + J_{k+1}[f_k(x_k, u_k, w_k)]\}, \end{aligned}$$

with $J_N(x_N) = g_N(x_N)$. Assume further that the functions J_k are real valued and the preceding expectations are well defined and finite. Show that π^* is optimal within $\tilde{\Pi}$ and

$$J_0(x_0) = \min_{\pi \in \tilde{\Pi}} J_\pi(x_0) = J_{\pi^*}(x_0).$$

13. *Semilinear Systems.* Consider a problem involving the system

$$x_{k+1} = A_k x_k + f_k(u_k) + w_k,$$

where $x_k \in R^n$, f_k are given functions, and A_k and w_k are random $n \times n$ matrices and n-vectors, respectively, with given probability distributions that do not depend on x_k, u_k or prior values of A_k and w_k. Assume that the cost functional is of the form

$$\mathop{E}_{\substack{A_k, w_k \\ k=0,1,\ldots,N-1}} \left\{ c_N' x_N + \sum_{k=0}^{N-1} [c_k' x_k + g_k[\mu_k(x_k)]] \right\},$$

where c_k are given vectors and g_k given functions. Show that if the optimal cost for this problem is finite and the control constraint sets $U_k(x_k)$ are independent of x_k, then the cost-to-go functions of the DP algorithm are affine (linear plus constant). Assuming that there is at least one optimal policy, show that there exists an optimal policy that consists of constant functions μ_k^*; that is, $\mu_k^*(x_k) =$ constant for all $x_k \in R^n$.

14. A farmer annually producing x_k units of a certain crop stores $(1 - u_k)x_k$ units of his production, where $0 \leq u_k \leq 1$, and invests the remaining $u_k x_k$ units, thus increasing the next year's production to a level x_{k+1} given by

$$x_{k+1} = x_k + w_k u_k x_k, \qquad k = 0, 1, \ldots, N-1.$$

The scalars w_k are independent random variables with identical probability distributions that do not depend either on x_k or u_k. Furthermore, $E\{w_k\} = \overline{w} > 0$. The problem is to find the optimal investment policy that maximizes the total expected product stored over N years

$$\underset{\substack{w_k \\ k=0,1,\ldots,N-1}}{E} \left\{ x_N + \sum_{k=0}^{N-1} (1 - u_k) x_k \right\}.$$

Show that one optimal control law is given by:

(a) If $\overline{w} > 1$, $\mu_0^*(x_0) = \cdots = \mu_{N-1}^*(x_{N-1}) = 1$.

(b) If $0 < \overline{w} < 1/N$, $\mu_0^*(x_0) = \cdots = \mu_{N-1}^*(x_{N-1}) = 0$.

(c) If $1/N \leq \overline{w} \leq 1$,

$$\mu_0^*(x_0) = \cdots = \mu_{N-\bar{k}-1}^*(x_{N-\bar{k}-1}) = 1,$$

$$\mu_{N-\bar{k}}^*(x_{N-\bar{k}}) = \cdots = \mu_{N-1}^*(x_{N-1}) = 0,$$

where $\bar{k}$ is such that $1/(\bar{k} + 1) < \overline{w} \leq 1/\bar{k}$. (Note that this control law consists of constant functions.)

15. Let x_k denote the number of educators in a certain country at time k and let y_k denote the number of research scientists at time k. New scientists (potential educators or research scientists) are produced during the kth period by educators at a rate γ_k per educator, while educators and research scientists leave the field due to death, retirement, and transfer at a rate δ_k. The scalars γ_k, $k = 0, 1, \ldots, N - 1$, are independent identically distributed random variables taking values within a closed and bounded interval of positive numbers. Similarly δ_k, $k = 0, 1, \ldots, N - 1$, are independent identically distributed and take values in an interval $[\delta, \delta']$ with $0 < \delta \leq \delta' < 1$. By means of incentives a science policy maker can determine the proportion u_k of new scientists produced at time k who become educators. Thus the number of research scientists and educators evolves according to the equations

$$x_{k+1} = (1 - \delta_k)x_k + u_k \gamma_k x_k,$$
$$y_{k+1} = (1 - \delta_k)y_k + (1 - u_k)\gamma_k x_k.$$

The initial numbers x_0, y_0 are known, and it is required to find a policy $\{\mu_0^*(x_0, y_0), \ldots, \mu_{N-1}^*(x_{N-1}, y_{N-1})\}$ with

$$0 < \alpha \leq \mu_k^*(x_k, y_k) \leq \beta < 1, \qquad \text{for all } x_k, y_k, \text{ and } k,$$

which maximizes $E_{\gamma_k, \delta_k}\{y_N\}$ (i.e., the expected final number of research scientists after N periods). The scalars α and β are given.

(a) Show that the cost-to-go functions $J_k(x_k, y_k)$ are linear; that is, for some scalars λ_k, μ_k

$$J_k(x_k, y_k) = \lambda_k x_k + \mu_k y_k.$$

(b) Derive an optimal policy $\{\mu_0^*, \ldots, \mu_{N-1}^*\}$ under the assumption $E\{\gamma_k\} > E\{\delta_k\}$, and show that this optimal policy can consist of constant functions.

(c) Assume that the proportion of new scientists who become educators at time k is $u_k + \varepsilon_k$ (rather than u_k), where ε_k are identically distributed independent random variables that are also independent of γ_k, δ_k and take values in the interval $[-\alpha, 1 - \beta]$. Derive the form of the cost-to-go functions and the optimal policy.

16. *DP on Two Parallel Processors* [*L1*]. Formulate a DP algorithm to solve the deterministic problem of Section 1.3 on a parallel computer with two processors. One processor should execute a forward algorithm and the other a backward algorithm.

17. The paragraphing problem deals with breaking up a sequence of N words $w_1, \ldots, w_N$ with lengths $L_1, \ldots, L_N$ into lines of length A. In a simple version of the problem, words are separated by blanks whose ideal width is b, but blanks can stretch or shrink if necessary, so that a line $w_i, w_{i+1}, \ldots, w_{i+k}$ has length exactly A. The cost associated with the line is $(k + 1)\,|b' - b|$, where $b' = (A - L_i - \cdots - L_{i+k})/(k + 1)$ is the actual average width of the blanks, except if we have the last line ($N = i + k$), in which case the cost is zero when $b' \geq b$. Formulate a DP algorithm for solving for the minimum cost separation. *Hint:* Consider the subproblems of optimally separating $w_i, \ldots, w_N$ for $i = 1, \ldots, N$.

18. *Computer Assignment.* In the classical game of blackjack the player draws cards knowing only one card of the dealer. The player loses upon reaching a sum of cards exceeding 21. If the player stops before exceeding 21, the dealer draws cards until reaching 17 or higher. The dealer loses upon reaching a sum exceeding 21 or a lower sum than the player's. If player and dealer end up with an equal sum no one wins, and in all other cases the dealer wins. An ace for the player may be counted as a 1 or an 11 as the player chooses. An ace for the dealer is counted as an 11 if this results in a sum from 17 to 21 and as a 1 otherwise. Jacks, queens, and kings count as 10 for both dealer and player. We assume an infinite card deck so the probability of a particular card showing up is independent of earlier cards.

(a) For every possible initial dealer card, calculate the probability that the dealer will reach a sum of 17, 18, 19, 20, 21, or over 21.

(b) Calculate the optimal choice of the player (draw or stop) for each of the possible combinations of dealer's card and player's sum of 12 to 20. Assume that the player's cards do not include an ace.

(c) Repeat part (b) for the case where the player's cards include an ace.

19. Consider a smaller version of a popular puzzle game. Three square tiles numbered 1, 2, and 3 are placed in a 2×2 grid with one space left empty. The two tiles adjacent to the empty space can be moved into that space, thereby creating new configurations. Use a DP argument to answer the question whether it is possible to generate a given configuration starting from any other configuration.

20. From a pile of eleven matchsticks, two players take turns removing one or four sticks. The player who removes the last stick wins. Use a DP argument to show that there is a winning strategy for the player who plays first.

21. *The Counterfeit Coin Problem.* We are given six coins, one of which is counterfeit and is known to be heavier or lighter than the rest. Construct a strategy to find the counterfeit coin using a two-pan scale in a minimum average number of tries. *Hint:* There are two initial decisions that make sense: (1) test two of the coins against two others, and (2) test one of the coins against one other.

22. Given a sequence of matrix multiplications

$$M_1 M_2 \cdots M_k M_{k+1} \cdots M_N,$$

where M_k, $k = 1, \ldots, N$, is of dimension $n_k \times n_{k+1}$, the order in which multiplications are carried out can make a difference. For example, if $n_1 = 1$, $n_2 = 10$, and $n_3 = 1$, the calculation $((M_1M_2)M_3)$ requires 20 multiplications, but the calculation $(M_1(M_2M_3))$ requires 200 multiplications. Derive a DP algorithm for finding the optimal multiplication order. Solve the problem for $n_1 = 2$, $n_2 = 10$, $n_3 = 5$, and $n_4 = 1$.

23. *Doubling Algorithms.* Consider a deterministic finite state problem that is time invariant in the sense that the state and control spaces, the cost per stage, and the system equation are the same for each time period. Let $J_k(x, y)$ be the optimal cost to reach state y at time k from state x at time 0. Show that for all k

$$J_{2k}(x, y) = \min_z\{J_k(x, z) + J_k(z, y)\}.$$

Discuss how this equation may be used with advantage to solve problems with a large number of stages.

24. *Complexity of DP for Shortest Paths.* Consider the shortest path algorithm

$$J_k(i) = \min_{j=1,\ldots,N} \{c_{ij} + J_{k+1}(j)\}$$

of Section 1.3. Suppose m is the largest number of arcs in a shortest path from any node $1, \ldots, N$ to the destination node t. Show that the algorithm can be terminated after m steps and that the number of arithmetic operations required is bounded by γmL, where L is the number of arcs and γ is a number that is independent of m, L, and N.

25. *Monotonicity Property of DP.* An evident, yet very important property of the DP algorithm is that if the terminal cost g_N is changed to a uniformly larger cost $\bar{g}_N$ [i.e., $g_N(x_N) \leq \bar{g}_N(x_N)$ for all x_N], then the corresponding costs $J_k(x_k)$ will be uniformly increased. More generally, given two functions J_{k+1} and $\bar{J}_{k+1}$ with $J_{k+1}(x_{k+1}) \leq \bar{J}_{k+1}(x_{k+1})$ for all x_{k+1}, we have, for all x_k and $u_k \in U_k(x_k)$,

$$\begin{aligned} &\underset{w_k}{E}\{g_k(x_k, u_k, w_k) + J_{k+1}[f_k(x_k, u_k, w_k)]\} \\ &\leq \underset{w_k}{E}\{g_k(x_k, u_k, w_k) + \bar{J}_{k+1}[f_k(x_k, u_k, w_k)]\}. \end{aligned}$$

Suppose now that in the basic problem the system and cost are time invariant; that is, $S_k \equiv S$, $C_k \equiv C$, $D_k \equiv D$, $f_k \equiv f$, $U_k(x_k) \equiv U(x_k)$, and $g_k \equiv g$. Show that if in the DP algorithm we have $J_{N-1}(x) \leq J_N(x)$ for all $x \in S$ then

$$J_k(x) \leq J_{k+1}(x), \qquad \text{for all } x \in S \text{ and } k.$$

Similarly, if we have $J_{N-1}(x) \geq J_N(x)$ for all $x \in S$, then

$$J_k(x) \geq J_{k+1}(x), \qquad \text{for all } x \in S \text{ and } k.$$

26. Modify the forward search algorithm of Section 1.4 so that it simultaneously finds the shortest paths from the origin s to several destination nodes. *Hint:* Connect the destination nodes with a new artificial node using arcs with very large length.

27. *Dijkstra's Algorithm for Shortest Paths.* Consider the best-first version of the forward search algorithm of Section 1.4. Here at each iteration we select a node j from OPEN that has minimum estimate d_j over all nodes in OPEN.

(a) Show that each node j will enter OPEN at most once and show that at the time it enters CLOSED its estimate d_j is equal to the shortest distance from s to j.

(b) Show that the number of arithmetic operations required for termination is bounded by cN^2 where N is the number of nodes and c is some constant.

28. *Distributed Asynchronous Shortest Path Computation* [B19]. Consider the problem of finding a shortest path from nodes 1, 2, . . ., N to node t, and assume that all arc lengths c_{ij} are positive. Consider the iteration

$$d_i^{k+1} = \min_j\{c_{ij} + d_j^k\}, \qquad i = 1, 2, \ldots, N,$$
$$d_t^{k+1} = 0. \tag{1.23}$$

(a) It was shown in Section 1.3 that, if the initial condition is $d_i^0 = \infty$ for $i = 1, \ldots, N$ and $d_t^0 = 0$, then (1.23) yields the shortest distances d_i^* in N steps. Show that if the initial condition is $d_i^0 = 0$, for all $i = 1, \ldots, N, t$, then (1.23) yields the shortest distances in a finite number of steps. Provide an upper bound for this number in terms of the problem data.

(b) Assume that the iteration

$$d_i := \min_j\{c_{ij} + d_j\} \tag{1.24}$$

is executed at node i in parallel with the corresponding iteration for d_j at every other node j. However, the times of execution of this iteration at the various nodes are not synchronized. Furthermore, each node i communicates the results of its latest computation of d_i at arbitrary times with potentially large communication delays. Therefore, there is the possibility of a node executing iteration (1.24) several times before receiving a communication from every other neighboring node. Assume that each node never stops executing iteration (1.24) and transmitting the result to the other nodes. Show that the estimates d_i^T available at time T at the corresponding nodes i equal the shortest distances d_i^* for all T after a finite time $\overline{T}$. *Hint:* Let $\overline{d}_i^k$ and $\underline{d}_i^k$ be the estimates generated by (1.23) when starting from the first and the second initial conditions in part (a), respectively. Show that for every k there exists a time T_k such that for all $T \geq T_k$ we have $\underline{d}_i^k \leq d_i^T \leq \overline{d}_i^k$.

CHAPTER TWO

Applications in Specific Areas

2.1 LINEAR SYSTEMS AND QUADRATIC COST: THE CERTAINTY EQUIVALENCE PRINCIPLE

In this section we consider the special case of a linear system

$$x_{k+1} = A_k x_k + B_k u_k + w_k, \qquad k = 0, 1, \dots, N-1,$$

where the objective is to find a control law minimizing the quadratic cost functional

$$\underset{\substack{w_k \\ k=0,\dots,N-1}}{E} \left\{ x_N' Q_N x_N + \sum_{k=0}^{N-1} (x_k' Q_k x_k + u_k' R_k u_k) \right\}.$$

In these expressions, x_k and u_k are vectors of dimension n and m, respectively, and the matrices A_k, B_k, Q_k, R_k are given and have appropriate dimension. We assume that Q_k are symmetric positive semidefinite matrices and R_k are symmetric and positive definite. The disturbances w_k are independent random vectors with given probability distributions that do not depend on x_k, u_k. Furthermore, the vectors w_k have zero mean and finite second moments. The control u_k is unconstrained.

This is a popular formulation of a regulation problem whereby we want to keep the state of the system close to the origin. Such problems are common in the theory of automatic control of a motion or a process. The quadratic cost functional is often reasonable since it induces a high penalty for large deviations of the state from the origin but a relatively small penalty for small deviations. However, the quadratic cost is frequently used even when it is not entirely justified, since it leads to an elegant analytical solution that can be easily implemented. A number of variations and generalizations have similar solutions. For example, the disturbances w_k could have nonzero means and the quadratic cost could have the form

$$E\left\{(x_N - \bar{x}_N)'Q_N(x_N - \bar{x}_N) + \sum_{k=0}^{N-1} [(x_k - \bar{x}_k)'Q_k(x_k - \bar{x}_k) + u_k'R_ku_k]\right\},$$

which expresses a desire to keep the state of the system close to a certain given trajectory $(\bar{x}_0, \bar{x}_1, \ldots, \bar{x}_N)$ rather than close to the origin. Another generalization is when A_k, B_k are independent random matrices, rather than being known. This case is considered at the end of this section.

Applying now the DP algorithm, we have

$$J_N(x_N) = x_N'Q_Nx_N, \tag{2.1}$$

$$J_k(x_k) = \min_{u_k} E\{x_k'Q_kx_k + u_k'R_ku_k + J_{k+1}(A_kx_k + B_ku_k + w_k)\}. \tag{2.2}$$

It turns out that the cost-to-go functions J_k are quadratic and as a result the optimal control law is a linear function of the state. These facts can be verified by straightforward calculation. By expansion of the quadratic form (2.1) in (2.2) for $k = N - 1$, and by using the fact $E\{w_{N-1}\} = 0$ to eliminate the term $E\{w_{N-1}'Q_N(A_{N-1}x_{N-1} + B_{N-1}u_{N-1})\}$, we have

$$\begin{aligned} J_{N-1}(x_{N-1}) = x_{N-1}'Q_{N-1}x_{N-1} + \min_{u_{N-1}}[&u_{N-1}'R_{N-1}u_{N-1} \\ &+ u_{N-1}'B_{N-1}'Q_NB_{N-1}u_{N-1} + x_{N-1}'A_{N-1}'Q_NA_{N-1}x_{N-1} \\ &+ 2x_{N-1}'A_{N-1}'Q_NB_{N-1}u_{N-1}] + E\{w_{N-1}'Q_Nw_{N-1}\}. \end{aligned}$$

By differentiating with respect to u_{N-1} and setting the derivative equal to zero, we obtain

$$(R_{N-1} + B_{N-1}'Q_NB_{N-1})u_{N-1} = -B_{N-1}'Q_NA_{N-1}x_{N-1}.$$

The matrix multiplying u_{N-1} on the left is positive definite (and hence invertible), since R_{N-1} is positive definite and $B_{N-1}'Q_NB_{N-1}$ is positive semidefinite. As a result, the minimizing control vector is given by

$$u_{N-1}^* = -(R_{N-1} + B_{N-1}'Q_NB_{N-1})^{-1}B_{N-1}'Q_NA_{N-1}x_{N-1}.$$

By substitution into the expression for J_{N-1}, we have

$$J_{N-1}(x_{N-1}) = x_{N-1}'K_{N-1}x_{N-1} + E\{w_{N-1}'Q_Nw_{N-1}\},$$

where the matrix K_{N-1} is obtained by straightforward calculation and is given by

$$\begin{aligned} K_{N-1} = A_{N-1}'[Q_N - Q_NB_{N-1}(B_{N-1}'Q_NB_{N-1} + R_{N-1})^{-1}B_{N-1}'Q_N]A_{N-1} \\ + Q_{N-1}. \end{aligned}$$

The matrix K_{N-1} is clearly symmetric. It is also positive semidefinite. To see this, note that from the preceding calculation we have for $x \in R^n$

$$x'K_{N-1}x = \min_u [x'Q_{N-1}x + u'R_{N-1}u + (A_{N-1}x + B_{N-1}u)'Q_N(A_{N-1}x + B_{N-1}u)].$$

Since Q_{N-1}, R_{N-1}, and Q_N are positive semidefinite, the expression within brackets is nonnegative. Minimization over u preserves nonnegativity, so it follows that $x'K_{N-1}x \geq 0$ for all $x \in R^n$. Hence K_{N-1} is positive semidefinite.

In view of the fact that J_{N-1} is a positive semidefinite quadratic function (plus an inconsequential constant term), we may proceed similarly and obtain from the DP equation (2.2) the optimal control law for stage $N - 2$. As earlier, we show that J_{N-2} is a positive semidefinite quadratic function, and proceeding sequentially we obtain the optimal control law for every k. It has the form

$$\mu_k^*(x_k) = L_k x_k, \tag{2.3}$$

where the gain matrices L_k are given by the equation

$$L_k = -(B_k'K_{k+1}B_k + R_k)^{-1}B_k'K_{k+1}A_k, \tag{2.4}$$

and where the symmetric positive semidefinite matrices K_k are given recursively by the algorithm

$$K_N = Q_N, \tag{2.5}$$

$$K_k = A_k'[K_{k+1} - K_{k+1}B_k(B_k'K_{k+1}B_k + R_k)^{-1}B_k'K_{k+1}]A_k + Q_k. \tag{2.6}$$

The optimal cost is given by

$$J_0(x_0) = x_0'K_0x_0 + \sum_{k=0}^{N-1} E\{w_k'K_{k+1}w_k\}.$$

The attractive aspect of the solution is the relative ease with which the control law (2.3) can be computed and implemented in engineering applications. The current state x_k is being fed back as input through the linear feedback gain matrix L_k as shown in Figure 2.1. This fact accounts for the great popularity of the linear–quadratic formulation. As we will

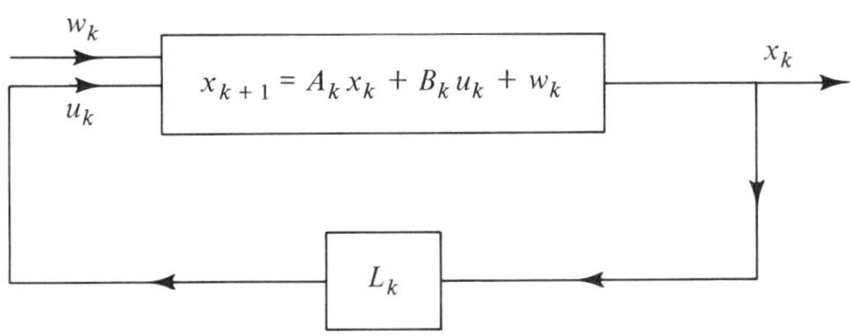

Figure 2.1 Linear feedback structure of the optimal controller for the linear–quadratic problem.

see in Chapter 3, the linearity of the control law is still maintained even for problems where the state x_k of the system is not completely observable (imperfect state information).

The Riccati Equation and Its Asymptotic Behavior

Equation (2.6) is called the *discrete-time Riccati equation.* It plays an important role in modern control theory. Its properties have been studied extensively and exhaustively. One interesting property of the Riccati equation is that whenever the matrices A_k, B_k, Q_k, R_k are constant and equal to A, B, Q, R, respectively, then as $k \to -\infty$ the solution K_k converges (under mild assumptions) to a steady-state solution K satisfying the *algebraic Riccati equation*

$$K = A'[K - KB(B'KB + R)^{-1}B'K]A + Q. \tag{2.7}$$

This property, to be proved shortly, indicates that when the system is

$$x_{k+1} = Ax_k + Bu_k + w_k, \qquad k = 0, 1, \ldots, N - 1, \tag{2.8}$$

and the number of stages N is large, one can reasonably approximate the control law (2.3) by a linear *stationary* control law of the form $\{\mu^*, \mu^*, \ldots, \mu^*\}$, where

$$\mu^*(x) = Lx, \tag{2.9}$$

$$L = -(B'KB + R)^{-1}B'KA, \tag{2.10}$$

and K is the steady-state solution of the Riccati equation (2.6) satisfying (2.7). This control law is even more attractive for implementation purposes.

We now turn to proving convergence of the sequence of matrices $\{K_k\}$ generated by the Riccati equations (2.5) and (2.6). We first introduce the notions of controllability and observability, which are of major importance in modern control theory.

Definition. A pair (A, B), where A is an $n \times n$ matrix and B an $n \times m$ matrix, is said to be *controllable* if the $n \times nm$ matrix

$$[B, AB, A^2B, \ldots, A^{n-1}B]$$

has full rank (i.e., has linearly independent rows). A pair (A, C), where A is an $n \times n$ matrix and C an $m \times n$ matrix, is said to be *observable* if the pair (A', C') is controllable, where A' and C' denote the transposes of A and C, respectively.

One may show that if the pair (A, B) is controllable, then for any initial state x_0 there exists a sequence of control vectors $u_0, u_1, \ldots, u_{n-1}$ that force the state x_n of the system

$$x_{k+1} = Ax_k + Bu_k \tag{2.11}$$

to be equal to zero at time n. To see this, note that from the system equation we obtain

$$x_n = A^n x_0 + Bu_{n-1} + ABu_{n-2} + \cdots + A^{n-1}Bu_0$$

or equivalently

$$x_n - A^n x_0 = [B, AB, \ldots, A^{n-1}B]\begin{bmatrix} u_{n-1} \\ \vdots \\ u_0 \end{bmatrix}. \tag{2.12}$$

If (A, B) is controllable, the matrix $[B, AB, \ldots, A^{n-1}B]$ has full rank and as a result the right side of (2.12) can be made equal to any vector in R^n by appropriate selection of $(u_0, u_1, \ldots, u_{n-1})$. In particular, one can choose $(u_0, u_1, \ldots, u_{n-1})$ so that the right side of (2.12) is equal to $-A^n x_0$, which implies $x_n = 0$. This property explains the name "controllable pair" and in fact is often used to define controllability. The notion of observability has an analogous interpretation in the context of estimation problems; that is, given measurements $z_0, z_1, \ldots, z_{N-1}$ of the form $z_k = Cx_k$, it is possible to infer the initial state x_0 of the system $x_{k+1} = Ax_k$.

Definition. We say that an $n \times n$ matrix D is *stable* if $\lim_{k\to\infty} D^k = 0$ (i.e., each sequence of elements of D^k converges to zero).

Note that if D is a stable matrix then the state x_k of the system $x_{k+1} = Dx_k$ tends to zero as $k \to \infty$ for an arbitrary state x_0. The notion of stability is of paramount importance in control theory. In the context of our problem it is important that the stationary control law (2.9) results in a stable system, that is, the matrix $(A + BL)$ is a stable matrix; then, in the absence of input disturbance, the state x_k of the corresponding closed-loop system

$$x_k = (A + BL)x_{k-1} = (A + BL)^k x_0, \qquad k = 0, 1, \ldots,$$

tends to zero as $k \to \infty$.

We give the following proposition, which shows that, for a stationary system and constant matrices Q_k, R_k, under controllability and observability conditions the solution of the Riccati equation (2.5) and (2.6) converges to a positive definite matrix K for an arbitrary positive semidefinite initial matrix. In addition, the proposition shows that the corresponding control law, (2.9) and (2.10), results in a stable system. To simplify notation, we have reversed the time indexing of the Riccati equation in the following proposition. Thus P_k in equation (2.13) corresponds to K_{N-k} in equation (2.6).

Proposition. Let A be an $n \times n$ matrix, B an $n \times m$ matrix, Q an $n \times n$ symmetric positive semidefinite matrix, and R an $m \times m$ symmetric positive definite matrix. Consider the discrete-time Riccati equation

$$P_{k+1} = A'[P_k - P_kB(B'P_kB + R)^{-1}B'P_k]A + Q, \qquad k = 0, 1, \ldots, \tag{2.13}$$

where the initial matrix P_0 is an arbitrary positive semidefinite symmetric matrix. Assume that the pair (A, B) is controllable. Assume also that Q may be written as $C'C$, where the pair (A, C) is observable.† Then:

(a) There exists a positive definite symmetric matrix P such that for every positive semidefinite symmetric initial matrix P_0 we have

$$\lim_{k\to\infty} P_k = P.$$

Furthermore, P is the unique solution of the algebraic matrix equation

$$P = A'[P - PB(B'PB + R)^{-1}B'P]A + Q \tag{2.14}$$

within the class of positive semidefinite symmetric matrices.

(b) The matrix

$$D = A + BL, \tag{2.15}$$

where

$$L = -(B'PB + R)^{-1}B'PA, \tag{2.16}$$

is a stable matrix.

Proof. The proof proceeds in several steps. First we show convergence of the sequence generated by (2.13) when the initial matrix P_0 is equal to zero. Next we show that the corresponding matrix D of (2.15) is stable. Subsequently, we show convergence of the sequence generated by (2.13) when P_0 is any positive semidefinite symmetric matrix, and finally we show uniqueness of the solution of (2.14).

Initial Matrix $P_0 = 0$. Consider the optimal control problem of finding a sequence $u_0, u_1, \ldots, u_{k-1}$ that minimizes

$$\sum_{i=0}^{k-1} (x_i'Qx_i + u_i'Ru_i) \tag{2.17}$$

subject to

$$x_{i+1} = Ax_i + Bu_i, \qquad i = 0, 1, \ldots, k-1, \tag{2.18}$$

where x_0 is given. The optimal value of this problem, according to the theory of this section, is

$$x_0'P_k(0)x_0,$$

where $P_k(0)$ is given by the Riccati equation (2.13) with $P_0 = 0$. We have

$$x_0'P_k(0)x_0 \le x_0'P_{k+1}(0)x_0, \qquad \text{for all } x_0 \in R^n, \quad k = 0, 1, \ldots,$$

since for any control sequence $(u_0, u_1, \ldots, u_k)$ we have

$$\sum_{i=0}^{k-1} (x_i'Qx_i + u_i'Ru_i) \le \sum_{i=0}^{k} (x_i'Qx_i + u_i'Ru_i)$$

† Notice that if r is the rank of Q, there exists an $r \times n$ matrix C of rank r such that $Q = C'C$ (see Appendix A).

and hence

$$x_0' P_k(0) x_0 = \min_{u_i, i=0,\ldots,k-1} \sum_{i=0}^{k-1} (x_i' Q x_i + u_i' R u_i)$$
$$\leq \min_{u_i, i=0,\ldots,k} \sum_{i=0}^{k} (x_i' Q x_i + u_i' R u_i) = x_0' P_{k+1}(0) x_0,$$

where both minimizations are subject to the system equation constraint $x_{i+1} = Ax_i + Bu_i$. Furthermore, for a fixed x_0 and for every k, $x_0' P_k(0) x_0$ is bounded above by the cost corresponding to a control sequence that forces x_0 to the origin in n steps and applies zero control after that. Such a sequence exists by the controllability assumption. Thus the sequence $\{x_0' P_k(0) x_0\}$ is increasing and bounded above and therefore converges to some real number for every $x_0 \in R^n$. It follows that the sequence $\{P_k(0)\}$ converges to some matrix P in the sense that each of the sequences of the elements of $P_k(0)$ converges to the corresponding elements of P. To see this, take $x_0 = (1, 0, \ldots, 0)$. It follows that the sequence of first diagonal elements of $P_k(0)$ converges to the first diagonal element of P. Similarly, by taking $x_0 = (0, \ldots, 0, 1, 0, \ldots, 0)$ with the one in the ith coordinate, for $i = 2, \ldots, n$, it follows that all the diagonal elements of $P_k(0)$ converge to the corresponding diagonal elements of P. Next take $x_0 = (1, 1, 0, \ldots, 0)$ to show that the second elements of the first row converge. Similarly proceeding, we obtain

$$\lim_{k \to \infty} P_k(0) = P,$$

where $P_k(0)$ are generated by (2.13) with $P_0 = 0$. Furthermore, the limit matrix P is positive semidefinite and symmetric. Now by taking the limit in (2.13) it follows that P satisifes

$$P = A'[P - PB(B'PB + R)^{-1}B'P]A + Q. \tag{2.19}$$

Furthermore, if we define

$$L = -(B'PB + R)^{-1}B'PA, \qquad D = A + BL \tag{2.20}$$

by direct calculation we can verify the following equality, which will be useful subsequently in the proof:

$$P = D'PD + Q + L'RL. \tag{2.21}$$

Stability of $D = A + BL$. Consider the system

$$x_{k+1} = (A + BL)x_k = Dx_k \tag{2.22}$$

for an arbitrary initial state x_0. Since

$$x_k = D^k x_0,$$

it will be sufficient to show that $x_k \to 0$ as $k \to \infty$. We have for all k, by using (2.21),

$$x_{k+1}' P x_{k+1} - x_k' P x_k = x_k'(D'PD - P)x_k = -x_k'(Q + L'RL)x_k.$$

Hence

$$x'_{k+1}Px_{k+1} = x'_0Px_0 - \sum_{i=0}^{k} x'_i(Q + L'RL)x_i. \tag{2.23}$$

Since the left side of the equation is bounded below by zero, it follows that

$$x'_k(Q + L'RL)x_k \to 0.$$

Using the fact that R is positive definite and Q may be written as $C'C$, we obtain

$$\lim_{k\to\infty} Cx_k = 0, \qquad \lim_{k\to\infty} Lx_k = 0. \tag{2.24}$$

From (2.22) we have

$$\begin{bmatrix} C\left(x_{k+n-1} - \sum_{i=1}^{n-1} A^{i-1}BLx_{k+n-i-1}\right) \\ C\left(x_{k+n-2} - \sum_{i=1}^{n-2} A^{i-1}BLx_{k+n-i-2}\right) \\ \vdots \\ C(x_{k+1} - BLx_k) \\ Cx_k \end{bmatrix} = \begin{bmatrix} CA^{n-1} \\ CA^{n-2} \\ \vdots \\ CA \\ C \end{bmatrix} x_k. \tag{2.25}$$

By (2.24) the left side tends to zero and hence the right side tends to zero also. By the observability assumption, however, the matrix multiplying x_k on the right side of (2.25) has full rank. It follows that $x_k \to 0$ and hence the matrix D of (2.21) is stable.

Positive Definiteness of P. Assume the contrary, i.e., there exists some $x_0 \neq 0$ such that $x'_0Px_0 = 0$. Then from (2.23) we obtain

$$x'_k(Q + L'RL)x_k = 0, \qquad k = 0, 1, \ldots,$$

where $x_k = D^kx_0$. This in turn implies [cf. Eq. (2.24)]

$$Cx_k = 0, \qquad Lx_k = 0, \qquad k = 0, 1, \ldots.$$

Consider now (2.25) for $k = 0$. By the preceding equalities, the left side is zero and hence

$$0 = \begin{bmatrix} CA^{n-1} \\ \vdots \\ CA \\ C \end{bmatrix} x_0.$$

Since the matrix multiplying x_0 has full rank by the observability assumption, we obtain $x_0 = 0$, which contradicts the hypothesis $x_0 \neq 0$. Hence P is positive definite.

Arbitrary Initial Matrix P_0. Next we show that the sequence of matrices $\{P_k(P_0)\}$, defined by (2.13) when the starting matrix is an arbitrary positive semidefinite matrix P_0, converges to $P = \lim_{k\to\infty} P_k(0)$. Indeed, the optimal cost of the problem of minimizing

$$x_k' P_0 x_k + \sum_{i=0}^{k-1} (x_i' Q x_i + u_i' R u_i) \tag{2.26}$$

subject to (2.18) equals $x_0' P_k(P_0) x_0$. Hence we have for every $x_0 \in R^n$

$$x_0' P_k(0) x_0 \leq x_0' P_k(P_0) x_0.$$

Consider now the cost (2.26) corresponding to the controller $\mu(x_k) = u_k = Lx_k$, where L is defined by (2.20). This cost is given by

$$x_0' \left[D'^k P_0 D^k + \sum_{i=0}^{k-1} [D'^i (Q + L'RL) D^i] \right] x_0$$

and is greater than $x_0' P_k(P_0) x_0$, which is, of course, the optimal value of (2.26). Hence we have for all k and $x \in R^n$

$$x' P_k(0) x \leq x' P_k(P_0) x \leq x' \left[D'^k P_0 D^k + \sum_{i=0}^{k-1} [D'^i (Q + L'RL) D^i] \right] x. \tag{2.27}$$

Now we have proved

$$\lim_{k\to\infty} P_k(0) = P, \tag{2.28}$$

and we also have (using the fact that $\lim_{k\to\infty} D'^k P_0 D^k = 0$)

$$\lim_{k\to\infty} \left\{ D'^k P_0 D^k + \sum_{i=0}^{k-1} [D'^i (Q + L'RL) D^i] \right\}$$

$$= \lim_{k\to\infty} \left\{ \sum_{i=0}^{k-1} [D'^i (Q + L'RL) D^i] \right\} = P, \tag{2.29}$$

where the last equality may be verified easily using (2.21). Combining (2.27) to (2.29), we obtain

$$\lim_{k\to\infty} P_k(P_0) = P,$$

for an arbitrary positive semidefinite symmetric P_0.

Uniqueness of Solution. If $\tilde{P}$ were another positive semidefinite solution of (2.14), we would have $P_k(\tilde{P}) = \tilde{P}$ for all $k = 0, 1, \ldots$. From the convergence result just proved we would also have

$$\lim_{k\to\infty} P_k(\tilde{P}) = P,$$

and it follows that $\tilde{P} = P$. Q.E.D.

The assumptions of the preceding proposition can be relaxed somewhat. Suppose that, instead of controllability of the pair (A, B), we assume that the system is *stabilizable* in the sense that there exists an $m \times n$ feedback gain matrix G such that the matrix $(A + BG)$ is stable. Then the proof of convergence of $P_k(0)$ to some positive semidefinite P given previously carries through. [We use the stationary control law $\mu(x) = Gx$ for which $(A + BG)$ is stable to ensure that $x_0'P_k(0)x_0$ is bounded.] Suppose that, instead of observability of the pair (A, C), the system is assumed *detectable* in the sense that A is such that if $u_k \to 0$ and $Cx_k \to 0$ then it follows that $x_k \to 0$. (This essentially means that instability of the system can be detected by looking at the measurement sequence $\{z_k\}$ with $z_k = Cx_k$.) Then Eq. (2.24) implies that $x_k \to 0$ and that the matrix $D = A + BL$ is stable. The other parts of the proof of the proposition follow similarly, with the exception of positive definiteness of P, which cannot be guaranteed anymore. (As an example take $A = 0$, $B = 0$, $C = 0$, $R > 0$. Then both the stabilizability and the detectability assumptions are satisfied, but $P = 0$.) To summarize, if the controllability and observability assumptions of the proposition are replaced by the previous stabilizability and detectability assumptions, the conclusions of the proposition hold with the exception of positive definiteness of the limit matrix P, which can now be guaranteed to be only positive semidefinite.

Random System Matrices

We consider now the more general case where $\{A_0, B_0\}, \{A_1, B_1\}, \ldots, \{A_{N-1}, B_{N-1}\}$ are not known but rather are independent random matrices that are also independent of $w_0, w_1, \ldots, w_{N-1}$. Their probability distributions are given and they are asssumed to have finite second moments. This problem falls again within the framework of the basic problem by considering as disturbance at each time k the triplet (A_k, B_k, w_k). The DP algorithm is written

$$J_N(x_N) = x_N'Q_Nx_N,$$

$$J_k(x_k) = \min_{u_k} \mathop{E}_{w_k, A_k, B_k} \{x_k'Q_kx_k + u_k'R_ku_k + J_{k+1}(A_kx_k + B_ku_k + w_k)\}.$$

Calculations very similar to those for the case where A_k, B_k are not random show that the optimal control law is of the form

$$\mu_k^*(x_k) = L_kx_k, \tag{2.30}$$

where the gain matrices L_k are given by

$$L_k = -[R_k + E\{B_k'K_{k+1}B_k\}]^{-1} E\{B_k'K_{k+1}A_k\}, \tag{2.31}$$

and where the matrices K_k are given by the recursive equation

$$K_N = Q_N, \tag{2.32}$$

$$\begin{aligned} K_k = E\{A_k'K_{k+1}A_k\} - E\{A_k'K_{k+1}B_k\}[R_k + E\{B_k'K_{k+1}B_k\}]^{-1} \\ \times E\{B_k'K_{k+1}A_k\} + Q_k. \end{aligned} \tag{2.33}$$

We close this section by making an observation related to the nature of the quadratic cost. Consider the minimization over u of the quadratic form

$$\underset{w}{E}\{(ax + bu + w)^2\},$$

where a, b are given scalars and w is a random variable. The optimum is attained for

$$u^* = -\left(\frac{a}{b}\right)x - \left(\frac{1}{b}\right)E\{w\}.$$

Thus u^* depends on the probability distribution of w only through the mean $E\{w\}$. In particular, the result of the optimization is the same as for the corresponding deterministic problem where w is replaced by $E\{w\}$. This property is called the *certainty equivalence principle* and appears in various forms in many (but not all) stochastic control problems involving linear systems and quadratic cost. For the first problem of this section (A_k, B_k known), the certainty equivalence principle is expressed by the fact that the control law (2.3) is the same as the one that would be obtained from the corresponding deterministic problem where w_k is not random but rather is known and equal to zero (its expected value). However, for the problem where A_k, B_k are random the certainty equivalence principle does not hold since if one replaces A_k, B_k with their expected values in Eq. (2.33), the resulting control law need not be optimal.

2.2 INVENTORY CONTROL

We consider now the inventory control problem discussed in Sections 1.1 and 1.2. We assume that excess demand at each period is backlogged and is filled when additional inventory becomes available. This is represented by negative inventory in the system equation

$$x_{k+1} = x_k + u_k - w_k, \qquad k = 0, 1, \ldots, N-1.$$

We also assume that the successive demands w_k are bounded and independent, the unfilled demand at the end of the Nth period is lost, and the inventory leftover at the end of the Nth period has zero value. Under these circumstances the total expected cost to be minimized is given by the expression

$$\underset{\substack{w_k \\ k=0,\ldots,N-1}}{E}\left\{\sum_{k=0}^{N-1}[cu_k + p\max(0, -x_{k+1}) + h\max(0, x_{k+1})]\right\},$$

or using the system equation

$$\underset{\substack{w_k \\ k=0,\ldots,N-1}}{E}\left\{\sum_{k=0}^{N-1}[cu_k + p\max(0, w_k - x_k - u_k) + h\max(0, x_k + u_k - w_k)]\right\}.$$

(A more general cost function may also be used as discussed in Section 1.1.) We assume that $c > 0$, $h \geqslant 0$, $p > c$. This is necessary in order for the problem to be well posed as will become apparent in what follows.

By applying the DP algorithm, we have

$$J_N(x_N) = 0 \tag{2.34}$$

$$J_k(x_k) = \min_{u_k \geqslant 0} [cu_k + L(x_k + u_k) + E\{J_{k+1}(x_k + u_k - w_k)\}], \tag{2.35}$$

where the function L is defined by

$$L(y) = p\,E\{\max(0, w_k - y)\} + h\,E\{\max(0, y - w_k)\}.$$

Actually, L depends on k whenever the probability distribution of w_k depends on k. To simplify notation, we do not show this dependence and assume that all demands are identically distributed.

By introducing the variable $y_k = x_k + u_k$, we can write the right side of (2.35) as

$$\min_{y_k \geqslant x_k} [cy_k + L(y_k) + E\{J_{k+1}(y_k - w_k)\}] - cx_k.$$

The function L can be seen to be convex. We will prove shortly that J_{k+1} is convex, but for the moment let us assume this fact. Then the function in brackets is convex. Suppose that this function has a minimum S_k. Then it is seen that (in view of the constraint $y_k \geqslant x_k$) a minimizing y_k equals x_k if $x_k \geqslant S_k$, and equals S_k otherwise. Using the equation $u_k = y_k - x_k$, we see that, under these circumstances, an optimal policy is determined by a sequence of scalars $\{S_0, S_1, \ldots, S_{N-1}\}$ and has the form

$$\mu_k^*(x_k) = \begin{cases} S_k - x_k, & \text{if } x_k < S_k, \\ 0, & \text{if } x_k \geqslant S_k. \end{cases} \tag{2.36}$$

For each k, the scalar S_k minimizes the function

$$G_k(y) = cy + L(y) + E\{J_{k+1}(y - w)\}. \tag{2.37}$$

Thus we can prove the optimality of the policy (2.36) by showing that the cost-to-go functions J_k [and hence also the functions G_k of (2.37)] are convex, and furthermore $\lim_{|y|\to\infty} G_k(y) = \infty$, so that the minimizing scalars S_k exist. We proceed to show these properties inductively.

We have that J_N is convex [cf. Eq. (2.34)]. Since the derivative of $L(y)$ as $y \to -\infty$, tends to $-p$, and $c < p$ we see that the derivative of $G_{N-1}(y)$ $(= (y + L(y))$ is negative and positive as $y \to -\infty$ and $y \to \infty$, respectively (see Figure 2.2). Therefore $\lim_{|y|\to\infty} G_{N-1}(y) = \infty$. An optimal policy at time $N - 1$ is given by

$$\mu_{N-1}^*(x_{N-l}) = \begin{cases} S_{N-1} - x_{N-1}, & \text{if } x_{N-1} < S_{N-1}, \\ 0, & \text{if } x_{N-1} \geqslant S_{N-1}. \end{cases}$$

Furthermore, from the DP equation (2.35) we have

$$J_{N-1}(x_{N-1}) = \begin{cases} c(S_{N-1} - x_{N-1}) + L(S_{N-1}), & \text{if } x_{N-1} < S_{N-1}, \\ L(x_{N-1}), & \text{if } x_{N-1} \geqslant S_{N-1}, \end{cases}$$

which is a convex function by the convexity of L and the fact that S_{N-1} minimizes $cy + L(y)$ (see Figure 2.2). Thus, given the convexity of J_N, we were able to prove the convexity of J_{N-1}. Furthermore $\lim_{|y|\to\infty} J_{N-1}(y) = \infty$.

Similarly, for $k = N - 2, \ldots, 0$, it is seen that $\lim_{|y|\to\infty} G_k(y) = \infty$, since $c < p$, and $\lim_{|y|\to\infty} J_{k+1}(y) = \infty$. We have

$$J_k(x_k) = \begin{cases} c(S_k - x_k) + L(S_k) + E\{J_{k+1}(S_k - w_k)\}, & \text{if } x_k < S_k, \\ L(x_k) + E\{J_{k+1}(x_k - w_k)\}, & \text{if } x_k \geqslant S_k, \end{cases}$$

where S_k minimizes $cy + L(y) + E\{J_{k+1}(y - w)\}$. Again we have $\lim_{|y|\to\infty} J_k(y) = \infty$, and the convexity of J_{k+1} [which implies convexity of $E\{J_{k+1}(x - w)\}$] shows the convexity of J_k. The optimality proof of the policy (2.36) is complete.

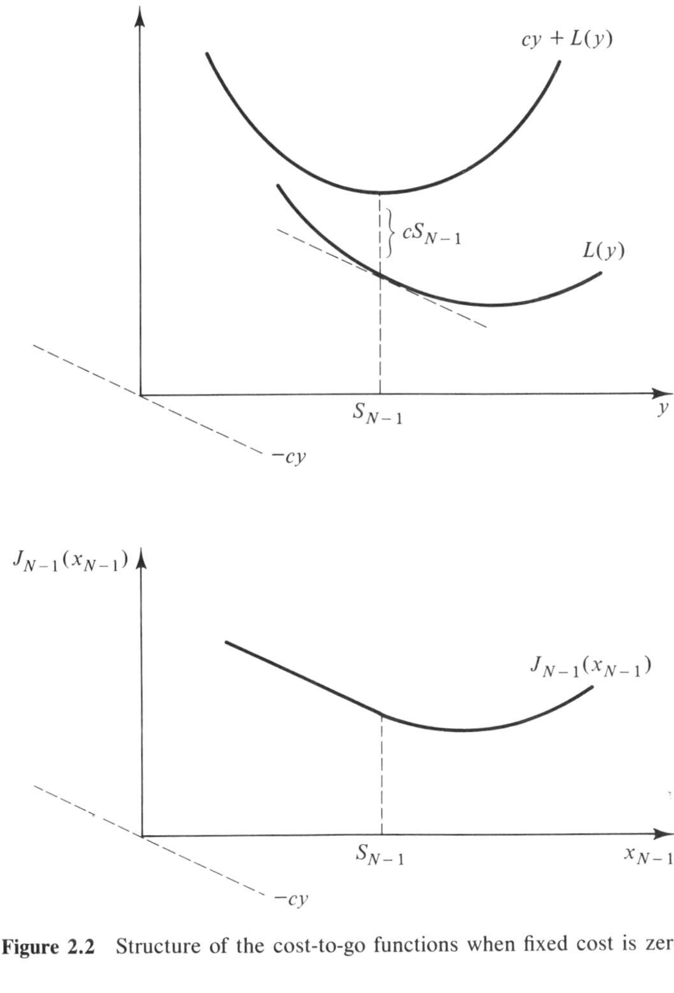

Figure 2.2 Structure of the cost-to-go functions when fixed cost is zero.

Positive Fixed Cost

We now turn to the more complicated case where there is a nonzero fixed cost $K > 0$ associated with a positive inventory order. Here the cost for ordering inventory $u \geq 0$ is

$$C(u) = \begin{cases} K + cu, & \text{if } u > 0, \\ 0, & \text{if } u = 0. \end{cases}$$

The DP algorithm takes the form

$$J_N(x_N) = 0,$$

$$J_k(x_k) = \min_{u_k \geq 0} [C(u_k) + L(x_k + u_k) + E\{J_{k+1}(x_k + u_k - w_k)\}],$$

with L defined as earlier by

$$L(y) = p\,E\{\max(0, w - y)\} + h\,E\{\max(0, y - w)\}.$$

Consider again the functions G_k:

$$G_k(y) = cy + L(y) + E\{J_{k+1}(y - w)\}. \tag{2.38}$$

If we could prove that the functions G_k were convex, then it would be easily verified that a policy of the (s, S) type

$$\mu_k^*(x_k) = \begin{cases} S_k - x_k, & \text{if } x < s_k, \\ 0, & \text{if } x \geq s_k, \end{cases} \tag{2.39}$$

is optimal, where S_k is a value of y that minimizes $G_k(y)$ and s_k is the smallest value of y for which $G_k(y) = K + G_k(S_k)$. Unfortunately, when $K > 0$ it is not necessarily true that J_k or G_k are convex functions. This opens the possibility of functions G_k having the form shown in Figure 2.3. For this case the optimal policy is to order $(S - x)$ in interval I, zero in

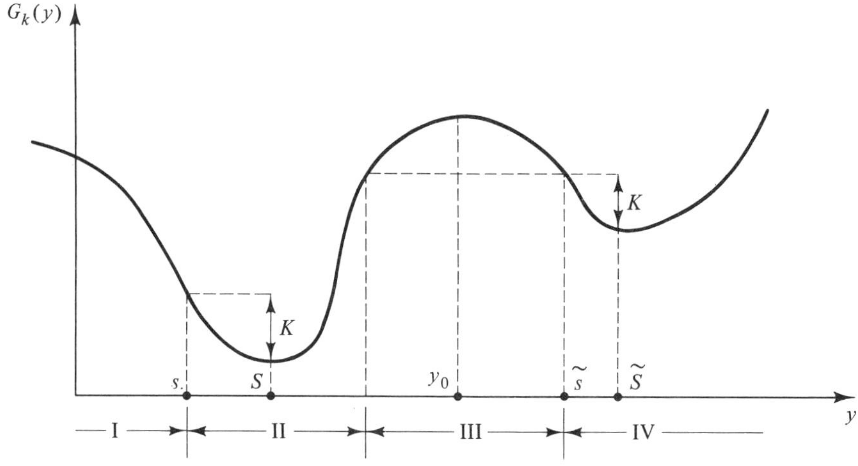

Figure 2.3 Potential form of the function G_k when fixed cost is nonzero.

intervals II and IV, and $(\tilde{S} - x)$ in interval III. However, we will show that even though the functions G_k may not be convex they have the property

$$K + G_k(z + y) \geqslant G_k(y) + z\left[\frac{G_k(y) - G_k(y - b)}{b}\right], \qquad \text{for all } z \geqslant 0, \quad b > 0, \quad y. \tag{2.40}$$

This property is called *K-convexity* and was first utilized by Scarf [S5] to show the optimality of multiperiod (s, S) policies. Now if (2.40) holds, then the situation shown in Figure 2.3 is impossible; for if y_0 is the local maximum in the interval III, then we must have, for sufficiently small $b > 0$,

$$\frac{G_k(y_0) - G_k(y_0 - b)}{b} \geqslant 0,$$

and from (2.40) it follows that

$$K + G_k(\tilde{S}) \geqslant G_k(y_0),$$

which contradicts the construction shown in Figure 2.3. More generally, it is easy to show by using part (d) of the following lemma that if (2.40) holds then an optimal policy takes the form (2.39).

Definition. We say that a function $g: R \to R$ is *K-convex*, where $K \geqslant 0$, if

$$K + g(z + y) \geqslant g(y) + z\left[\frac{g(y) - g(y - b)}{b}\right], \qquad \text{for all } z \geqslant 0, \quad b > 0, \quad y.$$

Some properties of K-convex functions are provided in the following lemma. The last part of the lemma essentially proves the optimality of the (s, S) policy (2.39) when G_k satisfies (2.40).

Lemma. (a) A convex function $g: R \to R$ is also 0-convex and hence also K-convex for all $K \geqslant 0$.

(b) If $g_1(y)$ and $g_2(y)$ are K-convex and L-convex $(K \geqslant 0, L \geqslant 0)$, respectively, then $\alpha g_1(y) + \beta g_2(y)$ is $(\alpha K + \beta L)$-convex for all positive α and β.

(c) If $g(y)$ is K-convex, then $E_w\{g(y - w)\}$ is also K-convex provided $E_w\{|g(y - w)|\} < \infty$ for all y.

(d) If $g: R \to R$ is a continuous K-convex function and $g(y) \to \infty$ as $|y| \to \infty$, then there exist scalars s and S with $s \leqslant S$ such that

(i) $g(S) \leqslant g(y)$, for all $y \in R$;

(ii) $g(S) + K = g(s) < g(y)$, for all $y < s$;

(iii) $g(y)$ is a decreasing function on $(-\infty, s)$;

(iv) $g(y) \leqslant g(z) + K$ for all y, z with $s \leqslant y \leqslant z$.

Proof. Part (a) follows from elementary properties of convex functions and parts (b) and (c) follow directly from the definition of a K-convex function. We will thus concentrate on proving part (d).

Since g is continuous and $g(y) \to \infty$ as $|y| \to \infty$, there exists a minimizing point of g. Let S be such a point. Also let s be the smallest scalar z for which $z \leq S$ and $g(S) + K = g(z)$. For all y with $y < s$, we have from the definition of K-convexity

$$K + g(S) \geq g(s) + \frac{S - s}{s - y}[g(s) - g(y)].$$

Since $K + g(S) - g(s) = 0$, we obtain $g(s) - g(y) \leq 0$. Since $y < s$ and s is the smallest scalar for which $g(S) + K = g(s)$, we must have $g(s) < g(y)$ and (ii) is proved. Now for $y_1 < y_2 < s$, we have

$$K + g(S) \geq g(y_2) + \frac{S - y_2}{y_2 - y_1}[g(y_2) - g(y_1)].$$

Also from (ii),

$$g(y_2) > g(S) + K = g(s),$$

and by adding these two inequalities we obtain

$$0 > \frac{S - y_2}{y_2 - y_1}[g(y_2) - g(y_1)],$$

from which $g(y_1) > g(y_2)$, thus proving (iii). To prove (iv), we note that it holds for $y = z$ as well as for either $y = S$ or $y = s$. There remain two other possibilities, $S < y < z$ and $s < y < S$. If $S < y < z$, then by K-convexity

$$K + g(z) \geq g(y) + \frac{z - y}{y - S}[g(y) - g(S)] \geq g(y),$$

and (iv) is proved. If $s < y < S$, then by K-convexity

$$g(s) = K + g(S) \geq g(y) + \frac{S - y}{y - s}[g(y) - g(s)],$$

from which

$$\left[1 + \frac{S - y}{y - s}\right]g(s) \geq \left[1 + \frac{S - y}{y - s}\right]g(y),$$

and $g(s) \geq g(y)$. Noting that

$$g(z) + K \geq g(S) + K = g(s),$$

it follows that $g(z) + K \geq g(y)$. Thus (iv) is proved for this case as well. Q.E.D.

Consider now the function G_{N-1} of (2.38):

$$G_{N-1}(y) = cy + L(y).$$

Clearly, G_{N-1} is convex and hence by part (a) of the previous lemma it is also K-convex. We have, from the analysis of the case where $K = 0$,

$$J_{N-1}(x) = \begin{cases} K + G_{N-1}(S_{N-1}) - cx, & \text{for } x < s_{N-1}, \\ G_{N-1}(x) - cx, & \text{for } x \geq s_{N-1}, \end{cases} \tag{2.41}$$

where S_{N-1} minimizes $G_{N-1}(y)$ and s_{N-1} is the smallest value of y for which $G_{N-1}(y) = K + G_{N-1}(S_{N-1})$. Notice that since $K > 0$ we have $s_{N-1} \neq S_{N-1}$ and furthermore the slope of G_{N-1} at s_{N-1} is negative. As a result the left slope of J_{N-1} at s_{N-1} is greater than the right slope, as shown in Figure 2.4, and J_{N-1} is not convex. However, we will show that J_{N-1} is K-convex based on the fact that G_{N-1} is K-convex. To this end we must verify that

$$K + J_{N-1}(y + z) \geqslant J_{N-1}(y) + z\left[\frac{J_{N-1}(y) - J_{N-1}(y - b)}{b}\right],$$
$$\text{for all } z \geqslant 0, \quad b > 0, \quad y. \tag{2.42}$$

We distinguish three cases:

Case 1 $y \geqslant s_{N-1}$ If $y - b \geqslant s_{N-1}$, then in this region of values of z, b, y the function J_{N-1}, by (2.41), is the sum of a K-convex function and a linear function. Hence by part (b) of the lemma it is K-convex and (2.42) holds. If $y - b < s_{N-1}$, then in view of (2.41) we can write (2.42) as

$$K + G_{N-1}(y + z) - c(y + z)$$
$$\geqslant G_{N-1}(y) - cy + z\left[\frac{G_{N-1}(y) - cy - G_{N-1}(s_{N-1}) + c(y - b)}{b}\right],$$

or equivalently

$$K + G_{N-1}(y + z) \geqslant G_{N-1}(y) + z\left[\frac{G_{N-1}(y) - G_{N-1}(s_{N-1})}{b}\right]. \tag{2.43}$$

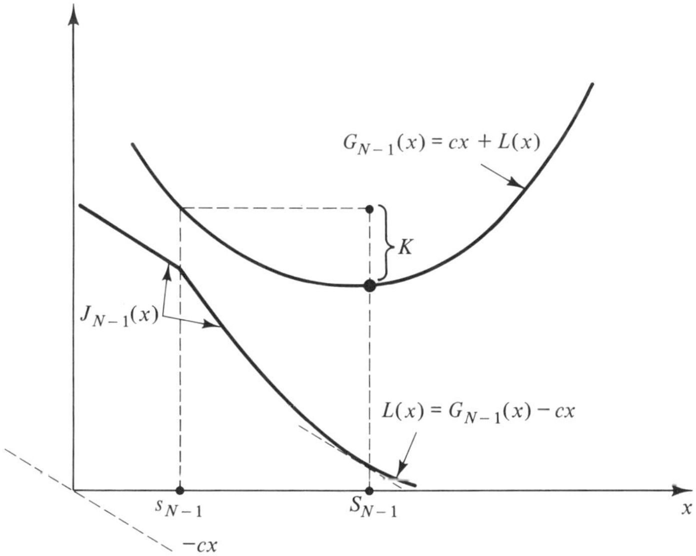

Figure 2.4 Structure of the cost-to-go function when fixed cost is nonzero.

Now if y is such that $G_{N-1}(y) \geqslant G_{N-1}(s_{N-1})$, then by K-convexity of G_{N-1} we have

$$K + G_{N-1}(y+z) \geqslant G_{N-1}(y) + z\left[\frac{G_{N-1}(y) - G_{N-1}(s_{N-1})}{y - s_{N-1}}\right]$$

$$\geqslant G_{N-1}(y) + z\left[\frac{G_{N-1}(y) - G_{N-1}(s_{N-1})}{b}\right].$$

Thus (2.43) and hence also (2.42) hold. If y is such that $G_{N-1}(y) < G_{N-1}(s_{N-1})$, then we have

$$K + G_{N-1}(y+z) \geqslant K + G_{N-1}(S_{N-1}) = G_{N-1}(s_{N-1}) > G_{N-1}(y)$$

$$\geqslant G_{N-1}(y) + z\left[\frac{G_{N-1}(y) - G_{N-1}(s_{N-1})}{b}\right].$$

So for this case (2.43), and hence also (2.42), hold.

Case 2 $y \leqslant y + z \leqslant s_{N-1}$ In this region, by (2.41), the function J_{N-1} is linear and hence (2.42) holds.

Case 3 $y < s_{N-1} < y + z$ For this case, in view of (2.41), we can write (2.42) as

$$K + G_{N-1}(y+z) - c(y+z)$$

$$\geqslant G_{N-1}(s_{N-1}) - cy + z\left[\frac{G_{N-1}(s_{N-1}) - cy - G_{N-1}(s_{N-1}) + c(y-b)}{b}\right],$$

or equivalently

$$K + G_{N-1}(y+z) \geqslant G_{N-1}(s_{N-1}),$$

which holds true by the definition of s_{N-1}.

We have thus proved that K-convexity and continuity of G_{N-1} together with the fact that $G_{N-1}(y) \to \infty$ as $|y| \to \infty$ imply K-convexity of J_{N-1}. In addition, J_{N-1} can be seen to be continuous. Now using the lemma it follows from (2.38) that G_{N-2} is a K-convex function. Furthermore, by using the boundedness of w_{N-2}, it follows that G_{N-2} is continuous and, in addition, $G_{N-2}(y) \to \infty$ as $|y| \to \infty$. Repeating the preceding argument, we obtain that J_{N-2} is K-convex and proceeding similarly we prove K-convexity and continuity of the functions G_k for all k, as well as that $G_k(y) \to \infty$ as $|y| \to \infty$. At the same time [by using part (d) of the lemma] we prove optimality of the multiperiod (s, S) policy of (2.39).

Optimality of policies of the (s, S) type can be proved for several other inventory problems (see Problems 3 to 6 and 14 to 17).

2.3 DYNAMIC PORTFOLIO ANALYSIS

Portfolio theory deals with the question of how to invest a certain amount of wealth among a collection of assets. Usually this problem is handled via the *mean–variance* formulation [M4, S18] whereby an investor is assumed to be maximizing the expected value of a utility function that depends on the mean and the variance of the return of the rate of investment. An alternative approach, to be discussed in this section, is to assume that an investor makes decisions over several time periods with the objective of maximizing final wealth. We will start with an analysis of a single-period model and then extend the results to the multiperiod case.

Let x_0 denote the initial wealth (measured in monetary units) of the investor and assume that there are n risky assets, with corresponding random rates of return $e_1, e_2, \ldots, e_n$ among which the investor can allocate his wealth. The investor can also invest in a riskless asset offering a sure rate of return s. If we denote by $u_1, \ldots, u_n$ the corresponding amounts invested in the n risky assets and by $(x_0 - u_1 - \cdots - u_n)$ the amount invested in the riskless asset, the final wealth is given by

$$x_1 = s(x_0 - u_1 - \cdots - u_n) + \sum_{i=1}^{n} e_i u_i,$$

or equivalently

$$x_1 = s x_0 + \sum_{i=1}^{n} (e_i - s) u_i. \tag{2.44}$$

The objective is to maximize over $u_1, \ldots, u_n$,

$$E\{U(x_1)\},$$

where U is a known utility function for the investor [A5]. We assume that the given expected value is well defined and finite for all x_0, u_i, and that U is concave and twice continuously differentiable. We will not impose constraints on $u_1, \ldots, u_n$. This is necessary in order to obtain the results in convenient form. A few additional assumptions will be made later.

Let us consider the preceding problem for every value of initial wealth and denote by $u_i^* = \mu^{i*}(x_0)$, $i = 1, \ldots, n$, the optimal amounts to be invested in the n risky assets when the initial wealth is x_0.

We say that the portfolio $\{\mu^{1*}(x_0), \ldots, \mu^{n*}(x_0)\}$ is *partially separated* if

$$\mu^{i*}(x_0) = \alpha^i h(x_0), \qquad i = 1, \ldots, n, \tag{2.45}$$

where α^i, $i = 1, \ldots, n$, are fixed constants and $h(x_0)$ is a function of x_0 (which is the same for all i).

When partial separation holds, the ratios of amounts invested in the risky assets are fixed and independent of the initial wealth; that is,

$$\frac{\mu^{i^*}(x_0)}{\mu^{j^*}(x_0)} = \frac{\alpha^i}{\alpha^j}, \qquad \text{for} \quad 1 \leq i, j \leq n, \quad \alpha^j \neq 0.$$

Actually, in the cases we will examine, when partial separation holds, the portfolio $\{\mu^{1^*}(x_0), \ldots, \mu^{n^*}(x_0)\}$ will be shown to consist of affine (linear plus constant) functions of x_0 that have the form

$$\mu^{i^*}(x_0) = \alpha^i[a + bsx_0], \qquad i = 1, \ldots, n, \tag{2.46}$$

where a and b are constants characterizing the utility function U. In the special case where $a = 0$ in (2.46), we say that the optimal portfolio is *completely separated* in the sense that the ratios of the amounts invested in both the risky asset *and* the riskless asset are fixed and independent of initial wealth.

We now show that when the utility function satisfies

$$-\frac{U'(x_1)}{U''(x_1)} = a + bx_1, \qquad \text{for all } x_1, \tag{2.47}$$

where U' and U'' denote the first and second derivatives of U, respectively, and a and b are some scalars, then the optimal portfolio is given by (2.46). Furthermore, if $J(x_0)$ is the optimal value of the problem

$$J(x_0) = \max_{u_i} E\{U(x_1)\}, \tag{2.48}$$

then we have

$$-\frac{J'(x_0)}{J''(x_0)} = \frac{a}{s} + bx_0, \qquad \text{for all } x_0. \tag{2.49}$$

Let us assume that an optimal portfolio exists and is of the form

$$\mu^{i*}(x_0) = \alpha^i(x_0)[a + bsx_0],$$

where $\alpha^i(x_0)$, $i = 1, \ldots, n$, are some differentiable functions. We will prove that $d\alpha^i(x_0)/dx_0 = 0$ for all x_0 and hence the functions α^i must be constant.

We have for every x_0, by the optimality of $\mu^{i*}(x_0)$, for $i = 1, \ldots, n$,

$$\frac{dE\{U(x_1)\}}{du_i} = E\left\{U'\left[sx_0 + \sum_{j=1}^{n} (e_j - s)\alpha^j(x_0)(a + bsx_0)\right](e_i - s)\right\} = 0. \tag{2.50}$$

Differentiating the n equations in (2.50) with respect to x_0 yields

$$E\left\{\begin{bmatrix} (e_1 - s)^2 \cdots (e_1 - s)(e_n - s) \\ \vdots \\ (e_n - s)(e_1 - s) \cdots (e_n - s)^2 \end{bmatrix} U''(x_1)(a + bsx_0)\right\} \begin{bmatrix} \dfrac{d\alpha^1(x_0)}{dx_0} \\ \vdots \\ \dfrac{d\alpha^n(x_0)}{dx_0} \end{bmatrix} \tag{2.51}$$

$$= -\begin{bmatrix} E\left\{U''(x_1)(e_1 - s)s\left[1 + \sum_{i=1}^{n}(e_i - s)\alpha^i(x_0)b\right]\right\} \\ \vdots \\ E\left\{U''(x_1)(e_n - s)s\left[1 + \sum_{i=1}^{n}(e_i - s)\alpha^i(x_0)b\right]\right\} \end{bmatrix}.$$

Using relation (2.47), we have

$$U''(x_1) = -\frac{U'(x_1)}{a + b\left[sx_0 + \sum_{i=1}^{n}(e_i - s)\alpha^i(x_0)(a + bsx_0)\right]}$$
$$= -\frac{U'(x_1)}{(a + bsx_0)\left[1 + \sum_{i=1}^{n}(e_i - s)\alpha^i(x_0)b\right]}. \tag{2.52}$$

Substituting in (2.51) and using (2.50), we have that the right side of (2.51) is the zero vector. The matrix on the left in (2.51), except for degenerate cases, can be shown to be nonsingular. Assuming that it is indeed nonsingular, we obtain

$$\frac{d\alpha^i(x_0)}{dx_0} = 0, \qquad i = 1, \ldots, n,$$

and $\alpha^i(x_0) = \alpha^i$, where α^i are some constants, thus proving (2.46).

We now turn our attention to proving relation (2.49). We have

$$J(x_0) = E\{U(x_1)\} = E\left\{U\left[s\left[1 + \sum_{i=1}^{n}(e_i - s)\alpha^i b\right]x_0 + \sum_{i=1}^{n}(e_i - s)\alpha^i a\right]\right\}$$

and hence

$$J'(x_0) = E\left\{U'(x_1)s\left[1 + \sum_{i=1}^{n}(e_i - s)\alpha^i b\right]\right\},$$
$$J''(x_0) = E\left\{U''(x_1)s^2\left[1 + \sum_{i=1}^{n}(e_i - s)\alpha^i b\right]^2\right\}. \tag{2.53}$$

The last relation after some calculation and using (2.52) yields

$$J''(x_0) = -\frac{E\left\{U'(x_1)s\left[1 + \sum_{i=1}^{n}(e_i - s)\alpha^i b\right]\right\}s}{a + bsx_0}. \tag{2.54}$$

By combining (2.53) and (2.54), we obtain the desired result:

$$-\frac{J'(x_0)}{J''(x_0)} = \frac{a}{s} + bx_0.$$

It can be shown that the following utility functions satisfy this condition

$$\begin{aligned} &\text{exponential:} \quad -e^{-x/a}, && \text{for} \quad b = 0, \\ &\text{logarithmic:} \quad \ln(x + a), && \text{for} \quad b = 1, \\ &\text{power:} \quad [1/(b - 1)](a + bx)^{1-(1/b)}, && \text{otherwise.} \end{aligned} \tag{2.55}$$

Naturally in our problem only concave utility functions from this class are admissible. Furthermore, if a utility function that is not defined over the whole real line is used, the problem should be formulated in a way that ensures that all possible values of the resulting final wealth are within the domain of definition of the utility function.

It is now easy to extend the one-period result of the preceding analysis to the multiperiod case. We will assume that the current wealth can be reinvested at the beginning of each of N consecutive time periods. We denote

- x_k the wealth of the investor at the begining of the kth period,
- u_i^k the amount invested at the beginning of the kth period in the ith risky asset,
- e_i^k the rate of return of the ith risky asset during the kth period,
- s_k the rate of return of the riskless asset during the kth period.

We have (in accordance with the single-period model) the system equation

$$x_{k+1} = s_k x_k + \sum_{i=1}^{n} (e_i^k - s_k) u_i^k, \qquad k = 0, 1, \ldots, N - 1. \tag{2.56}$$

We assume that the vectors $e^k = (e_1^k, \ldots, e_n^k)$, $k = 0, \ldots, N - 1$, are independent with given probability distributions that result in finite expected values throughout the following analysis.

The objective is to maximize $E\{U(x_N)\}$, the expected utility of the terminal wealth x_N, where we assume that U satisfies for all x

$$-\frac{U'(x)}{U''(x)} = a + bx.$$

Applying the DP algorithm to this problem, we have

$$J_N(x_N) = U(x_N), \tag{2.57}$$

$$J_k(x_k) = \max_{u_1^k, \ldots, u_n^k} E\left\{ J_{k+1}\left[s_k x_k + \sum_{i=1}^{n} (e_i^k - s_k) u_i^k \right] \right\}. \tag{2.58}$$

From the solution of the one-period problem we have that the optimal policy at the beginning of period $N - 1$ is of the form

$$\mu_{N-1}^*(x_{N-1}) = \alpha_{N-1}[a + b s_{N-1} x_{N-1}],$$

where α_{N-1} is an appropriate n-dimensional vector. Furthermore, we have

$$-\frac{J'_{N-1}(x)}{J''_{N-1}(x)} = \frac{a}{s_{N-1}} + bx. \tag{2.59}$$

Hence, applying the result of this section in (2.58) for the next to the last period, we obtain the optimal policy

$$\mu^*_{N-2}(x_{N-2}) = \alpha_{N-2}\left(\frac{a}{s_{N-1}} + bs_{N-2}x_{N-2}\right),$$

where α_{N-2} is again an appropriate n-dimensional vector.

Proceeding similarly, we have for the kth period

$$\mu^*_k(x_k) = \alpha_k\left(\frac{a}{s_{N-1}\cdots s_{k+1}} + bs_kx_k\right), \tag{2.60}$$

where α_k, $k = 0, 1, \ldots, N - 1$, are n-dimensional vectors that depend on the probability distributions of the rates of return e_i^k of the risky assets and are determined by optimization of the expected value of the optimal cost-to-go functions J_k. These functions satisfy

$$-\frac{J'_k(x)}{J''_k(x)} = \frac{a}{s_{N-1}\cdots s_k} + bx, \qquad k = 0, 1, \ldots, N-1. \tag{2.61}$$

Thus one can see that the investor, when faced with the opportunity to reinvest sequentially his wealth, uses a policy similar to that of the single-period case. Carrying the analysis one step further, one can see that if the utility function U is such that $a = 0$, that is, U has one of the forms

$$\ln x, \qquad \text{for} \quad b = 1,$$

$$\left(\frac{1}{b-1}\right)(bx)^{1-(1/b)}, \qquad \text{for} \quad b \neq 0, \quad b \neq 1,$$

then it follows from (2.60) that the investor acts at each stage k as if he were faced with a *single-period* investment characterized by the rates of return s_k, e_i^k, $i = 1, \ldots, n$, and the objective function $E\{U(x_{k+1})\}$. This policy whereby the investor can ignore the fact that he will have the opportunity to reinvest his wealth is called a *myopic policy* [M10].

Note that a myopic policy is also optimal when $s_k = 1$ for all k, which means that wealth is discounted at the rate of return of the riskless asset. Furthermore, it can be proved that when $a = 0$ a myopic policy is optimal even in the more general case where the rates of return s_k are independent random variables [M10], and for the case where forecasts on the probability distributions of the rates of return e_i^k of the risky assets become available during the investment process (see Problem 7).

It turns out that even for the more general case where $a \neq 0$ only a small amount of foresight is required on the part of the decision maker. It can be seen [compare (2.58) to (2.61)] that the optimal policy (2.60) at period k is the same as the one that would be used if the investor were faced with a single-period problem whereby he would maximize over u_i^k, $i = 1, \ldots, n$,

$$E\{U(s_{N-1} \cdots s_{k+1}x_{k+1})\}$$

subject to $x_{k+1} = s_k x_k + \sum_{i=1}^n (e_i^k - s_k)u_i^k$. In other words, the investor maximizes the expected utility of wealth that results if amounts u_i^k are invested in the risky assets in period k and the resulting wealth x_{k+1} is subsequently invested *exclusively* in the riskless asset during the remaining periods $k + 1, \ldots, N - 1$. This is known as a *partially myopic policy* [M10]. Such a policy can also be shown to be optimal when forecasts on the probability distributions of the rates of return of the risky assets become available during the investment process (see Problem 7).

Another interesting aspect of the case where $a \neq 0$ is that, when $s_k > 1$ for all k, then as the horizon becomes increasingly long ($N \to \infty$) the policy in the initial stages approaches a myopic policy [compare (2.60) and (2.61)]. Thus we can conclude that for $s_k > 1$ a partially myopic policy is asymptotically myopic as the horizon tends to infinity.

2.4 OPTIMAL STOPPING PROBLEMS

Optimal stopping problems of the type we will consider in this and subsequent sections are characterized by the availability, at each state, of a control that stops the evolution of the system. Thus at each stage the controller observes the current state of the system and decides whether to continue the process (perhaps at a certain cost) or stop the process and incur a certain loss.

Asset Selling Problem

As a first example, consider a person having an asset (say a piece of land) for which he is offered an amount of money from period to period. Let us assume that these random offers $w_0, w_1, \ldots, w_{N-1}$ are independent, identically distributed, and take values within some bounded interval. We consider a horizon of N stages and assume that if the person accepts the offer, he can invest the money at a fixed rate of interest $r > 0$, and if he rejects the offer, he waits until the next period to consider the next offer. Offers rejected are not renewed, and we assume that the last offer w_{N-1} must be accepted if every prior offer has been rejected. The objective is to find a policy for accepting and rejecting offers that maximizes the revenue of the person at the Nth period.

The DP algorithm for this problem can be derived by elementary reasoning. As a modeling exercise, however, we will try to embed the problem in the framework of the basic problem by defining the state space, control space, disturbance space, system equation, and cost functional. We consider as disturbance at time k the random offer w_k and as corresponding disturbance space the real line. The control space consists of two elements

u^1, u^2, which correspond to the decisions "sell" and "do not sell," respectively. We define the state space to be the real line, augmented with an additional state (call it T), which is a *termination state*. The system moves into the termination state as soon as the asset is sold. By writing that the system is at a state $x_k \neq T$ at time k, we mean that the asset has not been sold as yet and the current offer under consideration is equal to x_k. By writing that the system is at state $x_k = T$ at time k, we mean that the asset has already been sold. With these conventions we may write a system equation of the form

$$x_{k+1} = f_k(x_k, u_k, w_k), \qquad k = 0, \ldots, N-1,$$
$$x_0 = 0,$$

where $x_k \in R \cup \{T\}$ and the function f_k is defined via the relations

$$x_{k+1} = \begin{cases} T, & \text{if } \; u_k = u^1(\text{sell}) \;\text{ or }\; x_k = T, \\ w_k, & \text{otherwise.} \end{cases}$$

The corresponding reward function may be written

$$\underset{\substack{w_k \\ k=0,\ldots,N-1}}{E} \left\{ g_N(x_N) + \sum_{k=0}^{N-1} g_k(x_k, u_k, w_k) \right\}$$

where

$$g_N(x_N) = \begin{cases} x_N, & \text{if } \; x_N \neq T, \\ 0, & \text{otherwise,} \end{cases}$$

$$g_k(x_k, u_k, w_k) = \begin{cases} (1+r)^{N-k} x_k, & \text{if } \; x_k \neq T \;\text{ and }\; u_k = u^1, \\ 0, & \text{otherwise.} \end{cases}$$

Based on this formulation we can write the corresponding DP algorithm over the states x_k:

$$J_N(x_N) = \begin{cases} x_N, & \text{if } \; x_N \neq T, \\ 0, & \text{if } \; x_N = T, \end{cases} \tag{2.62}$$

$$J_k(x_k) = \begin{cases} \max[(1+r)^{N-k} x_k, E\{J_{k+1}(w_k)\}], & \text{if } \; x_k \neq T, \\ 0, & \text{if } \; x_k = T. \end{cases} \tag{2.63}$$

In Eq. (2.63), $(1 + r)^{N-k} x_k$ (where $x_k \neq T$) is the revenue resulting from decision u^1 (sell) when the offer under consideration is x_k, and $E\{J_{k+1}(w_k)\}$ represents the expected revenue corresponding to the decision u^2 (do not sell).

Now from the DP algorithm (2.62) and (2.63) we obtain the following optimal policy for the case where $x_k \neq T$:

$$\text{accept the offer } w_{k-1} = x_k \qquad \text{if} \quad (1+r)^{N-k} x_k > E\{J_{k+1}(w_k)\},$$

$$\text{reject the offer } w_{k-1} = x_k \qquad \text{if} \quad (1+r)^{N-k} x_k < E\{J_{k+1}(w_k)\}.$$

When $(1 + r)^{N-k} x_k = E\{J_{k+1}(w_k)\}$, both acceptance and rejection are optimal.

The result can be put into a more convenient form by some further analysis. Let us introduce the functions

$$V_k(x_k) = \frac{1}{(1+r)^{N-k}} J_k(x_k), \qquad x_k \neq T,$$

which represent discounted cost-to-go for the last $N - k$ stages. It can be seen from (2.62) and (2.63) that

$$V_N(x_N) = x_N, \tag{2.64}$$

$$V_k(x_k) = \max[x_k, (1+r)^{-1} E\{V_{k+1}(w_k)\}], \qquad k = 0, 1, \ldots, N-1. \tag{2.65}$$

By using the notation

$$\alpha_k = \frac{1}{1+r} E\{V_{k+1}(w_k)\},$$

the optimal policy is given by

$$\text{accept the offer } w_{k-1} = x_k \qquad \text{if} \quad x_k > \alpha_k,$$

$$\text{reject the offer } w_{k-1} = x_k \qquad \text{if} \quad x_k < \alpha_k,$$

while both acceptance and rejection are optimal for $x_k = \alpha_k$ (Figure 2.5). Thus the optimal policy is determined by the sequence $\alpha_1, \ldots, \alpha_{N-1}$.

From the algorithm (2.64) and (2.65) we have

$$V_k(x_k) = \begin{cases} x_k, & \text{if} \quad x_k > \alpha_k, \\ \alpha_k, & \text{if} \quad x_k < \alpha_k. \end{cases}$$

Hence we obtain

$$\alpha_k = \frac{1}{1+r} E\{V_{k+1}(w_k)\} = \frac{1}{1+r} \int_0^{\alpha_{k+1}} \alpha_{k+1} \, dP(w_k) + \frac{1}{1+r} \int_{\alpha_{k+1}}^{\infty} w_k \, dP(w_k),$$

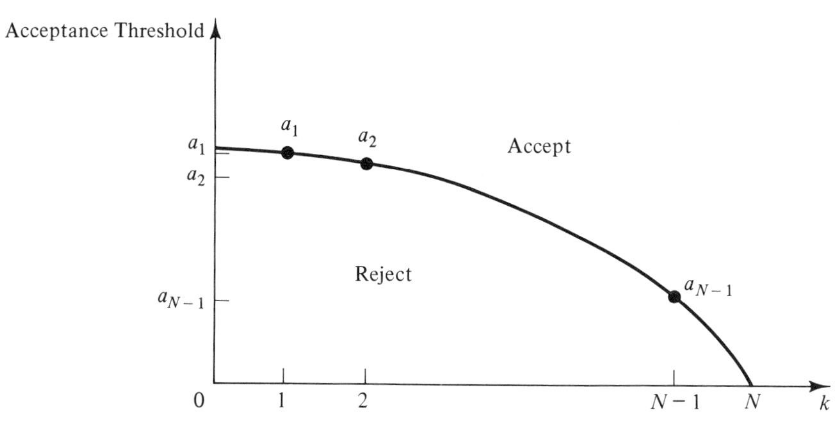

Figure 2.5 Threshold for accepting offers as a function of time.

where the function P is defined for all scalars λ by

$$P(\lambda) = \text{Prob}\{w < \lambda\}.$$

The difference equation for α_k may also be written

$$\alpha_k = \frac{P(\alpha_{k+1})}{1+r}\alpha_{k+1} + \frac{1}{1+r}\int_{\alpha_{k+1}}^{\infty} w_k \, dP(w_k), \qquad k = 1, \ldots, N-1, \tag{2.66}$$

with $\alpha_N = 0$. Let us first show that the solution of this equation is monotonically nonincreasing (as one would expect); that is,

$$\alpha_k \geq \alpha_{k+1}, \qquad \text{for all } k. \tag{2.67}$$

Indeed, from (2.64) and 2.65), we see that for all $x \geq 0$

$$V_{N-1}(x) \geq V_N(x), \qquad \text{for all } x \geq 0.$$

Applying (2.65) for $k = N - 2$ and $k = N - 1$, and using the preceding inequality, we obtain for all $x \geq 0$

$$\begin{aligned} V_{N-2}(x) &= \max\,[x, (1+r)^{-1}E_w\{V_{N-1}(w)\}] \\ &\geq \max\,[x, (1+r)^{-1}E_w\{V_N(w)\}] = V_{N-1}(x). \end{aligned}$$

Continuing in the same manner, we see that

$$V_k(x) \geq V_{k+1}(x), \qquad \text{for all } x \geq 0 \text{ and } k.$$

Since $\alpha_k = E\{V_{k+1}(w_k)\}/(1 + r)$, we obtain (2.67).

Now since we have

$$0 \leq \frac{P(\alpha)}{1+r} \leq \frac{1}{1+r} < 1, \qquad \text{for all } \alpha \geq 0,$$

$$0 \leq \frac{1}{1+r}\int_{\alpha_{k+1}}^{\infty} w \, dP(w_k) \leq \frac{E\{w_k\}}{1+r}, \qquad \text{for all } k,$$

it can be seen, using the monotonicity property (2.67), that the sequence $\{\alpha_k\}$ generated (backward) by the difference equation (2.66) converges (as $k \to -\infty$) to a constant $\overline{\alpha}$ satisfying

$$\overline{\alpha}(1+r) = P(\overline{\alpha})\overline{\alpha} + \int_{\overline{\alpha}}^{\infty} w \, dP(w).$$

This equation is obtained from (2.66) by taking limits as $k \to -\infty$ and by using the fact that P is continuous from the left.

Thus, when the horizon tends to become longer and longer (i.e., $N \to \infty$), the optimal policy for every fixed $k \geq 1$ approximates the stationary policy:

$$\text{accept the offer } w_{k-1} = x_k \qquad \text{if} \quad x_k > \overline{\alpha},$$

$$\text{reject the offer } w_{k-1} = x_k \qquad \text{if} \quad x_k < \overline{\alpha}.$$

The optimality of such a policy for the corresponding infinite horizon problem will be shown in Section 6.1.

Purchasing with a Deadline

Let us consider another problem of similar nature. Assume that a certain quantity of raw material is required by a certain time. If the price of this material fluctuates, then there arises the problem of deciding whether to purchase at the current price or wait a further period, during which the price may go up or down. We assume that successive prices w_k are independent and identically distributed with distribution $P(w_k)$, and that the purchase must be made within N time periods.

This problem and the earlier one have obvious similarities. Let us denote by

$$x_{k+1} = w_k$$

the price prevailing in the beginning of period $k + 1$. We have similarly as before the DP algorithm

$$J_N(x_N) = x_N,$$
$$J_k(x_k) = \min[x_k, E\{J_{k+1}(w_k)\}],$$

and the optimal policy is given by

$$\text{purchase if} \quad x_k < E\{J_{k+1}(w_k)\} = \alpha_k,$$
$$\text{do not purchase if} \quad x_k > E\{J_{k+1}(w_k)\} = \alpha_k.$$

We have similarly that the thresholds $\alpha_1, \alpha_2, \ldots, \alpha_{N-1}$ can be obtained from the discrete-time equation

$$\alpha_k = \alpha_{k+1}[1 - P(\alpha_{k+1})] + \int_0^{\alpha_{k+1}} w\, dP(w),$$

$$\alpha_{N-1} = \int_0^{\infty} wP(w) = E\{w\}.$$

Consider now a variation of this problem whereby we do not assume that the successive prices $w_0, \ldots, w_{N-1}$ are independent but rather that they are correlated and can be represented as

$$w_k = x_{k+1}, \qquad k = 0, 1, \ldots, N - 1,$$

with

$$x_{k+1} = \lambda x_k + \xi_k, \qquad x_0 = 0,$$

where λ is a scalar with $0 \leq \lambda < 1$ and $\xi_0, \xi_1, \ldots, \xi_{N-1}$ are independent identically distributed random variables taking positive values with given probability distribution. As discussed in Section 1.5, the DP algorithm under these circumstances takes the form

$$J_N(x_N) = x_N,$$
$$J_k(x_k) = \min[x_k, E\{J_{k+1}(\lambda x_k + \xi_k)\}],$$

where the cost associated with the purchasing decision is x_k and the cost associated with the waiting decision is $E\{J_{k+1}(\lambda x_k + \xi_k)\}$.

We will show that in this case the optimal policy is also of the same type as the one for independent prices. Indeed, we have

$$J_{N-1}(x_{N-1}) = \min [x_{N-1}, \lambda x_{N-1} + \bar{\xi}],$$

where $\bar{\xi} = E\{\xi_{N-1}\}$. As shown in Figure 2.6, an optimal policy at time $N - 1$ is given by

$$\text{purchase} \quad \text{if} \quad x_{N-1} < \alpha_{N-1},$$

$$\text{do not purchase} \quad \text{if} \quad x_{N-1} > \alpha_{N-1},$$

where α_{N-1} is defined from the equation $\alpha_{N-1} = \lambda\alpha_{N-1} + \bar{\xi}$; that is,

$$\alpha_{N-1} = \frac{1}{1-\lambda}\bar{\xi}.$$

Note that

$$J_{N-1}(x) \leq J_N(x), \qquad \text{for all } x,$$

and that J_{N-1} is concave and increasing in x. Using this fact in the DP algorithm, one may show (Problem 24 in Chapter 1) that

$$J_k(x) \leq J_{k+1}(x), \qquad \text{for all } x \text{ and } k,$$

and that J_k is concave and increasing in x for all k. Furthermore, in view of the fact that $\bar{\xi} = E\{\xi_k\} > 0$ for all k, one can show that

$$E\{J_{k+1}(\xi_k)\} > 0, \qquad \text{for all } k.$$

These facts imply (as shown in Figure 2.7) that the optimal policy for every

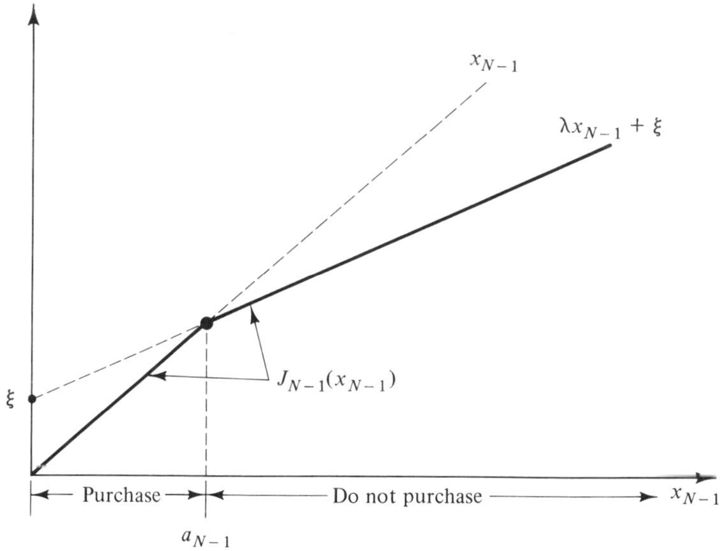

Figure 2.6 Structure of cost-to-go function $J_{N-1}(x_{N-1})$ when prices are correlated.

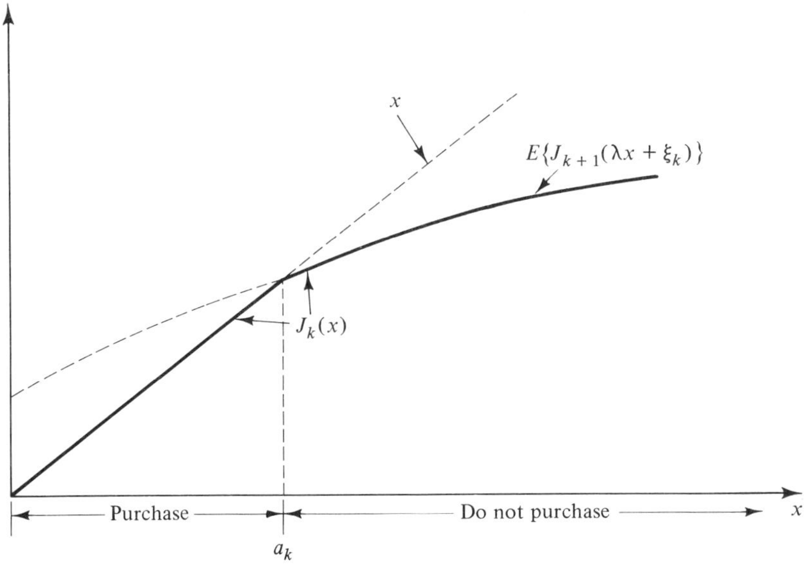

Figure 2.7 Determining the optimal policy when prices are correlated.

period k is of the form

$$\begin{aligned} &\text{purchase} && \text{if} \quad x_k < \alpha_k, \\ &\text{do not purchase} && \text{if} \quad x_k > \alpha_k, \end{aligned}$$

where the scalar α_k is obtained as the unique positive solution of the equation

$$x = E\{J_{k+1}(\lambda x + \xi_k)\}.$$

Note that $J_k(x) \leqslant J_{k+1}(x)$ implies

$$\alpha_{k-1} \leqslant \alpha_k \leqslant \alpha_{k+1}, \qquad \text{for all } k,$$

and hence (as one would expect) the threshold price below which one should purchase is lower in the early stages of the process and increases as the deadline comes nearer.

General Stopping Problems and the One-Step-Look-Ahead Rule

We now formulate a general type of N-stage problem where stopping is mandatory at or before stage N. Consider the stationary version of the basic problem of Section 1.1 (state, control, and disturbance spaces, disturbance distribution, control constraint set, and cost per stage are the same for all times). Assume that at each state x_k and time k there is available, in addition to the controls $u_k \in U(x_k)$, a stopping action that forces the system to enter a termination state at a cost $t(x_k)$ and subsequently remain there at no cost. The terminal cost, assuming stopping has not occurred by the last stage, is $t(x_N)$. Thus, in effect, we assume that the termination cost will always be incurred either at the last stage or earlier.

The DP algorithm is given by

$$J_N(x_N) = t(x_N) \tag{2.68}$$

$$J_k(x_k) = \min \Big[t(x_k), \min_{u \in U(x)} E\{g(x_k, u_k, w_k) \tag{2.69}$$
$$+ J_{k+1}[f(x_k, u_k, w_k)]\}\Big], \qquad k = 0, 1, \ldots, N-1,$$

and it is optimal to stop at time k for states x in the set

$$T_k = \{x | t(x) \leq \min_{u \in U(x)} E\{g(x, u, w) + J_{k+1}[f(x, u, w)]\}\}.$$

We have from (2.68) and (2.69)

$$J_{N-1}(x) \leq J_N(x), \qquad \text{for all } x \in S,$$

and using this fact in (2.69) we obtain inductively

$$J_k(x) \leq J_{k+1}(x), \qquad \text{for all } x \in S \text{ and } k.$$

[We are making use here of the stationarity of the problem and the monotonicity property of DP (Problem 24 in Chapter 1).] Using this fact and the definition of T_k, we see that

$$T_0 \subset \ldots \subset T_k \subset T_{k+1} \subset \ldots \subset T_{N-1}. \tag{2.70}$$

Consider now the case where the set T_{N-1} is *absorbing* in the sense that if a state belongs to T_{N-1} and termination is not selected, the next state will also be in T_{N-1}; that is,

$$f(x, u, w) \in T_{N-1}, \qquad \text{for } x \in T_{N-1}, \quad u \in U(x), \quad w \in D. \tag{2.71}$$

We will show that equality holds in (2.70) and for all k we have

$$T_k = T_{N-1} = \{x \in S | t(x) \leq \min_{u \in U(x)} E\{g(x, u, w) + t[f(x, u, w)]\}\}.$$

To see this, note that by definition of T_{N-1} we have

$$J_{N-1}(x) = t(x), \qquad x \in T_{N-1},$$

and using (2.71) we obtain for $x \in T_{N-1}$

$$\min_{u \in U(x)} E\{g(x, u, w) + J_{N-1}[f(x, u, w)]\}$$
$$= \min_{u \in U(x)} E\{g(x, u, w) + t[f(x, u, w)]\} \geq t(x).$$

Therefore, stopping is optimal for all $x_{N-2} \in T_{N-1}$ or equivalently $T_{N-1} \subset T_{N-2}$. This together with (2.70) implies $T_{N-2} = T_{N-1}$, and proceeding similarly we obtain $T_k = T_{N-1}$ for all k.

In conclusion, *if condition (2.71) holds (the one-step stopping set T_{N-1} is absorbing), then the stopping sets T_k are all equal to the set of states for which it is better to stop rather than continue for one more stage and then stop.* A policy of this type is known as a *one-step-look-ahead policy.* It turns out to be optimal in several types of applications. We provide next some examples. Additional examples are given in the problem section and in Sections 6.3 and 6.4 where the stopping problem is reexamined in an infinite horizon context.

Example 1

Asset Selling with Past Offers Retained. Consider the asset selling problem considered earlier in this section with the difference that rejected offers can be accepted at a later time. Then if the asset is not sold at time k the state evolves according to

$$x_{k+1} = \max[x_k, w_k]$$

instead of $x_{k+1} = w_k$. The DP equations (2.64) and (2.65) become then

$$V_N(x_N) = x_N$$

$$V_k(x_k) = \max[x_k, (1 + r)^{-1} E\{V_{k+1}(\max[x_k, w_k])\}].$$

The one-step-to-go stopping set is

$$T_{N-1} = \{x \mid x \geq (1 + r)^{-1} E\{\max[x, w]\}\}.$$

It is seen [compare with (2.66)] that an alternative characterization is

$$T_{N-1} = \{x \mid x \geq \overline{\alpha}\} \tag{2.72}$$

where $\overline{\alpha}$ is obtained from the equation

$$\overline{\alpha}(1 + r) = P(\overline{\alpha})\overline{\alpha} + \int_{\overline{\alpha}}^{\infty} w \, dp(w).$$

Since past offers can be accepted at a later date, the effective offer available cannot decrease with time, and it follows that the one-step stopping set (2.72) is absorbing in the sense of (2.71). Therefore, the one-step-look-ahead stopping rule that accepts the first offer that equals or exceeds $\overline{\alpha}$ is optimal. Note that this policy is independent of the horizon length N.

Example 2

The Rational Burglar [*W11*]. A burglar may at any night k choose to retire with his accumulated earnings x_k or enter a house and bring home an amount w_k. However, in the latter case he gets caught with probability p and then he is forced to terminate his activities and forfeit his earnings thus far. The amounts w_k are independent, identically distributed with mean $\overline{w}$. The problem is to find a policy that maximizes the burglar's expected earnings over N nights.

We can formulate this problem as a stopping problem with two actions (retire or continue) and a state space consisting of the real line, the retirement state, and a special state corresponding to the burglar getting caught. The DP algorithm is given by

$$J_N(x_N) = x_N$$

$$J_k(x_k) = \max[x_k, (1 - p)E\{J_{k+1}(x_k + w_k)\}].$$

The one-step-to-go stopping set is

$$T_{N-1} = \{x \mid x \geq (1 - p)(x + \overline{w})\} = \left\{x \;\middle|\; x \geq \frac{(1 - p)\overline{w}}{p}\right\},$$

(more accurately this set together with the special state corresponding to the burglar's arrest). Since this set is absorbing in the sense of (2.71), we conclude that the one-step-look-ahead policy by which the burglar retires when his earnings reach or exceed $(1 - p)\overline{w}/p$ is optimal. The optimality of this policy for the corresponding infinite horizon problem will be demonstrated in Section 6.3.

2.5 SCHEDULING AND THE INTERCHANGE ARGUMENT

Suppose one has a collection of tasks to perform but the ordering of the tasks is subject to optimal choice; for example, the ordering of operations in a construction project so as to minimize construction time or the scheduling of jobs in a workshop so as to minimize machine idle time. In such problems a useful technique is often to start with some schedule and then to interchange two adjacent tasks and see what happens.

As an example, consider a quiz contest whereby a person must answer questions from a given list of N in any order he chooses. Question i will be answered correctly with probability P_i, and the person will then receive a reward r_i. At the first incorrect answer, the quiz terminates and the person is allowed to keep his previous rewards. The problem is to choose the ordering of questions so as to maximize expected rewards.

Let i and j be two adjacent questions in an optimally ordered list $L = (i_0, \ldots, i_{k-1}, i, j, i_{k+2}, \ldots, i_{N-1})$. Consider the list $L' = (i_0, \ldots, i_{k-1}, j, i, i_{k+2}, \ldots, i_{N-1})$ obtained from L by interchanging the order of the kth and $(k + 1)$st questions i and j. We compare the expected rewards of L and L'. We have

$$\begin{aligned} E\{\text{reward of } L\} = {} & E\{\text{reward of } \{i_0, \ldots, i_{k-1}\}\} \\ & + p_{i_0} \cdots p_{i_{k-1}} (p_i r_i + p_i p_j r_j) \\ & + p_{i_0} \cdots p_{i_{k-1}} p_i p_j \, E\{\text{reward of } \{i_{k+2}, \ldots, i_{N-1}\}\} \\ E\{\text{reward of } L'\} = {} & E\{\text{reward of } \{i_0, \ldots, i_{k-1}\}\} \\ & + p_{i_0} \cdots p_{i_{k-1}} (p_j r_j + p_j p_i r_i) \\ & + p_{i_0} \cdots p_{i_{k-1}} p_j p_i \, E\{\text{reward of } \{i_{k+2}, \ldots, i_{N-1}\}\}. \end{aligned}$$

Since L is optimally ordered, it follows from these equations that

$$p_j r_j + p_j p_i r_i \leq p_i r_i + p_i p_j r_j$$

or equivalently

$$\frac{p_j r_j}{1 - p_j} \leq \frac{p_i r_i}{1 - p_i}.$$

Therefore, to maximize expected rewards, questions should be answered in decreasing order of $p_i r_i/(1 - p_i)$.

The Interchange Argument

Let us consider the basic problem of Chapter 1 and try to generalize the interchange argument given previously. The basic requirement is that the problem be such that *there exists an open-loop policy that is optimal*, that is, a sequence of controls that performs as well as any sequence of control functions. This is certainly true in deterministic problems as discussed in Chapter 1, but it is also true in some stochastic problems including the preceding example.

To apply the interchange argument, we start with an optimal sequence $\{u_0, \ldots, u_{k-1}, u^*, \tilde{u}, u_{k+2}, \ldots, u_{N-1}\}$ and focus attention on the controls u^* and $\tilde{u}$ applied at times k and $k + 1$, respectively ($k = 0, 1, \ldots, N - 1$). We then argue that if the order of u^* and $\tilde{u}$ is interchanged the expected cost cannot increase. In particular, if X_k is the set of states that can occur with positive probability starting from the given initial state x_0 and using the control subsequence $\{u_0, \ldots, u_{k-1}\}$, we must have for all $x_k \in X_k$

$$E\{g_k(x_k, u^*, w_k) + g_{k+1}(x^*_{k+1}, \tilde{u}, w_{k+1}) + J^*_{k+2}(x^*_{k+2})\}$$
$$\leq E\{g_k(x_k, \tilde{u}, w_k) + g_{k+1}(\tilde{x}_{k+1}, u^*, w_{k+1}) + J^*_{k+2}(\tilde{x}_{k+2})\}, \tag{2.73}$$

where x^*_{k+1} and x^*_{k+2} (or $\tilde{x}_{k+1}$ and $\tilde{x}_{k+2}$) are the states subsequent to x_k when $u_k = u^*$ and $u_{k+1} = \tilde{u}$ (or $u_k = \tilde{u}$ and $u_{k+1} = u^*$) are applied, and $J^*_{k+2}(\cdot)$ is the optimal cost-to-go function for time $k + 2$.

Relation (2.73) is a *necessary* condition for optimality. It holds for every k and every optimal policy that is open-loop. There is no guarantee that it is powerful enough to lead to an optimal solution in any given scheduling problem but it is certainly worth considering. We now provide two examples.

Job Scheduling on a Single Processor

Suppose we have N jobs to process in sequential order with the ith job requiring a random time T_i for its execution. The times $T_1, \ldots, T_N$ are independent. If job i is completed at time t, the reward is $a^t R_i$, where a is a discount factor with $0 < a < 1$. The problem is to find a schedule that maximizes the total expected reward.

It is evident that this problem can be formulated within the context of the basic problem. (Discrete time is incremented when a job is completed, the state at stage k is the collection of jobs completed thus far, and the admissible controls at time k are the jobs yet to be processed. The time of completion of the kth job need not be included in the state since the times T_i are independent.) It is clear also that there exists an open-loop policy that is optimal.

Consider an optimal job schedule $L = (i_0, \ldots, i_{k-1}, i, j, i_{k+2}, \ldots, i_{N-1})$, and the schedule $L' = (i_0, \ldots, i_{k-1}, j, i, i_{k+2}, \ldots, i_{N-1})$ obtained by interchanging i and j. Let t_k be the time of completion of job i_{k-1}. Since the reward for completing the remaining jobs $j_{k+2}, \ldots, i_{N-1}$ is independent of the order in which jobs i and j are executed, the necessary condition

(2.73) yields

$$E\{a^{t_k+T_i}R_i + a^{t_k+T_i+T_j}R_j\} \geq E\{a^{t_k+T_j}R_j + a^{t_k+T_j+T_i}R_i\}.$$

Since t_k, T_i, and T_j are independent, this relation can be written

$$E\{a^{t_k}\}(E\{a^{T_i}\}R_i + E\{a^{T_i}\}E\{a^{T_j}\}R_j) \geq E\{a^{T_k}\}(E\{a^{T_j}\}R_j + E\{a^{T_j}\}E\{a^{T_i}\}R_i),$$

from which we finally obtain

$$\frac{R_i\, E\{a^{T_i}\}}{1 - E\{a^{T_i}\}} \geq \frac{R_j\, E\{a^{T_j}\}}{1 - E\{a^{T_j}\}}.$$

It follows that scheduling jobs in order of decreasing $R_i\, E\{a^{T_i}\}/(1 - E\{a^{T_i}\})$ maximizes expected rewards.

Job Scheduling on Two Processors in Series [W3]

Consider scheduling of N jobs in two processors A and B, such that B accepts the output of A as input. Job i requires known times a_i and b_i for processing in A and B, respectively. The problem is to find a schedule that minimizes the total processing time.

To formulate the problem into the form of the basic problem, we increment discrete time at the moments when processing of a job is completed at machine A and the next job is started. We take as state at time k the collection of jobs X_k that remain to be processed at A together with the backlog of work τ_k at machine B, the amount of time needed to clear B if no further jobs were left. Thus if (X_k, τ_k) is the state at stage k and job i is completed at machine A, the state changes to (X_{k+1}, τ_{k+1}) given by

$$X_{k+1} = X_k - \{i\}, \qquad \tau_{k+1} = b_i + \min\,[0, \tau_k - a_i].$$

The corresponding DP algorithm is

$$J_k(X_k, \tau_k) = \min_{i \in X_k}\,[a_i + J_{k+1}(X_k - \{i\}, b_i + \min[0, \tau_k - a_i])]$$

with the terminal condition

$$J_N(\emptyset, \tau_N) = \tau_N$$

where $\emptyset$ is the empty set.

Since the problem is deterministic, there exists an optimal open-loop schedule $\{i_0, \ldots, i_{k-1}, i, j, i_{k+2}, \ldots, i_{N-1}\}$. Applying the necessary condition (2.73), we obtain

$$J_{k+2}(X_k - \{i\} - \{j\}, \tau_{ij}) \leq J_{k+2}(X_k - \{i\} - \{j\}, \tau_{ji}), \tag{2.74}$$

where τ_{ij} (τ_{ji}) is the backlog at machine B at time $k + 2$ when i is processed before j (j before i) and the backlog at time k was τ_k. A straightforward calculation shows that

$$\tau_{ij} = b_i + b_j - a_i - a_j + \max[\tau_k, a_i, a_i + a_j - b_i], \tag{2.75a}$$

$$\tau_{ji} = b_j + b_i - a_j - a_i + \max[\tau_k, a_j, a_j + a_i - b_j]. \tag{2.75b}$$

Clearly, J_{k+2} is monotonically increasing in τ, so from (2.74) we obtain

$$\tau_{ij} \leq \tau_{ji}.$$

In view of (2.75), this relation implies two possibilities. The first is

$$\tau_k \geq \max[a_i, a_i + a_j - b_i],$$

$$\tau_k \geq \max[a_j, a_j + a_i - b_j],$$

in which case $\tau_{ij} = \tau_{ji}$ and the order of i and j makes no difference. (This is the case where the backlog at time k is so large that both jobs i and j will find B working on an earlier job.) The second possibility is that

$$\max[a_i, a_i + a_j - b_i] \geq \max[a_j, a_j + a_i - b_j],$$

which can be seen to be equivalent to

$$\min[a_i, b_j] \leq \min[a_j, b_i].$$

A schedule satisfying these necessary conditions for optimality can be constructed by the following procedure:

1. Find $\min_i \min[a_i, b_i]$.
2. If the minimizing value is an a take the corresponding job first; if it is a b, take the corresponding job last.
3. Repeat the procedure with the remaining jobs until a complete schedule is constructed.

To show that this schedule is indeed optimal, we start with an optimal schedule. We consider the job i_0 that minimizes $\min[a_i, b_i]$ and by successive interchanges we move it to the same position as in the schedule constructed previously. It is seen from the preceding analysis that the resulting schedule is still optimal. Similarly, continuing through successive interchanges and maintaining optimality throughout, we can transform the optimal schedule into the schedule constructed earlier. We leave the details to the reader.

2.6 NOTES

The certainty equivalence principle for dynamic linear–quadratic problems was first discussed by Simon [S19]. His work was preceded by that of Theil [T2], who considered a single-period case, and Holt et al. [H11], who considered a deterministic case. Similar problems were considered somewhat later (and apparently independently) by Kalman and Koepcke [K2], Gunckel and Franklin [G5], and Joseph and Tou [J5]. Since their work, the literature on linear-quadratic problems has grown tremendously. The special issue on the linear–quadratic problem of the *IEEE Transactions on Automatic Control* [I1] contains most of the pertinent theory and variations thereof, together with hundreds of references. For a multidimensional version of Problem 2, see [J1].

The literature on inventory control stimulated by the pioneering paper of Arrow et al. [A7] is also voluminous. The 1966 survey paper by Veinott [V5] contains 118 references. An important work summarizing most of the research up to 1958 is the book by Arrow et al. [A8]. The ingenious line of argument for proving the optimality of (s, S) policies in the case of nonzero fixed costs is due to Scarf [S5]. The result of Problem 17 is due to Veinott [V7]. See also Tsitsiklis [T7].

Most of the material in Section 3.3 is taken from the paper by Mossin [M10].

PROBLEMS

1. *Linear–Quadratic Problems with Forecasts.* Consider the linear–quadratic problem first examined in Section 2.1 (A_k, B_k: known) for the case where at the beginning of period k there is available a forecast $y_k \in \{1, 2, \ldots, n\}$ consisting of an accurate prediction that w_k will be selected in accordance with a particular probability distribution $P_{k|y_k}$ (cf. Section 1.4). The vectors w_k need not have zero mean under the distributions $P_{k|y_k}$. Show that the optimal control law is of the form

$$\mu_k(x_k, y_k) = -(B_k' K_{k+1} B_k + R_k)^{-1} B_k' K_{k+1}[A_k x_k + E\{w_k | y_k\}] + \alpha_k,$$

where the matrices K_k are given by the Riccati equation (2.5) and (2.6) and α_k are appropriate vectors.

2. Consider a scalar linear system

$$x_{k+1} = a_k x_k + b_k u_k + w_k, \qquad k = 0, 1, \ldots, N-1,$$

where a_k, $b_k \in R$, and each w_k is a Gaussian random variable with zero mean and variance σ^2. Show that the control law $\{\mu_0^*, \mu_1^*, \ldots, \mu_{N-1}^*\}$ that minimizes the cost functional

$$E\left\{\exp\left[x_N^2 + \sum_{k=0}^{N-1}(x_k^2 + r u_k^2)\right]\right\}, \qquad r > 0,$$

is linear in the state variable. We assume no control constraints, independent disturbances, and that the optimal cost is finite for every x_0. Show by example that the Gaussian assumption is essential for the result to hold.

3. Consider an inventory control problem similar to the multistage inventory problem of Section 3.2. The only difference is that at the beginning of each period k the decision maker, in addition to knowing the current inventory level x_k, receives an accurate forecast that the demand w_k will be selected in accordance with one out of two possible probability distributions P_l, P_s (large demand, small demand). The a priori probability of a large demand forecast is known (cf. Section 1.4).

(a) Obtain the optimal inventory ordering policy for the case of a single-period problem.

(b) Extend the result to the N-period case.

(c) Extend the result to the case of any finite number of possible distributions.

4. Consider the inventory control problem where the purchase costs c_k, $k = 0,$

$1, \ldots, N-1$, are not known at the beginning of the process but instead they are independent random variables with a priori known probability distributions. The exact value of the cost c_k, however, becomes known to the decision maker at the beginning of the kth period, so that the inventory purchasing decision at time k is made with exact knowledge of the cost c_k. Characterize the optimal ordering policy.

5. Consider the multiperiod inventory model of Section 2.2 for the case where there is a one-period time lag between order and delivery of inventory; that is, the system equation is of the form

$$x_{k+1} = x_k + u_{k-1} - w_k, \qquad k = 1, \ldots, N-1,$$

$$x_1 = x_0 - w_0.$$

Show that an (s, S) policy is optimal.

6. Consider the inventory problem under the assumption that unfillled demand at each stage is not backlogged but rather is lost; that is, the system equation is $x_{k+1} = \max[0, x_k + u_k - w_k]$ instead of $x_{k+1} = x_k + u_k - w_k$. Show that a multiperiod (s, S) policy is optimal.

Abbreviated Proof (S. Shreve) Let $J_N(x) = 0$ and for all k

$$G_k(y) = cy + E\{h \max[0, y - w_k] + p \max[0, w_k - y]$$
$$+ J_{k+1}(\max[0, y - w_k])\},$$

$$J_k(x) = -cx + \min_{u \geq 0}[K\delta(u) + G_k(x + u)],$$

where $\delta(0) = 0$, $\delta(u) = 1$ for $u > 0$. The result will follow if we can show that G_k is K-convex, continuous, and $G_k(y) \to \infty$ as $|y| \to \infty$. The difficult part is to show K-convexity since K-convexity of G_{k+1} does not imply K-convexity of $E\{J_{k+1}(\max[0, y - w])\}$. It will be sufficient to show that K-convexity of G_{k+1} implies K-convexity of

$$H(y) = p \max[0, -y] + J_{k+1}(\max[0, y]), \tag{2.76}$$

or equivalently that

$$K + H(y + z) \geq H(y) + z\frac{H(y) - H(y - b)}{b}, \qquad z \geq 0, \quad b > 0, \quad y. \tag{2.77}$$

By K-convexity of G_{k+1} we have for appropriate scalars s_{k+1} and S_{k+1} such that $G_{k+1}(S_{k+1}) = \min_y G_{k+1}(y)$ and $K + G_{k+1}(S_{k+1}) = G_{k+1}(s_{k+1})$:

$$J_{k+1}(x) = -cx + \begin{cases} G_{k+1}(x), & \text{if } s_{k+1} \leq x, \\ K + G_{k+1}(S_{k+1}), & \text{if } x < s_{k+1}, \end{cases} \tag{2.78}$$

and J_{k+1} is K-convex by the theory of Section 2.2.

Case 1 $0 \leq y - b < y \leq y + z$ For this region, (2.77) follows from K-convexity of J_{k+1}.

Case 2 $y - b < y \leq y + z \leq 0$ In this region, H is linear and hence K-convex.

Case 3 $y - b < y \leq 0 \leq y + z$ In this region, (2.77) may be written [in view of (2.76)] as $K + J_{k+1}(y + z) \geq J_{k+1}(0) - p(y + z)$. We will show that

$$K + J_{k+1}(z) \geq J_{k+1}(0) - pz, \qquad z \geq 0. \tag{2.79}$$

If $0 < s_{k+1} \leq z$, then using (2.78) and the fact $p > c$,

$$K + J_{k+1}(z) = K - cz + G_{k+1}(z) \geq K - pz + G_{k+1}(S_{k+1}) = J_{k+1}(0) - pz.$$

If $0 \leq z \leq s_{k+1}$, then using (2.78) and the fact $p > c$,

$$K + J_{k+1}(z) = 2K - cz + G_{k+1}(S_{k+1}) \geq K - pz + G_{k+1}(S_{k+1})$$
$$= J_{k+1}(0) - pz.$$

If $s_{k+1} \leq 0 \leq z$, then using (2.78), the fact $p > c$, and part (iv) of the lemma in Section 2.2,

$$K + J_{k+1}(z) = K - cz + G_{k+1}(z) \geq G_{k+1}(0) - pz = J_{k+1}(0) - pz.$$

Thus (2.79) is proved and (2.77) follows for the case under consideration.

Case 4 $y - b < 0 < y \leq y + z$ Then $0 < y < b$. If

$$\frac{H(y) - H(0)}{y} \geq \frac{H(y) - H(y - b)}{b}, \tag{2.80}$$

then since H agrees with J_{k+1} on $[0, \infty)$ and J_{k+1} is K-convex,

$$K + H(y + z) \geq H(y) + z\frac{H(y) - H(0)}{y} \geq H(y) + z\frac{H(y) - H(y - b)}{b},$$

where the last step follows from (2.80). If

$$\frac{H(y) - H(0)}{y} < \frac{H(y) - H(y - b)}{b},$$

then we have

$$H(y) - H(0) < \frac{y}{b}[H(y) - H(y - b)] = \frac{y}{b}[H(y) - H(0) + p(y - b)].$$

It follows that

$$\left(1 - \frac{y}{b}\right)[H(y) - H(0)] < \left(\frac{y}{b}\right)p(y - b) = -py\left(1 - \frac{y}{b}\right),$$

and since $b > y$,

$$H(y) - H(0) < -py. \tag{2.81}$$

Now we have, using the definition of H, (2.79), and (2.81),

$$H(y) + z\frac{H(y) - H(y - b)}{b} = H(y) + z\frac{H(0) - py - H(0) + p(y - b)}{b}$$
$$= H(y) - pz < H(0) - p(y + z)$$
$$\leq K + H(y + z).$$

Hence (2.77) is proved for this case as well. Q.E.D.

7. Consider the dynamic portfolio problem of Section 2.3 for the case where at each period k there is a forecast that the rates of return of the risky assets for

that period will be selected in accordance with a particular probability distribution as in Section 1.5. Show that a partially myopic policy is optimal.

8. Consider a problem involving the linear system

$$x_{k+1} = A_k x_k + B_k u_k, \qquad k = 0, 1, \ldots, N-1,$$

where the $n \times n$ matrices A_k are given and the $n \times m$ matrices B_k are independent random matrices and have given probability distributions that do not depend on x_k, u_k. The problem is to find the optimal control law $\{\mu_0^*, \ldots, \mu_{N-1}^*\}$ that maximizes the cost functional $E\{U(c'x_N)\}$, where c is a given n-dimensional vector. We assume that U is a concave utility function satisfying for all y

$$-\frac{U'(y)}{U''(y)} = a + by,$$

and that the control is unconstrained. Show that the optimal control law consists of affine functions of the current state. *Hint:* Reduce the problem to a one-dimensional problem and use the results of Section 2.3.

9. An employer interviews N candidates for a position and must decide immediately after each interview whether to appoint the corresponding candidate. A score is given to a candidate after the interview, and scores are independent and identically distributed. Determine the policy that maximizes the expected score of the appointed candidate.

10. Suppose that an individual wants to sell a house and an offer comes at the beginning of each day. We assume that successive offers are independent and an offer is x_j with probability p_j, $j = 1, \ldots, n$, where x_j are given nonnegative scalars. Any offer not immediately accepted is not lost but may be accepted at any later date. Also, a maintenance cost c is incurred for each day that the house remains unsold. The objective is to maximize the price at which the house is sold minus the maintenance costs. Consider the problem when there is a deadline to sell the house within N days and characterize the optimal policy.

11. *Capacity Expansion Problem.* Consider a problem of expanding the capacity of a facility for production of a single type of nonstorable good or service over N time periods. Let us denote by x_k the production capacity at the beginning of the kth period and by $u_k \geq 0$ the addition to capacity during the kth period. Thus capacity evolves according to

$$x_{k+1} = x_k + u_k, \qquad k = 0, 1, \ldots, N-1.$$

The demand at the kth period is denoted w_k and has a known probability distribution that does not depend on either x_k or u_k. Also, successive demands are assumed to be independent and bounded. We denote

$C_k(u_k)$ expansion cost associated with adding capacity u_k,

$P_k(x_k + u_k - w_k)$ penalty cost associated with capacity $x_k + u_k$ and demand w_k,

$S(x_N)$ salvage value of final capacity x_N.

Thus the cost functional takes the form

$$\underset{\substack{w_k \\ k=0,1,\ldots,N-1}}{E} \left\{ -S(x_N) + \sum_{k=0}^{N-1} [C_k(u_k) + P_k(x_k + u_k - w_k)] \right\}.$$

(a) Derive the DP algorithm for solving this problem.

(b) Assume that S is a concave function with $\lim_{x\to\infty} dS(x)/dx = 0$, P_k are convex functions, and the expansion cost C_k is of the form

$$C_k(u) = \begin{cases} K + c_k u, & \text{if } u > 0, \\ 0, & \text{if } u = 0, \end{cases}$$

where $K \geq 0$, $c_k > 0$ for all k. Show that the optimal policy is of the (s, S) type assuming $c_k y + E\{P_k(y - w_k)\} \to \infty$ as $|y| \to \infty$.

12. *A Gambling Problem.* A gambler enters a game whereby he may at any time k stake any amount $u_k \geq 0$ that does not exceed his current fortune x_k (defined to be his initial capital plus his gain or minus his loss thus far). He wins his stake back and as much more with probability p, where $\frac{1}{2} < p < 1$, and he loses his stake with probability $(1 - p)$. Show that the gambling strategy that maximizes $E\{\ln x_N\}$, where x_N denotes his fortune after N plays, is to stake at each time k an amount $u_k = (2p - 1)x_k$. *Hint:* The problem is related to the portfolio problem of Section 2.3.

13. *Optimal Termination of Sampling.* A collection of $N \geq 2$ objects is observed randomly and sequentially one at a time. The observer may either select the current object observed, in which case the selection process is terminated, or reject the object and proceed to observe the next. The observer can rank each object relative to those already observed, and the objective is to maximize the probability of selecting the "best" object according to some criterion. It is assumed that no two objects can be judged to be equal. Let r^* be the smallest positive integer r such that

$$\frac{1}{N-1} + \frac{1}{N-2} + \cdots + \frac{1}{r} \leq 1.$$

Show that an optimal policy requires that the first r^* objects be observed. If the r^*th object has rank 1 relative to the others already observed, it should be selected; otherwise, the observation process should be continued until an object of rank 1 relative to those already observed is found. *Hint:* We assume that, if the rth object has rank 1 relative to the previous $(r - 1)$ objects, then the probability that it is best is r/N. For $k \geq r^*$, let $J_k(0)$ be the maximal probability of finding the best object assuming k objects have been selected and the kth object is not best relative to the previous $(k - 1)$ objects. Show that

$$J_k(0) = \frac{k}{N}\left(\frac{1}{N-1} + \cdots + \frac{1}{k}\right).$$

14. Consider the inventory control problem of Section 2.2 with the difference that successive demands are correlated and satisfy a relation of the form

$$w_k = e_k - ce_{k-1}, \qquad k = 0, 1, \ldots,$$

where c is a given scalar, e_k are independent random variables, and $e_{-1} = 0$.

(a) Show that this problem can be converted into an inventory problem with independent demands. *Hint:* Given $w_0, w_1, \ldots, w_{k-1}$, we can determine e_{k-1} in view of the relation

$$e_{k-1} - c^k e_{-1} = \sum_{i=0}^{k-1} c^i w_{k-1-i}.$$

Define $z_k = x_k + ce_{k-1}$ as a new state variable.

(b) Show that the same is true when in addition there is a one-period delay in the delivery of inventory (cf. Problem 5).

15. Consider the inventory control problem of Section 2.2 with zero fixed cost, the only difference being that there is an upper bound $\overline{b}$ and a lower bound $\underline{b}$ to the allowable values of the stock x_k. This imposes the additional constraint on u_k

$$\underline{b} + d \leq u_k + x_k \leq \overline{b},$$

where $d > 0$ is the maximum value that the demand w_k can take (we assume $\underline{b} + d < \overline{b}$). Show that there exist scalars $S_0, S_1, \ldots, S_{N-1}$ and an optimal policy $\{\mu_0^*, \ldots, \mu_{N-1}^*\}$ of the form

$$\mu_k^*(x_k) = \begin{cases} S_k - x_k, & \text{if } x_k < S_k, \\ 0, & \text{if } x_k \geq S_k. \end{cases}$$

16. Consider the inventory control problem of Section 2.2 (nonzero fixed cost) with the difference that demand is deterministic and must be met at each time period (i.e., the shortage cost per unit is ∞). Show that it is optimal to order a positive amount at period k if and only if the stock x_k is insufficient to meet the demand w_k. Furthermore, when a positive amount is ordered, it should bring up stock to a level that will satisfy demand for an integral number of periods.

17. Consider the inventory control problem of Section 2.2 for zero fixed cost with the only difference that the orders u_k are constrained to be nonnegative *integers*. Let J_k be the optimal cost-to-go function. Show that:

(a) J_k is continuous.

(b) $J_k(x + 1) - J_k(x)$ is a nondecreasing function of x.

(c) There exists a sequence $\{S_k\}$ of numbers such that the policy given by

$$\mu_k(x_k) = \begin{cases} n, & \text{if } x_k \in [S_k - n, S_k - n + 1), \quad n = 1, 2, \ldots, \\ 0, & \text{if } x_k \geq S_k \end{cases}$$

is optimal.

18. The Greek adventurer Theseus is trapped in King Minos' Labyrinth maze. He can try on each day one of N passages. If he enters passage i he will escape with probability p_i, he will be killed with probability q_i, and he will determine that the passage is a dead end with probability $(1 - p_i - q_i)$, in which case he will return to the point from which he started. Show that trying passages in order of decreasing p_i/q_i maximizes the probability of escape within N days. *Hint:* Use an interchange argument.

19. A driver is looking for a parking place on the way to his destination. Each parking place is free with probability p independently of whether other parking places are free or not. The driver cannot observe whether a parking place is free until he reaches it. If he parks k places from his destination, he incurs a cost k. If he reaches the destination without having parked the cost is C.

(a) Let F_k be the minimal expected cost if he is k parking places from his destination. Show that

$$F_0 = C$$

$$F_k = p \min[k, F_{k-1}] + qF_{k-1}, \qquad k = 1, 2, \ldots,$$

where $q = 1 - p$.

(b) Show that an optimal policy is of the form: never park if $k \geqslant k^*$, but take the first free place if $k < k^*$, where k is the number of parking places from the destination and k^* is the smallest integer i satisfying $q^{i-1} < (pC + q)^{-1}$.

20. *Hardy's Theorem.* Let $\{a_1, \ldots, a_n\}$ and $\{b_1, \ldots, b_n\}$ be monotonically nondecreasing sequences of numbers. Let us associate with each $i = 1, \ldots, n$ a distinct index j_i, and consider the expression $\Sigma_{i=1}^n a_i b_{j_i}$. Show that this expression is maximized when $j_i = i$ for all i, and is minimized when $j_i = n - i + 1$ for all i. *Hint:* Use an interchange argument.

21. A person may go hunting for a certain type of animal on a given day or stay home. When the animal population is x, the probability of capturing one animal is $p(x)$, a known increasing function, and the probability of capturing more than one is zero. A captured animal is worth one unit and a day of hunting costs c units. Show that it is optimal to hunt only when $p(x) \geqslant c$.

22. Consider the scalar linear system

$$x_{k+1} = ax_k + bu_k$$

where a and b are known. At each period k we have the option of using a control u_k and incur a cost $qx_k^2 + ru_k^2$, or else stop and incur a stopping cost tx_k^2. If we have not stopped by period N, the terminal cost is the stopping cost tx_N^2. We assume that $q \geqslant 0$, $r > 0$, $t > 0$. Show that there is a threshold value for t below which immediate stopping is optimal at every initial state and above which continuing at every state x_k and period k is optimal.

CHAPTER THREE

Problems with Imperfect State Information

3.1 REDUCTION TO THE PERFECT STATE INFORMATION CASE

We have assumed so far that the controller has access to the exact value of the current state, but this assumption is often unrealistic. For example, some state variables may be inaccessible, the sensors used for measuring them may be inaccurate, or the cost of obtaining the exact value of the state may be prohibitive. We model situations of this type by assuming that at each stage the controller receives some observations about the value of the current state, which may be corrupted by stochastic uncertainty. Mathematically, the observation z_k obtained at stage k has the form

$$z_k = h_k(x_k, u_{k-1}, v_k),$$

where h_k is some function and v_k is a random disturbance. We will provide a precise problem formulation shortly. We first look at an example.

Multiaccess Communication Example

Consider a collection of transmitting stations sharing a common channel, for example, a set of ground stations communicating with a satellite at a common frequency. The stations are synchronized to transmit packets of data at integer times. Each packet requires one time unit (also called a *slot*) for transmission. The total number a_k of packet arrivals during slot k is independent of prior arrivals and has a given probability distribution. The stations do not know the backlog x_k at the beginning of the kth slot (the number of packets waiting transmission). There is therefore some difficulty in scheduling packet transmissions. As a result, a strategy is adopted (known as *slotted Aloha*) whereby each packet in the system at the beginning of slot k is transmitted during that slot with probability u_k (common for all packets). If two or more packets are transmitted simultaneously, they collide and have to rejoin the backlog for retransmission at a later slot. However, the stations can observe the channel and determine whether in any one slot there was a collision (more than two packets), a success (one packet), or an idle (no packets). These observations provide information about the state of the system (the backlog x_k) and can be used to select appropriately the control (the transmission probability u_k). The objective is to keep the backlog small so that a cost per stage $g_k(x_k)$, which is a monotonically increasing function of x_k, is appropriate.

The state of the system here is the backlog x_k and evolves according to the equation

$$x_{k+1} = x_k + a_k - t_k,$$

where a_k is the number of new arrivals and t_k is the number of packets successfully transmitted during slot k. Both a_k and t_k may be viewed as stochastic disturbances, and the distribution of t_k depends on the state x_k and the control u_k. It can be seen that t_k is unity (a success) with probability $x_k u_k(1 - u_k)^{x_k - 1}$, and zero (idle or collision) otherwise. If we had perfect state information (i.e., the backlog x_k were known at the beginning of slot k), the optimal policy would be to select the value of u_k that maximizes the success probability $x_k u_k(1 - u_k)^{x_k - 1}$. By setting the derivative of this probability to zero, we find the optimal (perfect state information) policy to be

$$\mu_k(x_k) = \frac{1}{x_k}, \qquad \text{for all } x_k \geq 1.$$

However, x_k is not known (imperfect state information), and the optimal control must be chosen on the basis of the available observations (i.e., the entire channel history of successes, idles, and collisions). These observations relate to the backlog history (the past states) and the past transmission probabilities (the past controls), but are corrupted by stochastic uncertainty. Mathematically, we may write an equation $z_{k+1} = v_{k+1}$, where z_{k+1} is the observation obtained at the end of the kth slot, and the random variable v_{k+1} yields an idle with probability $(1 - u_k)^{x_k}$, a success with probability $x_k u_k(1 - u_k)^{x_k - 1}$, and a collision otherwise.

We now state precisely the problem of this chapter.

Basic Problem with Imperfect State Information

Consider the basic problem of Section 1.1 where the controller, instead of having perfect knowledge of the state, has access to observations z_k of the form

$$z_0 = h_0(x_0, v_0), \qquad z_k = h_k(x_k, u_{k-1}, v_k), \qquad k = 1, 2, \ldots, N-1. \tag{3.1}$$

The observation z_k belongs to a given observation space Z_k. The random observation disturbance v_k belongs to a given space V_k and is characterized by a given probability measure

$$P_{v_k}(\cdot|x_k, \ldots, x_0, u_{k-1}, \ldots, u_0, w_{k-1}, \ldots, w_0, v_{k-1} \ldots, v_0),$$

which depends explicitly on the current state and the past states, controls, and disturbances.

The initial state x_0 is also random and characterized by a given probability measure P_{x_0}. The probability measure $P_{w_k}(\cdot|x_k, u_k)$ of w_k is given and may depend explicitly on x_k and u_k but not on prior disturbances $w_0, \ldots, w_{k-1}, v_0, \ldots, v_{k-1}$. The control u_k is constrained to take values from a given nonempty subset U_k of the control space C_k. It is assumed that this subset does not depend on x_k.

Let us denote by I_k the information available to the controller at time k and call it the *information vector*. We have

$$\begin{aligned} I_k &= (z_0, z_1, \ldots, z_k, u_0, u_1, \ldots, u_{k-1}), \qquad k = 1, 2, \ldots, N-1, \\ I_0 &= z_0. \end{aligned} \tag{3.2}$$

We consider the class of control laws (or policies), which consist of a sequence of functions $\pi = \{\mu_0, \mu_1, \ldots, \mu_{N-1}\}$, where each function μ_k maps the information vector I_k into the control space C_k and

$$\mu_k(I_k) \in U_k, \qquad \text{for all } I_k, \quad k = 0, \ldots, N-1.$$

Such control laws are termed *admissible*. The problem is to find an admissible control law $\pi = \{\mu_0, \mu_1, \ldots, \mu_{N-1}\}$ that minimizes the cost functional

$$J_\pi = \underset{\substack{x_0, w_k, v_k \\ k=0,\ldots,N-1}}{E} \left\{ g_N(x_N) + \sum_{k=0}^{N-1} g_k[x_k, \mu_k(I_k), w_k] \right\} \tag{3.3}$$

subject to the system equation

$$x_{k+1} = f_k[x_k, \mu_k(I_k), w_k], \qquad k = 0, 1, \ldots, N-1,$$

and the measurement equation

$$\begin{aligned} z_0 &= h_0(x_0, v_0), \\ z_k &= h_k[x_k, \mu_{k-1}(I_{k-1}), v_k], \qquad k = 1, 2, \ldots, N-1. \end{aligned}$$

The cost functions g_k, $k = 0, 1, \ldots, N$, are given.

Notice the difference from the case of perfect state information. Whereas before we were trying to find a rule that would specify the control u_k to be applied for each state x_k and time k, now we are looking for a rule that gives the control to be applied for every possible information vector I_k (or state of information), that is, for every sequence of observations received and controls employed up to time k.

We now show how the problem can be reformulated into the framework of the basic problem with perfect state information. Similarly, as in the discussion of state augmentation in Section 1.5, it is intuitively clear that we should define a new system the state of which at time k consists of all variables the knowledge of which can be of benefit to the controller when making the kth decision. Thus a first candidate as the state of the new system is the information vector I_k. Indeed we will show that this choice is appropriate.

We have by definition [cf. Eq. (3.2)]

$$I_{k+1} = (I_k, z_{k+1}, u_k), \qquad k = 0, 1, \ldots, N-2, \qquad I_0 = z_0. \tag{3.4}$$

These equations can be viewed as describing the evolution of a system of the same nature as the one considered in the basic problem of Section 1.1. The state of the system is I_k, the control u_k, and z_{k+1} can be viewed as a random disturbance. Furthermore, we have

$$P(z_{k+1} \in \overline{Z}_{k+1} | I_k, u_k) = P(z_{k+1} \in \overline{Z}_{k+1} | I_k, u_k, z_0, z_1, \ldots, z_k), \tag{3.5}$$

for any event $\overline{Z}_{k+1}$ (a subset of Z_{k+1}) since $z_0, z_1, \ldots, z_k$ are part of the information vector I_k. Thus the probability measure of z_{k+1} depends explicitly only on the state I_k and control u_k of the new system (3.4) and not on the prior disturbances $z_k, \ldots, z_1$.

By writing

$$E\{g_k(x_k, u_k, w_k)\} = E\left\{ \underset{x_k, w_k}{E} \{g_k(x_k, u_k, w_k) | I_k, u_k\} \right\},$$

we can similarly reformulate the cost functional in terms of the variables of the new system. The cost per stage as a function of the new state I_k and the control u_k is

$$\tilde{g}_k(I_k, u_k) = \underset{x_k, w_k}{E} \{g_k(x_k, u_k, w_k) | I_k, u_k\}. \tag{3.6}$$

Thus the basic problem with imperfect state information has been reformulated to a problem with perfect state information that involves system (3.4) and cost per stage (3.6). By writing the DP algorithm for this latter problem and substituting the expressions (3.4) and (3.6), we obtain

$$J_{N-1}(I_{N-1}) = \min_{u_{N-1} \in U_{N-1}} \left[\underset{x_{N-1}, w_{N-1}}{E} \{g_N[f_{N-1}(x_{N-1}, u_{N-1}, w_{N-1})] \right.$$
$$\left. + g_{N-1}(x_{N-1}, u_{N-1}, w_{N-1}) | I_{N-1}\, u_{N-1}\} \right], \tag{3.7}$$

$$J_k(I_k) = \min_{u_k \in U_k} \left[\underset{x_k, w_k, z_{k+1}}{E} \{g_k(x_k, u_k, w_k) \right.$$
$$\left. + J_{k+1}(I_k, z_{k+1}, u_k) | I_k, u_k\} \right]. \tag{3.8}$$

Equations (3.7) and (3.8) constitute the basic DP algorithm for the problem of this section. An optimal control law $\{\mu_0^*, \mu_1^*, \ldots, \mu_{N-1}^*\}$ is obtained by first solving the minimization problem in (3.7) for every possible value of the information vector I_{N-1} to obtain $\mu^*_{N-1}(I_{N-1})$. Simultaneously, $J_{N-1}(I_{N-1})$ is computed and used in the computation of $J_{N-2}(I_{N-2})$ via the minimization in (3.8), which is carried out for every possible value of I_{N-2}. Proceeding similarly, one obtains $J_{N-3}(I_{N-3})$ and μ^*_{N-3} and so on until $J_0(I_0) = J_0(z_0)$ is computed. The optimal cost J^* is then obtained from

$$J^* = \underset{z_0}{E}\{J_0(z_0)\}. \tag{3.9}$$

3.2 LINEAR SYSTEMS AND QUADRATIC COST: SEPARATION OF ESTIMATION AND CONTROL

We now consider the imperfect state information analog of the linear system/quadratic cost problem of Section 2.1. We have the same linear system

$$x_{k+1} = A_k x_k + B_k u_k + w_k, \qquad k = 0, 1, \ldots, N-1, \tag{3.10}$$

and quadratic cost

$$E\left\{x'_N Q_N x_N + \sum_{k=0}^{N-1} (x'_k Q_k x_k + u'_k R_k u_k)\right\}, \tag{3.11}$$

but now the controller does not have access to the current system state. Instead it receives at the beginning of each period k an observation of the form

$$z_k = C_k x_k + v_k, \qquad k = 0, 1, \ldots, N-1, \tag{3.12}$$

where $z_k \in R^s$, C_k is a given $s \times m$ matrix, $k = 0, 1, \ldots, N-1$, and $v_k \in R^s$ is an observation noise vector with given probability distribution. Furthermore, the vectors v_k are independent, and independent from w_k and x_0 as well. We make the same assumptions as in Section 2.1 concerning the input disturbances w_k, and we assume that the system matrices A_k, B_k are known.

From Eq. (3.7) we have

$$\begin{aligned} J_{N-1}(I_{N-1}) = \min_{u_{N-1}}\Big[\underset{x_{N-1}, w_{N-1}}{E} &\{(A_{N-1}x_{N-1} + B_{N-1}u_{N-1} + w_{N-1})'Q_N \\ &\times (A_{N-1}x_{N-1} + B_{N-1}u_{N-1} + w_{N-1}) + x'_{N-1}Q_{N-1}x_{N-1} \\ &+ u'_{N-1}R_{N-1}u_{N-1} | I_{N-1}\}\Big]. \end{aligned}$$

Using the fact that $E\{w_{N-1}|I_{N-1}\} = E\{w_{N-1}\} = 0$, this expression can be written

$$\begin{aligned} J_{N-1}(I_{N-1}) = &\underset{x_{N-1}}{E}\{x'_{N-1}(A'_{N-1}Q_N A_{N-1} + Q_{N-1})x_{N-1}|I_{N-1}\} \\ &+ \underset{w_{N-1}}{E}\{w'_{N-1}Q_N w_{N-1}\} \end{aligned} \tag{3.13}$$

$$+ \min_{u_{N-1}}[u'_{N-1}(B'_{N-1}Q_N B_{N-1} + R_{N-1})u_{N-1}$$
$$+ 2E\{x_{N-1}|I_{N-1}\}'A_{N-1}Q_N B_{N-1}u_{N-1}].$$

The minimization yields the optimal control law for the last stage,

$$\begin{aligned} u^*_{N-1} &= \mu^*_{N-1}(I_{N-1}) \\ &= -(B'_{N-1}Q_N B_{N-1} + R_{N-1})^{-1}B'_{N-1}Q_N A_{N-1}\, E\{x_{N-1}|I_{N-1}\}, \end{aligned} \tag{3.14}$$

and upon substitution in (3.13) we obtain

$$\begin{aligned} J_{N-1}(I_{N-1}) = &\mathop{E}_{x_{N-1}}\{x'_{N-1}K_{N-1}x_{N-1}|I_{N-1}\} \\ &+ \mathop{E}_{x_{N-1}}\{[x'_{N-1} - E\{x_{N-1}|I_{N-1}\}]'P_{N-1}[x_{N-1} - E\{x_{N-1}|I_{N-1}\}]|I_{N-1}\} \\ &+ \mathop{E}_{w_{N-1}}\{w'_{N-1}Q_N w_{N-1}\}, \end{aligned} \tag{3.15}$$

where the matrices K_{N-1} and P_{N-1} are given by

$$P_{N-1} = A'_{N-1}Q_N B_{N-1}(R_{N-1} + B'_{N-1}Q_N B_{N-1})^{-1}B'_{N-1}Q_N A_{N-1},$$
$$K_{N-1} = A'_{N-1}Q_N A_{N-1} - P_{N-1} + Q_{N-1}.$$

Note that the control law (3.14) is identical to the corresponding optimal control law for the problem of Section 2.1 except that x_{N-1} is replaced by its conditional expectation $E\{x_{N-1}|I_{N-1}\}$. Notice also that the cost-to-go $J_{N-1}(I_{N-1})$ exhibits a corresponding similarity to the cost-to-go for the perfect information problem except that $J_{N-1}(I_{N-1})$ contains an additional middle term, which is in effect a penalty for estimation error.

Now the DP equation for period $N - 2$ is

$$\begin{aligned} J_{N-2}(I_{N-2}) &= \min_{u_{N-2}}\Big[\mathop{E}_{\substack{x_{N-2}w_{N-2}\\ z_{N-1}}}\{x'_{N-2}Q_{N-2}x_{N-2} + u'_{N-2}R_{N-2}u_{N-2} \\ &\qquad + J_{N-1}(I_{N-1})|I_{N-2}, u_{N-2}\}\Big] \\ &= \min_{u_{N-2}}\Big[\mathop{E}_{x_{N-2}w_{N-2}}\{x'_{N-2}Q_{N-2}x_{N-2} + u'_{N-2}R_{N-2}u_{N-2} \\ &\qquad + (A_{N-2}x_{N-2} + B_{N-2}u_{N-2} + w_{N-2})'K_{N-1}(A_{N-2}x_{N-2} \\ &\qquad + B_{N-2}u_{N-2} + w_{N-2})|I_{N-2}\}\Big] \\ &\qquad + E\{[x_{N-1} - E\{x_{N-1}|I_{N-1}\}]'P_{N-1}[x_{N-1} \\ &\qquad - E\{x_{N-1}|I_{N-1}\}]|I_{N-2}, u_{N-2}\} \\ &\qquad + \mathop{E}_{w_{N-1}}\{w'_{N-1}Q_N w_{N-1}\}. \end{aligned} \tag{3.16}$$

Note that we have excluded the next to last term from the minimization with respect to u_{N-2}. We have done so since this term will be shown to be independent of u_{N-2}, a fact that follows easily from the following lemma.

Lemma. For every k, there is a function F_k such that for all policies we have

$$x_k - E\{x_k|I_k\} = F_k(x_0, w_0, \ldots, w_{k-1}, v_0, \ldots, v_k).$$

Proof. Fix a policy and consider the following two systems with identical initial condition $x_0 = \bar{x}_0$. In the first system there is control as determined by the policy

$$x_{k+1} = A_k x_k + B_k u_k + w_k, \qquad z_k = C_k x_k + v_k,$$

while in the second system there is no control:

$$\bar{x}_{k+1} = A_k \bar{x}_k + w_k, \qquad \bar{z}_k = C_k \bar{x}_k + v_k.$$

Denote

$$z^k = (z_0, \ldots, z_k)', \qquad \bar{z}^k = (\bar{z}_0, \ldots, \bar{z}_k)',$$
$$w^k = (w_0, \ldots, w_k)', \qquad v^k = (v_0, \ldots, v_k)',$$
$$u^k = (u_0, \ldots, u_k)'.$$

Linearity implies the existence of matrices F_k, G_k, and H_k such that

$$x_k = F_k x_0 + G_k u^{k-1} + H_k w^{k-1},$$
$$\bar{x}_k = F_k x_0 + H_k w^{k-1}.$$

Since we have $u^{k-1} = E\{u^{k-1}|I_k\}$, these equations yield

$$x_k - E\{x_k|I_k\} = \bar{x}_k - E\{\bar{x}_k|I_k\}.$$

From the equations for z_k and $\bar{z}_k$, we see that the information provided by $I_k = (z^k, u^{k-1})$ regarding $\bar{x}_k$ is summarized in $\bar{z}^k$. Therefore, we have $E\{\bar{x}_k|I_k\} = E\{\bar{x}_k|\bar{z}^k\}$, and it follows that

$$x_k - E\{x_k|I_k\} = \bar{x}_k - E\{\bar{x}_k|\bar{z}^k\}. \quad \text{Q.E.D.}$$

The lemma says essentially that the quality of estimation as expressed by the statistics of the error $x_k - E\{x_k|I_k\}$ cannot be influenced by the choice of control. This is due to the linearity of both the system and the measurement equation.

Returning now to our problem, the minimization in Eq. (3.16) yields, using a similar type of argument as for the last stage,

$$u^*_{N-2} = \mu^*_{N-2}(I_{N-2}) = -(R_{N-2} + B'_{N-2}K_{N-1}B_{N-2})^{-1}$$
$$\times B'_{N-2}K_{N-1}A_{N-2}\, E\{x_{N-2}|I_{N-2}\},$$

and proceeding similarly we obtain the optimal control law for every stage:

$$\mu^*_k(I_k) = L_k\, E\{x_k|I_k\} \tag{3.17}$$

where

$$L_k = -(R_k + B_k' K_{k+1} B_k)^{-1} B_k' K_{k+1} A_k, \tag{3.18}$$

with the matrices K_k given recursively by the Riccati equation

$$K_N = Q_N \tag{3.19}$$

$$K_k = A_k'[K_{k+1} - K_{k+1} B_k (R_k + B_k' K_{k+1} B_k)^{-1} B_k' K_{k+1}] A_k + Q_k. \tag{3.20}$$

Generalizing an earlier observation, we note that the optimal control law (3.17) is identical to the optimal control law for the corresponding perfect state information problem of Section 2.1 except that the state x_k is replaced by its conditional expectation $E\{x_k|I_k\}$.

It is interesting to note that the optimal controller can be decomposed into the two parts shown in Figure 3.1, an estimator, which uses the data to generate the conditional expectation $E\{x_k|I_k\}$, and an actuator, which multiplies $E\{x_k|I_k\}$ by the gain matrix L_k and applies the control input $u_k = L_k E\{x_k|I_k\}$. Furthermore, the gain matrix L_k is independent of the statistics of the problem and is the same as the one that would be used if we were faced with the deterministic problem where w_k and x_0 would be fixed and equal to their expected values. On the other hand, it can be shown that the estimate $\hat{x}$ of a random vector x given some information (random vector) I, which minimizes the mean squared error $E_x\{\|x - \hat{x}\|^2|I\}$ is precisely the conditional expectation $E_x\{x|I\}$ (expand the quadratic form and set to zero the derivative with respect to $\hat{x}$). Thus the *estimator portion of the optimal controller is an optimal solution of the problem of estimating the state x_k assuming no control takes place, while the actuator portion is an optimal solution of the control problem assuming perfect state information prevails.*

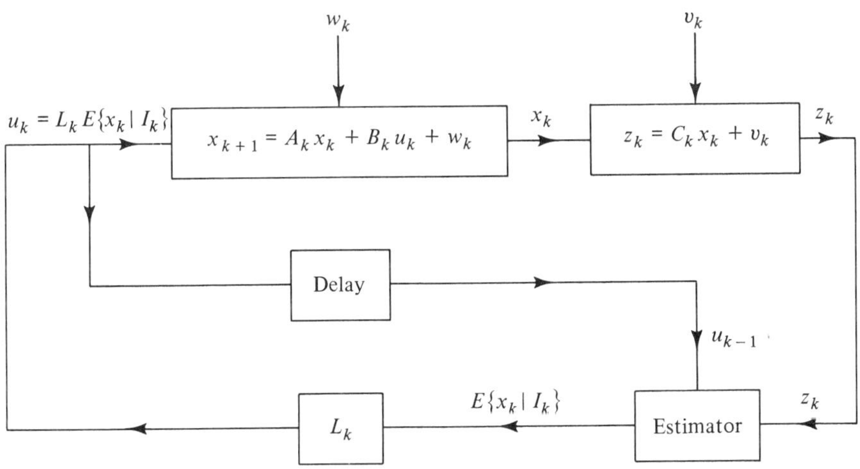

Figure 3.1 Structure of the optimal controller for the linear–quadratic problem.

This property, which shows that the two portions of the optimal controller can be designed independently as optimal solutions of an estimation and a control problem, has been called the *separation theorem for linear systems and quadratic cost* and occupies a central position in modern automatic control theory.

Another interesting observation is that the optimal controller applies at each time k the control that would be applied when faced with the deterministic problem of minimizing the cost-to-go

$$x_N' Q_N x_N + \sum_{i=k}^{N-1} (x_i' Q_i x_i + u_i' R_i u_i),$$

and the input disturbances $w_k, w_{k+1}, \ldots, w_{N-1}$ and current state x_k were known and fixed at their conditional expected values, which are zero and $E\{x_k|I_k\}$, respectively. This is another form of the *certainty equivalence principle*, which was referred to in Section 2.1. For a generalization of this fact to the case of correlated disturbances, see Problem 1.

Implementation Aspects: Steady-State Controller

As explained in the perfect information case, the linear form of the actuator portion of the optimal control law is particularly attractive for implementation. In the imperfect information case, however, we are faced with the additional problem of constructing an estimator that produces the conditional expectation $E\{x_k|I_k\}$. The implementation of such an estimator is not easy in general. However, in the important special case, when *the disturbances w_k, v_k, and the initial state x_0 are Gaussian random vectors,* a convenient implementation of the estimator is possible by means of the Kalman filtering algorithm [K1]. This algorithm provides the conditional expectation $E\{x_k|I_k\}$, which due to the Gaussian nature of the uncertainties turns out to be a linear function of the information vector I_k† (i.e., the measurements $z_0, z_1, \ldots, z_k$ and the controls $u_0, u_1 \ldots, u_{k-1}$). The computations, however, are organized recursively so that only the most recent measurement z_k and control u_{k-1} are needed at time k, together with $E\{x_{k-1}|I_{k-1}\}$ in order to produce $E\{x_k|I_k\}$. The form of the algorithm is (see [A1], [M6])

$$\begin{aligned} E\{x_{k+1}|I_{k+1}\} = A_k E\{x_k|I_k\} + B_k u_k \\ + \Sigma_{k+1|k+1} C_{k+1}' N_{k+1}^{-1} [z_{k+1} - C_{k+1}(A_k E\{x_k|I_k\} + B_k u_k)], \\ k = 0, 1, \ldots, N-1, \end{aligned} \tag{3.21}$$

† Actually, the conditional expectation $E\{x_k|I_k\}$ can be shown to be a linear function of I_k for a more general class of probability distributions of x_0, w_k, u_k that includes the Gaussian distribution as a special case, the class of *spherically invariant distributions* [V9, B31].

$$E\{x_0|I_0\} = E\{x_0\} + \Sigma_{0|0}C_0'N_0^{-1}[z_0 - C_0E\{x_0\}], \tag{3.22}$$

where the matrices $\Sigma_{k|k}$ are precomputable and given recursively by

$$\Sigma_{k+1|k+1} = \Sigma_{k+1|k} - \Sigma_{k+1|k}C_{k+1}'(C_{k+1}\Sigma_{k+1|k}C_{k+1}' + N_{k+1})^{-1}C_{k+1}\Sigma_{k+1|k}, \tag{3.23}$$

$$\Sigma_{k+1|k} = A_k\Sigma_{k|k}A_k' + M_k, \qquad k = 0, 1, \ldots, N - 1, \tag{3.24}$$

with

$$\Sigma_{0|0} = S - SC_0'(C_0SC_0' + N_0)^{-1}C_0S.$$

In this equation M_k, N_k, and S are the covariance matrices of w_k, v_k, and x_0, respectively, and we assume that w_k and v_k have zero mean; that is,

$$E\{w_k\} = E\{v_k\} = 0,$$
$$M_k = E\{w_kw_k'\}, \qquad N_k = E\{v_kv_k'\},$$
$$S = E\{[x_0 - E\{x_0\}][x - E\{x_0\}]'\}.$$

In addition, the matrices N_k are assumed to be positive definite.

Consider now the case where the system and measurement equations and the disturbance statistics are stationary. We can then drop subscripts from the system matrices. Assume that *the pair (A, B) is controllable and the pair (A, F) is observable, where F is a matrix such that $Q = F'F$*. By the theory of Section 2.1, if the horizon tends to infinity, the optimal controller tends to the steady-state control law

$$\mu^*(I_k) = L\hat{x}_k, \tag{3.25}$$

where we use the notation

$$E\{x_k|I_k\} = \hat{x}_k, \qquad L = -(R + B'KB)^{-1}B'KA, \tag{3.26}$$

and K is the unique positive semidefinite symmetric solution of the algebraic Riccati equation

$$K = A'[K - KB(R + B'KB)^{-1}B'K]A + Q. \tag{3.27}$$

By a similar argument, $\hat{x}_k$ can be generated in the limit as $k \to \infty$ by a steady-state Kalman filtering algorithm:

$$\hat{x}_{k+1} = (A + BL)\hat{x}_k + \bar{\Sigma}C'N^{-1}[z_{k+1} - C(A + BL)\hat{x}_k], \tag{3.28}$$

where $\bar{\Sigma}$ is given by

$$\bar{\Sigma} = \Sigma - \Sigma C'(C\Sigma C' + N)^{-1}C\Sigma, \tag{3.29}$$

and Σ is the unique positive semidefinite solution of the Riccati equation

$$\Sigma = A[\Sigma - \Sigma C'(C\Sigma C' + N)^{-1}C\Sigma]A' + M. \tag{3.30}$$

This can be shown using the theory of Section 2.1 provided *the pair (A, C) is observable and the pair (A, D) is controllable, where D is a matrix such that $M = DD'$*. The steady-state controller of Eqs. (3.25), (3.26), and (3.28) is particularly attractive for practical implementation in view of its simplicity.

3.3 MINIMUM VARIANCE CONTROL OF LINEAR SYSTEMS

We have considered so far control of linear systems in state variable form as in the previous section. However, linear systems are often modeled by means of an input–output equation, which is more economical in terms of number of parameters needed to describe the system dynamics. In this section we consider single-input, single-output, linear, time-invariant systems and a special type of quadratic cost functional. The resulting optimal control law is particularly simple and has found wide application. We first introduce some of the basic facts regarding linear systems in input–output form. Detailed discussions may be found in [A11], [A12], [G3], and [W12].

A single-input, single-output, linear, finite-dimensional, causal, time-invariant system is specified by an equation of the form

$$y_k + a_1 y_{k-1} + \cdots + a_m y_{k-m} = b_0 u_k + b_1 u_{k-1} + \cdots + b_m u_{k-m}, \tag{3.31}$$

where a_i, b_i are given scalars. The scalar sequences $\{u_k \mid k = 0, \pm 1, \pm 2, \ldots\}$, $\{y_k \mid k = 0, \pm 1, \pm 2, \ldots\}$ are viewed as the input and output of the system, respectively.

It is convenient to describe this type of system by means of the *backward shift operator,* denoted s, which when operating on a sequence $\{x_k \mid k = 0, \pm 1, \pm 2, \ldots\}$ shifts its index by one unit; that is,

$$s(x_k) = x_{k-1}, \qquad k = 0, \pm 1, \pm 2, \ldots.$$

We denote by s^r the operator resulting from r successive applications of s.

$$s^r(x_k) = x_{k-r}, \qquad k = 0, \pm 1, \pm 2, \ldots. \tag{3.32}$$

We also write for simplicity $s^r x_k = x_{k-r}$. The *forward shift operator,* denoted s^{-1}, is the inverse of s and is defined by

$$s^{-1}(x_k) = x_{k+1}, \qquad k = 0, \pm 1, \pm 2, \ldots.$$

Thus the notation (3.32) holds for all integers r. We can form linear combinations of operators of the form s^r. Thus, for example, the operator $(s + 2s^2)$ is defined by

$$(s + 2s^2)(x_k) = x_{k-1} + 2x_{k-2}, \qquad k = 0, \pm 1, \pm 2, \ldots.$$

With this notation, (3.31) can be written

$$A(s)y_k = B(s)u_k, \tag{3.33}$$

where $A(s)$, $B(s)$ are the operators

$$A(s) = 1 + a_1 s + \cdots + a_m s^m, \tag{3.34}$$

$$B(s) = b_0 + b_1 s + \cdots + b_m s^m. \tag{3.35}$$

Sometimes it is convenient to write (3.33) as

$$y_k = \frac{B(s)}{A(s)} u_k$$

or

$$\frac{A(s)}{B(s)} y_k = u_k.$$

The meaning of both equations is that the sequences $\{y_k\}$ and $\{u_k\}$ are related via (3.33). There is a certain ambiguity here in that, for a fixed $\{u_k\}$, Eq. (3.33) has an infinite number of solutions in $\{y_k\}$. For example, the equation

$$y_k + ay_{k-1} = u_k$$

for $u_k \equiv 0$ has as solutions all sequences of the form $y_k = \beta(-a)^k$, where β is any scalar. As will be discussed shortly, however, for stable systems and for a *bounded* sequence $\{u_k\}$ there is a unique solution $\{y_k\}$ that is *bounded*. It is this solution that will be denoted $(B(s)/A(s))u_k$ in what follows. Note that $B(s)/A(s)$ can be viewed as a *transfer function* in the usual linear system sense involving z-transforms.

We now introduce some terminology:

(a) When $\{y_k\}$, $\{u_k\}$ satisfy $A(s)y_k = B(s)u_k$, we say that *y_k is obtained by passing u_k through the filter $B(s)/A(s)$*. This comes from engineering terminology, where linear time-invariant systems are commonly referred to as filters. We also refer to the equation $A(s)y_k = B(s)u_k$ as the filter $B(s)/A(s)$.

(b) A filter $B(s)/A(s)$ is said to be *stable* if the polynomial $A(s)$ has all its (complex) roots strictly outside the unit circle of the complex plane, that is, $|\rho| > 1$ for all complex ρ satisfying $A(\rho) = 0$. *A stable filter $B(s)/A(s)$ has the following two properties:*

1. Every solution $\{y_k\}$ of
$$A(s)y_k = 0$$
satisfies $\lim_{k\to\infty} y_k = 0$; that is, the output y_k tends to zero if the input sequence $\{u_k\}$ is identically zero.
2. For every bounded sequence $\{\bar{u}_k\}$, the equation
$$A(s)y_k = B(s)\bar{u}_k$$
has a *unique* solution $\{\bar{y}_k\}$ within the class of bounded sequences. Furthermore, every solution $\{y_k\}$ (possibly unbounded) of the equation satisfies
$$\lim_{k\to\infty} (y_k - \bar{y}_k) = 0. \tag{3.36}$$

For example, consider the system
$$y_k - 0.5y_{k-1} = u_k.$$
Given the bounded input sequence $\bar{u}_k = \{\ldots, 1, 1, 1, \ldots\}$, the set of all solutions is given by
$$y_k = 2 + \frac{1}{2^k},$$
but of these the only bounded solution is $\bar{y}_k = \{\ldots, 2, 2, 2, \ldots\}$.

(c) The filter $B(s)/A(s)$ is said to be *minimum phase* when the polynomial $B(s)$ has all its roots strictly outside the unit circle. The terminology "minimum phase" is explained, for example, in [P5]. The reasons will not concern us here. If $b_0 \neq 0$ and the filter $B(s)/A(s)$ is minimum phase and stable, then the *inverse* filter $A(s)/B(s)$ is also minimum phase and stable. Under these circumstances, for every bounded output sequence $\{\overline{y}_k\}$, there is a unique bounded input sequence $\{\overline{u}_k\}$ satisfying

$$A(s)\overline{y}_k = B(s)\overline{u}_k.$$

Modeling of Linear Time-Invariant Systems with Stochastic Inputs

Consider now a stochastic, linear, time-invariant, finite-dimensional system with output $\{y_k\}$, control input $\{u_k\}$ and a zero-mean stochastic input $\{w_k\}$. We assume that $\{w_k\}$ is a stationary (up to second order) stochastic process. That is, $\{w_k\}$ is a sequence of random variables defined on the same probability space and satisfying, for all i, $k = 0, \pm 1, \pm 2, \ldots$,

$$E\{w_k\} = 0, \qquad E\{w_0 w_i\} = E\{w_k w_{k+i}\} < \infty.$$

(All references to stationary processes in this section are meant in the limited sense just described.) By linearity we have that y_k is the sum of one sequence due to the presence of $\{u_k\}$ and one due to the presence of $\{w_k\}$. In other words, we have

$$y_k = y_k^1 + y_k^2, \tag{3.37}$$

where y_k^1, y_k^2, satisfy

$$A_1(s)y_k^1 = B_1(s)u_k, \tag{3.38a}$$

$$A_2(s)y_k^2 = B_2(s)w_k \tag{3.38b}$$

for some filters $B_1(s)/A_1(s)$, $B_2(s)/A_2(s)$.

Operating on (3.38a) and (3.38b) with $A_2(s)$ and $A_1(s)$, respectively, adding, and using (3.37), we obtain

$$\overline{A}(s)y_k = \overline{B}(s)u_k + v_k, \tag{3.39}$$

where $\overline{A}(s)$ and $\overline{B}(s)$ are the polynomials

$$\overline{A}(s) = A_1(s)A_2(s),$$

$$\overline{B}(s) = A_2(s)B_1(s),$$

and $\{v_k\}$, given by

$$v_k = A_1(s)B_2(s)w_k, \tag{3.40}$$

is a zero-mean, generally correlated, stationary stochastic process.

We envision a situation where u_k is a control input applied *after* y_k, y_{k-1}, y_{k-2}, . . . have occurred and been observed. Thus we are interested in the case where in (3.38)

$$B_1(0) = 0.$$

Therefore, the polynomials $\overline{A}(s)$ and $\overline{B}(s)$ have the form

$$\overline{A}(s) = 1 + \overline{a}_1 s + \cdots + \overline{a}_{m_0} s^{m_0},$$

$$\overline{B}(s) = \overline{b}_1 s + \cdots + \overline{b}_{m_0} s^{m_0}$$

for some scalars $\overline{a}_i$ and $\overline{b}_i$ and some positive integer m_0.

To summarize, we have constructed a model of the form

$$\overline{A}(s)y_k = \overline{B}(s)u_k + v_k,$$

where $\overline{A}(s)$ and $\overline{B}(s)$ are polynomials of the preceding form and $\{v_k\}$ is some zero-mean, correlated, stationary stochastic process.

Stochastic Processes with Rational Spectrum

Let us now digress for a moment to discuss the nature of the stochastic process $\{v_k\}$ of (3.40). Given a zero-mean, stationary scalar process $\{v_k\}$, denote by $C(k)$ the autocorrelation function

$$C(k) = E\{v_i v_{i+k}\}, \qquad k = 0, \pm 1, \pm 2, \ldots.$$

We say that $\{v_k\}$ has *rational spectrum* if the transform of $\{C(k)\}$ defined by

$$S_v(\lambda) = \sum_{k=-\infty}^{\infty} C(k)\, e^{-jk\lambda} = C(0) + 2\sum_{k=1}^{\infty} C(k)\cos(k\lambda)$$

exists for $\lambda \in [-\pi, \pi]$ and can be expressed as

$$S_v(\lambda) = \sigma^2 \frac{|B(e^{j\lambda})|^2}{|A(e^{j\lambda})|^2}, \qquad \lambda \in [-\pi, \pi], \tag{3.41}$$

where σ is a scalar, $A(z)$ and $B(z)$ are some polynomials with real coefficients

$$A(z) = 1 + a_1 z + \cdots + a_m z^m, \tag{3.42a}$$

$$B(z) = 1 + b_1 z + \cdots + b_m z^m, \tag{3.42b}$$

and $A(z)$ has no roots on the unit circle $\{z \mid |z| = 1\}$.

We have the following facts:

(a) If $\{v_k\}$ is a white process with $C(0) = \sigma^2$, $C(k) = 0$ for $k \neq 0$, then

$$S_v(\lambda) = \sigma^2, \qquad \lambda \in [-\pi, \pi],$$

and clearly $\{v_k\}$ has rational spectrum.

(b) If $\{v_k\}$ has rational spectrum S_v given by (3.41), then S_v can be written as

$$S_v(\lambda) = \tilde{\sigma}^2 \frac{|\tilde{B}(e^{j\lambda})|^2}{|\tilde{A}(e^{j\lambda})|^2}, \qquad \lambda \in [-\pi, \pi],$$

where $\tilde{\sigma}$ is a scalar and $\tilde{A}(z)$, $\tilde{B}(z)$ are unique real polynomials of the form

$$\tilde{A}(z) = 1 + \tilde{a}_1 z + \cdots + \tilde{a}_m z^m,$$

$$\tilde{B}(z) = 1 + \tilde{b}_1 z + \cdots + \tilde{b}_m z^m$$

satisfying:

1. $\tilde{A}(z)$ has all its roots strictly outside the unit circle.
2. $\tilde{B}(z)$ has all its roots strictly outside or on the unit circle, and if $B(z)$ has no roots on the unit circle, then the same is true for $\tilde{B}(z)$.

These facts are seen by noting that if $\rho \neq 0$ is a root of $A(z)$ then $|A(e^{j\lambda})|^2 = A(e^{j\lambda})A(e^{-j\lambda})$ contains a factor $(1 - \rho^{-1}e^{j\lambda})(1 - \rho^{-1}e^{-j\lambda}) = \rho^{-2}(1 - \rho e^{j\lambda})(1 - \rho e^{-j\lambda})$. A little reflection shows that the roots of $\tilde{A}(z)$ should be ρ or ρ^{-1} depending on whether ρ is outside or inside the unit circle. Similarly, the roots of $\tilde{B}(z)$ are obtained from the roots of $B(z)$. Thus the polynomials $\tilde{A}(z)$ and $\tilde{B}(z)$ as well as $\tilde{\sigma}^2$ can be uniquely determined. We may thus assume without loss of generality that $A(z)$ and $B(z)$ in (3.41) have no roots inside the unit circle.

(c) If $\{v_k\}$ is stationary with rational spectrum $S_v(\lambda)$, and $\{w_k\}$ is another stationary process obtained by passing v_k through a stable linear filter $B_1(s)/A_1(s)$, that is,

$$A_1(s)w_k = B_1(s)v_k,$$

then $\{w_k\}$ has rational spectrum S_w given by

$$S_w(\lambda) = \frac{|B_1(e^{j\lambda})|^2}{|A_1(e^{j\lambda})|^2} S_v(\lambda), \qquad \lambda \in [-\pi, \pi].$$

In particular, if $\{v_k\}$ is white and $E\{v_k^2\} = \sigma^2$, then

$$S_w(\lambda) = \sigma^2 \frac{|B_1(e^{j\lambda})|^2}{|A_1(e^{j\lambda})|^2}, \qquad \lambda \in [-\pi, \pi].$$

The proof of this is straightforward using the definitions. It is a standard fact given, for example, in [P5].

(d) The next fact is hard to prove rigorously. We state it as a proposition. For a proof see, for example, [A10, pp. 75–76].

Proposition. If $\{v_k\}$ is a zero-mean, stationary stochastic process with rational spectrum

$$S_v(\lambda) = \sigma^2 \frac{|B(e^{j\lambda})|^2}{|A(e^{j\lambda})|^2}, \qquad \lambda \in [-\pi, \pi],$$

where A, B are given by (3.42) and are assumed (without loss of generality) to have no roots inside the unit circle, then there exists a zero-mean, white, stationary process $\{\epsilon_k\}$ (defined on the same probability space as $\{v_k\}$) with $E\{\epsilon_k^2\} = \sigma^2$ such that for all k

$$v_k + a_1 v_{k-1} + \cdots + a_m v_{k-m} = \epsilon_k + b_1\epsilon_{k-1} + \cdots + b_m\epsilon_{k-m}.$$

(For the mathematically advanced we note that this relation is meant in a P-almost everywhere sense, where P is the probability measure of the space.)

ARMAX Models

Let us now return to the problem of representation of a linear system with stochastic inputs. We had arrived at the model (3.39),

$$\bar{A}(s)y_k = \bar{B}(s)u_k + v_k.$$

If the zero-mean stationary process $\{v_k\}$ has rational spectrum, the preceding analysis and proposition show that there exists a zero-mean, white, stationary process $\{\epsilon_k\}$ satisfying

$$D(s)v_k = C(s)\epsilon_k, \tag{3.43}$$

where the polynomials $C(s)$ and $D(s)$ are of the form

$$C(s) = 1 + c_1 s + \cdots + c_{m_1} s^{m_1},$$

$$D(s) = 1 + d_1 s + \cdots + d_{m_1} s^{m_1},$$

and $C(s)$ has no roots inside the unit circle. Operating on both sides of (3.39) with $D(s)$ and using (3.43), we obtain

$$A(s)y_k = B(s)u_k + C(s)\epsilon_k, \tag{3.44}$$

where

$$A(s) = D(s)\overline{A}(s),$$

$$B(s) = D(s)\overline{B}(s).$$

In view of the fact that $\overline{A}(0) = 1$, $\overline{B}(0) = 0$, we can write, for some integer m and scalars $a_1, \ldots, a_m, b_1, \ldots, b_m, c_1, \ldots, c_m$,

$$A(s) = 1 + a_1 s + \cdots + a_m s^m,$$

$$B(s) = b_1 s + \cdots + b_m s^m,$$

$$C(s) = 1 + c_1 s + \cdots + c_m s^m,$$

and write (3.44) as

$$y_k + a_1 y_{k-1} + \cdots + a_m y_{k-m} = b_1 u_{k-1} + \cdots + b_m u_{k-m} + \epsilon_k + c_1 \epsilon_{k-1} + \cdots + c_m \epsilon_{k-m}. \tag{3.45}$$

The model (3.45) is the one that we will adopt, and *without loss of generality it will be assumed that $C(s)$ has no roots strictly inside the unit circle*. Equation (3.45) is known as an ARMAX model (AutoRegressive, Moving Average, with eXogenous input). For much of the analysis in subsequent sections, it will be necessary to exclude the critical case where $C(s)$ has roots *on* the unit circle and assume that the filter $C(s)/A(s)$ is minimum phase. This assumption is satisfied in most practical cases.

In several situations, analysis and algorithms relating to the ARMAX model

$$A(s)y_k = B(s)u_k + C(s)\epsilon_k$$

are greatly simplified if $C(s) = 1$ so that the noise term sequence $C(s)\epsilon_k = \epsilon_k$ is white. However, our earlier analysis showed that *this is typically an unrealistic assumption*. To emphasize this point and see how easily the noise can be correlated, suppose that we have a first-order system

$$x_{k+1} = a x_k + w_k,$$

where we observe

$$y_k = x_k + v_k.$$

Then

$$\begin{aligned} y_{k+1} &= x_{k+1} + v_{k+1} \\ &= ax_k + w_k + v_{k+1} \\ &= a(y_k - v_k) + w_k + v_{k+1}, \end{aligned}$$

so finally

$$y_{k+1} = ay_k + v_{k+1} - av_k + w_k.$$

However, the noise sequence $\{v_{k+1} - av_k + w_k\}$ is correlated even if $\{v_k\}$ and $\{w_k\}$ are white and mutually independent.

The ARMAX model (3.45) can be put into state space form. The process is based on state augmentation and can perhaps be best understood in terms of an example. Consider the system

$$y_k + a_1 y_{k-1} = b_1 u_{k-1} + b_2 u_{k-2} + \epsilon_k + c_1 \epsilon_{k-1}. \tag{3.46}$$

We have

$$\begin{bmatrix} y_{k+1} \\ u_k \\ \epsilon_{k+1} \end{bmatrix} = \begin{bmatrix} -a_1 & b_2 & c_1 \\ 0 & 0 & 0 \\ 0 & 0 & 0 \end{bmatrix} \begin{bmatrix} y_k \\ u_{k-1} \\ \epsilon_k \end{bmatrix} + \begin{bmatrix} b_1 \\ 1 \\ 0 \end{bmatrix} u_k + \begin{bmatrix} \epsilon_{k+1} \\ 0 \\ \epsilon_{k+1} \end{bmatrix}. \tag{3.47}$$

By setting

$$x_k = \begin{bmatrix} y_k \\ u_{k-1} \\ \epsilon_k \end{bmatrix}, \qquad w_k = \begin{bmatrix} \epsilon_{k+1} \\ 0 \\ \epsilon_{k+1} \end{bmatrix},$$

$$A = \begin{bmatrix} -a_1 & b_2 & c_1 \\ 0 & 0 & 0 \\ 0 & 0 & 0 \end{bmatrix}, \qquad B = \begin{bmatrix} b_1 \\ 1 \\ 0 \end{bmatrix},$$

we can write (3.47) as

$$x_{k+1} = Ax_k + Bu_k + w_k, \tag{3.48}$$

where $\{w_k\}$ is a stationary white process. We have arrived at this state space model through state augmentation. Notice that the state x_k includes ϵ_k. Thus if the controller is assumed to know at time k only the present and past outputs $y_k, y_{k-1}, \ldots$, and the past controls $u_{k-1}, u_{k-2}, \ldots$ (but not $\epsilon_{k-1}, \epsilon_{k-2}, \ldots$), we are faced with a model of imperfect state information. If $c_1 = 0$ in (3.46), then the state space model can be simplified so that

$$x_k = \begin{bmatrix} y_k \\ u_{k-1} \end{bmatrix}$$

in which case we have perfect state information. More generally, we have perfect state information in the ARMAX model (3.45) if and only if $b_1 \neq 0$ and $c_1 = c_2 = \cdots = c_m = 0$.

Minimum Variance Control: Perfect State Information Case

Consider the perfect state information case of the ARMAX model (3.45):

$$y_k + a_1 y_{k-1} + \cdots + a_m y_{k-m} = b_1 u_{k-1} + \cdots + b_m u_{k-m} + \epsilon_k, \tag{3.49}$$

where $b_1 \neq 0$. We wish to minimize the cost

$$E\left\{\sum_{k=1}^{N} |y_k|^2\right\}. \tag{3.50}$$

The controller at time k applies u_k knowing the present and past outputs $y_k, y_{k-1}, \ldots$, as well as the past controls $u_{k-1}, u_{k-2}, \ldots$. There are no constraints on u_k. By transforming the system to state space form, we see that this problem can be reduced to a perfect state information linear–quadratic problem involving a system of the form

$$x_{k+1} = Ax_k + Bu_k + w_k,$$

where x_k is the vector

$$[y_k, y_{k-1}, \ldots, y_{k-m+1}, u_{k-1}, \ldots, u_{k-m+1}]'.$$

The problem is of the same nature as the one of Section 2.1 except that the corresponding matrices R_k in the quadratic cost functional are zero here. Nonetheless, in Section 2.1 we used the invertibility of R_k only to ensure that various matrices in the optimal control law and the Riccati equation are invertible. If invertibility of these matrices can be guaranteed by other means, the same analysis applies even if R_k is not positive definite. This is indeed the case for the problem involving the system (3.49) and the cost functional (3.50). An analysis analogous to the one of Section 2.1 shows that *the optimal control u_k^* at time k (given $y_k, y_{k-1}, \ldots, y_{k-m+1}$, $u_{k-1}, \ldots, u_{k-m+1}$) is the same as the one that would be applied if all future disturbances $\epsilon_{k+1}, \ldots, \epsilon_N$ were set equal to zero, their expected value (certainty equivalence).* It follows that

$$\mu_k^*(y_k, \ldots, y_{k-m+1}, u_{k-1}, \ldots, u_{k-m+1})$$
$$= \frac{1}{b_1}(a_1 y_k + \cdots + a_m y_{k-m+1} - b_2 u_{k-1} - \cdots - b_m u_{k-m+1}),$$

and $\{u_k^*\}$ is generated via the equation

$$b_1 u_k^* + b_2 u_{k-1}^* + \cdots + b_m u_{k-m+1}^*$$
$$= a_1 y_k + a_2 y_{k-1} + \cdots + a_m y_{k-m+1}. \tag{3.51}$$

In other words, $\{u_k^*\}$ is generated by passing $\{y_k\}$ through the linear filter $\overline{A}(s)/\overline{B}(s)$, where

$$\overline{A}(s) = a_1 + a_2 s + \cdots + a_m s^{m-1}, \tag{3.52}$$

$$\overline{B}(s) = b_1 + b_2 s + \cdots + b_m s^{m-1}, \tag{3.53}$$

as shown in Figure 3.2. The resulting closed-loop system is

$$y_k = \epsilon_k \tag{3.54}$$

and the associated cost is

$$N\, E\{\epsilon_k^2\}.$$

Notice that the optimal policy, called *minimum variance control law,* is time invariant and does not depend on the horizon N.

Whereas the optimal closed-loop system as given by (3.54) is clearly stable, we can anticipate serious difficulties if the filter $\overline{A}(s)/\overline{B}(s)$ in the feedback loop is unstable. For if $\overline{B}(s)$ has some roots inside the unit circle, then the sequence $\{u_k\}$ will tend to be unbounded. This is illustrated by the following example.

Example

Consider the system

$$y_k + y_{k-1} = u_{k-1} - 2u_{k-2} + \epsilon_k.$$

The optimal control law is

$$u_k = y_k + 2u_{k-1}$$

and the optimal closed-loop system is

$$y_k = \epsilon_k,$$

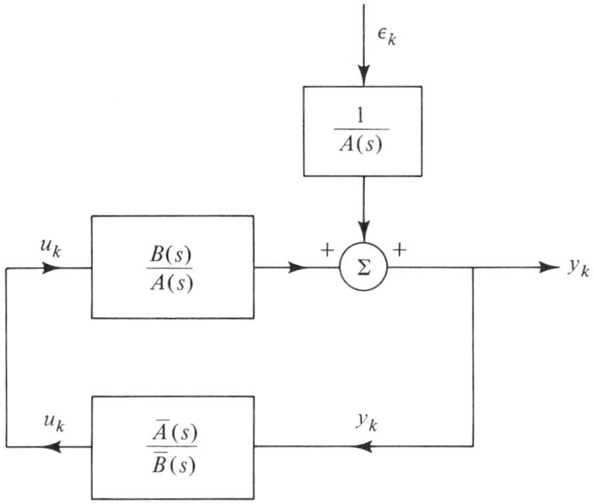

Figure 3.2 Minimum variance control with perfect state information. Structure of optimal closed-loop system, where $A(s) = 1 + a_1 s + \cdots + a_m s^m$, $B(s) = b_1 s + \cdots + b_m s^m$, $\overline{A}(s) = s^{-1}(A(s) - 1)$, and $\overline{B}(s) = s^{-1}B(s)$.

which is a stable system. On the other hand, these two equations yield

$$u_k = \epsilon_k + 2u_{k-1}.$$

It follows that u_k is generated by an *unstable* system and in fact is given by

$$u_k = \sum_{n=0}^{k} 2^n \epsilon_{k-n}.$$

Therefore, even though the output y_k stays bounded, the control u_k becomes unbounded with probability 1.

For another view of the same difficulty, suppose that the coefficients $b_1, \ldots, b_m$ of $\overline{B}(s)$ are slightly different from the ones of the true system. We will show that if the feedback filter $\overline{A}(s)/\overline{B}(s)$ is unstable then the closed-loop system is also unstable in the sense that both u_k and y_k become unbounded with probability one.

Assume that the system is governed by

$$A^0(s)y_k = B^0(s)u_k + \epsilon_k, \tag{3.55}$$

while the control law is calculated under the assumption that the system model is

$$A(s)y_k = B(s)u_k + \epsilon_k,$$

where the coefficients of $A(s)$ and $B(s)$ differ slightly from those of $A^0(s)$, $B^0(s)$. Define $\overline{A}^0(s)$, $\overline{B}^0(s)$ by

$$1 + s\overline{A}^0(s) = A^0(s), \tag{3.56a}$$

$$s\overline{B}^0(s) = B^0(s). \tag{3.56b}$$

Note that $\overline{A}^0(s) = \overline{A}(s)$ and $\overline{B}^0(s) = \overline{B}(s)$ if $A^0(s) = A(s)$, $B^0(s) = B(s)$. Multiplying (3.55) with $\overline{B}(s)$ and using the control law relation

$$\overline{B}(s)u_k = \overline{A}(s)y_k,$$

we obtain

$$\overline{B}(s)A^0(s)y_k = B^0(s)\overline{A}(s)y_k + \overline{B}(s)\epsilon_k.$$

Using (3.56) to eliminate $A^0(s)$ and $B^0(s)$ we obtain the closed-loop system

$$\{\overline{B}(s) + s[\overline{B}(s)\overline{A}^0(s) - \overline{B}^0(s)\overline{A}(s)]\}y_k = \overline{B}(s)\epsilon_k.$$

If the coefficients of $\overline{A}^0(s)$ and $\overline{B}^0(s)$ are close to those of $\overline{A}(s)$, $\overline{B}(s)$, then the roots of the polynomial

$$\overline{B}(s) + s[\overline{B}(s)\overline{A}^0(s) - \overline{B}^0(s)\overline{A}(s)]$$

are close to the roots of $\overline{B}(s)$, and *the closed-loop system is stable only if the roots of $\overline{B}(s)$ are outside the unit circle;* that is, the filter $\overline{A}(s)/\overline{B}(s)$ is stable. If our model is exact, the closed-loop system will be stable due to what is commonly referred to as a *pole-zero cancellation*. However, the slightest modeling discrepancy will induce instability.

The conclusion from the preceding analysis is that the minimum variance control law is advisable only if it can be realized through a stable filter

[$\overline{B}(s)$ has roots outside the unit circle]. Even if $\overline{B}(s)$ has its roots outside the unit circle, but some of these roots are near the unit circle, the performance of the minimum variance control law can be very sensitive to variations in the parameters of the polynomials $A(s)$ and $B(s)$. One way to overcome this sensitivity is to change the cost to

$$E\left\{\sum_{k=1}^{N}(|y_k|^2 + R|u_{k-1}|^2)\right\},$$

where R is some positive parameter. This requires solution via the Riccati equation as in Section 2.1. For a detailed derivation, see [A12].

In some problems the system equation includes an additional external input sequence $\{v_k\}$, the values of which can be measured by the controller as they occur. Consider the scalar system

$$y_k + a_1 y_{k-1} + \cdots + a_m y_{k-m}$$
$$= b_1 u_{k-1} + \cdots + b_m u_{k-m} + d_1 v_{k-1} + \cdots + d_m v_{k-m} + \epsilon_k,$$

where $\{v_k\}$ is an arbitrary sequence. The value v_k can be measured without error by the controller at time k. The minimum variance controller then takes the form

$$\mu_k^*(y_k, \ldots, y_{k-m+1}, u_{k-1}, \ldots, u_{k-m+1}, v_k, \ldots, v_{k-m+1})$$
$$= \frac{1}{b_1}(a_1 y_k + \cdots + a_m y_{k-m+1}$$
$$- d_1 v_k - \cdots - d_m v_{k-m+1} - b_2 u_{k-1} \cdots - b_m u_{k-m+1})$$

and $\{u_k^*\}$ is generated by

$$\overline{B}(s)u_k^* = \overline{A}(s)y_k - \overline{D}(s)v_k,$$

where

$$\overline{A}(s) = a_1 + a_2 s + \cdots + a_m s^{m-1},$$
$$\overline{B}(s) = b_1 + b_2 s + \cdots + b_m s^{m-1},$$
$$\overline{D}(s) = d_1 + d_2 s + \cdots + d_m s^{m-1}.$$

The closed-loop system is again $y_k = \epsilon_k$, but for practical purposes it is stable only if $\overline{B}(s)$ has its roots outside the unit circle. The process whereby external inputs are measured and used for control is commonly referred to as *feedforward control*.

Imperfect State Information Case

Consider now the general ARMAX model

$$y_k + a_1 y_{k-1} + \cdots + a_m y_{k-m}$$
$$= b_M u_{k-M} + \cdots + b_m u_{k-m} + \epsilon_k + c_1 \epsilon_{k-1} + \cdots + c_m \epsilon_{k-m}$$

or equivalently

$$A(s)y_k = B(s)u_k + C(s)\epsilon_k,$$

where

$$A(s) = 1 + a_1 s + \cdots + a_m s^m,$$
$$B(s) = b_M s^M + \cdots + b_m s^m,$$
$$C(s) = 1 + c_1 s + \cdots + c_m s^m.$$

We assume the following:

1. $b_M \neq 0$, and $1 \leq M \leq m$.
2. $\{\epsilon_k\}$ is a zero mean, white, stationary process.
3. The polynomial $C(s)$ has all its roots outside the unit circle. (As explained earlier, this assumption is not overly restrictive.)

The controller knows at each time k the present and past outputs $y_k, y_{k-1}, \ldots, y_{-m+1}, u_{k-1}, u_{k-2}, \ldots, u_{-m+M}$. Thus the information vector at time k is

$$I_k = (y_k, y_{k-1}, \ldots, y_{-m+1}, u_{k-1}, u_{k-2}, \ldots, u_{-m+M}). \tag{3.57}$$

There are no constraints on u_k. The problem is to find a control law $\{\mu_0(I_0), \ldots, \mu_{N-1}(I_{N-1})\}$ that minimizes

$$E\left\{\sum_{k=1}^{N} |y_k|^2\right\}.$$

This problem can be cast using state augmentation into the framework of the linear–quadratic problem of Section 3.2. The corresponding linear system in state space format involves a state x_k given by

$$x_k = (y_{k+M-1}, \ldots, y_{k+M-m}, u_{k-1}, \ldots, u_{k+M-m}, \epsilon_{k+M-1}, \ldots, \epsilon_{k+M-m}).$$

Because $y_{k+M-1}, \ldots, y_{k+1}$ and $\epsilon_{k+M-1}, \ldots, \epsilon_{k+M-m}$ are unknown to the controller, we are faced with a problem of imperfect state information.

An analysis analogous to the one of Section 3.2 shows that the *optimal control u_k^* at time k (given I_k) is the same as the one that would be applied in the deterministic problem where the current state*

$$x_k = (y_{k+M-1}, \ldots, y_{k+M-m}, u_{k-1}, \ldots, u_{k+M-m}, \epsilon_{k+M-1}, \ldots, \epsilon_{k+M-m})$$

is set equal to its conditional expected value given I_k, and the future disturbances $\epsilon_{k+M}, \ldots, \epsilon_N$ are set equal to zero (their expected value).

Thus the optimal control $u_k^* = \mu_k^*(I_k)$ is the one for which $E\{y_{k+M}|u_k, I_k\} = 0$ and is obtained by solving for u_k the equation

$$E\{y_{k+M}|y_k, \ldots, y_{-m+1}, u_k, u_{k-1}, \ldots, u_{-m+M}\} = 0. \tag{3.58}$$

This leads to the problem of calculating this conditional expected value, the *forecasting* or *prediction* problem, which is important in its own right.

Forecasting for ARMAX Models

Given $A(s)$ and $C(s)$, we can obtain polynomials $F(s)$ and $G(s)$ of the form

$$F(s) = 1 + f_1 s + \cdots + f_{M-1} s^{M-1}, \tag{3.59}$$

$$G(s) = g_0 + g_1 s + \cdots + g_{m-1} s^{m-1} \tag{3.60}$$

satisfying

$$C(s) = A(s)F(s) + s^M G(s). \tag{3.61}$$

The coefficients of $F(s)$ and $G(s)$ are uniquely determined from those of $C(s)$ and $A(s)$ by equating coefficients of both sides of the relation

$$\begin{aligned}1 + c_1 s + \cdots + c_m s^m = (1 + a_1 s + \cdots + a_m s^m)(1 + f_1 s + \cdots + f_{M-1} s^{M-1}) \\ + s^M (g_0 + g_1 s + \cdots + g_{m-1} s^{m-1}).\end{aligned}$$

Example

Let $m = 3$ and $M = 2$. Then the preceding equation takes the form

$$1 + c_1 s + c_2 s^2 + c_3 s^3 = (1 + a_1 s + a_2 s^2 + a_3 s^3)(1 + f_1 s) + s^2(g_0 + g_1 s + g_2 s^2),$$

and by equating coefficients we have

$$c_1 = a_1 + f_1, \qquad c_2 = a_2 + a_1 f_1 + g_0,$$

$$c_3 = a_3 + a_2 f_1 + g_1, \qquad a_3 f_1 + g_2 = 0,$$

from which f_1, g_0, g_1, and g_2 are uniquely determined.

The ARMAX model can be written as

$$A(s) y_{k+M} = \overline{B}(s) u_k + C(s) \epsilon_{k+M}, \tag{3.62}$$

where

$$\overline{B}(s) = s^{-M} B(s) = b_M + b_{M+1} s + \cdots + b_m s^{m-M}.$$

Multiplying both sides of (3.62) with $F(s)$, we have

$$F(s)A(s) y_{k+M} = F(s)\overline{B}(s) u_k + F(s)C(s)\epsilon_{k+M},$$

and using (3.61) we obtain

$$C(s)[y_{k+M} - F(s)\epsilon_{k+M}] = F(s)\overline{B}(s) u_k + G(s) y_k. \tag{3.63}$$

Let

$$\begin{aligned} z_{k+M} &= y_{k+M} - F(s)\epsilon_{k+M} \\ &= y_{k+M} - \epsilon_{k+M} - f_1 \epsilon_{k+M-1} - \cdots - f_{M-1}\epsilon_{k+1} \end{aligned} \tag{3.64}$$

$$w_k = F(s)\overline{B}(s) u_k + G(s) y_k. \tag{3.65}$$

Then (3.63) is written as

$$C(s) z_{k+M} = w_k$$

or

$$z_{k+M} + c_1 z_{k+M-1} + \cdots + c_m z_{k+M-m} = w_k. \tag{3.66}$$

We now make two basic observations regarding z_{k+M}:

(a) We have from (3.64) and the fact that $\{\epsilon_k\}$ is an independent, zero-mean sequence

$$E\{z_{k+M} | I_k, u_k\} = E\{y_{k+M} | I_k, u_k\},$$

so we can obtain the desired forecast of y_{k+M} by forecasting z_{k+M} in its place.

(b) The scalar w_k of (3.65) is available at time k (i.e., is determined from I_k and u_k). Therefore, (3.66) can serve as a basis for forecasting z_{k+M} using w_k. In particular, the forecast $E\{z_{k+M}|I_k\}$ can be approximated by $\hat{y}_{k+M}$ generated by

$$\hat{y}_{k+m} + c_1\hat{y}_{k+m-1} + \cdots + c_m\hat{y}_{k+M-m} = w_k \tag{3.67}$$

with initial condition

$$\hat{y}_{M-1} = \hat{y}_{M-2} = \cdots = \hat{y}_{M-m} = 0. \tag{3.68}$$

To see this, note that from (3.66) to (3.68) we have

$$z_{k+M} = \hat{y}_{k+M} + [\gamma_1(k)z_{M-1} + \cdots + \gamma_m(k)z_{M-m}] \tag{3.69}$$

and

$$E\{z_{k+M}|I_k, u_k\} = \hat{y}_{k+M} + \sum_{i=1}^{m} \gamma_i(k)E\{z_{M-i}|I_k, u_k\},$$

where $\gamma_1(k), \ldots, \gamma_m(k)$ are appropriate scalars depending on k. Since $C(s)$ has all its roots inside the unit circle, we have (compare with the discussion on stability earlier in this section)

$$\lim_{k\to\infty} \gamma_1(k) = \lim_{k\to\infty} \gamma_2(k) = \cdots = \lim_{k\to\infty} \gamma_m(k) = 0. \tag{3.70}$$

It follows that, for large values of k,

$$\hat{y}_{k+M} \simeq E\{z_{k+M}|I_k, u_k\} = E\{y_{k+M}|I_k, u_k\}.$$

(More precisely, we have $|\hat{y}_{k+M} - E\{y_{k+M}|I_k, u_k\}| \to 0$ as $k \to \infty$, where the convergence is in the mean-square sense.)

In conclusion, *an approximation to the optimal forecast* $E\{y_{k+M}|I_k, u_k\}$ *is given by* $\hat{y}_{k+M}$ *generated by the equation*

$$\hat{y}_{k+M} + c_1\hat{y}_{k+M-1} + \cdots + c_m\hat{y}_{k+M-m} = F(s)\overline{B}(s)u_k + G(s)y_k \tag{3.71}$$

with the initial condition

$$\hat{y}_{M-1} = \hat{y}_{M-2} = \cdots = \hat{y}_{M-m} = 0. \tag{3.72}$$

Minimum Variance Control: Imperfect State Information Case

From the earlier discussion, we have that the minimum variance control law is obtained by solving for u_k equation (3.58), repeated here:

$$E\{y_{k+M}|I_k, u_k\} = 0.$$

Thus a reasonable approximation is obtained by setting u_k to the value that makes $\hat{y}_{k+M} = 0$, that is, by solving for u_k the equation [cf. (3.71) and (3.72)]

$$F(s)\overline{B}(s)u_k + G(s)y_k = c_1\hat{y}_{k+M-1} + \cdots + c_m\hat{y}_{k+M-m}.$$

If this policy is followed, however, the earlier forecasts $\hat{y}_{k+M-1}, \ldots, \hat{y}_{k+M-m}$ will be equal to zero. Thus the (approximate) minimum variance control law is given by

$$F(s)\overline{B}(s)u_k + G(s)y_k = 0. \tag{3.73}$$

That is, u_k^* is generated by passing y_k through the linear filter $-G(s)/F(s)\overline{B}(s)$, as shown in Figure 3.3.

From (3.63) and (3.73), we obtain the equation for the closed-loop system:

$$C(s)[y_{k+M} - F(s)\epsilon_{k+M}] = 0.$$

Since $C(s)$ has its roots outside the unit circle, we obtain

$$y_{k+M} = F(s)\epsilon_{k+M} + \gamma(k),$$

where $\gamma(k) \to 0$ as $k \to \infty$. So asymptotically the closed-loop system takes the form

$$y_k = \epsilon_k + f_1\epsilon_{k-1} + \cdots + f_{M-1}\epsilon_{k-M+1}.$$

Let us consider now the stability properties of the closed-loop system when the true system parameters differ slightly from those of the assumed model. Let the true system be described by

$$A^0(s)y_k = s^M\overline{B}^0(s)u_k + C^0(s)\epsilon_k, \tag{3.74}$$

while u_k is given by the minimum variance control law

$$F(s)\overline{B}(s)u_k + G(s)y_k = 0, \tag{3.75}$$

where

$$C(s) = A(s)F(s) + s^MG(s).$$

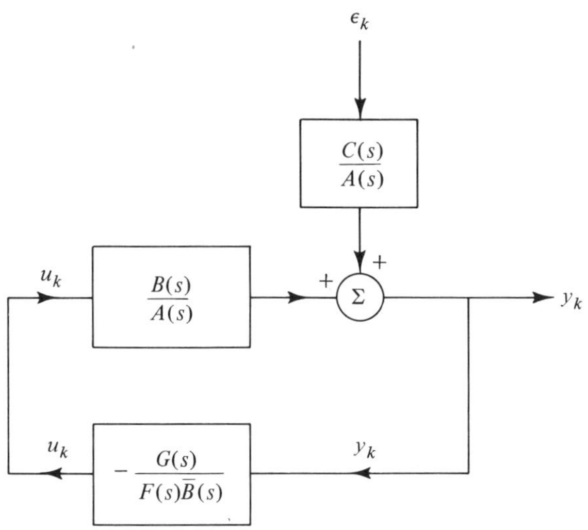

Figure 3.3 Minimum variance control with imperfect state information. Structure of optimal closed-loop system.

Operating on (3.74) with $F(s)\overline{B}(s)$ and using (3.75), we obtain

$$F(s)\overline{B}(s)A^0(s)y_k = -s^M\overline{B}^0(s)G(s)y_k + F(s)\overline{B}(s)C^0(s)\epsilon_k.$$

Combining the last two equations and collecting terms, we have

$$\{F(s)\overline{B}(s)A^0(s) + [C(s) - A(s)F(s)]\overline{B}^0(s)\}y_k = F(s)\overline{B}(s)C^0(s)\epsilon_k$$

or

$$\{\overline{B}^0(s)C(s) + F(s)[\overline{B}(s)A^0(s) - A(s)\overline{B}^0(s)]\}y_k = F(s)\overline{B}(s)C^0(s)\epsilon_k.$$

If the coefficients of $A^0(s)$, $\overline{B}^0(s)$, and $C^0(s)$ are near those of $A(s)$, $\overline{B}(s)$, and $C(s)$, then the poles of the closed-loop system will be near the roots of $\overline{B}(s)C(s)$. Thus *the closed-loop system will be in effect stable only if the roots of $\overline{B}(s)$ are strictly outside the unit circle,* similarly as for the perfect state information case examined earlier.

Example

Consider the case of no delay ($M = 1$). From (3.61) we have

$$G(s) = s^{-1}[C(s) - A(s)], \qquad F(s) = 1,$$

and from (3.73) we obtain, using $\overline{B}(s) = s^{-1}B(s)$,

$$B(s)u_k = [A(s) - C(s)]y_k.$$

Equivalently, u_k is generated via the equation

$$u_k = \frac{1}{b_1}[(a_1 - c_1)y_k + \cdots + (a_m - c_m)y_{k-m+1} - b_2u_{k-1} - \cdots - b_mu_{k-m+1}].$$

The closed-loop system is given by

$$y_k - \epsilon_k + c_1(y_{k-1} - \epsilon_{k-1}) + \cdots + c_m(y_{k-m} - \epsilon_{k-m}) = 0,$$

or equivalently $C(s)(y_k - \epsilon_k) = 0$. Since $C(s)$ has its roots outside the unit circle, this is a stable system, and we have

$$y_k = \epsilon_k + \gamma(k),$$

where $\gamma(k) \to 0$ as $k \to \infty$.

3.4 SUFFICIENT STATISTICS AND FINITE STATE MARKOV CHAINS: A PROBLEM OF INSTRUCTION

The main difficulty with the DP algorithm (3.7) and (3.8) is that it is carried out over a state space of expanding dimension. As a new measurement is added at each stage k, the dimension of the state (the information vector I_k) increases accordingly. This motivates an effort to reduce the data that are truly necessary for control purposes. In other words, it is of interest to look for quantities known as *sufficient statistics,* which ideally would be of smaller dimension than I_k and yet summarize all the essential content of I_k as far as control is concerned.

Consider the DP algorithm (3.7) and (3.8) restated here for convenience:

$$J_{N-1}(I_{N-1}) = \min_{u_{N-1}\in U_{N-1}} \left[\underset{x_{N-1}, w_{N-1}}{E} \{ g_N[f_{N-1}(x_{N-1}, u_{N-1}, w_{N-1})] + g_{N-1}(x_{N-1}, u_{N-1}, w_{N-1}) | I_{N-1}, u_{N-1} \} \right], \tag{3.76}$$

$$J_k(I_k) = \min_{u_k\in U_k} \left[\underset{x_k, w_k, z_{k+1}}{E} \{ g_k(x_k, u_k, w_k) + J_{k+1}(I_k, z_{k+1}, u_k) | I_k, u_k \} \right]. \tag{3.77}$$

Suppose that we can find a function $S_k(\cdot)$ of the information vector I_k, such that a minimizing control in (3.76) and (3.77) depends on I_k via $S_k(I_k)$. By this we mean that the minimization in the right side of the DP algorithm (3.76) and (3.77) can be written in terms of some function H_k as

$$\min_{u_k\in U_k} H_k[S_k(I_k), u_k].$$

Such a function $S_k(\cdot)$ will be called a *sufficient statistic*. Its salient feature is that an optimal control law obtained by the preceding minimization can be written as

$$\mu_k(I_k) = \overline{\mu}_k[S_k(I_k)],$$

where $\overline{\mu}_k$ is an appropriate function. Thus, if the sufficient statistic is characterized by a set of fewer numbers than the information vector I_k, it may be easier to implement the control law in the form $u_k = \overline{\mu}_k[S_k(I_k)]$ and take advantage of the resulting data reduction.

There are many different functions that can serve as sufficient statistics. The identity function $S_k(I_k) = I_k$ is certainly one of them. Another important sufficient statistic is obtained if we assume that *the probability distribution of the observation disturbance v_{k+1} depends explicitly only on the immediately preceding state, control, and system disturbance x_k, u_k, w_k, and not on $x_{k-1}, \ldots, x_0$, $u_{k-1}, \ldots, u_0$, $w_{k-1}, \ldots, w_0$, $v_{k-1}, \ldots, v_0$.* Under this assumption we can show that a sufficient statistic is given by the conditional probability measure $P_{x_k|I_k}$ of the state x_k, given the information vector I_k.

Proving that $P_{x_k|I_k}$ is a sufficient statistic requires a development that is of independent interest. A key fact is that $P_{x_k|I_k}$ is generated recursively in time and can be viewed as the state of a controlled discrete-time dynamic system. By using Bayes's rule, we can write for all k

$$P_{x_{k+1}|I_{k+1}} = \Phi_k(P_{x_k|I_k}, u_k, z_{k+1}), \tag{3.78}$$

where Φ_k is some function that can be determined from the data of the problem, u_k is the control of the system, and z_{k+1} plays the role of a random disturbance the statistics of which are known and depend explicitly on $P_{x_k|I_k}$ and u_k only and not on $z_k, \ldots, z_0$. This fact is perhaps best illustrated by an example.

Example

In a classical problem of search, one has to decide at each period whether to search a site that may contain a treasure. If a treasure is present, the search reveals it with probability β, in which case the treasure is removed from the site. Denote

p_k: probability a treasure is present at the beginning of period k.

This probability evolves according to the equation

$$p_{k+1} = \begin{cases} p_k, & \text{if the site is not searched at time } k, \\ 0, & \text{if the site is searched and a treasure is found at period } k, \\ \dfrac{p_k(1-\beta)}{p_k(1-\beta)+1-p_k}, & \text{if the site is searched but no treasure is found at period } k. \end{cases}$$

The second relation holds because the treasure is removed after a successful search. The third relation follows by application of Bayes's rule (p_{k+1} is the kth period probability of a treasure being present *and* the search being unsuccessful, divided by the probability of an unsuccessful search). The preceding equation above defines a dynamic system of the form (3.78). Here the control u_k takes two values: search and not search. If the site is searched, the observation z_{k+1} takes two values, treasure found or not found, while the value of z_{k+1} is irrelevant when the site is not searched.

The general form of equation (3.78) is developed in Problem 7 for the case where the state, control, observation, and disturbance spaces are finite sets. In the case where these spaces are the real line and all random variables involved possess probability density functions, the conditional density $p(x_{k+1}|I_{k+1})$ is generated from $p(x_k|I_k)$, u_k, and z_{k+1} by means of the equation

$$p(x_{k+1}|I_{k+1}) = p(x_{k+1}|I_k, u_k, z_{k+1}) = \frac{p(x_{k+1}, z_{k+1}|I_k, u_k)}{p(z_{k+1}|I_k, u_k)}$$
$$= \frac{p(x_{k+1}|I_k, u_k)p(z_{k+1}|I_k, u_k, x_{k+1})}{\int_{-\infty}^{\infty} p(x_{k+1}|I_k, u_k)p(z_{k+1}|I_k, u_k, x_{k+1})\, dx_{k+1}}.$$

In this equation all the probability densities appearing in the right side may be expressed in terms of $p(x_k|I_k)$, u_k, and z_{k+1} alone. In particular, the density $p(x_{k+1}|I_k, u_k)$ may be expressed through $p(x_k|I_k)$, u_k, and the system equation $x_{k+1} = f_k(x_k, u_k, w_k)$ using the given density $p(w_k|x_k, u_k)$ and the relation

$$p(w_k|I_k, u_k) = \int_{-\infty}^{\infty} p(x_k|I_k)p(w_k|x_k, u_k)dx_k.$$

Similarly, the density $p(z_{k+1}|I_k, u_k, x_{k+1})$ is expressed through the measurement equation $z_{k+1} = h_{k+1}(x_{k+1}, u_k, v_{k+1})$ using $p(x_k|I_k)$, $p(w_k|x_k, u_k)$ and the given probability density $p(v_{k+1}|x_k, u_k, w_k)$. By substituting these expressions in the equation for $p(x_{k+1}|I_{k+1})$, we obtain an equation of the form (3.78). Other explicit examples of equations of the form of (3.78) will be given in subsequent sections. A mathematically rigorous substantiation of (3.78) and the following DP algorithm can be found in [B23]. In any case, one can see that *the system described by (3.78) fits the framework of the basic problem.* Furthermore, the controller can calculate (at least in principle) at time k the conditional probability measure $P_{x_k|I_k}$. Therefore, in system (3.78), the controller has perfect state information.

Now the DP algorithm (3.76) and (3.77) can be written in terms of the sufficient statistic $P_{x_k|I_k}$ by making use of the new system equation (3.78) as follows:

$$\bar{J}_{N-1}(P_{x_{N-1}|I_{N-1}}) = \min_{u_{N-1}\in U_{N-1}} \Big[\underset{x_{N-1}, w_{N-1}}{E} \{g_N[f_{N-1}(x_{N-1}, u_{N-1}, w_{N-1})] + g_{N-1}(x_{N-1}, u_{N-1}, w_{N-1})|I_{N-1}, u_{N-1}\} \Big], \tag{3.79}$$

$$\bar{J}_k(P_{x_k|I_k}) = \min_{u_k\in U_k} \Big[\underset{x_k, w_k, z_{k+1}}{E} \{g_k(x_k, u_k, w_k) + \bar{J}_{k+1}[\Phi_k(P_{x_k|I_k}, u_k, z_{k+1})]|I_k, u_k\} \Big]. \tag{3.80}$$

Furthermore, this DP algorithm yields a control law of the form

$$u_k^* = \bar{\mu}_k^*(P_{x_k|I_k}), \qquad k = 0, 1, \dots, N-1.$$

In addition, the optimal cost is given by

$$J^* = \underset{z_0}{E}\{\bar{J}_0(P_{x_0|z_0})\},$$

where $\bar{J}_0$ is obtained by the last step of the algorithm (3.79) and (3.80), and the probability measure of z_0 is obtained from the statistics of x_0 and v_0 and the measurement equation $z_0 = h_0(x_0, v_0)$.

The preceding analysis is in effect an alternate reduction of the basic problem with imperfect state information to a problem with perfect state information that involves system (3.78), the state of which is $P_{x_k|I_k}$, and an appropriately reformulated cost functional. A conclusion that can be drawn is that *the conditional probability $P_{x_k|I_k}$ summarizes all the information that is necessary for control purposes at period k.* In the absence of perfect knowledge of the state, *the controller can be viewed as controlling the "probabilistic state" $P_{x_k|I_k}$ so as to minimize the expected cost-to-go conditioned on the information I_k available.*

Regardless of its computational value, the representation of the optimal control law as a sequence of functions of the conditional probability distribution $P_{x_k|I_k}$,

$$\mu_k(I_k) = \bar{\mu}_k(P_{x_k|I_k}), \qquad k = 0, 1, \dots, N-1,$$

is conceptually useful. It provides a decomposition of the optimal controller in two parts: (1) an *estimator,* which uses at time k the measurement z_k and the control u_{k-1} to generate the probability distribution $P_{x_k|I_k}$, and (2) an *actuator,* which generates a control input to the system as a function of the probability distribution $P_{x_k|I_k}$ (Figure 3.4). Aside from its conceptual and analytical importance, this interpretation has formed the basis for various suboptimal control schemes that separate a priori the controller into an estimator and an actuator and attempt to design each part in a manner that seems "reasonable." Schemes of this type will be presented in Chapter 4.

When the system is a finite state Markov chain, the conditional probability distribution $P_{x_k|I_k}$ is characterized by a finite set of numbers. This is particularly convenient, and the situation simplifies further when the control and observation spaces are also finite sets. It then turns out that the cost-to-go functions $\bar{J}_k$ in the DP algorithm (3.79) and (3.80) are *piecewise linear* and *concave.* The demonstration of this fact is straightforward, but tedious, and is outlined in Problem 7. The piecewise linearity of $\bar{J}_k$ is, however, an important property since it shows that $\bar{J}_k$ can be characterized by a finite set of scalars. Still, however, for fixed k, the number of these scalars can increase fast with N, and there may be no computationally efficient way to solve the problem (see [P3]). We will not discuss here any special procedures for computing $\bar{J}_k$ (see [S21], [S23]). Instead we will demonstrate the DP algorithm by means of examples. The first example, a problem of instruction, is considered in this section. The second, a hypothesis testing problem, is treated in the next.

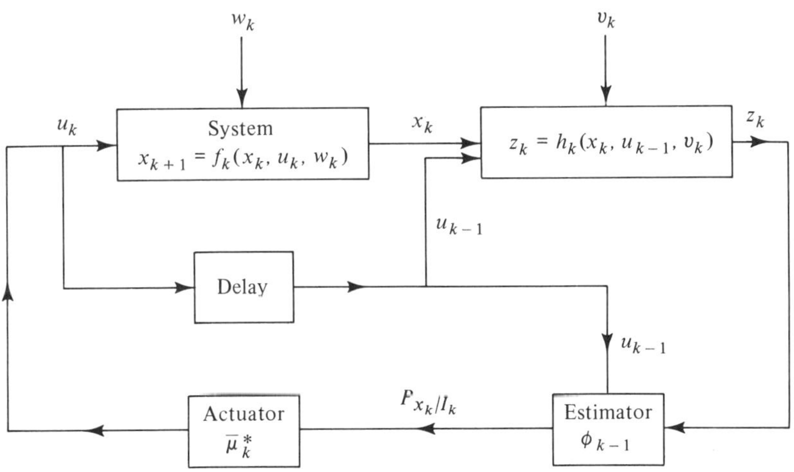

Figure 3.4 Conceptual separation of the optimal controller into an estimator and an actuator.

A Problem of Instruction

Consider a problem of instruction where the objective is to teach a student a certain simple item. At the beginning of each period, the student may be in one of two possible states:

x^1 item learned,
x^2 item not learned.

At the beginning of each period, the instructor must make one of two decisions

u^1 terminate the instruction,
u^2 continue the instruction for one period and then conduct a test that indicates whether the student has learned the item.

The test has two possible outcomes:

z^1 student gives a correct answer,
z^2 student gives an incorrect answer.

The transition probabilities from one state to the next if instruction takes place are given by

$$P(x_{k+1} = x^1 | x_k = x^1) = 1, \qquad P(x_{k+1} = x^2 | x_k = x^1) = 0,$$

$$P(x_{k+1} = x^1 | x_k = x^2) = t, \qquad P(x_{k+1} = x^2 | x_k = x^2) = 1 - t, \qquad 0 < t < 1.$$

The outcome of the test depends probabilistically on the state of knowledge of the student as follows:

$$P(z_k = z^1 | x_k = x^1) = 1, \qquad P(z_k = z^2 | x_k = x^1) = 0,$$

$$P(z_k = z^1 | x_k = x^2) = r, \qquad P(z_k = z^2 | x_k = x^2) = 1 - r, \qquad 0 < r < 1.$$

The cost of instruction and testing is I per period, the cost of terminating instruction is 0, and $C > 0$ if the student has learned or has not learned the item, respectively. The objective is to find the instruction–termination policy for each period k as a function of the test information accrued up to that period, which minimizes the total expected cost, assuming that there is a maximum of N periods of instruction.

It is easy to reformulate this problem into the framework of the basic problem with imperfect state information and conclude that the decision whether to terminate or continue instruction at period k should depend on the conditional probability that the student has learned the item given the test results so far. This probability is denoted

$$p_k = P(x_k = x^1 | z_0, z_1, \ldots, z_k).$$

In addition, we can use the DP algorithm (3.79) and (3.80) defined over the space of the sufficient statistic p_k to obtain an optimal policy. However, rather than proceeding with this elaborate reformulation, we prefer to argue and obtain directly this DP algorithm.

Concerning the evolution of the conditional probability p_k (assuming instruction occurs), we have by Bayes' rule

$$p_{k+1} = P(x_{k+1} = x^1 | z_0, \ldots, z_{k+1})$$
$$= \frac{P(x_{k+1} = x^1, z_{k+1} | z_0, \ldots, z_k)}{P(z_{k+1} | z_0, \ldots, z_k)}$$
$$= \frac{P(x_{k+1} = x^1 | z_0, \ldots, z_k) P(z_{k+1} | z_0, \ldots, z_k, x_{k+1} = x^1)}{\sum_{i=1}^{2} P(x_{k+1} = x^i | z_0, \ldots, z_k) P(z_{k+1} | z_0, \ldots, z_k, x_{k+1} = x^i)}.$$

From the probabilistic descriptions given, we have

$$P(z_{k+1} | z_0, \ldots, z_k, x_{k+1} = x^1) = P(z_{k+1} | x_{k+1} = x^1) = \begin{cases} 1, & \text{if } z_{k+1} = z^1, \\ 0, & \text{if } z_{k+1} = z^2, \end{cases}$$

$$P(z_{k+1} | z_0, \ldots, z_k, x_{k+1} = x^2) = P(z_{k+1} | x_{k+1} = x^2) = \begin{cases} r & \text{if } z_{k+1} = z^1, \\ 1 - r, & \text{if } z_{k+1} = z^2, \end{cases}$$

$$P(x_{k+1} = x^1 | z_0, \ldots, z_k) = p_k + (1 - p_k)t,$$
$$P(x_{k+1} = x^2 | z_0, \ldots, z_k) = (1 - p_k)(1 - t).$$

Combining these equations, we obtain

$$p_{k+1} = \Phi(p_k, z_{k+1}),$$

where the function Φ is defined by

$$\Phi(p_k, z_{k+1}) = \begin{cases} \dfrac{p_k + (1 - p_k)t}{p_k + (1 - p_k)t + (1 - p_k)(1 - t)r}, & \text{if } z_{k+1} = z^1, \\ 0, & \text{if } z_{k+1} = z^2, \end{cases}$$

or equivalently

$$\Phi(p_k, z_{k+1}) = \begin{cases} \dfrac{1 - (1 - t)(1 - p_k)}{1 - (1 - t)(1 - r)(1 - p_k)}, & \text{if } z_{k+1} = z^1, \\ 0, & \text{if } z_{k+1} = z^2. \end{cases} \tag{3.81}$$

A cursory examination of this equation shows that, as expected, the conditional probability p_{k+1} that the student has learned the item increases with every correct answer and drops to zero with every incorrect answer. We mention also that Eq. (3.81) is a special case of Eq. (3.78). The dependence of the function Φ on the control u_k is not explicitly shown since there is only one possible action aside from termination.

We turn now to the development of the DP algorithm for the problem. At the end of the Nth period, assuming instruction has continued to that period, the expected cost is

$$\bar{J}_N(p_N) = (1 - p_N)C. \tag{3.82}$$

At the end of period $N - 1$, the instructor has calculated the conditional probability p_{N-1} that the student has learned the item and wishes to decide whether to terminate instruction and incur an expected cost $(1 - p_{N-1})C$ or continue the instruction and incur an expected cost $I + E_{z_N}\{\bar{J}_N(p_N)\}$. This leads to the following equation for the optimal expected cost-to-go:

$$\bar{J}_{N-1}(p_{N-1}) = \min\left[(1 - p_{N-1})C, I + \underset{z_N}{E}\{\bar{J}_N[\Phi(p_{N-1}, z_N)]\}\right].$$

Similarly, the algorithm is written for every stage k by replacing N by $k + 1$:

$$\bar{J}_k(p_k) = \min\left[(1 - p_k)C, I + \underset{z_{k+1}}{E}\{\bar{J}_{k+1}[\Phi(p_k, z_{k+1})]\}\right].$$

Now using expression (3.81) for the function Φ and the probabilities

$$P(z_{k+1} = z^2 | p_k) = (1 - t)(1 - r)(1 - p_k),$$
$$P(z_{k+1} = z^1 | p_k) = 1 - (1 - t)(1 - r)(1 - p_k),$$

we have

$$\bar{J}_k(p_k) = \min[(1 - p_k)C, I + A_k(p_k)], \tag{3.83}$$

where

$$A_k(p_k) = [1 - (1 - t)(1 - r)(1 - p_k)]\bar{J}_{k+1}\left[\frac{1 - (1 - t)(1 - p_k)}{1 - (1 - t)(1 - r)(1 - p_k)}\right] + (1 - t)(1 - r)(1 - p_k)\bar{J}_{k+1}(0). \tag{3.84}$$

In particular, by using (3.82) to (3.84), we have by straightforward calculation

$$\begin{aligned}\bar{J}_{N-1}(p_{N-1}) &= \min[(1 - p_{N-1})C, I + A_{N-1}(p_{N-1})] \\ &= \min[(1 - p_{N-1})C, I + (1 - t)(1 - p_{N-1})C].\end{aligned}$$

Thus, as shown in Figure 3.5, if

$$I + (1 - t)C < C, \tag{3.85}$$

there exists a scalar α_{N-1} with $0 < \alpha_{N-1} < 1$ that determines an optimal policy for the last period:

$$\text{continue instruction} \quad \text{if } p_{N-1} \leq \alpha_{N-1},$$
$$\text{terminate instruction} \quad \text{if } p_{N-1} > \alpha_{N-1}.$$

It may be shown (Problem 8) using (3.84) that under condition (3.85) the functions $A_k(p)$ are concave and piecewise linear for each k and satisfy, for all k,

$$A_k(1) = 0. \tag{3.86}$$

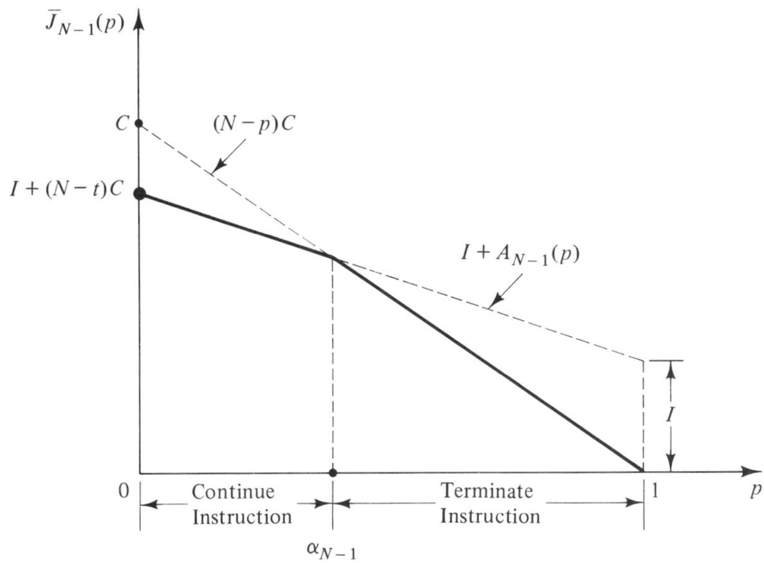

Figure 3.5 Determining the optimal instruction policy in the last period.

Furthermore, they satisfy, for all k,

$$A_k(p) \geq A_k(p'), \qquad \text{for } 0 \leq p < p' \leq 1, \tag{3.87}$$

$$A_{k-1}(p) \leq A_k(p) \leq A_{k+1}(p), \qquad \text{for all } p \in [0, 1]. \tag{3.88}$$

Thus, from the DP algorithm (3.83) and Eqs. (3.86) to (3.88), we obtain that the optimal policy for each period is determined by the unique scalars α_k, which are such that

$$(1 - \alpha_k)C = I + A_k(\alpha_k), \qquad k = 0, 1, \dots, N-1.$$

An optimal policy for period k is given by

$$\begin{aligned} &\text{continue instruction} && \text{if } p_k \leq \alpha_k, \\ &\text{terminate instruction} && \text{if } p_k > \alpha_k. \end{aligned}$$

Since the functions $A_k(p)$ are monotonically nondecreasing with respect to k, it follows from Figure 3.6 that

$$\alpha_{N-1} \leq \alpha_{N-2} \leq \cdots \leq \alpha_k \leq \alpha_{k-1} \leq \cdots \leq 1 - \frac{I}{C},$$

and therefore the sequence $\{\alpha_k\}$ converges to some scalar $\overline{\alpha}$ as $k \to -\infty$. Thus, as the horizon gets longer, the optimal policy (at least for the initial stages) can be approximated by the stationary policy

$$\begin{aligned} &\text{continue instruction} && \text{if } p_k \leq \overline{\alpha}, \\ &\text{terminate instruction} && \text{if } p_k > \overline{\alpha}. \end{aligned} \tag{3.89}$$

It turns out that this stationary policy has a convenient implementation that

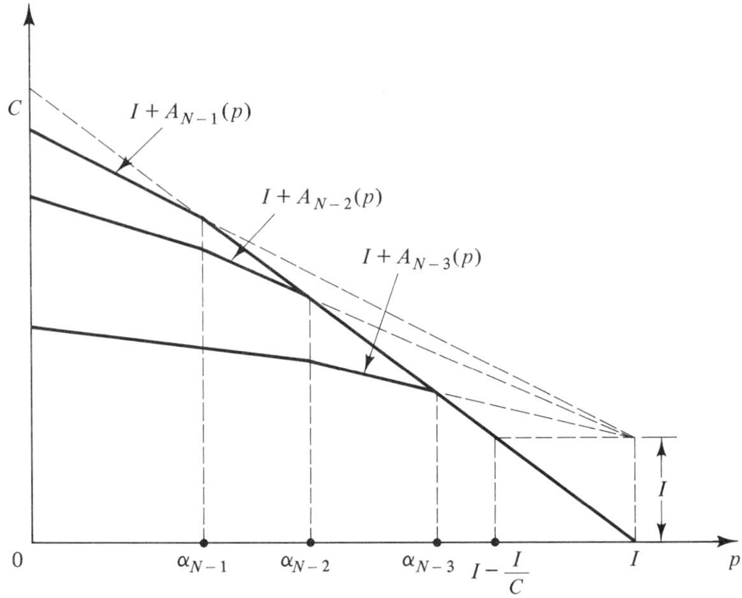

Figure 3.6 Demonstrating that the instruction thresholds are decreasing with time.

does not require the calculation of the conditional probability at each stage. From Eq. (3.81) we have that p_{k+1} increases over p_k, if a correct answer z^1 is given and drops to zero if an incorrect answer z^2 is given. Define recursively the probabilities

$$\pi_1 = \Phi(0, z^1), \pi_2 = \Phi(\pi_1, z^1), \ldots, \pi_{k+1} = \Phi(\pi_k, z^1), \ldots,$$

and let n be the smallest integer for which $\pi_n > \overline{\alpha}$. It is clear that the stationary policy (3.89) can be implemented as follows:

terminate instruction	if n successive correct answers have been received,
continue instruction	otherwise.

3.5 HYPOTHESIS TESTING: SEQUENTIAL PROBABILITY RATIO TEST

In this section we consider a hypothesis testing problem typical of statistical sequential analysis. A decision maker can make observations, at a cost C each, relating to two hypotheses. Given a new observation, he can either accept one of the hypotheses or delay the decision for one more period, pay the cost C, and obtain a new observation. At issue is trading off the cost of observation with the higher probability of accepting the wrong hypothesis.

Let $z_0, z_1, \ldots, z_{N-1}$ be the sequence of observations. We assume that they are independent, identically distributed random variables taking values on a finite set Z. Suppose we know that the probability distribution of the z_k's is either f_0 or f_1 and that we are trying to decide on one of these. Here, for any element $z \in Z$, $f_0(z)$ $[f_1(z)]$ denotes the probability of z when f_0 (f_1) is the true distribution. At time k after observing $z_0, \ldots, z_k$, we may either stop observing and accept either f_0 or f_1, or we may take an additional observation at a cost $C > 0$. If we stop observing and make a choice, then we incur zero cost if our choice is correct, and costs L_0, L_1 if we choose incorrectly f_0 and f_1, respectively. We are given the a priori probability p that the true distribution is f_0, and we assume that at most N observations are possible.

It is easy to see that we are faced with an imperfect state information problem involving the two states:

$$x^0: \quad \text{true distribution is } f_0,$$

$$x^1: \quad \text{true distribution is } f_1.$$

The sufficient statistic DP algorithm (3.79) and (3.80) is defined over the interval [0, 1] of possible values of the conditional probability

$$p_k = P(x_k = x^0 | z_0, \ldots, z_k).$$

Similarly, as in the previous section, we will obtain this algorithm directly.

The conditional probability p_k is generated recursively according to the following equation [assuming $f_0(z) > 0$, $f_1(z) > 0$ for all $z \in Z$]:

$$p_{k+1} = \frac{p_k f_0(z_{k+1})}{p_k f_0(z_{k+1}) + (1 - p_k) f_1(z_{k+1})}, \qquad k = 0, 1, \ldots, N-2, \tag{3.90}$$

$$p_0 = \frac{p f_0(z_0)}{p f_0(z_0) + (1 - p) f_1(z_0)}, \tag{3.91}$$

where p is the a priori probability that the true distribution is f_0. The optimal expected cost for the last period is

$$\bar{J}_{N-1}(p_{N-1}) = \min[(1 - p_{N-1})L_0, p_{N-1}L_1], \tag{3.92}$$

where $(1 - p_{N-1})L_0$ is the expected cost for accepting f_0 and $p_{N-1}L_1$ is the expected cost for accepting f_1. Taking into account (3.90) and (3.91), we can obtain the optimal expected cost-to-go for the kth period from the equation

$$\bar{J}_k(p_k) = \min\Bigg[(1 - p_k)L_0,\ p_k L_1,\ C + \mathop{E}_{z_{k+1}}\bigg\{\bar{J}_{k+1}\bigg[\frac{p_k f_0(z_{k+1})}{p_k f_0(z_{k+1}) + (1 - p_k) f_1(z_{k+1})}\bigg]\bigg\}\Bigg],$$

where the expectation over z_{k+1} is taken with respect to the probability distribution

$$p(z_{k+1}) = p_k f_0(z_{k+1}) + (1 - p_k) f_1(z_{k+1}), \qquad z_{k+1} \in Z.$$

Equivalently, for $k = 0, 1, \ldots, N - 2$,

$$\bar{J}_k(p_k) = \min[(1 - p_k)L_0, p_kL_1, C + A_k(p_k)], \tag{3.93}$$

where

$$A_k(p_k) = \underset{z_{k+1}}{E}\left\{\bar{J}_{k+1}\left[\frac{p_kf_0(z_{k+1})}{p_kf_0(z_{k+1}) + (1 - p_k)f_1(z_{k+1})}\right]\right\}. \tag{3.94}$$

An optimal policy for the last period (see Figure 3.7) is obtained from the minimization indicated in (3.92):

$$\text{accept } f_0 \qquad \text{if } p_{N-1} \geq \mu,$$

$$\text{accept } f_1 \qquad \text{if } p_{N-1} < \mu,$$

where μ is determined from the relation $(1 - \mu)L_0 = \mu L_1$ or equivalently

$$\mu = \frac{L_0}{L_0 + L_1}.$$

We now prove the following lemma.

Lemma. The functions A_k: $[0, 1] \to R$ of (3.94) are concave and satisfy for all k and $p \in [0, 1]$

$$A_k(0) = A_k(1) = 0,$$

$$A_{k-1}(p) \leq A_k(p).$$

Proof. We have for all $p \in [0, 1]$

$$\bar{J}_{N-2}(p) \leq \min[(1 - p)L_0, pL_0] = \bar{J}_{N-1}(p).$$

By making use of the stationarity of the system and the monotonicity

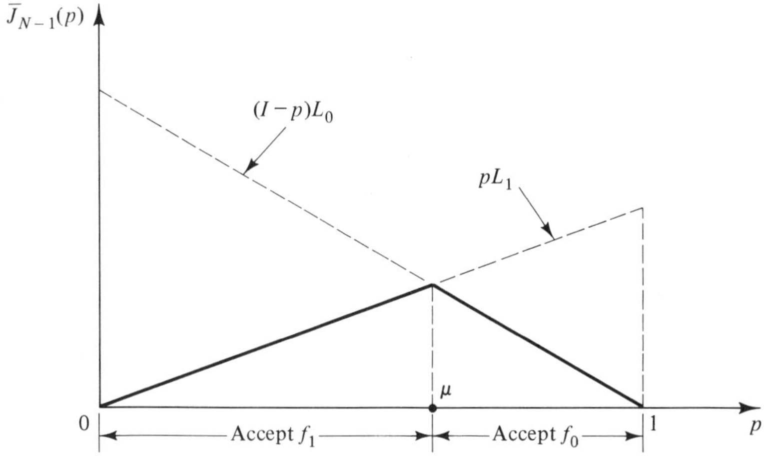

Figure 3.7 Determining the optimal policy in the last period.

property of DP (Problem 24 in Chapter 1), we obtain

$$\bar{J}_k(p) \leq \bar{J}_{k+1}(p)$$

for all k and $p \in [0, 1]$. Using (3.94), we obtain $A_{k-1}(p) \leq A_k(p)$ for all k and $p \in [0, 1]$.

To prove concavity of A_k in view of (3.92) and (3.93), it is sufficient to show that concavity of $\bar{J}_{k+1}$ implies concavity of A_k through relation (3.94). Indeed, assume that $\bar{J}_{k+1}$ is concave over $[0, 1]$. Let $z^1, z^2, \ldots, z^n$ denote the elements of the observation space Z. We have from (3.94) that

$$A_k(p) = \sum_{i=1}^{n} [pf_0(z^i) + (1 - p)f_1(z^i)]\bar{J}_{k+1}\left[\frac{pf_0(z^i)}{pf_0(z^i) + (1 - p)f_1(z^i)}\right].$$

Hence it is sufficient to show that concavity of $\bar{J}_{k+1}$ implies concavity of each of the functions

$$h_i(p) = [pf_0(z^i) + (1 - p)f_1(z^i)]\bar{J}_{k+1}\left[\frac{pf_0(z^i)}{pf_0(z^i) + (1 - p)f_1(z^i)}\right].$$

To show concavity of h_i, we must show that for every $\lambda \in [0, 1]$, p_1, $p_2 \in [0, 1]$ we have

$$\lambda h_i(p_1) + (1 - \lambda)h_i(p_2) \leq h_i[\lambda p_1 + (1 - \lambda)p_2].$$

Using the notation

$$\xi_1 = p_1 f_0(z^i) + (1 - p_1)f_1(z^i), \qquad \xi_2 = p_2 f_0(z^i) + (1 - p_2)f_1(z^i),$$

the preceding inequality is equivalent to

$$\frac{\lambda\xi_1}{\lambda\xi_1 + (1 - \lambda)\xi_2}\bar{J}_{k+1}\left[\frac{p_1 f_0(z^i)}{\xi_1}\right] + \frac{(1 - \lambda)\xi_2}{\lambda\xi_1 + (1 - \lambda)\xi_2}\bar{J}_{k+1}\left[\frac{p_2 f_0(z^i)}{\xi_2}\right]$$
$$\leq \bar{J}_{k+1}\left[\frac{(\lambda p_1 + (1 - \lambda)p_2)f_0(z^i)}{\lambda\xi_1 + (1 - \lambda)\xi_2}\right].$$

This relation, however, is implied by the concavity of $\bar{J}_{k+1}$. Q.E.D.

Using the lemma, we obtain (see Figure 3.8) that if

$$C + A_{N-2}[L_0/(L_0 + L_1)] < L_0 L_1/(L_0 + L_1),$$

then an optimal policy for each period k is of the form

accept f_0	if $p_k \geq \alpha_k$,
accept f_1	if $p_k \leq \beta_k$,
continue the observations	if $\beta_k < p_k < \alpha_k$,

where the scalars α_k, β_k are determined from the relations

$$\beta_k L_1 = C + A_k(\beta_k),$$
$$(1 - \alpha_k)L_0 = C + A_k(\alpha_k).$$

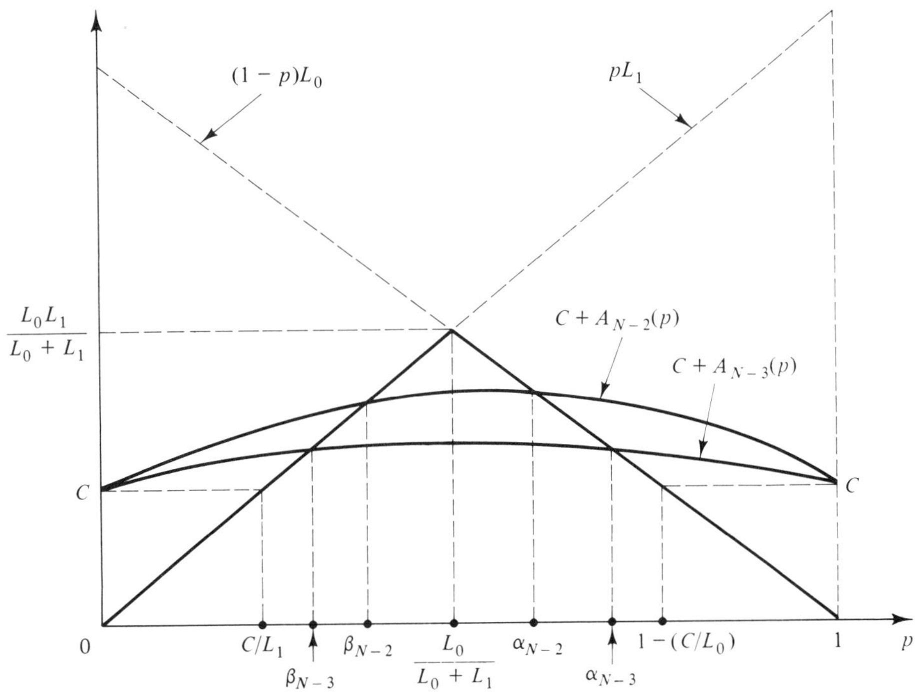

Figure 3.8 Determining the optimal hypothesis testing policy.

Furthermore, we have

$$\cdots \leqslant \alpha_{k+1} \leqslant \alpha_k \leqslant \alpha_{k-1} \leqslant \cdots \leqslant 1 - \frac{C}{L_0},$$

$$\cdots \geqslant \beta_{k+1} \geqslant \beta_k \geqslant \beta_{k-1} \geqslant \cdots \geqslant \frac{C}{L_1}.$$

Hence as $N \to \infty$ the sequences $\{\alpha_{N-i}\}$, $\{\beta_{N-i}\}$ converge to scalars $\overline{\alpha}$, $\overline{\beta}$, respectively, and the optimal policy is approximated by the stationary policy

$$\begin{aligned} &\text{accept } f_0 && \text{if } p_k \geqslant \overline{\alpha}, \\ &\text{accept } f_1 && \text{if } p_k \leqslant \overline{\beta}, \\ &\text{continue the observations} && \text{if } \overline{\beta} < p_k < \overline{\alpha}. \end{aligned} \tag{3.95}$$

Now the conditional probability p_k is given by

$$p_k = \frac{p f_0(z_0) f_0(z_1) \cdots f_0(z_k)}{p f_0(z_0) \cdots f_0(z_k) + (1 - p) f_1(z_0) \cdots f_1(z_k)}, \tag{3.96}$$

where p is the a priori probability that f_0 is the true hypothesis. Using

(3.96), the stationary policy (3.95) can be written in the form

$$\begin{aligned} &\text{accept } f_0 && \text{if } R_k \geq A = \frac{(1-p)\overline{\alpha}}{p(1-\overline{\alpha})}, \\ &\text{accept } f_1 && \text{if } R_k \leq B = \frac{(1-p)\overline{\beta}}{p(1-\overline{\beta})}, \\ &\text{continue the observations} && \text{if } B < R_k < A, \end{aligned} \tag{3.97}$$

where the *sequential probability ratio* R_k is given by

$$R_k = \frac{f_0(z_0)\cdots f_0(z_k)}{f_1(z_0)\cdots f_1(z_k)}.$$

Note that R_k can be easily generated by means of the recursive equation

$$R_{k+1} = \frac{f_0(z_{k+1})}{f_1(z_{k+1})}R_k.$$

The procedure (3.97) is known as the *sequential probability ratio test*. Procedures of this type were among the first formal methods of statistical sequential analysis [W1]. The optimality of policy (3.95) for the infinite horizon version of the problem will be shown in Section 6.3.

3.6 NOTES

For literature on linear–quadratic problems with imperfect state information, see the references quoted for Section 2.1 and Witsenhausen's survey paper [W16]. The Kalman filtering algorithm [K1] is a well-known and widely used tool. Detailed discussions can be found in many textbooks [A1, J3, L8, M6, M7, N1]. For linear–quadratic problems with Gaussian uncertainties and observation cost in the spirit of Problem 6, see [A4] and [C3]. Problem 1, indicating the form of the certainty equivalence principle when the random disturbances are correlated, is based on an unpublished report by the author [B8]. The minimum variance approach is also described in [A11], [A13], and [W12].

The idea of data reduction via a sufficient statistic gained wide attention following the 1965 paper by Striebel [S29] (see also [S27, S31]). For the analog of the sufficient statistic idea in sequential minimax problems, see [B22].

The possibility of analysis of the problem of control of a Markov chain with imperfect state information via sufficient statistics has been known for a long time. It has been exploited in [E2], [S21], and [S23]. The proof of piecewise linearity of the cost-to-go functions and an algorithm for their computation is given in [S21] and [S23]. The instruction model described in Section 3.4 has been considered (with some variations) by a number of authors [A14, G4, K3, S20].

For a discussion of the sequential probability ratio test and related subjects, see [C1], [D1], [W11], and the references quoted therein. The treatment given here stems from [A6].

PROBLEMS

1. Consider the linear system and measurement equation of Section 3.2 and consider the problem of finding a control law $\{\mu_0^*(I_0), \ldots, \mu_{N-1}^*(I_{N-1})\}$ that minimizes the quadratic cost

$$E\left\{x_N' Q x_N + \sum_{k=0}^{N-1} u_k' R_k u_k\right\}.$$

Assume, however, that the random vectors $x_0, w_0, \ldots, w_{N-1}, v_0, \ldots, v_{N-1}$ are correlated and have given joint probability distribution and finite first and second moments. Show that the optimal control law is given by

$$\mu_k^*(I_k) = L_k E\{y_k | I_k\},$$

where the gain matrices L_k are obtained from the recursive algorithm

$$L_k = -(B_k' K_{k+1} B_k + R_k)^{-1} B_k' K_{k+1} A_k,$$

$$K_N = Q,$$

$$K_k = A_k'[K_{k+1} - K_{k+1} B_k (B_k' K_{k+1} B_k + R_k)^{-1} B_k' K_{k+1}] A_k,$$

and the vectors y_k are given by

$$y_k = x_k + A_k^{-1} w_k + A_k^{-1} A_{k+1}^{-1} w_{k+1} + \cdots + A_k^{-1} \cdots A_{N-1}^{-1} w_{N-1}$$

(assuming the matrices $A_0, A_1, \ldots, A_{N-1}$ are invertible). *Hint:* Show that the cost can be written

$$E\left\{y_0' K_0 y_0 + \sum_{k=0}^{N-1} (u_k - L_k y_k)' P_k (u_k - L_k y_k)\right\},$$

where

$$P_k = B_k' K_{k+1} B_k + R_k.$$

2. Consider the scalar system

$$x_{k+1} = x_k + u_k + w_k,$$

$$z_k = x_k + v_k,$$

where the assumptions of Section 3.2 are in effect. Let the cost be

$$E\left\{x_N^2 + \sum_{k=0}^{N-1} (x_k^2 + u_k^2)\right\},$$

and let the given probability distributions be

$$p(x_0 = 2) = \tfrac{1}{2}, \qquad p(w_k = 1) = \tfrac{1}{2}, \qquad p(v_k = \tfrac{1}{4}) = \tfrac{1}{2},$$

$$p(x_0 = -2) = \tfrac{1}{2}, \qquad p(w_k = -1) = \tfrac{1}{2}, \qquad p(v_k = -\tfrac{1}{4}) = \tfrac{1}{2}.$$

(a) Determine the optimal control law. *Hint:* For this particular problem, $E\{x_k | I_k\}$ can be determined from $E\{x_{k-1} | I_{k-1}\}$, u_{k-1}, and z_k.

(b) Determine the control law that is optimal within the class of all control laws that are linear functions of the measurements.

(c) Determine the asymptotic form of the control laws in parts (a) and (b) as $N \to \infty$. Find the ratio of the corresponding long-term average costs

$$\lim_{N\to\infty} \frac{1}{N} E\left\{\sum_{k=0}^{N-1} (x_k^2 + u_k^2)\right\}.$$

3. A linear system with Gaussian disturbances

$$x_{k+1} = Ax_k + Bu_k + w_k, \qquad k = 0, 1, \ldots, N-1,$$

is to be controlled so as to minimize a quadratic cost similarly as in Section 3.2. The difference is that the controller has the option of choosing at each time k one of two types of measurements for the next stage $(k+1)$:

$$\textit{First type:} \qquad z_{k+1} = C^1 x_{k+1} + v_{k+1}^1$$

$$\textit{Second type:} \qquad z_{k+1} = C^2 x_{k+1} + v_{k+1}^2.$$

Here C^1 and C^2 are given matrices of appropriate dimension and $\{v_k^1\}$ and $\{v_k^2\}$ are zero-mean, white, random sequences with given finite covariances that are independent of x_0 and $\{w_k\}$. There is a cost g_1 (or g_2) each time a measurement of type 1 (or type 2) is taken. The problem is to find the optimal control and measurement selection policy that minimizes the expected value of the sum of the quadratic cost

$$x_N' Q x_N + \sum_{k=0}^{N-1} (x_k' Q x_k + u_k' R u_k)$$

and the total measurement cost. Assume for convenience that $N = 2$ and that the first measurement z_0 is of type 1. Show that the optimal measurement selection at $k = 0$ and $k = 1$ does not depend on the value of the information vectors I_0 and I_1 and can be determined a priori. Describe the nature of the optimal policy.

4. Consider a scalar single-input, single-output system given by

$$\begin{aligned} y_k + a_1 y_{k-1} + \cdots + a_m y_{k-m} \\ = b_M u_{k-M} + \cdots + b_m u_{k-m} + \epsilon_k + c_1 \epsilon_{k-1} + \cdots, \epsilon_{k-m} + v_{k-n} \end{aligned}$$

where $1 \le M \le m$, $0 \le n \le m$, and v_k is generated by an equation of the form

$$v_k + d_1 v_{k-1} + \cdots + d_m v_{k-m} = \zeta_k + e_1 \zeta_{k-1} + \cdots + e_m \zeta_{k-m},$$

and the polynomials $(1 + c_1 s + \cdots + c_m s^m)$, $(1 + d_1 s + \cdots + d_m s^m)$, and $(1 + e_1 s + \cdots + e_m s^m)$ have roots strictly outside the unit circle. The value of the scalar v_k is observed by the controller at time k together with y_k. The sequences $\{\epsilon_k\}$ and $\{\zeta_k\}$ are zero mean independent identically distributed with finite variances. Find an easily implementable approximation to the minimum variance controller minimizing $E\{\sum_{k=0}^N y_k^2\}$. Discuss the stability properties of the closed-loop system.

5. (a) Within the framework of the basic problem with imperfect state information, consider the case where the system and the observations are linear:

$$x_{k+1} = A_k x_k + B_k u_k + w_k, \qquad k = 0, 1, \ldots,$$

$$z_k = C_k x_k + v_k, \qquad k = 0, 1, \ldots.$$

The initial state x_0 and the disturbances w_k and v_k are assumed Gaussian and mutually independent. Their covariances are given, and w_k and v_k have zero mean. Show that $E\{x_0|I_0\}, \ldots, E\{x_{N-1}|I_{N-1}\}$ constitute a sufficient statistic for this problem.

(b) Use the result of part (a) to obtain an optimal control law for the special case of the single-stage problem involving the scalar system and observation

$$x_1 = x_0 + u_0,$$

$$z_0 = x_0 + v_0,$$

and the cost functional $E\{|x_1|\}$.

(c) Generalize part (b) for the case of the scalar system

$$x_{k+1} = ax_k + u_k, \qquad k = 0, 1, \ldots, N-1,$$

$$z_k = cx_k + v_k, \qquad k = 0, 1, \ldots, N-1$$

and the cost functional $E\{\Sigma_{k=1}^{N} |x_k|\}$. The scalars a and c are given. *Note:* You may find useful the following "differentiation of an integral" formula:

$$\frac{d}{dy}\int_{\alpha(y)}^{\beta(y)} f(y, \xi)\, d\xi = \int_{\alpha(y)}^{\beta(y)} \frac{df(y, \xi)}{dy}\, d\xi + f[y, \beta(y)]\frac{d\beta(y)}{dy} - f[y, \alpha(y)]\frac{d\alpha(y)}{dy}.$$

6. Consider a machine that can be in one of two states, good or bad. Suppose that the machine produces an item at the end of each period. The item produced is either good or bad depending on whether the machine is in a good or bad state, respectively. We suppose that once the machine is in a bad state it remains in that state until it is replaced. If the machine is in a good state at the beginning of a certain period, then with probability t it will be in the bad state at the end of the period. Once an item is produced, we may inspect the item at a cost I or not inspect. If an inspected item is found bad, the machine is replaced with a machine in good state at a cost R. The cost for producing a bad item is $C > 0$. Write a DP algorithm for obtaining an optimal inspection policy assuming an initial machine in good state and a horizon of N periods. Solve the problem for $t = 0.2$, $I = 1$, $R = 3$, $C = 2$, and $N = 8$. (The optimal policy is to inspect at the end of the third period and not inspect in any other period.) *Hint:* Search for a suitable sufficient statistic.

7. *Control of Finite-State Systems with Imperfect State Information.* Consider a system that at any time can be in any one of a finite number of states $1, 2, \ldots, n$. When a control u is applied, the system moves from state i to state j with probability $p_{ij}(u)$. The control u is chosen from a finite collection $u^1, u^2, \ldots, u^m$. Following each state transition, an observation is made by the controller. There is a finite number of possible observation outcomes $z^1, z^2, \ldots, z^q$. The probability of occurrence of z^θ, given that the current state is j and the previous control was u, is denoted $r_j(u, \theta)$, $\theta = 1, \ldots, q$.

(a) Consider the column vector of conditional probabilities

$$P_k = [p_k^1, \ldots, p_k^n]',$$

where

$$p_k^j = P(x_k = j | z_0, \ldots, z_k, u_0, \ldots, u_{k-1}), \qquad j = 1, \ldots, n,$$

and show that it can be updated according to

$$p_{k+1}^j = \frac{\sum_{i=1}^{n} p_k^i p_{ij}(u_k) r_j(u_k, z_{k+1})}{\sum_{s=1}^{n}\sum_{i=1}^{n} p_k^i p_{is}(u_k) r_s(u_k, z_{k+1})}, \qquad j = 1, \ldots, n.$$

Write this equation in the compact form

$$P_{k+1} = \frac{[r(u^k, z^{k+1})] * [P(u^k)'P_k]}{r(u^k, z^{k+1})'P(u^k)'P_k}, \qquad j = 1, \ldots, n,$$

where $P(u_k)$ is the $n \times n$ transition probability matrix with ijth element $p_{ij}(u_k)$, $r(u_k, z_{k+1})$ is the column vector with jth coordinate $r_j(u_k, z_{k+1})$, $[P(u_k)'P_k]_j$ is the jth coordinate of the vector $P(u_k)'P_k$, $[r(u_k, z_{k+1})] * [P(u_k)'P_k]$ denotes the vector with jth coordinate $r_j(u_k, z_{k+1})[P(u_k)'P_k]_j$, and prime denotes transposition.

(b) Assume there is a cost for each stage k denoted $g_k(i, u, j)$ and associated with the control u and a transition from i to j. There is no terminal cost. Consider the problem of finding an optimal policy minimizing the sum of costs per stage over N periods. Show that the corresponding DP algorithm is given by

$$\bar{J}_{N-1}(P_{N-1}) = \min_{u \in \{u^1, \ldots, u^m\}} P'_{N-1} G_{N-1}(u)$$

$$\bar{J}_k(P_k) = \min_{u \in \{u^1, \ldots, u^m\}} \left[P'_k G_k(u) + \sum_{\theta=1}^{q} r(u, \theta)'P(u)'P_k \bar{J}_{k+1}\left[\frac{[r(u, \theta)] * [P(u)'P_k]}{r(u, \theta)'P(u)'P_k}\right]\right],$$

$$k = 0, 1, \ldots, N-2,$$

where $G_k(u)$ is given by

$$G_k(u) = \begin{bmatrix} \sum_{j=1}^{n} p_{1j}(u) g_k(1, u, j) \\ \cdots \\ \sum_{j=1}^{n} p_{nj}(u) g_k(n, u, j) \end{bmatrix}, \qquad k = 0, 1, \ldots, N-1.$$

(c) Show by induction that, for all k, $\bar{J}_k$ when viewed as a function on the set of vectors with nonnegative coordinates is *positively homogeneous;* that is,

$$\bar{J}_k(\lambda P_k) = \lambda \bar{J}_k(P_k), \qquad \lambda > 0.$$

Use this fact to write $\bar{J}_k$, $k = 0, 1, \ldots, N-2$, in the alternative form

$$\bar{J}_k(P_k) = \min_{u \in \{u^1, \ldots, u^m\}} [P'_k G_k(u) + \sum_{\theta=1}^{q} \bar{J}_{k+1}[[r(u, \theta)] * [P(u)'P_k]]].$$

(d) Show by induction that, for all k, $\bar{J}_k$ is of the form

$$\bar{J}_k(P_k) = \min [P'_k \alpha_k^1, \ldots, P'_k \alpha_k^{m_k}],$$

where $\alpha_k^1, \ldots, \alpha_k^{m_k}$ are some vectors in R^n.

8. Consider the functions $\bar{J}_k(p_k)$ in the instruction problem. Show inductively that each of these functions is piecewise linear and concave of the form

$$\bar{J}_k(p_k) = \min[\alpha_k^1 + \beta_k^1 p_k, \alpha_k^2 + \beta_k^2 p_k, \ldots, \alpha_k^{m_k} + \beta_k^{m_k} p_k],$$

where $\alpha_k^1, \ldots, \alpha_k^{m_k}, \beta_k^1, \ldots, \beta_k^{m_k}$ are suitable scalars.

9. *Two-Armed Bandit Problem.* A person is offered N free plays to be distributed as he pleases between two slot machines A and B. Machine A pays α dollars with known probability s and nothing with probability $(1 - s)$. Machine B pays β dollars with probability p and nothing with probability $(1 - p)$. The person does not know p but instead has an a priori probability distribution $F(p)$ for p. The problem is to find a playing policy that maximizes expected profit. Let $(m + n)$ denote the number of plays in machine B after k free plays $(m + n \leq k)$, and let m denote the number of successes and n the number of failures. Show that a DP algorithm for this problem is given by

$$\bar{J}_{N-1}(m, n) = \max\{s\alpha, p(m, n)\beta\}, \qquad m + n \leq N - 1,$$

$$\bar{J}_k(m, n) = \max\{s[\alpha + \bar{J}_{k+1}m, n)] + (1 - s)\bar{J}_{k+1}(m, n),$$
$$p(m, n)[\beta + \bar{J}_{k+1}(m + 1, n)] + [1 - p(m, n)]\bar{J}_{k+1}(m, n + 1)\},$$
$$m + n \leq k,$$

where

$$p(m, n) = \frac{\int_0^1 p^{m+1}(1 - p)^n \, dF(p)}{\int_0^1 p^m(1 - p)^n \, dF(p)}.$$

Solve the problem for $N = 6$, $\alpha = \beta = 1$, $s = 0.6$, $dF(p)/dp = 1$ for $0 \leq p \leq 1$. [The answer is to play machine B for the following pairs (m, n):(0, 0), (1, 0), (2, 0), (3, 0), (4, 0), (5, 0), (2, 1), (3, 1), (4, 1). Otherwise, machine A should be played.]

10. A person is offered 2 to 1 odds in a coin-tossing game where he wins whenever a tail occurs. However, he suspects that the coin is biased and has an a priori probability distribution $F(p)$ for the probability p that a head occurs at each toss. The problem is to find an optimal policy of deciding whether to continue or stop participating in the game given the outcomes of the game so far. A maximum of N tossings is allowed. Indicate how such a policy can be found by means of DP.

CHAPTER FOUR

Suboptimal and Adaptive Control

We have seen that it is sometimes possible to obtain a closed-form solution of the DP algorithm or at least use the algorithm for characterization of an optimal policy. However, this tends to be the exception, and in most cases one has to solve the DP equations numerically in order to obtain an optimal policy. The computational requirements for doing so are often overwhelming, and for many problems a complete solution of the problem by DP is impossible. The reason lies in what Bellman has called the "curse of dimensionality." Consider, for example, a problem where the state space is R^n. To obtain the cost-to-go function $J_k(x_k)$, it is necessary first to discretize the state space. Taking, for example, 100 discretization points per axis results in a grid with 100^n points. For each of these points the minimization in the right side of the DP equation must be carried out numerically. Matters are further complicated by the requirement to carry out a numerical integration (the expectation operation) every time the function under minimization is evaluated. Computer storage also presents an acute problem. Thus, for problems with finite-dimensional state and control spaces, DP can be applied only if the dimension of these spaces is small. When the control space is one-dimensional, things sometimes are simplified through the use of one-dimensional minimization techniques [L9]. In other cases the special structure of the problem can be exploited to reduce the computational requirements.

When everything else fails, one has to settle for a control scheme that can be practically implemented and performs adequately (hopefully close to optimally). In this chapter we discuss several ideas for suboptimal control.

4.1 CERTAINTY EQUIVALENT CONTROL

The *certainty equivalent controller* (CEC) is a suboptimal control scheme that is motivated by linear–quadratic control theory. It applies at each stage the control that would be optimal if all the uncertain quantities were fixed at their expected values; that is, it acts as if a form of the certainty equivalence principle were holding.

We take as our model the basic problem with imperfect state information of Section 3.1 and we further assume that the probability measures of the input disturbances w_k do not depend on x_k and u_k. We assume that the state spaces and disturbance spaces are convex subsets of corresponding Euclidean spaces so that the expected values

$$\overline{x}_k = E\{x_k \mid I_k\}, \qquad \overline{w}_k = E\{w_k\},$$

belong to the corresponding state spaces and disturbance spaces. If this is not so, the following scheme may be implemented with $\overline{x}_k$ and $\overline{w}_k$ being some "typical" elements of the respective spaces.

The control input $\overline{\mu}_k(I_k)$ applied by the CEC at each time k is determined by the following rule:

1. Given the information vector I_k, compute
$$\overline{x}_k = E\{x_k \mid I_k\}.$$
2. Solve the deterministic problem of finding a control sequence $\{\overline{u}_k, \overline{u}_{k+1}, \ldots, \overline{u}_{N-1}\}$ that minimizes
$$g_N(x_N) + \sum_{i=k}^{N-1} g_i(x_i, u_i, \overline{w}_i)$$
subject to the constraints
$$u_i \in U_i, \qquad x_{i+1} = f_i(x_i, u_i, \overline{w}_i), \qquad i = k, k+1, \ldots, N-1, \qquad x_k = \overline{x}_k.$$
3. Apply the control input
$$\overline{\mu}_k(I_k) = \overline{u}_k.$$

Note that if the current state x_k is measured exactly (perfect state information), then step (1) is unnecessary. The deterministic optimization problem in step (2) must be solved at each time k as soon as the initial state $\overline{x}_k = E\{x_k \mid I_k\}$ becomes known by means of an estimation (or perfect observation) procedure. (In practice, one often uses a suboptimal estimation scheme that generates an approximation to $\overline{x}_k$). A total of N such problems must be solved in any actual operation of the CEC. Each of these problems, however, is a deterministic optimal control problem and is often of the type for which powerful numerical techniques such as steepest descent, conjugate gradient, and Newton's method [L10] are applicable. Thus the CEC requires the solution of N such problems in place of the solution of the DP algorithm required to obtain an optimal controller. Furthermore, the implementation of the CEC requires no storage of the type required for the optimal feedback controller, often a major advantage.

An alternative to solving N optimal control problems in an "on-line" fashion is to solve these problems a priori. This is accomplished by computing an optimal feedback controller for the deterministic optimal control problem obtained from the original problem by replacing all uncertain quantities by their expected values. It is easy to verify (based on the equivalence of open-loop and feedback implementation of optimal controllers for deterministic problems) that the implementation of the CEC given earlier is equivalent to the following:

Let $\{\mu_0^d(x_0), \ldots, \mu_{N-1}^d(x_{N-1})\}$ be an optimal controller obtained from the DP algorithm for the deterministic problem

$$\text{minimize} \quad g_N(x_N) + \sum_{k=0}^{N-1} g_k[x_k, \mu_k(x_k), \overline{w}_k], \qquad \text{over all } \{\mu_0, \ldots, \mu_{N-1}\}$$

$$\text{subject to} \quad \mu_k(x_k) \in U_k, \qquad \text{for all } x_k \in S_k, \qquad x_{k+1} = f_k[x_k, \mu_k(x_k), \overline{w}_k],$$
$$k = 0, 1, \ldots, N-1.$$

Then the control input $\tilde{\mu}_k(I_k)$ applied by the CEC at time k is given by

$$\tilde{\mu}_k(I_k) = \mu_k^d[E\{x_k \mid I_k\}] = \mu_k^d(\overline{x}_k)$$

as shown in Figure 4.1.

In other words *an alternative implementation of the CEC consists of finding a feedback controller* $\{\mu_0^d, \mu_1^d, \ldots, \mu_{N-1}^d\}$ *that is optimal for a corresponding deterministic problem, and subsequently using this controller*

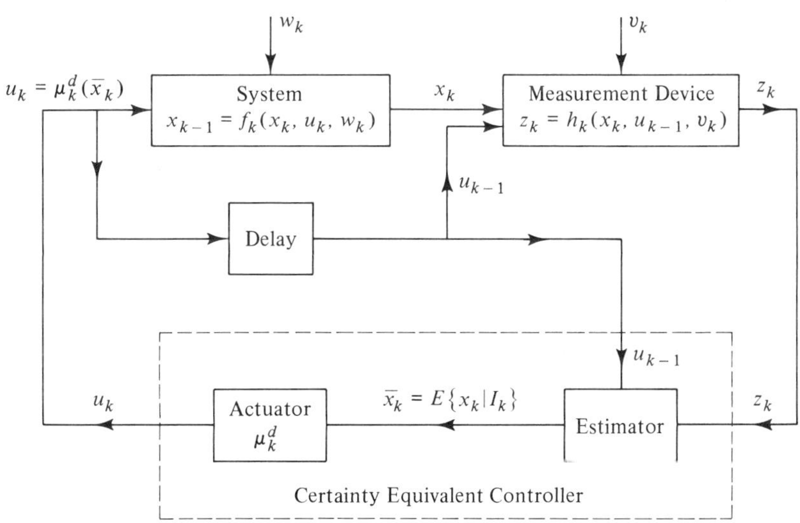

Figure 4.1 Structure of the certainty equivalent controller.

for control of the uncertain system (modulo substitution of the state by its expected value). Either of the definitions given for the CEC can serve as a basis for its implementation. Depending on the nature of the problem, one method may be preferable to the other.

The CEC often performs well in practice and results in a cost that is close to the optimal. In fact, for the linear–quadratic problems of Sections 2.1 and 3.2, it is identical to the optimal controller (certainty equivalence principle). It is possible, however, that it performs strictly worse than the optimal open-loop controller (see Problem 4).

Multiaccess Communication Example

Consider the slotted Aloha system described at the beginning of Section 3.1. It is very difficult to obtain an optimal policy for this problem primarily because there is no simple characterization of the conditional distribution of the backlog (state), given the channel transmission history. We therefore resort to a suboptimal policy. As discussed in Section 3.1, the perfect state information version of the problem admits a simple optimal policy:

$$\mu_k(x_k) = \frac{1}{x_k}, \qquad \text{for all } x_k \geq 1.$$

As a result, there is a natural CEC,

$$\bar{\mu}_k(I_k) = \min\left[1, \frac{1}{\bar{x}_k}\right],$$

where $\bar{x}_k$ is an estimate of the current packet backlog based on the entire past channel history of successes, idles, and collisions. Recursive estimators for generating $\bar{x}_k$ are given in [H2] and [R1]. The latter estimator obtains $\bar{x}_{k+1}$ by increasing $\bar{x}_k$ by a certain amount if a collision occurs in the kth slot and by decreasing it by unity otherwise. Then it adds the expected number of packet arrivals during the kth slot, which is estimated as the observed success rate (number of successes up to slot k divided by k). We refer to [H2] and [R1] for details. The stability of the overall control scheme is investigated in [T8].

4.2 OPEN-LOOP FEEDBACK CONTROLLER

The *open-loop feedback controller* (OLFC) is similar to the CEC except that it takes explicitly into account the uncertainty about $x_k, w_k, \ldots, w_{N-1}$ when calculating the control $\bar{\mu}_k(I_k)$ to be applied at time k. This control is determined by the following procedure:

1. Given the information vector I_k, compute the conditional probability measure $P_{x_k|I_k}$.

2. Find a control sequence $\{\bar{u}_k, \bar{u}_{k+1}, \ldots, \bar{u}_{N-1}\}$ that minimizes

$$\mathop{E}_{x_k, w_k, \ldots, w_{N-1}} \left\{ g_N(x_N) + \sum_{i=k}^{N-1} g_i(x_i, u_i, w_i) \mid I_k \right\}$$

subject to the constraints

$$u_i \in U_i, \qquad x_{i+1} = f_i(x_i, u_i, w_i), \qquad i = k, \ldots, N-1.\dagger$$

3. Apply the control input

$$\bar{\mu}_k(I_k) = \bar{u}_k.$$

The operation of the OLFC can be interpreted as follows: At each time k the controller uses the new measurement received to calculate the conditional probability distribution $P_{x_k|I_k}$. However, it selects the control input as if no further measurements will be received in the future.

Similarly to the CEC, the OLFC requires the solution of N optimal control problems in any actual operation of the system. Each problem may again be solved by deterministic optimal control or mathematical programming techniques. The computations are a little more complicated than those for the CEC since now the cost includes the expectation operation with respect to the uncertain quantities. The main difficulty in the implementation of the OLFC is the computation of $P_{x_k|I_k}$. In many cases one cannot compute $P_{x_k|I_k}$ exactly, in which case some "reasonable" approximation scheme must be used. Of course, if we have perfect state information, this difficulty does not arise.

In any suboptimal control policy, one would like to be assured that measurements are used with advantage. By this we mean that the scheme performs at least as well as any open-loop policy applying a sequence of controls that is independent of the values of the measurements received. An optimal open-loop policy can be obtained by finding a sequence $\{u_0^*, u_1^*, \ldots, u_{N-1}^*\}$ that minimizes

$$\bar{J}(u_0, u_1, \ldots, u_{N-1}) = \mathop{E}_{\substack{x_0, w_k \\ k=0,1,\ldots,N-1}} \left\{ g_N(x_N) + \sum_{k=0}^{N-1} g_k(x_k, u_k, w_k) \right\}$$

subject to the constraints $x_{k+1} = f_k(x_k, u_k, w_k)$, and $u_k \in U_k$, $k = 0, 1, \ldots, N-1$. A nice property of the OLFC is that, in contrast with the CEC (cf. Problem 4), it performs at least as well as an optimal open-loop policy.

Proposition. The cost $J_{\bar{\pi}}$ corresponding to an OLFC $\bar{\pi} = \{\bar{\mu}_0, \bar{\mu}_1, \ldots, \bar{\mu}_{N-1}\}$ satisfies

$$J^* \le J_{\bar{\pi}} \le J_0^*, \tag{4.1}$$

† Similarly as for the CEC, we assume that an optimal solution to this problem exists and ambiguities resulting from multiple solutions are resolved by some rule.

where J_0^* is the cost corresponding to an optimal open-loop policy.

Proof.† We have

$$J_{\bar{\pi}} = \underset{z_0}{E}\{\bar{J}_0(I_0)\} = \underset{z_0}{E}\{\bar{J}_0(z_0)\}, \tag{4.2}$$

where the function $\bar{J}_0$ is obtained from the recursive algorithm

$$\begin{aligned} \bar{J}_{N-1}(I_{N-1}) = \underset{x_{N-1}, w_{N-1}}{E} \{ & g_N[f_{N-1}(x_{N-1}, \bar{\mu}_{N-1}(I_{N-1}), w_{N-1})] \\ & + g_{N-1}[x_{N-1}, \bar{\mu}_{N-1}(I_{N-1}), w_{N-1}] \mid I_{N-1}\}, \end{aligned} \tag{4.3}$$

$$\begin{aligned} \bar{J}_k(I_k) = \underset{x_k, w_k, v_{k+1}}{E} \{ & g_k[x_k, \bar{\mu}_k(I_k), w_k] \\ & + \bar{J}_{k+1}[I_k, h_{k+1}[f_k(x_k, \bar{\mu}_k(I_k), w_k), \bar{\mu}_k(I_k), v_{k+1}], \bar{\mu}_k(I_k)] \mid I_k\}, \\ & k = 0, 1, \ldots, N-1. \end{aligned} \tag{4.4}$$

Consider also the functions $J_k^c(I_k)$, $k = 0, 1, \ldots, N-1$, defined by

$$J_k^c(I_k) = \min_{\substack{u_i \in U_i \\ i=k,\ldots,N-1}} \underset{\substack{x_k,\, w_i \\ x_{i+1}=f_i(x_i,u_i,w_i) \\ i=k,\ldots,N-1}}{E} \left\{ g_N(x_N) + \sum_{i=k}^{N-1} g_i(x_i, u_i, w_i) \mid I_k \right\}. \tag{4.5}$$

The minimization problem in this equation is precisely the one that must be solved at time k in order to calculate the control input $\bar{\mu}_k(I_k)$ of the OLFC. Clearly, $J_k^c(I_k)$ can be interpreted as the calculated open-loop optimal cost from time k to time N when the current information vector is I_k. It can be seen that

$$\underset{z_0}{E}\{J_0^c(z_0)\} \leq J_0^*. \tag{4.6}$$

We will prove that

$$\bar{J}_k(I_k) \leq J_k^c(I_k), \qquad \text{for all } I_k \text{ and } k. \tag{4.7}$$

Then from (4.2), (4.6), and (4.7) it will follow that

$$J_{\bar{\pi}} \leq J_0^*,$$

which is the relation to be proved. We show (4.7) by induction.

By the definition of the OLFC and (4.5), we have

$$\bar{J}_{N-1}(I_{N-1}) = J_{N-1}^c(I_{N-1}), \qquad \text{for all } I_{N-1},$$

and hence (4.7) holds for $k = N-1$. Assume

$$\bar{J}_{k+1}(I_{k+1}) \leq J_{k+1}^c(I_{k+1}), \qquad \text{for all } I_{k+1}. \tag{4.8}$$

† We assume throughout the proof that all expected values appearing are well defined and finite and the minimum in (4.5) is attained for every I_k.

Then from (4.4), (4.8), and (4.5), we have

$$\begin{aligned}
\overline{J}_k(I_k) &= \underset{x_k,\, w_k,\, v_{k+1}}{E} \{g_k[x_k, \overline{\mu}_k(I_k), w_k] \\
&\quad + \overline{J}_{k+1}\, [I_k, h_{k+1}[f_k(x_k, \overline{\mu}_k(I_k), w_k), \overline{\mu}_k(I_k), v_{k+1}], \overline{\mu}_k(I_k)] \mid I_k\} \\
&\leq \underset{x_k,\, w_k,\, v_{k+1}}{E} \{g_k[x_k\, \overline{\mu}_k(I_k), w_k] \\
&\quad + J^c_{k+1}\, [I_k, h_{k+1}[f_k(x_k, \overline{\mu}_k(I_k), w_k), \overline{\mu}_k(I_k), v_{k+1}], \overline{\mu}_k(I_k)] \mid I_k\} \\
&= \underset{x_k, w_k, v_{k+1}}{E} \Bigg\{ \min_{\substack{u_i \in U_i \\ i=k+1,\ldots,N-1}} \underset{\substack{x_{k+1}, w_i \\ x_{i+1}=f_i(x_i,u_i,w_i) \\ i=k+1,\ldots,N-1}}{E} \{g_k[x_k, \overline{\mu}_k(I_k), w_k] \\
&\quad + \sum_{i=k+1}^{N-1} g_i(x_i, u_i, w_i) + g_N(x_N) \mid I_{k+1}\} \mid I_k \Bigg\} \\
&\leq \min_{\substack{u_i \in U_i \\ i=k+1,\ldots,N-1}} \underset{\substack{x_k, w_k, w_i \\ x_{i+1}=f_i(x_i,u_i,w_i) \\ i=k+1,\ldots,N-1 \\ x_{k+1}=f_k[x_k,\mu_k(I_k),w_k]}}{E} \Bigg\{ g_N(x_N) + g_k[x_k, \overline{\mu}_k(I_k), w_k] \\
&\quad + \sum_{i=k+1}^{N-1} g_i(x_i, u_i, w_i) \mid I_k \Bigg\} = J^c_k(I_k).
\end{aligned}$$

The second inequality follows by interchanging expectation and minimization (notice that we always have $E\,\{\min[\cdot]\} \leq \min\,[E\,\{\cdot\}]$) and by "integrating out" v_{k+1}. The last equality follows from the definition of OLFC. Thus (4.7) is proved for all k and the desired result is shown. Q.E.D.

It is worth noting that by (4.7) the calculated open-loop optimal cost from time k to time N, $J^c_k(I_k)$, provides a readily obtainable performance bound for the OLFC.

The preceding proposition shows that the OLFC uses the measurements with advantage even though it selects at each period the present control input as if no further measurements will be taken in the future. Of course, this says nothing about how closely the resulting cost approximates the optimal. It appears, however, that the OLFC is a fairly satisfactory mode of control for many problems.

4.3 LIMITED LOOKAHEAD POLICIES: APPLICATIONS IN FLEXIBLE MANUFACTURING AND COMPUTER CHESS

A practical way to cut down the number of states examined by the DP algorithm is to truncate the time horizon and use at each stage a decision based on lookahead of a small number of stages. The simplest possibility is to use a *one-step lookahead policy* whereby at stage k and state x_k one uses the control $\bar{\mu}_k(x_k)$, which attains the minimum in the expression

$$\min_{u_k \in U_k(x_k)} E\{g_k(x_k, u_k, w_k) + \tilde{J}_{k+1}[f_k(x_k, u_k, w_k)]\},$$

where $\tilde{J}_{k+1}$ is some approximation of the true cost-to-go function J_{k+1}. Similarly, a *two-step lookahead policy* applies at time k and state x_k the control $\bar{\mu}_k(x_k)$, attaining the minimum in the preceding equation where now $\tilde{J}_{k+1}$ is obtained itself on the basis of a one-step lookahead approximation. In other words, for all possible states

$$x_{k+1} = f_k(x_k, u_k, w_k),$$

we have

$$\tilde{J}_{k+1}(x_{k+1}) = \min_{u_{k+1} \in U_{k+1}(x_{k+1})} E\{g_{k+1}(x_{k+1}, u_{k+1}, w_{k+1}) + \tilde{J}_{k+2}[f_{k+1}(x_{k+1}, u_{k+1}, w_{k+1})]\},$$

where $\tilde{J}_{k+2}$ is some approximation of the cost-to-go function J_{k+2}.

The computational savings of this approach are evident. For a one-step lookahead policy, only a single minimization problem has to be solved per stage, while in a two-step policy the number of states at which the DP equation has to be solved at stage k equals one plus the number of all possible next states x_{k+1} that can be generated from the current state x_k. Actually, the entire two-step lookahead computation can be formulated as a single mathematical programming problem that is often tractable (see Problems 1 and 2). Note also that the fixed lookahead approach can be combined with the certainty equivalent and open-loop-feedback control approaches of Sections 4.1 and 4.2 to simplify even further the calculations.

A key issue in implementing a limited lookahead policy is the selection of the cost-to-go approximation at the final step. It may appear important at first sight that the true cost-to-go function be approximated well over the range of relevant states; however, this is not necessarily true. What is important is that the *cost-to-go differentials (or relative values) be approximated well;* that is, for an n-step lookahead policy it is important to have

$$\tilde{J}_{k+n}(x) - \tilde{J}_{k+n}(x') \approx J_{k+n}(x) - J_{k+n}(x'),$$

for any two states x and x' that can be generated n steps ahead from the current state. For example, if equality were to hold for all x, x', then $\tilde{J}_{k+n}(x)$ and $J_{k+n}(x)$ would differ by the same constant for each relevant x and the n-step lookahead policy would be optimal.

The manner in which the cost-to-go approximation is selected depends very much on the problem solved. For example, in some games like chess, the approximate cost-to-go in a certain position (state) involves a heuristic incorporation of certain features of the position into a figure of merit. In other problems, a cost-to-go approximation may be based on solution of a simpler problem that is tractable computationally or analytically. The following examples illustrate these approaches.

Production Control in a Flexible Manufacturing System

Flexible manufacturing systems (FMS) provide a popular approach for increasing productivity in the manufacture of small- and medium-sized batches of related parts. There are several workstations in an FMS and each is capable of carrying out a variety of operations. This allows the simultaneous manufacturing of more than one part type, reduces idle time, and allows production to continue even when a workstation is out of service because of failure or maintenance.

Consider a work center in which n part types are produced. Denote

u_k^i: the amount of part i produced in period k.

d_k^i: a known demand for part i in period k.

x_k^i: the cumulative difference of amount of part i produced and demanded up to period k.

Let us denote also by x_k, u_k, d_k the n-dimensional vectors with coordinates x_k^i, u_k^i, d_k^i, respectively. We then have

$$x_{k+1} = x_k + u_k - d_k. \tag{4.9}$$

The work center consists of n workstations that fail and get repaired in random fashion, thereby affecting the productive capacity of the system (i.e., the constraints on u_k). Roughly, our problem is to schedule part production so that x_k is kept around zero to the extent possible.

The state of the workstations is described by an m-dimensional vector

$$\alpha_k = (\alpha_k^1, \ldots, \alpha_k^m),$$

where

$$\alpha_k^i = \begin{cases} 1, & \text{if station } i \text{ is operational at period } k, \\ 0, & \text{otherwise.} \end{cases}$$

We model the evolution of α_k by a Markov chain with known transition probabilities

$$p_{rs}^i = P(\alpha_{k+1}^i = s \mid \alpha_k^i = r), \qquad r, s = 0, 1, \text{and } i = 1, 2, \ldots, m.$$

In a practical context these probabilities must be estimated from individual station failure and repair rates, but we will not go into the matter further. Note also that in practice these probabilities may depend on u_k. This dependence is ignored for the purpose of development of a cost-to-go approximation [cf. (4.15)]. It may be taken into account when the actual suboptimal control is computed [cf. the minimization of (4.16)].

The productive capacity of the system is, by definition, the constraint set of the production vector u_k and depends on the workstation state α_k. We denote it by $U(\alpha_k)$.

We select as system state the pair (x_k, α_k), where x_k evolves according to (4.9) and α_k evolves according to the Markov chain described earlier. The problem is to find for every state (x_k, α_k) a production vector $u_k \in U(\alpha_k)$ such that a cost function of the form

$$J_\pi(x_0) = E\left\{\sum_{k=0}^{N-1}\sum_{i=1}^{n} g_i(x_k^i)\right\}$$

is minimized. The cost per stage g_i expresses the desire to keep the current backlog or surplus of part i near zero. Two examples are $g_i(x^i) = \beta_i|x^i|$ or $g_i(x^i) = \beta_i|x^i|^2$, with $\beta_i > 0$.

The DP algorithm for this problem is

$$J_k(x_k, \alpha_k) = \sum_{i=1}^{n} g_i(x_k^i) + \min_{u_k \in U(\alpha_k)} \underset{\alpha_{k+1}}{E}\{J_{k+1}(x_k + u_k - d_k, \alpha_{k+1}) \mid \alpha_k\}, \tag{4.10}$$

but unfortunately often requires a prohibitive amount of calculation for an FMS of realistic size (say for $n > 10$ part types). We therefore consider the possibility of a one-step lookahead policy with a suitable approximation $\tilde{J}_{k+1}$ replacing the cost-to-go J_{k+1}.

We now observe that our problem can to a large extent be decomposed with respect to individual part types. Indeed, the system equation (4.9) and the cost per stage have a decomposable structure and the only coupling between parts comes from the constraint $u_k \in U(\alpha_k)$. This constraint typically has a simplex-like structure

$$U(\alpha_k) = \{u_k \mid \gamma(\alpha_k)' u_k \leq \delta(\alpha_k),\ u_k^i \geq 0,\ i = 1, \ldots, n\}, \tag{4.11}$$

where $\gamma(\alpha_k)$ is a known n-dimensional vector and $\delta(\alpha_k)$ is a known scalar depending on α_k. Suppose we approximate $U(\alpha_k)$ by hypercubes $\underline{U}(\alpha_k)$ and $\overline{U}(\alpha_k)$ of the form

$$\begin{aligned} \underline{U}(\alpha_k) &= \{u_k^i \mid 0 \leq u_k^i \leq \underline{B}_i(\alpha_k)\}, \\ \overline{U}(\alpha_k) &= \{u_k^i \mid 0 \leq u_k^i \leq \overline{B}_i(\alpha_k)\}, \\ \underline{U}(\alpha_k) &\subset U(\alpha_k) \subset \overline{U}(\alpha_k), \end{aligned} \tag{4.12}$$

as shown in Figure 4.2. If $U(\alpha_k)$ is replaced for each workstation state α_k by either $\overline{U}(\alpha_k)$ or $\underline{U}(\alpha_k)$, then the problem is decomposed completely with respect to part types. For every part i the DP algorithm for the outer approximation is given by

$$\begin{aligned} \overline{J}_k^i(x_k^i, \alpha_k) = g_i(x_k^i) &+ \\ &\min_{0 \leq u_k^i \leq \overline{B}_i(\alpha_k)} \underset{\alpha_{k+1}}{E}\{\overline{J}_{k+1}^i(x_k^i + u_k^i - d_k^i, \alpha_{k+1}) \mid \alpha_k\}, \end{aligned} \tag{4.13}$$

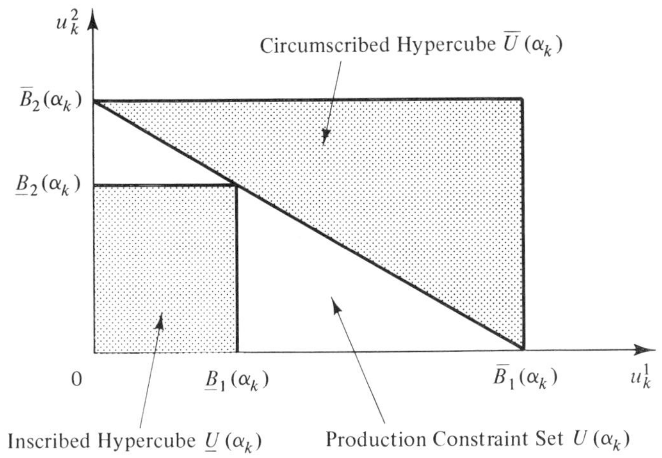

Figure 4.2 Inner and outer approximations of the production capacity constraint set by hypercubes.

and for the inner approximation it is given by

$$\underline{J}_k^i(x_k^i, \alpha_k) = g_i(x_k^i) + \min_{0 \le u_k^i \le \underline{B}_i(\alpha_k)} \mathop{E}_{\alpha_{k+1}} \{\underline{J}_{k+1}^i(x_k^i + u_k^i - d_k^i, \alpha_{k+1}) \mid \alpha_k\}. \tag{4.14}$$

Furthermore, in view of (4.12), the cost-to-go functions $\overline{J}_k^i$ and $\underline{J}_k^i$ provide lower and upper bounds to the true cost-to-go function J_k,

$$\sum_{i=1}^n \overline{J}_k^i(x_k^i, \alpha_k) \le J_k(x_k, \alpha_k) \le \sum_{i=1}^n \underline{J}_k^i(x_k^i, \alpha_k), \tag{4.15}$$

and can be used to construct approximations to J_k that are suitable for a one-step lookahead policy. The simplest possibility is to adopt the averaging approximation

$$\tilde{J}_k(x_k, \alpha_k) = \frac{1}{2}\sum_{i=1}^n [\overline{J}_k^i(x_k^i, \alpha_k) + \underline{J}_k^i(x_k^i, \alpha_k)]$$

and use at state (x_k, α_k) the suboptimal control $\tilde{u}_k$ that minimizes [cf. (4.10)]

$$E\left\{\sum_i [\overline{J}_{k+1}^i(x_k^i + u_k^i - d_k^i, \alpha_{k+1}) + \underline{J}_{k+1}^i(x_k^i + u_k^i - d_k^i, \alpha_{k+1})] \mid \alpha_k\right\} \tag{4.16}$$

over all $u_k \in U(\alpha_k)$.

To implement this scheme, it is necessary to carry out the DP algorithm (4.13) and (4.14) and to store the corresponding functions $\overline{J}_k^i$ and $\underline{J}_k^i$ in tables so that they can be used in the real-time computation of the suboptimal control via the minimization of expression (4.16). The calculations involved in the DP algorithm (4.13) and (4.14) are nontrivial but they can be carried out off-line, and in any case are much less than what would be required to compute the optimal controller. The feasibility and the benefits of the overall approach have been demonstrated by simulation for FMS of realistic size in [K8]. See also [T6] and [K7].

Computer Chess

Chess-playing computer programs are one of the more visible successes of artificial intelligence. Their underlying methodology provides an interesting case study in the use of suboptimal control. It involves the idea of limited lookahead, but also illustrates some DP ideas that we have not had much opportunity to look at in detail. These are the idea of a *forward search,* an important memory-saving technique that is common in artificial intelligence applications and was discussed in Section 1.4, and the idea of *alpha–beta pruning,* which is an effective method for reducing the amount of calculation required to find optimal game strategies.

The fundamental paper on which all computer chess programs are based was written by one of the most illustrious modern-day applied mathematicians, C. Shannon [S16]. It was argued by Shannon that whether the starting chess position is a win, loss, or draw is a question that can be answered in principle, but the answer will probably never be known. He estimated that, based on the chess rule requiring a pawn advance or a capture every 50 moves (otherwise a draw is declared), there are on the order of 10^{120} different possible sequences of moves in a chess game. He concluded that to examine these and select the best initial move for White would require 10^{90} years of a "fast" computer's time. As an alternative, Shannon proposed a *limited lookahead* of a few moves and *evaluating the end positions by means of a scoring function* that suitably takes into account the material balance, mobility, pawn structure, and other positional factors. The convention here is that White is favored in positions with high score, while Black is favored in positions with low score.

Consider first a *one-move lookahead strategy* for selecting the first move in a given position P. Let $M_1, \ldots, M_r$ be all the legal moves that can be made in position P by the side to move. Denote the resulting positions by $M_1P, M_2P, \ldots, M_rP$, and let $S(M_1P), \ldots, S(M_rP)$ be the corresponding scores. Then the move selected by White (Black) in position P is the move with maximum (minimum) score. This is known as the *backed-up score* of P and is given by

$$BS(P) = \begin{cases} \max\{S(M_1P), \ldots, S(M_rP)\}, & \text{if White is to move in position } P, \\ \min\{S(M_1P), \ldots, S(M_rP)\}, & \text{if Black is to move in position } P. \end{cases}$$

This process is illustrated in Figure 4.3.

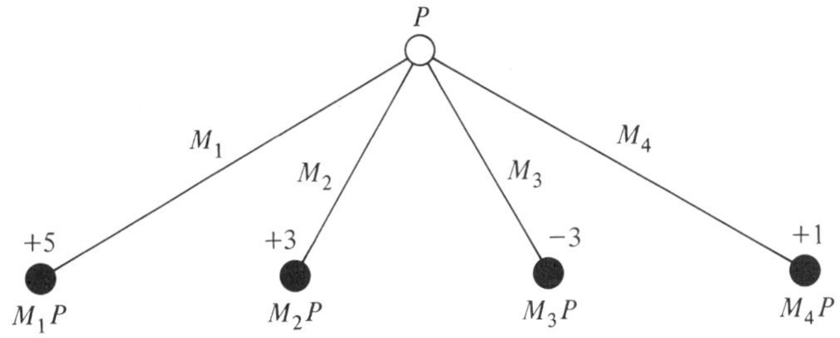

Figure 4.3 A one-move lookahead tree. If White moves at position P, the best move is M_1 and the backed-up score is $+5$. If Black moves at position P, the best move is M_3 and the backed-up score of P is -3.

Consider next a *two-move lookahead strategy* in a given position P. Assume for concreteness that White moves, and let the legal moves be M_1, . . ., M_r and the corresponding positions be M_1P, . . ., M_rP. Then in each of the positions M_iP, $i = 1, \ldots, r$, apply the one-move lookahead strategy with Black to move. This gives a best move and a backed-up score $BS(M_iP)$ for Black in each of the positions M_iP, $i = 1, \ldots, r$. Finally, based on the backed-up scores $BS(M_1P), \ldots, BS(M_rP)$, apply a one-move lookahead strategy for White, thereby obtaining the best move at position P and a backed-up score for position P of

$$BS(P) = \max \{BS(M_1P), \ldots, BS(M_rP)\}.$$

The sequence of best moves is known as the *principal continuation*. The process is illustrated in Figure 4.4.

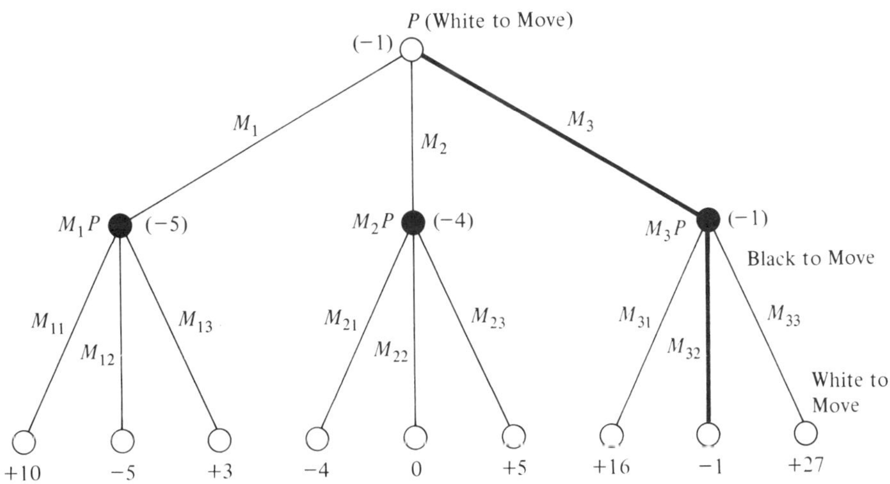

Figure 4.4 A two-move lookahead tree with White to move. The backed-up scores are shown in parentheses. The best initial move is M_3 and the principal continuation is (M_3, M_{32}).

It is clear that Shannon's method as just described (known as the type A minimax algorithm) can be generalized for an arbitrary number of lookahead moves (see Figure 4.5). The idea of solving one-step lookahead problems with a terminal cost (or backed-up score) that summarizes future costs is of course central in the DP algorithm. Indeed, it can be seen that the minimax algorithm described is nothing but the DP algorithm for minimax problems (see Problem 5 in Chapter 1). Here positions and moves can be identified with states and controls, respectively, there are only terminal costs (the scores of the terminal positions), and the backed-up score of a position is nothing but the optimal cost-to-go at the corresponding state.

Shannon recognized that with a type A strategy one still could not expect a computer to seriously challenge human players of even moderate strength. In a typical chess position there are around 30 to 35 legal moves. It follows that for an n-move lookahead there will be around 30^n to 35^n terminal positions to be scored. For $n = 6$ this gives roughly 10^6 positions, and assuming that a position can be scored in 10 μs, we conclude that for a six-move lookahead a computer would need about 2 hours and 45 minutes just to score terminal positions. Another drawback was that some chess positions require more analysis than others. For example, if in the last

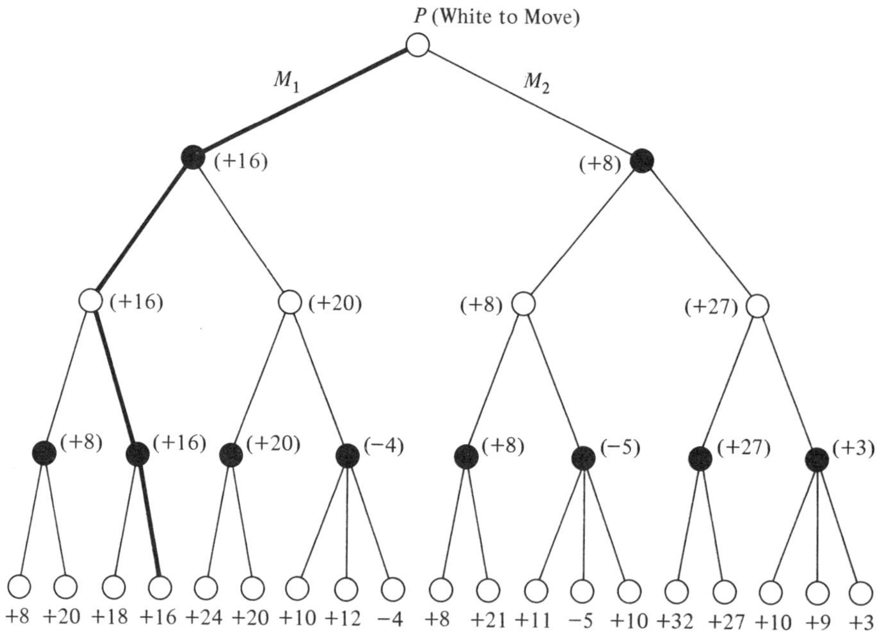

Figure 4.5 A four-move lookahead tree with White to move. The backed-up scores are shown in parentheses. The best initial move is M_1. The principal continuation is heavily shaded.

move of a search sequence a capture occurs, it is essential to consider whether the opponent will recapture and how.

These considerations led Shannon to consider a *type B strategy* whereby the depth of the search tree is variable. He suggested that at each position the computer give all legal moves a preliminary examination and discard those that are "obviously bad." A scoring function together with some heuristic strategy can be used for this purpose. Similarly, he suggested that some positions, involving for example captures or checkmate threats, be explored further beyond the nominal depth of the search.

Nearly all chess-playing computer programs utilize some form of Shannon's type B strategy. They differ in the choice of scoring function, the criteria for discarding moves in a given position, and the criteria for declaring a given position as terminal. A particularly effective algorithm known as *swapoff* is used to quickly analyze long sequences of captures and countercaptures, thereby making it possible to score realistically complex, dynamic positions [L2].

Shannon pointed out that, while the amount of computation per move grows exponentially with the depth of lookahead, the amount of memory required grows only *linearly,* thereby allowing chess programs to operate in limited-memory microprocessor systems. This is illustrated in Figures 4.6 and 4.7 and is accomplished by generating new moves only when needed, and by storing only the *one* move sequence under current examination together with one list of legal moves at each level of the search tree. Calculations and move generation are done in depth-first fashion. The precise algorithm can be described by the following routine, which calls itself recursively.

Minimax algorithm. To determine the backed-up score $BS(n)$ of position n, do the following:

1. If n is a terminal position return its score.
   Otherwise:
2. Generate the list of legal moves at position n and let the corresponding positions be $n_1, \ldots, n_r$. Set the tentative backed-up score $TBS(n)$ of position n to $+\infty$ if it is White's turn to move at n and to $-\infty$ if it is Black's turn to move at n.
3. For $i = 1, \ldots, r$, do:
   a. Determine the backed-up score $BS(n_i)$ of position n_i.
   b. If it is White's turn to move at position n, set $TBS(n) := \max\{TBS(n), BS(n_i)\}$.
      If it is Black's turn to move at position n, set $TBS(n) := \min\{TBS(n), BS(n_i)\}$.
4. Return $BS(n) = TBS(n)$.

Note that once the backed-up score of a position is calculated all of its successors in the search tree can be purged from memory, as indicated

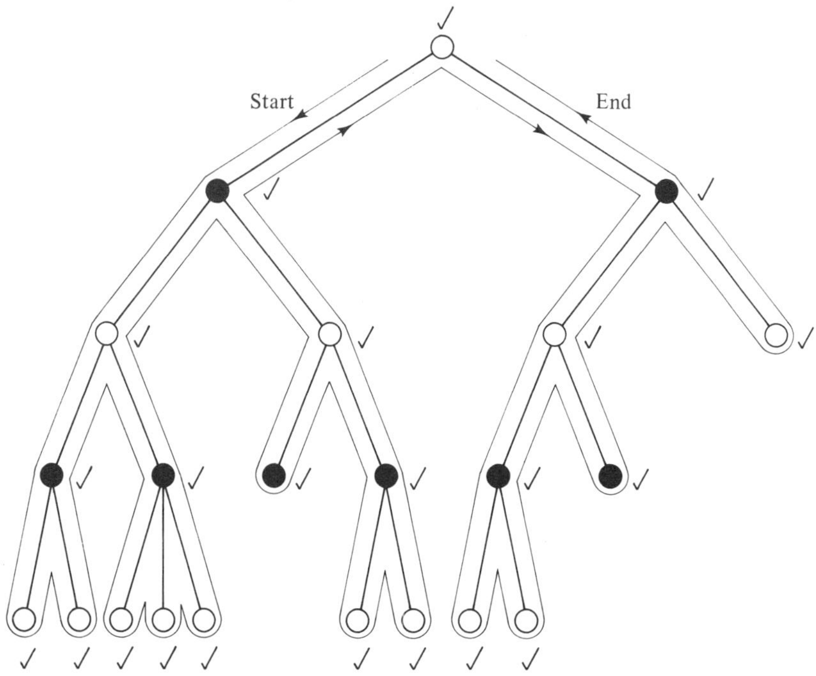

Figure 4.6 Traversing a tree in depth-first fashion. Checkmarks show the points where scores of terminal positions and backed-up scores of intermediate positions are evaluated.

in Figure 4.7. The substantial memory savings afforded by this forward method of calculation is very useful in search problems with a large number of terminal states, as discussed also in Section 1.4.

The efficiency of the minimax algorithm can be substantially improved by using the *alpha–beta pruning procedure* (denoted α–β for short), which can be used to forgo some calculations involving positions that cannot affect the selection of the best move. To understand the α–β procedure, consider a chess player pondering the next move at position P. Suppose that the player has already exhaustively analyzed one relatively good move M_1 with corresponding score $BS(M_1P)$ and proceeds to examine the next move M_2. Suppose that as the opponent's replies are examined a particularly strong response is found, which assures that the score of M_2 will be worse than that of M_1. Such a response, called a *refutation* of move M_2, makes further consideration of move M_2 unnecessary (i.e., the portion of the search tree that descends from move M_2 can be discarded). An example is shown in Figure 4.8.

The α–β procedure can be generalized to trees of arbitrary or irregular depth and can be incorporated very simply into the minimax algorithm.

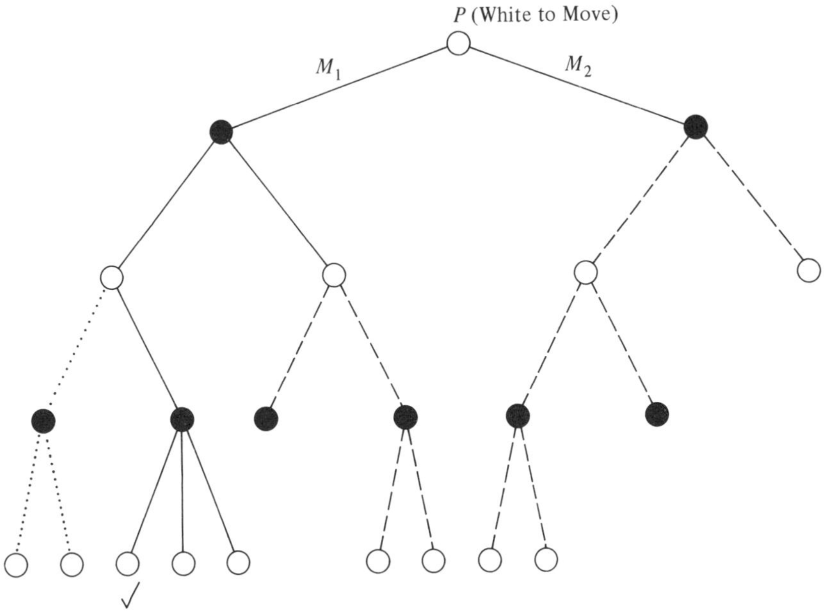

Figure 4.7 Storage requirements of the depth-first version of the minimax algorithm for the tree of Figure 4.6. At the time that the terminal position marked by a checkmark is scored, only the solid-line moves are stored in memory. The dotted-line moves have been generated and purged from memory. The broken-line moves have not been generated as yet. The memory requirements grow linearly with the depth of the lookahead.

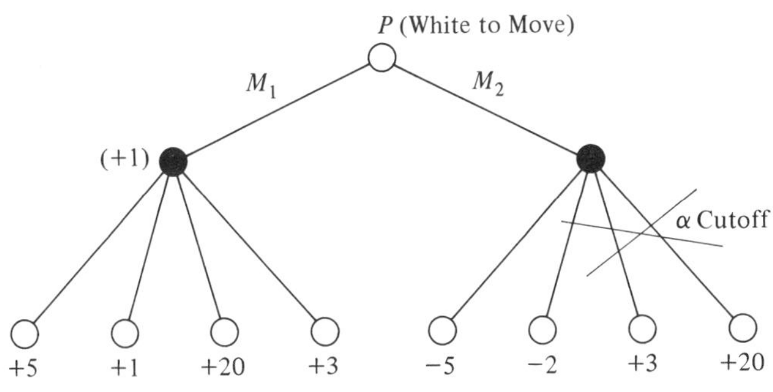

Figure 4.8 The α β procedure. White has evaluated move M_1 to have backed-up score $(+1)$, and starts evaluating move M_2. The first reply of Black is a refutation of M_2 since it leads to a temporary score of -5, less than the backed-up score of M_1. Since the backed-up score of M_2 will be -5 or less, M_2 will be inferior to M_1. Therefore, it is not necessary to evaluate move M_2 further.

Generally, if in the process of updating the backed-up score of a given position (step 3b) this score crosses a certain bound, then no further calculation is needed regarding that position. The cutoff bounds are adjusted dynamically and transmitted top-down as follows:

1. The cutoff bound for Black in position n is denoted α and equals the highest current score of all ancestor positions of n where White has to move. The exploration of position n can be terminated as soon as its temporary backed-up score equals or falls below α.
2. The cutoff bound for White in position n is denoted β and equals the lowest current value of all ancestor positions of n where Black has the move. The exploration of position n can be terminated as soon as its temporary backed-up score rises above β.

The process is illustrated in Figure 4.9. *It can be shown that the backed-up score and optimal move at the starting position are unaffected by the incorporation of the α–β procedure in the minimax algorithm.* We leave the verification of this fact to the reader (Problem 8). It can be seen

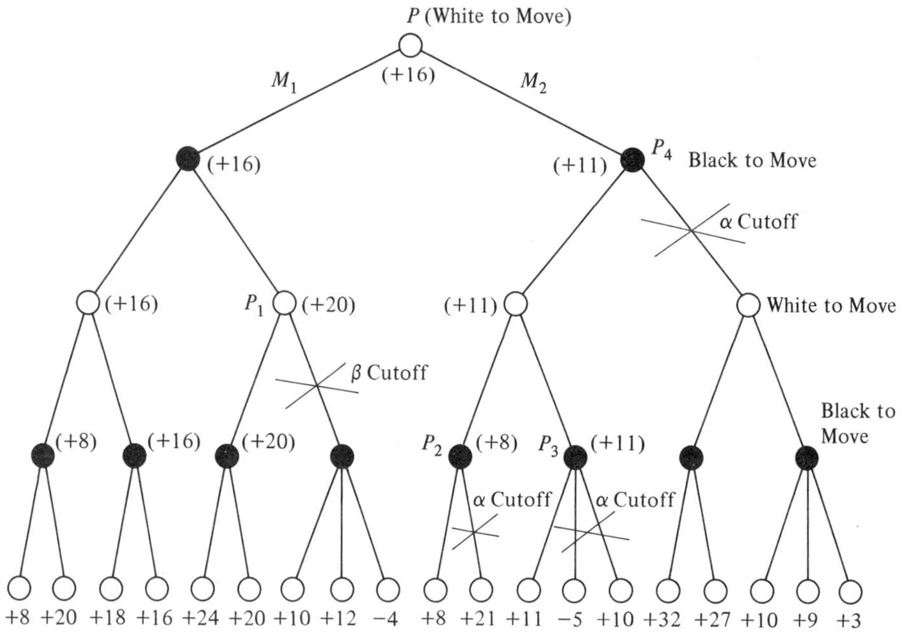

Figure 4.9 The α–β pruning procedure applied to the tree of Figure 4.5. For example, the β-cutoff in position P_1 is due to the fact that its temporary score (+20) exceeds its current β-bound (+16). The α-cutoffs in positions P_2, P_3, and P_4 are due to the fact that the corresponding temporary scores, +8, +11, and +11, have fallen below the current α-bound, which is +16, the current temporary score in position P.

that the α–β procedure will be more effective if the best moves in each position are explored first. This tends to keep the α bounds high and the β bounds low, thus saving a maximum amount of calculation. Much of the current level of success of chess programs is due to intelligent techniques for ordering moves so as to maximize the effectiveness of the α–β procedure. Two of these techniques, known as *iterative deepening* and the *killer heuristic*, will be discussed briefly.

Iterative deepening, in its pure form, consists of first conducting a search based on lookahead of one move; then carrying out (from scratch) a search based on lookahead of two moves; then carrying out a search based on lookahead of three moves, and so on. This process is continued either up to a fixed level of lookahead or until some limit on computation time is exceeded. At each iteration associated with a certain level of look-ahead, one obtains a best move at the starting position. This move is examined first in the subsequent iteration involving one extra move of lookahead. This enhances the power of the α–β procedure, thereby more than making up for the extra computation involved in doing a short lookahead search before doing a longer one. (Actually, given that the number of terminal positions increases on the average by more than a factor of about 30 with each additional level of lookahead, the extra computation is relatively small.) An additional benefit of this method is that a best move is maintained throughout the search and can be produced at any time as needed. This comes in handy in commercial programs that incorporate a feature whereby the computer is forced to move either upon exhausting a given time allocation or upon command by a human opponent. An improvement of the method is to obtain a thoroughly sorted list of moves at the starting position via a one-move lookahead, and then use the improved ordering in subsequent iterations to enhance the performance of the α–β procedure.

The killer heuristic is similar to iterative deepening in that it aims at examining first the most powerful moves at each position, thereby enhancing the pruning power of the α–β procedure. To understand the idea, suppose that in some position White selects the first move M_1 from a candidate list $\{M_1, M_2, M_3, \ldots\}$, and upon examining Black's responses to M_1 finds that a particular move, call it K, is by far Black's best. Then it is often true that K (commonly referred to as a *killer move*) is also Black's best response to the second and subsequent moves $M_2, M_3, \ldots$ in White's list. It is therefore a good idea from the point of view of α–β pruning to consider the killer move K first as a potential response to the remaining moves M_2, $M_3, \ldots$. Of course, this does not always work as hoped, in which case it is advisable to change the killer move depending on subsequent results of the computation. (Some programs actually maintain lists of more than one killer move at each level of lookahead.)

The α–β procedure is safe in the sense that searching a game tree with and without it will produce the same result. Some computer chess programs use more drastic tree-pruning procedures, which usually require less computation for a given level of lookahead, but may miss on occasion the strongest move. There is some debate at present regarding the merits of such procedures. References [L2] and [N4] consider this subject and provide a broader discussion of the limitations of computer chess programs.

4.4 ADAPTIVE CONTROL: SELF-TUNING REGULATORS

We have been dealing so far with systems having a known state equation. In practice, however, one is frequently faced with situations where the system equation contains parameters that are not known exactly. One possible approach, of course, is to conduct experiments and estimate the unknown parameters from input–output records of the system. This procedure, however, can be quite time consuming. Furthermore, it may be necessary to repeat the procedure if the parameters of the system change with time, as is often the case in many industrial processes.

The alternative is to formulate the stochastic control problem in a way that unknown parameters are dealt with directly. It is easy to show that problems involving unknown system parameters can be embedded within the framework of our basic problem with imperfect state information by using state augmentation. Indeed, let the system equation be of the form

$$x_{k+1} = f_k(x_k, \theta, u_k, w_k),$$

where θ is a vector of unknown parameters with a given a priori probability distribution. We introduce an additional state variable $y_k = \theta$ and obtain a system equation of the form

$$\begin{bmatrix} x_{k+1} \\ y_{k+1} \end{bmatrix} = \begin{bmatrix} f_k(x_k, y_k, u_k, w_k) \\ y_k \end{bmatrix}. \tag{4.17}$$

By defining $\tilde{x}_k = (x_k, y_k)$ as the new state, we obtain

$$\tilde{x}_{k+1} = \tilde{f}_k(\tilde{x}_k, u_k, w_k),$$

where $\tilde{f}_k$ is defined in an obvious manner from (4.17). The initial state is

$$\tilde{x}_0 = (x_0, \theta).$$

With a suitable reformulation of the cost functional, the resulting problem becomes one that fits our usual framework.

It is to be noted, however, that since $y_k = \theta$ is unobservable, we are faced with a problem of imperfect state information even if the controller receives an exact measurement of the state x_k. Furthermore, the parameter vector θ usually enters the state equation in a manner that makes the augmented system (4.17) nonlinear. As a result, in the great majority of cases it is practically impossible to obtain an optimal controller by means of a DP algorithm. Suboptimal controllers are thus called for and in this section we discuss some of the issues involved in their design. We then consider a form of the certainty equivalent controller for ARMAX models, called the *self-tuning regulator,* that has been used with success in practice.

Caution, Probing, and Dual Control

Suboptimal control is often guided by the qualitative nature of optimal control. It is therefore important to try to understand some of the characteristic features of the latter. One of these is the need for balance between "caution" and "probing," two notions that are best explained by means of an example.

Consider the linear scalar system

$$x_{k+1} = x_k + bu_k + w_k, \qquad k = 0, 1, \dots, N-1,$$

and the quadratic terminal cost $E\{x_N^2\}$. Here everything is as in Section 2.1 (perfect state information) except that the control coefficient b is unknown. Instead, it is known that the a priori probability distribution of b is Gaussian with mean and variance

$$\bar{b} = E\{b\} > 0, \qquad \sigma_b^2 = E\{(b - \bar{b})^2\}.$$

Furthermore, w_k is zero mean Gaussian with variance σ_w^2 for each k.

Consider first the case where $N = 1$ so the cost is

$$E\{x_1^2\} = E\{(x_0 + bu_0 + w_0)^2\}.$$

A straightforward calculation gives the minimizing value of u_0:

$$u_0 = -\frac{\bar{b}}{\bar{b}^2 + \sigma_b^2} x_0,$$

and the optimal cost is

$$\frac{\sigma_b^2}{\bar{b}^2 + \sigma_b^2} x_0^2 + \sigma_w^2.$$

Therefore, the optimal control here is *cautious* in that $|u_0|$ decreases as the uncertainty in b (i.e., σ_b^2) increases.

Consider next the case where $N = 2$. The optimal cost-to-go at stage 1 is obtained by the calculation given earlier:

$$J_1(I_1) = \frac{\sigma_b^2(1)}{[\bar{b}(1)]^2 + \sigma_b^2(1)} x_1^2 + \sigma_w^2, \tag{4.18}$$

where $I_1 = (x_0, u_0, x_1)$ is the information vector and

$$\bar{b}\,(1) = E\{b \mid I_1\}, \qquad \sigma_b^2(1) = E\{[(b - b(1)]^2 \mid I_1\}.$$

The value of $\sigma_b^2(1)$ can be obtained from the equation $x_1 = x_0 + bu_0 + w_0$ and standard least-squares estimation theory results (see [A1] and [L7]). The end result will be of no further use to us, so we just state it without going into the calculation:

$$\sigma_b^2(1) = \frac{\sigma_b^2 \sigma_w^2}{u_0^2 \sigma_b^2 + \sigma_w^2}. \tag{4.19}$$

From (4.18) we see that at stage 1 we would like to have small $\sigma_b^2(1)$, and it follows from (4.19) that to achieve this we must apply a control u_0 that is large in absolute value. A choice of large control to enhance parameter identification is called *probing*. On the other hand, if $|u_0|$ is large, $|x_1|$ will also be large, and this is not desirable in view of (4.18). Therefore, in choosing u_0 we must strike a balance between caution (a small value to keep x_1 reasonably small) and probing (a large value to improve the signal-to-noise ratio and enhance estimation of b). This tradeoff between the control objective and the parameter estimation objective is commonly referred to as *dual control*. It manifests itself often when system parameters are unknown, but unfortunately it cannot be quantified precisely in most cases.

Two-Phase Control and Identifiability

An apparently reasonable form of suboptimal control in the presence of unknown parameters is to separate the control process into two phases, a *parameter identification phase* and a *control phase*. In the first phase the unknown parameters are identified, while the control takes no account of the interim results of identification. The final parameter estimates from the first phase are then used to implement an optimal control law in the second phase. This alternation of identification and control phases may be repeated several times during any system run in order to take into account subsequent changes of the parameters.

One drawback of this approach is that information gathered during the identification phase is not used to adjust the control law until the beginning of the second phase. Furthermore, it is not always easy to determine when to terminate one phase and start the other.

A second difficulty, of a more fundamental nature, is due to the fact that the control process may make some of the unknown parameters invisible to the identification process. This is the problem of parameter *identifiability* [L7], which is best explained by means of an example.

Example 1

Consider the scalar system

$$x_{k+1} = ax_k + bu_k + w_k, \qquad k = 0, 1, \ldots, N-1$$

with the quadratic cost

$$E\left\{\sum_{k=1}^{N} x_k^2\right\}.$$

We assume perfect state information; so if the parameters a and b are known, this is a minimum variance control problem (cf. Section 3.3), and the optimal control law is

$$\mu_k^*(x_k) = -\frac{a}{b}x_k.$$

Assume now that the parameters a and b are unknown and consider the two-phase method. During the first phase the control law

$$\tilde{\mu}_k(x_k) = \gamma x_k \tag{4.20}$$

is used (γ is some scalar; for example, $\gamma = -\bar{a}/\bar{b}$ where $\bar{a}$, $\bar{b}$ are a priori estimates of a and b). At the end of the first phase, the control law is changed to

$$\bar{\mu}_k(x_k) = -\frac{\hat{a}}{\hat{b}}x_k,$$

where $\hat{a}$ and $\hat{b}$ are the estimates obtained from the identification process. However, with the control law (4.20), the closed-loop system is

$$x_{k+1} = (a + b\gamma)x_k + w_k,$$

so the identification process can at best identify the value of $(a + b\gamma)$ but not the values of both a and b. In other words, the identification process cannot discriminate between pairs of values (a_1, b_1) and (a_2, b_2) such that $a_1 + b_1\gamma = a_2 + b_2\gamma$. Therefore, a and b are not identifiable when feedback control of the form (4.20) is applied.

One way to correct the difficulty is to add an additional known input δ_k to the control law (4.20); that is, use

$$\overline{\mu}_k(x_k) = \gamma x_k + \delta_k.$$

Then the closed-loop system becomes

$$x_{k+1} = (a + b\gamma)x_k + b\delta_k + w_k,$$

and from knowledge of $\{x_k\}$ and $\{\delta_k\}$ it is possible to identify $(a + b\gamma)$ and b. Given γ, one can then obtain estimates of a and b. Actually, to guarantee this in a more general context where the system is of higher dimension, the sequence $\{\delta_k\}$ must satisfy certain conditions: it must be "persistently exciting" (see [L8]).

A second possibility to bypass the identifiability problem is to change the structure of the system by artificially introducing a one-unit delay in the control feedback. Thus, instead of considering control laws of the form $\tilde{\mu}_k(x_k) = \gamma x_k$, we consider controls of the form

$$u_k = \hat{\mu}_k(x_{k-1}) = \gamma x_{k-1}.$$

The closed-loop system then becomes

$$x_{k+1} = ax_k + b\gamma x_{k-1} + w_k,$$

and, given γ, it is possible to identify both parameters a and b. This technique can be generalized for systems of arbitrary order, but artificially introducing a control delay seems like a less than ideal solution to the identifiability problem.

Certainty Equivalent Control and Identifiability

A scheme that in some sense lies at the opposite extreme of the two-phase method is to incorporate into the control law the parameter estimates as they are generated, treating them as if they were true values. This scheme is essentially the certainty equivalent controller considered in Section 4.2. In terms of the system

$$x_{k+1} = f_k(x_k, \theta, u_k, w_k)$$

considered earlier, suppose that, for each possible value of θ, the control law $\pi^*(\theta) = \{\mu_0^*(\cdot, \theta), \ldots, \mu_{N-1}^*(\cdot, \theta)\}$ is optimal with respect to a certain cost $J_\pi(x_0, \theta)$. Then the (suboptimal) control used at time k is

$$\hat{\mu}_k(I_k) = \mu_k^*(x_k, \hat{\theta}_k),$$

where $\hat{\theta}_k$ is an estimate of θ based on the information

$$I_k = \{x_0, x_1, \ldots, x_k, u_0, \ldots, u_{k-1}\}$$

available at time k; for example,

$$\hat{\theta}_k = E\{\theta \mid I_k\}$$

or, more likely, an estimate obtained via an on-line system identification method.

Unfortunately, identifiability difficulties are associated with this scheme as well. Suppose for simplicity that the system is stationary with a priori known transition probabilities $P\{x_{k+1} \mid x_k, u_k, \theta\}$ and that the control law used is also stationary:

$$\hat{\mu}_k(I_k) = \mu^*(x_k, \hat{\theta}_k), \qquad k = 0, 1, \ldots.$$

Then at time k, given the estimate $\hat{\theta}_k$, the controller *thinks* that the probabilistic evolution of the system is governed by

$$P\{x_{k+1} \mid x_k, \mu^*(x_k, \hat{\theta}_k), \hat{\theta}_k\}.$$

However, the *true* probabilistic evolution is governed by

$$P\{x_{k+1} \mid x_k, \mu^*(x_k, \hat{\theta}_k), \theta^*\},$$

where θ^* is the true parameter value. Suppose now that for some $\hat{\theta} \neq \theta^*$ and all x_{k+1}, x_k, we have

$$P\{x_{k+1} \mid x_k, \mu^*(x_k, \hat{\theta}), \hat{\theta}\} = P\{x_{k+1} \mid x_k, \mu^*(x_k, \hat{\theta}), \theta^*\}. \tag{4.21}$$

That is, *there is a false value of parameter for which the system under closed-loop control looks exactly as if the false value were true*. Then, if the controller estimates at some time the parameter to be $\hat{\theta}$, subsequent data will tend to reinforce this erroneous estimate. As a result, a situation may develop where the identification procedure locks onto a wrong parameter value and the controls applied differ consistently from the optimal, regardless of how long information is collected.

Relation (4.21) indicates the nature of the identifiability problem under closed-loop control. *The true parameter value cannot be determined uniquely from the probabilistic evolution of the closed-loop system.* The following examples illustrate this difficulty.

Example 2 [B33]

Consider a two-state system with two controls u^1 and u^2. The transition probabilities depend on the control applied as well as a parameter θ, which is known to take one of two values θ^* and $\hat{\theta}$. They are as shown in Figure 4.10. There is zero cost for a transition from state 1 to itself and a unity cost for all other transitions. Therefore, the optimal control at state 1 is the one that maximizes the probability of the state remaining at 1. Assume the true parameter is θ^*. Then the optimal control is u^2, but if the controller *thinks* that the true parameter is $\hat{\theta}$, it will apply u^1. Because under u^1 the system looks identical for both values of the parameter, subsequent data will tend to reinforce the controller's belief that the true parameter is indeed $\hat{\theta}$.

More precisely, suppose that the parameter estimation method selects at each time k the value of θ that maximizes

$$P\{\theta \mid I_k\} = \frac{P\{I_k \mid \theta\}P(I_k)}{P(\theta)},$$

where $P(\theta)$ is the a priori probability that the true parameter is θ. (This scheme is almost the same as the maximum likelihood method.) Then if $P(\hat{\theta}) > P(\theta^*)$, it can be seen that the controller will at each time k estimate falsely θ to be $\hat{\theta}$ and apply the incorrect control u^1.

Example 3 [K11]

Consider the linear scalar system

$$x_{k+1} = ax_k + bu_k + w_k,$$

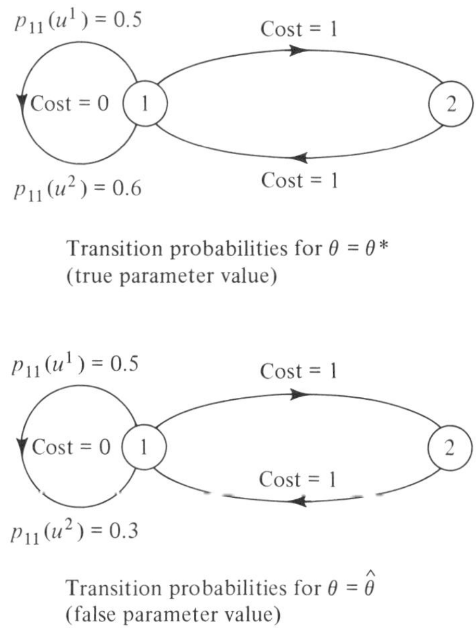

Figure 4.10 Transition probabilities for two-state system of Example 2. Under the nonoptimal control u^1, the system looks identical under the true and the false values of parameter θ.

where we know that the parameters are either $(a, b) = (1, 1)$ or $(a, b) = (0, -1)$. The sequence $\{w_k\}$ is independent, stationary, zero mean, and Gaussian. The cost is quadratic of the form

$$\sum_{k=0}^{N-1} (x_k^2 + 2u_k^2),$$

where N is very large, so the stationary form of the optimal control law is used (see Sections 2.1 and 7.4). This control law can be calculated via the Riccati equation to be

$$\mu^*(x_k) = \begin{cases} -\dfrac{x_k}{2}, & \text{if } (a, b) = (1, 1), \\ 0, & \text{if } (a, b) = (0, -1). \end{cases}$$

To estimate (a, b), we use a least-squares identification method. The value of the least-squares criterion at time k is given by

$$V_k(1, 1) = \sum_{i=0}^{k-1} (x_{i+1} - x_i - u_i)^2, \qquad \text{for } (a, b) = (1, 1), \tag{4.22a}$$

$$V_k(0, -1) = \sum_{i=0}^{k-1} (x_{i+1} + u_i)^2, \qquad \text{for } (a, b) = (0, -1). \tag{4.22b}$$

The control applied at time k is

$$u_k = \tilde{\mu}_k(I_k) = \begin{cases} -\dfrac{x_k}{2}, & \text{if } V_k(1, 1) < V_k(0, -1), \\ 0, & \text{if } V_k(1, 1) > V_k(0, -1). \end{cases}$$

Suppose the true parameters are $\theta^* = (0, -1)$. Then the true system evolves according to

$$x_{k+1} = -u_k + w_k. \tag{4.23}$$

If at time k the controller estimates incorrectly the parameters to be $\hat{\theta} = (1, 1)$ because $V_k(\hat{\theta}) < V_k(\theta^*)$, the control applied will be $u_k = -x_k/2$ and the *true* closed-loop system will evolve according to

$$x_{k+1} = \frac{x_k}{2} + w_k. \tag{4.24}$$

On the other hand, the controller *thinks* (given the estimate $\hat{\theta}$) that the closed-loop system will evolve according to

$$x_{k+1} = x_k + u_k + w_k = x_k - \frac{x_k}{2} + w_k = \frac{x_k}{2} + w_k, \tag{4.25}$$

so from (4.24) and (4.25) we see that *under the control law $u_k = -x_k/2$ the closed-loop system evolves identically for both the true and the false values of the parameters* [cf. (4.21)].

To see what can go wrong, note that if $V_k(\hat{\theta}) < V_k(\theta^*)$ for some k we will have, from (4.23) to (4.25),

$$x_{k+1} + u_k = x_{k+1} - x_k - u_k,$$

so from (4.22a) and (4.22b) we obtain

$$V_{k+1}(\hat{\theta}) < V_{k+1}(\theta^*).$$

Therefore, if $V_1(\hat{\theta}) < V_1(\theta^*)$, the least-squares identification method will yield the wrong estimate $\hat{\theta}$ for every k. To see that this can happen with positive probability, note that, since the true system is $x_{k+1} = -u_k + w_k$, we have

$$V_1(\hat{\theta}) = (x_1 - x_0 - u_0)^2 = (w_0 - x_0 - 2u_0)^2,$$

$$V_1(\theta^*) = (x_1 + u_0)^2 = w_0^2.$$

Therefore, the inequality $V_1(\hat{\theta}) < V_1(\theta^*)$ is equivalent to

$$(x_0 + 2u_0)^2 < 2w_0(x_0 + 2u_0),$$

which will occur with positive probability since w_0 is Gaussian.

Finally, we note that intuition suggests that, *if the parameter estimates converge to some $\hat{\theta} \neq \theta^*$, then for this $\hat{\theta}$ loss of identifiability in the sense of (4.21) is very likely,* since, generally, parameter estimate convergence in identification methods implies that the data obtained are asymptotically consistent with the view of the system one has based on the current estimates. This will be shown in the context of ARMAX models, least-squares identification, and minimum variance control in what follows. It can also be shown in other contexts (e.g., finite state systems and maximum likelihood identification; see [B32] and [B33], which were the first to clarify the issues just described). The conclusion is that loss of identifiability is a serious problem that typically arises in the context of certainty equivalent control.

Self-tuning Regulator

We described earlier the nature of the identifiability issue in certainty equivalent control; that is, under closed-loop control incorrect parameter estimates may make the system behave as if these estimates were correct [cf. (4.21)]. As a result, the identification scheme may lock onto false parameter values. This is not necessarily bad, however, since it may happen that the control law implemented on the basis of the false parameter values is near optimal. Indeed, through a fortuitous coincidence, it turns out that *in the practically important minimum variance control formulation (Section 3.3) when the parameter estimates converge, they typically converge to false values, but the resulting control law typically converges to the optimal.* We can get an idea about this phenomenon by means of an example:

Example 4

Consider the simplest ARMAX model:

$$y_{k+1} + ay_k = bu_k + \epsilon_{k+1}.$$

The minimum variance control law when a and b are known is

$$u_k = \mu_k(I_k) = \frac{a}{b} y_k.$$

Suppose now that a and b are not known but they are identified on-line by means of some scheme. The control applied is

$$u_k = \frac{\hat{a}_k}{\hat{b}_k} y_k, \tag{4.26}$$

where $\hat{a}_k$ and $\hat{b}_k$ are the estimates obtained at time k. Let the true parameter values be a^* and b^*. Then the difficulty with identifiability occurs when

$$\hat{a}_k \to \hat{a}, \qquad \hat{b}_k \to \hat{b},$$

where $\hat{a}$ and $\hat{b}$ are such that the true closed-loop system given by

$$y_{k+1} + a^* y_k = \frac{b^* \hat{a}}{\hat{b}} y_k + \epsilon_{k+1}$$

coincides with the closed-loop system that the controller thinks is true on the basis of the estimates $\hat{a}$ and $\hat{b}$. This latter system is

$$y_{k+1} = \epsilon_{k+1}.$$

For these two systems to be identical, we must have

$$\frac{a^*}{b^*} = \frac{\hat{a}}{\hat{b}},$$

which means that *the control law (4.26) asymptotically becomes optimal despite the fact that the asymptotic estimates* $\hat{a}$ *and* $\hat{b}$ *may be incorrect.*

Example 4 can be extended to the general ARMAX model of Section 3.3 with no delay:

$$y_k + \sum_{i=1}^{m} a_i y_{k-i} = \sum_{i=1}^{m} b_i u_{k-i} + \epsilon_k + \sum_{i=1}^{m} c_i \epsilon_{k-1}. \tag{4.27}$$

If the parameter estimates converge (regardless of the identification method used), then a minimum variance controller *thinks* that the closed-loop system is asymptotically

$$y_k = \epsilon_k \tag{4.28}$$

(cf. Section 3.3). So if the difficulty with identifiability occurs, the true closed-loop system must also asymptotically be given by (4.28) and this is clearly the optimal closed-loop system.

To summarize, we have shown that, if the parameter estimates converge to values for which loss of identifiability occurs in the sense of (4.21), then the resulting minimum variance control law for the ARMAX model (4.27) is asymptotically optimal regardless of the identification method used. We now strengthen this result by showing that *if identification methods of the least-squares type are used, then parameter estimate convergence can occur only at values that result in loss of identifiability (and therefore make the corresponding minimum variance control law asymptotically optimal).* In fact, this can occur even if the model adopted for identification is incorrect to some extent.

Assume that the true system is given by

$$y_k + \sum_{i=1}^{m} a_i^* y_{k-i} = \sum_{i=1}^{m} b_i^* u_{k-i} + \epsilon_k + \sum_{i=1}^{m} c_i^* \epsilon_{k-i}. \tag{4.29}$$

For simplicity, we require that $b_1^* \neq 0$ (this assumption can be relaxed using essentially the same proof as the one to be given shortly). The controller assumes a model of the form

$$y_k + \sum_{i=1}^{m} a_i y_{k-i} = \sum_{i=1}^{m} b_i u_{k-i} + \epsilon_k$$

and applies minimum variance control

$$u_k = \hat{\mu}_k(I_k) = \frac{1}{\hat{b}_1^k}\left(\sum_{i=1}^{m} \hat{a}_i^k y_{k-i+1} - \sum_{i=2}^{m} \hat{b}_i^k u_{k-i+1}\right), \tag{4.30}$$

where the estimates $\hat{a}_i^k$ $\hat{b}_i^k$ minimize over a_i and b_i:

$$\sum_{n=1}^{k} \left(y_n + \sum_{i=1}^{m} a_i y_{n-i} - \sum_{i=1}^{m} b_i u_{n-i}\right)^2.$$

Setting to zero the derivatives of this expression with respect to a_i, we obtain, for all $i = 1, \ldots, m$,

$$\sum_{n=1}^{k} y_{n-i}\left(y_n + \sum_{j=1}^{m} \hat{a}_j^k y_{n-j} - \sum_{j=1}^{m} \hat{b}_j^k u_{n-j}\right) = 0. \tag{4.31}$$

Assume now that the estimates $\hat{a}_i^k$ and $\hat{b}_i^k$ converge to some $\hat{a}_i$ and $\hat{b}_i$ as $k \to \infty$:

$$\hat{a}_i^k \to \hat{a}_i, \qquad \hat{b}_i^k \to \hat{b}_i, \qquad i = 1, \ldots, m.$$

Then, in view of the use of the minimum variance control (4.30), we have

$$\sum_{i=1}^{m} \hat{a}_i y_{n-i} - \sum_{i=1}^{m} \hat{b}_i u_{n-i} \to 0, \qquad \text{as } n \to \infty,$$

so from (4.31) we obtain for the closed-loop system

$$\lim_{k\to\infty} \frac{1}{k} \sum_{n=1}^{k} y_{n-i} y_n = 0, \qquad i = 1, \ldots, m.$$

Under mild (ergodicity) assumptions, the time average in the preceding equation can be replaced by an ensemble average, which implies that asymptotically, as $k \to \infty$, we have

$$E\{y_{k-i} y_k\} = 0, \qquad i = 1, \ldots, m.$$

Therefore, the output y_k is uncorrelated with past outputs y_{k-i}, $i = 1, 2, \ldots$, asymptotically as $k \to \infty$. It follows that the true closed-loop system asymptotically becomes

$$y_k = \epsilon_k. \tag{4.32}$$

This is the optimal that can be achieved with minimum variance control even when all system parameters are known.

Note that the asymptotic estimates $\hat{a}_i$ and $\hat{b}_i$ will not converge to the true values a_i^* and b_i^* if $c_i^* \neq 0$. Even in the simplest case where $m = 1$ and $c_1^* = 0$, the only relation implied by (4.32) is $a_1^*/b_1^* = \hat{a}_1/\hat{b}_1$.

The preceding argument can also be used to show a similar result for slightly different least-squares identification procedures. Similar results can also be shown for other identification methods, but the proof is somewhat different [K10]. To repeat, if the least-squares parameter estimates converge, then an asymptotically optimal minimum variance control law is obtained.

The next issue that arises is whether the least-squares parameter estimates indeed converge. Extensive simulations have shown that these estimates converge for many systems, and this has established the practicality of the overall control scheme. However, a complete analysis of the convergence issue has defied the efforts of numerous researchers. The partial results [L6] available at present have not yet been brought together into a comprehensive theory. We refer to the survey paper [K10] for an exposition of the status of research on this subject. However, the self-tuning regulator has proved sufficiently robust in practice to be widely marketed at present as a general-purpose process control algorithm.

4.5 NOTES

The problems caused by large dimensionality have long been recognized as the principal drawback of DP. A great deal of effort by Bellman and his associates, and by others, has been directed toward finding partial remedies (see for example [B5], [B6], and [N2]). A class of two-stage problems, called stochastic programming problems, can be solved by using mathematical programming techniques (see Problems 1, 2, references [V1], [B10], [B13], [R3], and [W2], and the references quoted therein).

The example of Problem 4 showing that the CEC may perform worse than the optimal open-loop controller is due to Witsenhausen (see [T1]). For an interesting sensitivity property of the CEC, see [M1]. The idea of open-loop feedback control is due to Dreyfus [D8]. Its superiority over open-loop control was established in [B17] in the context of minimax control. A generalization of this result is given in [W4]. Suboptimal controllers other than the ones given here have been suggested by a number of authors [B1, B21, T3, T4, T5, D5, S1, S2, S24, and S32]. Self-tuning regulators received wide attention following the paper by Astrom and Wittenmark [A14]. Kumar has considered the general linear quadratic problem with unknown parameters [K11] and has provided an excellent survey of adaptive control [K10]. See also [A12], [G3], [L6], and [L8]. Control of Markov chains with unknown parameters has been considered in [B32], [B33], [D7], [K12], and [M2].

Whenever a suboptimal controller is used in practice it is desirable to know how close the resulting cost approximates the optimal. Tight bounds on the performance of the suboptimal controller are useful but are usually quite hard to obtain. For some interesting results in this direction see [W14] and [W15].

PROBLEMS

1. *Two-Stage Problems and Deterministic Optimization.* The purpose of this problem is to show how certain stochastic control problems can be solved by (deterministic) mathematical programming techniques. Consider the basic problem of Chapter 1 for the case where there are only two stages ($N = 2$) and the disturbance space for the initial stage is a finite set $D_0 = \{w_0^1, \ldots, w_0^r\}$. The probability of w_0^i, $i = 1, \ldots, r$, is denoted p_i and does not depend on x_0 or u_0. Verify that the optimal cost function $J_0(x_0)$ given by

$$J_0(x_0) = \min_{u_0 \in U_0(x_0)} \sum_{i=1}^{r} p_i[g_0(x_0, u_0, w_0^i)$$
$$+ \min_{u_1 \in U_1[f_0(x_0, u_0, w_0^i)]} \mathop{E}_{w_1} \{g_1[f_0(x_0, u_0, w_0^i), u_1, w_1]$$
$$+ g_2[f_1[f_0(x_0, u_0, w_0^i), u_1, w_1]]\}]$$

is equal to the optimal cost of the problem

$$\underset{\substack{u_0, z_i, u_1^i \\ i=1,\ldots,r}}{\text{minimize}} \sum_{i=1}^{r} p_i[g_0(x_0, u_0, w_0^i) + z_i]$$

$$\text{subject to } z_i \geq \mathop{E}_{w_1} \{g_1[f_0(x_0, u_0, w_0^i), u_1^i, w_1]$$
$$+ g_2[f_1[f_0(x_0, u_0, w_0^i), u_1^i, w_1]]\},$$
$$u_0 \in U_0(x_0), \qquad u_1^i \in U_1[f_0(x_0, u_0, w_0^i)].$$

Show also how a solution of this mathematical programming problem may be used to yield an optimal control law.

2. *Stochastic Programming.* Consider the problem of minimizing over x:

$$g(x) + \mathop{E}_{r} \left\{ \min_{\substack{y \geq 0 \\ f(x) + Ay = r}} q'y \right\}$$

subject to $h_i(x) = 0$, $i = 1, \ldots, s$, $l_j(x) \leq 0$, $j = 1, \ldots, p$, where $x \in R^n$, $y \in R^m$, q is a given vector in R^m, $r \in R^k$ is a random vector taking a finite number of values $r_1, \ldots, r_t$ with given probabilities $p_1, \ldots, p_t$, g, h_i, l_j are given continuously differentiable real-valued functions, $f: R^n \to R^k$ is a continuously differentiable mapping, and A is a given $k \times m$ matrix. Show that this problem may be viewed as a two-stage problem that fits the framework of the basic problem of Chapter 1. Show also how the problem can be converted to a deterministic problem that can be solved by standard mathematical programming techniques.

3. Consider a problem with perfect state information involving the n-dimensional

linear system of Section 2.1:

$$x_{k+1} = A_k x_k + B_k u_k + w_k, \qquad k = 0, 1, \ldots, N-1,$$

and a cost functional of the form

$$\underset{\substack{w_k \\ k=0,\ldots,N-1}}{E} \left\{ g_N(c'x_N) + \sum_{k=0}^{N-1} g_k(u_k) \right\},$$

where $c \in R^n$ is a given vector. Show that the DP algorithm for this problem can be carried out over a one-dimensional state space.

4. Consider the following two-dimensional, two-stage linear system with scalar control and disturbance

$$x_{k+1} = x_k + bu_k + dw_k, \qquad k = 0, 1,$$

where $b = [1, 0]'$ and $d = [1/2, \sqrt{2}/2]'$. The initial state is $x_0 = 0$. The controls u_0 and u_1 are unconstrained, and the disturbances w_0 and w_1 are independent random variables with identical distribution. They take the values $+1$ and -1 each with probability 1/2. Perfect state information prevails. The cost is

$$\underset{w_0, w_1}{E} \{\|x_2\|\},$$

where $\|\cdot\|$ denotes the usual Euclidean norm. Show that the optimal open-loop cost and the optimal closed-loop cost are both $\sqrt{3}/2$, but the cost corresponding to the CEC is 1.

5. Consider a two-stage problem with perfect state information involving the scalar system

$$x_0 = 1, \qquad x_1 = x_0 + u_0 + w_0, \qquad x_2 = f(x_1, u_1).$$

The control constraints are $u_0, u_1 \in \{0, -1\}$. The random variable w_0 takes the values $+1$ and -1 with equal probability $\frac{1}{2}$. The function f is defined by

$$f(1, 0) = f(1, -1) = f(-1, 0) = f(-1, -1) = 0.5,$$

$$f(2, 0) = 0, \quad f(2, -1) = 2, \qquad f(0, -1) = 0.6, \qquad f(0, 0) = 2.$$

The cost functional is

$$\underset{w_0}{E} \{x_2\}.$$

(a) Show that one possible OLFC for this problem is

$$\bar{\mu}_0(x_0) = -1; \qquad \bar{\mu}_1(x_1) = \begin{cases} 0, & \text{if } x_1 = \pm 1, 2, \\ -1, & \text{if } x_1 = 0, \end{cases} \tag{4.33}$$

and the resulting cost is 0.5.

(b) Show that one possible CEC for this problem is

$$\tilde{\mu}_0(x_0) = 0, \qquad \tilde{\mu}_1(x_1) = \begin{cases} 0, & \text{if } x_1 = \pm 1, 2, \\ -1, & \text{if } x_1 = 0, \end{cases} \tag{4.34}$$

and the resulting cost is 0.3. Show also that this CEC is an optimal feedback controller.

6. Consider the system and cost functional of Problem 5 but with the difference that

$$f(0, -1) = 0.$$

(a) Show that the controller (4.33) of Problem 5 is both an OLFC and a CEC and that the corresponding cost is 0.5.

(b) Assume that the control constraint set for the first stage is $\{0\}$ rather than $\{0, -1\}$. Show that the controller (4.34) of Problem 5 is both an OLFC and a CEC and that the corresponding cost is 0.

Note: This problem illustrates a pathology that occurs generically in suboptimal control. To see this, consider a problem and a suboptimal control strategy that is not optimal for the problem. Let $\pi^* = \{\mu_0^*, \ldots, \mu_{N-1}^*\}$ be an optimal policy. Restrict the control constraint set so that only the optimal control $\mu_k^*(x_k)$ is allowed at state x_k. Then the cost attained by the suboptimal control strategy will be improved.

7. Show that the Astrom–Wittenmark result regarding the convergence properties of the self-tuning regulator also holds in either one of the following two situations:

(a) The value of the parameter b_1 is not estimated but rather is kept at some fixed nonzero value while all other parameters are estimated using least squares.

(b) The control delay is greater than 1.

8. Provide a careful argument showing that searching a chess position with and without α–β pruning will give the same result.

9. In a version of the game of Nim, two players start with a stack of five pennies and take turns removing one, two, or three pennies from the stack. The player who removes the last penny loses. Construct the game tree and verify that the second player to move can win with optimal play.

CHAPTER FIVE

Infinite Horizon Problems: Theory

The remainder of the text is devoted to problems that differ from those considered so far in two respects. First, the number of stages is infinite, and, second, the system is stationary: that is, the system equation, the cost per stage, and the random disturbance statistics do not change from one stage to the next. The assumption of an infinite number of stages is, of course, a mathematical formalization since it is never satisfied in practice. It constitutes a reasonable approximation for problems involving a finite but very large number of stages. The assumption of stationarity is often satisfied in practice, and in other cases it approximates reasonably a situation where the system parameters vary slowly with time.

Infinite horizon problems, as a general rule, require considerably more sophisticated analysis than their finite horizon counterparts. The difficulties are of a twofold nature. First, the consideration of an infinite horizon requires analysis of limiting behavior, for example, the convergence of the DP algorithm and the corresponding optimal policies. This analysis is often nontrivial and at times reveals surprising possibilities. Second, a rigorous consideration of the probabilistic aspects of problems involving uncountable disturbance spaces requires the sophisticated machinery of measure-theoretic probability theory. The resulting difficulties are considerably more severe than those of finite horizon problems and are far beyond the introductory scope of this text. For this reason and given that the need for precision is much greater in infinite horizon problems than in their finite horizon counterparts, *we will restrict ourselves exclusively to the case where the disturbance space is a countable set.* Reference [B23] addresses in detail the mathematical issues relating to uncountable disturbance spaces, and gives a more complete treatment of advanced topics.

On the positive side, the analysis of infinite horizon problems is often elegant, and the implementation of optimal policies is often simple. For example, optimal policies are typically stationary; that is, the optimal rule for applying controls does not change from one stage to the next.

Traditionally, there have been three classes of infinite horizon problems of major interest:

(a) In the *discounted case with bounded cost per stage,* the cost functional takes the form

$$J_\pi(x_0) = \lim_{N\to\infty} \underset{\substack{w_k \\ k=0,1,\ldots}}{E} \left\{ \sum_{k=0}^{N-1} \alpha^k g[x_k, \mu_k(x_k), w_k] \right\},$$

where $J_\pi(x_0)$ denotes the cost associated with an initial state x_0 and a policy $\pi = \{\mu_0, \mu_1, \ldots\}$, and α is a scalar with $0 < \alpha < 1$, called the *discount factor*. The cost per stage $g(x, u, w)$ is uniformly bounded from above and below. This case is examined in Sections 5.1 to 5.3 and is by far the simplest infinite horizon problem, primarily due to the presence of a contraction mapping underlying the DP iteration (Section 5.3). There are no pathologies here, and effective computational methods are available for solution.

(b) In the case of *unbounded costs per stage,* the cost functional has the same form as in (a) except that the scalar α is positive but not necessarily less than unity. Furthermore, the cost per stage is allowed to be unbounded either from above or from below. This case is treated in Section 5.4.

(c) Minimization of $J_\pi(x_0)$ in (a) makes sense only if $J_\pi(x_0)$ is finite for at least some admissible policies π and some initial states x_0. In many problems of interest, it turns out that $J_\pi(x_0) = +\infty$, but the limit

$$\lim_{N\to\infty} \frac{1}{N} \underset{\substack{w_k \\ k=0,1,\ldots}}{E} \left\{ \sum_{k=0}^{N-1} g[x_k, \mu_k(x_k), w_k] \right\}$$

is finite for every policy $\pi = \{\mu_0, \mu_1, \ldots\}$ and initial state x_0. Under these circumstances it is reasonable to try to minimize the preceding expression, which may be viewed as an *average cost per stage* associated with policy π. Such problems are the subject of Chapter 7, where we restrict attention mostly to finite state Markov chains.

Throughout the remainder of the text we concentrate on the perfect information case. Imperfect information problems can be treated, as in Chapter 3, by reformulation into perfect information problems involving a sufficient statistic. In this chapter we focus on the following infinite horizon, stationary version of the basic problem of Chapter 1.

Problem I: Total Expected Cost Infinite Horizon Problem. Consider the stationary discrete-time dynamic system

$$x_{k+1} = f(x_k, u_k, w_k), \qquad k = 0, 1, 2, \ldots, \tag{5.1}$$

where the state x_k, $k = 0, 1, \ldots$, is an element of a space S, the control u_k, $k = 0, 1, \ldots$, is an element of a space C, and the random disturbance w_k, $k = 0, 1, \ldots$, is an element of a space D. It is assumed that D is a countable set. The control u_k is constrained to take values in a given nonempty subset $U(x_k)$ of C, which depends on the current state x_k [$u_k \in U(x_k)$, for all $x_k \in S$, $k = 0, 1, \ldots$]. The random disturbances w_k, $k = 0, 1, \ldots$, have identical statistics and are characterized by probabilities $P(\cdot|x_k, u_k)$ defined on D, where $P(w_k|x_k, u_k)$ is the probability of occurrence of w_k, when the current state and control are x_k and u_k, respectively. The probability of w_k may depend explicitly on x_k and u_k but not on values of prior disturbances $w_{k-1}, \ldots, w_0$.

Given an initial state x_0, the problem is to find a policy $\pi = \{\mu_0, \mu_1, \ldots\}$ where $\mu_k: S \to C$, $\mu_k(x_k) \in U(x_k)$, for all $x_k \in S$, $k = 0, 1, \ldots$, that minimizes the cost functional†

$$J_\pi(x_0) = \lim_{N\to\infty} \underset{\substack{w_k \\ k=0,1,\ldots}}{E} \left\{ \sum_{k=0}^{N-1} \alpha^k g[x_k, \mu_k(x_k), w_k] \right\} \tag{5.2}$$

subject to the system equation constraint (5.1). The real-valued function $g: S \times C \times D \to R$ is given, and the scalar α is positive.

Note that, while we allow an arbitrary state and control space, we require that the disturbance space be a countable set. This is necessary to avoid the mathematical complications discussed in Section 1.1. Our assumption, however, is satisfied in many problems of interest, notably for deterministic optimal control problems and problems of control of finite and countable state Markov chains. For other problems, our main results can typically be proved (under additional technical conditions) by following the same line of argument as given here [B23].

The cost $J_\pi(x_0)$ given by (5.2) represents the limit of finite horizon costs. These costs are well defined as discussed in Section 1.1. Another possibility would be to minimize over π the expected infinite horizon cost

$$\underset{\substack{w_k \\ k=0,1,\ldots}}{E} \left\{ \sum_{k=0}^{\infty} \alpha^k g[x_k, \mu_k(x_k), w_k] \right\}.$$

Such a cost functional would require a far more complex mathematical formulation (a probability measure on the space of all disturbance sequences;

† In what follows we always assume that $g(x, u, w)$ is either nonnegative for all x, u, and w or nonpositive for all x, u, and w, so the limit in (5.2) is well defined as a real number or $\pm\infty$.

see [B23]). However, we mention that, under the assumptions that we will be using, the preceding expression is equal to the cost given by (5.2). This may be proved by using the monotone convergence theorem (see Section 5.4), which allows interchange of limit and expectation under conditions that in our case are satisfied.

In the first three sections of this chapter we will operate under the following assumption:

Assumption D (Discounted Cost). The cost per stage g satisfies

$$0 \leq g(x, u, w) \leq M, \qquad \text{for all } (x, u, w) \in S \times C \times D, \tag{5.3}$$

where M is some scalar. Furthermore, $0 < \alpha < 1$.

Notice that (5.3) could be replaced by an inequality of the form

$$M_2 \leq g(x, u, w) \leq M_1,$$

where M_1 and M_2 are arbitrary scalars, since addition of a constant r to g merely adds $(1 - \alpha)^{-1}r$ to the cost. Assumption D is not as restrictive as might appear. It holds for problems where the spaces S, C, and D are finite sets. Even if these spaces are not finite, during computational solution of the problem they will ordinarily be approximated by finite sets. In other cases it is often possible to reformulate the problem so that it is defined over bounded regions of the state and control spaces over which relation (5.3) holds.

Let us denote by Π the set of all *admissible* policies π, that is, the set of all sequences of functions $\pi = \{\mu_0, \mu_1, \ldots\}$ with $\mu_k : S \to C$, $\mu_k(x) \in U(x)$ for all $x \in S$, $k = 0, 1, \ldots$. The optimal cost function J^* given by

$$J^*(x) = \min_{\pi \in \Pi} J_\pi(x), \qquad x \in S,$$

is well defined as a real-valued function under Assumption D. In fact, using (5.2) and (5.3), it is easily seen that $0 \leq J^*(x) \leq M \sum_{k=0}^{\infty} \alpha^k = M/(1 - \alpha)$ for all $x \in S$.

A class of admissible policies of particular interest to us is the class of *stationary policies* of the form $\pi = \{\mu, \mu, \ldots\}$ for which the rule for control selection is the same at every stage. Throughout this chapter *a stationary policy is implicitly assumed to be admissible.* The cost associated with a stationary policy $\{\mu, \mu, \ldots\}$ and an initial state $x \in S$ will also be denoted by $J_\mu(x)$; that is, for $\pi = \{\mu, \mu, \ldots\}$, we write

$$J_\mu(x_0) = J_\pi(x_0) = \lim_{N \to \infty} \underset{\substack{w_k \\ k=0,1,\ldots}}{E} \left\{ \sum_{k=0}^{N-1} \alpha^k g[x_k, \mu(x_k), w_k] \right\}. \tag{5.4}$$

Similarly as for J^*, we have that J_μ is well defined as a real-valued function under Assumption D. *A statement that the stationary policy* $\{\mu^*, \mu^*, \ldots\}$

is optimal will mean throughout this chapter that $J^*(x) = J_{\mu^*}(x)$ *for all* $x \in S$.

The next section gives a characterization of the optimal cost function J^* and provides the basic results under Assumption D. Section 5.2 describes computational methods, assuming that the state, control, and disturbance spaces are finite sets. The results obtained in Sections 5.1 and 5.2 are interpreted by means of the notion of a contraction mapping in Section 5.3. In Section 5.4 we relax Assumption D and consider costs per stage that are unbounded above or below. Finally, in Section 5.5 we consider problems involving a nonstationary or periodic system and cost per stage. We show that such problems can be reformulated as problems involving a stationary system and cost per stage. Consequently, we are able to obtain in a simple manner results for nonstationary problems that are analogous to those for the stationary case.

5.1 BASIC RESULTS

Consider an N-stage problem obtained from the infinite horizon problem by truncation. This problem is to find a policy $\pi_N = \{\mu_0, \mu_1, \ldots, \mu_{N-1}\}$ with $\mu_k(x_k) \in U(x_k)$, for all $x_k \in S$ that minimizes

$$J_{\pi_N}(x_0) = \underset{\substack{w_k \\ k=0,1,\ldots,N-1}}{E} \left\{ \sum_{k=0}^{N-1} \alpha^k g[x_k, \mu_k(x_k), w_k] \right\} \tag{5.5}$$

subject to the system equation constraints. The optimal cost of this problem for each initial state x_0 is $V_0(x_0)$, where V_0 is given by the last step of the DP algorithm:

$$V_N(x) = 0, \qquad x \in S,$$

$$V_k(x) = \min_{u \in U(x)} \underset{w}{E}\{\alpha^k g(x, u, w) + V_{k+1}[f(x, u, w)]\},$$

$$x \in S, \quad k = 0, 1, \ldots, N-1.$$

Dividing both sides by α^k, and denoting

$$J_{N-k}(x) = \alpha^{-k} V_k(x), \qquad x \in S, \qquad k = 0, 1, \ldots, N,$$

these equations can be written as

$$J_0(x) = 0, \qquad x \in S \tag{5.6}$$

$$J_{k+1}(x) = \min_{u \in U(x)} \underset{w}{E}\{g(x, u, w) + \alpha J_k[f(x, u, w)]\},$$

$$x \in S, \qquad k = 0, 1, \ldots, N-1. \tag{5.7}$$

The optimal cost is $J_N(x_0)$.

The algorithm (5.6), (5.7) is equivalent to the ordinary DP algorithm. The main difference is that the indexing of the cost-to-go functions has been reversed so that now the algorithm proceeds from lower to higher values of the index k. We can interpret $J_k(x)$ as the minimal cost that can be obtained starting at state x and proceeding for k (rather than $N - k$) stages (i.e., it is the k-stage optimal cost). Since the number of stages is not fixed in an infinite horizon problem, working with J_k rather than V_k is convenient. For this reason, the form (5.6) and (5.7) of the DP algorithm will be adopted throughout the remainder of the text.

We want to develop relations between the N-stage problem with cost (5.5) and its infinite horizon counterpart, but before doing so we need to introduce some notation and preliminary facts.

For any functions $J: S \to R$, $\mu: S \to C$ with $\mu(x) \in U(x)$, for all $x \in S$, we denote:

$$T(J)(x) = \min_{u \in U(x)} \mathop{E}_{w}\{g(x, u, w) + \alpha J[f(x, u, w)]\}, \tag{5.8}$$

$$T_\mu(J)(x) = \mathop{E}_{w}\{g[x, \mu(x), w] + \alpha J[f(x, \mu(x), w)]\}. \tag{5.9}$$

(Whenever we write $T(J)(x)$ or $T_\mu(J)(x)$ we implicitly assume that the expected values are well defined.) Note that $T(J)(\cdot)$ and $T_\mu(J)(\cdot)$ are functions defined on the state space S, and T, T_μ may be viewed as mappings that transform a function J on S into another function $[T(J)$ or $T_\mu(J)]$ on S.

The mappings T and T_μ play an important theoretical role and provide a convenient shorthand notation in expressions that would be too complicated to write otherwise. For this reason the reader should gain a firm grasp of their meaning. From the definitions (5.8) and (5.9), it can be seen that *$T(J)(x)$ is the optimal cost for the one-stage problem with initial state x, stage cost g, and terminal cost function αJ*. Similarly, *$T_\mu(J)(x)$ is the cost corresponding to policy $\{\mu, \mu, \ldots\}$ for the same problem.*

We will denote by T^k the composition of the mapping T with itself k times; that is, for all x and k

$$T^k(J)(x) = T[T^{k-1}(J)](x), \qquad T^0(J)(x) = J(x).$$

Similarly, $T_\mu^k(J)$ is defined by

$$T_\mu^k(J)(x) = T_\mu[T_\mu^{k-1}(J)](x), \qquad T_\mu^0(J)(x) = J(x).$$

It is seen that *$T^k(J)(x)$ is the optimal cost for the k-stage, α-discounted problem with initial state x, cost per stage g, and terminal cost function $\alpha^k J$*. Similarly, *$T_\mu^k(J)(x)$ is the cost of a policy $\{\mu, \mu, \ldots\}$ for the same problem*. Note that in terms of this notation the DP algorithm (5.6), (5.7), which corresponds to a finite horizon problem with a zero terminal cost function, can be written

$$J_0(x) = 0, \tag{5.10}$$

$$J_k(x) = T^k(J_0)(x). \tag{5.11}$$

Finally, consider a k-stage policy for a k-stage problem $\{\mu_0, \mu_1, \ldots, \mu_{k-1}\}$. Then $(T_{\mu_0}T_{\mu_1} \ldots T_{\mu_{k-1}})(J)(x)$ is defined recursively for $i = 0, \ldots,$

$k - 2$ by

$$(T_{\mu_i} T_{\mu_{i+1}} \cdots T_{\mu_{k-1}})(J)(x) = T_{\mu_i}[(T_{\mu_{i+1}} \cdots T_{\mu_{k-1}})(J)](x)$$

and represents the cost of the policy for the k-stage, α-discounted problem with initial state x, cost per stage g, and terminal cost $\alpha^k J$.

The following monotonicity property plays a fundamental role in the developments of this chapter.

Lemma 1. For any functions $J:S \to R$, $J':S \to R$, such that

$$J(x) \leq J'(x), \qquad \text{for all } x \in S,$$

and for any function $\mu:S \to C$ with $\mu(x) \in U(x)$, for all $x \in S$, we have

$$T^k(J)(x) \leq T^k(J')(x), \qquad x \in S, \qquad k = 1, 2, \ldots,$$

$$T^k_\mu(J)(x) \leq T^k_\mu(J')(x), \qquad x \in S, \qquad k = 1, 2, \ldots .$$

Proof. The proof follows from the interpretations given previously of $T^k(J)(x)$ and $T^k_\mu(J)(x)$ as k-stage problem costs. (As the terminal cost function increases uniformly so will the k-stage costs.) Q.E.D.

For any two functions $J:S \to R$, $J':S \to R$, we write

$$J \leq J', \qquad \text{if } J(x) \leq J'(x) \text{ for all } x \in S.$$

With this notation, Lemma 1 is stated as

$$J \leq J' \Rightarrow T^k(J) \leq T^k(J'), \qquad k = 1, 2, \ldots,$$

$$J \leq J' \Rightarrow T^k_\mu(J) \leq T^k_\mu(J'), \qquad k = 1, 2, \ldots .$$

Denote also by $e:S \to R$ the unit function that takes the value 1 identically on S:

$$e(x) = 1, \qquad \text{for all } x \in S. \tag{5.12}$$

We have from (5.8) and (5.9) for any function $J:S \to R$ and any scalar r, and all $x \in S$,

$$T(J + re)(x) = T(J)(x) + \alpha r,$$

$$T_\mu(J + re)(x) = T_\mu(J)(x) + \alpha r.$$

More generally, by induction we can show the following lemma.

Lemma 2. For every k, function $J:S \to R$, stationary policy $\{\mu, \mu, \ldots\}$, and scalar r, we have

$$T^k(J + re)(x) = T^k(J)(x) + \alpha^k r, \qquad \text{for all } x \in S, \tag{5.13}$$

$$T^k_\mu(J + re)(x) = T^k_\mu(J)(x) + \alpha^k r, \qquad \text{for all } x \in S. \tag{5.14}$$

The following proposition shows that the DP algorithm (5.6) and (5.7) or (5.10) and (5.11) converges to the optimal cost function J^* for an *arbitrary* bounded starting function J. This will follow as a consequence of Assumption D, which implies that the "tail" of the cost $E\{\sum_{k=N}^{\infty} \alpha^k g(x_k, u_k, w_k)\}$ diminishes to zero as $N \to \infty$. Furthermore, even if a terminal cost $\alpha^N J(x_N)$ is added to the N-stage cost, its effect diminishes to zero as $N \to \infty$ when J is bounded.

Proposition 1: Convergence of the DP Algorithm. For any bounded function $J: S \to R$, there holds

$$J^*(x) = \lim_{k\to\infty} T^k(J)(x), \qquad \text{for all } x \in S. \tag{5.15}$$

Proof. From (5.3) we have, for any initial state $x \in S$ and every policy $\{\mu_0, \mu_1, \ldots\}$,

$$\lim_{N\to\infty} E\left\{\sum_{k=0}^{N-1} \alpha^k g[x_k, \mu_k(x_k), w_k]\right\} \leq E\left\{\sum_{k=0}^{N-1} \alpha^k g[x_k, \mu_k(x_k), w_k]\right\} + M \sum_{k=N}^{\infty} \alpha^k.$$

By taking minimum over $\{\mu_0, \mu_1, \ldots\}$ of both sides,

$$J^*(x) \leq J_N(x) + \left(\frac{\alpha^N}{1-\alpha}\right) M, \qquad \text{for all } x \in S, \quad N = 0, 1, \ldots, \tag{5.16}$$

where J_N is defined for all N by (5.6) and (5.7) [or (5.10) and (5.11)]. Also, since the cost per stage is nonnegative

$$J_N(x) \leq J^*(x), \qquad \text{for all } x \in S. \tag{5.17}$$

Combining the two inequalities, we obtain

$$J^*(x) = \lim_{N\to\infty} J_N(x), \qquad \text{for all } x \in S. \tag{5.18}$$

Now for an arbitrary bounded function $J: S \to R$, let r be a scalar such that

$$J_0 - re \leq J \leq J_0 + re, \tag{5.19}$$

where J_0 is the zero function. By applying T^k to this relation and using Lemma 2, we obtain

$$T^k(J_0) - \alpha^k re \leq T^k(J) \leq T^k(J_0) + \alpha^k re. \tag{5.20}$$

Since $T^k(J_0)$ converges to J^* [Eq. (5.18)] and $\alpha^k r$ converges to zero, the result follows. Q.E.D.

Given any stationary policy $\{\mu, \mu, \ldots\}$, we can consider a problem that is the same as Problem I except for the fact that the control constraint set contains only one element for each state x, the control $\mu(x)$, that is, a control constraint set of the form $\tilde{U}(x) = \{\mu(x)\}$, $x \in S$. Clearly, in this problem Assumption D is satisfied, and since there is only one admissible policy ($\{\mu, \mu, \ldots\}$), application of Proposition 1 yields the following corollary:

Corollary 1.1. Let $J_\mu(x)$ be the value of the cost functional (5.2) corresponding to a stationary policy $\{\mu, \mu, \ldots\}$ when the initial state is

x. Then for any bounded function $J: S \to R$ there holds

$$J_\mu(x) = \lim_{k\to\infty} T_\mu^k(J)(x), \qquad x \in S. \tag{5.21}$$

The next proposition shows that J^* is the unique solution of a functional equation. This equation, called *Bellman's equation*, provides the means for obtaining a stationary optimal policy.

Proposition 2: Bellman's Equation, Necessary and Sufficient Condition for Optimality (a) The optimal cost function J^* satisfies

$$J^*(x) = \min_{u\in U(x)} \underset{w}{E}\{g(x, u, w) + \alpha J^*[f(x, u, w)]\}, \qquad x \in S, \tag{5.22}$$

or equivalently

$$J^*(x) = T(J^*)(x), \qquad x \in S.$$

Furthermore, J^* is the unique bounded solution of this equation.

(b) A stationary policy $\{\mu^*, \mu^*, \ldots\}$ is optimal if and only if $\mu^*(x)$ attains the minimum in (5.22) for all $x \in S$; that is,

$$T(J^*)(x) = T_{\mu^*}(J^*)(x), \qquad x \in S.$$

Proof. (a) From (5.16) we have

$$J_k \leq J^* \leq J_k + \left(\frac{M\alpha^k}{1-\alpha}\right) e.$$

Applying the mapping T in this relation and using Lemma 2, we obtain

$$J_{k+1} \leq T(J^*) \leq J_{k+1} + \left(\frac{M\alpha^{k+1}}{1-\alpha}\right) e.$$

Since J_{k+1} converges to J^* (Proposition 1), we obtain $J^* = T(J^*)$ by taking the limit as $k \to \infty$ in the preceding relation.

To show uniqueness simply observe that if J is bounded and satisfies $J = T(J)$ then $J = \lim_{k\to\infty} T^k(J)$, so by Proposition 1 we have $J = J^*$.

(b) To show this part, let us state the following corollary, which follows from the part of Proposition 2 already proved by the same reasoning we used to obtain Corollary 1.1 from Proposition 1.

Corollary 2.1. Let $\{\mu, \mu, \ldots\}$ be a stationary policy. Then

$$J_\mu(x) = \underset{w}{E}\{g[x, \mu(x), w] + \alpha J_\mu[f(x, \mu(x), w)]\}, \qquad x \in S, \tag{5.23}$$

or equivalently

$$J_\mu(x) = T_\mu(J_\mu)(x), \qquad x \in S.$$

Furthermore, J_μ is the unique bounded solution of this equation.

Now if $\mu^*(x)$ minimizes the right side of (5.22) for each $x \in S$, then we have for all $x \in S$,

$$J^*(x) = \underset{w}{E}\{g[x, \mu^*(x), w] + \alpha J^*[f(x, \mu^*(x), w)]\}.$$

Hence, by the uniqueness part of the corollary, we must have $J^*(x) = J_{\mu^*}(x)$ for all $x \in S$, and it follows that $\{\mu^*, \mu^*, \ldots\}$ is optimal. Also, if $\{\mu^*, \mu^*, \ldots\}$ is optimal, then we have $J^* = J_{\mu^*}$, while from the corollary we obtain $J_{\mu^*} = T_{\mu^*}(J_{\mu^*})$. Hence $J^* = T_{\mu^*}(J^*)$, which implies that $\mu^*(x)$ attains the minimum in (5.22) for all $x \in S$. Q.E.D.

Note that Proposition 2 implies the existence of an optimal stationary policy when the minimum in the right side of (5.22) is attained for all $x \in S$. In particular, when $U(x)$ is finite for each $x \in S$, an optimal stationary policy is guaranteed to exist.

We finally show the following convergence rate estimate, which holds for any bounded function J:

$$\max_{x \in S}|T^k(J)(x) - J^*(x)| \leq \alpha^k \max_{x \in S}|J(x) - J^*(x)|, \qquad k = 0, 1, \ldots .$$

This relation is a special case of the following result:

Proposition 3. For any two bounded functions $J:S \to R$, $J':S \to R$, and for all $k = 0, 1, \ldots$, there holds

$$\max_{x \in S}|T^k(J)(x) - T^k(J')(x)| \leq \alpha^k \max_{x \in S}|J(x) - J'(x)|. \tag{5.24}$$

Proof. Denote

$$c = \max_{x \in S}|J(x) - J'(x)|.$$

Then we have

$$J - ce \leq J' \leq J + ce.$$

Applying T^k in this relation and using Lemma 2, we obtain

$$T^k(J) - \alpha^k ce \leq T^k(J') \leq T^k(J) + \alpha^k ce.$$

It follows that

$$|T(J)(x) - T(J')(x)| \leq \alpha^k c, \qquad x \in S,$$

which proves the result. Q.E.D.

As earlier, we have:

Corollary 3.1. For any two bounded functions $J:S \to R$, $J':S \to R$, and any stationary policy $\{\mu, \mu, \ldots\}$, we have

$$\max_{x \in S}|T_\mu^k(J)(x) - T_\mu^k(J')(x)| \leq \alpha^k \max_{x \in S}|J(x) - J'(x)|, \qquad k = 0, 1, \ldots.$$

The main conclusion from the propositions established so far is that the optimal cost function J^* is the unique bounded solution of Bellman's equation (5.22). This equation yields an optimal stationary policy provided the minimum in its right side is attained. Furthermore, the DP algorithm yields in the limit the function J^* starting from an arbitrary bounded function J, and the rate of convergence is at least as fast as the rate of a convergent geometric progression (Proposition 3). Thus the DP algorithm may be used for actual computation of at least an approximation to J^*. This computational method together with some additional methods will be examined in the next section. The remainder of this section is devoted to two examples.

Asset Selling Example

Consider the asset selling problem of Section 2.4. When the problem is viewed over an infinite horizon, it is essentially a discounted cost problem with discount factor $\alpha = 1/(1 + r)$ [cf. Eq. (2.65)]. If we assume that the offers x are bounded, then the analysis of the present section is applicable, and the optimal value function is the unique solution of Bellman's equation

$$J^*(x) = \max[x, (1 + r)^{-1} E\{J^*(w)\}].$$

The optimal policy is obtained from this equation and has the following form. If current offer $\geqslant (1 + r)^{-1} E\{J^*(w)\} = \overline{\alpha}$, sell; otherwise, do not sell. The critical number $\overline{\alpha} = (1 + r)^{-1} E\{J^*(w)\}$ is obtained as in Section 2.4.

Component Replacement Example

A certain component of a machine tool can be in any one of a continuum of states, which we represent by the interval $[0, 1]$. At the beginning of each period the component is inspected, its current state $x \in [0, 1]$ is determined, and a decision is made on whether or not to replace the component at a cost $R > 0$ by a new one at state $x = 0$. The expected cost of having the component at state x for a single period is $C(x)$, where $C(\cdot)$ is a nonnegative bounded and increasing function of x on $[0, 1]$. The conditional probability distribution $F(z|x)$ of the component being at a state less or equal to z at the end of the period, given that it was at state x at the beginning of the period, is known. Furthermore, for each nondecreasing function $J:[0, 1] \to R$, we have

$$\int_y^1 J(z)\, dF(z|x_1) \leqslant \int_y^1 J(z)\, dF(z|x_2), \qquad \text{for } 0 \leqslant x_1 \leqslant x_2 \leqslant 1.$$

This assumption implies that the component tends to turn worse gradually with use; that is, for each $y \in [0, 1]$ there is greater chance that the component will go to a final state in the interval $[y, 1]$ when at a worse initial state. Assuming a discount factor $\alpha \in (0, 1)$ and an infinite horizon, the problem is to determine the optimal replacement policy.

The problem clearly falls within the framework of this section, and the optimal cost function J^* is the unique bounded solution of Bellman's equation

$$J^*(x) = \min\left[R + C(0) + \alpha \int_0^1 J^*(z)\, dF(z|0),\ C(x) + \alpha \int_0^1 J^*(z)\, dF(z|x)\right].$$

An optimal replacement policy is given by

$$\text{Replace if} \quad R + C(0) + \alpha \int_0^1 J^*(z)\, dF(z|0) \le C(x) + \alpha \int_0^1 J^*(z)\, dF(z|x).$$

Do not replace otherwise.

Now consider the DP algorithm

$$J_0(x) = 0,$$
$$T(J_0)(x) = \min[R + C(0), C(x)],$$
$$T^k(J_0)(x) = \min\left[R + C(0) + \alpha \int_0^1 T^{k-1}(J_0)(z)\, dF(z|0),\right.$$
$$\left. C(x) + \alpha \int_0^1 T^{k-1}(J_0)(z)\, dF(z|x)\right], \qquad k = 1, 2, \ldots.$$

Since $C(x)$ is increasing in x, we have that $T(J_0)(x)$ is nondecreasing in x, and, in view of our assumption on the distributions $F(z|x)$, the same is true for $T^2(J_0)(x)$. Similarly, it is seen that, for all k, $T^k(J_0)(x)$ is nondecreasing in x and so is the limit

$$J^*(x) = \lim_{k\to\infty} T^k(J_0)(x).$$

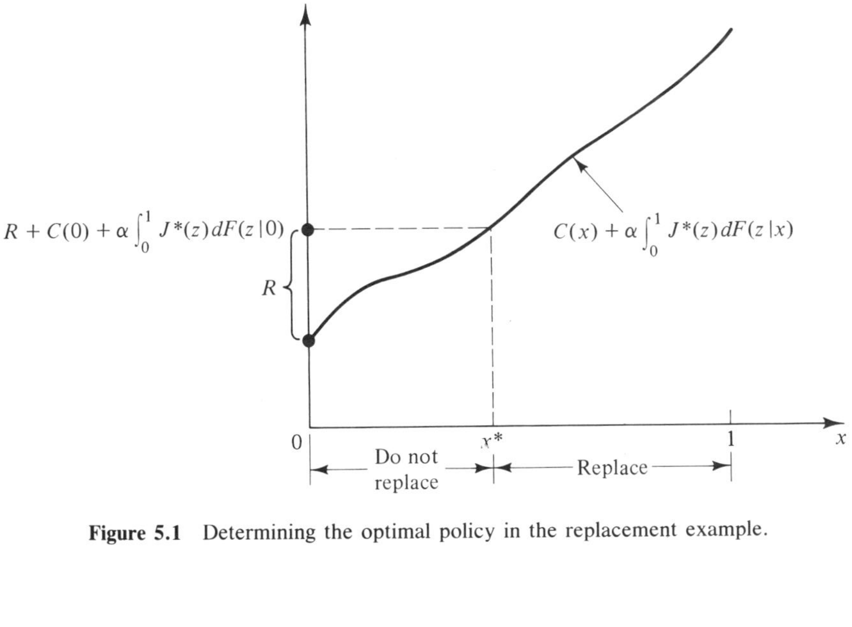

Figure 5.1 Determining the optimal policy in the replacement example.

It follows under our assumptions that the function $C(x) + \alpha \int_0^1 J^*(z)\, dF(z|x)$ is increasing in x. This is simply a reflection of the intuitively clear fact that the optimal cost cannot decrease as the initial state increases (i.e., we start at a worse initial state). Thus the optimal policy takes the form

$$\begin{aligned} &\text{Replace} && \text{if } x \geq x^* \\ &\text{Do not replace} && \text{if } x < x^*, \end{aligned}$$

where x^* is the scalar for which

$$R + C(0) + \alpha \int_0^1 J^*(z)\, dF(z|0) = C(x^*) + \alpha \int_0^1 J^*(z)\, dF(z|x^*),$$

as shown in Figure 5.1.

5.2 COMPUTATIONAL METHODS: SUCCESSIVE APPROXIMATION, POLICY ITERATION, ADAPTIVE AGGREGATION, LINEAR PROGRAMMING

This section presents alternative approaches for solving the infinite horizon problem (5.1) under Assumption D. The first approach, successive approximation, is essentially the DP algorithm and yields in the limit the optimal cost function and an optimal policy, as discussed in the previous section. We will describe some variations aimed at accelerating convergence. Two other approaches, policy iteration and linear programming, terminate in a finite number of iterations (assuming the spaces involved are finite sets). However, when the number of states is large, these approaches are impractical because of large overhead per iteration. Adaptive aggregation is a new approach [B20] that bridges the gap between successive approximation and policy iteration, and in a sense combines the best features of both methods.

Throughout this section we assume that Assumption D holds and that the spaces S, C, and D underlying the problem are finite sets. Thus we are dealing in effect with control of a finite state Markov chain.

Let S consist of n states denoted by $1, 2, \ldots, n$:

$$S = \{1, 2, \ldots, n\}.$$

Let us denote by $p_{ij}(u)$ the *transition probability*

$$p_{ij}(u) = P(x_{k+1} = j | x_k = i, u_k = u), \qquad i, j \in S, \quad u \in U(i).$$

Thus $p_{ij}(u)$ is the probability that the next state will be j given that the current state is i and control $u \in U(i)$ is applied. These transition probabilities may either be given a priori or calculated from the system equation

$$x_{k+1} = f(x_k, u_k, w_k)$$

and the known probability distribution $P(\cdot|x, u)$ of the input disturbance w_k. Indeed, we have

$$p_{ij}(u) = P[W_{ij}(u)|i, u],$$

where $W_{ij}(u)$ is the (finite) set

$$W_{ij}(u) = \{w \in D | f(i, u, w) = j\}.$$

To simplify notation when dealing with Markov chains, we assume that the cost per stage does not depend on w. This amounts to using expected cost per stage in all calculations, which makes no essential difference in either the definitions of the mappings T and T_μ of (5.8), (5.9), or the subsequent analysis. The basic expression

$$g(i, u) + \alpha E\{J[f(i, u, w)]\}$$

may be written in terms of $p_{ij}(u)$ as

$$g(i, u) + \alpha \sum_{j=1}^{n} p_{ij}(u) J(j), \qquad i \in S.$$

As a result, the mappings T and T_μ of (5.8) and (5.9) can be written

$$T(J)(i) = \min_{u \in U(i)} \left[g(i, u) + \alpha \sum_{j=1}^{n} p_{ij}(u) J(j) \right], \qquad i = 1, 2, \ldots, n,$$

$$T_\mu(J)(i) = g[i, \mu(i)] + \alpha \sum_{j=1}^{n} p_{ij}[\mu(i)] J(j), \qquad i = 1, 2, \ldots, n.$$

The functions J, $T_\mu(J)$ may be represented by the n-dimensional vectors

$$J = \begin{bmatrix} J(1) \\ \vdots \\ J(n) \end{bmatrix}, \qquad T_\mu(J) = \begin{bmatrix} T_\mu(J)(1) \\ \vdots \\ T_\mu(J)(n) \end{bmatrix}.$$

If we form the transition probability matrix

$$P_\mu = \begin{bmatrix} p_{11}[\mu(1)] & \ldots & p_{1n}[\mu(1)] \\ \vdots & & \vdots \\ p_{n1}[\mu(n)] & \ldots & p_{nn}[\mu(n)] \end{bmatrix},$$

and consider the n-dimensional vector g_μ defined by

$$g_\mu = \begin{bmatrix} g[1, \mu(1)] \\ \vdots \\ g[n, \mu(n)] \end{bmatrix},$$

then we can write in vector notation

$$T_\mu(J) = g_\mu + \alpha P_\mu J.$$

The cost function J_μ corresponding to a stationary policy $\{\mu, \mu, \ldots\}$ is, by Corollary 2.1, the unique solution of the equation

$$J_\mu = T_\mu(J_\mu) = g_\mu + \alpha P_\mu J_\mu. \tag{5.25}$$

This equation can also be written as

$$(I - \alpha P_\mu) J_\mu = g_\mu,$$

or equivalently

$$J_\mu = (I - \alpha P_\mu)^{-1} g_\mu,$$

where I denotes the $n \times n$ identity matrix. The invertibility of the matrix $I - \alpha P_\mu$ is assured since we have proved that the system of equations representing the equation $J_\mu = T_\mu(J_\mu)$ has a unique solution for any vector g_μ (cf. Corollary 2.1).

Successive Approximation and Error Bounds

Here we start with any n-dimensional vector J and successively compute $T(J), T^2(J), \ldots$, where the mapping T is defined by (5.8). By Proposition 1, we have

$$\lim_{k\to\infty} T^k(J)(i) = J^*(i), \qquad i \in S.$$

Furthermore, by Proposition 3, $|J^*(i) - T^k(J)(i)|$ is bounded by a multiple of a geometric progression for all $i \in S$. It is also of interest to note that the successive approximation method will yield an optimal policy after a finite number of iterations (see Problem 14). The method can be substantially improved thanks to the availability of certain error bounds, as we now proceed to explain.

As an aid in understanding the nature of these bounds, note that the cost of a stationary policy $\{\mu, \mu, \ldots\}$ is expressed as

$$J_\mu(i) = g[i, \mu(i)] + \sum_{k=1}^{\infty} \alpha^k E\{g[x_k, \mu(x_k)] | x_0 = i\}.$$

It follows that

$$g_\mu + \left(\frac{\alpha\beta}{1-\alpha}\right) e \le J_\mu \le g_\mu + \left(\frac{\alpha\overline{\beta}}{1-\alpha}\right) e, \tag{5.26}$$

where e is the unit vector, $e = [1, 1, \ldots, 1]'$, and β and $\overline{\beta}$ are the minimum and maximum cost per stage:

$$\beta = \min_i g_\mu[i, \mu(i)], \qquad \overline{\beta} = \max_i g_\mu[i, \mu(i)].$$

Using the definition of β and $\overline{\beta}$ we can strengthen (5.26) as follows

$$\begin{aligned}\left(\frac{\beta}{1-\alpha}\right) e \le g_\mu + \left(\frac{\alpha\beta}{1-\alpha}\right) e \le J_\mu \\ \le g_\mu + \left(\frac{\alpha\overline{\beta}}{1-\alpha}\right) e \le \left(\frac{\overline{\beta}}{1-\alpha}\right) e.\end{aligned} \tag{5.27}$$

These bounds will now be applied in the context of the successive approximation method. Suppose that we have a vector J and we compute

$$T_\mu(J) = g_\mu + \alpha P_\mu J.$$

By using this equation to eliminate g_μ from the equation

$$J_\mu = g_\mu + \alpha P_\mu J_\mu,$$

we obtain

$$J_\mu - J = T_\mu(J) - J + \alpha P_\mu(J_\mu - J),$$

which is a *variational* form of the equation $J_\mu = T_\mu(J_\mu)$. It follows from this equation that $J_\mu - J$ *is the cost vector associated with the policy* $\{\mu, \mu, \ldots\}$ *and a cost per stage vector equal to* $T_\mu(J) - J$. Therefore, the bounds (5.27) apply with J_μ replaced by $J_\mu - J$ and g_μ replaced by $T_\mu(J) - J$. It follows that

$$\left(\frac{\gamma}{1-\alpha}\right) e \leq T_\mu(J) - J + \left(\frac{\alpha\gamma}{1-\alpha}\right) e \leq J_\mu - J$$
$$\leq T_\mu(J) - J + \left(\frac{\alpha\overline{\gamma}}{1-\alpha}\right) e \leq \left(\frac{\overline{\gamma}}{1-\alpha}\right) e,$$

where

$$\gamma = \min_i [T_\mu(J)(i) - J(i)], \qquad \overline{\gamma} = \max_i [T_\mu(J)(i) - J(i)].$$

Equivalently, for every vector J, we have

$$J + \left(\frac{\gamma}{1-\alpha}\right) e \leq T_\mu(J) + \left(\frac{\alpha\gamma}{1-\alpha}\right) e \leq J_\mu$$
$$\leq T_\mu(J) + \left(\frac{\alpha\overline{\gamma}}{1-\alpha}\right) e \leq J + \left(\frac{\overline{\gamma}}{1-\alpha}\right) e.$$

The following proposition is obtained by a more sophisticated application of the preceding argument.

Proposition 4. For every vector J, state i, and k, we have

$$T^k(J)(i) + c_k \leq T^{k+1}(J)(i) + c_{k+1} \tag{5.28}$$
$$\leq J^*(i) \leq T^{k+1}(J)(i) + \overline{c}_{k+1} \leq T^k(J)(i) + \overline{c}_k,$$

where

$$c_k = \frac{\alpha}{1-\alpha} \min_{i \in S} [T^k(J)(i) - T^{k-1}(J)(i)], \tag{5.29}$$

$$\overline{c}_k = \frac{\alpha}{1-\alpha} \max_{i \in S} [T^k(J)(i) - T^{k-1}(J)(i)]. \tag{5.30}$$

Proof. Denote

$$\gamma = \min_{i \in S} [T(J)(i) - J(i)].$$

We have

$$J + \gamma e \leq T(J). \tag{5.31}$$

Applying T to both sides, using the monotonicity of T and (5.13),

$$T(J) + \alpha\gamma e \leq T^2(J), \tag{5.32}$$

and, because of (5.31),

$$J + (1 + \alpha)\gamma e \leq T(J) + \alpha\gamma e \leq T^2(J). \tag{5.33}$$

This process can be repeated, first applying T to obtain

$$T(J) + (\alpha + \alpha^2)\gamma e \leq T^2(J) + \alpha^2\gamma e \leq T^3(J), \tag{5.34}$$

and then using (5.31) to write

$$\begin{aligned} J + (1 + \alpha + \alpha^2)\gamma e &\leq T(J) + (\alpha + \alpha^2)\gamma e \\ &\leq T^2(J) + \alpha^2\gamma e \leq T^3(J). \end{aligned} \tag{5.35}$$

After k steps, this results in the inequalities

$$\begin{aligned} J + \left(\sum_{i=0}^{k} \alpha^i\right)\gamma e &\leq T(J) + \left(\sum_{i=1}^{k} \alpha^i\right)\gamma e \\ &\leq T^2(J) + \left(\sum_{i=2}^{k} \alpha^i\right)\gamma e \leq \cdots \leq T^{k+1}(J). \end{aligned}$$

Taking the limit as $k \to \infty$, we obtain

$$J + \left(\frac{c_1}{\alpha}\right)e \leq T(J) + c_1 e \leq T^2(J) + \alpha c_1 e \leq J^*, \tag{5.36}$$

where c_1 is defined by (5.29). Replacing J by $T^k(J)$ in this inequality, we have

$$T^{k+1}(J) + c_{k+1}e \leq J^*,$$

which is the second inequality in (5.28).

From (5.33), we have

$$\alpha\gamma \leq \min_{i \in S}[T^2(J)(i) - T(J)(i)],$$

and consequently

$$\alpha c_1 \leq c_2.$$

Using this in (5.36) yields

$$T(J) + c_1 e \leq T^2(J) + c_2 e,$$

and replacing J by $T^{k-1}(J)$, we have the first inequality in (5.28). An analogous argument shows the last two inequalities in (5.28). Q.E.D.

Notice that the error bounds (5.28) may be easily computed as a by-product of the computations in the successive approximation method. The following example demonstrates their nature.

Example

Consider a problem where there are two states and two controls

$$S = \{1, 2\}, \qquad C = \{u^1, u^2\}.$$

The transition probabilities corresponding to the controls u^1 and u^2 are as shown in Figure 5.2; that is, we have the transition probability matrices

$$P(u^1) = \begin{bmatrix} p_{11}(u^1) & p_{12}(u^1) \\ p_{21}(u^1) & p_{22}(u^1) \end{bmatrix} = \begin{bmatrix} \frac{3}{4} & \frac{1}{4} \\ \frac{3}{4} & \frac{1}{4} \end{bmatrix},$$

$$P(u^2) = \begin{bmatrix} p_{11}(u^2) & p_{12}(u^2) \\ p_{21}(u^2) & p_{22}(u^2) \end{bmatrix} = \begin{bmatrix} \frac{1}{4} & \frac{3}{4} \\ \frac{1}{4} & \frac{3}{4} \end{bmatrix}.$$

The transition costs are as follows:

$$g(1, u^1) = 2, \qquad g(1, u^2) = 0.5, \qquad g(2, u^1) = 1, \qquad g(2, u^2) = 3,$$

and the discount factor is $\alpha = 0.9$. The mapping T is given by

$$T(J)(i) = \min\left\{ g(i, u^1) + \alpha \sum_{j=1}^{2} p_{ij}(u^1)J(j), \right.$$
$$\left. g(i, u^2) + \alpha \sum_{j=1}^{2} p_{ij}(u^2)J(j) \right\}, \qquad i = 1, 2.$$

The scalars c_k and $\overline{c}_k$ of (5.29) and (5.30) are given by

$$c_k = \frac{\alpha}{1-\alpha} \min\{T^k(J)(1) - T^{k-1}(J)(1), T^k(J)(2) - T^{k-1}(J)(2)\},$$

$$\overline{c}_k = \frac{\alpha}{1-\alpha} \max\{T^k(J)(1) - T^{k-1}(J)(1), T^k(J)(2) - T^{k-1}(J)(2)\}.$$

The results of the successive approximation method starting with the zero function J_0 $[J_0(1) = J_0(2) = 0]$ are shown in Table 5.1 and illustrate the power and practicality of the error bounds.

In practice, one terminates the iterations of successive approximation when the difference $(\overline{c}_k - c_k)$ of the error bounds becomes sufficiently small. One can then take as final estimate of J^* the "median"

$$\tilde{J}_k = T^k(J) + \left(\frac{\overline{c}_k - c_k}{2}\right) e$$

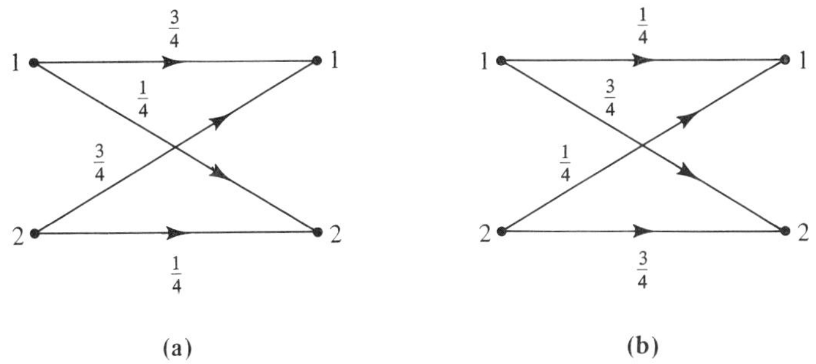

Figure 5.2 State transition diagram for Example 1: (a) $u = u^1$; (b) $u = u^2$.

TABLE 5.1 Performance of the Successive Approximation Method with and without the Error Bounds of Proposition 4

k	$T^k(J_0)(1)$	$T^k(J_0)(2)$	$T^k(J_0)(1) + c_k$	$T^k(J_0)(1) + \bar{c}_k$	$T^k(J_0)(2) + c_k$	$T^k(J_0)(2) + \bar{c}_k$
0	0.00000	0.00000				
1	0.50000	1.00000	5.00000	9.50000	5.50000	10.00000
2	1.28750	1.56250	6.35000	8.37500	6.62500	8.65000
3	1.84438	2.22063	6.85625	7.76750	7.23250	8.14375
4	2.41391	2.74459	7.12962	7.53969	7.46031	7.87038
5	2.89573	3.24692	7.23214	7.41667	7.58333	7.76786
6	3.34321	3.68517	7.28750	7.37054	7.62946	7.71250
7	3.73972	4.08583	7.30826	7.34563	7.65437	7.69174
8	4.09937	4.44362	7.31947	7.33628	7.66372	7.68053
9	4.42180	4.76689	7.32367	7.33124	7.66876	7.67633
10	4.71256	5.05727	7.32594	7.32935	7.67065	7.67406
11	4.97398	5.31886	7.32679	7.32833	7.67167	7.67321
12	5.20938	5.55418	7.32725	7.32794	7.67206	7.67275
13	5.42118	5.76602	7.32743	7.32774	7.67226	7.67257
14	5.61183	5.95665	7.32752	7.32766	7.67234	7.67248
15	5.78340	6.12823	7.32755	7.32762	7.67238	7.67245
16	5.93782	6.28265	7.32757	7.32760	7.67240	7.67243
17	6.07680	6.42163	7.32758	7.32759	7.67241	7.67242
18	6.20188	6.54670	7.32758	7.32759	7.67241	7.67242

or the "average"

$$\hat{J}_k = T^k(J) + \frac{\alpha}{n(1 - \alpha)} \sum_{i=1}^{n} [T^k(J)(i) - T^{k-1}(J)(i)]e.$$

Both of these vectors lie in the region delineated by the error bounds. If there is a unique optimal stationary policy $\{\mu^*, \mu^*, \ldots\}$, it can be shown [B20] that the rate at which $\hat{J}_k$ and $\tilde{J}_k$ approach the optimal cost vector J^* is governed by the *subdominant* eigenvalue of the transition probability matrix P_{μ^*}. More precisely, let $\lambda_1, \ldots, \lambda_n$ be the eigenvalues of P_{μ^*} ordered according to decreasing modulus; that is,

$$|\lambda_1| \geqslant |\lambda_2| \geqslant \cdots \geqslant |\lambda_n|,$$

with λ_1 equal to 1. Then λ_2 is the subdominant eigenvalue. The speed of convergence of $\hat{J}_k - J^*$ depends on how close $|\lambda_2|$ is to unity. If $|\lambda_2| \approx 1$ and $\alpha \approx 1$, then the rate of convergence is slow; essentially, $\hat{J}_k - J^*$ converges to zero like α^k. If $|\lambda_2| \approx 0$, the rate of convergence is fast. [The advanced reader will gain some understanding of the reason for this by first verifying the equation (for all J and μ^*)

$$T_{\mu^*}(J) - J_{\mu^*} = \alpha P_{\mu^*}(J - J_{\mu^*}),$$

and then assuming the existence of a set of linearly independent eigenvectors $e_1, e_2, \ldots, e_n$ corresponding to $\lambda_1, \lambda_2, \ldots, \lambda_n$ with $e_1 = e =$

$[1, 1, \ldots, 1]'$. Then we have

$$J - J_{\mu^*} = \xi_1 e + \sum_{j=2}^{n} \xi_j e_j$$

for some scalars $\xi_1, \xi_2, \ldots, \xi_n$, and the error of the successive approximation method can be written as

$$T_{\mu^*}^k(J) - J_{\mu^*} = \alpha^k \xi_1 e + \alpha^k \sum_{j=2}^{n} \lambda_j^k \xi_j e_j.$$

Using the error bounds of Proposition 4 amounts to a translation of $T_{\mu^*}^k(J)$ along the vector e. This can eliminate the component $\alpha^k \xi_1 e$ of the error, but cannot affect the remaining term $\alpha^k \sum_{j=2}^n \lambda_j^k \xi_j e_j$, which diminishes like $\alpha^k |\lambda_2|^k$ with λ_2 being the subdominant eigenvalue (see also [B20, M8], [M9], and Problem 26).

In the preceding example, it can be shown that $\mu^*(1) = u^2$, $\mu^*(2) = u^1$, and

$$P_{\mu^*} = \begin{bmatrix} \frac{1}{4} & \frac{3}{4} \\ \frac{3}{4} & \frac{1}{4} \end{bmatrix}.$$

The eigenvalues of P_{μ^*} are $\lambda_1 = 1$ and $\lambda_2 = -\frac{1}{2}$ and convergence is quite fast. On the other hand, there are situations where convergence of the method even with the use of error bounds is very slow. For example, suppose that P_{μ^*} is block diagonal with two or more blocks, or more generally corresponds to a system with more than one ergodic class (see Appendix D). Then it can be shown that the subdominant eigenvalue λ_2 is unity, and convergence is typically slow when α is near unity.

As an example, consider three simple deterministic problems with a single policy and more than one ergodic class:

Problem 1. $n = 3$, P_μ = three-dimensional identity, $g_\mu[i, \mu(i)] = i$.

Problem 2. $n = 5$, P_μ = five-dimensional identity, $g_\mu[i, \mu(i)] = i$.

Problem 3. $n = 6$, $g_\mu[i, \mu(i)] = i$ and

$$P_\mu = \begin{bmatrix} 1 & 0 & 0 & 0 & 0 & 0 \\ 0 & 0 & 1 & 0 & 0 & 0 \\ 0 & 1 & 0 & 0 & 0 & 0 \\ 0 & 0 & 0 & 0 & 1 & 0 \\ 0 & 0 & 0 & 0 & 0 & 1 \\ 0 & 0 & 0 & 1 & 0 & 0 \end{bmatrix}.$$

Table 5.2 shows the number of iterations needed by the successive approximation method with and without the error bounds of Proposition 4 to find J_μ within a maximum coordinatewise error of $10^{-6} \max_i |J_\mu(i)|$. The starting function in all cases was taken to be zero. The performance is

TABLE 5.2 Number of Iterations for Successive Approximation Method with and without Error Bounds. The Problems Are Deterministic. Because the Subdominant Eigenvalue of the Transition Matrix Is Unity, the Error Bounds Are Ineffective.

	Problem 1		Problem 2		Problem 3	
	$\alpha = 0.9$	$\alpha = 0.99$	$\alpha = 0.9$	$\alpha = 0.99$	$\alpha = 0.9$	$\alpha = 0.99$
Without error bounds	131	1374	131	1374	132	1392
With error bounds	127	1333	129	1352	131	1374

rather unsatisfactory but, nonetheless, is typical of situations where the subdominant eigenvalue modulus of the optimal transition probability matrix is near unity.

Gauss–Seidel Version of Successive Approximation

In the successive approximation method described earlier, the approximate cost function is iterated on for all states simultaneously. An alternative is to iterate one state at a time, while incorporating into the computation the interim results. This corresponds to using the Gauss–Seidel method for solving the nonlinear system of equations $J = T(J)$ (see [O4]).

For n-dimensional vectors J, define the mapping F by

$$F(J)(1) = \min_{u \in U(i)} [g(i, u) + \alpha \sum_{j=1}^{n} p_{ij}(u)J(j)] \tag{5.37}$$

and, for $i = 2, \ldots, n$,

$$F(J)(i) = \min_{u \in U(i)} \left[g(i, u) + \alpha \sum_{j=1}^{i-1} p_{ij}(u)F(J)(j) + \alpha \sum_{j=i}^{n} p_{ij}(u)J(j) \right]. \tag{5.38}$$

In words, $F(J)(i)$ is computed by the same equation as $T(J)(i)$ except that the previously calculated values $F(J)(1), \ldots, F(J)(i-1)$ are used in place of $J(1), \ldots, J(i-1)$. Evidently the computation of $F(J)$ is as easy as the computation of $T(J)$, unless a parallel computer is used.

Consider now the successive approximation method whereby we compute $J, F(J), F^2(J), \ldots$. The following propositions show that the method is valid and provide an indication of better performance over the earlier successive approximation method.

Proposition 5. Let J, J' be two n-dimensional vectors. Then for any $k = 0, 1, \ldots,$

$$\max_{i \in S} |F^k(J)(i) - F^k(J')(i)| \leq \alpha^k \max_{i \in S} |J(i) - J'(i)|. \tag{5.39}$$

Furthermore, we have

$$F(J^*)(i) = J^*(i), \qquad i \in S, \tag{5.40}$$

$$\lim_{k\to\infty} F^k(J)(i) = J^*(i), \qquad i \in S. \tag{5.41}$$

Proof. It is sufficient to prove (5.39) for $k = 1$. We have by the definition of F and Proposition 3,

$$|F(J)(1) - F(J')(1)| \le \alpha \max_{i\in S}|J(i) - J'(i)|.$$

Also, using this inequality,

$$\begin{aligned}|F(J)(2) - F(J')(2)| &\le \alpha \max\{|F(J)(1) - F(J')(1)|,\\ &\qquad |J(2) - J'(2)|, \ldots, |J(n) - J'(n)|\}\\ &\le \alpha \max_{i\in S}|J(i) - J'(i)|.\end{aligned}$$

Proceeding similarly, we have, for every i and $j \le i$,

$$|F(J)(j) - F(J')(j)| \le \alpha \max_{i\in S}|J(i) - J'(i)|,$$

so (5.39) is obtained for $k = 1$. Relation (5.40) follows from definition (5.37) to (5.38) and the fact that $J^* = T(J^*)$. Relation (5.41) follows from (5.39) and (5.40). Q.E.D.

Proposition 6. If a vector J satisfies

$$J(i) \le T(J)(i) \le J^*(i), \qquad i \in S,$$

then

$$T^k(J)(i) \le F^k(J)(i) \le J^*(i), \qquad i \in S, \quad k = 1, 2, \ldots. \tag{5.42}$$

Proof. The proof is immediate by using definition (5.37) to (5.38) and the monotonicity property of T. Q.E.D.

The preceding proposition provides the main motivation for employing the mapping F in place of T in the successive approximation method. A similar result may be proved for n-dimensional vectors J satisfying $J^* \le T(J) \le J$. The faster convergence of the Gauss–Seidel version over the ordinary successive approximation method has been confirmed in practice through extensive experimentation. This comparison is somewhat misleading, however, because the ordinary method will normally be used in conjunction with the error bounds of Proposition 4. One may also employ error bounds in the Gauss–Seidel version (see Problem 3). However, there is no clear superiority of one method over the other when bounds are introduced. Furthermore, the ordinary method is better suited for parallel computation than the Gauss–Seidel version.

Elimination of Nonoptimal Actions in Successive Approximation

We know from Proposition 2 that, if $\tilde{u} \in U(i)$ is such that

$$g(i, \tilde{u}) + \alpha \sum_{j=1}^{n} p_{ij}(\tilde{u})J^*(j) > J^*(i), \tag{5.43}$$

then $\tilde{u}$ cannot be optimal at state i; that is, for every optimal stationary policy $\{\mu^*, \mu^*, \ldots\}$, we have $\mu^*(i) \neq \tilde{u}$. Therefore, if we could be sure that (5.43) holds, we could safely eliminate $\tilde{u}$ from the admissible set $U(i)$. While we cannot check (5.43) directly since we do not know the optimal cost function J^*, we can guarantee that it holds if

$$g(i, \tilde{u}) + \alpha \sum_{j=1}^{n} p_{ij}(\tilde{u})\underline{J}(j) > \overline{J}(i), \tag{5.44}$$

where $\overline{J}$ and $\underline{J}$ are upper and lower bounds satisfying

$$\underline{J}(i) \leq J^*(i) \leq \overline{J}(i), \qquad i \in S.$$

The preceding observation is the basis for a useful application of the error bounds given earlier in this section. As these bounds are computed in the course of the successive approximation method, the inequality (5.44) can be simultaneously checked and nonoptimal actions can be eliminated from the admissible set with considerable savings in subsequent computations. Since the upper and lower bound functions $\overline{J}$ and $\underline{J}$ converge to J^*, it is easily seen [taking into account the finiteness of the constraint set $U(i)$] that eventually all nonoptimal $\tilde{u} \in U(i)$ will be eliminated, thereby reducing after a finite number of iterations the set $U(i)$ to the set of controls that are optimal at i. In this manner the computational requirements of successive approximation can be substantially reduced. However, the amount of computer memory required to maintain the set of controls not as yet eliminated at each $i \in S$ may be increased.

Policy Iteration

The policy iteration algorithm operates as follows. An initial stationary policy $\pi^0 = \{\mu^0, \mu^0, \ldots\}$ is adopted, and the corresponding cost function $J_{\mu^0} = J_{\pi^0}$ is calculated. Then an improved policy $\pi^1 = \{\mu^1, \mu^1, \ldots\}$ is computed by minimization in the DP equation corresponding to J_{μ^0} and the process is repeated.

The algorithm is based on the following proposition.

Proposition 7. Let $\pi = \{\mu, \mu, \ldots\}$ and $\overline{\pi} = \{\overline{\mu}, \overline{\mu}, \ldots\}$ be stationary policies such that

$$g[i, \overline{\mu}(i)] + \alpha \sum_{j=1}^{n} p_{ij}[\overline{\mu}(i)]J_{\mu}(j) = \min_{u \in U(i)} [g(i, u) + \alpha \sum_{j-1}^{n} p_{ij}(u)J_{\mu}(j)], \tag{5.45}$$

or equivalently

$$T_{\overline{\mu}}(J_\mu) = T(J_\mu).$$

Then we have

$$J_{\overline{\mu}}(i) \leq J_\mu(i), \qquad i \in S. \tag{5.46}$$

Furthermore, if π is not optimal, strict inequality holds in (5.46) for at least one state $i \in S$.

Proof. From Corollary 2.1 and (5.45), we have for every $i \in S$,

$$\begin{aligned} J_\mu(i) &= g[i, \mu(i)] + \alpha \sum_{j=1}^{n} p_{ij}[\mu(i)] J_\mu(j) \\ &\geq g[i, \overline{\mu}(i)] + \alpha \sum_{j=1}^{n} p_{ij}[\overline{\mu}(i)] J_\mu(j) \\ &= T_{\overline{\mu}}(J_\mu)(i). \end{aligned}$$

Applying repeatedly $T_{\overline{\mu}}$ on both sides of this inequality and using the monotonicity of $T_{\overline{\mu}}$ and Corollary 1.1, we obtain

$$J_\mu \geq T_{\overline{\mu}}(J_\mu) \geq \cdots \geq T^k_{\overline{\mu}}(J_\mu) \geq \cdots \geq \lim_{k\to\infty} T^k_{\overline{\mu}}(J_\mu) = J_{\overline{\mu}},$$

proving (5.46). If $J_\mu = J_{\overline{\mu}}$, then from the preceding relation $J_\mu = T_{\overline{\mu}}(J_\mu)$ and from (5.45) we have $T_{\overline{\mu}}(J_\mu) = T(J_\mu)$, so that $J_\mu = T(J_\mu)$ and hence $J_\mu = J^*$ by Proposition 2. Thus $\pi = \{\mu, \mu, \ldots\}$ must be optimal. It follows that strict inequality holds in (5.46) for some $i \in S$ if π is not optimal. Q.E.D.

Policy Iteration Algorithm

Step 1 (*Initialization*) Guess an initial stationary policy

$$\pi^0 = \{\mu^0, \mu^0, \ldots\}.$$

Step 2 (*Policy Evaluation*) Given the stationary policy

$$\pi^k = \{\mu^k, \mu^k, \ldots\},$$

compute the corresponding cost function J_{μ_k} from the linear system of equations

$$(I - \alpha P_{\mu^k}) J_{\mu^k} = g_{\mu^k}.$$

Step 3 (*Policy Improvement*) Obtain a new stationary policy $\pi^{k+1} = \{\mu^{k+1}, \mu^{k+1}, \ldots\}$ satisfying for all $i \in S$

$$g[i, \mu^{k+1}(i)] + \alpha \sum_{j=1}^{n} p_{ij}[\mu^{k+1}(i)] J_{\mu^k}(j) = \min_{u \in U(i)} [g(i, u) + \alpha \sum_{j=1}^{n} p_{ij}(u) J_{\mu^k}(j)]$$

or equivalently

$$T_{\mu^{k+1}}(J_{\mu^k}) = T(J_{\mu^k}).$$

If $J_{\mu^k} = T(J_{\mu^k})$ stop; else return to step 2 and repeat the process.

Since the collection of all stationary policies is finite (by the finiteness of S and C) and an improved policy is generated at every iteration, it follows that the algorithm will find an optimal stationary policy in a finite number of iterations and thereby terminate. This property of the policy iteration algorithm is its main advantage over successive approximation, which in general converges in an infinite number of iterations. On the other hand, finding the exact value of J_{μ^k} in step 2 of the algorithm requires solution of the system of linear equations representing $J_{\mu^k} = T_{\mu^k}(J_{\mu^k})$. The dimension of this system is equal to the number of states, and thus when this number is very large the method is not attractive.

We demonstrate the algorithm by means of the example considered earlier in this section.

Example (continued)

Step 1 Let us select an initial policy $\pi^0 = \{\mu^0, \mu^0, \ldots\}$, where

$$\mu^0(1) = u^1, \qquad \mu^0(2) = u^2.$$

Step 2 We obtain J_{μ^0} through the equation $J_{\mu^0} = T_{\mu^0}(J_{\mu^0})$ or equivalently

$$J_{\mu^0}(1) = g(1, u^1) + \alpha p_{11}(u^1)J_{\mu^0}(1) + \alpha p_{12}(u^1)J_{\mu^0}(2),$$

$$J_{\mu^0}(2) = g(2, u^2) + \alpha p_{21}(u^2)J_{\mu^0}(1) + \alpha p_{22}(u^2)J_{\mu^0}(2).$$

Substituting the data of the problem,

$$J_{\mu^0}(1) = 2 + 0.9 \times \tfrac{3}{4} \times J_{\mu^0}(1) + 0.9 \times \tfrac{1}{4} \times J_{\mu^0}(2),$$

$$J_{\mu^0}(2) = 3 + 0.9 \times \tfrac{1}{4} \times J_{\mu^0}(1) + 0.9 \times \tfrac{3}{4} \times J_{\mu^0}(2).$$

Solving this system of linear equations for $J_{\mu^0}(1)$ and $J_{\mu^0}(2)$, we obtain

$$J_{\mu^0}(1) \simeq 24.12, \qquad J_{\mu^0}(2) \simeq 25.96.$$

Step 3 We now find $\mu^1(1)$ and $\mu^1(2)$ satisfying $T_{\mu^1}(J_{\mu^0}) = T(J_{\mu^0})$. We have

$$\begin{aligned} T(J_{\mu^0})(1) &= \min\{2 + 0.9(\tfrac{3}{4} \times 24.12 + \tfrac{1}{4} \times 25.96), \\ &\qquad 0.5 + 0.9(\tfrac{1}{4} \times 24.12 + \tfrac{3}{4} \times 25.96)\} \\ &= \min\{24.12, 23.45\} = 23.45, \\ T(J_{\mu^0})(2) &= \min\{1 + 0.9(\tfrac{3}{4} \times 24.12 + \tfrac{1}{4} \times 25.96), \\ &\qquad 3 + 0.9(\tfrac{1}{4} \times 24.12 + \tfrac{3}{4} \times 25.96)\} \\ &= \min\{23.12, 25.95\} = 23.12. \end{aligned}$$

The minimizing controls are

$$\mu^1(1) = u^2, \qquad \mu^1(2) = u^1.$$

Step 2 We obtain J_{μ^1} through the equation $J_{\mu^1} = T_{\mu^1}(J_{\mu^1})$:

$$J_{\mu^1}(1) = g(1, u^2) + \alpha p_{11}(u^2)J_{\mu^1}(1) + \alpha p_{12}(u^2)J_{\mu^1}(2),$$

$$J_{\mu^1}(2) = g(2, u^1) + \alpha p_{21}(u^1)J_{\mu^1}(1) + \alpha p_{22}(u^1)J_{\mu^1}(2).$$

Substitution of the data of the problem and solution of the system of equations yields

$$J_{\mu^1}(1) \simeq 7.33, \qquad J_{\mu^1}(2) \simeq 7.67.$$

Step 3 We perform the minimization required to find $T(J_{\mu^1})$:

$$\begin{aligned} T(J_{\mu^1})(1) &= \min\{2 + 0.9(\tfrac{3}{4} \times 7.33 + \tfrac{1}{4} \times 7.67), \\ &\qquad 0.5 + 0.9(\tfrac{1}{4} \times 7.33 + \tfrac{3}{4} \times 7.67)\} \\ &= \min\{8.67, 7.33\} = 7.33, \\ T(J_{\mu^1})(2) &= \min\{1 + 0.9(\tfrac{3}{4} \times 7.33 + \tfrac{1}{4} \times 7.67), \\ &\qquad 3 + 0.9(\tfrac{1}{4} \times 7.33 + \tfrac{3}{4} \times 7.67)\} \\ &= \min\{7.67, 9.83\} = 7.67. \end{aligned}$$

Hence we have $J_{\mu^1} = T(J_{\mu^1})$, which implies that $\{\mu^1, \mu^1, \ldots\}$ is optimal and $J_{\mu^1} = J^*$:

$$\mu^*(1) = u^2, \quad \mu^*(2) = u^1, \qquad J^*(1) \simeq 7.33, \quad J^*(2) \simeq 7.67.$$

Approximate Policy Iteration and Adaptive State Aggregation

We remarked earlier that, when the number of states is large, the policy evaluation step of the policy iteration algorithm is time consuming and detracts from the practicality of the method. One way to get around this difficulty is to carry out policy evaluation approximately by finding for each k an *approximate* solution $\tilde{J}_{\mu^k}$ of the system

$$J_{\mu^k} = g_{\mu^k} + \alpha P_{\mu^k} J_{\mu^k}.$$

A natural way to do this is to carry out several successive approximation steps aimed at solving the preceding system. Here we enter the kth policy evaluation step with the result $T_{\mu^k}(\tilde{J}_{\mu^{k-1}}) = T(\tilde{J}_{\mu^{k-1}})$ of the policy improvement step, and approximate J_{μ^k} by

$$\tilde{J}_{\mu^k} = T^m_{\mu^k}(\tilde{J}_{\mu^{k-1}}),$$

where m is some positive integer. Error bounds such as the ones of Proposition 4 can be used to refine this process. Taking $m = 1$ corresponds to a successive approximation method where the policy evaluation step is skipped altogether, while taking $m = \infty$ corresponds to policy iteration whereby the policy evaluation step is performed iteratively via the successive approximation method. Analysis and computational experience ([P18], [P19]) suggest that it is usually best to take m an integer that is greater than unity and is determined by trial and error. A key idea here is that a successive approximation step involving a single policy [evaluating $T_\mu(J)$ for some μ and J] is much less expensive than a step involving all policies [evaluating $T(J)$ for some J], when the number of controls available at each state is large. Note that Gauss–Seidel steps can be used in place of the usual successive approximation steps, and this results typically in more efficient computation.

It is not essential to use successive approximation to solve approximately the system

$$J_\mu = T_\mu(J_\mu).$$

Another possibility is to solve instead a system of smaller dimension obtained by lumping together the states of the original system into a smaller set of aggregate states. More specifically, for a fixed stationary policy $\{\mu, \mu, \ldots\}$, we partition the state space S into m disjoint subsets $S_1, S_2, \ldots, S_m$,

$$S = S_1 \cup S_2 \cup \cdots \cup S_m,$$

called *aggregate states*. Suppose that we have an estimate J of J_μ and that *we postulate that over the states s of every aggregate state S_i the variation $J_\mu(s) - J(s)$ is constant*. This amounts to hypothesizing that for some m-dimensional vector y we have

$$J_\mu - J = Wy,$$

where the ith column of the $n \times m$ matrix W has unit entries at coordinates corresponding to states in S_i and all other entries equal to zero. From the equations $T_\mu(J) = g_\mu + \alpha P_\mu J$ and $J_\mu = g_\mu + \alpha P_\mu J_\mu$, we have

$$(I - \alpha P_\mu)(J_\mu - J) = T_\mu(J) - J.$$

This is the variational form of the equation $J_\mu = T_\mu(J_\mu)$ discussed earlier and can be used equally well for evaluating J_μ. Let us multiply both sides with the transpose W' and use the equation $J_\mu - J = Wy$. We obtain

$$W'(I - \alpha P_\mu)Wy = W'(T_\mu(J) - J),$$

and this equation can be solved for y, giving

$$y = [W'(I - \alpha P_\mu)W]^{-1}W'(T_\mu(J) - J).$$

Therefore, by substitution in the equation $J_\mu - J = Wy$, we have

$$J_\mu = J + W[W'(I - \alpha P_\mu)W]^{-1}W'(T_\mu(J) - J),$$

and, by applying T_μ to both sides,

$$J_\mu = T_\mu(J_\mu) = T_\mu(J) + \alpha P_\mu W[W'(I - \alpha P_\mu)W]^{-1}W'(T_\mu(J) - J).$$

We can conclude therefore that, if the variation of $J_\mu(s) - J(s)$ is roughly constant over each aggregate state, then a good approximation for J_μ is given by

$$J_\mu \simeq T_\mu(J) + \alpha P_\mu W[W'(I - \alpha P_\mu)W]^{-1}W'(T_\mu(J) - J).$$

To obtain this approximation, given J, we need to:

1. Compute $T_\mu(J)$.
2. Delineate the aggregate states (i.e., define W).
3. Solve for the vector y in the system

$$W'(I - \alpha P_\mu)Wy = W'(T_\mu(J) - J) \tag{5.47}$$

and approximate J_μ using

$$J_\mu \simeq T_\mu(J) + \alpha P_\mu Wy.$$

A key point is that the dimension of (5.47) is m (the number of aggregate states), which can be much smaller than n (the dimension of the system $J_\mu = T_\mu(J_\mu)$ arising in the policy evaluation phase of policy iteration). In fact, a small value of m, say 3 to 6, is often very effective (see [B20]).

Note that it is possible to use more than one successive aggregation step to approximate the policy evaluation step of the policy iteration algorithm. Furthermore, experimentation and analysis [B20] show that the most effective way to operate the method is to precede and follow each aggregation step with several successive approximation steps; that is, applications of the mapping T_μ on the current iterate. The number of successive approximation steps following an aggregation step is either fixed or is based on algorithmic progress; that is, an aggregation step is performed when the progress of the successive approximation steps becomes relatively small.

There is no proof of convergence of the scheme just described. On the basis of computational experimentation, it appears reliable in practice. Its convergence nonetheless can be guaranteed by introducing a feature whereby the error bounds of Proposition 4 are calculated at the successive approximation step (step 1), and a requirement is imposed that the subsequent aggregation step is skipped if these error bounds do not improve by a certain factor over the bounds computed prior to the preceding aggregation step.

The system (5.47) has an interesting interpretation. Suppose we multiply both sides with the diagonal matrix

$$N = \begin{bmatrix} n_1^{-1} & & & & 0 \\ & n_2^{-1} & & & \\ & & \cdot & & \\ & & & \cdot & \\ 0 & & & & n_m^{-1} \end{bmatrix},$$

where n_i is the number of states in the aggregate state S_i. Then a straightforward calculation shows that the system (5.47) takes the form

$$(I - \alpha\overline{P})y = r,$$

where $\overline{P}$ is a transition probability $m \times m$ matrix for the aggregate Markov chain with elements

$$\overline{p}_{ij} = \frac{1}{n_i} \sum_{s \in S_i} \sum_{t \in S_j} p_{st}(\mu), \qquad i, j, = 1, \ldots, m,$$

and r is the vector having as ith coordinate the average value of $T_\mu(J) - J$ over the ith aggregate state

$$r_i = \frac{1}{n_i} \sum_{j \in S_i} [T_\mu(J)(j) - J(j)],$$

(see Figure 5.3). Thus we can *view solution of system (5.47) as a policy evaluation step for the aggregate Markov chain, and for cost per stage for each aggregate state i equal to r_i – the average $T_\mu(J) - J$ over that state.*

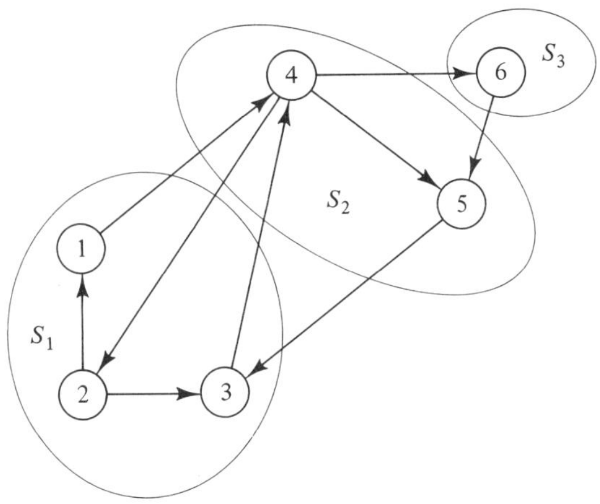

Figure 5.3 Interpretation of the adaptive aggregation method. In this example the aggregate states are $S_1 = \{1, 2, 3\}$, $S_2 = \{4, 5\}$, and $S_3 = \{6\}$. The aggregate Markov chain has transition probabilities $\overline{p}_{11} = \frac{1}{3}(p_{21} + p_{23})$, $\overline{p}_{12} = \frac{1}{3}(p_{14} + p_{34})$, $\overline{p}_{13} = 0$, $\overline{p}_{21} = \frac{1}{2}(p_{42} + p_{53})$, $\overline{p}_{22} = \frac{1}{2}p_{45}$, $\overline{p}_{23} = \frac{1}{2}p_{46}$, $\overline{p}_{31} = 0$, $\overline{p}_{32} = p_{56}$, and $\overline{p}_{33} = 0$. An aggregation step can be interpreted as a policy evaluation step involving the aggregate Markov chain.

The key issue is how to identify the aggregate states $S_1, \ldots, S_m$ in a way that the error $J_\mu - J$ is of similar magnitude on each one. One way to resolve this is to group states according to magnitude of the differences $T_\mu(J)(i) - J(i)$. By this we mean that for each state i, we set $i \in S_1$ if $T_\mu(J)(i) - J(i) = c$, and

$$i \in S_k \qquad \text{if} \qquad T_\mu(J)(i) - J(i) - c - (k-1)\Delta \in (0, \Delta],$$

where

$$c = \min_i [T_\mu(J)(i) - J(i)], \quad \overline{c} = \max_i [T_\mu(J)(i) - J(i)], \quad \Delta = \frac{\overline{c} - c}{m}.$$

This choice is based on the conjecture that, at least near convergence, $T_\mu(J)(i) - J(i)$ will be of comparable magnitude for states i for which $J_\mu(i) - J(i)$ is of comparable magnitude. This is certainly true if P is the identity matrix, but it turns out to be true also in other situations exemplified by the case when the Markov chain has more than one ergodic class, which is precisely the type of problem where the successive approximation method converges slowly. We refer to [B20] for detailed analysis and computational results. In particular, for problems involving several ergodic classes it is important to carry out several (pure) successive approximation steps before carrying out a single aggregation step. This has the effect of making both $J_\mu(i) - J(i)$ and $T_\mu(J)(i) - J(i)$ of comparable magnitude within each ergodic class prior to the aggregation step.

It is worth noting that the aggregate states can change from one iteration to the next, and this is our reason for characterizing the aggregation scheme as adaptive. Furthermore, the criterion used to delineate the aggregate states does not exploit any special problem structure. In some cases it is possible to take advantage of existing special structure and modify accordingly the method used to form the aggregate states.

To illustrate the effectiveness of the adaptive aggregation method, consider the three deterministic problems described earlier (cf. Table 5.2), and the performance of the method with two, three, and four aggregate states, starting from the zero function. The results given in Table 5.3 should be compared with those of Table 5.2.

It is intuitively clear that the performance of the aggregation method should improve as the number of aggregate states increases, and indeed the computational results bear this out. The two extreme cases where $m = n$ and $m = 1$ are of interest. When $m = n$, each aggregate state has a single state and we obtain the policy iteration algorithm. When $m = 1$, there is only one aggregate state; we have

$$W = \begin{bmatrix} 1 \\ 1 \\ \vdots \\ 1 \end{bmatrix},$$

and a straightforward calculation shows that equation (5.47) yields

$$y = \frac{1}{n(1 - \alpha)} \sum_{i=1}^{n} [T_\mu(J)(i) - J(i)].$$

From this equation we obtain the approximation

$$J_\mu \simeq T_\mu(J) + W \frac{\alpha}{n(1 - \alpha)} \sum_{i=1}^{n} [T_\mu(J)(i) - J(i)],$$

which amounts to shifting the result $T_\mu(J)$ of successive approximation to a vector that lies somewhere in the middle of the error bound range given by Proposition 4. Thus we may view the aggregation scheme as a continuum of algorithms with policy iteration and successive approximation (coupled with the error bounds of Proposition 4) included as the two extreme special cases.

TABLE 5.3 Number of Iterations of Adaptive Aggregation Methods with Two, Three, and Four Aggregate States to Solve the Problems of Table 5.2

Number of Aggregate States	Problem 1		Problem 2		Problem 3	
	$\alpha = 0.9$	$\alpha = 0.99$	$\alpha = 0.9$	$\alpha = 0.99$	$\alpha = 0.9$	$\alpha = 0.99$
2	14	13	9	9	83	505
3	1	1	3	3	64	367
4	—	—	3	3	26	354

Linear Programming

As discussed earlier, we have

$$J \leq T(J) \Rightarrow J \leq J^* = T(J^*).$$

Thus it is clear that $J^*(1), \ldots, J^*(n)$ solve the following maximization problem (in $\lambda_1, \ldots, \lambda_n$):

$$\max \sum_{i=1}^{n} \lambda_i$$

subject to

$$\lambda_i \leq T(J_\lambda)(i), \qquad i = 1, \ldots, n,$$

where the function $J_\lambda : S \to R$ is defined by

$$J_\lambda(i) = \lambda_i, \qquad i = 1, \ldots, n.$$

The problem is written

$$\max \sum_{i=1}^{n} \lambda_i$$

subject to

$$\lambda_i \leq g(i, u) + \alpha \sum_{j=1}^{n} p_{ij}(u)\lambda_j, \qquad i = 1, \ldots, n, \quad u \in U(i).$$

This is a linear program with n variables and as many as $n \times m$ constraints, where m is the maximum number of elements of the sets $U(i)$. As n increases, its solution becomes more complex, and for very large n and m (in the order of several hundreds) the linear programming approach becomes impractical.

For the example considered in this section, the linear programming problem takes the form

$$\text{maximize } \lambda_1 + \lambda_2$$

subject to $\lambda_1 \leq 2 + 0.9(\tfrac{3}{4}\lambda_1 + \tfrac{1}{4}\lambda_2), \qquad \lambda_1 \leq 0.5 + 0.9(\tfrac{1}{4}\lambda_1 + \tfrac{3}{4}\lambda_2),$

$$\lambda_2 \leq 1 + 0.9(\tfrac{3}{4}\lambda_1 + \tfrac{1}{4}\lambda_2), \qquad \lambda_2 \leq 3 + 0.9(\tfrac{1}{4}\lambda_1 + \tfrac{3}{4}\lambda_2).$$

5.3 THE ROLE OF CONTRACTION MAPPINGS

Two key structural properties in DP models are responsible for most of the mathematical results one can prove about them. The first is the *monotonicity property* of the mappings T and T_μ (cf. Lemma 1 in Section 5.1). This property is fundamental for the model of this chapter. For example, it forms the basis for the results to be shown in the next section.

When the cost per stage is bounded and there is discounting, however, we have another property that strengthens the effects of monotonicity, the fact that the mappings T and T_μ are *contraction mappings*. In this section we explain the meaning and implications of this property. The material in this section is conceptually very important since contraction mappings are present in several additional DP models. However, the reader can also skip this section without loss of continuity. Abstract DP models and the implications of monotonicity and contraction are explored in detail in [D2], [B16], and [B23].

Let $B(S)$ denote the set of all bounded real-valued functions on S. With every function $J:S \to R$ that belongs to $B(S)$ we associate the scalar

$$\|J\| = \max_{x \in S} |J(x)|.$$

(For the benefit of the advanced reader we mention that the function $\|\cdot\|$ may be shown to be a norm on the linear space $B(S)$, and with this norm $B(S)$ becomes a complete normed linear space, i.e., a Banach space [L9].) The following definition and theorem are specializations to $B(S)$ of a more general notion and result (see, e.g., references [L5] and [L9]).

Definition. A mapping $H:B(S) \to B(S)$ is said to be a *contraction mapping* if there exists a scalar $\rho < 1$ such that

$$\|H(J) - H(J')\| \leq \rho \|J - J'\|, \qquad \text{for all } J, J' \in B(S),$$

where $\|\cdot\|$ is as in (5.47). It is said to be an *m-stage contraction mapping* if there exists a positive integer m and some $\rho < 1$ such that

$$\|H^m(J) - H^m(J')\| \leq \rho \|J - J'\|, \qquad \text{for all } J, J' \in B(S),$$

where H^m denotes the composition $H \ldots H$ of H with itself m times.

The main result concerning contraction mappings is as follows.

Contraction Mapping Fixed-Point Theorem. If $H:B(S) \to B(S)$ is a contraction mapping or an m-stage contraction mapping, then there exists a unique fixed point of H; that is, there exists a unique function $J^* \in B(S)$ such that

$$H(J^*) = J^*.$$

Furthermore, if J is any function in $B(S)$ and H^k is the composition of H with itself k times, then

$$\lim_{k \to \infty} \|H^k(J) - J^*\| = 0.$$

Proof. See reference [L5] or [L9].

Now consider the mappings T and T_μ defined by (5.8) and (5.9). Proposition 3 and Corollary 3.1 show that T and T_μ are contraction mappings ($\rho = \alpha$). As a result, the convergence of the successive approximation method to the unique fixed point of T follows directly from the contraction mapping theorem. Notice also that, by Proposition 5, the mapping F defined by (5.37) and (5.38) is also a contraction mapping with $\rho = \alpha$, and the convergence result of Proposition 5 is again a special case of the fixed-point theorem.

5.4 UNBOUNDED COSTS PER STAGE AND UNDISCOUNTED PROBLEMS

In this section we consider Problem I but relax Assumption D by allowing $\alpha \geqslant 1$ and costs per stage that are unbounded above or below. The complications resulting are substantial, and the analysis required is considerably more sophisticated than the one under Assumption D. The main difficulty is that Proposition 1 and the results that depend on it need not be true anymore even if $\alpha < 1$. We will assume that one of the following two assumptions is in effect in place of Assumption D.

Assumption P (Positivity).† The function g in the cost functional (5.2) satisfies

$$0 \leqslant g(x, u, w), \qquad \text{for all } (x, u, w) \in S \times C \times D. \tag{5.48}$$

Assumption N (Negativity). The function g in the cost functional (5.2) satisfies

$$g(x, u, w) \leqslant 0, \qquad \text{for all } (x, u, w) \in S \times C \times D. \tag{5.49}$$

In problems where reward or utility per stage is nonnegative and total discounted expected reward is to be *maximized,* we may consider minimization of negative reward, thus coming within the framework of Assumption N.

Note that when $\alpha < 1$, and g is either bounded above or below, we may add a scalar to g so that either (5.48) or (5.49) is satisfied. An optimal policy will not be affected by this change since, in view of the presence of the discount factor, the addition of a constant r to g merely adds $(1 - \alpha)^{-1}r$ to the cost associated with every policy.

One complication arising from unbounded costs per stage is that, for some initial states x_0 and some admissible policies $\pi = \{\mu_0, \mu_1, \ldots\}$, the cost $J_\pi(x_0)$ may be $+\infty$ (in the case of Assumption P) or $-\infty$ (in the case of Assumption N). Consider the following example.

Example 1

Let the system equation be

$$x_{k+1} = \beta x_k + u_k, \qquad k = 0, 1, 2, \ldots,$$

where $x_k, u_k \in R$, $k = 0, 1, \ldots$, and β is a positive scalar. The control constraint

† Problems corresponding to Assumption P are sometimes referred to in the research literature as negative DP problems [S28]. In these problems the objective function is maximized and the reward per stage is negative. Similarly, problems corresponding to Assumption N are sometimes referred to as positive DP problems [B28, S28].

is $|u_k| \leq 1$ and the cost is

$$J_\pi(x_0) = \lim_{N\to\infty} \sum_{k=0}^{N-1} \alpha^k |x_k|.$$

Consider the policy $\bar{\pi} = \{\bar{\mu}, \bar{\mu}, \ldots\}$, where $\bar{\mu}(x) = 0$ for all $x \in R$. Then

$$J_{\bar{\pi}}(x_0) = \lim_{N\to\infty} \sum_{k=0}^{N-1} \alpha^k \beta^k |x_0|,$$

and hence

$$J_{\bar{\pi}}(x_0) = \infty, \qquad \text{if} \qquad x_0 \neq 0, \quad \alpha\beta \leq 1,$$

and $J_{\bar{\pi}}(x_0)$ is finite otherwise. It is also possible to verify that when $\beta > 1$ and $\alpha\beta \geq 1$ the optimal cost $J^*(x_0)$ is equal to $+\infty$ for $|x_0| > 1/(\beta - 1)$ and is finite for $|x_0| \leq 1/(\beta - 1)$. The problem here is that when $\beta > 1$ the system is unstable, and in view of the restriction on the control it may not be possible to force the state near zero once it has reached sufficiently large magnitude.

There is not much that can be done about the possibility of the cost function being infinite for some policies. The presence of a discount factor $\alpha < 1$ does not help very much since the product $\alpha^k g(x_k, u_k, w_k)$ may still be bounded away from zero as $k \to \infty$ for some state and control trajectories. To cope with this situation, we conduct our analysis with the notational understanding that the costs $J_\pi(x_0)$ and $J^*(x_0)$ may be $+\infty$ $(-\infty)$ under P (N) for some initial states x_0 and policies $\pi \in \Pi$. In other words, we consider $J_\pi(\cdot)$ and $J^*(\cdot)$ to be extended real-valued functions. In fact, the entire subsequent analysis is valid even if the cost $g(x, u, w)$ is $+\infty$ $(-\infty)$ for some (x, u, w).

The results to be presented provide characterizations of the optimal cost function J^*, as well as optimal stationary policies. They also provide conditions under which the successive approximation method yields in the limit the optimal cost function J^*. In the proofs we will often need to interchange expectation and limit in various relations. This interchange is valid under the assumptions of the following theorem.

Monotone Convergence Theorem. Let $P = (p_1, p_2, \ldots)$ be a probability distribution over a countable set S denoted by $S = \{1, 2, \ldots\}$. Let $\{h_N\}$ be a sequence of extended real-valued functions on S such that

$$0 \leq h_N(i) \leq h_{N+1}(i), \qquad i, N = 1, 2, \ldots.$$

Let $h: S \to [0, +\infty]$ be the limit function

$$h(i) = \lim_{N\to\infty} h_N(i).$$

Then

$$\lim_{N\to\infty} \sum_{i=1}^{\infty} p_i h_N(i) = \sum_{i=1}^{\infty} p_i \lim_{N\to\infty} h_N(i) = \sum_{i=1}^{\infty} p_i h(i).$$

Proof. We have

$$\sum_{i=1}^{\infty} p_i h_N(i) \leq \sum_{i=1}^{\infty} p_i h(i).$$

By taking the limit, we obtain

$$\lim_{N\to\infty} \sum_{i=1}^{\infty} p_i h_N(i) \leq \sum_{i=1}^{\infty} p_i h(i),$$

so it remains to prove the reverse inequality. For every integer $M \geq 1$, we have

$$\lim_{N\to\infty} \sum_{i=1}^{\infty} p_i h_N(i) \geq \lim_{N\to\infty} \sum_{i=1}^{M} p_i h_N(i) = \sum_{i=1}^{M} p_i h(i),$$

and by taking the limit as $M \to \infty$ the reverse inequality follows. Q.E.D.

Bellman's Equation: Conditions for Optimality

Proposition 8. Under either Assumption P or N the optimal cost function J^* satisfies

$$J^*(x) = \min_{u\in U(x)} \underset{w}{E}\{g(x, u, w) + \alpha J^*[f(x, u, w)]\}, \qquad x \in S \tag{5.50a}$$

or, in terms of the mapping T of (5.8),

$$J^* = T(J^*). \tag{5.50b}$$

Proof. Let $\pi = \{\mu_0, \mu_1, \ldots\}$ be an admissible policy, and consider the cost $J_\pi(x)$ corresponding to π when the initial state is x. We have

$$J_\pi(x) = \underset{w}{E}\{g[x, \mu_0(x), w] + V_\pi[f(x, \mu_0(x), w)]\}, \tag{5.51}$$

where, for all $x_1 \in S$,

$$V_\pi(x_1) = \lim_{N\to\infty} \underset{\substack{w_k \\ k=1,2,\ldots}}{E} \left\{ \sum_{k=1}^{N-1} \alpha^k g[x_k, \mu_k(x_k), w_k] \right\}.$$

In this equation, x_{k+1} is generated from x_k, $\mu_k(x_k)$, w_k by the system equation (5.1). In other words, $V_\pi(x_1)$ is the cost from stage 1 to infinity using π when the initial state is x_1. We have clearly

$$V_\pi(x_1) \geq \alpha J^*(x_1), \qquad \text{for all } x_1 \in S.$$

Hence from (5.51)

$$\begin{aligned} J_\pi(x) &\geq \underset{w}{E}\{g[x, \mu_0(x), w] + \alpha J^*[f(x, \mu_0(x), w)]\} \\ &\geq \min_{u\in U(x)} \underset{w}{E}\{g(x, u, w) + \alpha J^*[f(x, u, w)]\}. \end{aligned}$$

Taking the minimum over all admissible policies, we have

$$\min_{\pi} J_\pi(x) = J^*(x) \geq \min_{u \in U(x)} E_w\{g(x, u, w) + \alpha J^*[f(x, u, w)]\} = T(J^*)(x).$$

Thus it remains to prove that the reverse inequality also holds.

Assume P, let $\{\epsilon_i\}$ be a positive sequence, and consider an admissible policy $\overline{\pi} = \{\overline{\mu}_0, \overline{\mu}_1, \ldots\}$ such that

$$T_{\overline{\mu}_k}(J^*)(x) \leq T(J^*)(x) + \epsilon_k, \qquad x \in S, \quad k = 0, 1, \ldots .$$

It was shown earlier that $T(J^*) \leq J^*$, so from the preceding inequality we obtain

$$T_{\overline{\mu}_k}(J^*)(x) \leq J^*(x) + \epsilon_k, \qquad x \in S, \quad k = 0, 1, \ldots .$$

Applying $T_{\overline{\mu}_{k-1}}$ on both sides of this relation, we have

$$\begin{aligned}(T_{\overline{\mu}_{k-1}} T_{\overline{\mu}_k})(J^*)(x) &\leq T_{\overline{\mu}_{k-1}}(J^*)(x) + \alpha\epsilon_k \\ &\leq T(J^*)(x) + \epsilon_{k-1} + \alpha\epsilon_k \\ &\leq J^*(x) + \epsilon_{k-1} + \alpha\epsilon_k .\end{aligned}$$

Continuing this process, we obtain

$$(T_{\overline{\mu}_0} T_{\overline{\mu}_1} \cdots T_{\overline{\mu}_k})(J^*)(x) \leq T(J^*)(x) + \sum_{i=0}^{k} \alpha^i \epsilon_i .$$

Taking the limit as $k \to \infty$, it follows that

$$J^*(x) \leq J_{\overline{\pi}}(x) \leq T(J^*)(x) + \sum_{i=0}^{\infty} \alpha^i \epsilon_i , \qquad x \in S.$$

Since the sequence $\{\epsilon_i\}$ is arbitrary, we can take $\Sigma_{i=0}^{\infty} \alpha^i \epsilon_i$ as small as desired, and we obtain $J^*(x) \leq T(J^*)(x)$ for all $x \in S$. Combining this with the inequality $J^*(x) \geq T(J^*)(x)$ shown earlier, the result follows (under Assumption P).

Assume N and let J_N be the optimal cost function for the corresponding N-stage problem

$$J_N(x_0) = \min_{\pi} E\left\{\sum_{k=0}^{N-1} \alpha^k g[x_k, \mu_k(x_k), w_k]\right\}. \tag{5.52}$$

We first show that

$$J^*(x) = \lim_{N \to \infty} J_N(x), \qquad x \in S. \tag{5.53}$$

Indeed, in view of Assumption N we have $J^* \leq J_N^*$ for all N, so

$$J^*(x) \leq \lim_{N \to \infty} J_N(x), \qquad x \in S. \tag{5.54}$$

Also, for all $\pi = \{\mu_0, \mu_1, \ldots\}$, we have

$$E\left\{\sum_{k=0}^{N-1} \alpha^k g[x_k, \mu_k(x_k), w_k]\right\} \geq J_N(x_0)$$

and by taking the limit as $N \to \infty$

$$J_\pi(x) \geq \lim_{N\to\infty} J_N(x), \qquad x \in S.$$

Taking minima over $\pi \in \Pi$, we obtain $J^*(x) \geq \lim_{N\to\infty} J_N(x)$, and combining this relation with (5.54) we obtain (5.53).

For every admissible μ, we have

$$T_\mu(J_N) \geq J_{N+1}$$

and by taking the limit as $N \to \infty$ and using the monotone convergence theorem and (5.53), we obtain

$$T_\mu(J^*) \geq J^*.$$

Taking minimum over μ, we obtain $T(J^*) \geq J^*$, which combined with the inequality $J^* \geq T(J^*)$ shown earlier proves the result under Assumption N. Q.E.D.

Similarly as in Corollaries 1.1, 2.1, and 3.1, we have:

Corollary 8.1. Let $\pi = \{\mu, \mu, \ldots\}$ be a stationary policy. Then under Assumption P or N, we have

$$J_\mu(x) = \underset{w}{E}\{g[x, \mu(x), w] + \alpha J_\mu[f(x, \mu(x), w)]\}$$

or, in terms of the mapping T_μ of (5.9),

$$J_\mu = T_\mu(J_\mu). \tag{5.55}$$

Contrary to the case of Assumption D, the optimal cost function J^* under Assumption P or N need not be the unique solution of Bellman's equation

$$J(x) = T(J)(x) = \min_{u\in U(x)} \underset{w}{E}\{g(x, u, w) + \alpha J[f(x, u, w)]\}. \tag{5.56}$$

Consider the following example.

Example 2

Let $S = [0, +\infty)$ (or $S = (-\infty, 0]$) and

$$g(x, u, w) = 0, \qquad f(x, u, w) = \frac{x}{\alpha}.$$

Then for every β, the function J given by

$$J(x) = \beta x, \qquad x \in S,$$

is a solution of (5.56) and hence T has an infinite number of fixed points in this case. Note, however, that there is a unique fixed point within the class of bounded functions, the zero function $J_0(x) \equiv 0$, which is the optimal cost function for this problem. More generally, it can be shown by using the following Proposition 9 that if $\alpha < 1$ and there exists a bounded function that is a fixed point of T, then that function must be equal to the optimal cost function J^* (see Problem 15). When $\alpha = 1$, Eq. (5.56) may have an infinity of solutions even within the class of bounded functions. This is clear since if $\alpha = 1$ and $J(\cdot)$ is any solution of (5.56), then $J(\cdot) + r$, where r is any scalar, is also a solution.

The optimal cost function J^*, however, has the property that it is the smallest (under Assumption P) or largest (under Assumption N) fixed point of T in the sense described in the following proposition.

Proposition 9. (a) Under Assumption P, if $\tilde{J}: S \to (-\infty, +\infty]$ satisfies $\tilde{J} \geq T(\tilde{J})$ and either $\tilde{J}$ is bounded below and $\alpha < 1$, or $\tilde{J} \geq 0$, then $\tilde{J} \geq J^*$.

(b) Under Assumption N, if $\tilde{J}: S \to [-\infty, +\infty)$ satisfies $\tilde{J} \leq T(\tilde{J})$ and either $\tilde{J}$ is bounded above and $\alpha < 1$, or $\tilde{J} \leq 0$, then $\tilde{J} \leq J^*$.

Proof. (a) Under Assumption P, let r be a scalar such that $\tilde{J}(x) + r \geq 0$ for all $x \in S$ and if $\alpha \geq 1$ let $r = 0$. For any sequence $\{\epsilon_k\}$ with $\epsilon_k > 0$, let $\tilde{\pi} = \{\tilde{\mu}_0, \tilde{\mu}_1, \ldots\}$ be an admissible policy for which we have for every $x \in S$ and k,

$$\underset{w}{E}\{g[x, \tilde{\mu}_k(x), w] + \alpha\tilde{J}[f(x, \tilde{\mu}_k(x), w)]\} \leq T(\tilde{J})(x) + \epsilon_k. \tag{5.57}$$

Such a policy exists since $T(\tilde{J})(x) > -\infty$ for all $x \in S$. We have for any initial state $x_0 \in S$,

$$\begin{aligned} J^*(x_0) &= \min_{\pi} \lim_{N\to\infty} \underset{w_k}{E}\left\{\sum_{k=0}^{N-1} \alpha^k g[x_k, \mu_k(x_k), w_k]\right\} \\ &\leq \min_{\pi} \liminf_{N\to\infty} \underset{w_k}{E}\left\{\alpha^N[\tilde{J}(x_N) + r] + \sum_{k=0}^{N-1} \alpha^k g[x_k, \mu_k(x_k), w_k]\right\} \\ &\leq \liminf_{N\to\infty} \underset{w_k}{E}\left\{\alpha^N[\tilde{J}(x_N) + r] + \sum_{k=0}^{N-1} \alpha^k g[x_k, \tilde{\mu}_k(x_k), w_k]\right\}. \end{aligned}$$

Using (5.57) and the assumption $\tilde{J} \geq T(\tilde{J})$, we obtain

$$\begin{aligned} &E\left\{\alpha^N\tilde{J}(x_N) + \sum_{k=0}^{N-1} \alpha^k g[x_k, \tilde{\mu}_k(x_k), w_k]\right\} \\ &= \underset{w_k}{E}\left\{\alpha^N\tilde{J}[f(x_{N-1}, \tilde{\mu}_{N-1}(x_{N-1}), w_{N-1})] + \sum_{k=0}^{N-1} \alpha^k g[x_k, \tilde{\mu}_k(x_k), w_k]\right\} \\ &\leq \underset{w_k}{E}\left\{\alpha^{N-1}T(\tilde{J})(x_{N-1}) + \sum_{k=0}^{N-2} \alpha^k g[x_k, \tilde{\mu}_k(x_k), w_k]\right\} + \alpha^{N-1}\epsilon_{N-1} \\ &\leq \underset{w_k}{E}\left\{\alpha^{N-1}\tilde{J}(x_{N-1}) + \sum_{k=0}^{N-2} \alpha^k g[x_k, \tilde{\mu}_k(x_k), w_k]\right\} + \alpha^{N-1}\epsilon_{N-1} \\ &\leq \underset{w_k}{E}\left\{\alpha^{N-2}\tilde{J}(x_{N-2}) + \sum_{k=0}^{N-3} \alpha^k g[x_k, \tilde{\mu}_k(x_k), w_k]\right\} + \alpha^{N-2}\epsilon_{N-2} + \alpha^{N-1}\epsilon_{N-1} \\ &\;\vdots \\ &\leq \tilde{J}(x_0) + \sum_{k=0}^{N-1} \alpha^k \epsilon_k. \end{aligned}$$

Combining these inequalities, we obtain

$$J^*(x_0) \leq \tilde{J}(x_0) + \lim_{N\to\infty}\left(\alpha^N r + \sum_{k=0}^{N-1} \alpha^k \epsilon_k\right).$$

Since the sequence $\{\epsilon_k\}$ is arbitrary (except for $\epsilon_k > 0$), we may select $\{\epsilon_k\}$ so that $\lim_{N\to\infty} \sum_{k=0}^{N-1} \alpha^k \epsilon_k$ is arbitrarily close to zero, and the result follows.

(b) Under Assumption N, let r be a scalar such that $\tilde{J}(x) + r \leq 0$ for all $x \in S$, and if $\alpha \geq 1$, let $r = 0$. We have for every initial state $x_0 \in S$,

$$\begin{aligned} J^*(x_0) &= \min_\pi \lim_{N\to\infty} \underset{w_k}{E}\left\{\sum_{k=0}^{N-1} \alpha^k g[x_k, \mu_k(x_k), w_k]\right\} \\ &\geq \min_\pi \limsup_{N\to\infty} \underset{w_k}{E}\left\{\alpha^N[\tilde{J}(x_N) + r] + \sum_{k=0}^{N-1} \alpha^k g[x_k, \mu_k(x_k), w_k]\right\} \qquad (5.58) \\ &\geq \limsup_{N\to\infty} \min_\pi \underset{w_k}{E}\left\{\alpha^N[\tilde{J}(x_N) + r] + \sum_{k=0}^{N-1} \alpha^k g[x_k, \mu_k(x_k), w_k]\right\}, \end{aligned}$$

where the last inequality follows from the fact that for any sequence $\{h_N(\lambda)\}$ of functions of a parameter λ we have

$$\min_\lambda \limsup_{N\to\infty} h_N(\lambda) \geq \limsup_{N\to\infty} \min_\lambda h_N(\lambda).$$

This inequality follows by writing

$$h_N(\lambda) \geq \min_\lambda h_N(\lambda)$$

and by subsequently taking the limit superior of both sides and the minimum over λ of the left side.

Now we have, by using the assumption $\tilde{J} \leq T(\tilde{J})$,

$$\begin{aligned} &\min_\pi \underset{w_k}{E}\left\{\alpha^N \tilde{J}(x_N) + \sum_{k=0}^{N-1} \alpha^k g[x_k, \mu_k(x_k), w_k]\right\} \\ &\quad = \min_\pi \underset{w_k}{E}\Bigg\{\sum_{k=0}^{N-2} \alpha^k g[x_k, \mu_k(x_k), w_k] \\ &\qquad + \alpha^{N-1} \min_{u_{N-1}\in U(x_{N-1})} \underset{w_{N-1}}{E}\{g(x_{N-1}, u_{N-1}, w_{N-1}) \\ &\qquad + \alpha \tilde{J}[f(x_{N-1}, u_{N-1}, w_{N-1})]\}\Bigg\} \\ &\quad \geq \min_\pi \underset{w_k}{E}\left\{\alpha^{N-1}\tilde{J}(x_{N-1}) + \sum_{k=0}^{N-2} \alpha^k g[x_k, \mu_k(x_k), w_k]\right\} \\ &\quad \vdots \\ &\quad \geq \tilde{J}(x_0). \end{aligned}$$

Using this relation in (5.58), we obtain

$$J^*(x_0) \geq \tilde{J}(x_0) + \lim_{N\to\infty} \alpha^N r = \tilde{J}(x_0). \quad \text{Q.E.D.}$$

As before, we have the following corollary:

Corollary 9.1. Let $\pi = \{\mu, \mu, \ldots\}$ be an admissible stationary policy.

(a) Under Assumption P, if $\tilde{J}: S \to (-\infty, +\infty]$ satisfies $\tilde{J} \geq T_\mu(\tilde{J})$ and either $\tilde{J}$ is bounded below and $\alpha < 1$, or $\tilde{J} \geq 0$, then $\tilde{J} \geq J_\mu$.

(b) Under Assumption N, if $\tilde{J}: S \to [-\infty, +\infty)$ satisfies $\tilde{J} \leq T_\mu(\tilde{J})$ and either $\tilde{J}$ is bounded above and $\alpha < 1$, or $\tilde{J} \leq 0$, then $\tilde{J} \leq J_\mu$.

Under Assumption N, Proposition 9 yields also the following characterization of an optimal stationary policy.

Proposition 10: Necessary and Sufficient Condition for Optimality under Assumption N. For a stationary policy $\pi^* = \{\mu^*, \mu^*, \ldots\}$ to be optimal under Assumption N, it is necessary and sufficient that

$$J_{\mu^*} = T_{\mu^*}(J_{\mu^*}) = T(J_{\mu^*}),$$

or equivalently

$$\begin{aligned} J_{\mu^*}(x) &= E_w\{g[x, \mu^*(x), w] + \alpha J_{\mu^*}[f(x, \mu^*(x), w)]\} \\ &= \min_{u\in U(x)} E_w\{g(x, u, w) + \alpha J_{\mu^*}[f(x, u, w)]\}, \qquad x \in S. \end{aligned}$$

Proof. Assume that the preceding condition holds. Then, since J_{μ^*} is a fixed point of T, we have by Proposition 9 that $J_{\mu^*} \leq J^*$, which implies that π^* is optimal. Conversely, if π^* is optimal, we have $J^* = J_{\mu^*}$ and hence we obtain $T_{\mu^*}(J_{\mu^*}) = J_{\mu^*} = J^* = T(J^*) = T(J_{\mu^*})$, which proves the desired result. Q.E.D.

The interpretation of the preceding optimality condition is that persistently using μ^* is optimal if and only if it performs at least as well as using any μ at the first stage and using μ^* thereafter. While this condition is necessary under Assumption P, it is not sufficient, as the following example shows.

Example 3

Let $S = (-\infty, +\infty)$, $U(x) = (0, 1]$ for all $x \in S$,

$$g(x, u, w) = |x|, \qquad f(x, u, w) = \alpha^{-1}ux,$$

for all $(x, u, w) \in S \times C \times D$. Let $\mu^*(x) = 1$ for all $x \in S$. Then $J_{\mu^*}(x) = +\infty$ if $x \neq 0$ and $J_{\mu^*}(0) = 0$. Furthermore, we have $J_{\mu^*} = T_{\mu^*}(J_{\mu^*}) = T(J_{\mu^*})$, as the reader can easily verify. It is also easy to verify that $J^*(x) = |x|$, and hence the policy $\{\mu^*, \mu^*, \ldots\}$ is not optimal.

On the other hand, under Assumption P we have a different optimality condition.

Proposition 11: Necessary and Sufficient Condition for Optimality under Assumption P. For a stationary policy $\pi^* = \{\mu^*, \mu^*, \ldots\}$ to be optimal under Assumption P, it is necessary and sufficient that

$$J^* = T_{\mu^*}(J^*) = T(J^*),$$

or equivalently

$$J^*(x) = \underset{w}{E}\{g[x, \mu^*(x), w] + \alpha J^*[f(x, \mu^*(x), w)]\}$$
$$= \min_{u \in U(x)} E\{g(x, u, w) + \alpha J^*[f(x, u, w)]\}, \qquad x \in S.$$

Proof. We have by Corollary 8.1 that $J_{\mu^*} = T_{\mu^*}(J_{\mu^*})$. If the preceding condition holds [i.e., $J^* = T_{\mu^*}(J^*)$], then we obtain from Corollary 9.1 that $J_{\mu^*} \leq J^*$, which implies optimality of π^*. Conversely, if π^* is optimal, we have $J^* = J_{\mu^*}$ and hence we obtain $T_{\mu^*}(J^*) = T_{\mu^*}(J_{\mu^*}) = J_{\mu^*} = J^* = T(J^*)$, which proves the desired result. Q.E.D.

Again the sufficiency part of the proposition need not be true under Assumption N, as the following example shows.

Example 4

Let $S = C = (-\infty, 0]$, $U(x) = C$ for all $x \in S$, and

$$g(x, u, w) = f(x, u, w) = u,$$

for all $(x, u, w) \in S \times C \times D$. Then $J^*(x) = -\infty$ for all $x \in S$, and every stationary policy $\pi^* = \{\mu^*, \mu^*, \ldots\}$ satisfies the condition of the preceding proposition. On the other hand, for $\mu^*(x) \equiv 0$ we have $J_{\mu^*}(x) = 0$ for all $x \in S$ and hence $\{\mu^*, \mu^*, \ldots\}$ is not optimal.

It is worth noting that Proposition 11 implies the existence of an optimal stationary policy under Assumption P when $U(x)$ is a finite set for every $x \in S$. This need not be true under Assumption N (see Problem 7 in Chapter 6).

The Successive Approximation Method

We now turn to the question whether the DP algorithm converges to the optimal cost function J^*. Let J_0 be the zero function on S; that is,

$$J_0(x) = 0, \qquad \text{for all } x \in S.$$

Then under Assumption P we have

$$J_0 \leq T(J_0) \leq T^2(J_0) \leq \cdots \leq T^k(J_0) \leq \cdots,$$

while under Assumption N we have

$$J_0 \geq T(J_0) \geq T^2(J_0) \geq \cdots \geq T^k(J_0) \geq \cdots.$$

In either case the limit function

$$J_\infty(x) = \lim_{k\to\infty} T^k(J_0)(x), \qquad x \in S \tag{5.59}$$

is well defined provided we allow the possibility that J_∞ can take the value $+\infty$ (under Assumption P) or $-\infty$ (under Assumption N). There arises the question of whether the successive approximation method is valid in the sense

$$J_\infty = J^*. \tag{5.60}$$

This question is, of course, of computational interest, but it is also of analytical interest since, if one knows that $J^* = \lim_{k\to\infty} T^k(J_0)$, one can infer properties of the unknown function J^* from properties of $T^k(J_0)$ that are functions defined in a concrete algorithmic manner.

Under Assumption D, we proved that we always have $J_\infty = J^*$. We will show that this is true under Assumption N as well. It turns out, however, that under Assumption P we may have $J_\infty \neq J^*$ (see Problem 9). In what follows we will provide easily verifiable conditions that guarantee that $J_\infty = J^*$ under Assumption P. We have the following proposition.

Proposition 12. (a) Let Assumption P hold and assume that

$$J_\infty(x) = T(J_\infty)(x), \qquad x \in S.$$

Then if $J: S \to R$ is any bounded function and $\alpha < 1$, or otherwise $J_0 \leq J \leq J^*$, we have

$$\lim_{k\to\infty} T^k(J)(x) = J^*(x), \qquad x \in S. \tag{5.61}$$

(b) Let Assumption N hold. Then if $J: S \to R$ is any bounded function and $\alpha < 1$, or otherwise $J^* \leq J \leq J_0$, we have

$$\lim_{k\to\infty} T^k(J)(x) = J^*(x), \qquad x \in S. \tag{5.62}$$

Proof. (a) Since under Assumption P we have

$$J_0 \leq T(J_0) \leq \cdots \leq T^k(J_0) \leq \cdots \leq J^*,$$

it follows that $\lim_{k\to\infty} T^k(J_0) = J_\infty \leq J^*$. Since J_∞ is also a fixed point of T by assumption, we obtain from Proposition 9 that $J^* \leq J_\infty$. It follows that

$$J_\infty = J^* \tag{5.63}$$

and hence (5.61) is proved for the case $J = J_0$.

For the case where $\alpha < 1$ and J is bounded, let r be a scalar such that

$$J_0 - re \leq J \leq J_0 + re. \tag{5.64}$$

Applying T^k to this relation and using Lemmas 1 and 2, we obtain

$$T^k(J_0) - \alpha^k re \leq T^k(J) \leq T^k(J_0) + \alpha^k re. \tag{5.65}$$

Since $T^k(J_0)$ converges to J^*, as shown, this relation shows that $T^k(J)$ converges also to J^*.

In the case where $J_0 \leq J \leq J^*$, we have by applying T^k

$$T^k(J_0) \leq T^k(J) \leq J^*, \qquad k = 0, 1, \ldots . \tag{5.66}$$

Since $T^k(J_0)$ converges to J^*, so does $T^k(J)$.

(b) It was shown earlier [cf. (5.53)] that under Assumption N we have

$$J_\infty(x) = \lim_{k\to\infty} T^k(J_0)(x) = J^*(x). \tag{5.67}$$

The proof from this point is identical to that for part (a). Q.E.D.

We now proceed to obtain conditions that guarantee under Assumption P that $J_\infty = T(J_\infty)$ (and hence, by Proposition 12, $J_\infty = J^*$) holds. We prove two propositions. The first admits an easy proof but requires a restrictive assumption. The second is a little harder to prove but requires a much weaker assumption.

Proposition 13. Let Assumption P hold and assume that the control constraint set is finite for every $x \in S$. Then

$$J_\infty = T(J_\infty) = J^*. \tag{5.68}$$

Proof. As shown in the proof of part (a) of Proposition 12, we have, for all k, $T^k(J_0) \leq J_\infty \leq J^*$. Applying T in this relation we obtain

$$\begin{aligned} T^{k+1}(J_0)(x) &= \min_{u\in U(x)} \mathop{E}_{w}\{g(x, u, w) + \alpha T^k(J_0)[f(x, u, w)]\} \\ &\leq T(J_\infty)(x), \end{aligned} \tag{5.69}$$

and taking the limit in (5.69), $J_\infty \leq T(J_\infty)$. Suppose that there existed a state $\bar{x} \in S$ such that

$$J_\infty(\bar{x}) < T(J_\infty)(\bar{x}). \tag{5.70}$$

Let u_k minimize in (5.69) when $x = \bar{x}$. Since $U(\bar{x})$ is finite, there must exist some $\bar{u} \in U(\bar{x})$ such that $u_k = \bar{u}$ for all k in some infinite subset $\mathscr{K}$ of the positive integers. By (5.69) we have for all $k \in \mathscr{K}$

$$T^{k+1}(J_0)(\bar{x}) = \mathop{E}_{w}\{g(\bar{x}, \bar{u}, w) + \alpha T^k(J_0)[f(\bar{x}, \bar{u}, w)]\} \leq T(J_\infty)(\bar{x}).$$

Taking the limit as $k \to \infty$, $k \in \mathscr{K}$, we obtain

$$\begin{aligned} J_\infty(\bar{x}) &= \mathop{E}_{w}\{g(\bar{x}, \bar{u}, w) + \alpha J_\infty[f(\bar{x}, \bar{u}, w)]\} \\ &\leq T(J_\infty)(\bar{x}) = \min_{u\in U(\bar{x})} \mathop{E}_{w}\{g(\bar{x}, u, w) + \alpha J_\infty[f(\bar{x}, u, w)]\}. \end{aligned}$$

It follows that $J_\infty(\bar{x}) = T(J_\infty)(\bar{x})$, contradicting (5.70). Q.E.D.

The following proposition strengthens Proposition 13 in that it requires a compactness rather than a finiteness assumption. We recall (see Appendix

A) that a subset X of an n-dimensional Euclidean space R^n is said to be *compact* if every sequence $\{x_k\}$ with $x_k \in X$ contains a subsequence $\{x_k\}_{k\in\mathcal{K}}$ that converges to a point $x \in X$. Equivalently, X is compact if and only if it is closed and bounded. The empty set is (trivially) considered compact. Given any collection of compact sets, their intersection is a compact set (possibly empty). Given a sequence of nonempty compact sets $X_1, X_2, \ldots, X_k, \ldots$ such that

$$X_1 \supset X_2 \supset \cdots \supset X_k \supset X_{k+1} \supset \cdots, \tag{5.71}$$

their intersection $\cap_{k=1}^{\infty} X_k$ is both nonempty and compact. In view of this fact, it follows that if $f: R^n \to [-\infty, +\infty]$ is a function such that the set

$$F_\lambda = \{x \in R^n | f(x) \leq \lambda\} \tag{5.72}$$

is compact for every $\lambda \in R$, then there exists a point x^* minimizing f; that is, there exists an $x^* \in R^n$ such that

$$f(x^*) = \min_{x\in R^n} f(x). \tag{5.73}$$

To see this, take a sequence $\{\lambda_k\}$ such that $\lambda_k \to \min_{x\in R^n} f(x)$ and $\lambda_k \geq \lambda_{k+1}$ for all k. If $\min_{x\in R^n} f(x) < +\infty$, such a sequence exists and the sets

$$F_{\lambda_k} = \{x \in R^n | f(x) \leq \lambda_k\} \tag{5.74}$$

are nonempty and compact. Furthermore, $F_{\lambda_k} \supset F_{\lambda_{k+1}}$ for all k, and hence the intersection $\cap_{k=1}^{\infty} F_{\lambda_k}$ is also nonempty and compact. Let x^* be any point in $\cap_{k=1}^{\infty} F_{\lambda_k}$. Then

$$f(x^*) \leq \lambda_k, \qquad k = 1, 2, \ldots, \tag{5.75}$$

and taking the limit as $k \to \infty$ we obtain $f(x^*) \leq \min_{x\in R^n} f(x)$, proving that x^* minimizes $f(x)$. The most common case where we can guarantee that the set F_λ of (5.72) is compact for all λ is when f is continuous and $f(x) \to \infty$ as $\|x\| \to \infty$.

Proposition 14. Let Assumption P hold, and assume that the sets

$$U_k(x, \lambda) = \left\{u \in U(x) \,\middle|\, \underset{w}{E}\{g(x, u, w) + \alpha T^k(J_0)[f(x, u, w)]\} \leq \lambda\right\} \tag{5.76}$$

are compact subsets of a Euclidean space for every $x \in S$, $\lambda \in R$, and for all k greater than some integer $\bar{k}$. Then

$$J_\infty = T(J_\infty) = J^*. \tag{5.77}$$

Furthermore, there exists a stationary optimal policy.

Proof. As in Proposition 13, we have $J_\infty \leq T(J_\infty)$. Suppose that there existed a state $\tilde{x} \in S$ such that

$$J_\infty(\tilde{x}) < T(J_\infty)(\tilde{x}). \tag{5.78}$$

Clearly, we must have $J_\infty(\tilde{x}) < +\infty$. For every $k \geq \bar{k}$, consider the sets

$$U_k[\tilde{x}, J_\infty(\tilde{x})] = \{u \in U(\tilde{x}) | \underset{w}{E}\{g(\tilde{x}, u, w) + \alpha T^k(J_0)[f(\tilde{x}, u, w)]\} \leq J_\infty(\tilde{x})\}.$$

Let also u_k be a point attaining the minimum in

$$T^{k+1}(J_0)(\bar{x}) = \min_{u \in U(\bar{x})} \underset{w}{E}\{g(\bar{x}, u, w) + \alpha T^k(J_0)[f(\bar{x}, u, w)]\}.$$

That is, u_k is such that

$$T^{k+1}(J_0)(\bar{x}) = \underset{w}{E}\{g(\bar{x}, u_k, w) + \alpha T^k(J_0)[f(\bar{x}, u_k, w)]\}.$$

Such minimizing points u_k exist by our compactness assumption. For every $k \geq \bar{k}$, consider the sequence $\{u_i\}_{i=k}^{\infty}$. Since $T^k(J_0) \leq T^{k+1}(J_0) \leq \cdots \leq J_\infty$, it follows that

$$\begin{aligned} &\underset{w}{E}\{g(\bar{x}, u_i, w) + \alpha T^k(J_0)[f(\bar{x}, u_i, w)]\} \\ &\quad \leq \underset{w}{E}\{g(\bar{x}, u_i, w) + \alpha T^i(J_0)[f(\bar{x}, u_i, w)]\} \\ &\quad \leq J_\infty(\bar{x}), \qquad i \geq k. \end{aligned}$$

Hence $\{u_i\}_{i=k}^{\infty} \subset U_k[\bar{x}, J_\infty(\bar{x})]$, and since $U_k[\bar{x}, J_\infty(\bar{x})]$ is compact, all the limit points of $\{u_i\}_{i=k}^{\infty}$ belong to $U_k[\bar{x}, J_\infty(\bar{x})]$ and at least one such limit point exists. Hence the same is true of the limit points of the whole sequence $\{u_i\}_{i=\bar{k}}^{\infty}$. It follows that if $\tilde{u}$ is a limit point of $\{u_i\}_{i=\bar{k}}^{\infty}$ then

$$\tilde{u} \in \bigcap_{k=\bar{k}}^{\infty} U_k[\bar{x}, J_\infty(\bar{x})].$$

This implies by (5.76) that for all $k \geq \bar{k}$

$$J_\infty(\bar{x}) \geq \underset{w}{E}\{g(\bar{x}, \tilde{u}, w) + \alpha T^k(J_0)[f(\bar{x}, \tilde{u}, w)]\} \geq T^{k+1}(J_0)(\bar{x}).$$

Taking the limit as $k \to \infty$, we obtain

$$J_\infty(\bar{x}) = \underset{w}{E}\{g(\bar{x}, \tilde{u}, w) + \alpha J_\infty[f(\bar{x}, \tilde{u}, w)]\}.$$

Since the right side is greater or equal to $T(J_\infty)(\bar{x})$, (5.78) is contradicted. Hence $J_\infty = T(J_\infty)$ and (5.77) is proved in view of Proposition 12(a).

To show that there exists an optimal stationary policy, observe that (5.77) and the last relation imply that $\tilde{u}$ attains the minimum in

$$J^*(\bar{x}) = \min_{u \in U(\bar{x})} \underset{w}{E}\{g(\bar{x}, u, w) + \alpha J^*[f(\bar{x}, u, w)]\}$$

for a state $\bar{x} \in S$ with $J^*(\bar{x}) < +\infty$. For states $\bar{x} \in S$ such that $J^*(\bar{x}) = +\infty$, every $u \in U(\bar{x})$ attains the preceding minimum. Hence by Proposition 11 an optimal stationary policy exists. Q.E.D.

The reader may verify by inspection of the proof that if $\mu_k(\bar{x})$, $k = 0, 1, \ldots$, attains the minimum in the relation

$$T^{k+1}(J_0)(\bar{x}) = \min_{u \in U(x)} \underset{w}{E}\{g(\bar{x}, u, w) + \alpha T^k(J_0)[f(\bar{x}, u, w)]\}$$

then if $\mu^*(\bar{x})$ is a limit point of $\{\mu_k(\bar{x})\}$, for every $\bar{x} \in S$, the policy $\pi^* = \{\mu^*, \mu^*, \ldots\}$ is optimal. Furthermore, $\{\mu_k(\bar{x})\}$ has at least one limit point for every $\bar{x} \in S$ for which $J^*(\bar{x}) < +\infty$. Thus *the successive approximation method under the assumptions of Proposition 13 or 14 yields in the limit not only the optimal cost function* J^* *but also an optimal stationary policy.*

Other Computational Methods

Under Assumption D we discussed three methods for computational solution: successive approximation, policy iteration, and linear programming. We have already seen that the validity of successive approximation carries over under Assumptions P and N. (Actually, under P an additional condition is needed such as finiteness of the control space, but this will typically be satisfied when computational solution is attempted.)

Unfortunately, policy iteration is not a valid procedure under either P or N in the absence of further conditions. If $\{\mu, \mu, \ldots\}$ and $\{\bar{\mu}, \bar{\mu}, \ldots\}$ are admissible policies and $T_{\bar{\mu}}(J_\mu) = T(J_\mu)$, then it can be shown that under Assumption P we have

$$J_{\bar{\mu}}(x) \leqslant J_\mu(x), \qquad x \in S. \tag{5.79}$$

To see this, note that $T_{\bar{\mu}}(J_\mu) = T(J_\mu) \leqslant T_\mu(J_\mu) = J_\mu$ from which we obtain $\lim_{N\to\infty} T_{\bar{\mu}}^N(J_\mu) \leqslant J_\mu$. Since $J_{\bar{\mu}} = \lim_{N\to\infty} T_{\bar{\mu}}^N(J_0)$ and $J_0 \leqslant J_\mu$, we obtain (5.79). However, (5.79) by itself is not sufficient to guarantee the validity of policy iteration. For example, it is not clear that strict inequality holds in (5.79) for at least one state $x \in S$ when μ is not optimal. The difficulty here is that the equality $J_\mu = T(J_\mu)$ does not imply that $\{\mu, \mu, \ldots\}$ is optimal as it does under Assumption D, and additional conditions are needed to guarantee the validity of policy iteration. However, for several types of problems such conditions can be verified (see Sections 6.1 and 6.4).

It is possible to devise a computational method based on mathematical programming when S, C, and D are finite sets by making use of Proposition 9. Under N and $\alpha = 1$, the corresponding (linear) program is (compare with the end of Section 6.2)

$$\max \sum_{i=1}^{n} \lambda_i$$

subject to

$$\lambda_i \leqslant g(i, u) + \sum_{j=1}^{n} p_{ij}(u)\lambda_j, \qquad i = 1, 2, \ldots, n, \quad u \in U(i).$$

Under P and $\alpha = 1$, the corresponding program takes the form

$$\min \sum_{i=1}^{n} \lambda_i$$

subject to

$$\lambda_i \geqslant \min_{u \in U(i)} [g(i, u) + \sum_{j=1}^{n} p_{ij}(u)\lambda_j], \qquad i = 1, \ldots, n,$$

but unfortunately this program is not linear or even convex.

The reader should keep in mind, however, that problems involving finite state Markov chains (S, C, and D finite) and no discounting ($\alpha \geq 1$) are of two basic types. One possibility is that the optimal total expected cost is infinite for some initial states, in which case the formulation of this chapter is very likely not meaningful and the problem should be cast in the average cost per stage framework of Chapter 7. The other possibility is that the optimal total expected cost is finite for all initial states, in which case Assumption P or N implies that, with probability one, some cost-free state (or set of cost-free states) is eventually entered and never left subsequently. There is a special theory for problems of this type (see Section 6.4), which guarantees the validity of policy iteration under normally satisfied assumptions.

5.5 NONSTATIONARY AND PERIODIC PROBLEMS

The standing assumption so far in this chapter has been that the problem involves a stationary system and a stationary cost per stage (except for the presence of the discount factor). Problems where the system or the cost per stage are nonstationary arise occasionally in practice or in theoretical studies and are thus of some interest. It turns out that such problems can be embedded by means of a simple reformulation within the framework of Problem I for which stationarity prevails. Once this reformulation is considered, one obtains results analogous to those of Sections 5.1 and 5.4.

Consider a nonstationary system of the form

$$x_{k+1} = f_k(x_k, u_k, w_k), \qquad k = 0, 1, \ldots,$$

and a cost functional of the form

$$J_\pi(x_0) = \lim_{N\to\infty} \underset{\substack{w_k \\ k=0,1,\ldots,N-1}}{E} \left\{ \sum_{k=0}^{N-1} \alpha^k g_k[x_k, \mu_k(x_k), w_k] \right\}. \tag{5.80}$$

In these equations, for each k, x_k belongs to a space S_k, u_k belongs to a space C_k and satisfies $u_k \in U_k(x_k)$ for all $x_k \in S_k$, and w_k belongs to a countable space D_k. The sets S_k, C_k, $U_k(x_k)$, D_k may differ from one stage to the next. The random disturbances w_k are characterized by probabilities $P_k(\cdot|x_k, u_k)$, which depend on x_k and u_k as well as the time index k. The set of admissible policies Π is the set of all sequences $\pi = \{\mu_0, \mu_1, \ldots\}$ with $\mu_k: S_k \to C_k$ and $\mu_k(x_k) \in U_k(x_k)$ for all $x_k \in S_k$ and $k = 0, 1, \ldots$. The functions $g_k: S_k \times C_k \times D_k \to R$ are given and are assumed to satisfy one of the following three assumptions, which are analogous to Assumptions D, P, and N considered earlier in this chapter:

Assumption D′. The functions g_k satisfy, for all $k = 0, 1, \ldots,$

$$0 \leq g_k(x_k, u_k, w_k) \leq M, \qquad \text{for all } (x_k, u_k, w_k) \in S_k \times C_k \times D_k,$$

where M is some scalar and $\alpha < 1$.

Assumption P′. The functions g_k satisfy, for all $k = 0, 1, \ldots,$

$$0 \leq g_k(x_k, u_k, w_k), \qquad \text{for all } (x_k, u_k, w_k) \in S_k \times C_k \times D_k.$$

Assumption N′. The functions g_k satisfy, for all $k = 0, 1, \ldots,$

$$g_k(x_k, u_k, w_k) \leq 0, \qquad \text{for all } (x_k, u_k, w_k) \in S_k \times C_k \times D_k.$$

We will refer to the problem formulated as the *nonstationary problem* (NSP). We can get an idea on how the NSP can be converted to a stationary problem by considering the special case where the state space is the same for each stage (i.e., $S_k = S$ for all k). We consider an augmented state

$$\tilde{x} = (x, k),$$

where $x \in S$, and k is the time index. The new state space is $\tilde{S} = S \times K$, where K denotes the set of nonnegative integers. The augmented system evolves according to

$$(x, k) \to [f_k(x, u_k, w_k), k + 1], \qquad (x, k) \in \tilde{S}.$$

Similarly, we can define a cost per stage as

$$\tilde{g}[(x, k), u_k, w_k] = g_k(x, u_k, w_k), \qquad (x, k) \in \tilde{S}.$$

It is evident that the problem corresponding to the augmented system is stationary. If we restrict attention to initial states $\tilde{x}_0 \in S \times \{0\}$, it can be seen that this stationary problem is equivalent to the NSP.

Let us now consider the more general case. To simplify notation, we will assume that the state spaces S_i, $i = 0, 1, \ldots$, the control spaces C_i, $i = 0, 1, \ldots$, and the disturbance spaces D_i, $i = 0, 1, \ldots$, are all mutually disjoint. This assumption does not involve a loss of generality since, if necessary, we may relabel the elements of S_i, C_i, and D_i without affecting the structure of the problem. Define now a new state space S, a new control space C, and a new (countable) disturbance space D by

$$S = \bigcup_{i=0}^{\infty} S_i, \qquad C = \bigcup_{i=0}^{\infty} C_i, \qquad D = \bigcup_{i=0}^{\infty} D_i.$$

Introduce a new (stationary) system

$$\tilde{x}_{k+1} = f(\tilde{x}_k, \tilde{u}_k, \tilde{w}_k), \qquad k = 0, 1, \ldots, \tag{5.81}$$

where $\tilde{x}_k \in S$, $\tilde{u}_k \in C$, $\tilde{w}_k \in D$, and the system function $f: S \times C \times D \to S$ is defined by

$$f(\tilde{x}, \tilde{u}, \tilde{w}) = f_i(\tilde{x}, \tilde{u}, \tilde{w}), \qquad \text{if } \tilde{x} \in S_i, \quad \tilde{u} \in C_i, \quad \tilde{w} \in D_i, \quad i = 0, 1, \ldots.$$

For triplets $(\tilde{x}, \tilde{u}, \tilde{w})$, where for some $i = 0, 1, \ldots$ we have $\tilde{x} \in S_i$ but $\tilde{u} \notin C_i$, or $\tilde{w} \notin D_i$, the definition of f is immaterial; any definition is adequate for our purposes in view of the control constraints to be introduced. The control constraint is taken to be $\tilde{u} \in U(\tilde{x})$ for all $\tilde{x} \in S$, where $U(\cdot)$ is defined by

$$U(\tilde{x}) = U_i(\tilde{x}), \qquad \text{if } \tilde{x} \in S_i, \quad i = 0, 1, \ldots.$$

The disturbance $\tilde{w}$ is characterized by probabilities $P(\tilde{w}|\tilde{x}, \tilde{u})$ such that

$$P(\tilde{w} \in D_i|\tilde{x} \in S_i, \tilde{u} \in C_i) = 1, \qquad i = 0, 1, \ldots,$$

$$P(\tilde{w} \notin D_i|\tilde{x} \in S_i, \tilde{u} \in C_i) = 0, \qquad i = 0, 1, \ldots.$$

Furthermore, for any $w_i \in D_i$, $x_i \in S_i$, $u_i \in C_i$, $i = 0, 1, \ldots$, we have

$$P(w_i|x_i, u_i) = P_i(w_i|x_i, u_i).$$

We also intoduce a new cost functional

$$\tilde{J}_{\tilde{\pi}}(\tilde{x}_0) = \lim_{N\to\infty} \underset{\substack{\tilde{w}_k \\ k=0,1,\ldots,N-1}}{E} \left\{ \sum_{k=0}^{N-1} \alpha^k g[\tilde{x}_k, \tilde{\mu}_k(\tilde{x}_k), \tilde{w}_k] \right\}, \tag{5.82}$$

where the (stationary) cost per stage $g: S \times C \times D \to R$ is defined by

$$g(\tilde{x}, \tilde{u}, \tilde{w}) = g_i(\tilde{x}, \tilde{u}, \tilde{w}), \qquad \text{if } \tilde{x} \in S_i, \quad \tilde{u} \in C_i, \quad \tilde{w} \in D_i, \quad i = 0, 1, \ldots.$$

For triplets $(\tilde{x}, \tilde{u}, \tilde{w})$, where for some $i = 0, 1, \ldots$ we have $\tilde{x} \in S_i$ but $\tilde{u} \notin C_i$ or $\tilde{w} \notin D_i$, any definition of g is adequate provided $0 \leq g(\tilde{x}, \tilde{u}, \tilde{w}) \leq M$ for all $(\tilde{x}, \tilde{u}, \tilde{w})$ when Assumption D′ holds, $0 \leq g(\tilde{x}, \tilde{u}, \tilde{w})$ when P' holds, and $g(\tilde{x}, \tilde{u}, \tilde{w}) \leq 0$ when N' holds. The set of admissible policies $\tilde{\Pi}$ for the new problem consists of all sequences $\tilde{\pi} = \{\tilde{\mu}_0, \tilde{\mu}_1, \ldots\}$, where $\tilde{\mu}_k: S \to C$ and $\tilde{\mu}_k(\tilde{x}) \in U(\tilde{x})$ for all $\tilde{x} \in S$ and $k = 0, 1, \ldots$.

The construction given defines a problem that clearly fits the framework of Problem I. We will refer to this problem as the *stationary problem* (SP).

It is important to understand the nature of the intimate connection between the NSP and the SP formulated here. Let $\pi = \{\mu_0, \mu_1 \ldots\}$ be an admissible policy for the NSP. Also, let $\tilde{\pi} = \{\tilde{\mu}_0, \tilde{\mu}_1, \ldots\}$ be an admissible policy for the SP such that

$$\tilde{\mu}_i(\tilde{x}) = \mu_i(\tilde{x}), \qquad \text{if } \tilde{x} \in S_i, \quad i = 0, 1, \ldots. \tag{5.83}$$

Let $x_0 \in S_0$ be the initial state for the NSP and consider the same initial state for the SP (i.e., $\tilde{x}_0 = x_0 \in S_0$). Then the sequence of states $\{\tilde{x}_i\}$ generated in the SP will satisfy $\tilde{x}_i \in S_i$, $i = 0, 1, \ldots$, with probability 1 (i.e., the system will move from the set S_0 to the set S_1, then to S_2, etc., just as in the NSP). Furthermore, the probabilistic law of generation of states and costs is identical in the NSP and the SP. As a result, it is easy to see that for any admissible policies π and $\tilde{\pi}$ satisfying (5.83) and initial states x_0, $\tilde{x}_0$ satisfying $x_0 = \tilde{x}_0 \in S_0$, the sequence of generated states in the NSP and the SP is the same ($x_i = \tilde{x}_i$, for all i) provided the generated disturbances w_i and $\tilde{w}_i$ are also the same for all i ($w_i = \tilde{w}_i$, for all i). Furthermore, if π and $\tilde{\pi}$ satisfy (5.83) we have $J_\pi(x_0) = \tilde{J}_\pi(\tilde{x}_0)$ if $x_0 = \tilde{x}_0 \in S_0$. Let us also consider the optimal cost functions for the NSP and the SP:

$$J^*(x_0) = \min_{\pi\in\Pi} J_\pi(x_0), \qquad x_0 \in S_0,$$

$$\tilde{J}^*(\tilde{x}_0) = \min_{\tilde{\pi}\in\tilde{\Pi}} \tilde{J}_{\tilde{\pi}}(\tilde{x}_0), \qquad \tilde{x}_0 \in S.$$

Then it follows from the construction of the SP that

$$\tilde{J}^*(\tilde{x}_0) = \tilde{J}^*(\tilde{x}_0, i), \qquad \text{if } \tilde{x}_0 \in S_i, \quad i = 0, 1, \ldots, \tag{5.84}$$

where

$$\tilde{J}^*(\tilde{x}_0, i) = \min_{\pi\in\Pi} \lim_{N\to\infty} \underset{\substack{w_k \\ k=i,\ldots,N-1}}{E} \left\{ \sum_{k=i}^{N-1} \alpha^{k-i} g_k[x_k, \mu_k(x_k), w_k] \right\},$$

$$\text{if } \tilde{x}_0 = x_i \in S_i, \quad i = 0, 1, \ldots. \tag{5.85}$$

Note that in this equation the right side is defined in terms of the data of the NSP. As a special case of this equation, we obtain

$$\tilde{J}^*(\tilde{x}_0) = \tilde{J}^*(\tilde{x}_0, 0) = J^*(x_0), \qquad \text{if } \tilde{x}_0 = x_0 \in S_0. \tag{5.86}$$

Thus *the optimal cost function J^* of the NSP can be obtained from the optimal cost function $\tilde{J}^*$ of the SP.* Furthermore, if $\tilde{\pi}^* = \{\tilde{\mu}_0^*, \tilde{\mu}_1^*, \ldots\}$ is an optimal policy for the SP, then the policy $\pi^* = \{\mu_0^*, \mu_1^*, \ldots\}$ defined by

$$\mu_i^*(x_i) = \tilde{\mu}_i^*(x_i), \qquad \text{for all } x_i \in S_i, \quad i = 0, 1, \ldots, \tag{5.87}$$

is an optimal policy for the NSP. *Thus optimal policies for the SP yield optimal policies for the NSP via (5.87).* Another point to be noted is that *if Assumption D′ (P′, N′) is satisfied for the NSP, then Assumption D (P, N) introduced earlier in this chapter is satisfied for the SP.*

These observations show that one may analyze the NSP by means of the SP. Every result given in Sections 5.1 and 5.4 when applied to the SP yields a corresponding result for the NSP. We will just provide the form of the optimality equation for the NSP in the following proposition.

Proposition 15. Under Assumption D′ (P′, N′), there holds

$$J^*(x_0) = \tilde{J}^*(x_0, 0), \qquad x_0 \in S_0,$$

where for all $i = 0, 1, \ldots$, the functions $\tilde{J}^*(\cdot, i)$ map S_i into $[0, \infty)$ ($[0, \infty]$, $[-\infty, 0]$), are given by (5.85), and satisfy

$$\tilde{J}^*(x_i, i) = \min_{u_i\in U_i(x_i)} \underset{w_i}{E}\{g_i(x_i, u_i, w_i) + \alpha\tilde{J}^*[f_i(x_i, u_i, w_i), i + 1]\},$$

$$x_i \in S_i, \quad i = 0, 1, \ldots. \tag{5.88}$$

Under Assumption D′ the functions $\tilde{J}^*(\cdot, i)$, $i = 0, 1, \ldots$, are the unique bounded solutions of the set of equations (5.88). Furthermore, under Assumption D′ or P′, if $\mu_i^*(x_i) \in U_i(x_i)$ attains the minimum in (5.88) for all $x_i \in S_i$, and i, then the policy $\pi^* = \{\mu_0^*, \mu_1^*, \ldots\}$ is optimal for the NSP.

Proof. Apply Propositions 2, 8, and 11 to the SP. Then the result follows by using definitions (5.84) to (5.86). Q.E.D.

Periodic Problems

Assume within the framework of the NSP that there exists an integer $p \geq 2$ (called the *period*) such that for all integers i and j with $|i - j| =$

λp, $\lambda = 1, 2, \ldots$, we have

$$S_i = S_j, \qquad C_i = C_j, \qquad D_i = D_j, \qquad U_i(\cdot) = U_j(\cdot),$$

$$f_i = f_j, \qquad g_i = g_j, \qquad P_i(\cdot|x, u) = P_j(\cdot|x, u), \qquad (x, u) \in S_i \times C_i.$$

We assume that the spaces S_i, C_i, D_i, $i = 0, 1, \ldots, p-1$, are mutually disjoint. We define new state, control, and disturbance spaces by

$$S = \bigcup_{i=0}^{p-1} S_i, \qquad C = \bigcup_{i=0}^{p-1} C_i, \qquad D = \bigcup_{i=0}^{p-1} D_i.$$

The optimality equation for the equivalent stationary problem reduces to the system of p equations:

$$\tilde{J}^*(x_0, 0) = \min_{u_0 \in U_0(x_0)} \mathop{E}_{w_0}\{g_0(x_0, u_0, w_0) + \alpha \tilde{J}^*[f_0(x_0, u_0, w_0), 1]\},$$

$$\tilde{J}^*(x_1, 1) = \min_{u_1 \in U_1(x_1)} \mathop{E}_{w_1}\{g_1(x_1, u_1, w_1) + \alpha \tilde{J}^*[f_1(x_1, u_1, w_1), 2]\},$$

$$\vdots$$

$$\tilde{J}^*(x_{p-1}, p-1) = \min_{u_{p-1} \in U_{p-1}(x_{p-1})} \mathop{E}_{w_{p-1}}\{g_{p-1}(x_{p-1}, u_{p-1}, w_{p-1}) + \alpha \tilde{J}^*[f_{p-1}(x_{p-1}, u_{p-1}, w_{p-1}), 0]\}.$$

These equations may be used to obtain (under Assumption D′ or P′) a periodic policy of the form $\{\mu_0^*, \ldots, \mu_{p-1}^*, \mu_0^*, \ldots, \mu_{p-1}^*, \ldots\}$ whenever the minimum of the right side is attained for all x_i, $i = 0, 1, \ldots, p-1$.

When all spaces involved are finite, an optimal policy may be found in a finite number of arithmetic operations by means of the policy iteration algorithm or linear programming. The form of these algorithms may be obtained by applying them to the corresponding SP.

Finally, we provide the form of the successive approximation method with starting functions equal to zero:

$$\tilde{J}_0(x_i, i) = 0, \qquad x_i \in S_i, \quad i = 0, 1, \ldots, p-1.$$

The $(k+1)$st iteration is given by

$$\tilde{J}_{k+1}(x_i, i) = \min_{u_i \in U_i(x_i)} \mathop{E}_{w_i}\{g_i(x_i, u_i, w_i) + \alpha \tilde{J}_k[f_i(x_i, u_i, w_i), i+1]\}, \qquad i = 0, 1, \ldots, p-2,$$

$$\tilde{J}_{k+1}(x_{p-1}, p-1) = \min_{u_{p-1} \in U_{p-1}(x_{p-1})} \mathop{E}_{w_{p-1}}\{g_{p-1}(x_{p-1}, u_{p-1}, w_{p-1}) + \alpha \tilde{J}_k[f_{p-1}(x_{p-1}, u_{p-1}, w_{p-1}), 0]\}.$$

Under Assumptions D′ and N′, we have (by applying Proposition 1 or 12 to the corresponding SP)

$$\lim_{k \to \infty} \tilde{J}_k(x_i, i) = \tilde{J}^*(x_i, i), \qquad x_i \in S_i, \quad i = 0, \ldots, p-1,$$

while under Assumption P′ the same equations hold, provided the sets

$$U_k(x_i, \lambda, i) = \left\{ u_i \in U_i(x_i) \,\middle|\, \underset{w_i}{E}\{g_i(x_i, u_i, w_i) + \alpha \tilde{J}_k[f_i(x_i, u_i, w_i), i + 1]\} \le \lambda \right\}, \qquad i = 0, \ldots, p - 2,$$

$$U_k(x_{p-1}, \lambda, p - 1) = \left\{ u_{p-1} \in U_{p-1}(x_{p-1}) \,\middle|\, \underset{w_{p-1}}{E}\{g_{p-1}(x_{p-1}, u_{p-1}, w_{p-1}) + \alpha \tilde{J}_k[f_{p-1}(x_{p-1}, u_{p-1}, w_{p-1}), 0]\} \le \lambda \right\}$$

are compact subsets of Euclidean spaces for all $x_i \in S_i$, $\lambda \in R$, and k greater than some integer $\bar{k}$ (Proposition 14 applied to the SP). Under the same compactness condition, an optimal periodic policy is guaranteed to exist.

5.6 NOTES

The discounted problem with bounded cost per stage is by far the simplest and most well-behaved infinite horizon problem. This is due to the contraction property induced by the discount factor. Many authors have contributed to its analysis, most notably Bellman [B5] and Blackwell [B27]. The mapping F of Section 5.2 and the corresponding algorithms are given in [K14], where the connection with Gauss–Seidel iterations is pointed out (see also [H5]). The linear programming approach of Section 5.2 was proposed in [D3]. The error bounds given in Section 5.2 and Problem 3 are improvements on results from [M5] (see [P13], [P14], and [B17]). For discretization procedures that approximate infinite state space problems with finite state Markov chains, see [B18], [F5], [H6], [W8], [W9], and [W10]. Surveys of computational research can be found in [P16]. Discounted semi-Markov decision problems are similar to those considered in this chapter except that the time needed for a transition between successive states is random and affects the cost through the discount factor. Their analysis follows closely the one given here (see [R6]). In particular, when costs per stage are bounded, a contraction property such as the one of Section 5.3 can be established and used to derive results analogous to the ones of Section 5.1 and 5.2. The material on adaptive aggregation is new (see [B20]). Our approach differs from other approaches [S11] in that aggregate states change adaptively from one iteration to the next depending on the progress of the computation. This has a significant effect in the efficiency of the computation, particularly for problems involving multiple ergodic classes.

Undiscounted problems and discounted problems with unbounded cost per stage were first analyzed systematically in [D9], [B28], and [S28]. An extensive treatment, which also resolves the associated measurability questions, is [B23]. Sufficient conditions for convergence of the successive approximation method under Assumption N (cf. Proposition 14) were derived independently in [B16] and [S6]. Reference [B16] also derives necessary and sufficient conditions for convergence.

While the primary objective in this text has been the analysis of stochastic optimal control problems with additive cost structure, at various points we have indicated that DP is applicable to other types of problems (see, e.g., Problems 5, 7, 9 in Chapter 1, and Problems 4 and 6 in this chapter). While the nature of these problems may vary widely, their underlying structure turns out to be very similar. We can capture this structure by taking as a starting point an abstract mapping describing the corresponding DP algorithm. In this way, most basic results of an analytical or computational nature relating to DP can be developed in a unified manner. This analysis is given in detail in [B16] and [B23].

The structure of the successive approximation method is very well suited for parallel or distributed computation. It turns out that the method can be carried out by multiple processors in an asynchronous, in effect chaotic, manner allowing arbitrary communication delays between processors regarding the results of their respective computations. See Problem 8 and [B19].

In the formulation of Problem I we can take into account the possibility of constraints on the state x_k of the form $x_k \in X \subset S$ by adjusting the control constraint set $U(x_{k-1})$ if necessary so that we have

$$x_k = f(x_{k-1}, u_{k-1}, w_{k-1}) \in X, \qquad \text{for all } w_{k-1} \in D,\ u_{k-1} \in U(x_{k-1}).$$

An alternative possibility is to take the state constraint $x_k \in X$ directly into account under Assumption P by adding to the cost per stage g the indicator function $\delta(x|X)$ of the set X:

$$\delta(x|X) = \begin{cases} 0, & \text{if} \quad x \in X, \\ +\infty, & \text{if} \quad x \notin X. \end{cases}$$

This formulation, however, requires that g can take the value $+\infty$. Nonetheless, all the results of Section 5.4 shown under Assumption P may be proved for g satisfying

$$0 \leq g(x, u, w) \leq +\infty \qquad (x, u, w) \in S \times C \times D,$$

that is, whenever g is allowed to take the value $+\infty$. For an analysis and treatment of state constraints, see references [B12] and [B14] or Problem 10 in Chapter 6.

We have bypassed a number of complex theoretical issues relating to stationary policies that historically have played an important role in the development of the subject of this chapter. The main question is to what extent is it possible to restrict attention to stationary policies. Some aspects of this question are still open. Suppose, for example, that we are given an $\epsilon > 0$. One issue is whether there exists an ϵ-optimal stationary policy, that is, a policy $\{\mu, \mu, \ldots\}$ such that

$$J_\mu(x) \leq J^*(x) + \epsilon, \qquad \text{for all } x \in S \text{ with } J^*(x) > -\infty,$$

$$J_\mu(x) \leq -\frac{1}{\epsilon}, \qquad \text{for all } x \in S \text{ with } J^*(x) = -\infty.$$

The answer is positive under any one of the following conditions:

1. Assumption P holds and $\alpha < 1$ (see Problem 22).
2. Assumption N holds, S is a finite set, $\alpha = 1$, and $J^*(x) > -\infty$ for all $x \in S$ (see Problem 25 or [B28], [B29], and [O3]).
3. Assumption N holds, S is a countable set, $\alpha = 1$, and the problem is deterministic (see [B24]).

The answer can be negative under any one of the following conditions:

4. Assumption P holds and $\alpha = 1$ (see Problem 22).
5. Assumption N holds and $\alpha < 1$ (see Problem 25 or [B24]).

Another issue is whether there exists an optimal stationary policy whenever there exists an optimal policy for each initial state. This is true under Assumption P (see Problem 23). It is also true (but very hard to prove) under Assumption N if $J^*(x) > -\infty$ for all $x \in S$, $\alpha = 1$, and the disturbance space D is countable [B29], [D9], [O3]. Simple two-state examples can be constructed showing that the result fails to hold if $\alpha = 1$ and $J^*(x) = -\infty$ for some state x (see Problem 24). However, these examples rely on the presence of a stochastic element in the problem. If the problem is deterministic, stronger results are available; one can find an optimal stationary policy if there exists an optimal policy at each initial state and either $\alpha = 1$ or $\alpha < 1$ and $J^*(x) > -\infty$ for all $x \in S$. These results also require a difficult proof [B24].

Finally, we note that even though the problem of this chapter requires a countable disturbance space, it may still serve as the starting point of analysis of a problem with uncountable disturbance space. This can be done by reducing such a problem to a deterministic problem (i.e., one where the disturbance space consists of a single element) with state space a set of probability measures. The basic idea of this reduction is demonstrated in Problem 18. The advanced reader may consult [B23] and see how a related reduction can be effected for a very broad class of finite and infinite horizon problems.

PROBLEMS

1. A computer manufacturer can be in two states. In state 1 he has a successful product that sells well, while in state 2 his product sells poorly. While in state 1 he can advertise his product in which case the one-stage reward is 4 units,

and the transition probabilities are $p_{11} = 0.8$ and $p_{12} = 0.2$. If in state 1 he does not advertise, the reward is 6 units and the transition probabilities are $p_{11} = p_{12} = 0.5$. While in state 2 he can do research to improve his product, in which case the one-stage reward is -5 units and the transition probabilities are $p_{21} = 0.7$ and $p_{22} = 0.3$. If in state 2 he does not do research, the reward is -3 and the transition probabilities are $p_{21} = 0.4$ and $p_{22} = 0.6$. Consider the infinite horizon, discounted version of this problem.

(a) Show that when the discount factor α is sufficiently small the computer manufacturer should follow the "shortsighted" policy of not advertising (not doing research) while in state 1 (state 2). By contrast, when α is sufficiently close to unity he should follow the "farsighted" policy of advertising (doing research) while at state 1 (state 2).

(b) Calculate the optimal cost and policy when $\alpha = 0.9$.

2. An energetic salesman works every day of the week. He can work in only one of two towns A and B on each day. For each day he works in town A (B) his expected reward is r_A (r_B). The cost for changing towns is c. Assume that $c > r_A > r_B$ and that there is a discount factor $\alpha < 1$.

(a) Show that for α sufficiently small the optimal policy is to stay in the town he starts in, and that for α sufficiently close to unity the optimal policy is to move to town A (if not starting there) and stay in A for all subsequent times.

(b) Solve the problem for $c = 3$, $r_A = 2$, $r_B = 1$, and $\alpha = 0.9$.

(c) Suppose that on Sundays only the expected reward for working in towns A and B is changed to R_A and R_B, respectively. Assuming that $R_A < R_B$, discuss the nature of the optimal policy. Solve the problem for the data in part (b) and $R_A = 1$, $R_B = 4.5$. *Hint:* This part requires the theory of periodic problems of Section 5.5.

3. *Generalized Error Bounds* [P14], [P15], [B17]. Let S be a set and $B(S)$ be the set of all bounded real-valued functions on S. Let $T: B(S) \to B(S)$ be a mapping with the following two properties:

(1) $T(J) \leq T(J')$ for all $J, J' \in B(S)$ with $J \leq J'$.

(2) For every scalar $r \neq 0$ and all $x \in S$

$$\alpha_1 \leq \frac{[T(J + re)(x) - T(J)(x)]}{r} \leq \alpha_2,$$

where α_1, α_2 are two scalars with $0 \leq \alpha_1 \leq \alpha_2 < 1$.

(a) Show that T is a contraction mapping on $B(S)$, and hence for every $J \in B(S)$ we have

$$\lim_{k\to\infty} T^k(J)(x) = J^*(x), \qquad x \in S,$$

where J^* is the unique fixed point of T in $B(S)$.

(b) Show that for all $J \in B(S)$, $x \in S$, and $k = 1, 2, \ldots,$

$$T^k(J)(x) + c_k \leq T^{k+1}(J)(x) + c_{k+1} \leq J^*(x)$$
$$\leq T^{k+1}(J)(x) + \overline{c}_{k+1} \leq T^k(J)(x) + \overline{c}_k,$$

where for all k

$$c_k = \min\left\{\frac{\alpha_1}{1-\alpha_1}\min_{x\in S}[T^k(J)(x) - T^{k-1}(J)(x)],\right.$$

$$\left.\frac{\alpha_2}{1-\alpha_2}\min_{x\in S}[T^k(J)(x) - T^{k-1}(J)(x)]\right\},$$

$$\overline{c}_k = \max\left\{\frac{\alpha_1}{1-\alpha_1}\max_{x\in S}[T^k(J)(x) - T^{k-1}(J)(x)],\right.$$

$$\left.\frac{\alpha_2}{1-\alpha_2}\max_{x\in S}[T^k(J)(x) - T^{k-1}(J)(x)]\right\}.$$

A geometric interpretation of these relations for the case where S consists of a single element is provided in Figure 5.4.

(c) Show that the Gauss–Seidel mapping F defined by (5.37) and (5.38) satisfies

$$\alpha^n \leq \frac{[F(J + re)(x) - F(J)(x)]}{r} \leq \alpha,$$

where n is the number of elements in S.

(d) Let J be an n-dimensional vector and consider solution of the equation $J = T(J)$. The mapping $T: R^n \to R^n$ is given by

$$T(J) = g + MJ$$

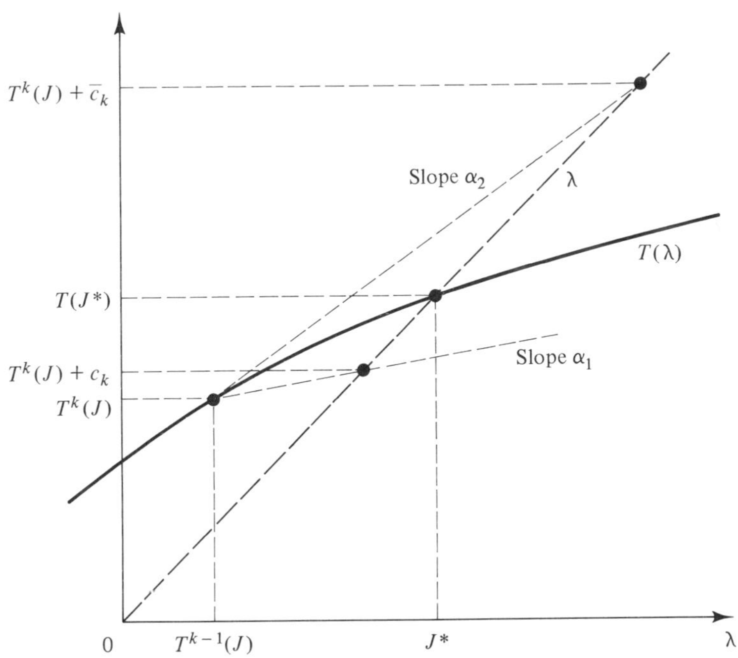

Figure 5.4 Graphical interpretation of the error bounds of Problem 3.

where the vector $g \in R^n$ and the matrix M are given. Let s_i be the ith row sum of M, that is,

$$s_i = \sum_{j=1}^{n} m_{ij},$$

and let $\alpha_1 = \min_i s_i$, $\alpha_2 = \max_i s_i$. Show that if the elements m_{ij} of M are all nonnegative and $\alpha_2 < 1$ then the conclusions of parts (a) and (b) hold.

(e) Consider the Gauss–Seidel method for solving the system $J = g + \alpha PJ$, where $0 < \alpha < 1$ and P is a transition probability matrix. Use part (d) to construct bounds that are sharper than the ones implied by the inequality of part (c).

4. *Minimax Problems.* Provide analogs for the results and algorithms of Sections 5.1 and 5.2 for the minimax problem where the cost is

$$J_\pi(x_0) = \lim_{N\to\infty} \max_{\substack{w_k \in W[x_k, \mu_k(x_k)] \\ k=0,1,\ldots}} \sum_{k=0}^{N-1} \alpha^k g[x_k, \mu_k(x_k), w_k],$$

g satisfies Assumption D, x_k is generated by $x_{k+1} = f[x_k, \mu_k(x_k), w_k]$, and $W(x, u)$ is a given nonempty subset of D for each $(x, u) \in S \times C$. (Compare with Problem 5, Chapter 1.)

5. Consider a problem similar to that of Section 5.1 except for the fact that when we are at state x_k there is a probability β, where $0 < \beta < 1$, that the next state x_{k+1} will be determined according to $x_{k+1} = f(x_k, u_k, w_k)$ and a probability $(1 - \beta)$ that the system will move to a termination state where it stays permanently thereafter at no cost. Show that even if $\alpha = 1$ (no discounting) the problem can be put into the discounted cost framework.

6. Consider a problem similar to Problem I under Assumption D except for the fact that the discount factor α depends on the current state x_k, the control u_k, and the disturbance w_k, that is, the cost functional has the form

$$J_\pi(x_0) = \lim_{N\to\infty} \mathop{E}_{\substack{w_k \\ k=0,1,\ldots}} \left\{ \sum_{k=0}^{N-1} \alpha_{\pi,k} g[x_k, \mu_k(x_k), w_k] \right\},$$

where

$$\alpha_{\pi,k} = \alpha[x_0, \mu_0(x_0), w_0]\alpha[x_1, \mu_1(x_1), w_1] \cdots \alpha[x_k, \mu_k(x_k), w_k],$$

with $\alpha(x, u, w)$ a given function satisfying

$$0 \le \min\{\alpha(x, u, w) | x \in S, u \in C, w \in D\}$$
$$\le \max\{\alpha(x, u, w) | x \in S, u \in C, w \in D\} < 1.$$

Show that the results and algorithms of Sections 5.1 and 5.2 have direct counterparts for such problems.

7. Let $\bar{J}: S \to R$ be any bounded function on S and consider the successive approximation method of Section 5.2 with a starting function $J: S \to R$ of the form

$$J(x) = \bar{J}(x) + r, \qquad x \in S,$$

where r is some scalar. Show that the bounds $T^k(J)(x) + c_k$ and $T^k(J)(x) + \bar{c}_k$ on $J^*(x)$ of Proposition 4 are independent of the scalar r for all $x \in S$. Show also that if S consists of a single element $\bar{x}$ (i.e., $S = \{\bar{x}\}$) then

$$T(J)(\bar{x}) + c_1 = T(J)(\bar{x}) + \bar{c}_1 = J^*(\bar{x}).$$

8. *Distributed Asynchronous Dynamic Programming* [B19]. The successive approximation method is well suited for distributed (or parallel) computation since the iteration

$$J(i) := T(J)(i) \tag{5.89}$$

corresponding to state i can be carried out in parallel with the iteration corresponding to any other state. Consider the finite state discounted problem of Section 5.2 and assume that iteration (5.89) is executed *asynchronously* at a different processor i for each state i. By this we mean that the ith processor executes at *arbitrary* times an iteration of the form

$$J^i(i) := T(J^i)(i),$$

and at *arbitrary* times transmits the results of the latest computation to other processors m who then update $J^m(i)$ according to

$$J^m(i) := J^i(i).$$

Assume that all processors never stop computing and transmitting the results of their computation to the other processors. Show that the estimates J_t^i of the optimal cost function available at each processor i at time t converge to the optimal solution function J^* as $t \to \infty$. *Hint:* Let $\bar{J}$ and $\underline{J}$ be two functions such that $\underline{J} \leq T(\underline{J})$ and $T(\bar{J}) \leq \bar{J}$, and suppose that for all initial estimates J_0^i of the processors we have $\underline{J} \leq J_0^i \leq \bar{J}$. Show that the estimates J_t^i of the processors at time t satisfy $\underline{J} \leq J_t^i \leq \bar{J}$, for all $t \geq 0$ and $T(\underline{J}) \leq J_t^i \leq T(\bar{J})$ for t sufficiently large.

9. Let $S = [0, \infty)$ and $C = U(x) = (0, \infty)$ be the state and control spaces, respectively, let the system equation be

$$x_{k+1} = \left(\frac{2}{\alpha}\right) x_k + u_k, \qquad k = 0, 1, \ldots,$$

where α is the discount factor, and let

$$g(x_k, u_k) = x_k + u_k$$

be the cost per stage. Show that for this deterministic problem Assumption P is satisfied and that $J^*(x) = \infty$ for all $x \in S$, but $T^k(J_0)(0) = 0$ for all k [J_0 is the zero function, $J_0(x) = 0$, for all $x \in S$].

10. Let Assumption P hold and consider the finite state case $S = D = \{1, 2, \ldots, n\}$, $\alpha = 1$, $x_{k+1} = w_k$. The mapping T is represented as

$$T(J)(i) = \min_{u \in U(i)} [g(i, u) + \sum_{j=1}^{n} p_{ij}(u) J(j)], \qquad i = 1, \ldots, n,$$

where $p_{ij}(u)$ denotes the transition probability that the next state will be j when the current state is i and control u is applied. Assume that $p_{ij}(u)$ and $g(i, u)$ are continuous on $U(i)$ for all i, j and that the sets $U(i)$ are compact subsets of R^m for all i. Show that we have $\lim_{k\to\infty} T^k(J_0)(i) = J^*(i)$, where $J_0(i) = 0$, $i = 1, \ldots, n$. Show also that there exists an optimal stationary policy.

11. Consider a deterministic problem involving a linear system

$$x_{k+1} = Ax_k + Bu_k, \qquad k = 0, 1, \ldots,$$

where the pair (A, B) is controllable and $x_k \in R^n$, $u_k \in R^m$. Assume no constraints on the control and a cost per stage g satisfying

$$0 \leq g(x, u), \qquad (x, u) \in R^n \times R^m.$$

Assume furthermore that g is continuous in x and u, and that $g(x_n, u_n) \to +\infty$ if $\{x_n\}$ is bounded and $|u_n| \to +\infty$.

(a) Show that for a discount factor $\alpha < 1$ the optimal cost satisfies $0 \leq J^*(x) < +\infty$, for all $x \in R^n$. Furthermore, there exists an optimal stationary policy and

$$\lim_{k\to\infty} T^k(J_0)(x) = J^*(x), \qquad x \in R^n.$$

(b) Show that the same holds true except perhaps for $J^*(x) < +\infty$ when the system is of the form $x_{k+1} = f(x_k, u_k)$, with $f: R^n \times R^m \to R^n$ being a continuous function.

(c) Prove the same results assuming that the control is constrained to lie in a compact set $U \subset R^m$ $(U(x) \equiv U)$ in place of the assumption $g(x_n, u_n) \to +\infty$ if $\{x_n\}$ is bounded and $|u_n| \to +\infty$. *Hint:* Show that $T^k(J_0)$ is real valued and continuous for every k and use Proposition 14.

12. Under Assumption P, let μ be such that $\mu(x) \in U(x)$, for all $x \in S$, and

$$T_\mu(J^*)(x) \leq T(J^*)(x) + \epsilon, \qquad x \in S.$$

Show that, if $\alpha < 1$,

$$J_\mu(x) \leq J^*(x) + \frac{\epsilon}{1 - \alpha}, \qquad x \in S.$$

Hint: Show that $T_\mu^k(J^*)(x) \leq J^*(x) + \Sigma_{i=0}^{k-1} \alpha^i \epsilon$. Alternatively, let $\tilde{J} = J^* + [\epsilon/(1 - \alpha)]e$, show that $T_\mu(\tilde{J}) \leq \tilde{J}$, and use Corollary 9.1.

13. *Generalized Policy Iteration Algorithm.* The purpose of this problem is to provide a policy iteration algorithm for the case where the state space and the control space are not necessarily finite sets. Under Assumption D, let $\{\mu, \mu, \ldots\}$ be an admissible stationary policy and let $\tilde{J}_\mu: S \to R$ be such that

$$\max_{x\in S} |\tilde{J}_\mu(x) - J_\mu(x)| \leq \gamma.$$

Let $J': S \to R$ be such that

$$\max_{x\in S} |J'(x) - T(\tilde{J}_\mu)(x)| \leq \delta$$

and assume that

$$\max_{x\in S} |J'(x) - \tilde{J}_\mu(x)| \leq \epsilon.$$

Show that for all $x \in S$ there holds

$$J^*(x) \leq J_\mu(x) \leq J^*(x) + \frac{\delta + \epsilon}{1 - \alpha} + \gamma. \tag{5.90}$$

Consider the following policy iteration algorithm, for fixed $\gamma, \delta, \epsilon > 0$.

1. Start with an admissible stationary policy $\pi^0 = \{\mu^0, \mu^0, \ldots\}$.
2. Given $\{\mu^i, \mu^i, \ldots\}$, find $\tilde{J}_{\mu^i}: S \to R$ such that $|\tilde{J}_{\mu^i}(x) - J_{\mu^i}(x)| \leq \gamma\alpha^i$ for all $x \in S$.

3. Find $\mu^{i+1}: S \to C$ with $\mu^{i+1}(x) \in U(x)$ for all $x \in S$ such that

$$T_{\mu^{i+1}}(\tilde{J}_{\mu^i})(x) \leq T(\tilde{J}_{\mu^i})(x) + \delta\alpha^i, \qquad x \in S.$$

If $\max_{x\in S}|T_{\mu^{i+1}}(\tilde{J}_{\mu^i})(x) - \tilde{J}_{\mu^i}(x)| \leq \epsilon$, stop. Otherwise, replace μ^i by μ^{i+1} and go to step 2.

Show that the algorithm will terminate after a finite number of iterations (say k) and that

$$J^*(x) \leq J_{\mu^k}(x) \leq J^*(x) + \frac{\alpha^{k-1}\delta + \epsilon}{1 - \alpha} + \gamma\alpha^{k-1}, \qquad x \in S.$$

Hint: To show inequality (5.90), use the fact that for any $\beta > 0$ there exists a k such that for all $x \in S$

$$|T^{k+1}(\tilde{J}_\mu)(x) - J^*(x)| \leq \beta.$$

Then use the inequalities

$$\begin{aligned}|\tilde{J}_\mu(x) - J^*(x)| &\leq |\tilde{J}_\mu(x) - T(\tilde{J}_\mu)(x)| + |T(\tilde{J}_\mu)(x) - T^2(\tilde{J}_\mu)(x)| \\ &\quad + \cdots + |T^{k+1}(\tilde{J}_\mu)(x) - J^*(x)| \\ &\leq \max_{x\in S}|\tilde{J}_\mu(x) - T(\tilde{J}_\mu)(x)|(1 + \alpha + \cdots + \alpha^k) + \beta \\ &\leq \frac{1}{1-\alpha}\max_{x\in S}|\tilde{J}_\mu(x) - T(\tilde{J}_\mu)(x)| + \beta,\end{aligned}$$

to show that

$$|\tilde{J}_\mu(x) - J^*(x)| \leq \frac{1}{1-\alpha}\max_{x\in S}|\tilde{J}_\mu(x) - T(\tilde{J}_\mu)(x)|, \qquad x \in S.$$

To show that the policy iteration algorithm will terminate in a finite number of iterations, assume the contrary; that is, we have

$$\max_{x\in S}|T_{\mu^{i+1}}(\tilde{J}_{\mu^i})(x) - \tilde{J}_{\mu^i}(x)| > \epsilon$$

for all i, and the algorithm generates an infinite sequence of policies $\{\pi^i\}$. Show first that, for all $x \in S$ and $i = 0, 1, \ldots$, we have

$$T_{\mu^{i+1}}(J_{\mu^i})(x) \leq T(J_{\mu^i})(x) + (\delta + 2\gamma\alpha)\alpha^i \leq J_{\mu^i}(x) + (\delta + 2\gamma\alpha)\alpha^i.$$

Use this inequality to show that, for all $x \in S$ and i, k,

$$T^k_{\mu^{i+1}}(J_{\mu^i})(x) \leq T(J_{\mu^i})(x) + (\delta + 2\gamma\alpha)\alpha^i \sum_{j=0}^{k-1} \alpha^j,$$

and conclude that, for all $x \in S$ and $i = 0, 1, \ldots$,

$$J^*(x) \leq J_{\mu^{i+1}}(x) \leq T(J_{\mu^i})(x) + \lambda\alpha^i,$$

where

$$\lambda = \frac{\delta + 2\gamma\alpha}{1 - \alpha}.$$

Show that, for all $x \in S$ and $i = 1, 2, \ldots$,

$$J^*(x) \leq J_{\mu^i}(x) \leq T^i(J_{\mu^0})(x) + i\alpha^{i-1}\lambda,$$

and conclude that

$$\lim_{i\to\infty} \max_{x\in S} |J_{\mu^i}(x) - J^*(x)| = 0.$$

Use this equality to reach a contradiction.

14. The purpose of this problem is to show that the successive approximation method of Section 5.2 will yield an optimal policy after a finite number of iterations when S, C, and D are finite sets. Under Assumption D, let $J:S \to R$ be a function such that for some $\epsilon > 0$ and all $x \in S$ we have

$$|J(x) - J^*(x)| \leq \epsilon.$$

Let $\mu(x)$ be such that for all $x \in S$ we have $\mu(x) \in U(x)$ and

$$\begin{aligned} T_\mu(J)(x) &= \underset{w}{E}\{g[x, \mu(x), w] + \alpha J[f(x, \mu(x), w)]\} \\ &= \min_{u\in U(x)} \underset{w}{E}\{g(x, u, w) + \alpha J[f(x, u, w)]\} = T(J)(x). \end{aligned}$$

(a) Show that, for all $x \in S$,

$$|T_\mu(J)(x) - J(x)| \leq (1 + \alpha)\epsilon.$$

(b) Using the preceding inequality, show that, for all $x \in S$,

$$|T_\mu(J)(x) - J_\mu(x)| \leq \frac{\alpha(1 + \alpha)}{1 - \alpha}\epsilon.$$

(c) Show that, for all $x \in S$,

$$J^*(x) \leq J_\mu(x) \leq J^*(x) + \frac{2\epsilon}{1 - \alpha}.$$

(d) Assume that the state, control, and disturbance spaces are finite sets. Show that the successive approximation method after some index will yield an optimal policy at every iteration; that is, for any starting function $J:S \to R$ there exists an index $\bar{k}$ such that if μ^* is such that

$$T_{\mu^*}[T^k(J)] = T^{k+1}(J) \quad \text{and} \quad k \geq \bar{k},$$

then $\{\mu^*, \mu^*, \ldots\}$ is optimal.

15. Under Assumption P or N, show that if $\alpha < 1$ and $\tilde{J}:S \to R$ is a *bounded* function satisfying $\tilde{J} = T(\tilde{J})$, then $\tilde{J} = J^*$.

16. *Policy Iteration and Newton's Method* [P17]. The purpose of this problem is to demonstrate a relation between policy iteration and Newton's method for solving nonlinear equations. Consider an equation of the form $F(J) = 0$, where $F:R^n \to R^n$. Given a vector $J_k \in R^n$, Newton's method determines J_{k+1} by solving the linear system of equations

$$F(J_k) + \frac{\partial F(J_k)}{\partial J}(J_{k+1} - J_k) = 0,$$

where $\partial F(J_k)/\partial J$ is the Jacobian matrix of F evaluated at J_k.

(a) Consider the discounted finite-state problem of Section 5.2 and define

$$F(J) = T(J) - J.$$

Show that if there is a unique policy μ such that

$$T_\mu(J) = T(J)$$

then the Jacobian matrix of F at J is

$$\frac{\partial F(J)}{\partial J} = \alpha P_\mu - I,$$

where I is the $n \times n$ identity.

(b) Show that the policy iteration algorithm can be identified with Newton's method for solving $F(J) = 0$ (assuming it gives a unique policy at each step).

17. Consider the problem of finding a scalar sequence $\{u_0, u_1, \ldots\}$ satisfying $\sum_{k=0}^{\infty} u_k \leq c$, $u_k \geq 0$, for all k, and maximizing $\sum_{k=0}^{\infty} g(u_k)$, where $c > 0$ and $g(u) \geq 0$ for all $u \geq 0$, $g(0) = 0$. Assume that g is monotonically nondecreasing on $[0, \infty)$. Show that the optimal value of the problem is $J^*(c)$, where J^* is a monotonically nondecreasing function on $[0, \infty)$ satisfying $J^*(0) = 0$ and

$$J^*(x) = \max_{0 \leq u \leq x}\{g(u) + J^*(x-u)\}, \qquad x \in [0, \infty).$$

18. *Transforming a Stochastic Problem into a Deterministic Problem.* Consider the problem of this chapter under Assumption D for the case where the sets S, C, and D are finite sets. Using the notation of Section 5.2, consider the controlled system

$$p_{k+1} = p_k P_{\mu_k}, \qquad k = 0, 1, \ldots,$$

where p_k is a probability distribution over S viewed as a row vector, and P_{μ_k} is the transition probability matrix corresponding to a function $\mu_k : C \to S$ with $\mu_k(i) \in U(i)$ for all $i \in S$. The state is p_k and the control is μ_k. Consider also the cost functional

$$\lim_{N\to\infty} \sum_{k=0}^{N-1} \alpha^k p_k g_{\mu_k}.$$

Show that the optimal cost and an optimal policy for the deterministic problem involving the system and the preceding cost functional yield the optimal cost and an optimal policy for the problem of this chapter.

19. *Jacobi Version of the Successive Approximation Method.* Consider the problem of Section 5.2 and the version of the successive approximation method that starts with an arbitrary function $J: S \to R$ and generates recursively $F(J)$, $F^2(J)$, . . . , where F is the mapping given by

$$F(J)(i) = \min_{u\in U(i)} \frac{g(i, u) + \alpha \sum_{j \neq i} p_{ij}(u) J(j)}{1 - \alpha p_{ii}(u)}.$$

Show that $F^k(J)(i) \to J^*(i)$ as $k \to \infty$ and provide a rate of convergence estimate that is at least as favorable as the one for the ordinary method (cf. Proposition 3).

20. *Data Transformations* [S9]. A finite state problem where the discount factor at each stage depends on the state can be transformed into a problem with state independent discount factor. To see this, consider the following set of equations in the variables J_i:

$$J_i = g_i + \sum_{j=1}^{n} M_{ij} J_j, \qquad i = 1, \ldots, n, \tag{5.91}$$

where we assume that for all i, j we have $M_{ij} \geq 0$ and

$$m_i \triangleq \sum_{j=1}^{n} M_{ij} < 1.$$

(a) Let

$$\alpha = \max_{i=1,\ldots,n} \left\{ \frac{m_i - M_{ii}}{1 - M_{ii}} \right\}$$

$$\delta_{ij} = \begin{cases} 1, & \text{if} \quad i = j, \\ 0, & \text{if} \quad i \neq j, \end{cases}$$

and define, for all i and j,

$$\overline{g}_i = \frac{g_i(1 - \alpha)}{1 - m_i},$$

$$\overline{M}_{ij} = \delta_{ij} + \frac{(1 - \alpha)(M_{ij} - \delta_{ij})}{1 - m_i}.$$

Show that, for all i and j,

$$\sum_{j=1}^{n} \overline{M}_{ij} = \alpha < 1, \qquad \overline{M}_{ij} \geq 0,$$

and that a solution $\{J_i \mid i = 1, \ldots, n\}$ of (5.91) is also a solution of the equations

$$J_i = \overline{g}_i + \sum_{j=1}^{n} \overline{M}_{ij} J_j, \qquad i = 1, \ldots, n.$$

(b) Provide a version of this result applying to an equation like (5.91) that involves minimization over a control set, and relate it to an infinite horizon problem like the one of Section 5.2.

21. Let Assumption P hold and assume that $\pi^* = \{\mu_0^*, \mu_1^*, \ldots\} \in \Pi$ satisfies $J^* = T_{\mu_k^*}(J^*)$ for all k. Show that π^* is optimal; that is, $J_{\pi^*} = J^*$.

22. Under Assumption P, show that, given $\epsilon > 0$, there exists a policy $\pi_\epsilon \in \Pi$ such that $J_{\pi_\epsilon}(x) \leq J^*(x) + \epsilon$ for all $x \in S$, and that for $\alpha < 1$ the policy π_ϵ can be taken stationary. Give an example where $\alpha = 1$ and for each stationary policy π we have $J_\pi(x) = \infty$, while $J^*(x) = 0$ for all x. *Hint:* See the proof of Proposition 8.

23. Under Assumption P, show that if there exists an optimal policy (a policy $\pi^* \in \Pi$ such that $J_{\pi^*} = J^*$), then there exists an optimal stationary policy.

24. Use the following counterexample to show that the result of Problem 23 may fail to hold under Assumption N if $J^*(x) = -\infty$ for some $x \in S$. Let $S = D = \{0, 1\}$, $f(x, u, w) = w$, $g(x, u, w) = u$, $U(0) = (-\infty, 0]$, $U(1) = \{0\}$, $p(w = 0 \mid x = 0, u) = \frac{1}{2}$, and $p(w = 1 \mid x = 1, u) = 1$. Show that $J^*(0) = -\infty$, $J^*(1) = 0$, and that the admissible nonstationary policy $\{\mu_0^*, \mu_1^*, \ldots\}$ with $\mu_k^*(0) = -(2/\alpha)^k$ is optimal. Show that any admissible stationary policy $\{\mu, \mu, \ldots\}$ satisfies $J_\mu(0) = [2/(2 - \alpha)]\mu(0)$, $J_\mu(1) = 0$ (see [B29], [D9], and [O3] for related analysis).

25. Show that the result of Problem 22 holds under Assumption N if S is a finite set, $\alpha = 1$, and $J^*(x) > -\infty$ for all $x \in S$. Construct a counterexample to show that the result can fail to hold if S is countable and $\alpha < 1$ (even if $J^*(x) > -\infty$ for all $x \in S$). *Hint:* Consider an integer N such that the N-stage optimal cost J_N satisfies $J_N(x) \leq J^*(x) + \epsilon$ for all x. For a counterexample, see [B24].

26. *Convergence Rate of Successive Approximation Method with Error Bounds.* Let P be an $n \times n$ transition probability matrix, g be a vector in R^n, e be the unit vector in R^n, and $\alpha < 1$ be a discount factor. Define for $J \in R^n$

$$T(J) = g + \alpha PJ,$$

$$A(J) = J + \frac{e'(T(J) - J)}{n(1 - \alpha)} e,$$

$$F(J) = T(A(J)) = T(J) + \frac{\alpha e'(T(J) - J)}{n(1 - \alpha)} e,$$

and consider the method that generates $\{F^k(J)\}$. (It is similar to the successive approximation method coupled with the error bounds of Proposition 4.)

(a) Show that

$$T(F(J)) - F(J) = \alpha P(F(J) - A(J)) = \alpha P\left(I - \frac{ee'}{n}\right)(T(J) - J).$$

(b) Define for $k \geq 1$

$$r_k = T(F^k(J)) - F^k(J).$$

Show that for all k

$$r_k = (\alpha P - I)[F^k(J) - J^*]$$

where J^* is the unique fixed point of T. Furthermore,

$$r_k = \alpha P\left(I - \frac{ee'}{n}\right) r_{k-1}$$

$$r_k = \alpha^k P\left(I - \frac{ee'}{n}\right) P^{k-1}(T(J) - J).$$

Hint: Show that $\left(I - \frac{ee'}{n}\right)P\left(I - \frac{ee'}{n}\right) = \left(I - \frac{ee'}{n}\right)P.$

(c) Assume for simplicity that P has a set of linearly independent eigenvectors, and consider a decomposition of $P^{k-1}(T(J) - J)$ into a linear combination of these eigenvectors. Show that r_k will converge to zero geometrically at a rate determined by the subdominant eigenvalue of αP. *Note:* If P does not have a set of linearly independent eigenvectors, a similar argument applies by considering a decomposition of $P^{k-1}(T(J) - J)$ along a set of invariant subspaces corresponding to the eigenvalues of P.

CHAPTER SIX

Infinite Horizon Problems: Applications

In this chapter we consider various special cases of the infinite horizon Problem I of Chapter 5. Most of these represent classes of problems that are important in their own right. Other applications have been selected because they illustrate interesting features of the theory of Chapter 5. The problem section touches on several related topics.

Each problem discussed in this chapter satisfies one of the Assumptions D, P, or N of Sections 5.1 and 5.4. To be strictly within the framework of Chapter 5, we also assume that the underlying disturbance space is countable, although we will not explicitly state this assumption in each individual case. Most of the results can be shown for a more general disturbance space, albeit at the expense of considerable technical complications (see [B23]).

6.1 LINEAR SYSTEMS AND QUADRATIC COST

Consider the case where in Problem I the system is linear:

$$x_{k+1} = Ax_k + Bu_k + w_k, \qquad k = 0, 1, \ldots,$$

where $x_k \in R^n$, $u_k \in R^m$ for all k and the matrices A, B are known. As in Sections 2.1 and 3.2, we assume that the random disturbances w_k are independent with zero mean and finite second moments. The cost functional is quadratic and has the form

$$J_\pi(x_0) = \lim_{N\to\infty} \underset{\substack{w_k \\ k=0,\ldots,N-1}}{E} \left\{ \sum_{k=0}^{N-1} \alpha^k [x_k' Q x_k + \mu_k(x_k)' R \mu_k(x_k)] \right\},$$

where Q is a positive semidefinite symmetric $n \times n$ matrix and R is a positive definite symmetric $m \times m$ matrix. The problem clearly falls under the framework of Assumption P.

Our approach will be to use the DP algorithm to obtain the functions $T(J_0)$, $T^2(J_0)$, . . ., as well as the pointwise limit function $J_\infty = \lim_{k\to\infty} T^k(J_0)$. Subsequently, we show that J_∞ satisfies $J_\infty = T(J_\infty)$ and hence, by Proposition 12 of Section 5.4, $J_\infty = J^*$. The optimal policy is then obtained from the optimal cost function J^* using Bellman's equation and Proposition 11 of Section 5.4.

As in Section 2.1, we have

$$J_0(x) = 0, \qquad x \in R^n,$$

$$T(J_0)(x) = \min_u (x'Qx + u'Ru) = x'Qx, \qquad x \in R^n,$$

$$T^2(J_0)(x) = \min_u \underset{w}{E}\{x'Qx + u'Ru + \alpha(Ax + Bu + w)'Q(Ax + Bu + w)\}$$

$$= x'K_1x + \alpha \underset{w}{E}\{w'Qw\}, \qquad x \in R^n,$$

$$T^{k+1}(J_0)(x) = x'K_kx + \sum_{m=0}^{k-1} \alpha^{k-m} \underset{w}{E}\{w'K_mw\}, \qquad x \in R^n, \quad k = 1, 2, \ldots,$$

where the matrices K_0, K_1, K_2, . . . are given recursively by

$$K_0 = Q,$$

$$K_{k+1} = A'[\alpha K_k - \alpha^2 K_k B(\alpha B'K_kB + R)^{-1}B'K_k]A + Q, \qquad k = 0, 1, \ldots.$$

By writing $\tilde{R} = R/\alpha$ and $\tilde{A} = \sqrt{\alpha}A$, the preceding equation may be written

$$K_{k+1} = \tilde{A}'[K_k - K_kB(B'K_kB + \tilde{R})^{-1}B'K_k]\tilde{A} + Q,$$

and is of the form considered in Section 2.1. By making use of the result shown there, we have

$$K_k \to K$$

provided the pairs $(\tilde{A}, B)$ and $(\tilde{A}, C)$, where $Q = C'C$, are controllable and observable, respectively. Since $\tilde{A} = \sqrt{\alpha}A$, controllability and observability of (A, B) or (A, C) are clearly equivalent to controllability and observability of $(\tilde{A}, B)$ or $(\tilde{A}, C)$. The matrix K is positive definite and is the unique solution of the equation

$$K = A'[\alpha K - \alpha^2 KB(\alpha B'KB + R)^{-1}B'K]A + Q \tag{6.1}$$

within the class of positive semidefinite symmetric matrices.

As a result of the preceding analysis, we have that the pointwise limit of the functions $T^k(J_0)$ is given by

$$J_\infty(x) = \lim_{k\to\infty} T^k(J_0)(x) = x'Kx + c, \tag{6.2}$$

where

$$c = \lim_{k\to\infty} \sum_{m=0}^{k-1} \alpha^{k-m} \underset{w}{E}\{w'K_m w\}.$$

This limit is well defined because $K_m \to K$. In fact, it can be verified that

$$c = \frac{\alpha}{1-\alpha} \underset{w}{E}\{w'Kw\}. \tag{6.3}$$

Using (6.1) to (6.3), it can be seen that for all $x \in S$

$$J_\infty(x) = T(J_\infty)(x) = \min_u \left[x'Qx + u'Ru + \alpha \underset{w}{E}\{J_\infty(Ax + Bu + w)\} \right] \tag{6.4}$$

and hence, by Proposition 12 of Section 5.4, $J_\infty = J^*$. Another method for proving that $J_\infty = T(J_\infty)$ is to show that the assumption of Proposition 14 of Section 5.4 is satisfied; that is, the sets

$$U_k(x, \lambda) = \left\{ u \,\middle|\, \underset{w}{E}\{x'Qx + u'Ru + \alpha T^k(J_0)(Ax + Bu + w)\} \leq \lambda \right\}$$

are compact. This can be easily verified using the fact that $T^k(J_0)$ is a quadratic function and R is positive definite. The optimal policy is obtained by minimization in (6.4) and has the form $\pi^* = \{\mu^*, \mu^*, \ldots\}$, where μ^* is given by

$$\mu^*(x) = -\alpha(\alpha B'KB + R)^{-1}B'KAx, \qquad x \in R^n.$$

The linearity and stationarity of this policy makes it very attractive for engineering applications. A number of generalized versions of the problem of this section, including the case of imperfect state information, are treated in the problem section. An interesting fact is that the problem can be solved by policy iteration (see Problem 5), even though, as discussed in Section 5.4, policy iteration is not valid in general under Assumption P.

6.2 INVENTORY CONTROL

Let us consider an infinite horizon version of the inventory control problem of Section 2.2 where costs per stage are discounted. Inventory stock evolves according to the equation

$$x_{k+1} = x_k + u_k - w_k, \qquad k = 0, 1, \ldots. \tag{6.5}$$

Again we assume that the successive demands w_k are independent and bounded and have identical probability distributions. We will assume for simplicity that there is no fixed cost. A similar analysis may be carried out for the case of a nonzero fixed cost. The function to be minimized is given by

$$J_\pi(x_0) = \lim_{N\to\infty} \underset{\substack{w_k \\ k=0,1,\ldots}}{E} \left\{ \sum_{k=0}^{N-1} \alpha^k [c\mu_k(x_k) + p \max(0, w_k - x_k - \mu_k(x_k)) \right.$$

$$\left. + h \max(0, x_k + \mu_k(x_k) - w_k)] \right\}.$$

The DP algorithm is given by

$$J_0(x) = 0,$$

$$T^{k+1}(J_0)(x) = \min_{0\le u} \underset{w}{E}\{cu + p \max(0, w - x - u) + h \max(0, x + u - w)$$

$$+ \alpha T^k(J_0)(x + u - w)\}.$$

Let us first show that

$$J^*(x_0) = \min_\pi J_\pi(x_0) < +\infty, \qquad \text{for all } x_0 \in S. \tag{6.6}$$

Indeed, consider the policy $\tilde{\pi} = \{\tilde{\mu}, \tilde{\mu}, \ldots\}$, where $\tilde{\mu}$ is defined by

$$\tilde{\mu}(x) = \begin{cases} 0, & \text{if } x \ge 0, \\ -x, & \text{if } x < 0. \end{cases}$$

Since w_k is nonnegative and bounded, it follows that the inventory stock x_k when the policy $\tilde{\pi}$ is used satisfies

$$-w_{k-1} \le x_k \le \max[0, x_0], \qquad k = 1, 2, \ldots,$$

and is bounded. Hence $\tilde{\mu}(x_k)$ is also bounded. Hence the cost per stage incurred when $\tilde{\pi}$ is used is bounded, and in view of the presence of the discount factor we have

$$J_{\tilde{\pi}}(x_0) < +\infty, \qquad x_0 \in S.$$

Since $J^* \le J_{\tilde{\pi}}$, (6.6) follows.

Next let us observe that, under the assumption $c < p$, the functions $T^k(J_0)$ are real-valued and convex. Indeed, we have

$$J_0 \le T(J_0) \le \cdots \le T^k(J_0) \le \cdots \le J^*,$$

which implies that $T^k(J_0)$ is real-valued. Convexity follows easily by induction as shown in Section 2.2. Consider now the sets

$$U_k(x, \lambda) = \{u \ge 0 | E\{cu + p \max(0, w - x - u) + h \max(0, x + u - w)$$

$$+ \alpha T^k(J_0)(x + u - w)\} \le \lambda\}. \tag{6.7}$$

These sets are bounded since the expected value tends to $+\infty$ as $u \to +\infty$. Also, the sets $U_k(x, \lambda)$ are closed since the expected value in (6.7) is a continuous function of u [recall that $T^k(J_0)$ is a real-valued convex and hence continuous function]. Thus we may invoke Proposition 14 of Section

5.4 and assert that

$$J_\infty(x) = \lim_{k\to\infty} T^k(J_0)(x) = J^*(x), \qquad x \in S.$$

It follows from the convexity of the functions $T^k(J_0)$ that the limit function J^* is a real-valued convex function. Furthermore, we have from Proposition 8 of Section 5.4 the optimality equation

$$J^*(x) = \min_{u\geq 0} \mathop{E}_{w}\{cu + p\max(0, w - x - u) + h\max(0, x + u - w) + \alpha J^*(x + u - w)\}.$$

An optimal stationary policy $\pi^* = \{\mu^*, \mu^*, \ldots\}$ can be obtained from this equation as in Section 2.2. We have

$$\mu^*(x) = \begin{cases} S^* - x, & \text{if} \quad x \leq S^*, \\ 0, & \text{otherwise}, \end{cases}$$

where S^* is a minimizing point of

$$G^*(y) = cy + L(y) + \mathop{E}_{w}\{J^*(y - w)\},$$

with

$$L(y) = p\mathop{E}_{w}\{\max(0, w - y)\} + h\mathop{E}_{w}\{\max(0, y - w)\}.$$

It is easy to see that if $p > c$ we have $\lim_{|y|\to\infty} G^*(y) = +\infty$ so that such a minimizing point exists. Furthermore, by utilizing the observation made near the end of Section 5.4, it follows that minimizing points S^* of $G^*(y)$ may be obtained as limit points of sequences $\{S_k\}$, where for each k the scalar S_k minimizes

$$G_k(y) = cy + L(y) + \alpha\mathop{E}_{w}\{T^k(J_0)(y - w)\}$$

and is obtained by means of the successive approximation method.

It turns out that the critical level S^* has a simple characterization. It can be shown that S^* maximizes the expression $(1 - \alpha)cy + L(y)$ over y, and it can be essentially obtained in closed form (see Problem 25 and [H8], Ch. 2).

In the case where there is a positive fixed cost $(K > 0)$, the same line of argument may be used. Similarly, we prove that J^* is a real-valued K-convex function. A separate argument is necessary to prove that J^* is also continuous (this is intuitively clear and is left for the reader). Once K-convexity and continuity of J^* are established, the optimality of a stationary (s^*, S^*) policy follows from the equation

$$J^*(x) = \min_{u\geq 0} \mathop{E}_{w}\{C(u) + p\max(0, w - x - u) + h\max(0, x + u - w) + \alpha J^*(x + u - w)\},$$

where $C(u) = K + cu$ if $u > 0$ and $C(0) = 0$.

6.3 OPTIMAL STOPPING

Consider a situation where at each state x two possible actions are available. We may either *stop* and pay a terminal cost $t(x)$ or pay a cost $c(x)$ and *continue* the process according to the system equation

$$x_{k+1} = f_c(x_k, w_k), \qquad k = 0, 1, \ldots. \tag{6.8}$$

The objective is to find the optimal stopping policy that minimizes the total expected cost over an infinite number of stages. It is assumed that the input disturbances w_k have the same probability distribution for all k, which depends only on the current state x_k.

To put this problem within the framework of Problem I, we introduce an additional state s (termination state) and we complete the system equation (6.8) as in Section 2.4 by letting

$$x_{k+1} = s, \qquad \text{if} \quad u_k = \text{stop} \quad \text{or} \quad x_k = s.$$

Once the system reaches the termination state, it remains there permanently at no cost.

We will assume in this section that

$$t(x) \geq 0, \qquad c(x) \geq 0, \qquad \text{for all } x \in S. \tag{6.9}$$

The case where $t(x) \leq 0$ and $c(x) \leq 0$ for all $x \in S$ is treated in Problem 7. Actually, whenever there exists an $\epsilon > 0$ such that $c(x) \geq \epsilon$ for all $x \in S$, the results to be obtained apply also to the case where

$$\min_{x \in S} t(x) > -\infty,$$

that is, when $t(x)$ is bounded below by some scalar rather than bounded by zero. The reason is that, if $c(x)$ is assumed to be greater than $\epsilon > 0$ for all $x \in S$, any policy that will not stop within a finite expected number of stages results in infinite cost and can be excluded from consideration. As a result, if we reformulate the problem and add a constant r to $t(x)$ so that $t(x) + r \geq 0$ for all $x \in S$, the optimal cost $J^*(x)$ will merely be increased by r, while optimal policies will remain unaffected.

Under our assumptions the problem clearly falls within the framework of Problem I provided the disturbance space D is a countable set. Furthermore, Assumption P is satisfied by virtue of (6.9). The mapping T that defines the DP algorithm takes the form

$$T(J)(x) = \min[t(x), c(x) + E\{J[f_c(x, w)]\}], \qquad x \in S, \tag{6.10}$$

where $t(x)$ is the cost of the stopping action, and $c(x) + E_w\{J[f_c(x, w)]\}$ is the cost of the continuation action. To be precise, we should also define $T(J)(s) = 0$, where s is the termination state. However, in what follows the value of various functions at s is immaterial and will not be explicitly considered.

By Proposition 8 of Section 5.4, the optimal cost function J^* satisfies

$$J^* = T(J^*).$$

Since the control space has only two elements, by Proposition 13 of Section 5.4 we have

$$\lim_{k\to\infty} T^k(J_0)(x) = J^*(x), \qquad x \in S, \tag{6.11}$$

where J_0 is the zero function ($J_0(x) = 0$, for all $x \in S$). By Proposition 11 of Section 5.4, there exists a stationary optimal policy given by:

$$\text{Stop} \qquad \text{if } t(x) < c(x) = E\{J^*[f_c(x, w)]\},$$

$$\text{Continue} \qquad \text{if } t(x) \geq c(x) + E\{J^*[f_c(x, w)]\}.$$

Let us denote by S^* the optimal stopping set (which may be empty)

$$S^* = \{x \in S | t(x) < c(x) + E\{J^*[f_c(x, w)]\}\}.$$

Consider also the sets

$$S_k = \{x \in S | t(x) < c(x) + E\{T^k(J_0)[f_c(x, w)]\}\}$$

that determine the optimal policy for finite horizon versions of the stopping problem. Since we have

$$J_0 \leq T(J_0) \leq \cdots \leq T^k(J_0) \leq \cdots \leq J^*,$$

it follows that

$$S_1 \subset \cdots \subset S_k \subset \cdots \subset S^*$$

and therefore $\cup_{k=1}^{\infty} S_k \subset S^*$. Also, if $\bar{x} \notin \cup_{k=1}^{\infty} S_k$, then we have

$$t(\bar{x}) \geq c(\bar{x}) + E\{T^k(J_0)[f_c(\bar{x}, w)]\}, \qquad k = 0, 1, \ldots,$$

and by taking limits and using (6.11) we obtain

$$t(\bar{x}) \geq c(\bar{x}) + E\{J^*[f_c(\bar{x}, w)]\},$$

from which $\bar{x} \notin S^*$. Hence

$$S^* = \bigcup_{k=1}^{\infty} S_k. \tag{6.12}$$

In other words, the *optimal stopping set S^* for the infinite horizon problem is equal to the union of all the finite horizon stopping sets S_k*. In particular, when the state space is finite, the infinite and finite horizon stopping sets coincide when the horizon is sufficiently large.

Hypothesis Testing Example: Sequential Probability Ratio Test

Consider the hypothesis testing problem of Section 3.5 for the case where the number of possible observations is unlimited. Here the set S is the interval $[0, 1]$ and corresponds to the sufficient statistic

$$p_k = P(x_k = x^0 | z_0, z_1, \ldots, z_k).$$

To each $p \in [0, 1]$ we may assign the termination cost

$$t(p) = \min[(1 - p)L_0, pL_1],$$

that is, the cost associated with optimal choice between the distributions f_0 and f_1. The mapping T of (6.10) takes the form

$$T(J)(p) = \min\left[(1 - p)L_0, pL_1, c + \mathop{E}_{z}\left\{J\left[\frac{pf_0(z)}{pf_0(z) + (1 - p)f_1(z)}\right]\right\}\right], \tag{6.13}$$

where the expectation over z is taken with respect to the probability distribution

$$P(z) = pf_0(z) + (1 - p)f_1(z), \qquad z \in Z.$$

The optimal cost function J^* satisfies

$$J^*(p) = \min\left[(1 - p)L_0, pL_1, c + \mathop{E}_{z}\left\{J^*\left[\frac{pf_0(z)}{pf_0(z) + (1 - p)f_1(z)}\right]\right\}\right] \tag{6.14}$$

and is obtained in the limit through the equation

$$J^*(p) = \lim_{k\to\infty} T^k(J_0)(p), \qquad p \in [0, 1],$$

where J_0 is the zero function on $[0, 1]$.

Now consider the functions $T^k(J_0)$, $k = 0, 1, \ldots$. It is clear that

$$J_0 \leq T(J_0) \leq \cdots \leq T^k(J_0) \leq \cdots \leq \min[(1 - p)L_0, pL_1].$$

Furthermore, in view of the analysis of Section 3.5, we have that the function $T^k(J_0)$ is concave on $[0, 1]$ for all k. Hence the pointwise limit function J^* is also concave on $[0, 1]$. In addition, (6.14) implies that

$$J^*(0) = J^*(1) = 0 \quad \text{and} \quad J^*(p) \leq \min[(1 - p)L_0, pL_1].$$

It follows from (6.14) and Figure 6.1 that [provided $c < L_0L_1/(L_0 + L_1)$] there exist two scalars $\overline{\alpha}, \overline{\beta}$ with $0 < \overline{\beta} \leq \overline{\alpha} < 1$, that determine an optimal stationary policy of the form

Accept f_0	if $p \geq \overline{\alpha}$.
Accept f_1	if $p \leq \overline{\beta}$.
Continue the observations	if $\overline{\beta} < p < \overline{\alpha}$.

In view of the optimality of the preceding stationary policy, the sequential probability ratio test described in Section 3.5 is justified when the number of possible observations is infinite.

One-Step Lookahead Policies

We have already considered one valid version of the successive approximation method that starts with the zero function J_0 and progressively calculates $T^N(J_0)$, $N = 0, 1, \ldots$. We can view $T^N(J_0)(x_0)$ as the optimal

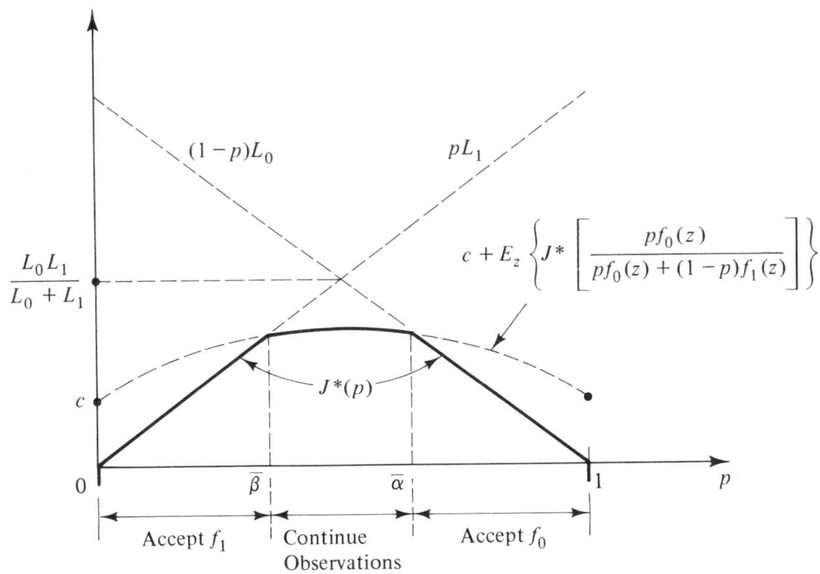

Figure 6.1 Derivation of the sequential probability ratio test.

cost at initial state x_0 of an N-stage stopping problem whereby at the Nth stage the terminal cost is zero if stopping has not already occurred.

Another interesting N-stage problem (already considered in more general form in Section 2.5) is one whereby the terminal cost is $t(x_N)$ (i.e., termination is forced at the Nth stage if it has not already occurred). The corresponding successive approximation method progressively calculates $T^N(t)(x)$, for all $x \in S$, $N = 0, 1, \ldots$. However, this method is *not* valid in general in the sense that $T^N(t)(x)$ need not converge to $J^*(x)$ as $N \to \infty$ for any x. To see this, consider a case where the continuation cost $c(x)$ is zero for all x, while the termination cost $t(x)$ is bounded below by $\epsilon > 0$. Then we will have $T^N(t)(x) \geqslant \epsilon$ for all x while $J^*(x) = 0$ for all x since the policy that always continues at no cost will be optimal. It would appear, however, that if the problem is such that optimal policies terminate eventually with probability one then the pathology described will not occur and $T^N(t)$ will converge to J^*. One way to guarantee this ([R6]) is to assume that for some $\epsilon > 0$ we have

$$c(x) \geqslant \epsilon, \qquad \text{for all } x \in S, \tag{6.15}$$

in which case, as discussed earlier, we can also relax the positivity assumption on t to one of boundedness from below. For a different set of assumptions, see Example 4 at the end of the next section.

Proposition 1. In the problem of this section assume (6.15) and that

$t(x)$ is bounded above over $x \in S$. Then for all $x_0 \in S$ and $N = 0, 1, \ldots,$

$$0 \leq T^N(t)(x_0) - J^*(x_0) \leq \frac{(\bar{t} - \epsilon)t(x_0)}{(N + 1)\epsilon}, \tag{6.16}$$

where ϵ is the lower bound in (6.15) and $\bar{t}$ is given by

$$\bar{t} = \max\,[\epsilon, \max_{x \in S} t(x)].$$

Proof. Let π^* be an optimal policy and let π_N be the policy that chooses the same actions as π^* for $k = 0, 1, \ldots, N - 1$ and stops at time N if it has not previously done so. Then if k_s is the random time at which π^* stops, and J_{π_N} is the cost corresponding to using π_N, we have, for all $x_0 \in S$,

$$\begin{aligned} J^*(x_0) = J^*_\pi(x_0) &= E\{C|k_s \leq N, \pi^*\}P(k_s \leq N) \\ &\quad + E\{C|k_s > N, \pi^*\}P(k_s > N), \\ T^N(t)(x_0) \leq J_{\pi_N}(x_0) &= E\{C|k_s \leq N, \pi^*\}P(k_s \leq N) \\ &\quad + E\{C|k_s > N, \pi_N\}P(k_s > N), \end{aligned}$$

where C denotes total cost incurred and the expectations are conditional on the initial state x_0. From the preceding relations, we obtain

$$\begin{aligned} T^N(t)(x_0) - J^*(x_0) &\leq [E\{C|k_s > N, \pi_N\} \\ &\quad - E\{C|k_s > N, \pi^*\}]\, P(k_s > N) \\ &\leq (\bar{t} - \epsilon)P(k_s > N). \end{aligned} \tag{6.17}$$

To obtain a bound on $P(k_s > N)$, we note that

$$t(x_0) \geq J^*(x_0) \geq (N + 1)\epsilon P(k_s > N),$$

so

$$P(k_s > N) \leq \frac{t(x_0)}{(N + 1)\epsilon}. \tag{6.18}$$

From (6.17) and (6.18), we obtain the right side of (6.16). The left side is obtained by applying the mapping T repeatedly on both sides of the relation $t \geq J^*$. Q.E.D.

Note that relation (6.16) not only guarantees the validity of the successive approximation method that starts from the termination cost t, but also provides a rate of convergence estimate, as well as precomputable error bounds.

Consider now, as in Section 2.4, the one-step-to-go stopping set

$$\tilde{S}_1 - \{x \in S | t(x) \leq c(x) + E\{t[f_c(x, w)]\}\} \tag{6.19}$$

and assume that $\tilde{S}_1$ is *absorbing* in the sense

$$f_c(x, w) \in \tilde{S}_1, \qquad \text{for all } x \in \tilde{S}_1, \quad w \in D. \tag{6.20}$$

Then, as in Section 2.4, it follows that the one-step lookahead policy

$$\text{Stop if and only if } x \in \tilde{S}_1$$

is optimal. We now provide some examples.

Asset Selling

Consider the asset-selling example of Sections 2.4 and 5.1, where the rate of interest r is zero and there is instead a maintenance cost $c > 0$ per period for which the house remains unsold. Furthermore, past offers can be accepted at any future time. We have the following optimality equation:

$$J^*(x) = \max[x, \, -c + E\{J^*(\max[x, w])\}].$$

In this case we consider maximization of total expected reward, the continuation cost is strictly negative, and the termination reward x is positive. Hence assumption (6.9) is not satisfied. If, however, we assume that x takes values in a bounded interval $[0, M]$, where M is an upper bound on the possible values of offers, our analysis is still applicable [cf. the discussion following (6.9)]. Consider the one-step-to-go stopping set of (6.19). It is given by

$$\tilde{S}_1 = \{x | x \geqslant -c + E\{\max[x, w]\}\}.$$

After a calculation similar to the one given in Section 2.4, we see that

$$\tilde{S}_1 = \{x | x \geqslant \overline{\alpha}\},$$

where $\overline{\alpha}$ is the scalar satisfying

$$\overline{\alpha} = P(\overline{\alpha})\overline{\alpha} + \int_{\overline{\alpha}}^{\infty} w \, dP(w) - c.$$

Clearly, $\tilde{S}_1$ is absorbing in the sense of (6.20) and therefore the one-step lookahead policy that accepts the first offer greater than or equal to $\overline{\alpha}$ is optimal.

The Rational Burglar

This example was considered at the end of Section 2.4 where it was shown that a one-step lookahead policy is optimal for any horizon length. The optimality equation is

$$\begin{aligned} J^*(x) &= \max[x, (1 - p)E\{J^*(x + w)\}] \\ &= \max[x, c(x) + E\{J^*(x + w)\}], \end{aligned}$$

where

$$c(x) = -pE\{J^*(x + w)\}.$$

We may view $c(x)$ as a strictly negative continuation cost corresponding to the possibility of the burglar's arrest. Therefore, the successive approximation method that starts from the termination cost is valid, equation

(6.20) holds, and it is easily seen that the finite horizon optimal policy whereby the burglar retires when his accumulated earnings reach or exceed $(1 - p)\overline{w}/p$ is optimal for an infinite horizon as well.

6.4 THE FIRST PASSAGE PROBLEM†

In the stopping problem of the previous section there were only two possible actions at each stage, stop or continue. We consider now a generalized version where the controller cannot stop the system, but instead can influence the probability of termination as well as the transition probabilities from one state to the next. We distinguish two different versions of the problem. In the first we assume that termination is inevitable with probability one under *all* policies. In the second version we assume that termination is eventually certain under *some* policies, but assume that the cost structure is such that there is an incentive to try to terminate. One can describe roughly the control objective as trying to terminate at minimum cost, and in this sense the problem of this section can be viewed as a stochastic generalization of the shortest path problem of Section 1.3.

Unless otherwise specified, in this section we assume that the system is a finite state Markov chain with state space

$$S = \{0, 1, \ldots, n\}.$$

The control space C is also assumed finite. The transition probabilities associated with control u are denoted

$$p_{ij}(u) = P\{x_{k+1} = j | x_k = i, u_k = u\}.$$

State 0 is a termination state in the sense

$$p_{00}(u) = 1, \qquad u \in U(0).$$

The cost per stage at state $i = 1, \ldots, n$ when control u is applied is denoted $g(i, u)$, and there is no cost incurred while in the termination state; that is, $g(0, u) = 0$ for all u.

Termination Inevitable under All Policies

Here we assume that there exists a positive integer m such that for every admissible policy $\pi = \{\mu_0, \mu_1, \ldots\}$ there holds

$$P(x_m = 0 | x_0 = i, \pi) > 0, \qquad i = 1, 2, \ldots, n. \tag{6.21}$$

In words, there is a positive probability of reaching the termination state under every policy from every initial state. A little thought should convince the reader that this is equivalent to assuming that termination will occur

† This section requires some familiarity with the basic notions associated with finite state Markov chains. A summary, together with references, is given in Appendix D.

with probability one under every policy. Actually, it is sufficient to assume that (6.21) holds for all *stationary* policies π; see Problems 12 and 13.

Under this assumption, one may prove a number of important results that are not available under either Assumption P or N. In fact, it turns out that *it is not necessary to assume Assumption P or N* (i.e., the costs per stage g need not be all either nonnegative or nonpositive). The basic reason is that the mapping T defining the DP algorithm is an m-stage contraction mapping over the set of all functions $J: S \to R$ with $J(0) = 0$, where m is the positive integer in (6.21) (see Section 5.3).

Proposition 2. There exists a scalar $\rho < 1$ such that for all $J, J': S \to R$ with $J(0) = J'(0) = 0$ we have

$$\max_{i=0,1,\dots,n} |T^m(J)(i) - T^m(J')(i)| \leq \rho \max_{i=0,1,\dots,n} |J(i) - J'(i)|, \tag{6.22}$$

where

$$T(J)(i) = \min_{u \in U(i)} \left[g(i, u) + \sum_{j=1}^{n} p_{ij}(u) J(j) \right], \qquad i = 1, 2, \dots, n,$$

$$T(J)(0) = 0.$$

Proof. Let $\pi_m = \{\mu_0, \mu_1, \dots, \mu_{m-1}\}$ be such that

$$T^m(J') = (T_{\mu_0} T_{\mu_1} \cdots T_{\mu_{m-1}})(J').$$

By subtracting this equation from the inequality

$$T^m(J) \leq (T_{\mu_0} T_{\mu_1} \cdots T_{\mu_{m-1}})(J),$$

we obtain, for every i,

$$T^m(J)(i) - T^m(J')(i) \leq (T_{\mu_0} \cdots T_{\mu_{m-1}})(J)(i) - (T_{\mu_0} \cdots T_{\mu_{m-1}})(J')(i). \tag{6.23}$$

The two terms on the right are m-stage costs corresponding to initial state i, policy π_m, and terminal costs $J(x_m)$ and $J'(x_m)$, respectively. Therefore, the right side of (6.23) equals

$$\sum_{j=1}^{n} P(x_m = j | x_0 = i, \pi_m)[J(j) - J'(j)], \tag{6.24}$$

and we obtain, for all i,

$$T^m(J)(i) - T^m(J')(i) \leq \sum_{j=1}^{n} P(x_m = j | x_0 = i, \pi_m) \max_s |J(s) - J'(s)|.$$

By reversing the roles of J and J', we similarly obtain, for some policy π'_m,

$$T^m(J')(i) - T^m(J)(i) \leq \sum_{j=1}^{n} P(x_m = j | x_0 = i, \pi'_m) \max_s |J(s) - J'(s)|.$$

From (6.21), we have

$$\rho = \max_{\pi} \max_{i} \sum_{j=1}^{n} P(x_m = j | x_0 = i, \pi) < 1 \tag{6.25}$$

and the last three relations prove (6.22). Q.E.D.

The argument used in this proof also proves the following corollary.

Corollary 2.1. Let $\pi = \{\mu_0, \mu_1, \ldots\}$ be an admissible policy. Then we have, for all $J, J': S \to R$ with $J(0) = J'(0) = 0$,

$$\max_{i=0,1,\ldots,n} |(T_{\mu_0} T_{\mu_1} \cdots T_{\mu_{m-1}})(J)(i) - (T_{\mu_0} T_{\mu_1} \cdots T_{\mu_{m-1}})(J')(i)|$$
$$\leq \rho \max_{i=0,1,\ldots,n} |J(i) - J'(i)|,$$

where ρ is given by (6.25).

Having established the m-stage contraction properties of Proposition 2 and Corollary 2.1, we are able to state a number of important analytical and computational results. The following proposition guarantees the convergence of the successive approximation method to the optimal cost function J^* starting from an arbitrary function $J: S \to R$ with $J(0) = 0$. Also, J^* and J_μ can be obtained as unique solutions of the equations $J = T(J)$ and $J = T_\mu(J)$, respectively.

Proposition 3. For every $J: S \to R$ with $J(0) = 0$,

$$J^*(x) = \lim_{k\to\infty} T^k(J)(x), \qquad x \in S,$$

and for every stationary policy $\{\mu, \mu, \ldots\}$,

$$J_\mu(x) = \lim_{k\to\infty} T_\mu^k(J)(x), \qquad x \in S.$$

Furthermore, J^* and J_μ are unique solutions of the equations $J = T(J)$ and $J = T_\mu(J)$, respectively, within the class of functions $J: S \to R$ with $J(0) = 0$. In addition, if $\mu^*(i)$ attains for $i = 1, \ldots, n$, the minimum in the right side of the equation

$$J^*(i) = \min_{u \in U(i)} \left[g(i, u) + \sum_{j=1}^{n} p_{ij}(u) J^*(j) \right], \qquad i = 1, \ldots, n,$$

then $\pi^* = \{\mu^*, \mu^*, \ldots\}$ is an optimal stationary policy.

The proof of Proposition 3 may be obtained through arguments similar to those used in Section 5.1. It is also possible to compute optimal stationary policies by using the method of policy iteration or linear programming (cf. Section 5.2). The development and proof of validity of these algorithms is again left as an exercise for the reader.

Example 1

Minimizing the Average Time to Termination. The case where

$$g(i, u) = 1, \qquad i = 1, \dots, n, \quad u \in U(i),$$

corresponds to a problem where the objective is to terminate as fast as possible on the average, while the corresponding optimal cost $J^*(i)$ is the minimum average time to termination starting from state i. From Proposition 3, we see that these times are the unique solution of the equations

$$J^*(i) = \min_{u \in U(i)} \left[1 + \sum_{j=1}^{n} p_{ij}(u) J^*(j) \right], \qquad i = 1, \dots, n.$$

In the special case where there is only one control at each state, $J^*(i)$ represents the mean first passage time from i to 0 (see Appendix D). These times, denoted t_i, are the unique solution of the equations

$$t_i = 1 + \sum_{j=1}^{n} p_{ij} t_j, \qquad i = 1, \dots, n,$$

which is a well-known result in Markov chain theory.

The following example demonstrates a pathology and shows that the assumption of a finite control space cannot be easily relaxed.

Example 2

The Blackmailer's Dilemma [W11]. Consider a problem where there are two states, the termination state 0 and another state $x = 1$. At state 1, we can choose a control u in (0, 1]; we then move to state 0 with probability u^2 and no cost, and stay in state 1 with probability $1 - u^2$ and a cost $-u$.

We may regard u as a demand made by a blackmailer, and state 1 as the situation where the victim complies. State 0 is the situation where the victim refuses to yield to the blackmailer's demand. The problem then can be seen as one whereby the blackmailer tries to maximize his total gain by balancing his desire for increased demands with keeping his victim compliant.

If controls were chosen from a *finite* subset of the interval (0, 1], the problem would come under the framework of this section, with assumption (6.21) being satisfied for every admissible policy. The optimal cost would then be finite, and there would exist an optimal stationary policy. It turns out, however, that *without the finiteness restriction the optimal cost starting at state 1 is $-\infty$ and there exists no optimal stationary policy*. To see this, first note that Assumption N is satisfied for this problem. The mapping T defining the DP algorithm is given by

$$T(J)(0) = 0$$

$$T(J)(1) = \min_{u \in (0,1]} [-u + (1 - u^2) J(1)].$$

For any stationary policy $\{\mu, \mu, \dots\}$ with $\mu(1) = u$, we have

$$J_\mu(1) = -u + (1 - u^2) J_\mu(1)$$

from which

$$J_\mu(1) = -\frac{1}{u}.$$

Therefore, $\min_\mu J_\mu(1) = -\infty$ and $J^*(1) = -\infty$, but there is no optimal stationary policy. Note also that this situation would not change if the constraint set were $u \in [0, 1]$ (i.e. $u = 0$ were an allowable control), although in this case the condition (6.21) would be violated.

Termination Inevitable under Some Policies: Shortest Paths Revisited

Here we impose assumptions that ensure that nothing is lost if attention is restricted to policies that lead to termination with probability one. Then, in effect, the theory just developed based on the contraction property of Proposition 2 comes into play.

A stationary policy π is called *proper* if there exists an integer m such that

$$P(x_m = 0 | x_0 = i, \pi) > 0, \qquad \text{for all } i = 1, 2, \dots, n. \tag{6.26}$$

We will assume that *there exists at least one optimal proper policy*. Under these circumstances the case where Assumption N holds can be reduced to the case already examined [(6.21) holds for all i and π]; see Problem 13(b). We will therefore restrict ourselves to the case where *Assumption P holds* [$g(i, u) \geqslant 0$ for all $i = 1, \dots, n$ and $u \in U(i)$]. Note that if there exists at least one proper policy and

$$g(i, u) > 0, \qquad i = 1, \dots, n, \quad u \in U(i), \tag{6.27}$$

then there must exist an optimal proper policy, since under (6.27), every stationary policy that is not proper results in infinite cost for some initial state and cannot be optimal.

Let us denote by P_μ the transition probability matrix

$$P_\mu = \begin{bmatrix} 1 & 0 & \cdots & 0 \\ p_{10}[\mu(1)] & p_{11}[\mu(1)] & \cdots & p_{1n}[\mu(1)] \\ \cdots & & \cdots & \\ p_{n0}[\mu(n)] & p_{n1}[\mu(n)] & \cdots & p_{nn}[\mu(n)] \end{bmatrix}. \tag{6.28}$$

The first row of P_μ is $(1, 0, \dots, 0)$ since $x = 0$ is an absorbing state. The following corollary is obtained from Proposition 3 by restricting the control constraint set at i to be $\{\mu(i)\}$.

Corollary 3.1. If $\pi = \{\mu, \mu, \dots\}$ is a proper policy, then

$$J_\mu = \{J_\mu(0), J_\mu(1), \dots, J_\mu(n)\}$$

satisfies $J_\mu = T_\mu(J_\mu)$, or equivalently

$$J_\mu = g_\mu + P_\mu J_\mu, \tag{6.29}$$

where P_μ is matrix (6.28) and g_μ is the vector

$$g_\mu = \begin{bmatrix} g[0, \mu(0)] \\ g[1, \mu(1)] \\ \cdots \\ g[n, \mu(n)] \end{bmatrix}.$$

Furthermore, J_μ is the unique real-valued J satisfying $J = T_\mu(J)$ and $J(0) = 0$. In addition, for every real-valued J with $J(0) = 0$, we have

$$\lim_{k\to\infty} T_\mu^k(J)(i) = J_\mu(i), \qquad i = 0, 1, \ldots, n. \tag{6.30}$$

Since Assumption P holds, by Proposition 10 in Section 5.4 we have that a stationary policy $\{\mu^*, \mu^*, \ldots\}$ is optimal if and only if $\mu^*(x)$ attains the minimum in Bellman's equation; that is,

$$T_{\mu^*}(J^*) = T(J^*). \tag{6.31}$$

The following proposition provides an alternative necessary and sufficient condition.

Proposition 4. Let $\pi^* = \{\mu^*, \mu^*, \ldots\}$ be a stationary policy with $J_{\mu^*}(i) < \infty$ for all i. In order for π^* to be optimal, it is necessary and sufficient that

$$T_{\mu^*}(J_{\mu^*}) = T(J_{\mu^*}), \tag{6.32}$$

or equivalently

$$g[i, \mu^*(i)] + \sum_{j=0}^{n} p_{ij}[\mu^*(i)]J_{\mu^*}(j)$$
$$= \min_{u\in U(i)} [g(i, u) + \sum_{j=0}^{n} p_{ij}(u)J_{\mu^*}(j)], \qquad i = 0, 1, \ldots, n.$$

Proof. Necessity of (6.32) follows from (6.31). Conversely, for any optimal proper policy $\overline{\pi} = \{\overline{\mu}, \overline{\mu}, \ldots\}$ the condition $J_{\mu^*} = T(J_{\mu^*})$ implies using (6.30) (which can be used because J_{μ^*} is assumed real-valued)

$$J_{\mu^*} \leqslant T_{\overline{\mu}}(J_{\mu^*}) \leqslant T_{\overline{\mu}}^2(J_{\mu^*}) \leqslant \cdots \leqslant \lim_{k\to\infty} T_{\overline{\mu}}^k(J_{\mu^*}) = J_{\overline{\mu}} = J^*.$$

Hence π^* is optimal. Q.E.D.

Another result is the following:

Proposition 5. The optimal cost function J^* is the only real-valued function J with $J(0) = 0$, $J(i) \geqslant 0$, $i = 1, \ldots, n$, that satisfies the equation $J = T(J)$.

Proof. Let $J: S \to R$ be a real-valued function with $J(0) = 0$, $J(i) \geqslant 0$, such that $J = T(J)$. By Proposition 9 of Section 5.4, we have $J \geqslant J^*$, so there remains to show the reverse inequality. Let $\{\mu^*, \mu^*, \ldots\}$ be an optimal proper policy. Then we have

$$J = T(J) \leqslant T_{\mu^*}(J) \leqslant \cdots \leqslant T_{\mu^*}^k(J) \leqslant \cdots.$$

Using (6.30), it follows that $J \leqslant J_{\mu^*}$. Since μ^* is optimal, we obtain $J \leqslant J^*$. Q.E.D.

This result can be used to show the following strengthened version of Proposition 12(a) regarding the validity of the successive approximation method:

Corollary 5.1. If J is a real-valued function with $J(0) = 0$, $J(i) \geq 0$, $i = 1, \ldots, n$, such that either

$$J(i) \leq J^*(i), \qquad i = 0, 1, \ldots, n,$$

or else

$$T(J)(i) \leq J(i), \qquad i = 0, 1, \ldots, n,$$

then

$$\lim_{k \to \infty} T^k(J)(i) = J^*(i), \qquad i = 0, 1, \ldots, n.$$

Proof. Under the first hypothesis, the result follows from Proposition 12(a) of Chapter 5. Under the second hypothesis, it is easily seen that the limit $J_\infty(i) = \lim_{k \to \infty} T^k(J)(i)$ exists and satisfies $J_\infty = T(J_\infty)$ (use the finiteness of the control space and compare with the proof of Proposition 13 in Chapter 5). The result now follows from Proposition 5. Q.E.D.

It is possible to show the validity of the policy iteration algorithm for the first passage problem under our present assumptions. Indeed, let $\pi = \{\mu, \mu, \ldots\}$ be a stationary policy with $J_\mu(i) < \infty$ for all i, and let $\bar{\mu}$ be such that $\bar{\mu}(i) \in U(i)$, $i = 0, 1, \ldots, n$, and

$$T_{\bar{\mu}}(J_\mu) = T(J_\mu).$$

Then $T_{\bar{\mu}}(J_\mu) \leq T_\mu(J_\mu) = J_\mu$, so from Corollary 9.1(a) of Section 5.4 we obtain $J_{\bar{\mu}} \leq J_\mu$. If we had $J_{\bar{\mu}} = J_\mu$, then, in view of the relations

$$J_{\bar{\mu}} = T_{\bar{\mu}}(J_{\bar{\mu}}) \leq T_{\bar{\mu}}(J_\mu) = T(J_\mu) \leq T_\mu(J_\mu) = J_\mu,$$

we would obtain $T(J_\mu) = J_\mu$, and by Proposition 4, $\pi = \{\mu, \mu, \ldots\}$ would be optimal. Therefore, either $\pi = \{\mu, \mu, \ldots\}$ is optimal or $\bar{\pi} = \{\bar{\mu}, \bar{\mu}, \ldots\}$ is a strictly better policy. It follows that *by policy iteration we can obtain an optimal proper policy in a finite number of steps provided that we start with a stationary policy that yields finite cost for all initial states.*

Example 3

Shortest Path Problem. Consider a directed graph and the problem of finding a shortest path from all nodes $i = 1, 2, \ldots, n$ to a special node 0. We assume that the length a_{ij} of each arc is strictly positive and that there exists a path from every node $i \neq 0$ to node 0. For convenience we write $a_{ij} = \infty$ if (i, j) is not an arc. A little thought should convince the reader that we are faced with a first passage problem where nodes are identified with states, outgoing arcs from a node are identified with controls available at the corresponding state, and costs per stage are identified with arc lengths. Furthermore, there exists an optimal proper policy. If we denote by $J^*(i)$ the minimum distance from node i to node 0, Bellman's equation yields

$$J^*(i) = \min_j [a_{ij} + J^*(j)], \qquad i = 1, 2, \dots, n,$$

$$J^*(0) = 0.$$

By Proposition 5 the minimum distances are the unique solution to Bellman's equation. Furthermore, these distances can be obtained by policy iteration, or by successive approximation starting from arbitrary nonnegative initial distances $J(i)$ with $J(0) = 0$ (Corollary 5.1).

Consider now what can happen if we relax the length positivity assumption to nonnegativity [$a_{ij} \geq 0$ for all (i, j)]. Then it may be shown that the shortest path distances solve Bellman's equation, but these distances need not be the unique solution or equal the optimal cost of the corresponding first passage problem. As an example, consider the network shown in Figure 6.2 and the arc lengths $a_{10} = 1$, $a_{12} = 0$, $a_{21} = 0$. The shortest distances are $J(1) = J(2) = 1$ and satisfy Bellman's equation together with $J(0) = 0$. However the optimal cost of the associated first passage problem is $J^*(0) = J^*(1) = J^*(2) = 0$ which also solves Bellman's equation as predicted by the theory of Section 5.4. What is happening here is that the optimal policy is to move from node 1 to node 2, and from node 2 back to node 1 at zero cost. This policy is not proper and does not correspond to a set of paths from nodes 1 and 2 to node 0. As a result, Proposition 5 does not hold. Furthermore, the proper policy that moves from 1 to 0, and from 2 to 1, satisfies the condition (6.32) but is not optimal. In addition, policy iteration, when started with that policy, and successive approximation, when started with the shortest distances $J(1) = J(2) = 1$, $J(0) = 0$ make no progress.

It is possible to allow zero lengths as long as we assume that every directed cycle not containing node 0 includes at least one arc with positive length. Then it is seen that every optimal policy is proper and, by Proposition 5, the shortest distances are the unique solution of Bellman's equation.

Example 4

Optimal Stopping. Assume that at each state i there is available a special control u^s that drives the system to the termination state with certainty; that is,

$$p_{i0}(u^s) = 1, \qquad i = 1, \dots, n.$$

We then obtain a stopping problem that is more special than the one of the previous section in that the state space is finite, but also more general in that the number of controls available at each state aside from termination may be more than one. Note that there exists at least one proper policy, the one that stops at each state. We will assume that $g(i, u) \geq 0$ for all i and u, and that there exists at least one

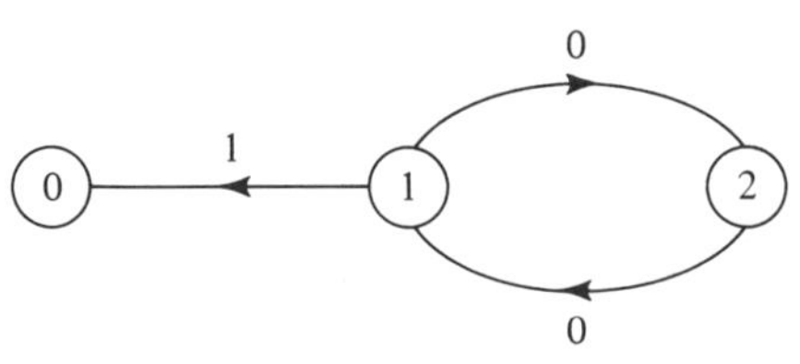

Figure 6.2 Shortest path problem involving a cycle of zero length. The shortest distances are $J(1) = J(2) = 1$ and satisfy, together with $J(0) = 0$, Bellman's equation. However, the optimal costs of the associated first passage problem are $J^*(0) = J^*(1) = J^*(2) = 0$.

optimal proper policy. [This will be true, for example, if (6.27) holds.] Then the results of Corollary 3.1 and Propositions 4 and 5 apply.

Let $t(i)$ denote the termination cost at state i,

$$t(i) = g(i, u^s), \qquad i = 1, \ldots, n,$$

and $\tilde{U}(i)$ be the set of admissible controls at state i other than stopping:

$$\tilde{U}(i) = \{u \in U(i) | u \neq u^s\}, \qquad i = 1, \ldots, n.$$

Bellman's equation takes the form

$$J^*(i) = T(J^*)(i) = \min\left[t(i), \min_{u \in \tilde{U}(i)}\left[g(i, u) + \sum_{j=1}^{n} p_{ij}(u)J^*(j)\right]\right], \tag{6.33}$$

$$J^*(0) = T(J^*)(0) = 0. \tag{6.34}$$

We know from Corollary 5.1 that the successive approximation method starting from the zero function converges to J^*. On the other hand, it is seen from (6.33) and (6.34) that the termination cost function t satisfies $T(t)(i) \leq t(i)$ for all i. It follows from Corollary 5.1 that the successive approximation method starting from t converges to the optimal cost; that is,

$$\lim_{k \to \infty} T^k(t)(i) = J^*(i), \qquad i = 0, 1, \ldots, n.$$

This fact parallels the conclusion of Proposition 1 for pure stopping problems.

Consider now the one-step-to-go stopping set

$$\tilde{S}_1 = \{i | t(i) \leq T(t)(i), i = 0, 1, \ldots, n\},$$

and assume that it is absorbing in the sense that, for all $u \neq u_s$,

$$p_{ij}(u) = 0, \qquad \text{if } i \in \tilde{S}_1, \quad j \notin \tilde{S}_1.$$

Then it is seen, similarly as in the previous section, that there is an optimal one-step lookahead policy that stops if and only if the current state is in $\tilde{S}_1$.

6.5 STOCHASTIC SCHEDULING AND THE MULTIARMED BANDIT

In the problem of this section there are n projects (or activities) of which only one can be worked on at any time period. Each project i is characterized at time k by its state x_k^i. If project i is worked on at time k, one receives an expected reward $\alpha^k R^i(x_k^i)$, where $\alpha \in (0, 1)$ is a discount factor; the state x_k^i then evolves according to the equation

$$x_{k+1}^i = f^i(x_k^i, w_k^i), \qquad \text{if } i \text{ is worked on at time } k, \tag{6.35}$$

where w_k^i is a random disturbance with probability distribution depending on x_k^i but not on prior disturbances. The states of all idle projects are unaffected; that is,

$$x_{k+1}^i = x_k^i, \qquad \text{if } i \text{ is idle at time } k. \tag{6.36}$$

We assume perfect state information and that the reward functions $R^i(\cdot)$

are uniformly bounded above and below, so the problem comes under Assumption D of Chapter 5.

We assume also that at any time k there is the option of permanently retiring from all projects, in which case a reward $\alpha^k M$ is received and no additional rewards are obtained in the future. The retirement reward M is given and provides a parameterization of the problem, which will prove very useful. Note that for M sufficiently small it is never optimal to retire, thereby allowing the possibility of modeling problems where retirement is not a real option.

The key characteristic of the problem is the independence of the projects manifested in our three basic assumptions:

1. States of idle projects remain fixed.
2. Rewards received depend only on the state of the project currently engaged.
3. Only one project can be worked on at a time.

The rich structure implied by these assumptions makes possible a powerful methodology. It turns out that optimal policies have the form of an *index rule;* that is, for each project i, there is a function $m^i(x^i)$ such that an optimal policy at time k is to

$$\text{Retire} \qquad \text{if} \quad M > \max_j \{m^j(x_k^j)\}. \tag{6.37a}$$

$$\text{Work on project } i \qquad \text{if} \quad m^i(x_k^i) = \max_j \{m^j(x_k^j)\} \geq M. \tag{6.37b}$$

Thus $m^i(x_k^i)$ may be viewed as an index of profitability of operating the ith project, while M represents profitability of retirement at time k. The optimal policy is to exercise the option of maximum profitability.

The problem of this section is traditionally known as a *multiarmed bandit problem*. An analogy here is drawn between project scheduling and selecting a sequence of plays on a slot machine that has several arms corresponding to different but unknown probability distributions of payoff. With each play the distribution of the selected arm is better identified, so the tradeoff here is between playing arms with high expected payoff and exploring the winning potential of other arms. By associating project states with distributions of payoff of arms, we see that the fundamental characteristics 1 to 3 are all present in multiarmed bandit problems.

Index of a Project

Let $J(x, M)$ denote the optimal reward attainable when the initial state is $x = (x^1, \ldots, x^n)$ and the retirement reward is M. From Section 5.1 we know that, for each M, $J(\cdot, M)$ is the unique bounded solution of Bellman's equation:

$$J(x, M) = \max\left[M, \max_i L^i(x, M, J)\right], \qquad \text{for all } x, \tag{6.38}$$

where L^i is defined by

$$L^i(x, M, J) = R^i(x^i) + \alpha \underset{w^i}{E}\{J[x^1, \ldots, x^{i-1}, f^i(x^i, w^i), x^{i+1}, \ldots, x^n, M]\}. \tag{6.39}$$

The next proposition gives some useful properties of J.

Proposition 6. Let $B = \max_i \max_{x^i} |R^i(x^i)|$. For fixed x, the optimal reward function $J(x, M)$ has the following properties as a function of M:

(a) $J(x, M)$ is convex and monotonically nondecreasing.
(b) $J(x, M)$ is constant for $M \leq -B/(1 - \alpha)$.
(c) $J(x, M) = M$ for all $M \geq B/(1 - \alpha)$.

Proof. Consider the successive approximation method starting with the function

$$J_0(x, M) = \max [0, M].$$

Successive iterations are generated by

$$J_{k+1}(x, M) = \max \left[M, \max_i L^i(x, M, J_k) \right], \qquad k = 0, 1, \ldots, \tag{6.40}$$

and we know from Proposition 1 of Section 5.1 that

$$\lim_{k \to \infty} J_k(x, M) = J(x, M), \qquad \text{for all } x, M. \tag{6.41}$$

We show inductively that $J_k(x, M)$ has the properties (a) to (c) stated in the proposition and, by taking the limit as $k \to \infty$, we establish the same properties for J. Clearly, $J_0(x, M)$ satisfies properties (a) to (c). Assume that $J_k(x, M)$ satisfies (a) to (c). Then from (6.39) and (6.40) it follows that $J_{k+1}(x, M)$ is convex and monotonically nondecreasing in M since the expectation and maximization operations preserve these properties. Verification of (b) and (c) is straightforward and is left for the reader. Q.E.D.

Consider now a problem where there is only one project that can be worked on, say project i. This is a stopping problem such as the one of Section 6.3 except for the presence of the discount factor. The optimal reward function for this problem is denoted $J^i(x^i, M)$ and has the properties indicated in Proposition 6. A typical form for $J^i(x^i, M)$ viewed as a function of M for fixed x^i is shown in Figure 6.3. Clearly, there is a minimal value $m^i(x^i)$ of M for which $J^i(x^i, M) = M$; that is,

$$m^i(x^i) = \min\{M | J^i(x^i, M) = M\}, \qquad \text{for all } x^i. \tag{6.42}$$

The function $m^i(x^i)$ is called the *index function* (or simply index) of project i. It provides an indifference threshold at each state; that is $m^i(x^i)$ is the retirement reward for which we are indifferent between retiring and operating the project when at state x^i.

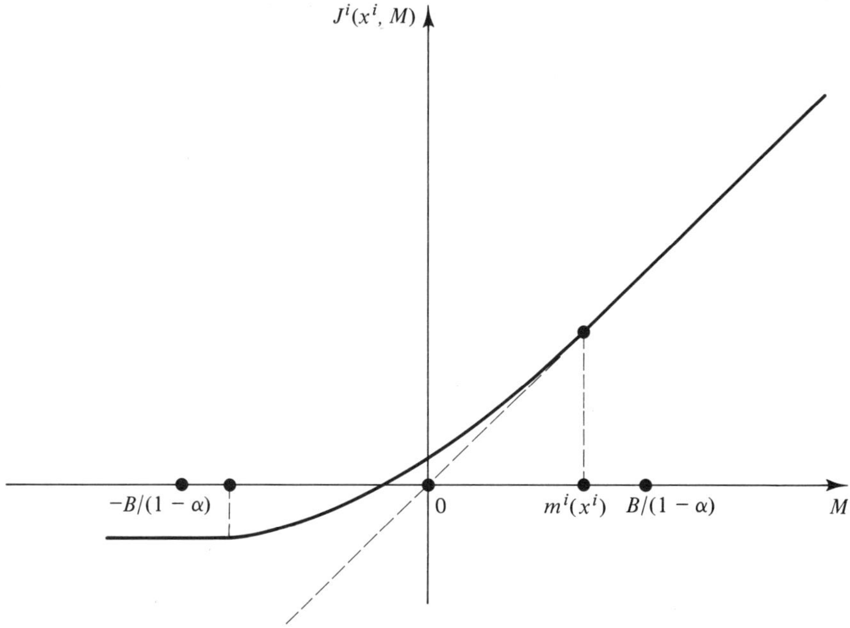

Figure 6.3 Form of the ith project reward function $J^i(x^i, M)$ for fixed x^i and definition of the index $m^i(x^i)$.

Our objective is to show the optimality of the index rule (6.37) for the index function defined by (6.42).

Project-by-Project Retirement Policies

Consider first a problem with a single project, say project i, and a fixed retirement reward M. Then by definition (6.42) of the index, an optimal policy is to

$$\text{Retire project } i \quad \text{if} \quad m^i(x^i) < M, \tag{6.43a}$$

$$\text{Work on project } i \quad \text{if} \quad m^i(x^i) \geq M. \tag{6.43b}$$

In other words, the project is operated continuously up to the time that its state falls into the *retirement set*

$$S^i = \{x^i | m^i(x^i) < M\}. \tag{6.44}$$

At that time the project is permanently retired.

Consider now the multiproject problem for fixed retirement reward M. Suppose at some time we are at state $x = (x^1, \ldots, x^n)$. Let us ask two questions:

1. Does it make sense to retire (from all projects) when there is still a project i with state x^i such that $m^i(x^i) > M$? The answer is negative. Retiring when

$m^i(x^i) > M$ cannot be optimal, since if we operate project i exclusively up to the time that its state x^i falls within the retirement set S^i of (6.44) and then retire, we will gain a higher expected reward. [This follows from the definition (6.42) of the index and the nature of the optimal policy (6.43) for the single-project problem.]

2. Does it ever make sense to work on a project i with state in the retirement set S^i of (6.44)? Intuitively, the answer is negative; it seems unlikely that a project unattractive enough to be retired if it were the only choice would become attractive merely because of the availability of other projects that are independent in the sense assumed here.

We are led therefore to the conjecture that there is an optimal *project-by-project retirement (PPR) policy* that permanently retires projects in the same way as if they were the only projects available. Thus at each time a PPR policy, when at state $x = (x^1, \ldots, x^n)$,

$$\text{Permanently retires project } i \qquad \text{if} \quad x^i \in S^i, \tag{6.45a}$$

$$\text{Works on some project} \qquad \text{if} \quad x^j \notin S^j \text{ for some } j, \tag{6.45b}$$

where S^i is the ith project retirement set of (6.44). Note that a PPR policy decides about retirement of projects but does not specify the project to be worked on out of those not yet retired.

The following proposition substantiates our conjecture. The proof is lengthy but quite simple.

Proposition 7. There exists an optimal PPR policy.

Proof. In view of (6.38), (6.39), and (6.45), existence of a PPR policy is equivalent to having, for all i,

$$M > L^i(x, M, J), \qquad \text{for all } x \text{ with } x^i \in S^i, \tag{6.46a}$$

$$M \leq L^i(x, M, J), \qquad \text{for all } x \text{ with } x^i \notin S^i, \tag{6.46b}$$

where L^i is given by

$$L^i(x, M, J) = R^i(x^i) + \alpha \mathop{E}_{w^i} \{J[x^1, \ldots, x^{i-1}, f^i(x^i, w^i), x^{i+1}, \ldots, x^n, M]\}, \tag{6.47}$$

and $J(x, M)$ is the optimal reward function corresponding to x and M.

The ith single-project optimal reward function J^i clearly satisfies, for all x^i,

$$J^i(x^i, M) \leq J(x^1, \ldots, x^{i-1}, x^i, x^{i+1}, \ldots, x^n, M), \tag{6.48}$$

since having the option of working at projects other than i cannot decrease the optimal reward. Furthermore, from the definition (6.44) of the retirement set S^l,

$$x^i \notin S^i, \qquad \text{if} \quad M \leq R^i(x^i) + \alpha \mathop{E}_{w^i} \{J^i[f^i(x^i, w^i), M]\}. \tag{6.49}$$

Using (6.47) to (6.49), we obtain (6.46b).

It will suffice to show (6.46a) for $i = 1$. Denote:

$\underline{x} = (x^2, \ldots, x^n)$: The state of all projects other than project 1.

$\underline{J}(\underline{x}, M)$: The optimal reward function for the problem resulting after project 1 is permanently retired.

$J(x^1, \underline{x}, M)$: The optimal reward function for the problem involving all projects and corresponding to state $x = (x^1, \underline{x})$.

We will show the following inequality for all $x = (x^1, \underline{x})$:

$$\underline{J}(\underline{x}, M) \leq J(x^1, \underline{x}, M) \leq \underline{J}(\underline{x}, M) + [J^1(x^1, M) - M]. \tag{6.50}$$

[In words this expresses the intuitively clear fact that at state $(x^1, \underline{x})$ one would be happy to retire project 1 permanently if one gets in return the maximum reward that can be obtained from project 1 in excess of the retirement reward M.] We claim that to show (6.46a) for $i = 1$ it will suffice to show (6.50). Indeed, when $x^1 \in S^1$, then $J^1(x^1, M) = M$, so from (6.50) we obtain $J(x^1, \underline{x}, M) = \underline{J}(\underline{x}, M)$, which is in turn equivalent to (6.46a) for $i = 1$.

We now turn to the proof of (6.50). Its left side is evident. To show the right side, we proceed by induction on the successive approximation recursions

$$J_{k+1}(x^1, \underline{x}) = \max\Big[M, R^1(x^1) + \alpha E\{J_k[f^1(x^1, w^1), \underline{x}]\}, \tag{6.51a}$$

$$\max_{i \neq 1}\{R^i(x^i) + \alpha E\{J_k[x^1, F^i(\underline{x}, w^i)]\}\Big],$$

$$\underline{J}_{k+1}(\underline{x}) = \max\Big[M, \max_{i \neq 1} [R^i(x^i) + \alpha E\{\underline{J}_k[F^i(\underline{x}, w^i)]\}\Big], \tag{6.51b}$$

$$J^1_{k+1}(x^1) = \max[M, R^1(x^1) + \alpha E\{J^1_k[f^1(x^1, w^1)]\}], \tag{6.51c}$$

where, for all $i \neq 1$ and $\underline{x} = (x^2, \ldots, x^n)$,

$$F^i(\underline{x}, w^i) = (x^2, \ldots, x^{i-1}, f^i(x^i, w^i), x^{i+1}, \ldots, x^n). \tag{6.52}$$

The initial conditions for the recursions (6.51) are

$$J_0(x^1, \underline{x}) = M, \qquad \text{for all } (x^1, \underline{x}), \tag{6.53a}$$

$$\underline{J}_0(\underline{x}) = M, \qquad \text{for all } \underline{x}, \tag{6.53b}$$

$$J^1_0(x^1) = M, \qquad \text{for all } x^1. \tag{6.53c}$$

We know that $J_k(x^1, \underline{x}) \to J(x^1, \underline{x}, M)$, $\underline{J}_k(\underline{x}) \to \underline{J}(\underline{x}, M)$, and $J^1_k(x^1) \to J^1(x^1, M)$, so to show (6.50) it will suffice to show that for all k and $x = (x^1, \underline{x})$ we have

$$J_k(x^1, \underline{x}) \leq \underline{J}_k(\underline{x}) + [J^1_k(x^1) - M]. \tag{6.54}$$

In view of the definitions (6.53), we see that (6.54) holds for $k = 0$. Assume that it holds for some k. We will show that it holds for $k + 1$. From

(6.51a) and the induction hypothesis (6.54), we have

$$J_{k+1}(x^1, \underline{x}) \leq \max\Bigg[M, R^1(x^1) + \alpha\, E\{\underline{J}_k(\underline{x}) + J_k^1[f^1(x^1, w^1)] - M\},$$

$$\max_{i \neq 1}\left\{R^i(x^i) + \alpha\, E\{\underline{J}_k[F^i(\underline{x}, w^i)] + J_k^1(x^1) - M\}\right\}\Bigg].$$

Using the facts $\underline{J}_k(\underline{x}) \geq M$ and $J_k^1(x^1) \geq M$ [cf. (6.51)] and the preceding equation, we see that

$$J_{k+1}(x^1, \underline{x}) \leq \max[\beta_1, \beta_2],$$

where

$$\beta_1 = \max\,[M, R^1(x^1) + \alpha\, E\{J_k^1[f^1(x^1, w^1)]\}] + \alpha[\underline{J}_k(\underline{x}) - M],$$

$$\beta_2 = \max\left[M, \max_{i \neq 1}\,[R^i(x^i) + \alpha\, E\{\underline{J}_k[F^i(\underline{x}, w^i)]\}]\right] + \alpha[J_k^1(x^1) - M].$$

Using (6.51b), (6.51c), and the preceding equations, we see that

$$J_{k+1}(x^1, \underline{x}) \leq \max[J_{k+1}^1(x^1) + \underline{J}_k(\underline{x}) - M, \underline{J}_{k+1}(\underline{x}) + J_k^1(x^1) - M]. \tag{6.55}$$

It can be seen from (6.51) and (6.53) that $J_k^1(x^1) \leq J_{k+1}^1(x^1)$ and $\underline{J}_k(\underline{x}) \leq \underline{J}_{k+1}(\underline{x})$ for all k, x^1, and $\underline{x}$; so from (6.55) we obtain that (6.54) holds for $k + 1$. The induction is complete. Q.E.D.

Form of the Optimal Reward Function

Armed with the knowledge of the existence of an optimal PPR policy, we can relate the optimal reward function $J(x, M)$ of the multiproject problem to the optimal reward functions of the single-project problems [see Eq. (6.56), which follows]. This will set the stage for the proof of optimality of the index rule. We first obtain an expression for the partial derivative of $J(x, M)$ with respect of M.

Lemma. For fixed x, let K_M denote the retirement time under an optimal policy when the retirement reward is M. Then for all M for which $\partial J(x, M)/\partial M$ exists we have

$$\frac{\partial J(x, M)}{\partial M} = E\{\alpha^{K_M} | x_0 = x\}.$$

Proof. Fix x and M. Let π^* be an optimal policy and let K_M be the retirement time under π^*. If π^* is used for a problem with retirement reward $M + \epsilon$, we receive

$$E\{\text{reward prior to retirement}\} + (M + \epsilon)\, E\{\alpha^{K_M}\} = J(x, M) + \epsilon\, E\{\alpha^{K_M}\}.$$

The optimal reward $J(x, M + \epsilon)$ when the retirement reward is $M + \epsilon$ is no less than the preceding expression, so

$$J(x, M + \epsilon) \geq J(x, M) + \epsilon\, E\{\alpha^{K_M}\}.$$

Similarly, we obtain

$$J(x, M - \epsilon) \geq J(x, M) - \epsilon\, E\{\alpha^{K_M}\}.$$

For $\epsilon > 0$, these two relations yield

$$\frac{J(x, M) - J(x, M - \epsilon)}{\epsilon} \leq E\{\alpha^{K_M}\} \leq \frac{J(x, M + \epsilon) - J(x, M)}{\epsilon}.$$

The result follows by taking $\epsilon \to 0$. Q.E.D.

Note that the convexity of $J(x, \cdot)$ with respect to M (Proposition 6) implies that the derivative $\partial J(x, M)/\partial M$ exists almost everywhere with respect to Lebesgue measure [R2]. Furthermore, it can be shown that $\partial J(x, M)/\partial M$ exists for all M for which the optimal policy is unique.

For a given M, initial state x, and optimal policy, let T_i be the retirement time of project i if it were the only project available, and let T be the retirement time for the multiproject problem. Both T_i and T take values that are either nonnegative or $+\infty$. The existence of an optimal PPR policy implies that we must have

$$T = \sum_{i=1}^{n} T_i$$

and in addition T_i, $i = 1, \ldots, n$, are independent random variables. Therefore,

$$E\{\alpha^T\} = E\{\alpha^{\Sigma_i T_i}\} = \prod_{i=1}^{n} E\{\alpha^{T_i}\}.$$

Using the Lemma, we obtain

$$\frac{\partial J(x, M)}{\partial M} = \prod_{i=1}^{n} \frac{\partial J^i(x^i, M)}{\partial M}. \tag{6.56}$$

Expression (6.56) is sufficient for our purpose of showing optimality of the index rule. It is interesting, however, to show how (6.56) can be used to obtain an expression for the optimal reward function. Integrating from M to some constant $C \geq M$, we obtain

$$J(x, M) = J(x, C) - \int_M^C \prod_{i=1}^{n} \frac{\partial J^i(x^i, m)}{\partial m}\, dm.$$

For $C \geq B/1 - \alpha$, we know from Proposition 6(c) that $J(x, C) = C$, so the preceding equation becomes

$$J(x, M) = C - \int_M^C \prod_{i=1}^{n} \frac{\partial J^i(x^i, m)}{\partial m}\, dm, \qquad \text{for all } x,\ C \geq B/(1 - \alpha).$$

This expresses the optimal reward function of the multiperiod problem in terms of the single-project optimal reward functions.

Optimality of the Index Rule

We are now ready to show our main result.

Proposition 8. The index rule (6.37) is an optimal stationary policy.

Proof. Fix $x = (x^1, \ldots, x^n)$ and let i be such that

$$m^i(x^i) = m(x) \triangleq \max_j \{m^j(x^j)\}.$$

If $m(x) < M$, the optimality of the index rule (6.37a) at state x follows from the existence of an optimal PPR policy. If $m(x) \geq M$, we first note that

$$J^i(x^i, M) = R^i(x^i) + \alpha\, E\{J^i[f^i(x^i, w^i), M]\},$$

and then use this relation together with (6.56) to write

$$\begin{aligned}
\frac{\partial J(x, M)}{\partial M} &= \frac{\partial J^i(x^i, M)}{\partial M} \cdot \prod_{j \neq i} \frac{\partial J^j(x^j, M)}{\partial M} \\
&= \alpha \frac{\partial}{\partial M} E\left\{ J^i[f^i(x^i, w^i), M] \cdot \prod_{j \neq i} \frac{\partial J^j(x^j, M)}{\partial M} \right\} \\
&= \alpha\, E\left\{ \frac{\partial}{\partial M} J^i[f^i(x^i, w^i), M] \cdot \prod_{j \neq i} \frac{\partial J^j(x^j, M)}{\partial M} \right\} \\
&= \alpha\, E\left\{ \frac{\partial}{\partial M} J[x^1, \ldots, x^{i-1}, f^i(x^i, w^i), x^{i+1}, \ldots, x^n, M] \right\} \\
&= \alpha \frac{\partial}{\partial M} E\{J[x^1, \ldots, x^{i-1}, f^i(x^i, w^i), x^{i+1}, \ldots, x^n, M]\},
\end{aligned}$$

and finally

$$\frac{\partial J(x, M)}{\partial M} = \frac{\partial}{\partial M} L^i(x, M, J),$$

where

$$L^i(x, M, J) = R^i(x^i) + \alpha\, E\{J[x^1, \ldots, x^{i-1}, f^i(x^i, w^i), x^{i+1}, \ldots, x^n, M]\}.$$

(The interchange of differentiation and expectation can be justified for almost all M; see [B13].) By the existence of an optimal PPR policy, we also have

$$J[x, m(x)] = L^i[x, m(x), J].$$

Therefore, the convex functions $J(x, M)$ and $L^i(x, M, J)$ viewed as functions of M for fixed x are equal for $M = m(x)$ and have equal derivative for almost all $M \leq m(x)$. It follows that for all $M \leq m(x)$ we have

$$J(x, M) = L^i(x, M, J).$$

This implies that the index rule (6.37b) is optimal for all x with $m(x) \geq M$. Q.E.D.

Deteriorating and Improving Cases

It is evident that great simplification results from optimality of the index rule (6.37) since optimization of a multiproject problem has been reduced into n separate single-project optimization problems. Nonetheless, solution of each of these single-project problems can be complicated. Under certain circumstances, however, the situation simplifies.

Suppose that for all i, x^i, and w^i that can occur with positive probability we have either

$$m^i(x^i) \leq m^i[f^i(x^i, w^i)] \tag{6.57}$$

or

$$m^i(x^i) \geq m^i[f^i(x^i, w^i)]. \tag{6.58}$$

Under (6.57) [or (6.58)], projects become more (less) profitable as they are worked on. We call these the *improving* and *deteriorating* cases, respectively.

In the improving case the nature of the optimal policy is evident: Either retire at the first period or else select a project with maximal index at the first period and continue engaging that project for all subsequent periods.

In the deteriorating case the form of the optimal policy is less evident but actually turns out to be simpler. To see what happens, note that (6.58) implies that if retirement is optimal when at state x^i then it is also optimal at each state $f^i(x^i, w^i)$. Therefore, for all x^i such that $M = m^i(x^i)$ we have, for all w^i,

$$J^i(x^i, M) = M, \qquad J^i[f^i(x^i, w^i), M] = M.$$

From Bellman's equation

$$J^i(x^i, M) = \max[M, R^i(x^i) + \alpha\, E\{J^i[f^i(x^i, w^i), M]\}]$$

we obtain

$$m^i(x^i) = R^i(x^i) + \alpha\, m^i(x^i)$$

or

$$m^i(x^i) = \frac{R^i(x^i)}{1-\alpha}. \tag{6.59}$$

The optimal policy in the deteriorating case in now evident from (6.59):

> Retire if $M > \max_i \dfrac{R^i(x^i)}{1-\alpha}$ and otherwise engage the project i with maximal one-step reward $R^i(x^i)$.

Example

Treasure Hunting. Consider a search problem involving N sites. Each site i may contain a treasure with expected value v_i. A search at site i costs c_i and reveals the treasure with probability β_i (assuming a treasure is there). Let P_i be the probability that there is a treasure at site i. We take P_i as the state of the project corresponding to searching site i. Then the corresponding one-step reward is

$$R^i(P_i) = \beta_i P_i v_i - c_i. \tag{6.60}$$

If a search at site i does not reveal the treasure, the probability P_i drops to

$$P_i^* = \frac{P_i(1 - \beta_i)}{P_i(1 - \beta_i) + 1 - P_i},$$

as can be easily verified using Bayes' rule. If the search finds the treasure, the probability P_i drops to zero since the treasure is removed from the site. Based on this and the fact that $R^i(P_i)$ is increasing with P_i [cf. (6.60)], it is easily shown that the deteriorating condition (6.58) holds. Therefore, searching the site for which expression (6.60) is maximal is an optimal index rule.

6.6 OPTIMAL GAMBLING STRATEGIES

A gambler enters a certain game played as follows. The gambler may stake at any time k any amount $u_k \geq 0$ that does not exceed his current fortune x_k (defined to be his initial capital plus his gain or minus his loss thus far). He wins his stake back and as much more with probability p and he loses his stake with probability $(1 - p)$. Thus the gambler's fortune evolves according to the equation

$$x_{k+1} = x_k + w_k u_k, \qquad k = 0, 1, \ldots, \tag{6.61}$$

where $w_k = 1$ with probability p and $w_k = -1$ with probability $(1 - p)$. Several games, such as playing red and black in roulette, fit this description.

The gambler enters the game with an initial capital x_0, and his goal is to increase his fortune up to a level X. He continues gambling until he either reaches his goal or loses his entire initial capital, at which point he leaves the game. The problem is to determine the optimal gambling strategy for maximizing the probability of reaching his goal. By a gambling strategy, we mean a rule that specifies what the stake should be at time k when the gambler's fortune is x_k for every x_k with $0 < x_k < X$.

The problem may be cast within the framework of Problem I, where we consider maximization in place of minimization. Let us assume for convenience that fortunes are normalized so that $X = 1$. The state space is the set $[0, 1] \cup \{s\}$, where s is a termination state to which the system moves with certainty from both states 0 and 1 with corresponding rewards 0 and 1. When $x_k \neq 0$, $x_k \neq 1$, the system evolves according to Eq. (6.61). The control constraint set is specified by

$$0 \leq u_k \leq x_k, \qquad 0 \leq u_k \leq 1 - x_k.$$

The reward per stage when $x_k \neq 0$ and $x_k \neq 1$ is zero. Under these circumstances the probability of reaching the goal is equal to the total expected reward. Assumption N holds since our problem is equivalent to a problem of minimizing expected total cost with nonpositive costs per stage.

The mapping T defining the DP algorithm takes the form

$$T(J)(x) = \max_{\substack{0 \le u \le x \\ 0 \le u \le 1-x}} [pJ(x+u) + (1-p)J(x-u)], \qquad x \in (0, 1), \tag{6.62}$$

$$T(J)(0) = 0, \qquad T(J)(1) = 1$$

for any function $J:[0, 1] \to [0, +\infty]$. Actually, for this problem one may restrict attention to functions J taking values in the interval $[0, 1]$ with $J(0) = 0$ and $J(1) = 1$.

Consider now the case where

$$0 < p < \tfrac{1}{2},$$

that is, the game is unfair to the gambler. A discretized version of the case where $\frac{1}{2} \le p < 1$ is considered in Problem 15. When $0 < p < \frac{1}{2}$, it is intuitively clear that if the gambler follows a very conservative strategy and stakes a very small amount at each time, he is all but certain to lose his capital. For example, if the gambler adopts a strategy of betting $1/n$ at each time, then it may be shown (see Problem 15 or [A9, p. 182]) that his probability of attaining the target fortune of unity starting with an initial capital i/n, $0 < i < n$, is given by

$$\left[\left(\frac{1-p}{p}\right)^i - 1\right]\left[\left(\frac{1-p}{p}\right)^n - 1\right]^{-1}.$$

If $0 < p < \frac{1}{2}$, n tends to infinity, i/n tends to a constant, and the probability given tends to zero, thus indicating that placing consistently small bets is a bad strategy.

From the preceding discussion one is led to consider a policy of placing large bets and, in particular, the *bold strategy* whereby the gambler stakes at each time k his entire fortune x_k or just enough to reach his goal, whichever is least. In other words, the bold strategy is the stationary policy $\pi^* = \{\mu^*, \mu^*, \ldots\}$ with μ^* given by

$$\mu^*(x) = \begin{cases} x, & \text{if } 0 < x \le \frac{1}{2}, \\ 1 - x, & \text{if } \frac{1}{2} \le x < 1. \end{cases}$$

We will prove that the bold strategy is indeed an optimal policy. To this end it is sufficient to show that for every initial fortune $x \in [0, 1]$ the value of the reward function $J_{\mu^*}(x)$ corresponding to the bold strategy $\{\mu^*, \mu^*, \ldots\}$ satisfies the sufficiency condition (cf. Proposition 10, Section 5.4)

$$T(J_{\mu^*}) = J_{\mu^*},$$

or equivalently

$$J_{\mu^*}(0) = 0, \qquad J_{\mu^*}(1) = 1,$$

$$J_{\mu^*}(x) \ge pJ_{\mu^*}(x+u) + (1-p)J_{\mu^*}(x-u) \tag{6.63}$$

$$\text{for all } x \in (0, 1),\ u \in [0, x] \cap [0, 1-x].$$

By using the definition of the bold strategy and the fact that

$$J_{\mu^*} = T_{\mu^*}(J_{\mu^*}),$$

we obtain that the function J_{μ^*} must satisfy

$$J_{\mu^*}(0) = 0, \qquad J_{\mu^*}(1) = 1, \tag{6.64}$$

$$J_{\mu^*}(x) = \begin{cases} pJ_{\mu^*}(2x), & \text{if } 0 < x \le \frac{1}{2}, \\ p + (1 - p)J_{\mu^*}(2x - 1), & \text{if } \frac{1}{2} \le x < 1. \end{cases} \tag{6.65}$$

We prove the following lemma showing that J_{μ^*} is uniquely defined from these relations.

Lemma. For every p, with $0 < p \le \frac{1}{2}$, there is only one bounded function on [0, 1] satisfying (6.64) and (6.65), the function J_{μ^*}. Furthermore, J_{μ^*} is continuous and strictly increasing on [0, 1].

Proof. Suppose that there existed two bounded functions $J_1:[0, 1] \to R$ and $J_2:[0, 1] \to R$ such that $J_i(0) = 0$, $J_i(1) = 1$, $i = 1, 2$, and

$$J_i(x) = \begin{cases} pJ_i(2x), & \text{if } 0 < x \le \frac{1}{2}, \\ p + (1 - p)J_i(2x - 1), & \text{if } \frac{1}{2} \le x < 1, \end{cases} \qquad i = 1, 2.$$

Then we have

$$J_1(2x) - J_2(2x) = \frac{J_1(x) - J_2(x)}{p}, \qquad \text{if } 0 \le x \le \tfrac{1}{2}, \tag{6.66}$$

$$J_1(2x - 1) - J_2(2x - 1) = \frac{J_1(x) - J_2(x)}{1 - p}, \qquad \text{if } \tfrac{1}{2} \le x \le 1. \tag{6.67}$$

Let z be any real number with $0 \le z \le 1$. Define

$$z_1 = \begin{cases} 2z, & \text{if } 0 \le z \le \frac{1}{2}, \\ 2z - 1, & \text{if } \frac{1}{2} < z \le 1, \end{cases}$$

$$\vdots$$

$$z_k = \begin{cases} 2z_{k-1} & \text{if } 0 \le z_{k-1} \le \frac{1}{2}, \\ 2z_{k-1} - 1, & \text{if } \frac{1}{2} < z_{k-1} \le 1, \end{cases}$$

for $k = 1, 2, \ldots$. Then from (6.66) and (6.67) it follows (using $p \le \frac{1}{2}$) that

$$|J_1(z_k) - J_2(z_k)| \ge \frac{|J_1(z) - J_2(z)|}{(1 - p)^k}, \qquad k = 1, 2, \ldots.$$

Since $J_1(z_k) - J_2(z_k)$ is bounded, it follows that $J_1(z) - J_2(z) = 0$, for otherwise the right side of the inequality would tend to $+\infty$. Since $z \in [0, 1]$ is arbitrary, we obtain $J_1 = J_2$. Hence J_{μ^*} is the unique bounded function on [0, 1] satisfying (6.64) and (6.65).

To show that J_{μ^*} is strictly increasing and continuous, we consider the mapping T_{μ^*}, which operates on functions $J:[0, 1] \to [0, 1]$ and is defined by

$$T_{\mu^*}(J)(x) = \begin{cases} pJ(2x) + (1 - p)J(0), & \text{if } 0 < x \leq \frac{1}{2}, \\ pJ(1) + (1 - p)J(2x - 1), & \text{if } \frac{1}{2} \leq x < 1, \end{cases}$$

$$T_{\mu^*}(J)(0) = 0, \qquad T_{\mu^*}(J)(1) = 1. \tag{6.68}$$

Consider the functions J_0, $T_{\mu^*}(J_0)$, . . ., $T^k_{\mu^*}(J_0)$, . . ., where J_0 is the zero function ($J_0(x) = 0$ for all $x \in [0, 1]$). We have

$$J_{\mu^*}(x) = \lim_{k\to\infty} T^k_{\mu^*}(J_0)(x), \qquad x \in [0, 1]. \tag{6.69}$$

Furthermore, the functions $T^k_{\mu^*}(J_0)$ can be shown to be monotonically nondecreasing in the interval [0, 1]. Hence, by (6.69), J_{μ^*} is also monotonically nondecreasing.

Consider now for $n = 0, 1, \ldots$ the sets

$$S_n = \{x \in [0, 1] | x = k2^{-n}, k = \text{nonnegative integer}\}.$$

It is straightforward to verify that:

$$T^m_{\mu^*}(J_0)(x) = T^n_{\mu^*}(J_0)(x), \qquad x \in S_{n-1}, \quad m \geq n \geq 1.$$

As a result of this equality and (6.69),

$$J_{\mu^*}(x) = T^n_{\mu^*}(J_0)(x), \qquad x \in S_{n-1}, \quad n \geq 1. \tag{6.70}$$

A further fact that may be verified by using induction and (6.68) and (6.70) is that for any nonnegative integers k, n for which $0 \leq k2^{-n} < (k + 1)2^{-n} \leq 1$, we have

$$p^n \leq J_{\mu^*}[(k + 1)2^{-n}] - J_{\mu^*}(k2^{-n}) \leq (1 - p)^n. \tag{6.71}$$

Since any number in [0, 1] can be approximated arbitrarily closely from above and below by numbers of the form $k2^{-n}$, and since J_{μ^*} has been shown to be monotonically nondecreasing, it follows immediately from (6.71) that J_{μ^*} is continuous and strictly increasing. Q.E.D.

We are now in a position to prove the following proposition.

Proposition 9. The bold strategy is an optimal stationary gambling policy.

Proof. We will prove the sufficiency condition

$$J_{\mu^*}(x) \geq pJ_{\mu^*}(x + u) + (1 - p)J_{\mu^*}(x - u),$$

$$x \in [0, 1], u \in [0, x] \cap [0, 1 - x]. \tag{6.72}$$

In view of the continuity of J_{μ^*} established in the previous lemma, it is sufficient to establish (6.72) for all $x \in [0, 1]$ and $u \in [0, x] \cap [0, 1 - x]$ that belong to the union $\cup_{n=0}^{\infty} S_n$ of the sets S_n defined by

$$S_n = \{z \in [0, 1] | z = k2^{-n}, k = \text{nonnegative integer}\}.$$

We will use induction. By using the fact that $J_{\mu^*}(0) = 0$, $J_{\mu^*}(\frac{1}{2}) = p$, and $J_{\mu^*}(1) = 1$, we can show that (6.72) holds for all x and u in S_0 and S_1. Assume that (6.72) holds for $x, u \in S_n$ and $n \geq 1$. We will show that it holds for all $x, u \in S_{n+1}$.

For any $x, u \in S_{n+1}$ with $u \in [0, x] \cap [0, 1 - x]$, there are four possibilities:

1. $x + u \leq \frac{1}{2}$,
2. $x - u \geq \frac{1}{2}$,
3. $x - u \leq x \leq \frac{1}{2} \leq x + u$,
4. $x - u \leq \frac{1}{2} \leq x \leq x + u$.

We will prove (6.72) for each of these cases.

Case 1. If $x, u \in S_{n+1}$, then $2x \in S_n$, and $2u \in S_n$, and by the induction hypothesis

$$J_{\mu^*}(2x) - pJ_{\mu^*}(2x + 2u) - (1 - p)J_{\mu^*}(2x - 2u) \geq 0. \tag{6.73}$$

If $x + u \leq \frac{1}{2}$, then by (6.65)

$$J_{\mu^*}(x) - pJ_{\mu^*}(x + u) - (1 - p)J_{\mu^*}(x - u)$$
$$= p[J_{\mu^*}(2x) - pJ_{\mu^*}(2x + 2u) - (1 - p)J_{\mu^*}(2x - 2u)]$$

and using (6.73) the desired relation (6.72) is proved for the case under consideration.

Case 2. If $x, u \in S_{n+1}$, then $(2x - 1) \in S_n$, and $2u \in S_n$, and by the induction hypothesis

$$J_{\mu^*}(2x - 1) - pJ_{\mu^*}(2x + 2u - 1) - (1 - p)J_{\mu^*}(2x - 2u - 1) \geq 0.$$

If $x - u \geq \frac{1}{2}$, then by (6.65)

$$\begin{aligned} J_{\mu^*}(x) &- pJ_{\mu^*}(x + u) - (1 - p)J_{\mu^*}(x - u) \\ &= p + (1 - p)J_{\mu^*}(2x - 1) - p[p + (1 - p)J_{\mu^*}(2x + 2u - 1)] \\ &\quad - (1 - p)[p + (1 - p)J_{\mu^*}(2x - 2u - 1)] \\ &= (1 - p)[J_{\mu^*}(2x - 1) - pJ_{\mu^*}(2x + 2u - 1) \\ &\quad - (1 - p)J_{\mu^*}(2x - 2u - 1)] \geq 0, \end{aligned}$$

and (6.72) follows from the preceding relations.

Case 3. Using (6.65), we have

$$\begin{aligned} J_{\mu^*}(x) &- pJ_{\mu^*}(x + u) - (1 - p)J_{\mu^*}(x - u) \\ &= pJ_{\mu^*}(2x) - p[p + (1 - p)J_{\mu^*}(2x + 2u - 1)] - p(1 - p)J_{\mu^*}(2x - 2u) \\ &= p[J_{\mu^*}(2x) - p - (1 - p)J_{\mu^*}(2x + 2u - 1) - (1 - p)J_{\mu^*}(2x - 2u)]. \end{aligned}$$

Now we must have $x \geq \frac{1}{4}$, for otherwise $u < \frac{1}{4}$ and $x + u < \frac{1}{2}$. Hence

$2x \geqslant \frac{1}{2}$ and the sequence of equalities can be continued as follows:

$$J_{\mu^*}(x) - pJ_{\mu^*}(x + u) - (1 - p)J_{\mu^*}(x - u)$$
$$= p[p + (1 - p)J_{\mu^*}(4x - 1) - p$$
$$- (1 - p)J_{\mu^*}(2x + 2u - 1) - (1 - p)J_{\mu^*}(2x - 2\text{u})]$$
$$= p(1 - p)[J_{\mu^*}(4x - 1) - J_{\mu^*}(2x + 2u - 1)$$
$$- J_{\mu^*}(2x - 2\text{u})]$$
$$= (1 - p)[J_{\mu^*}(2x - \tfrac{1}{2}) -$$
$$pJ_{\mu^*}(2x + 2u - 1) - pJ_{\mu^*}(2x - 2\text{u})].$$

Since $p \leqslant (1 - p)$, the last expression is greater than or equal to both

$$(1 - p)[J_{\mu^*}(2x - \tfrac{1}{2}) - pJ_{\mu^*}(2x + 2u - 1) - (1 - p)J_{\mu^*}(2x - 2u)]$$

and

$$(1 - p)[J_{\mu^*}(2x - \tfrac{1}{2}) - (1 - p)J_{\mu^*}(2x + 2u - 1) - pJ_{\mu^*}(2x - 2u)].$$

Now for $x, u \in S_{n+1}$ and $n \geqslant 1$, we have $(2x - \frac{1}{2}) \in S_n$ and $(2u - \frac{1}{2}) \in S_n$ if $(2u - \frac{1}{2}) \in [0, 1]$, and $(\frac{1}{2} - 2u) \in S_n$ if $(\frac{1}{2} - 2u) \in [0, 1]$. By the induction hypothesis, the first or the second of the preceding expressions is nonnegative, depending on whether $2x + 2u - 1 \geqslant 2x - \frac{1}{2}$ or $2x - 2u \geqslant 2x - \frac{1}{2}$ (i.e., $u \geqslant \frac{1}{4}$ or $u \leqslant \frac{1}{4}$). Hence (6.72) is proved for case 3.

Case 4. The proof resembles the one for case 3. Using (6.65), we have

$$J_{\mu^*}(x) - pJ_{\mu^*}(x + u) - (1 - p)J_{\mu^*}(x - u)$$
$$= p + (1 - p)J_{\mu^*}(2x - 1) - p[p + (1 - p)J_{\mu^*}(2x + 2u - 1)]$$
$$- (1 - p)pJ_{\mu^*}(2x - 2u) = p(1 - p) + (1 - p)[J_{\mu^*}(2x - 1)$$
$$- pJ_{\mu^*}(2x + 2u - 1) - pJ_{\mu^*}(2x - 2u)].$$

We must have $x \leqslant \frac{3}{4}$ for otherwise $u < \frac{1}{4}$ and $x - u > \frac{1}{2}$. Hence $0 \leqslant 2x - 1 \leqslant \frac{1}{2} \leqslant 2x - \frac{1}{2} \leqslant 1$, and using (6.65) we have

$$(1 - p)J_{\mu^*}(2x - 1) = (1 - p)pJ_{\mu^*}(4x - 2) = p[J_{\mu^*}(2x - \tfrac{1}{2}) - p].$$

Using the preceding relations, we obtain

$$J_{\mu^*}(x) - pJ_{\mu^*}(x + u) - (1 - p)J_{\mu^*}(x - u)$$
$$= p(1 - p) + p[J_{\mu^*}(2x - \tfrac{1}{2}) - p] - p(1 - p)J_{\mu^*}(2x + 2u - 1)$$
$$- p(1 - p)J_{\mu^*}(2x - 2u)$$
$$= p[(1 - 2p) + J_{\mu^*}(2x - \tfrac{1}{2}) - (1 - p)J_{\mu^*}(2x + 2u - 1)$$
$$- (1 - p)J_{\mu^*}(2x - 2u)].$$

These relations are equal to both

$$p[(1 - 2p)[1 - J_{\mu^*}(2x + 2u - 1)] + J_{\mu^*}(2x - \tfrac{1}{2})$$
$$- pJ_{\mu^*}(2x + 2u - 1) - (1 - p)J_{\mu^*}(2x - 2u)]$$

and

$$p[(1 - 2p)[1 - J_{\mu^*}(2x - 2u)] + J_{\mu^*}(2x - \tfrac{1}{2}) - (1 - p)J_{\mu^*}(2x + 2u - 1) - pJ_{\mu^*}(2x - 2u)].$$

Since $0 \leq J_{\mu^*}(2x + 2u - 1) \leq 1$ and $0 \leq J_{\mu^*}(2x - 2u) \leq 1$, these expressions are greater than or equal to both

$$p[J_{\mu^*}(2x - \tfrac{1}{2}) - pJ_{\mu^*}(2x + 2u - 1) - (1 - p)J_{\mu^*}(2x - 2u)]$$

and

$$p[J_{\mu^*}(2x - \tfrac{1}{2}) - (1 - p)J_{\mu^*}(2x + 2u - 1) - pJ_{\mu^*}(2x - 2u)]$$

and the result follows as in case 3. Q.E.D.

We note that the bold strategy is not the unique optimal stationary gambling strategy. For a characterization of all optimal strategies, see [D9, p. 90]. Several other gambling situations where strategies of the bold type are optimal are described in reference [D9, Chapters 5 and 6].

6.7 CONTINUOUS-TIME MARKOV CHAINS AND THEIR UNIFORMIZATION: APPLICATIONS IN QUEUEING SYSTEMS†

We have been considering so far problems where the cost per stage does not depend on the time required for transition from one state to the next. Such problems have a natural discrete-time representation. On the other hand, there are situations where controls are applied at discrete times but cost is defined as a time integral. Furthermore, the time between transitions is variable; it may be random or it may depend on the current state. For example, in queueing systems state transitions correspond to arrivals or departures of customers, and the corresponding times of transition are random. In this section we show that for an important class of continuous-time optimization models the issues relating to the transition times can be worked out in a way that these models may be analyzed within the discrete-time framework discussed up to now.

We will restrict ourselves to systems modeled by continuous-time Markov chains involving a finite or countable number of states. Here state transitions and control selections take place at discrete times, but the time from one transition to the next is random. Specifically we assume that:

1. If the system is in state i and control u is applied, the next state will be j with probability $p_{ij}(u)$.
2. The time interval τ between the transition to state i and the transition to the

† This section requires familiarity with the Poisson process and the basic notions of continuous-time Markov chains (see, e.g., [R8]).

next state is exponentially distributed with parameter $\nu_i(u)$; that is, the probability density function of τ is

$$p(\tau) = \nu_i(u)\, e^{-\nu_i(u)\tau}, \qquad \tau \geq 0.$$

Furthermore, τ is independent of earlier transition times, states, and controls. The parameters $\nu_i(u)$ are uniformly bounded in the sense that for some ν we have

$$\nu_i(u) \leq \nu, \qquad \text{for all } i, u.$$

The state and control at any time t are denoted by $x(t)$ and $u(t)$, respectively, and stay constant between transitions. The cost is given by

$$E\left\{\int_0^\infty e^{-\beta t}\, g[x(t), u(t)]\, dt\right\}, \tag{6.74}$$

where g is a given function and $\beta \geq 0$ is a given scalar discount parameter. The parameter $\nu_i(u)$ will be referred to as the *rate of transition* associated with state i and control u. It can be verified that the corresponding average transition time is

$$E\{\tau\} = \int_0^\infty \tau\nu_i(u)\, e^{-\nu_i(u)\tau}\, d\tau = \frac{1}{\nu_i(u)},$$

so $\nu_i(u)$ can be interpreted as the average number of transitions per unit time.

We first consider the case where the rate of transition is the same for all states and controls; that is,

$$\nu_i(u) = \nu, \qquad \text{for all } i, u.$$

We then show how models with state- or control-dependent transition rates can be reduced to this case by means of a process called *uniformization*.

Assume that $\nu_i(u) = \nu$ for all i and u and denote

t_k: The time of occurrence of the kth transition ($t_0 = 0$ by convention).

$\tau_k = t_k - t_{k-1}$: the kth transition time interval.

$x_k = x(t_k)$: the state after the kth transition [$x(t) = x_k$ for $t_k \leq t < t_{k+1}$].

$u_k = u(t_k)$: the control for the kth transition [$u(t) = u_k$ for $t_k \leq t < t_{k+1}$].

A little thought should convince the reader that this problem is essentially the same as one where transition times are fixed. The intuitive reason is that the control cannot influence the cost through the transition time intervals. More specifically, the cost (6.74) corresponding to a sequence $\{(x_k, u_k) | k = 0, 1, \ldots\}$ can be expressed as

$$\sum_{k=0}^\infty E\left\{\int_{t_k}^{t_{k+1}} e^{-\beta t} g[x(t), u(t)] dt\right\} = \sum_{k=0}^\infty E\left\{\int_{t_k}^{t_{k+1}} e^{-\beta t}\, dt\right\} E\{g(x_k, u_k)\}. \tag{6.75}$$

If $\beta > 0$, we have (using the independence of the transition time intervals)

$$E\left\{\int_{t_k}^{t_{k+1}} e^{-\beta t}\,dt\right\} = \frac{E\{e^{-\beta t_k}\}(1 - E\{e^{-\beta\tau_{k+1}}\})}{\beta} = \frac{\alpha^k(1-\alpha)}{\beta}, \tag{6.76}$$

where

$$\alpha = E\{e^{-\beta\tau}\} = \int_0^\infty e^{-\beta\tau}\nu e^{-\nu\tau}d\tau = \frac{\nu}{\beta+\nu}.$$

If $\beta = 0$, then

$$E\left\{\int_{t_k}^{t_{k+1}} dt\right\} = E\{\tau_{k+1}\} = \frac{1}{\nu}.$$

From (6.75) and (6.76) and the fact $(1-\alpha)/\beta = 1/(\beta+\nu)$, it follows that the cost of the problem can be expressed as

$$\frac{1}{\beta+\nu}\sum_{k=0}^{\infty}\alpha^k E\{g(x_k, u_k)\}, \qquad \text{if} \quad \beta > 0,$$

and

$$\frac{1}{\nu}\sum_{k=0}^{\infty} E\{g(x_k, u_k)\}, \qquad \text{if} \quad \beta = 0.$$

It can be seen that we are faced in effect with an ordinary discrete-time problem where expected total cost is to be minimized. If $\beta > 0$, then $\alpha < 1$ and the problem is discounted. If $\beta = 0$, the problem is undiscounted. The effect of randomness of the transition times has been simply to appropriately scale the cost per stage.

To summarize, a continuous-time Markov chain problem with cost

$$E\left\{\int_0^\infty e^{-\beta t} g[x(t), u(t)]\,dt\right\}$$

and rate of transition ν that is independent of state and control is equivalent to a discrete-time Markov chain problem with discount factor

$$\alpha = \frac{\nu}{\beta+\nu}, \tag{6.77}$$

and cost per stage given by

$$\tilde{g}(i, u) = \frac{1}{\beta+\nu} g(i, u). \tag{6.78}$$

In particular, Bellman's equation takes the form

$$J(i) = \frac{1}{\beta+\nu}\min_{u\in U(i)}[g(i, u) + \nu\sum_j p_{ij}(u)J(j)]. \tag{6.79}$$

Example 1

A manufacturer of a specialty item processes orders in batches. We assume that orders arrive according to a Poisson process with rate λ per unit time, and for each order there is a positive cost c per unit time that the order is unfilled. The setup cost for processing the orders is K. Upon arrival of a new order, the manufacturer must decide whether to process the current batch or wait for the next order.

In this example the time between transitions is exponentially distributed with parameter λ independently of state and control as shown in Figure 6.4. Assuming a positive discount parameter β, the effective discount factor is $\alpha = \lambda/(\beta + \lambda)$ [cf. (6.77)], and the average cost of a transition when i orders stay unfilled is $(ci)/(\beta + \lambda)$ [cf. (6.78)], while the cost of a transition where the orders are processed is K. (Note that the setup cost K is assumed to be incurred immediately after a decision to process the orders is made, so K is not discounted over the time interval up to the next transition.) We are faced with a discounted problem with positive but unbounded cost per stage. Assumption P holds (cf. Section 5.4), and Bellman's equation takes the form

$$J(i) = \min\left[K + \alpha J(1), \frac{ci}{\beta + \lambda} + \alpha J(i+1)\right], \qquad i = 1, 2, \ldots.$$

[Note that the optimal costs $J(i)$ cannot exceed the cost $K/(1 - \alpha)$ of the policy that fills each order at the moment it arrives. Therefore, from Problem 15 in Chapter 5, we see that the optimal cost function J is the *unique* bounded solution of Bellman's equation.] Reasoning from first principles, we see that $J(i)$ is a monotonically nondecreasing function of i, so from Bellman's equation it follows that there exists a threshold i^* such that it is optimal to process the orders if and only if their number i equals or exceeds i^*. There is a version of this result when there is no discounting ($\beta = 0$); see Problem 11 in Chapter 7.

Nonuniform Transition Rates

We now argue that the more general case where the transition rate $\nu_i(u)$ depends on the state, and control can be converted to the previous case of uniform transition rate by using the trick of *allowing fictitious*

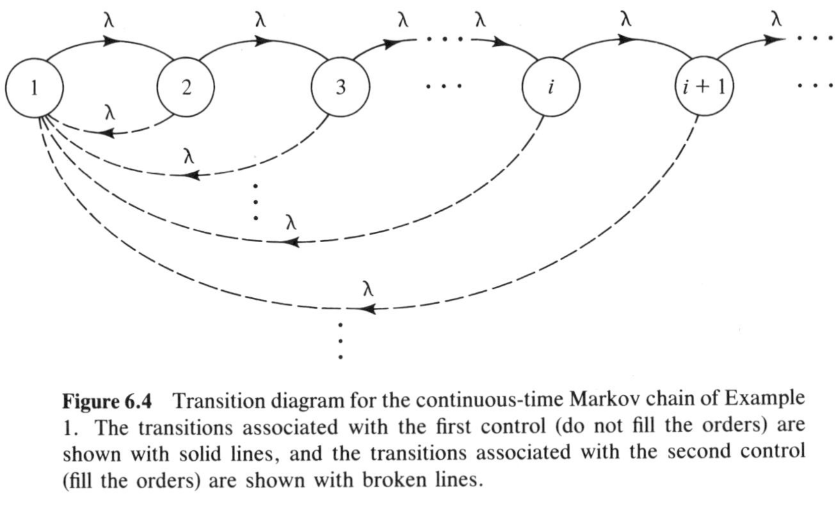

Figure 6.4 Transition diagram for the continuous-time Markov chain of Example 1. The transitions associated with the first control (do not fill the orders) are shown with solid lines, and the transitions associated with the second control (fill the orders) are shown with broken lines.

transitions from a state to itself. Roughly, transitions that are slow on the average are speeded up with the understanding that sometimes after a transition the state may stay unchanged. To see how this works, let ν be a new uniform transition rate with $\nu_i(u) \leq \nu$ for all i and u [cf. (6.75)] and define new transition probabilities

$$\tilde{p}_{ij}(u) = \begin{cases} \dfrac{\nu_i(u)}{\nu} p_{ij}(u), & \text{if } i \neq j, \\ 1 - \dfrac{\nu_i(u)}{\nu}, & \text{if } i = j. \end{cases}$$

We refer to this process as the *uniform* version of the original (see Figure 6.5). We argue now that the original process leaving state i at a rate $\nu_i(u)$

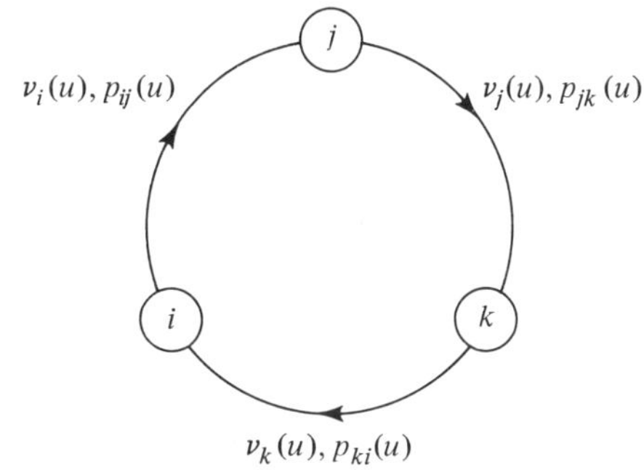

Transition rates and probabilities for continuous-time chain

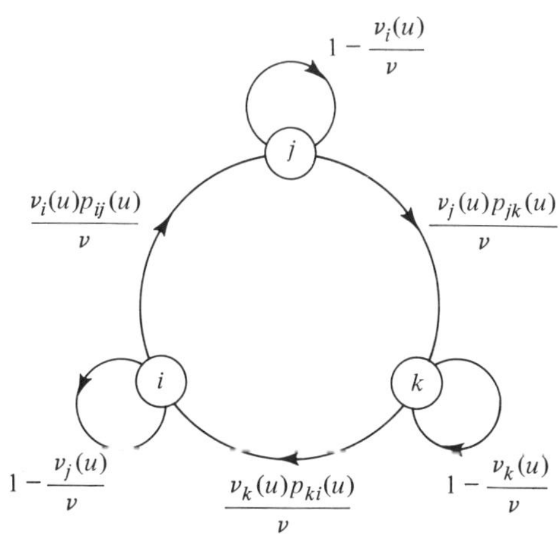

Transition probabilities for uniform version

Figure 6.5 Transforming a continuous-time Markov chain into its uniform version through the use of fictitious self-transitions. The uniform version has a uniform transition rate ν, which is an upper bound for all transition rates $\nu_i(u)$ of the original, and transition probabilities $\tilde{p}_{ij}(u) = (\nu_i(u)/\nu)p_{ij}(u)$, $i \neq j$, and $\tilde{p}_{ii}(u) = 1 - \nu_i(u)/\nu$.

is statistically identical to the new process leaving state i at the faster rate ν, but returning back to i with probability $(1 - \nu_i(u))/\nu$. Equivalently, transitions are real (lead to a different state) with probability $\nu_i(u)/\nu < 1$. By statistical equivalence, we mean that, for any given policy π, initial state x_0, time t, and state i, the probability $P\{x(t) = i|\pi, x_0\}$ is identical for the original process and its uniform version. We give a proof of this fact in Problem 22 for the case of a finite number of states (see also [L4], [S14], and [R8] for further discussion). In what follows we will illustrate the ideas by examples from queueing theory.

To summarize, we can convert a continuous-time Markov chain problem with transition rates $\nu_i(u)$, transition probabilities $p_{ij}(u)$, and cost

$$E\left\{\int_0^\infty e^{-\beta t} g[x(t), u(t)]\, dt\right\},$$

into a discrete-time Markov chain problem with discount factor

$$\alpha = \frac{\nu}{\beta + \nu}, \tag{6.80}$$

where ν is a uniform transition rate chosen so that

$$\nu_i(u) \leq \nu, \qquad \text{for all } i, u. \tag{6.81}$$

The transition probabilities are

$$\tilde{p}_{ij}(u) = \begin{cases} \dfrac{\nu_i(u)}{\nu} p_{ij}(u), & \text{if } i \neq j, \\ 1 - \dfrac{\nu_i(u)}{\nu}, & \text{if } i = j, \end{cases} \tag{6.82}$$

and the cost per stage is

$$\tilde{g}(i, u) = \frac{1}{\beta + \nu} g(i, u), \qquad \text{for all } i, u. \tag{6.83}$$

Bellman's equation in particular takes the form

$$\begin{aligned} J(i) = \frac{1}{\beta + \nu} \min_{u \in U(i)} \Big[& g(i, u) + [\nu - \nu_i(u)] J(i) \\ & + \nu_i(u) \sum_j p_{ij}(u) J(j) \Big]. \end{aligned} \tag{6.84}$$

Queueing Applications

Example 2

M/M/1 Queue with Controlled Service Rate. Consider a single-server queueing system where customers arrive according to a Poisson process with rate λ. The service time of a customer is exponentially distributed with parameter μ (called the service rate). Service times of customers are independent and are also independent of customer interarrival times. The service rate μ can be selected from a closed subset M of an interval $[0, \bar{\mu}]$ and can be changed at the times when a customer departs the system. There is a cost $q(\mu)$ per unit time for using rate μ and a waiting cost $c(i)$ per unit time when there are i customers in the system (waiting in queue or undergoing service). The idea is that one should be able to cut down on the customer waiting costs by choosing a faster service rate, which presumably costs more. The problem, roughly, is to select the service rate so that the service cost is optimally traded off with the customer waiting cost.

We assume the following:

1. For some $\mu \in M$ we have $\mu > \lambda$. (In words, a service rate is available that is fast enough to keep up with the arrival rate, thereby maintaining the queue length bounded.)
2. The waiting cost function c is nonnegative, monotonically nondecreasing, and "convex" in the sense
$$c(i + 2) - c(i + 1) \geq c(i + 1) - c(i), \qquad i = 0, 1, \ldots.$$
3. The service rate cost function q is nonnegative and continuous on $[0, \bar{\mu}]$, and $q(0) = 0$.

The problem fits the framework of this section. The state is the number of customers in the system, and the control is the choice of service rate following a customer departure. The Markov chain, together with the transition probabilities and transition rates, is shown in Figure 6.6, which also shows the corresponding uniform version for the choice

$$\nu = \lambda + \bar{\mu}.$$

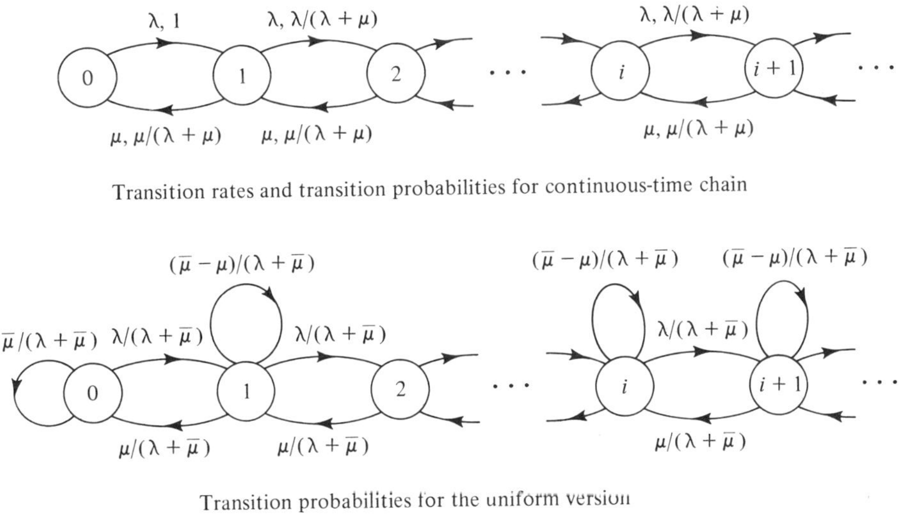

Figure 6.6 Continuous-time Markov chain and uniform version for Example 2 when the service rate is equal to μ. The transition rate for the uniform version is $\nu = \lambda + \bar{\mu}$.

The effective discount factor is

$$\alpha = \frac{\nu}{\beta + \nu}$$

and the cost per stage is

$$\frac{1}{\beta + \nu}[c(i) + q(\mu)].$$

Bellman's equation takes the form [cf. (6.84)]

$$J(0) = \frac{1}{\beta + \nu}[c(0) + (\nu - \lambda)J(0) + \lambda J(1)]$$

$$J(i) = \frac{1}{\beta + \nu} \min_{\mu \in M} [c(i) + q(\mu) + \mu J(i - 1) \tag{6.85}$$

$$+ (\nu - \lambda - \mu)J(i) + \lambda J(i + 1)], \quad i = 1, 2, \ldots.$$

An optimal policy is to use at state i the service rate that minimizes the expression on the right. Thus it is optimal to use at state i the service rate

$$\mu^*(i) = \arg \min_{\mu \in M} \{q(\mu) - \mu\Delta(i)\}, \tag{6.86}$$

where $\Delta(i)$ is the optimal cost differential

$$\Delta(i) = J(i) - J(i - 1), \qquad i = 1, 2, \ldots.$$

[When the minimum in (6.86) is attained by more than one service rate μ we choose by convention the smallest.] We will demonstrate shortly that *$\Delta(i)$ is monotonically nondecreasing*. It will then follow from (6.86) (see Figure 6.7) that the *optimal service rate $\mu^*(i)$ is monotonically nondecreasing;* so as the queue length increases, it is optimal to use a faster service rate.

To show that $\Delta(i)$ is monotonically nondecreasing, we use the successive approximation method to generate a sequence of functions J_k where the starting function is

$$J_0(i) = 0, \qquad i = 0, 1, \ldots,$$

and, for $k = 0, 1, \ldots$ [cf. (6.85)],

$$J_{k+1}(0) = \frac{1}{\beta + \nu}[c(0) + (\nu - \lambda)J_k(0) + \lambda J_k(1)],$$

$$J_{k+1}(i) = \frac{1}{\beta + \nu} \min_{\mu \in M} [c(i) + q(\mu) + \mu J_k(i - 1) \tag{6.87}$$

$$+ (\nu - \lambda - \mu)J_k(i) + \lambda J_k(i + 1)], \qquad i = 1, 2, \ldots.$$

For $k = 0, 1, \ldots$ and $i = 1, 2, \ldots$, let

$$\Delta_k(i) = J_k(i) - J_k(i - 1).$$

For completeness of notation, define also $J_k(-1) = J_k(0)$ and $\Delta_k(0) = 0$. From the theory of Section 5.4 (see Proposition 14, and compare with Problem 10 of Chapter 5), we have $J_k(i) \to J(i)$ as $k \to \infty$. It follows that we have

$$\lim_{k \to \infty} \Delta_k(i) = \Delta(i), \qquad i = 1, 2, \ldots.$$

Therefore, it will suffice to show for every k that $\Delta_k(i)$ is monotonically nondecreasing. For this we use induction. The assertion is trivially true for $k = 0$. Assuming that

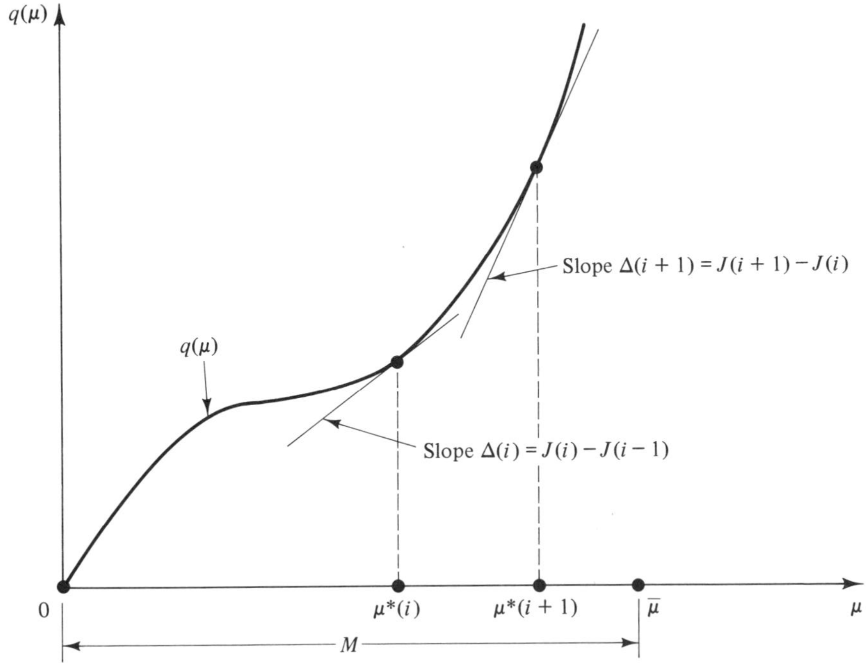

Figure 6.7 Determining the optimal service rate at states i and $(i + 1)$ in Example 2. The optimal cost differential $\Delta(i)$ is monotonically nondecreasing with i. As a result, the optimal service rate $\mu^*(i)$ tends to increase as the system becomes more crowded (i increases).

$\Delta_k(i)$ is monotonically nondecreasing, we show that the same is true for $\Delta_{k+1}(i)$. Let

$$\mu^k(0) = 0$$
$$\mu^k(i) = \arg\min_{\mu \in M} \{q(\mu) - \mu\Delta_k(i)\}, \qquad i = 1, 2, \ldots.$$

From (6.87) we have, for all $i = 0, 1, \ldots,$

$$\begin{aligned}
\Delta_{k+1}(i+1) &= J_{k+1}(i+1) - J_{k+1}(i) \\
&\geq \frac{1}{\beta + \imath}\Big[c(i+1) + q[\mu^k(i+1)] + \mu^k(i+1)J_k(i) \\
&\quad + [\nu - \lambda - \mu^k(i+1)]J_k(i+1) \\
&\quad + \lambda J_k(i+2) - c(i) - q[\mu^k(i+1)] - \mu^k(i+1)\, J_k(i-1) \\
&\quad - [\nu - \lambda - \mu^k(i+1)]J_k(i) - \lambda J_k(i+1)\Big] \\
&= \frac{1}{\beta + \nu}\Big[c(i+1) - c(i) + \lambda\, \Delta_k(i+2) + (\nu - \lambda)\, \Delta_k(i+1) \\
&\quad - \mu^k(i+1)[\Delta_k(i+1) - \Delta_k(i)]\Big].
\end{aligned} \tag{6.88}$$

Similarly, we obtain, for $i = 1, 2, \ldots,$

$$\Delta_{k+1}(i) \leq \frac{1}{\beta + \nu}\Big[c(i) - c(i-1) + \lambda\Delta_k(i+1) + (\nu - \lambda)\,\Delta_k(i) - \mu^k(i-1)[\Delta_k(i) - \Delta_k(i-1)]\Big].$$

Subtracting the last two inequalities, we obtain, for $i = 1, 2, \ldots,$

$$\begin{aligned}(\beta + \nu)[\Delta_{k+1}(i+1) - \Delta_{k+1}(i)] &\geq [c(i+1) - c(i)] - [c(i) - c(i-1)] + \lambda[\Delta_k(i+2) - \Delta_k(i+1)] \\ &\quad + [\nu - \lambda - \mu^k(i+1)][\Delta_k(i+1) - \Delta_k(i)] \\ &\quad + \mu^k(i-1)[\Delta_k(i) - \Delta_k(i-1)].\end{aligned}$$

Using our convexity assumption on $c(i)$, the fact $\nu - \lambda - \mu^k(i+1) = \overline{\mu} - \mu^k(i+1) \geq 0$, and the induction hypothesis, we see that every term on the right side of the preceding inequality is nonnegative. Therefore, $\Delta_{k+1}(i+1) \geq \Delta_{k+1}(i)$ for $i = 1, 2, \ldots$. From (6.88) we can also easily show that $\Delta_{k+1}(1) \geq 0 = \Delta_{k+1}(0)$, and the induction proof is complete.

To summarize, the optimal service rate $\mu^*(i)$ is given by (6.86) and tends to become faster as the system becomes more crowded (i increases).

Example 3

M/M/1 Queue with Controlled Arrival Rate. Consider the same queueing system as in the previous example with the difference that the service rate μ is fixed, but the arrival rate λ can be controlled. We assume that λ is chosen from a closed subset Λ of an interval $[0, \overline{\lambda}]$, and there is a continuous cost $q(\lambda)$ per unit time. All other assumptions of Example 2 are also in effect. What we have here is a problem of flow control. The cost for throttling the arrival process is to be traded off optimally with the customer waiting cost.

This problem is very similar to the one of Example 2. We choose as uniform transition rate

$$\nu = \overline{\lambda} + \mu$$

and construct the uniform version of the Markov chain. Bellman's equation takes the form

$$J(0) = \frac{1}{\beta + \nu}\min_{\lambda\in\Lambda}[c(0) + q(\lambda) + (\nu - \lambda)J(0) + \lambda J(1)],$$

$$J(i) = \frac{1}{\beta + \nu}\min_{\lambda\in\Lambda}[c(i) + q(\lambda) + \mu J(i-1) + (\nu - \lambda - \mu)J(i) + \lambda J(i+1)].$$

An optimal policy is to use at state i the arrival rate

$$\lambda^*(i) = \arg\min_{\lambda\in\Lambda}\{q(\lambda) + \lambda\Delta(i+1)\}, \tag{6.89}$$

where, as before, $\Delta(i)$ is the optimal cost differential

$$\Delta(i) = J(i) - J(i-1), \qquad i = 1, 2, \ldots.$$

As in Example 2, we can show that $\Delta(i)$ is monotonically nondecreasing; so from (6.89) we see that *the optimal arrival rate tends to decrease as the system becomes more crowded* (i increases).

Example 4

Priority Assignment and the μc Rule. Consider n queues that share a single server. There is a positive cost c_i per unit time and per customer in each queue i. The service time of a customer of queue i is exponentially distributed with parameter μ_i, and all customer service times are independent. Assuming we start with a given number of customers in each queue and no further arrivals occur, what is the optimal order for serving the customers? The cost here is

$$E\left\{\int_0^\infty e^{-\beta t}\sum_{i=1}^n c_i x_i(t)\,dt\right\},$$

where $x_i(t)$ is the number of customers in the ith queue at time t, and β is a positive discount parameter.

We first construct the uniform version of this continuous-time Markov chain problem based on the uniform rate

$$\mu = \max_i \{\mu_i\}.$$

The construction is shown in Figure 6.8. The discount factor is

$$\alpha = \frac{\mu}{\beta + \mu}, \tag{6.90}$$

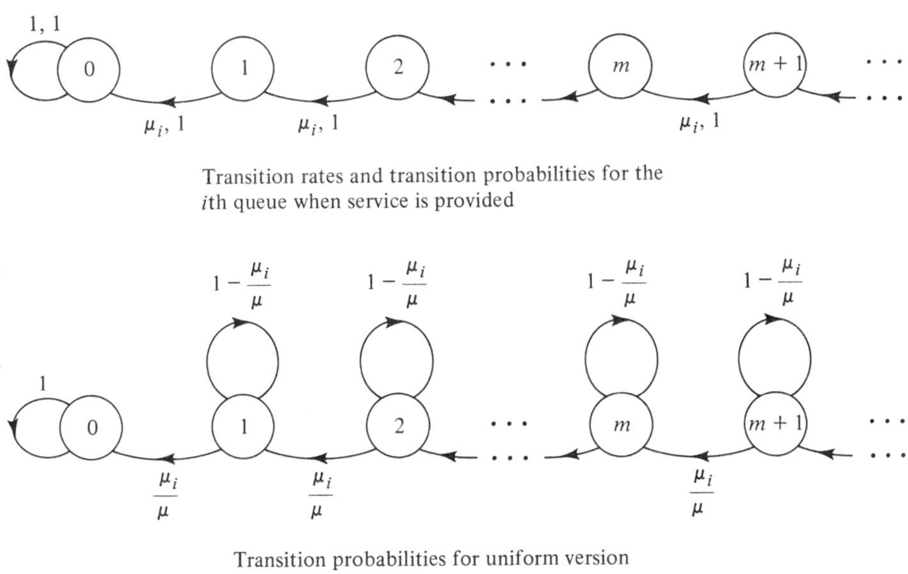

Figure 6.8 Continuous-time Markov chain and uniform version for the ith queue of Example 4 when service is provided. The transition rate for the uniform version is $\mu = \max \{\mu_i\}$.

and the corresponding cost is

$$\frac{1}{\beta + \mu} \sum_{k=0}^{\infty} \alpha^k E\left\{\sum_{i=1}^{n} c_i x_k^i\right\}, \tag{6.91}$$

where x_k^i is the number of customers in the ith queue after the kth transition (real or fictitious).

We now rewrite the cost in a way that is more convenient for analysis. The idea is to transform the problem from one of minimizing waiting costs to one of maximizing savings in waiting costs through customer service. For $m = 0, 1, \ldots,$ define

$$i_k = \begin{cases} i, & \text{if the } k\text{th transition corresponds to} \\ & \text{a customer departure from queue } i, \\ 0, & \text{if the } k\text{th transition is fictitious.} \end{cases}$$

Denote also

$$c_{i0} = 0,$$

$$x_0^i: \quad \text{the initial number of customers in queue } i.$$

Then the cost (6.91) can also be written as

$$\frac{1}{\beta + \mu}\left[\sum_{i=1}^{n} c_i x_0^i + \sum_{k=1}^{\infty} \alpha^k E\left\{\sum_{i=1}^{n} c_i x_0^i - \sum_{m=0}^{k-1} c_{i_m}\right\}\right]$$

$$= \frac{1}{\beta + \mu}\left[\sum_{k=0}^{\infty} \alpha^k\left(\sum_{i=1}^{n} c_i x_0^i\right) - E\left\{\sum_{m=0}^{\infty} \sum_{k=m+1}^{\infty} \alpha^k c_{i_m}\right\}\right]$$

$$= \frac{1}{(\beta + \mu)(1 - \alpha)} \sum_{i=1}^{n} c_i x_0^i - \frac{\alpha}{(\beta + \mu)(1 - \alpha)} \sum_{k=0}^{\infty} \alpha^k E\{c_{i_k}\}$$

$$= \frac{1}{\beta} \sum_{i=1}^{n} c_i x_0^i - \frac{\alpha}{\beta} \sum_{k=0}^{\infty} \alpha^k E\{c_{i_k}\}.$$

Therefore, instead of minimizing the cost (6.91), we can equivalently

$$\text{maximize} \sum_{k=0}^{\infty} \alpha^k E\{c_{i_k}\}, \tag{6.92}$$

where c_{i_k} can be viewed as the *savings in waiting cost rate* obtained from the kth transition. The problem equivalence just established expresses the intuitively clear idea that by serving a customer we save the corresponding waiting cost in queue.

We now recognize problem (6.92) as a multiarmed bandit problem. The n queues can be viewed as separate projects. At each time, a nonempty queue, say i, is selected and served. Since a customer departure occurs with probability μ_i/μ, and a fictitious transition that leaves the state unchanged occurs with probability $1 - \mu_i/\mu$, the corresponding expected reward is

$$\frac{\mu_i}{\mu} c_i. \tag{6.93}$$

It is evident that the problem falls in the deteriorating case examined at the end of Section 6.5. Therefore, after each customer departure an optimal policy is to serve the queue with maximum expected reward per stage (i.e. engage the project with maximal index; cf. the end of Section 6.5). Equivalently [cf. (6.93)], *it is optimal* *to serve the nonempty queue i for which $\mu_i c_i$ is maximum.* This policy is known as the *μc rule.* It plays an important role in several other formulations of the priority assignment problem (see [B2], [H3], and [H4]). We can view $\mu_i c_i$ as the ratio of the waiting cost rate c_i by the average time $1/\mu_i$ needed to serve a customer, thereby saving c_i in cost rate. Therefore, the μc rule amounts to serving the queue for which the savings in waiting cost rate per unit average service time are maximized.

Example 5

Threshold Policies for Routing in a Two-Station Queueing System. Consider the system consisting of two queues shown in Figure 6.9. Customers arrive according to a Poisson process with rate λ and are routed upon arrival to one of the two queues. Service times are independent and exponentially distributed with parameter μ_1 in the first queue and μ_2 in the second queue. The cost is

$$E\left\{\int_0^\infty e^{-\beta t}\,[c_1 x_1(t) + c_2 x_2(t)]\,dt\right\},$$

where β, c_1, and c_2 are given positive scalars, and $x_1(t)$ and $x_2(t)$ denote the number of customers at time t in queues 1 and 2, respectively.

As earlier, we construct the uniform version of this problem with uniform rate

$$\nu = \lambda + \mu_1 + \mu_2$$

and the transition probabilities shown in Figure 6.10. We take as state space the set of pairs (i, j) of customers in queues 1 and 2. Bellman's equation takes the form

$$\begin{aligned} J(i,j) = {} & \frac{1}{\beta + \nu}\,[c_1 i + c_2 j + \mu_1 J[(i-1)^+, j] + \mu_2 J[i, (j-1)^+]] \\ & + \frac{\lambda}{\beta + \nu} \min\,[J(i+1, j), J(i, j+1)], \end{aligned} \tag{6.94}$$

where for any x we denote

$$(x)^+ = \max\,[0, x].$$

From this equation we see that an optimal policy is to

Route an arriving customer to queue 1
iff the state (i, j) at the time of arrival belongs to S_1, (6.95)

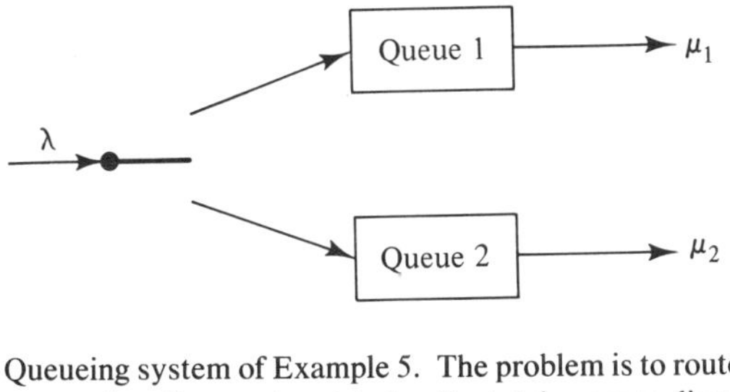

Figure 6.9 Queueing system of Example 5. The problem is to route each arriving customer to queue 1 or 2 so as to minimize the total average discounted waiting cost.

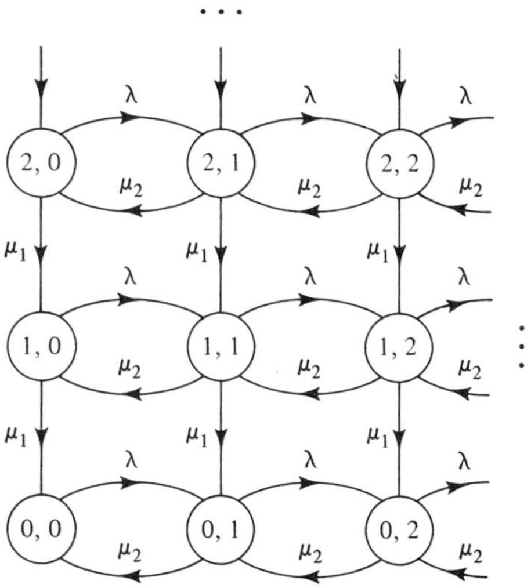

Transition rates when customers are routed to Queue 1

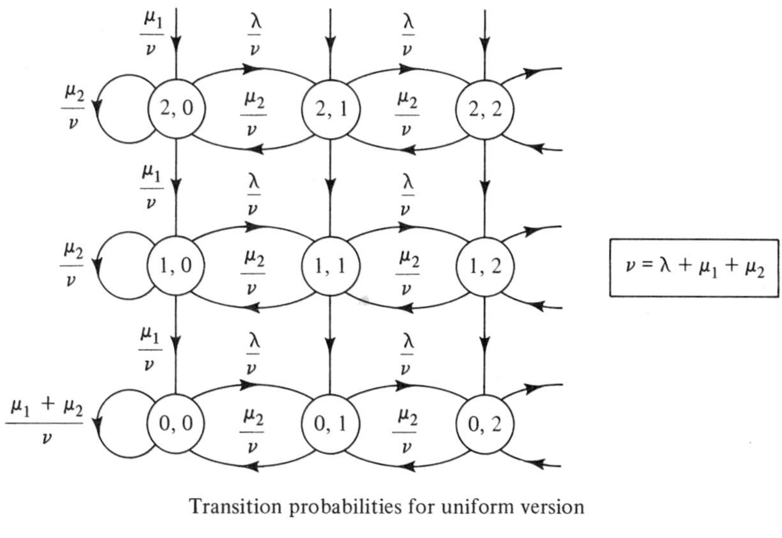

Transition probabilities for uniform version

Figure 6.10 Continuous-time Markov chain and uniform version for Example 5 when customers are routed to the first queue. The states are the pairs of customer numbers in the two queues.

where S_1 is the set of states for which routing a new customer to queue 1 results in at least as favorable cost-to-go as routing the customer to queue 2,

$$S_1 = \{(i, j) | J(i + 1, j) \leq J(i, j + 1)\}. \tag{6.96}$$

This optimal policy can be characterized better by some further analysis.

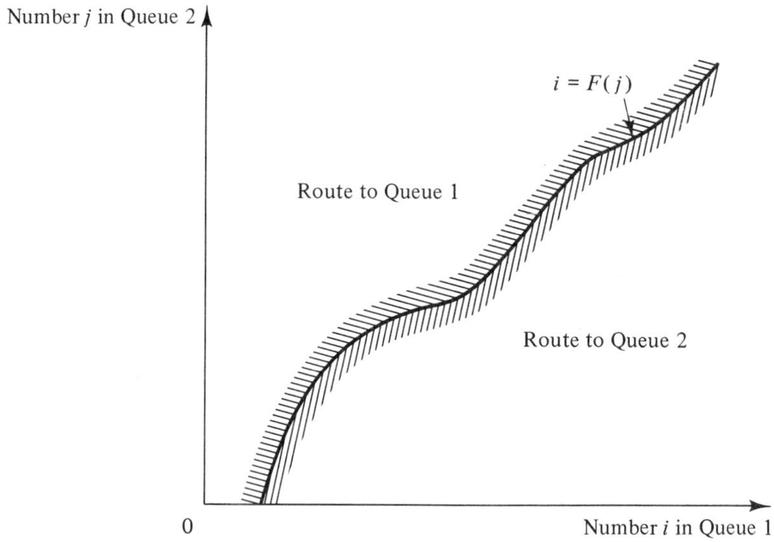

Figure 6.11 Typical threshold policy characterized by a threshold function F.

Intuitively, one expects that optimal routing can be achieved by sending a customer to the queue that is "less crowded" in some sense. It is therefore natural to conjecture that, if it is optimal to route to the first queue when the state is (i, j), it must be optimal to do the same when the first queue is even less crowded; that is, the state is $(i - m, j)$ with $m \geq 1$. This is equivalent to saying that the set of states S_1 for which it is optimal to route to the first queue is characterized by a monotonically nondecreasing *threshold function F* by means of

$$S_1 = \{(i, j) | \, i = F(j)\} \tag{6.97}$$

(see Figure 6.11). Accordingly, we call the corresponding optimal policy a *threshold policy*.

We will demonstrate the existence of a threshold optimal policy by showing that the variations

$$\Delta_1(i, j) = J(i + 1, j) - J(i, j + 1),$$

$$\Delta_2(i, j) = J(i, j + 1) - J(i + 1, j)$$

are monotonically nondecreasing in i for each fixed j, and in j for each fixed i, respectively. It will be sufficient to show that for all $k = 0, 1, \ldots$ the functions

$$\Delta_1^k(i, j) = J_k(i + 1, j) - J_k(i, j + 1) \tag{6.98}$$

are monotonically nondecreasing in i for each fixed j, where J_k is generated by the successive approximation method starting from the zero function; that is, $J_{k+1}(i, j) = T(J_k)(i, j)$, where T is the DP mapping defining Bellman's equation (6.94) and $J_0 = 0$. This is true because $J_k(i, j) \to J(i, j)$ for all i, j as $k \to \infty$ (Proposition 13 in Section 5.4). To prove that $\Delta_1^k(i, j)$ has the desired property, it is useful to first verify that $J_k(i, j)$ is monotonically nondecreasing in i (or j) for fixed j (or i). This is elementary to show by induction or by arguing from first principles using the fact that $J_k(i, j)$ has a k-stage optimal cost interpretation. Next we use (6.94) and (6.98) to write

$$\begin{aligned}(\beta + \nu)\,\Delta_1^{k+1}(i,j) = c_1 - c_2 & \\ + \mu_1\,[J_k(i,j) - J_k[(i-1)^+, j+1]] & \\ + \mu_2\,[J_k[i+1, (j-1)^+] - J_k(i,j)] & \qquad (6.99)\\ + \lambda\,[\min[J_k(i+2,j), J_k(i+1,j+1)] & \\ - \min[J_k(i+1,j+1), J_k(i,j+2)]]. &\end{aligned}$$

We now argue by induction. We have $\Delta_1^0(i, j) = 0$ for all (i, j). We assume that $\Delta_1^k(i, j)$ is monotonically nondecreasing in i for fixed j, and show that the same is true for $\Delta_1^{k+1}(i, j)$. This can be verified by showing that each of the terms in the right side of (6.99) is monotonically nondecreasing in i for fixed j. Indeed, the first term is constant, and the second and third terms are easily seen to be monotonically nondecreasing in i using the induction hypothesis for the case where $i, j > 0$ and the earlier shown fact that $J_k(i, j)$ is monotonically nondecreasing in i for the case where $i = 0$ or $j = 0$. The last term on the right side of (6.99) can be written

$$\begin{aligned}\lambda[J_k(i+1,j+1) + \min[J_k(i+2,j) - J_k(i+1,j+1), 0] &\\ - J_k(i+1,j+1) - \min[0, J_k(i,j+2) - J_k(i+1,j+1)]] &\\ = \lambda[\min[0, J_k(i+2,j) - J_k(i+1,j+1)] &\\ + \max[0, J_k(i+1,j+1) - J_k(i,j+2)]] &\\ = \lambda[\min[0, \Delta_1^k(i+1,j)] &\\ + \max[0, \Delta_1^k(i,j+1)]]. &\end{aligned}$$

Since $\Delta_1^k(i + 1, j)$ and $\Delta_1^k(i, j + 1)$ are monotonically nondecreasing in i by the induction hypothesis, the same is true for the preceding expression. Therefore, each of the terms on the right side of (6.99) is monotonically nondecreasing in i, and the induction proof is complete. Thus the existence of an optimal threshold policy is established.

There are a number of generalizations of the routing problem of this example that admit a similar analysis and for which there exist optimal policies of the threshold type. For example, suppose that there are additional Poisson arrival processes with rates λ_1 and λ_2 at queues 1 and 2, respectively. Then the existence of an optimal threshold policy can be shown by a nearly verbatim repetition of our analysis. A more substantive extension is obtained when there is additional service capacity μ that can be switched at the times of transition due to an arrival or service completion to serve a customer in queue 1 or 2. Then a similar proof as the earlier one can be used to show that it is optimal to route to queue 1 if and only if $(i, j) \in S_1$ and to switch the additional service capacity to queue 2 if and only if $(i + 1, j + 1) \in S_1$, where S_1 is given by (6.96) and is characterized by a threshold function as in (6.97). For a proof of this and further extensions, we refer to [H1], which generalizes and unifies several earlier results on the subject.

6.8 NOTES

The first passage problem was first formulated in [E1]. Our presentation sharpens results from several sources, including [D4], [K14], and [P1].

The index rule solution of the multiarmed bandit problem is due to [G1] and [G2]. The proof given here is due to Tsitsiklis [T9], and improves substantially on an earlier proof by Whittle [W11]. Reference [V3] analyzes extensions of the bandit problem. References [K10] and [K13] describe much additional work on the subject.

The gambling problem and its solution are taken from [D9]. In [B25] a surprising property of the optimal reward function J^* for this problem is shown; it is almost everywhere differentiable with derivative zero, yet it is strictly increasing, taking values ranging from 0 to 1.

The idea of using uniformization to convert stochastic control problems involving continuous-time Markov chains into discrete-time problems gained wide attention following [L4]. Control of queueing systems has been researched extensively. For additional material on the problem of control of arrival rate or service rate (cf. Examples 2 and 3 in Section 6.7), see [C4], [R4], [S15], [S22], [S25], and [S26]. For more on priority assignment and routing (cf. Examples 4 and 5 in Section 6.7), see [B2], [B3], [C4], [H3], [H4], and [E3], [H1], [L3], respectively.

PROBLEMS

1. *Deterministic Linear–Quadratic Problems.* Consider the deterministic linear–quadratic problem involving the system

$$x_{k+1} = Ax_k + Bu_k$$

and the cost functional

$$J_\pi(x_0) = \sum_{k=0}^{\infty} x_k'Qx_k + \mu_k(x_k)'R\mu_k(x_k).$$

It is assumed that R is positive definite symmetric, Q is of the form $C'C$, and the pairs (A, B), (A, C) are controllable and observable, respectively. Use the theory of Sections 2.1 and 6.1 to show that the stationary policy $\pi^* = \{\mu^*, \mu^*, \ldots\}$ with

$$\mu^*(x) = -(B'KB + R)^{-1}B'KAx$$

is optimal, where K is the unique positive semidefinite symmetric solution of the algebraic Riccati equation (cf. Section 2.1):

$$K = A'[K - KB(B'KB + R)^{-1}B'K]A + Q.$$

Provide a similar result under an appropriate controllability assumption for the case of a periodic deterministic linear system and a periodic quadratic cost functional (cf. Section 5.5 and Problem 3).

2. *Linear–Quadratic Problems with Nonstationary Disturbances.* Consider the linear–quadratic problem of Section 6.1 with the only difference that the disturbances w_k have zero mean, but their covariance matrices are nonstationary and uniformly bounded over k. Show that the optimal control law remains unchanged.

3. *Periodic Linear–Quadratic Problems.* Consider the linear system

$$x_{k+1} = A_k x_k + B_k u_k + w_k, \qquad k = 0, 1, \ldots,$$

and the quadratic cost functional

$$J_\pi(x_0) = \lim_{N\to\infty} \underset{\substack{w_k \\ k=0,\ldots,N-1}}{E} \left\{ \sum_{k=0}^{N-1} \alpha^k [x_k' Q_k x_k + \mu_k(x_k)' R_k \mu_k(x_k)] \right\},$$

where the matrices have appropriate dimensions, Q_k and R_k are positive semidefinite and positive definite, respectively, for all k, and $0 < \alpha < 1$. Assume that the system and cost functional are periodic with period p (cf. Section 5.5), that the controls are unconstrained, and that the disturbances are independent, have zero mean, and finite covariance matrices. Assume further that the following (controllability) condition is in effect.

Given any initial state $\bar{x}_0$, there exists a finite sequence of controls $\{\bar{u}_0, \bar{u}_1, \ldots, \bar{u}_r\}$ such that $\bar{x}_{r+1} = 0$, where $\bar{x}_{r+1}$ is generated by

$$\bar{x}_{k+1} = A_k \bar{x}_k + B_k \bar{u}_k, \qquad k = 0, 1, \ldots, r.$$

Show that there is an optimal periodic policy π^* of the form

$$\pi^* = \{\mu_0^*, \mu_1^*, \ldots, \mu_{p-1}^*, \mu_0^*, \mu_1^*, \ldots, \mu_{p-1}^*, \ldots\},$$

where $\mu_0^*, \ldots, \mu_{p-1}^*$ are given by

$$\mu_i^*(x) = -\alpha(\alpha B_i' K_{i+1} B_i + R_i)^{-1} B_i' K_{i+1} A_i x, \qquad i = 0, \ldots, p-2,$$

$$\mu_{p-1}^*(x) = -\alpha(\alpha B_{p-1}' K_0 B_{p-1} + R_{p-1})^{-1} B_{p-1}' K_0 A_{p-1} x,$$

and the matrices $K_0, K_1, \ldots, K_{p-1}$ satisfy the coupled set of p algebraic Riccati equations given by

$$K_i = A_i'[\alpha K_{i+1} - \alpha^2 K_{i+1} B_i (\alpha B_i' K_{i+1} B_i + R_i)^{-1} B_i' K_{i+1}] A_i + Q_i, \qquad i = 0, 1, \ldots, p-2,$$

$$K_{p-1} = A_{p-1}'[\alpha K_0 - \alpha^2 K_0 B_{p-1} (\alpha B_{p-1}' K_0 B_{p-1} + R_{p-1})^{-1} B_{p-1}' K_0] A_{p-1} + Q_{p-1}.$$

4. *Discounted Linear–Quadratic Problems with Imperfect State Information.* Consider the linear–quadratic problem of Section 6.1 with the difference that the controller, instead of having perfect state information, has access to measurements of the form

$$z_k = C x_k + v_k, \qquad k = 0, 1, \ldots.$$

As in Section 3.2, the disturbances v_k are independent and have identical statistics, zero mean, and finite covariance matrix. Assume that for every admissible policy π the matrices

$$E\{[x_k - E\{x_k | I_k\}][x_k - E\{x_k | I_k\}]' | \pi\}$$

are uniformly bounded over k, where I_k is the information vector defined in Section 3.2. Show that the optimal policy is $\pi^* = \{\mu^*, \mu^*, \ldots\}$, where μ^* is given by

$$\mu^*(I_k) = -\alpha(\alpha B'KB + R)^{-1}B'KA\, E\{x_k|I_k\}, \qquad \text{for all } I_k, \qquad k = 0, 1, \ldots.$$

Show also that the same is true if w_k and v_k are nonstationary with zero mean and covariance matrices that are uniformly bounded over k. *Hint:* Combine the theory of Sections 3.2 and 6.1.

5. *Policy Iteration for Discounted Linear-Quadratic Problems* [K9]. Consider the problem of Section 6.1 and let L_0 be an $m \times n$ matrix such that the matrix $(A + BL_0)$ is stable.

(a) Show that the cost corresponding to the stationary policy $\{\mu_0, \mu_0, \ldots\}$, where $\mu_0(x) = L_0 x$ is of the form

$$J_{\mu_0}(x) = x'K_0x + \text{constant},$$

where K_0 is a positive semidefinite matrix satisfying the (linear) equation

$$K_0 = \alpha(A + BL_0)'K_0(A + BL_0) + Q + L_0'RL_0.$$

(b) Let $\mu_1(x)$ attain the minimum for each x in the expression

$$\min_u \{u'Ru + (Ax + Bu)'K_0(Ax + Bu)\}.$$

Show that for all x

$$J_{\mu_1}(x) = x'K_1x + \text{constant} \leq J_{\mu_0}(x),$$

where K_1 is some positive semidefinite matrix.

(c) Show that the policy iteration process described in parts (a) and (b) yields a sequence $\{K_k\}$ such that

$$K_k \to K,$$

where K is the optimal cost matrix of the problem.

6. *Periodic Inventory Control Problems.* In the inventory control problem of Section 6.2, consider the case where the statistics of the demands w_k, the prices c_k, and the holding and the shortage costs are periodic with period p. Show that there exists an optimal periodic policy of the form $\pi^* = \{\mu_0^*, \ldots, \mu_{p-1}^*, \mu_0^*, \ldots, \mu_{p-1}^*, \ldots\}$,

$$\mu_i^*(x) = \begin{cases} S_i^* - x, & \text{if } x \leq S_i^*, \\ 0, & \text{otherwise,} \end{cases} \qquad i = 0, 1, \ldots, p-1,$$

where $S_0^*, \ldots, S_{p-1}^*$ are appropriate scalars.

7. Consider the stopping problem of Section 6.3 under the assumption that

$$t(x) \leq 0, \qquad c(x) \leq 0, \qquad \text{for all } x \in S.$$

Consider the mapping T defined by

$$T(J)(x) = \min\left[t(x), c(x) + \underset{w}{E}\{J[f_c(x, w)]\}\right].$$

(a) Show that the optimal cost function J^* satisfies

$$J^* = T(J^*), \qquad J^* = \lim_{k\to\infty} T^k(J_0),$$

where J_0 is the zero function.

(b) Let $S = \{1, 2, \ldots\}$, $f_c(i, w) = i + 1$, and $c(i) = 0$ for all $i \in S$, $w \in D$, and $t(i) = -1 + (1/i)$ for all $i \in S$. Show that $J^*(i) = -1$ for all i and that there does not exist an optimal policy for this problem (even though the control space is a finite set).

8. Let $z_0, z_1, \ldots$ be a sequence of independent and identically distributed random variables taking values on a finite set Z. We know that the probability distribution of the z_k's is one out of n distributions $f_1, f_2, \ldots, f_n$, and we are trying to decide which distribution is the correct one. At each time k after observing $z_1, \ldots, z_k$, we may either stop the observations and accept one of the n distributions as correct or take another observation at a cost $c > 0$. The cost for accepting f_i given that f_j is correct is L_{ij}, $i, j = 1, \ldots, n$. We assume $L_{ij} > 0$ for $i \neq j$, $L_{ii} = 0$, $i = 1, \ldots, n$. The a priori distribution of $f_1, \ldots, f_n$ is denoted

$$P_0 = \{p_0^1, p_0^2, \ldots, p_0^n\}, \qquad p_0^i \geq 0, \qquad \sum_{i=1}^{n} p_0^i = 1.$$

Show that the optimal cost $J^*(P_0)$ is a concave function of P_0. Characterize the optimal acceptance regions and show how they can be obtained in the limit by means of a successive approximation method.

9. Show that a finite horizon problem with N stages that falls within the framework of the basic problem of Chapter 1 can be viewed as a (stationary) first passage problem (not necessarily with finite state, control, and disturbance space) for which assumptions similar to those of Section 6.4 are satisfied. Show also that a contraction condition such as (6.22) holds for this problem. *Hint:* If $S_0, S_1, \ldots, S_N$ are the state spaces for the stages $0, 1, \ldots, N$, define a new state space S by $S = \{(x, k) | x \in S_k, k = 0, 1, \ldots, N\} \cup \{T\}$, where T is a termination (absorbing) state to which the system is driven with certainty from every state in $\{(x, N) | x \in S_N\}$ similar to the constructions of Section 5.5.

10. *Infinite Time Reachability* [B9], [B12]. Consider the stationary system

$$x_{k+1} = f(x_k, u_k, w_k), \qquad k = 0, 1, \ldots,$$

of the problem of this chapter, where the disturbance space D is an arbitrary (not necessarily countable) set. The disturbances w_k can take values in a subset $W(x_k, u_k)$ of D that may depend on x_k and u_k. This problem deals with the following question: Given a nonempty subset X of the state space S, under what conditions does there exist an admissible policy $\{\mu_0, \mu_1, \ldots\}$ with $\mu_k(x_k) \in U(x_k)$ for all $x_k \in S$ and $k = 0, 1, \ldots$, such that the state of the (closed-loop) system

$$x_{k+1} = f[x_k, \mu_k(x_k), w_k] \tag{6.100}$$

belongs to the set X for all k and all possible values $w_k \in W[x_k, \mu_k(x_k)]$, that is,

$$x_k \in X, \qquad \text{for all } w_k \in W[x_k, \mu_k(x_k)], \qquad k = 0, 1, \ldots? \tag{6.101}$$

The set X is said to be *infinitely reachable* if there exists an admissible policy $\{\mu_0, \mu_1, \ldots\}$ and *some* initial state $x_0 \in X$ for which relations (6.100) and (6.101) are satisfied. It is said to be *strongly reachable* if there exists an admissible policy $\{\mu_0, \mu_1 \ldots\}$ such that for *all* initial states $x_0 \in X$ relations (6.100) and (6.101) are satisfied.

Consider the function R mapping any subset Z of the state space S into a subset $R(Z)$ of S defined by

$$R(Z) = \{x \mid \text{there is } u \in U(x) \text{ with } f(x, u, w) \in Z, \text{ for all } w \in W(x, u)\} \cap Z.$$

(a) Show that the set X is strongly reachable if and only if $R(X) = X$. Given X, consider the set X^* defined as follows: $x_0 \in X^*$ if and only if $x_0 \in X$ and there exists an admissible policy $\{\mu_0, \mu_1, \ldots\}$ such that (6.100) and (6.101) are satisfied when x_0 is taken as the initial state of the system.

(b) Show that a set X is infinitely reachable if and only if it contains a nonempty strongly reachable set. Furthermore, the largest such set is X^* in the sense that X^* is strongly reachable whenever nonempty, and if $\tilde{X} \subset X$ is another strongly reachable set, then $\tilde{X} \subset X^*$.

(c) Show that if X is infinitely reachable there exists an admissible stationary policy $\{\mu, \mu, \ldots\}$ such that if the initial state x_0 belongs to X^*, then all subsequent states of the closed-loop system $x_{k+1} = f[x_k, \mu(x_k), w_k]$ are guaranteed to belong to X^*.

(d) Given X, consider the sets $R(X), \ldots, R^k(X), \ldots$, where $R^k(X)$ denotes the set obtained after k applications of the mapping R on X. Show that

$$X^* \subset \bigcap_{k=1}^{\infty} R^k(X).$$

(e) Given X, consider for each $x \in X$ and $k = 1, 2, \ldots$ the set

$$U_k(x) = \{u \mid f(x, u, w) \in R^k(X), \text{ for all } w \in W(x, u)\}.$$

Show that, if there exists an index $\bar{k}$ such that for all $x \in X$ and $k \geq \bar{k}$ the set $U_k(x)$ is a compact subset of a Euclidean space, then $X^* = \cap_{k=1}^{\infty} R^k(X)$.

11. *Infinite Time Reachability for Linear Systems.* Consider the linear stationary system

$$x_{k+1} = Ax_k + Bu_k + Gw_k,$$

where $x_k \in R^n$, $u_k \in R^m$, and $w_k \in R^r$, and the matrices A, B, and G are known and have appropriate dimensions. The matrix A is assumed invertible. The controls u_k and the disturbances w_k are restricted to take values in the ellipsoids $U = \{u \mid u'Ru \leq 1\}$ and $W = \{w \mid w'Qw \leq 1\}$, respectively, where R and Q are positive definite symmetric matrices of appropriate dimensions. Show that in order for the ellipsoid $X = \{x \mid x'Kx \leq 1\}$, where K is a positive definite symmetric matrix, to be strongly reachable (in the terminology of Problem 10), it is sufficient that for some positive definite matrix M and for some scalar $\beta \in (0, 1)$ we have

$$K = A'\left[(1 - \beta)K^{-1} - \frac{1 - \beta}{\beta} GQ^{-1}G' + BR^{-1}B'\right]^{-1} A + M, \tag{6.102}$$

$$K^{-1} - \frac{1}{\beta} GQ^{-1}G': \text{ positive definite.} \tag{6.103}$$

Show also that if (6.102) and (6.103) are satisfied, the stationary policy $\{\mu^*, \mu^*, \ldots\}$, where

$$\mu^*(x) = -(R + B'FB)^{-1}B'FAx = Lx,$$

$$F = \left[(1 - \beta)K^{-1} - \frac{1 - \beta}{\beta} GQ^{-1}G'\right]^{-1},$$

achieves reachability of the ellipsoid $X = \{x|x'Kx \leq 1\}$. Furthermore, the matrix $(A + BL)$ is a stable matrix. (For a proof together with a computational procedure for finding matrices K satisfying (6.102) and (6.103), see [B9] and [B12]).

12. In the context of the first passage problem of Section 6.4, assume that there exists $m > 0$ such that

$$P(x_m = 0|x_0 = i, \pi) > 0 \tag{6.104}$$

for all $i = 1, \ldots, n$ and stationary policies π. Show that this relation also holds for all nonstationary policies π. *Hint:* Argue by contradiction. Assume that there exists a nonstationary $\pi = \{\mu_0, \mu_1, \ldots\}$ and an initial state i such that (6.104) does not hold for any m. Define, for $k = 1, 2, \ldots,$

$$S_k(i) = \{j|P(x_k = j|x_0 = i, \pi) > 0\}.$$

Let S_∞ be the set of states that belong to infinitely many sets $S_k(i)$, and for each $j \in S_\infty$, let μ^j be such that simultaneously $\mu_k = \mu^j$ and $j \in S_k(i)$ for infinitely many integers k. Consider any stationary policy μ such that $\mu(j) = \mu^j(j)$ for $j \in S_\infty$. Show that (6.104) is violated for $\pi = \{\mu, \mu, \ldots\}$.

13. Consider the first passage problem of Section 6.4.

(a) Suppose that for some stationary policy π there exist $m > 0$ and $\epsilon > 0$ such that for all i

$$P(x_m = 0|x_0 = i, \pi) \geq \epsilon.$$

Show by induction that for all k

$$P(x_{km} = 0|x_0 = i, \pi) \geq 1 - (1 - \epsilon)^k$$

and therefore $P(x_k = 0|x_0 = i, \pi) \to 1$ as $k \to \infty$.

(b) Under Assumption N show that either the optimal cost is $-\infty$ for some initial state, or else, under every policy, the system eventually enters with probability one a set of cost-free states and never leaves that set thereafter.

(c) Under Assumption P, show that if there exists an optimal nonstationary policy for each initial state that is proper in the sense of (6.26), then there exists an optimal stationary policy that is proper.

14. A gambler engages in a game of successive coin flipping over an infinite horizon. He wins one dollar each time heads comes up, and loses $m > 0$ dollars each time two successive tails come up (so the sequence TTTT loses $3m$ dollars). The gambler at each time period either flips a fair coin or else cheats by flipping a two-headed coin. In the latter case, however, he gets caught with probability $p > 0$ before he flips the coin, the game terminates, and the gambler keeps his earnings thus far. The gambler wishes to maximize his expected earnings.

(a) Show that there is a critical value $\overline{m}$ for m below which it is optimal to flip the fair coin at all times.

(b) Assume that $m > \overline{m}$ and argue that it is then optimal to try to cheat if the last flip was tails and to play fair otherwise. *Hint:* This is a first passage problem; however, the assumptions of Section 6.4 are not quite satisfied.

15. *Gambling Strategies for Favorable Games.* A gambler plays a game such as the one of Section 6.6, but where the probability of winning p satisfies $\frac{1}{2} \leq p < 1$. His objective is to reach a final fortune n, where n is a positive integer with $n \geq 2$. His initial fortune is a positive integer i with $0 < i < n$, and his stake at time k can take only integer values u_k satisfying $0 \leq u_k \leq x_k$, $0 \leq u_k \leq n - x_k$, where x_k is his fortune at time k. Show that the strategy that always stakes one unit is optimal [i.e., $\mu^*(x) = 1$ for all integers x with $0 < x < n$ is optimal]. *Hint:* Use Proposition 3 to show that

$$J_{\mu^*}(i) = \left[\left(\frac{1-p}{p}\right)^i - 1\right]\left[\left(\frac{1-p}{p}\right)^n - 1\right]^{-1}, \qquad 0 \leq i \leq n, \ \tfrac{1}{2} < p < 1,$$

$$J_{\mu^*}(i) = \frac{i}{n}, \qquad 0 \leq i \leq n, \ p = \tfrac{1}{2}$$

(or see [A9, p. 182] for a proof). Then use the sufficiency condition of Proposition 10 of Section 5.4.

16. *Computer Assignment.* A quarterback can choose between running and passing the ball on any given play. The number of yards gained by running is Poisson distributed with parameter λ_r. A pass is incomplete with probability p, is intercepted with probability q, and is completed with probability $1 - p - q$. When completed, a pass gains a number of yards that is Poisson distributed with parameter λ_p. We assume that the yardage gained in each play is integer and that the probability of scoring a touchdown on a single play starting x yards from the goal equals the probability of gaining a number of yards greater or equal to x. We assume also that yardage cannot be lost on any play and that there are no penalties. The ball is turned over to the other team on a fourth down or when an interception occurs. Formulate the problem as a first passage problem, and use successive approximation and policy iteration to compute the quarterback's play-selection policy that maximizes the probability of scoring a touchdown on any single drive for $\lambda_r = 3$, $\lambda_p = 10$, $p = 0.4$, and $q = 0.05$.

17. *Optimal Serve Selection in Tennis* [N4]. A tennis player has a Fast serve and a Slow serve, denoted F and S, respectively. The probability of $F(S)$ landing in bounds is p_F (p_S). The probability of winning the point assuming the serve landed in bounds is q_F (q_S). We assume $p_F < p_S$ and $q_F > q_S$. The problem is to find the serve to be used at each possible scoring situation during a single game that maximizes the probability of winning that game.

(a) Formulate this as a first passage problem with 36 states (plus the absorbing state) and write down Bellman's equation.

(b) Show analytically that it is optimal (regardless of score) to use F on both serves if $(p_F q_F)/(p_S q_S) > 1$, to use S on both serves if $(p_F q_F)/(p_S q_S) < 1 + p_F - p_S$, and to use F on the first serve and S on the second otherwise.

(c) Optional computer assignment: Assume that $q_F = 0.6$, $q_S = 0.4$, and $p_S = 0.95$. Plot (in increments of 0.05) the probability of the server winning a game with optimal serve selection as a function of p_F.

18. *The Tax Problem* [V3]. This problem is similar to the multiarmed bandit problem. The only difference is that, if we engage project i at period k, we pay a tax $\alpha^k C^j(x^j)$ for every other project j [for a total of $\alpha^k \Sigma_{j \neq i} C^j(x^j)$], instead of earning a reward $\alpha^k R^i(x^i)$. The objective is to find a project selection policy that minimizes the total tax paid. Show that the problem can be converted into a bandit problem with reward function for project i equal to

$$R^i(x^i) = C^i(x^i) - \alpha E\{C^i[f^i(x^i, w^i)]\}.$$

19. *The Restart Problem* [K4]. The purpose of this problem is to show that the index of a project in the multiarmed bandit context can be calculated by solving an associated infinite horizon discounted cost problem. In what follows we consider a single project with reward function $R(x)$, a fixed initial state x_0, and the calculation of the value of index $m(x_0)$ for that state. Consider the problem where at state x_k and time k there are two options: (1) Continue, which brings reward $\alpha^k R(x_k)$ and moves the project to state $x_{k+1} = f(x_k, w)$, or (2) restart the project, which moves the state to x_0, brings reward $\alpha^k R(x_0)$, and moves the project to state $x_{k+1} = f(x_0, w)$. Show that the optimal reward functions of this problem and of the bandit problem with $M = m(x_0)$ are identical, and therefore the optimal reward for both problems when starting at x_0 equals $m(x_0)$. *Hint:* Show that Bellman's equation for both problems takes the form

$$J(x) = \max\,[R(x_0) + \alpha E\{J[f(x_0, w)]\},\ R(x) + \alpha E\{J[f(x, w)]\}].$$

20. *Alternative Characterization of the Index of a Project.* In the multiarmed bandit context, fix a project and an initial state x_0, and let $m(x_0)$ be the value of index at that state. Consider the single-project problem with retirement reward equal to $m(x_0)$. For any stationary policy $\{\mu, \mu, \ldots\}$, for this problem let K_μ be the corresponding (random) retirement time. Show that

$$m(x_0) = \max_{\mu} \frac{E\{\text{discounted reward prior to } K_\mu\}}{1 - E\{\alpha^{K_\mu}\}},$$

with the maximum attained when μ is an optimal retirement policy.

21. *Determining the Bottleneck Links in an Open Network of Queues with a Single Customer Class* [S8]. Consider a network of n queues whereby a customer at queue i upon completion of service is routed to queue j with probability p_{ij}, and exits the network with probability $1 - \Sigma_j p_{ij}$. For each queue i denote:

r_i: the external customer arrival rate,

$\dfrac{1}{\mu_i}$: the average customer service time,

λ_i: the customer departure rate,

a_i: the total customer arrival rate (sum of external rate and departure rates from upstream queues weighted by the corresponding probabilities).

We have

$$a_i = r_i + \sum_{j=1}^{n} \lambda_j p_{ji}, \qquad \text{for all } i,$$

and we assume that any portion of the arrival rate a_i in excess of the service rate μ_i is lost; so the departure rate at queue i satisfies

$$\lambda_i = \min\,[\mu_i, a_i] = \min\left[\mu_i,\ r_i + \sum_{j=1}^{n} \lambda_j p_{ji}\right].$$

Assume that $r_i > 0$ for at least one i, and that for every queue i_1 with $r_{i_1} > 0$ there is a queue i with $1 - \Sigma_j p_{ij} > 0$, and a sequence $i_1, i_2, \ldots, i_k, i$ such that $p_{i_1 i_2} > 0, \ldots, p_{i_k i} > 0$. Show that the departure rates λ_i satisfying the preceding equations are unique and can be found by successive approximation or policy iteration. *Hint:* This is *not* a Markovian decision problem because we may have $\Sigma_j p_{ji} > 1$ for some i. However, it is possible to carry out an analysis based on m-stage contraction mappings that is similar to the one for the first passage problem (cf. Proposition 2).

22. *Proof of Validity of Uniformization.* Complete the details of the following argument, showing the validity of the uniformization procedure for the case of a finite number of states $i = 1, \ldots, n$. We fix a policy, and for notational simplicity we do not show the dependence of transition rates on the control. Let $p(t)$ be the row vector with coordinates

$$p_i(t) = P\{x(t) = i | x_0\}, \qquad i = 1, \ldots, n.$$

We have

$$dp(t)/dt = p(t)A,$$

where $p(0)$ is the row vector with ith coordinate equal to one if $x_0 = i$ and zero otherwise, and the matrix A has elements

$$a_{ij} = \begin{cases} \nu_i p_{ij}, & \text{if } i \neq j, \\ -\nu_i, & \text{if } i = j. \end{cases}$$

From this we obtain

$$p(t) = p(0)e^{At},$$

where

$$e^{At} = \sum_{k=0}^{\infty} \frac{A^n}{k!}.$$

Consider the transition probability matrix B of the uniform version

$$B = I + \frac{A}{\nu},$$

where $\nu \geq \nu_i$, $i = 1, \ldots, n$. Consider also the following equation:

$$\begin{aligned} e^{At} &= e^{-\nu t} e^{B\nu t} \\ &= e^{-\nu t} \sum_{k=0}^{\infty} \frac{(B\nu t)^k}{k!}. \end{aligned}$$

Use these relations to write

$$p(t) = p(0) \sum_{k=0}^{\infty} \Gamma(k, t) B^k,$$

where

$$\begin{aligned} \Gamma(k, t) &= \frac{(\nu t)^k}{k!} e^{-\nu t} \\ &= \text{Prob}\{k \text{ transitions occur between } 0 \text{ and } t \text{ in the uniform Markov chain}\}. \end{aligned}$$

Verify that for $i = 1, \ldots, n$ we have

$$p_i(t) = \text{Prob}\{x(t) = i \text{ in the uniform Markov chain}\}.$$

23. Consider the $M/M/1$ queueing problem with variable service rate (Example 2 in Section 6.7). Assume that no arrivals are allowed ($\lambda = 0$), and one can either serve a customer at rate μ or refuse service ($M = \{0, \mu\}$). Let the cost rates for customer waiting and service be $c(i) = ci$ and $q(\mu)$, respectively. Show that an optimal policy is to always serve an available customer if

$$\frac{q(\mu)}{\mu} \leqslant \frac{c}{\beta},$$

and to always refuse service otherwise.

24. Consider a machine that may break down and can be repaired. Over a time unit where it is in operation it produces a negative cost (benefit) of -1 unit, and it may break down with probability 0.1. When it is in the breakdown mode, we may repair it with an effort u. The probability of making it operative over one time unit is then u, and the cost is Cu^2. Determine the optimal repair effort over an infinite time horizon with discount factor $\alpha < 1$. (This problem can be solved analytically.)

25. Show that the critical level S^* for the inventory problem with zero fixed cost of Section 6.2 maximizes $(1 - \alpha)cy + L(y)$ over y. *Hint:* Show that the cost can be expressed as

$$J_\pi(x_0) = E\left\{\sum_{k=0}^{\infty} \alpha^k[(1 - \alpha)cy_k + L(y_k)] + \frac{c\alpha}{1 - \alpha} E\{w\} - cx_0\right\}$$

where $y_k = x_k + \mu_k(x_k)$.

CHAPTER SEVEN

Minimization of Average Cost per Stage

The results of the last two chapters are applicable to problems for which the total expected cost is finite for at least some initial states. We saw that this is possible for several types of problems either through discounting or through the presence of cost-free absorbing states that the system eventually enters or approaches. On the other hand, in many situations it turns out that for every policy and initial state the total expected cost

$$\lim_{N\to\infty} E\left\{\sum_{k=0}^{N-1} g[x_k, \mu_k(x_k), w_k]\right\} \tag{7.1}$$

is infinite, but the limit

$$\lim_{N\to\infty} \frac{1}{N} E\left\{\sum_{k=0}^{N-1} g[x_k, \mu_k(x_k), w_k]\right\} \tag{7.2}$$

exists and is finite. Expression (7.2) may be viewed as average cost per stage and is a reasonably meaningful criterion for optimization. This chapter will deal with a problem similar to that of Chapter 5, except for the fact that the average cost per stage (7.2) is minimized in place of the total expected cost of (7.1). Furthermore, *in the first three sections we will restrict ourselves to the case of finite state space, control space, and disturbance space*. For this reason it is convenient to switch at the outset to a notation that is better suited for finite state systems.

Let $S = \{1, \ldots, n\}$ denote the state space. To each state $i \in S$ and control u in the finite control space C there corresponds a set of transition probabilities $p_{ij}(u)$, $j = 1, \ldots, n$, as discussed in Section 5.2. Each time the system is in state i and control u is applied, we incur an expected cost denoted by $g(i, u)$, and the system moves to state j with probability $p_{ij}(u)$. The objective is to minimize over all admissible policies $\pi = \{\mu_0, \mu_1, \ldots\}$ with $\mu_k : S \to C$, $\mu_k(i) \in U(i)$, for all $i \in S$, the average cost per stage†

$$J_\pi(x_0) = \lim_{N\to\infty} \frac{1}{N} E\left\{ \sum_{k=0}^{N-1} g[x_k, \mu_k(x_k)] \right\}, \tag{7.3}$$

for any given initial state $x_0 \in S$.

An Expression for Average Cost

Let us now provide a preliminary discussion of the problem that motivates some of the results to be obtained in the next section. Given any stationary policy $\pi = \{\mu, \mu, \ldots\}$, let us denote by P_μ the transition probability matrix having elements $p_{ij}[\mu(i)]$:

$$P_\mu = \begin{bmatrix} p_{11}[\mu(1)] & \ldots & p_{1n}[\mu(1)] \\ & \ldots & \\ p_{n1}[\mu(n)] & \ldots & p_{nn}[\mu(n)] \end{bmatrix}. \tag{7.4}$$

The matrix P_μ may be used to express the m-step transition probabilities corresponding to a stationary policy $\pi = \{\mu, \mu, \ldots\}$. We have

$$p_{ij}[\mu(i)] = P(x_{k+1} = j \mid x_k = i, \pi),$$

and it is an elementary matter to show (see Appendix D) that

$$[P_\mu^m]_{ij} = P(x_{k+m} = j \mid x_k = i, \pi),$$

where $[P_\mu^m]_{ij}$ is the element of the ith row and jth column of the matrix P_μ^m (i.e., P_μ raised to the mth power).

These probabilities can be used to express the cost $J_\pi(x_0)$ of (7.3). As before, we use the notation

$$J_\pi(i) = J_\mu(i), \qquad i = 1, \ldots, n,$$

for stationary policies $\pi = \{\mu, \mu, \ldots\}$. Denote

$$J_\mu = \begin{bmatrix} J_\mu(1) \\ J_\mu(2) \\ \vdots \\ J_\mu(n) \end{bmatrix}, \qquad g_\mu = \begin{bmatrix} g[1, \mu(1)] \\ g[2, \mu(2)] \\ \vdots \\ g[n, \mu(n)] \end{bmatrix}. \tag{7.5}$$

† When the limit in (7.3) is not known to exist, we define average cost by

$$J_\pi(x_0) = \limsup_{N\to\infty} \frac{1}{N} E\left\{ \sum_{k=0}^{N-1} g[x_k, \mu_k(x_k)] \right\}.$$

We will show, however, as part of our subsequent analysis that the limit in (7.3) exists at least for those policies π that are of interest.

With this notation it is seen that

$$J_\mu = \lim_{N\to\infty} \frac{1}{N} \sum_{k=0}^{N-1} P_\mu^k g_\mu. \tag{7.6}$$

The following result shows that J_μ is well defined. It is a standard result on transition probability matrices, and its proof is given in the appendix to this chapter (Proposition A7.1).

Lemma 1. For any $n \times n$ stochastic matrix P, that is, a matrix with elements p_{ij} satisfying

$$p_{ij} \geq 0, \qquad i, j = 1, \ldots, n, \qquad \sum_{j=1}^{n} p_{ij} = 1, \quad i = 1, \ldots, n,$$

we have

$$\lim_{N\to\infty} \frac{1}{N} \sum_{k=0}^{N-1} P^k = P^*, \tag{7.7}$$

where P^* is a stochastic matrix with the following properties:

(a) $P^* = PP^* = P^*P = P^*P^*$.

(b) $(I - P + P^*)$ is an invertible matrix, where I denotes the $n \times n$ identity matrix.

Using Lemma 1 to write

$$P_\mu^* = \lim_{N\to\infty} \frac{1}{N} \sum_{k=0}^{N-1} P_\mu^k, \tag{7.8}$$

we have from (7.6) that

$$J_\mu = P_\mu^* g_\mu. \tag{7.9}$$

Thus for every admissible stationary policy the corresponding average cost per stage is well defined and conveniently characterized by (7.9). This equation has a natural interpretation. Using (7.8), we see that the (i, j)th element of P_μ^* is the long-term fraction of time the system visits state j when the initial state is i. Therefore, (7.9) states that $J_\mu(i)$ is the sum over all j of the cost $g[j, \mu(j)]$ incurred when at state j, weighted by the fraction of time state j is visited when the initial state is i.

Dependence of Average Cost on the Initial State

An important fact to keep in mind regarding the average cost per stage (7.2) is that it primarily expresses cost incurred in the long term. Costs incurred in the initial stages (say the first K) do not matter since their contribution to the average cost per stage is reduced to zero as $N \to \infty$; that is,

$$\lim_{N\to\infty} \frac{1}{N} E\left\{ \sum_{k=0}^{K} g[x_k, \mu_k(x_k)] \right\} = 0. \tag{7.10}$$

Consider now a stationary policy $\{\mu, \mu, \ldots\}$ and two states i and j such that the system will, under μ, eventually reach j starting from i with probability one. Then intuitively it is clear that the average costs per stage starting from either i or j cannot be different, since the costs incurred in the process of reaching j from i do not essentially contribute to the average cost per stage [cf. (7.10)]. More precisely, let $K_{ij}(\mu)$ be the first passage time from i to j under μ, that is, the first index k for which $x_k = j$ starting from $x_0 = i$ under μ (see Appendix D). Then the average cost per stage corresponding to initial condition $x_0 = i$ can be expressed as

$$J_\mu(i) = \lim_{N\to\infty} \frac{1}{N} E\left\{ \sum_{k=0}^{K_{ij}(\mu)-1} g[x_k, \mu(x_k)] \right\} + \lim_{N\to\infty} E\left\{ \frac{1}{N} \sum_{k=K_{ij}(\mu)}^{N} g[x_k, \mu(x_k)] \right\}.$$

If $E\{K_{ij}(\mu)\} < \infty$ (which is equivalent to assuming that the system eventually reaches j starting from i with probability one; see Appendix D), then it is easily seen that the first limit is zero, while the second limit equals $J_\mu(j)$. Therefore,

$$J_\mu(i) = J_\mu(j), \qquad \text{for all } i, j \text{ with } E\{K_{ij}(\mu)\} < \infty.$$

The preceding argument suggests that the optimal cost

$$J^*(i) = \min_\pi J_\pi(i), \qquad i = 1, \ldots, n$$

should also be independent of the initial state under normal circumstances. To see this, suppose that for two states i and j there exists a stationary policy $\{\mu,\mu, \ldots\}$ such that $E\{K_{ij}(\mu)\} < \infty$. Then it is impossible that

$$J^*(j) < J^*(i),$$

since when starting from i we can adopt the policy $\{\mu, \mu, \ldots\}$ up to the time when j is first reached and then switch to a policy that is optimal when starting from j, thereby achieving an average cost starting from i equaling $J^*(j)$. Indeed, we will show in Proposition 4 that we have

$$J^*(i) = J^*(j), \qquad \text{for all } i, j = 1, \ldots, n$$

under the rather weak assumption that for every pair of states i and j there exists a stationary policy (dependent on i and j) under which state j is reached starting from i with positive probability.

We thus conclude that *for most problems of interest the optimal average cost per stage is independent of the initial state*. As a result, we view this as the normal case and concentrate exclusively on it in the main body of this chapter. We provide an analysis of the more general case in the chapter appendix.

The Analog of Bellman's Equation

Let us try to speculate next on the proper form of Bellman's equation for the average cost problem. Consider a stationary policy $\{\mu, \mu, \ldots\}$ and the N-horizon cost corresponding to initial state x_0:

$$J_\mu^N(x_0) = E\left\{\sum_{k=0}^{N-1} g[x_k, \mu(x_k)]\right\}.$$

We have already seen [cf. (7.6)] that $\lim_{N\to\infty} (1/N)\, J_\mu^N(i) = J_\mu(i)$, so it follows that

$$J_\mu^N(i) = NJ_\mu(i) + \epsilon_N(i), \tag{7.11}$$

where $\epsilon_N(i)$ is such that $\lim_{N\to\infty} [\epsilon_N(i)/N] = 0$. By denoting J_μ^N and ϵ_N the vectors with coordinates $J_\mu^N(i)$ and $\epsilon_N(i)$, $i = 1, \ldots, n$, we can write this relation as

$$J_\mu^N = NJ_\mu + \epsilon_N.$$

By substituting this equation in the usual recursion for the N-stage costs

$$J_\mu^{N+1} = g_\mu + P_\mu J_\mu^N,$$

we obtain

$$(N + 1)J_\mu + \epsilon_{N+1} = g_\mu + NP_\mu J_\mu + P_\mu \epsilon_N. \tag{7.12}$$

Dividing by N and taking the limit as $N \to \infty$, we see that

$$J_\mu = P_\mu J_\mu. \tag{7.13}$$

Note that this relation [which follows also from (7.9) and Lemma 1(a)] holds regardless of whether $J_\mu(i)$ is independent of the initial state i. Furthermore, from (7.12) and (7.13) we have

$$J_\mu + \epsilon_{N+1} = g_\mu + P_\mu\, \epsilon_N, \qquad N = 1, 2, \ldots. \tag{7.14}$$

If $\epsilon_N(i)$ converges to a limit as $N \to \infty$, that is,

$$\lim_{N\to\infty} \epsilon_N(i) = h_\mu(i), \qquad i = 1, 2, \ldots, n, \tag{7.15}$$

for some $h_\mu(i)$, $i = 1, \ldots, n$, then from (7.14) we obtain

$$J_\mu + h_\mu = g_\mu + P_\mu h_\mu,$$

and this turns out to be the proper form of the functional equation satisfied by J_μ [i.e., the analog of $J_\mu = T_\mu(J_\mu)$ in Chapter 5]. Note from (7.11) and (7.15) that, when $J_\mu(i)$ is independent of the initial state i, we have, for any i and j,

$$h_\mu(i) - h_\mu(j) = \lim_{N\to\infty} [J_\mu^N(i) - J_\mu^N(j)].$$

Thus we may view $h_\mu(i) - h_\mu(j)$ as a long-term *differential cost* expressing the long-term difference in *total* cost (not average cost per stage) due to starting at state i rather than state j.

It is not true in general that $\epsilon_N(i)$ converges to a limit as in (7.15), basically because $\epsilon_N(i)$ may have a periodic component (see the following example). However, it can be shown using the definition (7.11) of ϵ_N and

Lemma 1 (see Problem 5) that

$$\lim_{N\to\infty} \frac{1}{N} \sum_{k=1}^{N} \epsilon_k = \lim_{N\to\infty} \frac{1}{N} \sum_{k=1}^{N} \epsilon_{k+1} = (I - P_\mu + P_\mu^*)^{-1} (I - P_\mu^*) g_\mu \triangleq h_\mu, \tag{7.16}$$

where P_μ^* is given by (7.8). By adding (7.14) for $N = 1, 2, \ldots$, we obtain

$$J_\mu + \frac{1}{N} \sum_{k=1}^{N} \epsilon_{k+1} = g_\mu + P_\mu \left(\frac{1}{N} \sum_{k=1}^{N} \epsilon_k \right).$$

So we see, using (7.16), that the equation

$$J_\mu + h_\mu = g_\mu + P_\mu h_\mu$$

holds always regardless of whether the limit in (7.15) exists. From (7.11) and (7.16), we see that for any two states i and j with $J_\mu(i) = J_\mu(j)$

$$h_\mu(i) - h_\mu(j) = \lim_{N\to\infty} \frac{1}{N} \sum_{k=1}^{N} [J_\mu^k(i) - J_\mu^k(j)].$$

Therefore, when $J_\mu(i)$ is independent of the initial state i, we may again view h_μ as a differential cost vector.

Example

Assume that there are two states and the cost per stage vector is

$$g_\mu = \begin{bmatrix} 0 \\ 2 \end{bmatrix}.$$

Case 1: Let the transition probability matrix be

$$P_\mu = \begin{bmatrix} \frac{1}{2} & \frac{1}{2} \\ \frac{1}{2} & \frac{1}{2} \end{bmatrix}.$$

Then it is easily seen from (7.8) and (7.9) that

$$P_\mu^* = \begin{bmatrix} \frac{1}{2} & \frac{1}{2} \\ \frac{1}{2} & \frac{1}{2} \end{bmatrix}, \qquad J_\mu = \begin{bmatrix} 1 \\ 1 \end{bmatrix}.$$

The N-stage cost vector J_μ^N can be calculated from the recursion

$$J_\mu^{N+1} = g_\mu + P_\mu J_\mu^N, \qquad J_\mu^0 = \begin{bmatrix} 0 \\ 0 \end{bmatrix},$$

and by induction it can be verified that

$$J_\mu^N = NJ_\mu + \epsilon_N, \qquad N = 1, 2, \ldots,$$

where

$$\epsilon_N = \begin{bmatrix} -1 \\ 1 \end{bmatrix}.$$

The costs $J_\mu^N(1)$ and $J_\mu^N(2)$ are shown in Figure 7.1. In this case ϵ_N converges to the differential cost vector

$$h_\mu = \begin{bmatrix} -1 \\ 1 \end{bmatrix},$$

and the relation $J_\mu + h_\mu = g_\mu + P_\mu h_\mu$ can be easily verified.

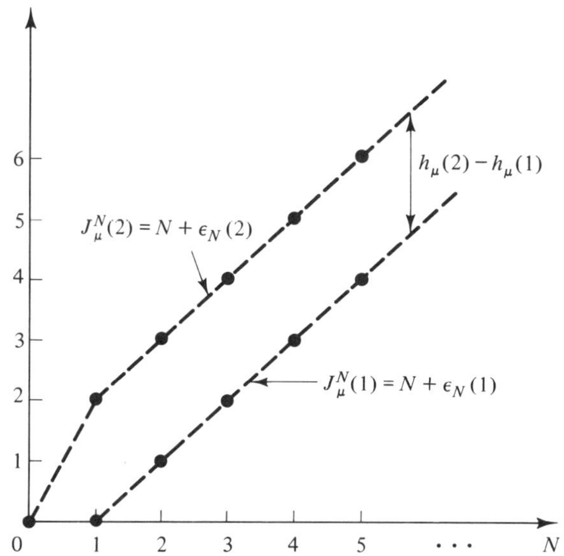

Figure 7.1 Interpretation of differential cost as a limit of difference of finite horizon costs.

Case 2: Let the transition probability matrix be

$$P_\mu = \begin{bmatrix} 0 & 1 \\ 1 & 0 \end{bmatrix}.$$

Here again we see from (7.8) and (7.9) that

$$P_\mu^* = \begin{bmatrix} \frac{1}{2} & \frac{1}{2} \\ \frac{1}{2} & \frac{1}{2} \end{bmatrix}, \qquad J_\mu = \begin{bmatrix} 1 \\ 1 \end{bmatrix}.$$

By induction it can be verified that

$$J_\mu^N = NJ_\mu + \epsilon_N, \qquad N = 1, 2, \ldots,$$

where

$$\epsilon_N = \begin{cases} \begin{bmatrix} 0 \\ 0 \end{bmatrix}, & \text{if } N \text{ is even}, \\ \begin{bmatrix} -1 \\ 1 \end{bmatrix}, & \text{if } N \text{ is odd}. \end{cases}$$

The costs $J_\mu^N(1)$ and $J_\mu^N(2)$ are shown in Figure 7.2. In this case ϵ_N does not converge and reflects the periodic behavior of the Markov chain. However, ϵ_N converges in the sense of (7.16) to the differential cost vector

$$h_\mu = \begin{bmatrix} -\frac{1}{2} \\ \frac{1}{2} \end{bmatrix},$$

satisfying the equation $J_\mu + h_\mu = g_\mu + P_\mu h_\mu$.

Prompted by the form of the functional equation for J_μ, it is natural

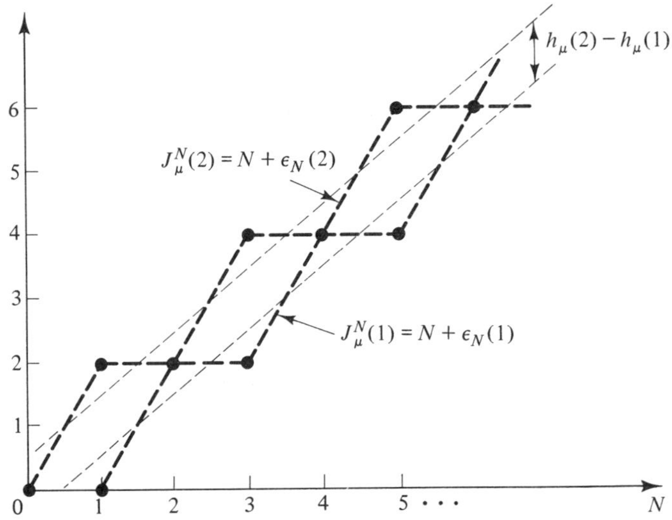

Figure 7.2 Differential cost interpretation when finite horizon cost differences do not converge to a limit.

to speculate that, when optimal average cost is independent of the initial state, Bellman's optimality equation for the average cost problem takes the form

$$\lambda + h(i) = \min_{u \in U(i)} \left[g(i, u) + \sum_{j=1}^{n} p_{ij}(u)\, h(j) \right], \qquad i = 1, \ldots, n, \tag{7.17}$$

where $\lambda = J^*(i)$ for all i, and $h(i)$, $i = 1, \ldots, n$, are some scalars having a differential cost interpretation as discussed previously. Furthermore, it should be possible to obtain an optimal stationary policy via the minimization in (7.17). We will demonstrate this fact in the next section. Sections 7.2 and 7.3 deal with computational methods, while Section 7.4 discusses the case of infinite state space and the average cost version of the linear–quadratic problem in particular.

The main body of the chapter is devoted exclusively to the case where the optimal cost is equal for all initial states. This is the case that normally appears in practice, as discussed earlier. However, the analysis of the more general case, where optimal costs can be different for different initial states, is genuinely interesting as it provides insights and methods of proof for the simpler case that would be very hard to obtain by other means. This analysis, directed primarily at the advanced reader, is carried out in the chapter appendix.

7.1 OPTIMALITY CONDITIONS

We first introduce the mappings T and T_μ that were used extensively in Chapters 5 and 6. Thus T maps an n-dimensional vector h into another n-dimensional vector $T(h)$ according to the equation

$$T(h)(i) = \min_{u \in U(i)} \left[g(i, u) + \sum_{j=1}^{n} p_{ij}(u)\, h(j) \right], \qquad i = 1, \ldots, n. \tag{7.18}$$

For any stationary policy $\{\mu, \mu, \ldots\}$, the corresponding mapping T_μ is given by

$$T_\mu(h)(i) = g[i, \mu(i)] + \sum_{j=1}^{n} p_{ij}[\mu(i)]\, h(j), \qquad i = 1, \ldots, n. \tag{7.19}$$

Denoting M the set of all admissible control functions μ, we can write these mappings in more compact form as

$$T(h) = \min_{\mu \in M} [g_\mu + P_\mu h], \tag{7.20}$$

$$T_\mu(h) = g_\mu + P_\mu h, \qquad \text{for all } \mu \in M, \tag{7.21}$$

where g_μ and P_μ are given by (7.4) and (7.5), and the minimization in (7.20) is meant to be separate for each state.

These mappings have the fundamental monotonicity property

$$h \leq h' \;\Rightarrow\; T(h) \leq T(h'),$$

$$h \leq h' \;\Rightarrow\; T_\mu(h) \leq T_\mu(h'), \qquad \mu \in M,$$

where, as earlier, the inequalities are assumed separate for each state. In what follows we will make use of the unit n-dimensional vector

$$e = \begin{bmatrix} 1 \\ 1 \\ \vdots \\ 1 \end{bmatrix}.$$

Note that if r is a scalar then

$$T(h + re) = T(h) + re, \tag{7.22a}$$

$$T_\mu(h + re) = T_\mu(h) + re, \qquad \mu \in M. \tag{7.22b}$$

Our first result introduces the analog of Bellman's equation for the case of equal optimal cost for each initial state. The proposition shows that all solutions of this equation can be identified with the optimal cost and an associated differential cost. However, it provides no assurance that the equation has a solution. Further assumptions are required for this and will be given in the sequel.

Proposition 1. If a scalar λ and an n-dimensional vector h satisfy

$$\lambda + h(i) = \min_{u \in U(i)} \left[g(i, u) + \sum_{j=1}^{n} p_{ij}(u)\, h(j) \right], \qquad i = 1, \ldots, n, \tag{7.23}$$

or equivalently

$$\lambda e + h = T(h), \tag{7.24}$$

then λ is the optimal value of the cost $J_\pi(i)$ for all i:

$$\lambda = \min_\pi J_\pi(i) = J^*(i), \qquad i = 1, 2, \ldots, n. \tag{7.25}$$

Furthermore, if $\mu^*(i)$ attains the minimum in (7.23) for each i, the stationary policy $\{\mu^*, \mu^*, \ldots\}$ is optimal; that is, $J_{\mu^*}(i) = J^*(i) = \lambda$ for all i.

Proof. Let $\pi = \{\mu_0, \mu_1, \ldots\}$ be any admissible policy and $N > 0$ be an integer. We have, from (7.23),

$$\lambda e + h \leq T_{\mu_{N-1}}(h).$$

In view of the monotonicity property, if $T_{\mu_{N-2}}$ is applied on both sides, the inequality is preserved. Therefore, by using (7.22) and (7.23) we obtain

$$2\lambda e + h \leq \lambda e + T_{\mu_{N-2}}(h) \leq (T_{\mu_{N-2}} T_{\mu_{N-1}})(h).$$

Continuing in the same manner, we finally obtain

$$N\lambda e + h \leq (T_{\mu_0} T_{\mu_1} \cdots T_{\mu_{N-1}})(h) \tag{7.26}$$

with equality if each μ_k, $k = 0, 1, \ldots, N - 1$, attains the minimum in (7.23). We have

$$(T_{\mu_0} T_{\mu_1} \cdots T_{\mu_{N-1}})(h)(i) = E\left\{ h(x_N) + \sum_{k=0}^{N-1} g[x_k, \mu_k(x_k)] | x_0 = i, \pi \right\}.$$

Using this equation in (7.26), we obtain

$$\lambda + \frac{1}{N} h(i) \leq \frac{1}{N} E\{h(x_N) \mid x_0 = i, \pi\} + \frac{1}{N} E\left\{ \sum_{k=0}^{N-1} g[x_k, \mu_k(x_k)] | x_0 = i, \pi \right\},$$

and by taking the limit as $N \to \infty$,

$$\lambda \leq J_\pi(i), \qquad i = 1, \ldots, n$$

with equality if $\mu_k(i)$, $k = 0, 1, \ldots$, attains the minimum in (7.23). Q.E.D.

Note that this proof carries through even if the state space and control space are infinite as long as the function h is bounded and the minimum in (7.23) is attained for each i. Also, the converse of Proposition 1 turns out to be true; that is, if $J^*(i) = \lambda$, $i = 1, \ldots, n$, for some scalar λ, then λ together with a vector h satisfies the optimality equation (7.23). However, the proof of this requires the machinery developed in the chapter appendix (see Propositions A7.3 and A7.4).

Now given a stationary policy $\pi = \{\mu, \mu, \ldots\}$, we may consider, as in the past two chapters, a problem where the constraint set $U(i)$ is replaced by the set $\tilde{U}(i) = \{\mu(i)\}$; that is, $\tilde{U}(i)$ contains a single element, the control $\mu(i)$. Since for the resulting problem there is only one admissible policy, the policy $\{\mu, \mu, \ldots\}$, application of Proposition 1 yields the following corollary.

Corollary 1.1. Let $\pi = \{\mu, \mu, \ldots\}$ be a stationary policy. If a scalar λ_μ and an n-dimensional vector h_μ satisfy, for all $i \in S$,

$$\lambda_\mu + h_\mu(i) = g[i, \mu(i)] + \sum_{j=1}^{n} p_{ij}[\mu(i)]h_\mu(j),$$

or equivalently

$$\lambda_\mu e + h_\mu = T_\mu(h_\mu),$$

then

$$\lambda_\mu = J_\mu(i), \qquad i = 1, 2, \ldots, n.$$

We now turn to obtaining conditions that guarantee the existence of λ and h satisfying Bellman's equation (7.23). At the same time we will establish a connection with the discounted cost problem of Chapter 5.

Consider the discounted cost

$$\lim_{N\to\infty} E\left\{\sum_{k=0}^{N-1} \alpha^k g[x_k, \mu_k(x_k)]\right\}, \qquad 0 < \alpha < 1.$$

Let $J_\alpha(i)$ be the optimal value of this cost corresponding to initial state i. Proposition 2 in Section 5.1 shows that J_α is the unique solution of the optimality equation

$$J_\alpha(i) = \min_{u\in U(i)} \left[g(i, u) + \alpha \sum_{j=1}^{n} p_{ij}(u)J_\alpha(j)\right], \qquad i = 1, \ldots, n. \tag{7.27}$$

Let s be an arbitrary state in S, and let us define

$$h_\alpha(i) = J_\alpha(i) - J_\alpha(s), \qquad i = 1, \ldots, n. \tag{7.28}$$

Using (7.27) to eliminate $J_\alpha(i)$ from (7.28), we have

$$h_\alpha(i) + J_\alpha(s) = \min_{u\in U(i)} \left[g(i, u) + \alpha \sum_{j=1}^{n} p_{ij}(u)[h_\alpha(j) + J_\alpha(s)]\right]$$

$$= \alpha J_\alpha(s) + \min_{u\in U(i)} \left[g(i, u) + \alpha \sum_{j=1}^{n} p_{ij}(u)h_\alpha(j)\right]$$

from which

$$(1 - \alpha)J_\alpha(s) + h_\alpha(i) = \min_{u\in U(i)} \left[g(i, u) + \alpha \sum_{j=1}^{n} p_{ij}(u)h_\alpha(j)\right]. \tag{7.29}$$

This equation looks very similar to the optimality equation (7.23). In particular, if for some sequence $\{\alpha_m\}$ with $0 < \alpha_m < 1$ and $\alpha_m \to 1$ we have

$$\lim_{m\to\infty} (1 - \alpha_m)\, J_{\alpha_m}(s) = \lambda, \tag{7.30}$$

$$\lim_{m\to\infty} h_{\alpha_m}(i) = h(i), \qquad i = 1, \ldots, n \tag{7.31}$$

(i.e., the preceding limits exist), then from (7.29),

$$\lambda + h(i) = \min_{u \in U(i)} \left[g(i, u) + \sum_{j=1}^{n} p_{ij}(u) h(j) \right], \qquad i = 1, \ldots, n,$$

and condition (7.23) is satisfied. The following proposition states that a sufficient condition for existence of a sequence $\{\alpha_m\}$ such that the limits in (7.30) and (7.31) exist is that the differences $[J_\alpha(i) - J_\alpha(s)]$ are uniformly bounded over α.

Proposition 2. Assume that there exists a constant L such that for some state $s \in S$ we have

$$|J_\alpha(i) - J_\alpha(s)| \leq L, \qquad \text{for all } i \in S,\ \alpha \in (0, 1). \tag{7.32}$$

Then for some sequence $\{\alpha_m\}$ with $\alpha_m \in (0, 1)$ and $\alpha_m \to 1$, we have for all i

$$h(i) = \lim_{m \to \infty} [J_{\alpha_m}(i) - J_{\alpha_m}(s)],$$

$$\lim_{m \to \infty} (1 - \alpha_m) J_{\alpha_m}(i) = \lambda,$$

and λ and h satisfy the optimality equation (7.23).

Proof. Let $\{\alpha_k\}$ be any sequence such that $\alpha_k \to 1$. By (7.32), the sequences $\{J_{\alpha_k}(i) - J_{\alpha_k}(s)\}$ are bounded. Hence there exists a subsequence of $\{\alpha_k\}$, say $\{\alpha_m\}$, such that $\{J_{\alpha_m}(i) - J_{\alpha_m}(s)\}$ converges to a limit $h(i)$ for each i. If B is a constant such that $|g(i, u)| \leq B$ for all i and $u \in U(i)$, then

$$|J_{\alpha_m}(s)| \leq B(1 - \alpha_m)^{-1}.$$

Hence the sequence $\{(1 - \alpha_m)|J_{\alpha_m}(s)|\}$ is bounded. Thus there exists a subsequence of $\{\alpha_m\}$, say $\{\alpha_{m'}\}$ such that

$$(1 - \alpha_{m'}) J_{\alpha_{m'}}(s) \to \lambda.$$

From (7.29) we have

$$(1 - \alpha_{m'}) J_{\alpha_{m'}}(s) + h_{\alpha_{m'}}(i) = \min_{u \in U(i)} \left[g(i, u) + \alpha_{m'} \sum_{j=1}^{n} p_{ij}(u) h_{\alpha_{m'}}(j) \right].$$

Taking the limit and interchanging limit and minimization [using the finiteness of $U(i)$], we obtain (7.23). Q.E.D.

Recall that a Markov chain is said to be *irreducible* if every two states communicate with each other. This is equivalent to the existence of a single ergodic class that includes all states, as well as to the mean first passage time between any two states being finite (Appendix D). The following proposition provides the simplest (and most restrictive) condition under which the optimal cost is the same for all initial states.

Proposition 3. Assume that every stationary policy gives rise to an irreducible Markov chain. Then there exists a scalar λ and a vector h

such that, for all $i \in S$,

$$\lambda + h(i) = \min_{u \in U(i)} \left[g(i, u) + \sum_{j=1}^{n} p_{ij}(u)h(j) \right],$$

and (by Proposition 1)

$$\lambda = J^*(i), \qquad i = 1, \ldots, n,$$

while if $\mu^*(i)$ attains the preceding minimum for each i, the stationary policy $\{\mu^*, \mu^*, \ldots\}$ is optimal.

Proof. For any $\alpha \in (0, 1)$, let $\{\mu_\alpha, \mu_\alpha, \ldots\}$ be a policy that minimizes the corresponding discounted cost. If B is such that $|g(i, u)| \leq B$ for all $i \in S$ and $u \in U(i)$, we have, for every $i \in S$ and $s \in S$,

$$J_\alpha(i) = E\left\{ \sum_{k=0}^{K_{is}(\mu_\alpha)-1} \alpha^k g[x_k, \mu_\alpha(x_k)] + \sum_{k=K_{is}(\mu_\alpha)}^{\infty} \alpha^k g[x_k, \mu_\alpha(x_k)] \mid x_0 = i \right\}$$
$$\leq B\, E\{K_{is}(\mu_\alpha)\} + J_\alpha(s),$$

where $K_{is}(\mu_\alpha)$ is the first passage time from i to s under μ_α. The hypothesis implies that $E\{K_{is}(\mu_\alpha)\}$ is uniformly bounded over i, s, and μ_α. Therefore, the difference $J_\alpha(i) - J_\alpha(s)$ is uniformly bounded over i, s, and α, and the hypothesis of Proposition 2 is satisfied. The result follows from Propositions 1 and 2. Q.E.D.

Proposition 3 can be shown under weaker hypotheses. The following strengthened version will be proved in the chapter appendix.

Proposition 4. Assume that one of the following conditions holds:

(a) Every stationary policy gives rise to a Markov chain with a single ergodic class.

(b) For every two states i and j, there exists a stationary policy π such that, for some k,

$$P(x_k = j \mid x_0 = i, \pi) > 0.$$

Then the conclusions of Proposition 3 hold.

Proof. See the chapter appendix. An independent proof under condition (a) is also obtained from Proposition 8 that follows.

The conditions listed are probably the weakest that guarantee that the optimal average cost per stage is independent of the initial state. It is clear, of course, that some sort of accessibility condition must be satisfied by the transition probability matrices corresponding to stationary policies or at least to optimal stationary policies. For if there existed two states none of which could be reached from the other no matter which policy we use, then it can be only by accident that the same optimal cost per state will correspond to each one. An extreme example is a problem where the state is forced to stay the same regardless of the control applied (i.e., each state is absorbing). Then the optimal average cost per stage for each state i is $\min_{u \in U(i)} g(i, u)$, and this cost may be different for different states.

For any stationary policy $\{\mu, \mu, \ldots\}$, we can consider the problem where there is only the control $\mu(i)$ available at state i. Then we obtain the following corollary to Proposition 4. A proof of this corollary may also be obtained by a small modification of the proof of Proposition 3.

Corollary 4.1. Let $\pi = \{\mu, \mu, \ldots\}$ be a stationary policy giving rise to a Markov chain with a single ergodic class. Then there exists a constant λ_μ and a vector h_μ such that

$$J_\mu(i) = \lambda_\mu, \qquad i = 1, \ldots, n, \tag{7.33}$$

and

$$\lambda_\mu + h_\mu(i) = g[i, \mu(i)] + \sum_{j=1}^{n} p_{ij}[\mu(i)]h_\mu(j), \qquad i = 1, \ldots, n. \tag{7.34}$$

Equation (7.34) represents a system of n linear equations with $(n + 1)$ unknowns: the scalars λ_μ, $h_\mu(1)$, $h_\mu(2)$, . . ., $h_\mu(n)$. We may add one additional equation to this system by requiring that

$$h_\mu(s) = 0, \tag{7.35}$$

where s is any one of the states. This eliminates the degree of freedom due to the fact that if $\{\lambda_\mu, h_\mu(1), \ldots, h_\mu(n)\}$ is a solution of (7.34), so is $\{\lambda_\mu, h_\mu(1) + r, \ldots, h_\mu(n) + r\}$, where r is any scalar. Corollary 4.1 under the condition stated asserts that system (7.34) and (7.35) has at least one solution. We now show that this solution is unique.

Proposition 5. For every stationary policy $\pi = \{\mu, \mu, \ldots\}$ that gives rise to a Markov chain with a single ergodic class, the system of equations (7.34) and (7.35) has a unique solution.

Proof. Let $\{\lambda, h(1), \ldots, h(n)\}$ and $\{\lambda', h'(1), \ldots, h'(n)\}$ be two solutions. We have $\lambda = \lambda' = \lambda_\mu$ by Corollary 1.1. Hence from (7.34) we obtain, for every $m \geq 1$,

$$h - h' = P_\mu(h - h') = P_\mu^m(h - h'),$$

or equivalently

$$h(i) - h'(i) = \sum_{j=1}^{n} p_{ij}^m(\mu)[h(j) - h'(j)], \qquad i = 1, \ldots, n.$$

Assume first that the state s in (7.35) belongs to the ergodic class. Then we obtain, for some $m_i \geq 1$ and $\epsilon > 0$,

$$p_{is}^{m_i}(\mu) \geq \epsilon > 0,$$

and, from (7.35) $h(s) - h'(s) = 0$. Hence

$$\begin{aligned} |h(i) - h'(i)| &\leq \sum_{j=1}^{n} p_{ij}^{m_i}(\mu)|h(j) - h'(j)| \\ &= \sum_{j \neq s} p_{ij}^{m_i}(\mu)|h(j) - h'(j)| \\ &\leq (1 - \epsilon) \max_j |h(j) - h'(j)|. \end{aligned}$$

Thus we obtain

$$\max_j |h(j) - h'(j)| \leq (1 - \epsilon) \max_j |h(j) - h'(j)|,$$

and $h(j) = h'(j)$ for all j.

Consider now the case where the state s in (7.35) does not belong to the ergodic class. We choose another state $\bar{s}$ in the ergodic class and define

$$\bar{h}(i) = h(i) - h(\bar{s}), \qquad \bar{h}'(i) = h'(i) - h'(\bar{s}).$$

Then $\{\lambda, \bar{h}(1), \ldots, \bar{h}(n)\}$ and $\{\lambda', \bar{h}'(1), \ldots, \bar{h}'(n)\}$ are solutions of (7.34) together with $h_\mu(\bar{s}) = 0$. By the argument given earlier, we then have $\bar{h} = \bar{h}'$, which implies that $h = h'$. Q.E.D.

We close this section with an example.

Machine Replacement. Consider a machine that can be in any one of n states, $S = \{1, 2, \ldots, n\}$. The implication here is that state i is better than state $i + 1$, and state 1 corresponds to a machine in perfect condition. The operating cost per unit time when the machine is in state i is denoted g_i, and we assume

$$0 \leq g_1 \leq g_2 \leq \cdots \leq g_n. \tag{7.36}$$

During a time period of operation, the transition probabilities satisfy

$$\begin{aligned} p_{ij} &= 0, \qquad \text{if} \quad j < i, \\ p_{ii} &< 1, \qquad i = 1, \ldots, n - 1. \end{aligned}$$

That is, the machine cannot go to a better state with usage. We also assume that for any nondecreasing function J we have

$$i \leq i' \Rightarrow \sum_{j=1}^{n} p_{ij} J(j) \leq \sum_{j=1}^{n} p_{i'j} J(j). \tag{7.37}$$

At the beginning of each period the state of the machine is determined and a decision is made whether to replace the machine at a cost $R > 0$ with a new machine that is in state 1 or to continue operation. Thus there are two possible controls: replace and do not replace. The problem is to find a policy that minimizes the average cost per period.

Note that the hypotheses of Propositions 3 and 4 are not satisfied for this problem. For example, consider the stationary policy that replaces at every state except the worst state n (a poor but legitimate choice). The corresponding Markov chain has two ergodic classes, $\{1, 2, \ldots, n-1\}$ and $\{n\}$. It can be also seen that one cannot guarantee in the absence of further assumptions that condition (b) of Proposition 4 is satisfied. We will be able, however, to argue in terms of Proposition 2.

Consider the corresponding discounted problem with a discount factor $\alpha < 1$. Then we have for all i

$$J_\alpha(i) = \min\left[R + g_1 + \alpha \sum_{j=1}^{n} p_{1j} J_\alpha(j),\ g_i + \alpha \sum_{j=1}^{n} p_{ij} J_\alpha(j)\right].$$

It follows that

$$J_\alpha(i) - J_\alpha(1) = \min\left[R,\ (g_i - g_1) + \alpha \sum_{j=1}^{n} (p_{ij} - p_{1j}) J_\alpha(j)\right] \leq R.$$

It is easily shown using (7.36) and (7.37) that we have, for all $\alpha \in (0, 1)$,

$$0 \leq J_\alpha(i) - J_\alpha(1), \qquad i = 1, 2, \ldots, n.$$

Furthermore, $J_\alpha(i) - J_\alpha(1)$ is nondecreasing in i. Hence, by Proposition 2, there exists a scalar λ and a nondecreasing function h, such that

$$\lambda + h(i) = \min\left[R + g_1 + \sum_{j=1}^{n} p_{1j} h(j),\ g_i + \sum_{j=1}^{n} p_{ij} h(j)\right], \qquad i = 1, 2, \ldots, n,$$

and the policy that chooses the minimizing action is average cost optimal. Let

$$i^* = \max\left\{i \,\middle|\, g_i + \sum_{j=1}^{n} p_{ij} h(j) \leq R + g_1 + \sum_{j=1}^{n} p_{1j} h(j)\right\}.$$

Then the policy that replaces if the current state is greater than i^* and does not replace otherwise is optimal.

7.2 SUCCESSIVE APPROXIMATION, ERROR BOUNDS, AND LINEAR PROGRAMMING SOLUTION

The natural version of the successive approximation method for the average cost problem is simply to generate successively the N-stage optimal costs $J_0, T(J_0), \ldots, T^k(J_0), \ldots$, starting with the zero function $J_0 \equiv 0$. We can gain some insight regarding the nature and proper implementation of this method by concentrating on a single stationary policy $\{\mu, \mu, \ldots\}$ and considering the iteration

$$J_\mu^0 = 0, \qquad J_\mu^{k+1} = T_\mu(J_\mu^k) = g_\mu + P_\mu J_\mu^k. \tag{7.38}$$

Clearly, J_μ^k is the k-stage cost vector corresponding to μ. As discussed in the introduction to this chapter, we have

$$J_\mu^k = kJ_\mu + \epsilon_k, \tag{7.39}$$

where J_μ is the average cost vector for μ, and ϵ_k is a vector that converges to some h_μ in the sense

$$h_\mu = \lim_{N\to\infty} \frac{1}{N} \sum_{k=1}^{N} \epsilon_k \tag{7.40}$$

(and in many cases in the sense $\lim_{k\to\infty} \epsilon_k = h_\mu$). Furthermore, we have

$$J_\mu + h_\mu = T_\mu(h_\mu) \tag{7.41}$$

and the differences $h_\mu(i) - h_\mu(j)$ have the interpretation of long-term differential cost.

We could determine J_μ by recursively generating J_μ^k, $k = 0, 1, \ldots$, and taking the limit $\lim_{k\to\infty} (1/k)J_\mu^k$, but this has two drawbacks. First, J_μ^k typically diverges to $+\infty$ or $-\infty$, so direct calculation of $\lim_{k\to\infty} (1/k) J_\mu^k$ is numerically impractical. Second, this will not provide us with a corresponding differential cost vector h_μ. We can bypass both difficulties by recursively generating instead a sequence $\{h^k\}$ converging to h_μ. The average cost vector J_μ can then be obtained by (7.41). Actually, for this we do not really need the vector h_μ of (7.40); any vector h_μ differing from the one of (7.40) by the same constant for each coordinate is sufficient to determine J_μ from (7.41). To eliminate this degree of freedom we therefore require that

$$h_\mu^k(s) = 0 \tag{7.42}$$

for some fixed state s. With this in mind, consider the iteration

$$h^{k+1} = T_\mu(h^k) - T_\mu(h^k)(s)e \tag{7.43}$$

where for all i

$$T_\mu(h^k)(i) = g[i, \mu(i)] + \sum_{j=1}^{n} p_{ij}[\mu(i)]h^k(j), \tag{7.44}$$

and $e = [1, 1, \ldots, 1]'$ is the unit vector. A key observation is that if the sequence $\{h^k\}$ converges, say to a vector h_μ, then we must have [cf. (7.43)]

$$T_\mu(h_\mu)(s)e + h_\mu = T_\mu(h_\mu).$$

By Corollary 1.1, this implies that $T_\mu(h_\mu)(s)$ is the average cost corresponding to μ, and h_μ is an associated differential cost vector.

Consider also the multiple policy version of iteration (7.43) given by

$$h^{k+1} = T(h^k) - T(h^k)(s)e \tag{7.45}$$

where for all i

$$T(h^k)(i) = \min_{u\in U(i)} \left[g(i, u) + \sum_{j=1}^{n} p_{ij}(u)h^k(j) \right]. \tag{7.46}$$

If this iteration converges to some vector h, then we must have

$$T(h)(s)e + h = T(h).$$

By Proposition 1, this implies that $T(h)(s)$ is the optimal value of average cost, and h is a corresponding differential cost vector.

The following proposition provides conditions under which convergence of (7.45) is assured. As an aid in understanding the hypotheses of this proposition, we first note that convergence can only be expected when the optimal average cost is independent of the initial state. Therefore, at least the hypotheses of one of Propositions 2, 3, or 4 are needed for convergence. It turns out, however, that a stronger hypothesis such as the one given in the proposition is required. The advanced reader can understand the reason for this by considering iteration (7.43). Using (7.44), it can be written as

$$h^{k+1} = (I - ee_s')\, g_\mu + \tilde{P}_\mu h^k \tag{7.47}$$

where

$$\tilde{P}_\mu = (I - ee_s')P_\mu$$

and e_s is the sth coordinate vector, having all coordinates zero except for the sth coordinate which is unity. Therefore, convergence of iteration (7.43) depends on whether all the eigenvalues of $\tilde{P}_\mu$ lie strictly within the unit circle. We have, using the facts $P_\mu e = e$ and $e_s'e = 1$,

$$\begin{aligned}\tilde{P}_\mu^2 &= (P_\mu - ee_s'P_\mu)(P_\mu - ee_s'P_\mu) = P_\mu^2 - P_\mu ee_s'P_\mu - ee_s'P_\mu^2 + ee_s'P_\mu ee_s'P_\mu \\ &= P_\mu^2 - ee_s'P_\mu^2 = P_\mu \tilde{P}_\mu,\end{aligned}$$

and it follows that for all $k > 1$

$$\tilde{P}_\mu^k = P_\mu^{k-1}\tilde{P}_\mu. \tag{7.48}$$

Using this equation, it can be shown that $\tilde{P}_\mu$ and P_μ have the same eigenvalues except that $\tilde{P}_\mu$ has a zero eigenvalue in place of a single unity eigenvalue of P_μ. Therefore, for convergence of (7.43), P_μ should have all its eigenvalues other than a single unity eigenvalue strictly inside the unit circle. This condition is violated when P_μ has multiple ergodic classes in which case unity is a multiple eigenvalue, but it is also violated when P_μ has a periodic structure and some of its nonunity eigenvalues are on the unit circle.

Proposition 6. Assume there exists a positive integer m such that for every set of control functions $\mu_0, \mu_1, \ldots, \mu_m$ with $\mu_k(i) \in U(i)$, $i = 1, \ldots, n$, $k = 0, \ldots, m$, there exists an $\epsilon > 0$ and a state x such that

$$[P_{\mu_m} P_{\mu_{m-1}} \cdots P_{\mu_1}]_{ix} \geqslant \epsilon, \qquad i = 1, \ldots, n, \tag{7.49}$$

$$[P_{\mu_{m-1}} P_{\mu_{m-2}} \cdots P_{\mu_0}]_{ix} \geqslant \epsilon, \qquad i = 1, \ldots, n, \tag{7.50}$$

where $[\cdot]_{ix}$ denotes the element of the ith row and xth column of the corresponding matrix. Fix a state $s \in S$ and consider the algorithm

$$h^{k+1}(i) = T(h^k)(i) - T(h^k)(s), \qquad i = 1, \ldots, n, \tag{7.51}$$

where $h^0(i)$ are arbitrary scalars and the mapping T is given by (7.46). Then the limits

$$h(i) = \lim_{k\to\infty} h^k(i), \qquad i = 1, 2, \ldots, n, \tag{7.52}$$

exist, and we have

$$\lambda = J^*(i), \qquad i = 1, \ldots, n, \tag{7.53}$$

and

$$\lambda + h(i) = T(h)(i), \qquad i = 1, \ldots, n, \tag{7.54}$$

where $\lambda = T(h)(s)$.

Proof. Denote

$$q^k(i) = h^{k+1}(i) - h^k(i), \qquad i = 1, 2, \ldots, n. \tag{7.55}$$

We will show that for all i and $k \geq m$ we have

$$\max_i q^k(i) - \min_i q^k(i) \leq (1 - \epsilon)\,[\max_i q^{k-m}(i) - \min_i q^{k-m}(i)], \tag{7.56}$$

where m and ϵ are as stated in the hypothesis. From (7.56) we then obtain, for some $B > 0$ and all k,

$$\max_i q^k(i) - \min_i q^k(i) \leq B(1 - \epsilon)^{k/m}.$$

Since $q^k(s) = 0$, it follows that, for all i,

$$|h^{k+1}(i) - h^k(i)| = |q^k(i)| \leq \max_j q^k(j) - \min_j q^k(j) \leq B(1 - \epsilon)^{k/m}.$$

Therefore, for every $r > 1$ and i we have

$$\begin{aligned} |h^{k+r}(i) - h^k(i)| &\leq B(1 - \epsilon)^{k/m} \sum_{t=0}^{r-1} (1 - \epsilon)^{t/m} \\ &= \frac{B(1 - \epsilon)^{k/m}[1 - (1 - \epsilon)^{r/m}]}{1 - (1 - \epsilon)^{1/m}}, \end{aligned} \tag{7.57}$$

and it follows that $\{h^k(i)\}$ is a Cauchy sequence and converges to a limit $h(i)$. From (7.51) we see then that

$$T(h)(s) + h(i) = T(h)(i), \qquad i = 1, \ldots, n,$$

so by Proposition 1 we obtain $\lambda = T(h)(s) = J^*(i)$ for all i.

To prove (7.56), we denote by $\mu_k(i)$ the control attaining the minimum in

$$T(h^k)(i) = \min_{u \in U(i)} \left[g(i, u) + \sum_{j=1}^{n} p_{ij}(u) h^k(j) \right]$$

for every k and i. Denote

$$w_k = T(h^k)(s).$$

Then we have

$$h^{k+1} = g_{\mu_k} + P_{\mu_k} h^k - w_k e \leq g_{\mu_{k-1}} + P_{\mu_{k-1}} h^k - w_k e,$$

$$h^k = g_{\mu_{k-1}} + P_{\mu_{k-1}} h^{k-1} - w_{k-1} e \leq g_{\mu_k} + P_{\mu_k} h^{k-1} - w_{k-1} e,$$

where $e = [1, 1, \ldots, 1]'$ is the unit vector. From these relations, using the definition $q^k = h^{k+1} - h^k$, we obtain

$$P_{\mu_k} q^{k-1} + (w_{k-1} - w_k) e \leq q^k \leq P_{\mu_{k-1}} q^{k-1} + (w_{k-1} - w_k) e.$$

Since this relation holds for every $k \geq 1$, by iterating we obtain

$$P_{\mu_k} \cdots P_{\mu_{k-m+1}} q^{k-m} + (w_{k-m} - w_k)e \leq q^k$$
$$\leq P_{\mu_{k-1}} \cdots P_{\mu_{k-m}} q^{k-m} + (w_{k-m} - w_k)e. \quad (7.58)$$

First, let us assume that the special state x corresponding to μ_{k-m}, . . ., μ_k as in (7.49) and (7.50) is the fixed state s used in iteration (7.51); that is,

$$[P_{\mu_k} \cdots P_{\mu_{k-m+1}}]_{is} \geq \epsilon, \qquad i = 1, \ldots, n, \quad (7.59)$$

$$[P_{\mu_{k-1}} \cdots P_{\mu_{k-m}}]_{is} \geq \epsilon, \qquad i = 1, \ldots, n. \quad (7.60)$$

Then the right side of (7.58) yields

$$q^k(i) \leq \sum_{j=1}^{n} [P_{\mu_{k-1}} \cdots P_{\mu_{k-m}}]_{ij} q^{k-m}(j) + w_{k-m} - w_k.$$

Using (7.60) and the fact $q^{k-m}(s) = 0$, we obtain from the preceding equation

$$q^k(i) \leq (1 - \epsilon) \max_j q^{k-m}(j) + w_{k-m} - w_k, \qquad i = 1, \ldots, n,$$

and therefore

$$\max_j q^k(j) \leq (1 - \epsilon) \max_j q^{k-m}(j) + w_{k-m} - w_k. \quad (7.61)$$

Similarly, from the left side of (7.58) we obtain

$$\min_j q^k(j) \geq (1 - \epsilon) \min_j q^{k-m}(j) + w_{k-m} - w_k, \quad (7.62)$$

and combining (7.61) and (7.62), we obtain the desired relation (7.56).

When the special state x corresponding to μ_{k-m}, . . ., μ_k as in (7.49) and (7.50) is not equal to s, we define a related iterative process

$$\tilde{h}^{k+1}(i) = T(\tilde{h}^k)(i) - T(\tilde{h}^k)(x), \qquad i = 1, \ldots, n,$$
$$\tilde{h}^0(i) = h^0(i), \qquad i = 1, \ldots, n. \quad (7.63)$$

Then, as earlier, we have

$$\max_i \tilde{q}^k(i) - \min_i \tilde{q}^k(i) \leq (1 - \epsilon)\left[\max_i \tilde{q}^{k-m}(i) - \min_i \tilde{q}^{k-m}(i)\right], \quad (7.64)$$

where

$$\tilde{q}^k = \tilde{h}^{k+1} - \tilde{h}^k.$$

It is straightforward to show, using (7.51) and (7.63), that for all i and k we have

$$h^k(i) = \tilde{h}^k(i) + T(\tilde{h}^{k-1})(x) - T(\tilde{h}^{k-1})(s).$$

Therefore, the coordinates of both h^k and q^k differ from the coordinates of $\tilde{h}^k$ and $\tilde{q}^k$, respectively, by a constant. It follows that

$$\max_i q^k(i) - \min_i q^k(i) = \max_i \tilde{q}^k(i) - \min_i \tilde{q}^k(i),$$

and from (7.64) we obtain the desired relation (7.56). Q.E.D.

Note that as a by-product of the proof we obtain a rate of convergence estimate. By taking the limit in (7.57) as $r \to \infty$, we obtain

$$\max_i |h^k(i) - h(i)| \leq \frac{B(1 - \epsilon)^{k/m}}{1 - (1 - \epsilon)^{1/m}}, \qquad k = 0, 1, \ldots,$$

so *the rate of convergence is at least linear with convergence ratio* $(1 - \epsilon)^{1/m}$. A sharper rate of convergence result can be obtained by considering the eigenvalue structure of the matrices $\tilde{P}_\mu$ in (7.47).

Error Bounds

As for discounted problems, the successive approximation method can be strengthened by the calculation of monotonic error bounds.

Proposition 7. Under the assumption of Proposition 6 for algorithm (7.51), there holds for every k

$$c_k \leq c_{k+1} \leq \lambda \leq \bar{c}_{k+1} \leq \bar{c}_k, \tag{7.65}$$

where $\lambda = J^*(i)$ for $i = 1, \ldots, n$ and

$$c_k = \min_i [T(h^k)(i) - h^k(i)],$$

$$\bar{c}_k = \max_i [T(h^k)(i) - h^k(i)].$$

Proof. Let $\mu_k(i)$ attain the minimum in

$$T(h^k)(i) = \min_{u \in U(i)} \left[g(i, u) + \sum_{j=1}^n p_{ij}(u) h^k(j) \right]$$

for each k and i. We have, using (7.51),

$$T(h^k)(i) = g[i, \mu_k(i)] + \sum_{j=1}^n p_{ij}[\mu_k(i)] T(h^{k-1})(j) - T(h^{k-1})(s),$$

$$h^k(i) \leq g[i, \mu_k(i)] + \sum_{j=1}^n p_{ij}[\mu_k(i)] h^{k-1}(j) - T(h^{k-1})(s).$$

From these we obtain

$$T(h^k)(i) - h^k(i) \geq \sum_{j=1}^n p_{ij}[\mu_k(i)][T(h^{k-1})(j) - h^{k-1}(j)],$$

and it follows that

$$\min_i [T(h^k)(i) - h^k(i)] \geq \min_i [T(h^{k-1})(j) - h^{k-1}(j)]$$

or equivalently

$$c_{k-1} \leq c_k.$$

A similar argument shows that

$$\bar{c}_k \leq \bar{c}_{k-1}.$$

By Proposition 6 we have $h^k(i) \to h(i)$ and $T(h)(i) - h(i) = \lambda$ for all i, so that $c_k \to \lambda$. Since $\{c_k\}$ is also nondecreasing, we must have $c_k \leq \lambda$ for all k. Similarly, $\bar{c}_k \geq \lambda$ for all k. Q.E.D.

We now demonstrate the successive approximation algorithm and the error bounds (7.65) by means of an example.

Example

Consider an undiscounted version of the example of Section 6.2. We have

$$S = \{1, 2\}, \qquad C = \{u^1, u^2\},$$

$$P(u^1) = \begin{bmatrix} p_{11}(u^1) & p_{12}(u^1) \\ p_{21}(u^1) & p_{22}(u^1) \end{bmatrix} = \begin{bmatrix} \frac{3}{4} & \frac{1}{4} \\ \frac{3}{4} & \frac{1}{4} \end{bmatrix},$$

$$P(u^2) = \begin{bmatrix} p_{11}(u^2) & p_{12}(u^2) \\ p_{21}(u^2) & p_{22}(u^2) \end{bmatrix} = \begin{bmatrix} \frac{1}{4} & \frac{3}{4} \\ \frac{1}{4} & \frac{3}{4} \end{bmatrix},$$

and

$$g(1, u^1) = 2, \qquad g(1, u^2) = 0.5, \qquad g(2, u^1) = 1, \qquad g(2, u^2) = 3.$$

Letting $s = 1$ be the reference state, algorithm (7.51) takes the form

$$T(h^k)(i) = \min\left\{ g(i, u^1) + \sum_{j=1}^{2} p_{ij}(u^1)h^k(j),\ g(i, u^2) + \sum_{j=1}^{2} p_{ij}(u^2)h^k(j) \right\}, \qquad i = 1, 2,$$

$$h^{k+1}(1) = 0$$

$$h^{k+1}(2) = T(h^k)(2) - T(h^k)(1).$$

The results of the computation starting with $h^0(1) = h^0(2) = 0$ are shown in Table 7.1.

TABLE 7.1

k	$h^k(1)$	$h^k(2)$	c_k	$\bar{c}_k$
0	0.00000	0.00000		
1	0.00000	0.50000	0.62500	0.87500
2	0.00000	0.25000	0.68750	0.81250
3	0.00000	0.37500	0.71875	0.78125
4	0.00000	0.31250	0.73438	0.76563
5	0.00000	0.34375	0.74219	0.75781
6	0.00000	0.32813	0.74609	0.75391
7	0.00000	0.33594	0.74805	0.75195
8	0.00000	0.33203	0.74902	0.75098
9	0.00000	0.33398	0.74951	0.75049
10	0.00000	0.33301	0.74976	0.75024
11	0.00000	0.33350	0.74988	0.75012
12	0.00000	0.33325	0.74994	0.75006
13	0.00000	0.33337	0.74997	0.75003
14	0.00000	0.33331	0.74998	0.75002
15	0.00000	0.33334	0.74999	0.75001
16	0.00000	0.33333	0.75000	0.75000

Other Versions of the Successive Approximation Method

We mentioned earlier that the condition for convergence of the successive approximation method given in Proposition 6 is stronger than conditions for the optimal average cost to be independent of the initial state given in Propositions 3 and 4. In fact, the example given in the introduction of this chapter shows that the successive approximation method does not converge when applied to a problem with a single policy and corresponding transition matrix

$$P_\mu = \begin{bmatrix} 0 & 1 \\ 1 & 0 \end{bmatrix}.$$

The matrix P_μ is irreducible, but the difficulty here is that the associated Markov chain has a periodic character. We can bypass this difficulty by modifying the problem without affecting either the optimal cost or optimal policies and by applying the successive approximation method to the modified problem.

Let τ be any scalar with

$$0 < \tau < 1,$$

and consider the problem that results when each transition matrix P_μ corresponding to a stationary policy $\{\mu, \mu, \ldots\}$ is replaced by

$$\tilde{P}_\mu = \tau P_\mu + (1 - \tau)I, \tag{7.66}$$

where I is the identity matrix. Note that $\tilde{P}_\mu$ is a transition probability matrix with the property that, at every state, a self-transition occurs with probability at least $(1 - \tau)$. This destroys any periodic character that P_μ may have. For another view of the same point, note that the eigenvalues of $\tilde{P}_\mu$ are $\tau\lambda_k + (1 - \tau)$ where λ_k are the eigenvalues of P_μ. Therefore, all eigenvalues $\lambda_k \neq 1$ of P_μ that lie on the unit circle are mapped into eigenvalues of $\tilde{P}_\mu$ strictly inside the unit circle. The equation

$$J_\mu + h_\mu = g_\mu + P_\mu h_\mu$$

can also be written

$$J_\mu + \tilde{h}_\mu = g_\mu + \tilde{P}_\mu \tilde{h}_\mu$$

with

$$\tilde{h}_\mu = \frac{h_\mu}{\tau}.$$

It follows from Corollary 1.1 that if $J_\mu(i)$ is independent of i for every μ then the same is true for the modified problem. Furthermore, the costs of all stationary policies, as well as the optimal cost, are equal for both the original and the modified problem.

Consider now the successive approximation method for the modified problem. A straightforward calculation shows that it takes the form

$$h^{k+1}(i) = (1 - \tau)h^k(i) + \min_{u \in U(i)} \left[g(i, u) + \tau \sum_{j=1}^{n} p_{ij}(u)h^k(j) \right]$$

$$- \min_{u \in U(s)} \left[g(s, u) + \tau \sum_{j=1}^{n} p_{sj}(u)h^k(j) \right] \tag{7.67}$$

where s is some fixed state with $h^0(s) = 0$. Note that this iteration is as easy to execute as the original version. It is convergent, however, under weaker conditions than those required in Proposition 6.

Proposition 8. Assume that each stationary policy gives rise to a Markov chain with a single ergodic class. Then, for $0 < \tau < 1$, the sequences $\{h^k(i)\}$ generated by iteration (7.67) satisfy

$$\lim_{k \to \infty} h^k(i) = \frac{h(i)}{\tau},$$

$$\lim_{k \to \infty} \min_{u \in U(i)} \left[g(s, u) + \tau \sum_{j=1}^{n} p_{sj}(u)h^k(j) \right] = \lambda, \tag{7.68}$$

where λ and h are optimal average and differential costs satisfying

$$\lambda + h(i) = \min_{u \in U(i)} \left[g(i, u) + \sum_{j=1}^{n} p_{ij}(u)h(j) \right], \qquad i = 1, \ldots, n.$$

Proof. The proof consists of showing that the conditions of Proposition 6 are satisfied for the modified problem involving the transition probability matrices $\tilde{P}_\mu$ of (7.66).

Indeed, let $m > nn_M$, where n is the number of states and n_M is the number of distinct stationary policies. Consider a set of control functions $\mu_0, \mu_1, \ldots, \mu_m$. Then in the subset $\mu_1, \ldots, \mu_{m-1}$ at least one $\mu \in M$ is repeated n times. Let x be a state belonging to the ergodic class of the Markov chain corresponding to μ. Then the conditions

$$[\tilde{P}_{\mu m} \cdots \tilde{P}_{\mu 1}]_{ix} \geqslant \epsilon, \qquad i = 1, \ldots, n,$$

$$[\tilde{P}_{\mu m-1} \cdots \tilde{P}_{\mu 0}]_{ix} \geqslant \epsilon, \qquad i = 1, \ldots, n,$$

are satisfied for some ϵ because, in view of (7.66), when there is a positive probability of reaching x from i at some stage there is also a positive probability of reaching it at any subsequent stage. Q.E.D.

Note that, since the modified successive approximation method is nothing but the ordinary method applied to a modified problem, the error bounds of Proposition 7 apply in appropriately modified form.

Error Bounds and Linear Programming

It is possible to bound the optimal cost from above and below in a more general manner than the one indicated in Proposition 7. If h is any n-dimensional vector and μ is such that

$$T_\mu(h) = T(h),$$

we will show that, for all i,

$$\min_j [T(h)(j) - h(j)] \leq J^*(i) \leq J_\mu(i) \leq \max_j [T(h)(j) - h(j)]. \qquad (7.69)$$

These bounds hold regardless of whether $J^*(i)$ is independent of the initial state i.

Indeed, let

$$\delta(i) = T(h)(i) - h(i), \qquad i = 1, \ldots, n,$$

and let δ be the vector with coordinates $\delta(i)$. Since $T_\mu(h) = T(h)$, we have

$$T_\mu(h) = \delta + h, \qquad T_\mu^2(h) = T_\mu(h) + P_\mu\delta = \delta + P_\mu\delta + h$$

and, continuing in the same manner,

$$T_\mu^N(h) = \sum_{k=0}^{N-1} P_\mu^k\delta + h, \qquad N = 1, 2, \ldots.$$

It follows that

$$J_\mu = \lim_{N\to\infty} \frac{1}{N} T_\mu^N(h) = P_\mu^*\delta,$$

where

$$P_\mu^* = \lim_{N\to\infty} \frac{1}{N} \sum_{k=0}^{N-1} P_\mu^k.$$

Therefore, $J_\mu(i) \leq \max_j \delta(j)$, and the right side of (7.69) is proved.

Also, let $\pi = \{\mu_0, \mu_1, \ldots\}$ be any policy. We have

$$T_{\mu_N}(h) \geq \delta + h$$

and, applying $T_{\mu_{N-1}}$ to both sides of this inequality, we obtain

$$\begin{aligned}(T_{\mu_{N-1}}T_{\mu_N})(h) &\geq P_{\mu_{N-1}}\delta + T_{\mu_{N-1}}(h)\\ &\geq P_{\mu_{N-1}}\delta + \delta + h\\ &\geq 2\,[\min_j \delta(j)]e + h.\end{aligned}$$

Continuing in the same manner, we have, for all i,

$$\frac{1}{N+1}(T_{\mu_0} \cdots T_{\mu_N})(h)(i) \geq \min_j \delta(j) + \frac{h(i)}{N+1}$$

and, taking the limit as $N \to \infty$, we obtain

$$J_\pi(i) \geq \min_j \delta(j).$$

Since π is arbitrary, we obtain the left side of (7.69).

From the error bounds (7.69), we obtain the inequalities

$$\max_h \min_j [T(h)(j) - h(j)] \leq J^*(i)$$
$$\leq \min_h \max_j [T(h)(j) - h(j)], \qquad i = 1, \ldots, n. \tag{7.70}$$

If a scalar λ and a vector h satisfy $\lambda e + h = T(h)$ (cf. Proposition 1), then h attains the extrema indicated in (7.70), and we have $J^*(i) = \lambda$ for all i. In other words, under these circumstances h solves the problem

$$\text{maximize } \min_j [T(h)(j) - h(j)].$$

This problem is seen to be equivalent to the problem

$$\begin{aligned} &\text{maximize} && \lambda \\ &\text{subject to} && \lambda \leq T(h)(i) - h(i), \qquad i = 1, \ldots, n. \end{aligned}$$

It then follows that λ and $h(i)$, $i = 1, \ldots, n$, solve the linear program

$$\text{maximize} \quad \lambda$$
$$\text{subject to} \quad \lambda + h(i) \leq g(i, u) + \sum_{j=1}^{n} p_{ij}(u)h(j), \quad i = 1, \ldots, n, \quad u \in U(i).$$

Unfortunately, when the number of states and/or controls is very large, the solution of this program becomes very difficult.

7.3 POLICY ITERATION

The policy iteration algorithm for the average cost problem is similar to those described in the past two chapters. Given a stationary policy, one obtains an improved policy by means of a minimization process until no further improvement is possible. *We will assume throughout this section that every stationary policy encountered in the course of the algorithm gives rise to a Markov chain with a single ergodic class.*

At the kth step of the policy iteration algorithm, we have a stationary policy $\{\mu^k, \mu^k, \ldots\}$. We determine corresponding average and differential costs λ^k and h^k satisfying

$$\lambda^k + h^k(i) = g[i, \mu^k(i)] + \sum_{j=1}^{n} p_{ij}[\mu^k(i)]\, h^k(j), \qquad i = 1, \ldots, n, \tag{7.71}$$

or equivalently

$$\lambda^k e + h^k = T_{\mu^k}(h^k) = g_{\mu^k} + P_{\mu^k}h^k,$$

where $e = [1, 1, \ldots, 1]'$ is the unit vector. Note that λ^k and h^k can be determined by solving for the unique solution of the linear system of equations (7.71) together with the normalizing equation $h^k(s) = 0$, where s is any state (cf. Proposition 5). This system can be solved either directly or iteratively using successive approximation and adaptive aggregation (see

Section 5.2 and [B20]). We subsequently find a stationary policy $\pi^{k+1} = \{\mu^{k+1}, \mu^{k+1}, \ldots\}$, where $\mu^{k+1}(i)$ is such that

$$g[i, \mu^{k+1}(i)] + \sum_{j=1}^{k} p_{ij}[\mu^{k+1}(i)]h^k(j)$$
$$= \min_{u \in U(i)} \left[g(i, u) + \sum_{j=1}^{n} p_{ij}(u)h^k(j) \right], \qquad i = 1, \ldots, n, \tag{7.72}$$

or equivalently

$$T_{\mu^{k+1}}(h^k) = T(h^k).$$

There is a restriction here; *if $\mu^k(i)$ attains the minimum in (7.72), we choose $\mu^{k+1}(i) = \mu^k(i)$ even if there are other controls attaining the minimum in addition to $\mu^k(i)$.* If $\mu^{k+1} = \mu^k$, the algorithm terminates; otherwise, the process is repeated with μ^{k+1} replacing μ^k.

The validity of the algorithm is established in the following proposition.

Proposition 9. The policy iteration algorithm described previously terminates in a finite number of steps with an optimal stationary policy.

It is convenient to state the main argument needed for the proof of Proposition 9 as a lemma:

Lemma 2. Let $\{\mu, \mu, \ldots\}$ be a stationary policy, and let λ and h be corresponding average and differential costs satisfying

$$\lambda e + h = T_\mu(h), \tag{7.73}$$

as well as the normalization condition

$$P_\mu^* h = \lim_{N \to \infty} \frac{1}{N} \sum_{k=0}^{N-1} P_\mu^k h = 0. \tag{7.74}$$

Let $\{\bar{\mu}, \bar{\mu}, \ldots\}$ be the policy obtained from μ via the policy iteration step described previously, and let $\bar{\lambda}$ and $\bar{h}$ be corresponding average and differential costs satisfying

$$\bar{\lambda} e + \bar{h} = T_{\bar{\mu}}(\bar{h}) \tag{7.75}$$

and

$$P_{\bar{\mu}}^* \bar{h} = \lim_{N \to \infty} \frac{1}{N} \sum_{k=0}^{N-1} P_{\bar{\mu}}^k \bar{h} = 0. \tag{7.76}$$

Then if $\bar{\mu} \neq \mu$ we must have either (1) $\bar{\lambda} < \lambda$, or (2) $\bar{\lambda} = \lambda$ and $\bar{h}(i) \leq h(i)$ for all $i = 1, \ldots, n$ with strict inequality for at least one state i.

We note that, once Lemma 2 is established, it can be easily shown that the policy iteration algorithm will terminate in a finite number of steps. The reason is that the vector h corresponding to μ via (7.73) and (7.74) is unique by Proposition 5, and therefore the conclusion of Lemma 2 guarantees that no policy will be encountered more than once during the course of the algorithm. Since the number of stationary policies is finite, the algorithm must terminate finitely. If the algorithm stops at the kth step with $\mu^{k+1} = \mu^k$, we see from (7.71) and (7.72) that

$$\lambda^k e + h^k = T(h^k),$$

which by Proposition 1 implies that $\{\mu^k, \mu^k, \ldots\}$ is an optimal stationary policy. So to prove Proposition 9 there remains to prove Lemma 2.

Proof of Lemma 2. For notational convenience, denote

$$P = P_\mu, \qquad \overline{P} = P_{\overline{\mu}}, \qquad P^* = P^*_\mu, \qquad \overline{P}^* = P^*_{\overline{\mu}},$$

$$g = g_\mu, \qquad \overline{g} = g_{\overline{\mu}}.$$

Define the vector δ by

$$\delta = \lambda e + h - \overline{g} - \overline{P}h. \tag{7.77}$$

We have, by assumption, $T_{\overline{\mu}}(h) = T(h) \leqslant T_\mu(h) = \lambda e + h$, or equivalently

$$\overline{g} + \overline{P}h \leqslant g + Ph = \lambda e + h \tag{7.78}$$

from which we obtain

$$\delta(i) \geqslant 0, \qquad i = 1, \ldots, n. \tag{7.79}$$

Define also

$$\Delta = h - \overline{h}. \tag{7.80}$$

By combining (7.77) with the equation $\overline{\lambda} e + \overline{h} = \overline{g} + \overline{P}\overline{h}$, we obtain

$$\delta = (\lambda - \overline{\lambda})e + \Delta - \overline{P}\Delta.$$

Multiplying this relation with $\overline{P}^k$ and adding from 0 to $N - 1$, we obtain

$$\sum_{k=0}^{N-1} \overline{P}^k \delta = N(\lambda - \overline{\lambda})e + \Delta - \overline{P}^N \Delta. \tag{7.81}$$

Dividing by N and taking the limit as $N \to \infty$, we obtain

$$\overline{P}^* \delta = \lim_{N\to\infty} \frac{1}{N} \sum_{k=0}^{N-1} \overline{P}^k \delta = (\lambda - \overline{\lambda})e. \tag{7.82}$$

In view of the fact $\delta \geqslant 0$ [cf. (7.79)], we see that

$$\lambda \geqslant \overline{\lambda}.$$

If $\lambda > \overline{\lambda}$, we are done; so assume that $\lambda = \overline{\lambda}$. A state i is called $\overline{P}$-*recurrent* ($\overline{P}$-*transient*) if i belongs (does not belong) to the single ergodic class of the Markov chain corresponding to $\overline{P}^*$. From (7.82) $\overline{P}^*\delta = 0$ and, since $\delta \geqslant 0$ and the elements of $\overline{P}^*$ that are positive are those columns corresponding to $\overline{P}$-recurrent states, we obtain

$$\delta(i) = 0, \qquad \text{for all } i \text{ that are } \overline{P}\text{-recurrent}. \tag{7.83}$$

It follows by construction of the algorithm that if i is $\overline{P}$-recurrent then the ith rows of P and $\overline{P}$ are identical [since $\overline{\mu}(i) = \mu(i)$ for all i with $\delta(i) = 0$]. Since P and $\overline{P}$ have a single ergodic class, it follows that this ergodic class is identical for both P and $\overline{P}$. From the normalization conditions (7.74) and (7.76), we then obtain $h(i) = \overline{h}(i)$ for all i that are $\overline{P}$-recurrent. Equivalently,

$$\Delta(i) = 0, \qquad \text{for all } i \text{ that are } \overline{P}\text{-recurrent.} \tag{7.84}$$

From (7.81) we obtain

$$\lim_{N\to\infty} \overline{P}^N\Delta = \Delta - \lim_{N\to\infty} \sum_{k=0}^{N-1} \overline{P}^k\delta \leq \Delta - \delta.$$

In view of (7.84), the coordinates of $\overline{P}^N\Delta$ corresponding to $\overline{P}$-transient states tend to zero. Therefore, we have

$$\delta(i) \leq \Delta(i), \qquad \text{for all } i \text{ that are } \overline{P}\text{-transient.} \tag{7.85}$$

From (7.79) and (7.83) to (7.85), we see now that either $\delta = 0$, in which case $\mu = \overline{\mu}$, or else $\Delta \geq 0$ with strict inequality $\Delta(i) > 0$ for at least one $\overline{P}$-transient state i. Q.E.D.

We now demonstrate the policy iteration algorithm by means of the example of the previous section.

Example (continued)
Let

$$\mu^0(1) = u^1, \qquad \mu^0(2) = u^2.$$

We take $s = 1$ as a reference state and obtain λ_{μ^0}, $h_{\mu^0}(1)$, and $h_{\mu^0}(2)$ from the system of equations

$$\lambda_{\mu^0} + h_{\mu^0}(1) = g(1, u^1) + p_{11}(u^1)h_{\mu^0}(1) + p_{12}(u^1)h_{\mu^0}(2),$$
$$\lambda_{\mu^0} + h_{\mu^0}(2) = g(2, u^2) + p_{21}(u^2)h_{\mu^0}(1) + p_{22}(u^2)h_{\mu^0}(2),$$
$$h_{\mu^0}(1) = 0.$$

Substituting the data of the problem,

$$\lambda_{\mu^0} = 2 + \tfrac{1}{4}h_{\mu^0}(2), \qquad \lambda_{\mu^0} + h_{\mu^0}(2) = 3 + \tfrac{3}{4}h_{\mu^0}(2),$$

from which

$$\lambda_{\mu^0} = 2.5, \qquad h_{\mu^0}(1) = 0, \qquad h_{\mu^0}(2) = 2.$$

We now find $\mu^1(1)$ and $\mu^1(2)$ by the minimization indicated in (7.72). We determine

$$\min[g(1, u^1) + p_{11}(u^1)h_{\mu^0}(1) + p_{12}(u^1)h_{\mu^0}(2),$$
$$g(1, u^2) + p_{11}(u^2)h_{\mu^0}(1) + p_{12}(u^2)h_{\mu^0}(2)]$$
$$= \min[2 + \tfrac{1}{4} \times 2, 0.5 + \tfrac{3}{4} \times 2] = \min[2.5, 2],$$
$$\min[g(2, u^1) + p_{21}(u^1)h_{\mu^0}(1) + p_{22}(u^1)h_{\mu^0}(2),$$
$$g(2, u^2) + p_{21}(u^2)h_{\mu^0}(1) + p_{22}(u^2)h_{\mu^0}(2)]$$
$$= \min[1 + \tfrac{1}{4} \times 2, 3 + \tfrac{3}{4} \times 2] = \min[1.5, 4.5].$$

The minimization yields

$$\mu^1(1) = u^2, \qquad \mu^1(2) = u^1.$$

We obtain λ_{μ^1}, $h_{\mu^1}(1)$, and $h_{\mu^1}(2)$ from the system of equations

$$\lambda_{\mu^1} + h_{\mu^1}(1) = g(1, u^2) + p_{11}(u^2)h_{\mu^1}(1) + p_{12}(u^2)h_{\mu^1}(2),$$
$$\lambda_{\mu^1} + h_{\mu^1}(2) = g(2, u^1) + p_{21}(u^1)h_{\mu^1}(1) + p_{22}(u^1)h_{\mu^1}(2),$$
$$h_{\mu^1}(1) = 0.$$

By substitution of the data of the problem, we obtain

$$\lambda_{\mu^1} = 0.75, \qquad h_{\mu^1}(1) = 0, \qquad h_{\mu^1}(2) = \tfrac{1}{3}.$$

We find $\mu^2(1)$ and $\mu^2(2)$ by determining the minimum in

$$\min[g(1, u^1) + p_{11}(u^1)h_{\mu^1}(1) + p_{12}(u^1)h_{\mu^1}(2),$$
$$g(1, u^2) + p_{11}(u^2)h_{\mu^1}(1) + p_{12}(u^2)h_{\mu^1}(2)]$$
$$= \min[2 + \tfrac{1}{4} \times \tfrac{1}{3}, 0.5 + \tfrac{3}{4} \times \tfrac{1}{3}] = \min[2.08, 0.75],$$
$$\min[g(2, u^1) + p_{21}(u^1)h_{\mu^1}(1) + p_{22}(u^1)h_{\mu^1}(2),$$
$$g(2, u^2) + p_{21}(u^2)h_{\mu^1}(1) + p_{22}(u^2)h_{\mu^1}(2)]$$
$$= \min[1 + \tfrac{1}{4} \times \tfrac{1}{3}, 3 + \tfrac{3}{4} \times \tfrac{1}{3}] = \min[1.08, 3.25].$$

The minimization yields

$$\mu^2(1) = \mu^1(1) = u^2, \qquad \mu^2(2) = \mu^1(2) = u^1,$$

and hence the preceding policy is optimal and the optimal average cost per stage is $\lambda_{\mu^1} = 0.75$.

7.4 INFINITE STATE SPACE: LINEAR SYSTEMS WITH QUADRATIC COST FUNCTIONALS

The standing assumption in the preceding sections has been that the state space is finite and thus the underlying system is a controlled finite state Markov chain. Once one removes the finiteness assumption on the state space, many of the results presented in the past three sections no longer hold. For example, whereas one could restrict attention to stationary policies for finite state systems, this is not true anymore when the state space is infinite. The following example [R6] shows that for a countable state space the optimal policy may be nonstationary.

Example

Let the state space be $S = \{1, 2, 3, \ldots\}$ and let there be two control actions $C = \{u^1, u^2\}$. The transition probabilities under u^1 and u^2 are specified by

$$p_{i(i+1)}(u^1) = p_{ii}(u^2) = 1.$$

The costs per stage are

$$g(i, u^1) = 1, \qquad g(i, u^2) = \frac{1}{i}, \qquad i = 1, 2, 3, \ldots.$$

In other words, at state i we may either move to state $(i + 1)$ at the cost of one unit or stay at i at a cost $1/i$.

For any stationary policy $\pi = \{\mu, \mu, \ldots\}$ other than the policy for which

$\mu(i) = u^1$ for all i, let $n(\pi)$ be the smallest integer for which

$$\mu[n(\pi)] = u^2.$$

Then the corresponding average cost per stage satisfies

$$J_\pi(i) = \frac{1}{n(\pi)} > 0, \qquad i \leq n(\pi).$$

For the policy where $\mu(i) = u^1$ for all i, we have $J_\pi(i) = 1$ for all i. Since the optimal cost per stage cannot be less than zero, it is clear that

$$\min_\pi J_\pi(i) = 0, \qquad i = 1, 2, \ldots.$$

However, the optimal cost is not attained by any stationary policy, so no stationary policy is optimal. On the other hand, consider the nonstationary policy π^* that on entering state i chooses u^2 for i consecutive times and then chooses u^1. If the starting state is i, the sequence of costs incurred is

$$\underbrace{\frac{1}{i}, \frac{1}{i}, \ldots, \frac{1}{i}}_{i \text{ times}}, \quad 1, \quad \underbrace{\frac{1}{i+1}, \frac{1}{i+1}, \ldots, \frac{1}{i+1}}_{(i+1) \text{ times}}, \quad 1, \quad \frac{1}{i+2}, \frac{1}{i+2}, \ldots.$$

The average cost corresponding to this policy is

$$J_{\pi^*}(i) = \lim_{m\to\infty} \frac{2m}{\sum_{k=1}^{m} (i+k)} = 0, \qquad i = 1, 2, 3, \ldots.$$

Hence the nonstationary policy π^* is optimal while, as shown previously, no stationary policy is optimal.

Generally, the analysis of average cost problems with an infinite state space is difficult. However, certain particular special cases can be satisfactorily analyzed, and one such case is the average cost version of the linear–quadratic problem examined in Chapters 2, 3, and 6.

Consider an undiscounted version ($\alpha = 1$) for the linear–quadratic problem of Section 6.1 involving the system

$$x_{k+1} = Ax_k + Bu_k + w_k, \qquad k = 0, 1, \ldots, \tag{7.86}$$

and the cost functional

$$J_\pi(x_0) = \lim_{N\to\infty} \frac{1}{N} \mathop{E}_{\substack{w_k \\ k=0,1,\ldots}} \left\{ \sum_{k=0}^{N-1} [x_k'Qx_k + \mu_k(x_k)'R\mu_k(x_k)] \right\}. \tag{7.87}$$

We make the same assumptions as in Section 6.1; that is, w_k are independent and have zero mean and finite second moments. We also assume that the pair (A, b) is controllable and that the pair (A, C), where $Q = C'C$, is observable. Under these assumptions, it was shown in Section 2.1 that the Riccati equation

$$K_0 = 0, \tag{7.88}$$

$$K_{k+1} = A'[K_k - K_kB(B'K_kB + R)^{-1}B'K_k]A + Q \tag{7.89}$$

yields in the limit a matrix K,

$$K = \lim_{k\to\infty} K_k, \tag{7.90}$$

which is the unique solution of the equation

$$K = A'[K - KB(B'KB + R)^{-1}B'K]A + Q \tag{7.91}$$

within the class of positive semidefinite symmetric matrices.

The optimal value of the N-stage costs

$$\frac{1}{N} \underset{\substack{w_k \\ k=0,1,\ldots,N-1}}{E} \left\{ \sum_{k=0}^{N-1} (x_k'Qx_k + u_k'Ru_k) \right\} \tag{7.92}$$

has been derived earlier and was seen to be equal to

$$\frac{1}{N}\left[x_0'K_Nx_0 + \sum_{k=0}^{N-1} E\{w'K_kw\} \right].$$

Thus using (7.90) and the fact

$$\lim_{N\to\infty} \frac{1}{N} \sum_{k=0}^{N-1} E\{w'K_kw\} = E\{w'Kw\},$$

the optimal finite horizon costs tend in the limit as $N \to \infty$ to

$$\lambda = E\{w'Kw\}. \tag{7.93}$$

In addition, the N-stage optimal policy in its initial stages tends to the stationary policy

$$\mu^*(x) = -(B'KB + R)^{-1}B'KAx. \tag{7.94}$$

Furthermore, a simple calculation shows that, by the definition of λ, K, and $\mu^*(x)$, we have

$$\lambda + x'Kx = \min_u E\{x'Qx + u'Ru + (Ax + Bu + w)'K(Ax + Bu + w)\},$$

while the minimum in the right side of the equation is attained at $u^* = \mu^*(x)$ as given by (7.94).

By repeating the proof of Proposition 1 of this chapter, we obtain

$$\lambda \leq \frac{1}{N} E\{x_N'Kx_N|x_0, \pi\} - \frac{1}{N}x_0'Kx_0 + \frac{1}{N}E\left\{ \sum_{k=0}^{N-1} (x_k'Qx_k + u_k'Ru_k)|x_0, \pi \right\},$$

with equality if $\pi = \{\mu^*, \mu^*, \ldots\}$. Hence, if π is such that $E\{x_N'Kx_N|x_0, \pi\}$ is uniformly bounded over N, we have, by taking the limit as $N \to \infty$ in the preceding relation,

$$\lambda \leq J_\pi(x), \qquad x \in R^n,$$

with equality if $\pi = \{\mu^*, \mu^*, \ldots\}$. Thus the linear stationary policy given by (7.94) is optimal over all policies π with $E\{x_N'Kx_N|x_0, \pi\}$ bounded uniformly over N.

7.5 NOTES

The average cost problem was formulated and analyzed in [H15]. Several authors have contributed to the problem ([B34, R6, S7, V4, V6]), most notably Blackwell ([B26]).

In our approach to the results of Section 7.1, we follow [R6]. This approach is generalizable to situations where the state space is infinite. The result of Proposition 4(b) was shown in [B4]. The successive approximation method of Section 7.2 was given in [W6]. The error bounds of Proposition 7 are due to Odoni ([O1]). The successive approximation method has been analyzed exhaustively in [S10], [S12], and [S13]. The error bounds (7.69) are due to Varaiya ([V2]), who used them to construct a differential form of the successive approximation method. Discrete time versions of Varaiya's method are given in [P12]. Platzman ([P10]) points out relations between this method and earlier work ([S10]) and shows convergence under slightly weaker conditions than those given here ([P11]).

The policy iteration algorithm can be generalized for problems where the optimal average cost per stage is not the same for every initial state (see [B26], [V4], and [D4]). Adaptive aggregation can be used similarly as in Section 5.2 to carry out iteratively the policy evaluation phase of the policy iteration algorithm [B20].

For analysis of infinite horizon versions of inventory control problems, such as the ones of Section 2.2, see [I3], [H13], [H14], and [V7]. [K15] considers more general average cost problems with infinite state space.

Problem 3, also known as the streetwalker's dilemma, is adapted from [R6], which considers also semi-Markov decision problems involving continuous time Markov chains.

PROBLEMS

1. *Optimal Control of Deterministic Finite-State Systems.* Consider a stationary deterministic control system

$$x_{k+1} = f(x_k, u_k), \qquad k = 0, 1, \ldots,$$

where the state x_k belongs to a finite state space $S = \{1, 2, \ldots, n\}$ and the control u_k is constrained in a subset $U(x_k)$ of a finite control space C. We say that the system is *completely controllable* if, given any two states $i, j \in S$, there exists a sequence of admissible controls that drives the state of the system from the state i to the state j within at most $(n - 1)$ steps. For a completely controllable system and a given initial state $x_0 = i$, consider the problem of finding an admissible control sequence $\{u_0, u_1, \ldots\}$ that minimizes

$$J_\pi(i) = \lim_{N\to\infty} \frac{1}{N} \sum_{k=0}^{N-1} g(x_k, u_k),$$

where $g: S \times C \to R$ is given. Show that the optimal cost is the same for every initial state. Show also that there exist optimal control sequences that after a certain time index are periodic.

2. Consider a stationary inventory control problem of the type considered in Section 3.2 but with the difference that the stock x_k can only take integer values from 0 to some integer M. The amount of the order u_k can take integer values with $0 \leq u_k \leq M - x_k$, and the random demand w_k can only take nonnegative integer values with $P(w_k = 0) > 0$ and $P(w_k = 1) > 0$. Unsatisfied demand is lost, so stock evolves according to the equation $x_{k+1} = \max(0, x_k + u_k - w_k)$. The problem is to find an inventory policy that minimizes the average cost per stage. Show that there exists an optimal stationary policy and that the optimal cost is independent of the initial stock x_0.

3. Consider a businessperson (B) providing a certain type of service to customers. B receives at the beginning of each time period with probability p_i a proposal by a customer of type i, where $i = 1, 2, \ldots, n$, who offers an amount of money M_i. We assume $\Sigma_{i=1}^{n} p_i \leq 1$. B may reject the offer, in which case the customer leaves and B remains idle during that period, or B may accept the offer in which case B spends some time with that customer determined according to a Markov process with transition probabilities β_{ik}, where, for $k = 1, 2, \ldots,$

β_{ik} = probability that the type i customer will leave after k periods, given that the customer has already stayed with B for $(k - 1)$ periods.

The problem is to determine an acceptance–rejection policy that maximizes

$$\lim_{N\to\infty} \frac{1}{N} \{\text{Expected payment over } N \text{ periods}\}.$$

Consider two cases:

1. $\beta_{ik} = \beta_i \in (0, 1)$ for all k.
2. For each i there exists $\bar{k}_i$ such that $\beta_{i\bar{k}_i} = 1$.

(a) Formulate the businessperson's problem as an average cost Markovian decision problem and show that the optimal value is independent of the initial state.

(b) Show that there exists a scalar λ^* and an optimal policy that accepts the offer of a type i customer if and only if

$$\lambda^* T_i \leq M_i,$$

where T_i is the expected time spent with the type i customer given by

$$T_i = \beta_{i1} + \sum_{k=2}^{\infty} k\beta_{ik-1}(1 - \beta_{ik-2}) \ldots (1 - \beta_{i0}).$$

4. *Policy Iteration for Linear–Quadratic Problems.* The purpose of this problem is to show that policy iteration works for linear–quadratic problems (even though neither the state space nor the control space are finite). Consider the problem of Section 7.4 under the usual controllability, observability, and positive (semi)definiteness assumptions. Let L_0 be an $m \times n$ matrix such that the matrix $(A + BL_0)$ is stable.

(a) Show that the average cost per stage corresponding to the stationary policy $\{\mu_0, \mu_0, \ldots\}$, where $\mu_0(x) = L_0 x$, is of the form

$$J_{\mu 0} = E\{w' K_0 w\},$$

where K_0 is a positive semidefinite matrix satisfying the (linear) equation

$$K_0 = (A + BL_0)' K_0 (A + BL_0) + Q + L_0' R L_0.$$

(b) Let $\mu_1(x) = L_1 x = (R + B'K_0B)^{-1} B' K_0 A x$ be the control function attaining the minimum for each x in the expression

$$\min_u \{u'Ru + (Ax + Bu)' K_0 (Ax + Bu)\}.$$

Show that

$$J_{\mu 1} = E\{w' K_1 w\} \leq J_{\mu 0},$$

where K_1 is some positive semidefinite matrix.

(c) Consider repeating the (policy iteration) process described in parts (a) and (b), thereby obtaining a sequence of positive semidefinite matrices $\{K_k\}$. Show that

$$K_k \to K,$$

where K is the optimal cost matrix of the problem.

5. Show Eq. (7.16). *Sketch of proof:* From the definition (7.11) we have

$$\epsilon_N = \sum_{k=0}^{N-1} P_\mu^k g_\mu - N J_\mu,$$

and multiplication with P_μ^* yields $P_\mu^* \epsilon_N = 0$. It follows that $(I - P_\mu + P_\mu^*)\epsilon_N = (I - P_\mu)\epsilon_N = g_\mu - P_\mu^N g_\mu$. By adding this relation from 1 to N, we obtain (7.16).

6. Consider a deterministic system with two states 0 and 1. Upon entering state 0, the system stays there permanently at no cost. In state 1 there is a choice of staying there at no cost or moving to state 0 at unity cost. Show that every policy is average cost optimal, but the only stationary policy that is Blackwell optimal (see the chapter appendix) is the one that keeps the system in the state it currently is in.

7. Show that a Blackwell optimal policy is optimal over all policies (not just those that are stationary). *Hint:* Use the following fact: If $\{c_n\}$ is a nonnegative bounded sequence, then

$$\liminf_{N\to\infty} \frac{1}{N} \sum_{n=1}^{N} c_n \leq \liminf_{\beta \uparrow 1} (1 - \beta) \sum_{n=1}^{\infty} \beta^{n-1} c_n$$

$$\leq \limsup_{\beta \uparrow 1} (1 - \beta) \sum_{n=1}^{\infty} \beta^{n-1} c_n \leq \limsup_{N\to\infty} \frac{1}{N} \sum_{n=1}^{N} c_n.$$

This fact is a corollary of the following Tauberian theorem, which can be found in D. V. Widder, *The Laplace Transform,* Princeton University Press, Princeton, N.J., 1941, pages 181–182.

If $K(\cdot)$ is nondecreasing on $[0, \infty)$ and

$$f(x) = \int_0^\infty e^{-xt}\, dK(t), \qquad x > 0$$

is convergent, then

$$\liminf_{t\to\infty} \frac{K(t)}{t} \le \liminf_{x\downarrow 0} xf(x) \le \limsup_{x\downarrow 0} xf(x) \le \limsup_{t\to\infty} \frac{K(t)}{t}.$$

8. *Reduction to the Discounted Case.* For the problem of Sections 7.1 to 7.3, suppose there is a state s such that for some $\beta > 0$ we have $p_{is}(u) \ge \beta$ for all states i and controls u. Consider the $(1 - \beta)$-discounted problem with the same state and control space and transition probabilities

$$\overline{p}_{ij}(u) = \begin{cases} (1 - \beta)^{-1} p_{ij}(u), & \text{if } j \ne s, \\ (1 - \beta)^{-1}[p_{ij}(u) - \beta], & \text{if } j = s. \end{cases}$$

Show that $\beta \overline{J}(s)$ and $\overline{J}(i)$ are optimal average and differential costs respectively, where $\overline{J}$ is the optimal cost of the $(1 - \beta)$-discounted problem.

9. Solve the average cost version ($\alpha = 1$) of the computer manufacturer's problem (Problem 1 in Chapter 5), and verify that the result of Proposition 2(c) holds.

10. *Continuous-Time Markov Chains.* Consider a continuous-time Markov chain problem of the type discussed in Section 6.7 for the case where the cost is

$$\lim_{T\to\infty} E\left\{\frac{1}{T}\int_0^T g[x(t), u(t)]\, dt\right\}.$$

Use arguments analogous to those in Section 6.7 to show the following:

(a) There is an equivalent discrete-time Markov chain problem with average cost

$$\lim_{N\to\infty} \frac{1}{N} E\left\{\sum_{k=0}^{N-1} \frac{g(x_k, u_k)}{\nu}\right\},$$

where ν is an upper bound to all transition rates $\nu_i(u)$.

(b) Show that for this problem Bellman's equation takes the form

$$\lambda + h(i) = \frac{1}{\nu} \min_{u\in U(i)} \left[g(i, u) + [\nu - \nu_i(u)]h(i) + \nu_i(u) \sum_j p_{ij}(u)h(j) \right].$$

11. Consider the manufacturer's problem of Example 1, Section 6.7, for the case where $\beta = 0$, and the cost is

$$\lim_{T\to\infty} \frac{1}{T} E\left\{\int_0^T g[x(t), u(t)]\, dt\right\}.$$

(a) Show that Bellman's equation takes the form

$$\lambda + h(i) = \min\left[K + h(1), \frac{ci}{\lambda} + h(i + 1) \right].$$

(b) Show that there exists a threshold i^* such that it is optimal to process the orders if and only if i equals or exceeds i^*. *Hint:* Use Proposition 2.

APPENDIX: EXISTENCE RESULTS AND PROOFS

In this appendix we provide proofs of some of the results of the main body of the chapter (Lemma 1 and Proposition 4). In the process we will demonstrate the existence of an optimal stationary policy. The proof of this result is based on the relationship between the average cost problem and its discounted version. We have already made use of this relation in the process of showing Propositions 2 and 3 for the case where the optimal average cost is independent of the initial state. We now consider the general case. Throughout the appendix we consider the finite state Markov chain case and make use of the notation established in the introduction to this chapter.

For any stationary policy $\{\mu, \mu, \ldots\}$, the corresponding α-discounted cost is given in vector form by

$$J_{\alpha,\mu} = \sum_{k=0}^{\infty} \alpha^k P_\mu^k g_\mu = (I - \alpha P_\mu)^{-1} g_\mu, \qquad \alpha \in (0, 1). \tag{A7.1}$$

The following proposition provides an expression for $(I - \alpha P_\mu)^{-1}$ and at the same time shows Lemma 1.

Proposition A7.1. For any stochastic matrix P and $\alpha \in (0, 1)$, there holds

$$(I - \alpha P)^{-1} = (1 - \alpha)^{-1} P^* + H + 0(|1 - \alpha|), \tag{A7.2}$$

where $0(|1 - \alpha|)$ is an α-dependent matrix such that

$$\lim_{\alpha \to 1} 0(|1 - \alpha|) = 0, \tag{A7.3}$$

and the matrices P^* and H are given by

$$P^* = \lim_{N \to \infty} \frac{1}{N} \sum_{k=0}^{N-1} P^k, \tag{A7.4}$$

$$H = (I - P + P^*)^{-1} - P^*. \tag{A7.5}$$

[It will be shown as part of the proof that the limit in (A7.4) and the inverse in (A7.5) exist.] Furthermore, P^* and H satisfy the following equations:

$$P^* = PP^* = P^*P = P^*P^* \tag{A7.6}$$

$$P^*H = 0 \tag{A7.7}$$

$$P^* + H = I + PH. \tag{A7.8}$$

Proof. From the usual matrix inversion formula, it follows that $(I - \alpha P)^{-1}$ can be expressed as a matrix with elements that are either zero or fractions with numerator and denominator being polynomials in α with no common divisor. The denominator polynomial of each nonzero element cannot have unity as a multiple root since otherwise we would have some elements of the matrix $(1 - \alpha)(I - \alpha P)^{-1}$ tending to infinity as $\alpha \to 1$, which is not possible in view of the discounted cost interpretation (A7.1) and the fact $|J_{\alpha,\mu}(j)| \leq (1 - \alpha)^{-1} \max_i |g_\mu(i)|$. Therefore, $(I - \alpha P)^{-1}$ has an expansion in a neighborhood of $\alpha = 1$ of the form (A7.2) and (A7.3) with the identifications

$$P^* = \lim_{\alpha \to 1} (1 - \alpha)(I - \alpha P)^{-1}, \tag{A7.9}$$

$$H = \lim_{\alpha \to 1} [(I - \alpha P)^{-1} - (1 - \alpha)^{-1} P^*]. \tag{A7.10}$$

We will now show equations (A7.6), (A7.5), (A7.7), and (A7.8), in that order, and finally equation (A7.4). We have

$$(I - \alpha P)(I - \alpha P)^{-1} = I \tag{A7.11}$$

and

$$\alpha(I - \alpha P)(I - \alpha P)^{-1} = \alpha I. \tag{A7.12}$$

Subtracting these two equations and rearranging terms, we obtain

$$\alpha P(1 - \alpha)(I - \alpha P)^{-1} = (1 - \alpha)(I - \alpha P)^{-1} + (\alpha - 1)I.$$

By taking the limit as $\alpha \to 1$ and using the definition (A7.9), it follows that

$$PP^* = P^*.$$

Also, by reversing the order of $(I - \alpha P)$ and $(I - \alpha P)^{-1}$ in (A7.11) and (A7.12), it follows similarly that $P^*P = P^*$. From $PP^* = P^*$, we also obtain $(I - \alpha P)P^* = (1 - \alpha)P^*$ or $P^* = (1 - \alpha)(I - \alpha P)^{-1}P^*$, and taking the limit as $\alpha \to 1$, we have $P^* = P^*P^*$. Thus (A7.6) has been proved.

We have, using (A7.6), $(P - P^*)^2 = P^2 - P^*$ and similarly

$$(P - P^*)^k = P^k - P^*, \qquad k > 0.$$

Therefore,

$$\begin{aligned}(I - \alpha P)^{-1} - (1 - \alpha)^{-1} P^* &= \sum_{k=0}^{\infty} \alpha^k(P^k - P^*) \\ &= I - P^* + \sum_{k=1}^{\infty} \alpha^k(P - P^*)^k \\ &= [I - \alpha(P - P^*)]^{-1} - P^*.\end{aligned}$$

Taking the limit as $\alpha \to 1$ and using (A7.10), we obtain (A7.5).

From (A7.5), we obtain

$$(I - P + P^*)H = I - (I - P + P^*)P^*$$

or, using (A7.6),

$$H - PH + P^*H = I - P^*. \tag{A7.13}$$

Multiplying this relation by P^* and using (A7.6), we obtain $P^*H = 0$, which is (A7.7). Equation (A7.8) then follows from (A7.13).

Multiplying (A7.8) with P^k and using (A7.6), we obtain

$$P^* + P^kH = P^k + P^{k+1}H, \qquad k = 0, 1, \ldots.$$

Adding over $k = 0, \ldots, N - 1$ this relation, we have

$$NP^* + H = \sum_{k=0}^{N-1} P^k + P^NH.$$

Dividing by N and taking the limit as $N \to \infty$, we obtain (A7.4). Q.E.D.

From the expression (A7.1) and Proposition A7.1, we obtain the following relation between α-discounted and average cost corresponding to a stationary policy.

Proposition A7.2. For any stationary policy $\{\mu, \mu, \ldots\}$ and $\alpha \in (0, 1)$, there holds

$$J_{\alpha,\mu} = (1 - \alpha)^{-1} J_\mu + h_\mu + 0(|1 - \alpha|), \tag{A7.14}$$

where

$$J_\mu = P_\mu^* g_\mu = \left(\lim_{N\to\infty} \frac{1}{N} \sum_{k=0}^{N-1} P_\mu^k \right) g_\mu$$

is the average cost vector corresponding to μ, and h_μ is a differential cost vector satisfying

$$J_\mu + h_\mu = g_\mu + P_\mu h_\mu.$$

Proof. The proof follows from (A7.1) and Proposition A7.1 with the identifications $P = P_\mu$, $P^* = P_\mu^*$, and $h_\mu = Hg_\mu$. Q.E.D.

We know from Section 5.1 that there exists an optimal stationary policy for the α-discounted problem for every $\alpha \in (0, 1)$. We say that a stationary policy $\{\mu, \mu, \ldots\}$ is *Blackwell optimal* if it is simultaneously optimal for all the α-discounted problems with α in an interval $(\overline{\alpha}, 1)$, where $\overline{\alpha} \in (0, 1)$ is some scalar. This notion and the following line of analysis were first introduced in [B26]. From Proposition A7.2, it follows that *a Blackwell optimal policy is optimal for the average cost problem within the class of all stationary policies*. To see this, note that if $\{\mu^*, \mu^*, \ldots\}$ is Blackwell optimal then for all stationary policies $\{\mu, \mu, \ldots\}$ and α in an interval $(\overline{\alpha}, 1)$ we have $J_{\alpha,\mu^*} \leq J_{\alpha,\mu}$. Equivalently, using (A7.14),

$$(1 - \alpha)^{-1} J_\mu^* + h_\mu^* + 0(|1 - \alpha|)$$
$$\leq (1 - \alpha)^{-1} J_\mu + h_\mu + 0(|1 - \alpha|), \qquad \alpha \in (\overline{\alpha}, 1)$$

or

$$J_{\mu^*} \leq J_\mu + (1 - \alpha)(h_\mu - h_{\mu^*}) + (1 - \alpha)0(|1 - \alpha|), \qquad \alpha \in (\overline{\alpha}, 1).$$

By taking the limit as $\alpha \to 1$, we obtain $J_{\mu^*} \leq J_\mu$. The reverse is not true; that is, it is possible that a stationary average cost optimal policy is not Blackwell optimal (see Problem 6). We mention also that one can show the stronger result that a Blackwell optimal policy is average cost optimal within the class of all policies (not just those that are stationary; see Problem 7).

The following proposition is of major importance and provides the basis for the proof of Proposition 4.

Proposition A7.3. There exists a Blackwell optimal policy.

Proof. From (A7.1), we know that, for each μ and state i, $J_{\alpha,\mu}(i)$ is a rational function of α. Therefore, for any two policies μ and μ' the graphs of $J_{\alpha,\mu}(i)$ and $J_{\alpha,\mu'}(i)$ either coincide or cross only a finite number of times in the interval (0, 1). Since there are only a finite number of policies, we conclude that for state i there is a policy μ^i and a scalar $\overline{\alpha}_i \in (0, 1)$ such that μ^i is optimal for the α-discounted problem for $\alpha \in (\overline{\alpha}_i, 1)$ when the initial state is i. Consider the stationary policy defined for each i by $\mu^*(i) = \mu^i(i)$. It can be seen that $\{\mu^*, \mu^*, \ldots\}$ is a stationary optimal policy for the α-discounted problem for all α with $\max_i \overline{\alpha}_i < \alpha < 1$. Therefore, $\{\mu^*, \mu^*, \ldots\}$ is Blackwell optimal. Q.E.D.

The next proposition provides a characterization of Blackwell optimal policies:

Proposition A7.4. If $\{\mu^*, \mu^*, \ldots\}$ is Blackwell optimal, then for all stationary policies $\{\mu, \mu, \ldots\}$ we have

$$J_{\mu^*} = P_{\mu^*}J_{\mu^*} \leq P_\mu J_{\mu^*}. \tag{A7.15}$$

Furthermore, for all μ such that $P_{\mu^*}J_{\mu^*} = P_\mu J_{\mu^*}$, we have

$$J_{\mu^*} + h_{\mu^*} = g_{\mu^*} + P_{\mu^*}h_{\mu^*} \leq g_\mu + P_\mu h_{\mu^*}, \tag{A7.16}$$

where h_{μ^*} is a differential cost vector corresponding to μ^* (cf. Proposition A7.2).

Proof. Since $\{\mu^*, \mu^*, \ldots\}$ is optimal for the α-discounted problem for all α in an interval $(\overline{\alpha}, 1)$, we must have, for every μ,

$$J_{\alpha,\mu^*} = g_{\mu^*} + \alpha P_{\mu^*}J_{\alpha,\mu^*} \leq g_\mu + P_\mu J_{\alpha,\mu^*}. \tag{A7.17}$$

From Proposition A7.2, we have, for all $\alpha \in (\overline{\alpha}, 1)$,

$$J_{\alpha,\mu^*} = (1 - \alpha)^{-1}J_{\mu^*} + h_{\mu^*} + 0(|1 - \alpha|).$$

Substituting this expression in (A7.17) and taking the limit as $\alpha \to 1$, we obtain the desired relations. Q.E.D.

Note that if the average cost $J_{\mu^*}(i)$ corresponding to a Blackwell optimal policy $\{\mu^*, \mu^*, \ldots\}$ is independent of the initial state i [i.e., $J_{\mu^*}(i) = \lambda$ for all i], then, for every μ, each element of the vector $P_\mu J_{\mu^*}$ equals λ. From (A7.16), we then obtain

$$\lambda e + h_{\mu^*} = T(h_{\mu^*}) = \min_\mu [g_\mu + P_\mu h_{\mu^*}],$$

which is the sufficiency condition of Proposition 1. Therefore, to show Proposition 4 it will suffice to show that its hypotheses guarantee that a Blackwell optimal policy yields average cost that is independent of the initial state. This is the basis of our proof.

Proof of Proposition 4

If a stationary policy $\{\mu, \mu, \ldots\}$ gives rise to a Markov chain with a single ergodic class, the corresponding average cost $J_\mu(i)$ is independent of the initial state i. (This was shown in Proposition 8 and can also be shown by extending the proof of Proposition 3.) Therefore, under hypothesis (a) of the proposition, a Blackwell optimal policy yields average cost that is independent of the initial state and the result follows as discussed previously.

Assume hypothesis (b), that is, every pair of states communicates under some stationary policy. Consider a Blackwell optimal policy $\{\mu^*, \mu^*, \ldots\}$. If it yields average cost that is independent of the initial state, we are done, as earlier. Assume the contrary; that is, the sets M and $\overline{M}$ are nonempty, where

$$M = \left\{ i \middle| J_{\mu^*}(i) = \max_j J_{\mu^*}(j) \right\}$$

and $\overline{M}$ is the complement of M. The idea now is that it should be possible to reduce the average cost corresponding to states in M by opening communication to the states in $\overline{M}$, thereby creating a contradiction. Take any states $i \in M$ and $j \in \overline{M}$ and a stationary policy $\{\mu, \mu, \ldots\}$ such that, for some k, $P(x_k = j | x_0 = i, \mu) > 0$. Then there must exist states $m \in M$ and $\overline{m} \in \overline{M}$ such that there is a positive transition probability from m to $\overline{m}$ under μ; that is, $[P_\mu]_{m\overline{m}} = P(x_{k+1} = \overline{m} | x_k = m, \mu) > 0$. It is easily seen that the mth component of $P_\mu J_{\mu^*}$ is strictly less than $\max_i J_{\mu^*}(i)$, which is equal to the mth component of J_{μ^*}. This contradicts the necessary condition (A7.15). Q.E.D.

APPENDIX A

Mathematical Review

The purpose of this and the following appendixes is to provide a list of mathematical and probabilistic definitions, notations, relations, and results that are used frequently in the text. For detailed expositions, the reader may consult the references given in each appendix.

A.1 SETS

If x is a member of the set S, we write $x \in S$. We write $x \notin S$ if x is not a member of S. A set S may be specified by listing its elements within braces. For example, by writing $S = \{x_1, x_2, \ldots, x_n\}$ we mean that the set S consists of the elements $x_1, \ldots, x_n$. A set S may also be specified in the generic form

$$S = \{x | x \text{ satisfies } P\}$$

as the set of elements satisfying property P. For example,

$$S = \{x | x : \text{real}, 0 \leq x \leq 1\}$$

denotes the set of all real numbers x satisfying $0 \leq x \leq 1$.

The *union* of two sets S and T is denoted by $S \cup T$ and the *intersection* of S and T is denoted by $S \cap T$. The union and intersection of a sequence of sets $S_1, S_2, \ldots, S_k, \ldots$ is denoted by $\cup_{k=1}^{\infty} S_k$ and $\cap_{k=1}^{\infty} S_k$, respectively. If S is a subset of T (i.e., if every element of S is also an element of T), we write $S \subset T$ or $T \supset S$.

Finite and Countable Sets

A set S is said to be *finite* if it consists of a finite number of elements. It is said to be *countable* if one can associate with each element of S a nonnegative integer in a way that to each pair of distinct elements of S there correspond two distinct integers. Thus, according to our definition, a finite set is also countable but not conversely. A countable set S that is not finite may be represented by listing its elements $x_0, x_1, x_2, \ldots$ (i.e., $S = \{x_0, x_1, x_2, \ldots\}$. If $A = \{a_0, a_1, \ldots\}$ is a countable set and S_{a_0}, $S_{a_1}, \ldots$ are each countable sets, then the union $\cup_{k=0}^{\infty} S_{a_k}$ (otherwise denoted $\cup_{a \in A} S_a$) is also a countable set.

Sets of Real Numbers

If a and b are real numbers or $+\infty$, $-\infty$, we denote by $[a, b]$ the set of numbers x satisfying $a \leq x \leq b$ (including the possibility $x = +\infty$ or $x = -\infty$). A rounded, instead of square, bracket denotes strict inequality in the definition. Thus $(a, b]$, $[a, b)$, and (a, b) denote the set of all x satisfying $a < x \leq b$, $a \leq x < b$, and $a < x < b$, respectively.

If S is a set of real numbers bounded above, then there is a smallest real number y such that $x \leq y$ for all $x \in S$. This number is called the *least upper bound or supremum* of S and is denoted $\sup\{x|x \in S\}$ or $\max\{x|x \in S\}$. (This is somewhat inconsistent with normal mathematical usage, where the use of max in place of sup indicates that the supremum is attained by some element of S.) Similarly, the greatest real number z such that $z \leq x$ for all $x \in S$ is called the *greatest lower bound or infimum* of S and is denoted $\inf\{x|x \in S\}$ or $\min\{x|x \in S\}$. If S is unbounded above, we write $\sup\{x|x \in S\} = +\infty$, and if it is unbounded below, $\inf\{x|x \in S\} = -\infty$. If S is the empty set, then by convention we write $\inf\{x|x \in S\} = +\infty$ and $\sup\{x|x \in S\} = -\infty$.

A.2 EUCLIDEAN SPACE

The set of all n-tuples $x = (x_1, \ldots, x_n)$, where $x_1, \ldots, x_n$ are real numbers, constitutes the *n-dimensional Euclidean space* denoted R^n.The elements of R^n are referred to as n-dimensional vectors or simply vectors when confusion cannot arise. The one-dimensional Euclidean space R^1 consists of all the real numbers and is denoted R. Vectors in R^n can be added by adding their corresponding components. They can be multiplied by a scalar by multiplication of each component by the scalar. The *inner product* (or scalar product) of two vectors $x = (x_1, \ldots, x_n)$, $y = (y_1, \ldots, y_n)$ is denoted $x'y$ and is equal to $\Sigma_{i=1}^{n} x_i y_i$. The *norm* of a vector $x = (x_1, \ldots, x_n) \in R^n$ is denoted $\|x\|$ and is equal to $(x'x)^{1/2} = (\Sigma_{i=1}^{n} x_i^2)^{1/2}$.

A set of vectors $a_1, a_2, \ldots, a_k$ is said to be *linearly dependent* if there exist scalars $\lambda_1, \lambda_2, \ldots, \lambda_k$, not all zero, such that $\sum_{i=1}^{k} \lambda_i a_i = 0$. If no such set of scalars exists, the vectors are said to be *linearly independent*.

A.3 MATRICES

An *$m \times n$ matrix* is a rectangular array of numbers, called *elements*, arranged in m rows and n columns. The element in the ith row and jth column of a matrix A is denoted by a subscript ij, such as a_{ij}, in which case we write $A = [a_{ij}]$. A square matrix (one with $m = n$) with elements $a_{ij} = 0$ for $i \neq j$ and $a_{ii} = 1$, for $i = 1, \ldots, n$, is said to be an *identity matrix*. The *sum* of two $m \times n$ matrices A and B is written as $A + B$ and is the matrix whose elements are the sum of the corresponding elements in A and B. The *product of a matrix A and a scalar λ*, written as λA or $A\lambda$, is obtained by multiplying each element of A by λ. The *product AB* of an $m \times n$ matrix A and an $n \times p$ matrix B is the $m \times p$ matrix C with elements $c_{ij} = \sum_{k=1}^{n} a_{ik} b_{kj}$. If b is an $n \times 1$ matrix (i.e., an n-dimensional column vector), and A is an $m \times n$ matrix, then Ab is an m-dimensional (column) vector.

The *transpose* of an $m \times n$ matrix A is the $n \times m$ matrix A' with elements $a'_{ij} = a_{ji}$. A square matrix A is *symmetric* if $A' = A$. A square $n \times n$ matrix A is *nonsingular* if there is an $n \times n$ matrix called the *inverse* of A, denoted by A^{-1} such that $A^{-1}A = I = AA^{-1}$, where I is the $n \times n$ identity matrix. A square $n \times n$ matrix is nonsingular if and only if the n vectors that constitute its rows are linearly independent or, equivalently, if the n vectors that constitute its columns are linearly independent.

Partitioned Matrices

It is often convenient to partition a matrix into submatrices by drawing partitioning lines through the matrix. For example, the matrix

$$A = \left[\begin{array}{cc|cc} a_{11} & a_{12} & a_{13} & a_{14} \\ \hline a_{21} & a_{22} & a_{23} & a_{24} \\ a_{31} & a_{32} & a_{33} & a_{34} \end{array}\right]$$

may be partitioned into

$$A = \begin{bmatrix} A_{11} & A_{12} \\ A_{21} & A_{22} \end{bmatrix},$$

where

$$A_{11} = [a_{11} \quad a_{12}], \qquad A_{12} = [a_{13} \quad a_{14}],$$

$$A_{21} = \begin{bmatrix} a_{21} & a_{22} \\ a_{31} & a_{32} \end{bmatrix}, \qquad A_{22} = \begin{bmatrix} a_{23} & a_{24} \\ a_{33} & a_{34} \end{bmatrix}.$$

For a partitioned matrix $A = [B \mid C]$, we use interchangeably the notation $[B, C]$ or $[B\ C]$. The transpose of the partitioned matrix A is

$$A' = \begin{bmatrix} A'_{11} & A'_{21} \\ A'_{12} & A'_{22} \end{bmatrix}.$$

Partitioned matrices may be multiplied just as nonpartitioned matrices provided the dimensions involved in the partitions are compatible. Thus if

$$A = \begin{bmatrix} A_{11} & A_{12} \\ A_{21} & A_{22} \end{bmatrix}, \qquad B = \begin{bmatrix} B_{11} & B_{12} \\ B_{21} & B_{22} \end{bmatrix},$$

then

$$AB = \begin{bmatrix} A_{11}B_{11} + A_{12}B_{21} & A_{11}B_{12} + A_{12}B_{22} \\ A_{21}B_{11} + A_{22}B_{21} & A_{21}B_{12} + A_{22}B_{22} \end{bmatrix},$$

provided the dimensions of the submatrices are such that the preceding products $A_{ij}B_{jk}$, $i, j, k = 1, 2$ can be formed.

Rank of a Matrix

The *rank* of a matrix A is equal to the maximum number of linearly independent row vectors of A. It is also equal to the maximum number of linearly independent column vectors. An $m \times n$ matrix is said to be of *full rank* if the rank of A is equal to the minimum of m and n. A square matrix is of full rank if and only if it is invertible (i.e., nonsingular).

Positive Definite and Semidefinite Matrices

A square symmetric $n \times n$ matrix A is said to be *positive semidefinite* if $x'Ax \geq 0$ for all $x \in R^n$. It is said to be *positive definite* if $x'Ax > 0$ for all nonzero $x \in R^n$. The matrix A is said to be *negative semidefinite* (*definite*) if $(-A)$ is *positive semidefinite* (*definite*).

A positive (negative) definite matrix is invertible and its inverse is also positive (negative) definite. Conversely, an invertible positive (negative) semidefinite matrix is positive (negative) definite. If A and B are $n \times n$ positive semidefinite (definite) matrices, then the matrix $\lambda A + \mu B$ is also positive semidefinite (definite) for all $\lambda > 0$ and $\mu > 0$. If A is an $n \times n$ positive semidefinite matrix and C is an $m \times n$ matrix, then the matrix CAC' is positive semidefinite. If A is positive definite, C has full rank, and $m \leq n$, then CAC' is positive definite.

An $n \times n$ positive definite matrix A can be written as CC' where C is a square invertible matrix. If A is positive semidefinite and its rank is m, then it can be written CC', where C is an $n \times m$ matrix of full rank.

Matrix Inversion Formulas

The following formulas expressing the inverses of various matrices are often very useful. Let A and B be square invertible matrices and C be a matrix of appropriate dimension. Then, if all the following inverses exist,

$$(A + CBC')^{-1} = A^{-1} - A^{-1}C(B^{-1} + C'A^{-1}C)^{-1}C'A^{-1}.$$

The equation can be verified by multiplying the right side by $A + CBC'$ and showing that the product is the identity matrix.

Consider a partitioned matrix M of the form

$$M = \begin{bmatrix} A & B \\ C & D \end{bmatrix}.$$

Then we have

$$M^{-1} = \left[\begin{array}{c|c} Q & -QBD^{-1} \\ \hline -D^{-1}CQ & D^{-1} + D^{-1}CQBD^{-1} \end{array}\right],$$

where

$$Q = (A - BD^{-1}C)^{-1},$$

provided all the inverses exist. The proof is obtained by multiplying M with the expression given for M^{-1} and verifying that the product yields the identity matrix.

A.4 TOPOLOGICAL CONCEPTS IN R^n

Convergence of Sequences

A sequence of vectors $x_0, x_1, \ldots, x_k, \ldots$ in R^n, denoted $\{x_k\}$, is said to *converge to a limit vector* x if $\|x_k - x\| \to 0$ as $k \to \infty$ (i.e., if, given $\epsilon > 0$, there is an N such that for all $k \geq N$ we have $\|x_k - x\| < \epsilon$). If $\{x_k\}$ converges to x, we write $x_k \to x$ or $\lim_{k\to\infty} x_k = x$. As can be easily verified, we have $Ax_k + By_k \to Ax + By$ if $x_k \to x$, $y_k \to y$, and A, B are matrices of appropriate dimension.

A vector x is said to be a *limit point* of a sequence $\{x_k\}$ if there is a subsequence of $\{x_k\}$ that converges to x, that is, if there is an infinite subset K of the nonnegative integers such that $\{x_k\}_{k\in K}$ converges to x.

A sequence of real numbers $\{r_k\}$ that is monotonically nondecreasing (nonincreasing), that is, satisfies $r_k \leq r_{k+1}$ $(r_k \geq r_{k+1})$ for all k, must either converge to a real number or be unbounded above (below), in which case we write $\lim_{k\to\infty} r_k = +\infty$ $(-\infty)$. Given any bounded sequence of real numbers $\{r_k\}$, we may consider the sequence $\{s_k\}$, where $s_k = \sup\{r_i | i \geq k\}$. Since this sequence is monotonically nonincreasing and bounded, it must have a limit called the *limit superior* of $\{r_k\}$ and denoted $\limsup_{k\to\infty} r_k$. We define similarly the *limit inferior* of $\{r_k\}$ and denote it $\liminf_{k\to\infty} r_k$. If $\{r_k\}$ is unbounded above, we write $\limsup_{k\to\infty} r_k = +\infty$, and if it is unbounded below, we write $\liminf_{k\to\infty} r_k = -\infty$. We also use this notation if $r_k \in [-\infty, \infty]$ for all k.

Open, Closed, and Compact Sets

A subset S of R^n is said to be *open* if for every vector $x \in S$ one can find an $\epsilon > 0$ such that $\{z \mid \|z - x\| < \epsilon\} \subset S$. A set S is *closed* if and only if its complement in R^n is open. Equivalently, S is closed if and only if every convergent sequence $\{x_k\}$ with elements in S converges to a point that also belongs to S. A set S is said to be *compact* if and only if it is both closed and bounded (i.e., it is closed and for some $M > 0$ we have $\|x\| \leq M$ for all $x \in S$). A set S is compact if and only if every sequence $\{x_k\}$ with elements in S has at least one limit point that belongs to S. Another important fact is that if $S_0, S_1, \ldots, S_k, \ldots$ is a sequence of nonempty compact sets in R^n such that $S_k \supset S_{k+1}$ for all k, then the intersection $\bigcap_{k=0}^{\infty} S_k$ is a nonempty and compact set.

Continuous Functions

A function f mapping a set S_1 into a set S_2 is denoted by $f : S_1 \to S_2$. A function $f{:}R^n \to R^m$ is said to be *continuous* if $f(x_k) \to f(x)$ whenever $x_k \to x$. Equivalently, f is continuous if, given $x \in R^n$ and $\epsilon > 0$, there is a $\delta > 0$ such that whenever $\|y - x\| < \delta$ we have $\|f(y) - f(x)\| < \epsilon$. The function

$$(a_1 f_1 + a_2 f_2)(\bullet) = a_1 f_1(\bullet) + a_2 f_2(\bullet)$$

is continuous for any two scalars a_1, a_2 and any two continuous functions $f_1, f_2{:}R^n \to R^m$. If S_1, S_2, S_3 are any sets and $f_1{:}S_1 \to S_2, f_2{:}S_2 \to S_3$ are functions, the function $f_2 \bullet f_2{:}S_1 \to S_3$ defined by $(f_2 \bullet f_1)(x) = f_2[f_1(x)]$ is called the *composition* of f_1 and f_2. If $f_1{:}R^n \to R^m$ and $f_2{:} R^m \to R^p$ are continuous, then $f_2 \bullet f_1$ is also continuous.

A.5 CONVEX SETS AND FUNCTIONS

A subset C of R^n is said to be *convex* if for every $x_1, x_2 \in C$ and every scalar α with $0 \leq \alpha \leq 1$ we have $\alpha x_1 + (1 - \alpha)x_2 \in C$. In words, C is convex if the line segment connecting any two points in C belongs to C. A function $f{:}C \to R$ defined over a convex subset C of R^n is said to be *convex* if for every $x_1, x_2 \in C$ and every scalar α with $0 \leq \alpha \leq 1$ we have

$$f[\alpha x_1 + (1 - \alpha)x_2] \leq \alpha f(x_1) + (1 - \alpha)f(x_2).$$

The function f is said to be *concave* if $(-f)$ is convex. If $f{:}C \to R$ is convex, then the sets $\Gamma_\lambda = \{x \mid x \in C, f(x) \leq \lambda\}$ are also convex for every scalar λ. An important property is that a real-valued convex function on R^n is always a continuous function.

If $f_1, f_2, \ldots, f_m$ are convex functions over a convex subset C of R^n and $\alpha_1, \alpha_2, \ldots, \alpha_m$ are nonnegative scalars, then the function $\alpha_1 f_1 + \cdots + \alpha_m f_m$ is also convex over C. If $f{:}R^m \to R$ is convex, A is an $m \times n$

matrix, and b is a vector in R^m, the function $g:R^n \to R$ defined by $g(x) = f(Ax + b)$ is also convex. If $f:R^n \to R$ is convex, then the function $g(x) = E_w \{f(x + w)\}$, where w is a random vector in R^n, is a convex function provided the expected value is well defined and finite for every $x \in R^n$.

For functions $f:R^n \to R$ that are differentiable, there are alternative characterizations of convexity. Thus, if $\nabla f(x)$ denotes the gradient of f at x, that is, the column vector

$$\nabla f(x) = \left[\frac{\partial f(x)}{\partial x^1}, \ldots, \frac{\partial f(x)}{\partial x^n}\right]',$$

the function f is convex if and only if

$$f(y) \geq f(x) + \nabla f(x)'(y - x), \qquad \text{for all } x, y \in R^n.$$

If $\nabla^2 f(x)$ denotes the Hessian matrix of f at x, that is, the matrix

$$\nabla^2 f(x) = \left[\frac{\partial^2 f(x)}{\partial x^i \partial x^j}\right]$$

the elements of which are the second derivatives of f at x, then f is convex if and only if $\nabla^2 f(x)$ is a positive semidefinite matrix for every $x \in R^n$.

For detailed presentations of the material in this appendix, see references [H10], [S27], [R2], [R9], and [R10].

APPENDIX B

On Optimization Theory

Given a real-valued function $f: S \to R$ defined on a set S and a subset $X \subset S$, by the optimization problem

$$\begin{array}{ll} \text{minimize} & f(x) \\ \text{subject to} & x \in X, \end{array} \tag{B.1}$$

we mean the problem of finding an element $x^* \in X$ (called a *minimizing element* or an *optimal solution*) such that

$$f(x^*) \leq f(x), \qquad \text{for all } x \in X.$$

Such an element need not exist. For example, the scalar functions $f(x) = x$ and $f(x) = e^x$ have no minimizing elements over the set of real numbers. The first function decreases without bound to $-\infty$ as x tends toward $-\infty$, while the second decreases toward 0 as x tends toward $-\infty$ but always takes positive values. Given the range of values that $f(x)$ takes as x ranges over X, that is, the set of real numbers

$$\{f(x) | x \in X\}$$

there are two possibilities:

1. The set $\{f(x) | x \in X\}$ is unbounded below (i.e., contains arbitrarily small real numbers) in which case we write

$$\min\{f(x) | x \in X\} = -\infty \quad \text{or} \quad \min_{x \in X} f(x) = -\infty.$$

2. The set $\{f(x) | x \in X\}$ is bounded below; that is, there exists a scalar M such that $M \leq f(x)$ for all $x \in X$. The greatest lower bound of $\{f(x) | x \in X\}$ is

also denoted by

$$\min\{f(x) \mid x \in X\} \quad \text{or} \quad \min_{x \in X} f(x).$$

In either case we call $\min_{x \in X} f(x)$ the *optimal value* of problem (B.1).

A maximization problem of the form

$$\begin{array}{ll} \text{maximize} & f(x) \\ \text{subject to} & x \in X \end{array}$$

may be converted into the minimization problem

$$\begin{array}{ll} \text{minimize} & -f(x) \\ \text{subject to} & x \in X, \end{array}$$

in the sense that both problems have the same optimal solutions, and the optimal value of one is equal to minus the optimal value of the other. The optimal value for the maximization problem is denoted $\max_{x \in X} f(x)$.

Existence of Optimal Solutions

We are often interested in verifying the existence of at least one minimizing element in problem (B.1). Such an element clearly exists when X is a finite set. When X is not finite, the existence of a minimizing point in problem (B.1) is guaranteed if $f: R^n \to R$ is a continuous function and X is a compact subset of R^n. This is the *Weierstrass theorem*. By a related result, existence of a minimizing point is guaranteed if $f: R^n \to R$ is a continuous function, $X = R^n$, and $f(x) \to +\infty$ if $\|x\| \to +\infty$.

Necessary and Sufficient Conditions for Optimality

Such conditions are available when f is a differentiable function on R^n and X is a convex subset of R^n (possibly $X = R^n$). Thus, if x^* is a minimizing point in problem (B.1), $f : R^n \to R$ is a continuously differentiable function on R^n, and X is convex, we have

$$\nabla f(x^*)'(x - x^*) \geq 0, \qquad \text{for all } x \in X, \tag{B.2}$$

where $\nabla f(x^*)$ denotes the gradient of f at x^*. When $X = R^n$ (i.e., the minimization is unconstrained), the necessary condition (B.2) is equivalent to the familiar condition

$$\nabla f(x^*) = 0. \tag{B.3}$$

When f is in addition twice continuously differentiable and $X = R^n$, an additional necessary condition is that the *Hessian matrix* $\nabla^2 f(x^*)$ *be positive semidefinite at* x^*. An important fact is that *if* $f: R^n \to R$ *is a convex function and* X *is convex then (B.2) is both a necessary and a sufficient condition for optimality of a point* x^*.

Minimization of Quadratic Forms

Let $f : R^n \to R$ be a quadratic form

$$f(x) = \tfrac{1}{2}x'Qx + b'x,$$

where Q is a symmetric $n \times n$ matrix and $b \in R^n$. If Q is a positive definite matrix, then f is a convex function. Its gradient is given by

$$\nabla f(x) = Qx + b.$$

By (B.3), a point x^* is a minimizing point of f if and only if

$$\nabla f(x^*) = Qx^* + b = 0,$$

which yields

$$x^* = -Q^{-1}b.$$

For detailed expositions, see references [A3], [L9], [L10], and [Z1].

APPENDIX C

On Probability Theory

This appendix lists selectively some of the basic probabilistic notions we will be using. Its main purpose is to familiarize the reader with some of the terminology we will adopt. It is not meant to be exhaustive, and the reader should consult references [A9], [F2], [P6], and [P7] for detailed treatments, particularly regarding operations with random variables, conditional probability, Bayes' rule, and so on. For a treatment of measure theoretic probability theory see the textbook by R. B. Ash, *Real Analysis and Probability,* Academic Press, New York, 1972.

Probability Space

A *probability space* consists of

(a) a set Ω,

(b) a collection $\mathcal{F}$ of subsets of Ω, called *events*, which includes Ω and has the following properties:

  (1) If A is an event, then the complement $\overline{A} = \{\omega \in \Omega | \omega \notin A\}$ is also an event. (The complement of Ω is the empty set and is considered to be an event.)

  (2) If A_1, A_2 are events, then $A_1 \cap A_2$, $A_1 \cup A_2$ are also events.

  (3) If $A_1, A_2, \ldots, A_k, \ldots$ are events, then $\cup_{k=1}^{\infty} A_k$ and $\cap_{k=1}^{\infty} A_k$ are also events.

(c) a function $P(\cdot)$ assigning to each event A a real number $P(A)$, called the *probability of the event* A, and satisfying

  (1) $P(A) \geq 0$ for every event A.

(2) $P(\Omega) = 1$.
(3) $P(A_1 \cup A_2) = P(A_1) + P(A_2)$ for every pair of disjoint events A_1, A_2.
(4) $P(\cup_{k=1}^{\infty} A_k) = \Sigma_{k=1}^{\infty} P(A_k)$ for every sequence of mutually disjoint events $A_1, A_2, \ldots, A_k, \ldots$.

The function P is referred to as a *probability measure*.

Convention for Finite and Countable Probability Spaces

The case of a probability space where the set Ω is a countable (possibly finite) set is encountered frequently in this text. Where we specify that Ω is finite or countable, we implicitly assume that the associated collection of events is the collection of *all* subsets of Ω (including Ω and the empty set). Under these circumstances, the probability of all events is specified by the probability of the elements of Ω (i.e., of the events consisting of single elements in Ω). Thus, if Ω is a finite set $\Omega = \{\omega_1, \omega_2, \ldots, \omega_n\}$, the probability space is specified by the probabilities $p_1, p_2, \ldots, p_n$, where p_i denotes the probability of the event consisting of ω_i. Similarly, if $\Omega = \{\omega_1, \omega_2, \ldots, \omega_k, \ldots\}$, the probability space is specified by the corresponding probabilities $p_1, p_2, \ldots, p_k, \ldots$. In either case we refer to $(p_1, p_2, \ldots, p_n)$ or $(p_1, p_2, \ldots, p_k, \ldots)$ as a *probability distribution over* Ω.

Random Variables

Given a probability space $(\Omega, \mathcal{F}, P)$, a *random variable* on the probability space is a function $x: \Omega \to R$ such that for every scalar λ the set

$$\{\omega \in \Omega | x(\omega) \leq \lambda\}$$

is an event (i.e., belongs to the collection $\mathcal{F}$).

An n-dimensional *random vector* $x = (x_1, \ldots, x_n)$ is an n-tuple of random variables $x_1, x_2, \ldots, x_n$ each defined on the same probability space.

The *distribution function* $F: R \to R$ of a random variable x is defined by

$$F(z) = P(\{\omega \in \Omega | x(\omega) \leq z\}),$$

that is, $F(z)$ is equal to the probability that the random variable takes a value less than or equal to z.

The distribution function $F: R^n \to R$ of a random vector $x = (x_1, x_2, \ldots, x_n)$ is defined by

$$F(z_1, z_2, \ldots, z_n) = P(\{\omega \in \Omega | x_1(\omega) \leq z_1, x_2(\omega) \leq z_2, \ldots, x_n(\omega) \leq z_n\}).$$

Given the distribution function of a random vector $x = (x_1, \ldots, x_n)$, the (marginal) distribution function of each random variable x_i is obtained from

$$F_i(z_i) = \lim_{z_j \to \infty, j \neq i} F(z_1, z_2, \ldots, z_n).$$

The random variables $x_1, \ldots, x_n$ are said to be *independent* if

$$F(z_1, \ldots, z_n) = F_1(z_1)F_2(z_2) \cdots F_n(z_n),$$

for all scalars $z_1, \ldots, z_n$.

The *expected value of a random variable* x with distribution function F is defined as

$$E\{x\} = \int_{-\infty}^{\infty} z \, dF(z)$$

provided the integral is well defined.

The *expected value of a random vector* $x = (x_1, \ldots, x_n)$ is the vector $E\{x\} = (E\{x_1\}, E\{x_2\}, \ldots, E\{x_n\})$.

The *covariance matrix* of a random vector $x = (x_1, \ldots, x_n)$ with expected value $E\{x\} = (\bar{x}_1, \ldots, \bar{x}_n)$ is defined to be the $n \times n$ symmetric positive semidefinite matrix

$$Q_x = \begin{bmatrix} E\{(x_1 - \bar{x}_1)^2\} & \cdots & E\{(x_1 - \bar{x}_1)(x_n - \bar{x}_n)\} \\ & \vdots & \\ E\{(x_n - \bar{x}_n)(x_1 - \bar{x}_1)\} & \cdots & E\{(x_n - \bar{x}_n)^2\} \end{bmatrix},$$

provided the expectations are well defined.

Two random vectors x and y are said to be *uncorrelated* if

$$E\{(x - E\{x\})(y - E\{y\})'\} = 0,$$

where $(x - E\{x\})$ is viewed as a column vector and $(y - E\{y\})'$ is viewed as a row vector.

The random vector $x = (x_1, \ldots, x_n)$ is said to be characterized by a piecewise continuous *probability density function* $f: R^n \to R$ if f is piecewise continuous and

$$F(z_1, \ldots, z_n) = \int_{-\infty}^{z_1} \int_{-\infty}^{z_2} \cdots \int_{-\infty}^{z_n} f(y_1, \ldots, y_n) \, dy_1 \cdots dy_n,$$

for every $z_1, \ldots, z_n$.

Conditional Probability

We shall restrict ourselves to the case where the underlying probability space Ω is a countable (possibly finite) set and the set of events is the set of all subsets of Ω.

Given two events A and B, we define the *conditional probability of B given A* by

$$P(B|A) = \begin{cases} \dfrac{P(A \cap B)}{P(A)}, & \text{if } P(A) > 0, \\ 0, & \text{if } P(A) = 0. \end{cases}$$

If $B_1, B_2, \ldots$ are a countable (possibly finite) collection of mutually exclusive and exhaustive events (i.e., the sets B_i are disjoint and their union is Ω)

and A is an event, then we have

$$P(A) = \sum_i P(A \cap B_i).$$

From the two preceding relations it is seen that

$$P(A) = \sum_i P(B_i)P(A|B_i).$$

From these expressions we obtain, for every k,

$$P(B_k|A) = \frac{P(A \cap B_k)}{P(A)} = \frac{P(B_k)P(A|B_k)}{\sum_i P(B_i)P(A|B_i)},$$

provided $P(A) > 0$. This relation is referred to as *Bayes' rule*.

Consider now two random vectors x and y on the (countable) probability space taking values in R^n and R^m, respectively [i.e., $x(\omega) \in R^n$, $y(\omega) \in R^m$ for all $\omega \in \Omega$]. Given two subsets X and Y of R^n and R^m, respectively, we denote

$$P(X|Y) = P(\{\omega|x(\omega) \in X\}|\{\omega|y(\omega) \in Y\}).$$

For a fixed vector $w \in R^n$, we define the *conditional distribution function* of x given w by

$$F(z|w) = P(\{\omega|x(\omega) \leq z\}|\{\omega|y(\omega) = w\}),$$

and the *conditional expectation* of x given w by

$$E\{x|w\} = \int_{R^n} z \, dF(z|w),$$

provided the integral is well defined. Note that $E\{x|w\}$ is a function mapping w into R^n.

Finally, let us derive Bayes' rule for random vectors. If $\omega_1, \omega_2, \ldots$ are the elements of Ω, denote

$$z_i = x(\omega_i), \qquad w_i = y(\omega_i), \qquad i = 1, 2, \ldots.$$

Also, for any vectors $z \in R^n$, $w \in R^m$, let us denote

$$P(z) = P(\{\omega|x(\omega) = z\}), \qquad P(w) = P(\{\omega|y(\omega) = w\}).$$

We have $P(z) = 0$ if $z \neq z_i$, $i = 1, 2, \ldots$, and $P(w) = 0$ if $w \neq w_i$, $i = 1, 2, \ldots$. Denote also

$$P(z|w) = P(\{\omega|x(\omega) = z\}|\{\omega|y(\omega) = w\}).$$

Then, if $P(w) > 0$, Bayes' rule yields

$$P(z_i|w) = \frac{P(z_i)P(w|z_i)}{\sum_j P(z_j)P(w|z_j)}, \qquad i = 1, 2, \ldots,$$

$$P(z|w) = 0, \qquad \text{if} \quad z \neq z_i, \quad i = 1, 2, \ldots,$$

where $P(w|z) = P(\{\omega|y(\omega) = w\}|\{\omega|x(\omega) = z\})$.

APPENDIX D

On Finite State Markov Chains

A square $n \times n$ matrix $[p_{ij}]$ is said to be a *stochastic* matrix if all its elements are nonnegative, that is, $p_{ij} \geqslant 0$, $i, j = 1, \ldots, n$, and the sum of the elements of each of its rows equals unity, that is, $\Sigma_{j=1}^{n} p_{ij} = 1$ for all $i = 1, \ldots, n$.

Stationary Finite State Markov Chains

Suppose we are given a stochastic $n \times n$ matrix P together with a finite set $S = \{1, \ldots, n\}$ called the *state space*. The elements of S are called *states*. The pair (S, P) will be referred to as a *stationary finite state Markov chain*. We associate with (S, P) a process whereby an initial state $x_0 \in S$ is chosen in accordance with some initial probability distribution

$$p_0 = (p_0^1, p_0^2, \ldots, p_0^n).$$

Subsequently, a transition is made from state x_0 to a new state $x_1 \in S$ in accordance with a probability distribution specified by P as follows. The probability that the new state will be j is equal to p_{ij} whenever the initial state is i; that is,

$$P(x_1 = j | x_0 = i) = p_{ij}, \qquad i, j = 1, \ldots, n.$$

Similarly, subsequent transitions produce states $x_2, x_3, \ldots$ in accordance with

$$P(x_{k+1} = j | x_k = j) = p_{ij}, \qquad i, j = 1, \ldots, n. \tag{D.1}$$

The probability that after the kth transition the state x_k will be equal to j, given that the initial state x_0 is equal to i, is denoted

$$p_{ij}^k = P(x_k = j|x_0 = i), \qquad i, j = 1, \ldots, n. \tag{D.2}$$

These probabilities are easily seen to be equal to the elements of the matrix P^k (P raised to the kth power), in the sense that p_{ij}^k is the element in the ith row and jth column of P^k:

$$P^k = [p_{ij}^k]. \tag{D.3}$$

Given the initial probability distribution p_0 of the state x_0 (viewed as a row vector in R^n), the probability distribution of the state x_k after k transitions

$$p_k = (p_k^1, p_k^2, \ldots, p_k^n)$$

(viewed again as a row vector) is given by

$$p_k = p_0 P^k, \qquad k = 1, 2, \ldots. \tag{D.4}$$

This relation follows immediately from (D.2) and (D.3) once we write

$$p_k^j = \sum_{i=1}^n P(x_k = j|x_0 = i)p_0^i = \sum_{i=1}^n p_{ij}^k p_0^i.$$

Classification of States of a Markov Chain

Given a stationary finite state Markov chain (S, P), we say that two states i and j *communicate* if there exist two positive integers k_1 and k_2 such that $p_{ij}^{k_1} \geqslant 0$ and $p_{ji}^{k_2} > 0$. In words, states i and j communicate if one can be reached from the other with positive probability.

Let $\tilde{S} \subset S$ be a subset of states such that

1. All states in $\tilde{S}$ communicate.
2. If $i \in \tilde{S}$ and $j \notin \tilde{S}$, then $p_{ij}^k = 0$ for all k.

Then we say that $\tilde{S}$ forms an *ergodic class* of states.

If S forms by itself an ergodic class (i.e., all states communicate with each other), then we say that the Markov chain is *irreducible*. It is possible that there exist several ergodic classes. It is also possible to prove that at least one ergodic class must exist. States that do not belong to any ergodic class are called *transient*. Transient states are characterized by the fact that

$$\lim_{k\to\infty} p_{ii}^k = 0, \qquad \text{if and only if } i \text{ is transient.}$$

In other words, if the process starts at a transient state, the probability of returning to the same state after k transitions diminishes to zero as k tends to infinity.

The definitions imply that once an ergodic class is entered then the process remains within this ergodic class for every subsequent transition. Thus, if the process starts within an ergodic class, it stays within that class.

If it starts at a transient state, it eventually (with probability one) enters an ergodic class after a number of transitions and subsequently remains there.

Limiting Probabilities

An important property of any stochastic matrix P is that the matrix P^* defined by

$$P^* = \lim_{N\to\infty} \frac{1}{N} \sum_{k=0}^{N-1} P^k$$

exists [in the sense that the sequences of the elements of $(1/N) \sum_{k=0}^{N-1} P^k$ converge to the corresponding elements of P^*]. The elements p_{ij}^* of P^* satisfy

$$p_{ij}^* \geq 0, \qquad \sum_{j=1}^{n} p_{ij}^* = 1, \qquad i = 1, \ldots, n.$$

That is, P^* is a stochastic matrix. A proof of this fact is given in Proposition A7.1 in the appendix of Chapter 7.

If $\tilde{S} \subset S$ is an ergodic class and $i, j \in \tilde{S}$, then it may be proved that, for all $k \in \tilde{S}$,

$$p_{ik}^* = p_{jk}^* > 0,$$

so that *if a Markov chain is irreducible, the matrix P^* has identical rows.* Also, if j is a transient state, we have

$$p_{ij}^* = 0, \qquad \text{for all } i \in S,$$

so the columns of the matrix P^* corresponding to transient states are identically zero.

First Passage Times

Let us denote by q_{ij}^k the probability that the state will be j for the first time after exactly $k \geq 1$ transitions given that the initial state is i; that is,

$$q_{ij}^k = P(x_k = j, x_m \neq j, 1 \leq m < k | x_0 = i).$$

Denote also, for fixed i and j,

$$K_{ij} = \min\{k \geq 1 | x_k = j, x_0 = i\}.$$

Then K_{ij}, called the *first passage time from i to j*, may be viewed as a random variable. We have, for every $k = 1, 2, \ldots,$

$$P(K_{ij} = k) = q_{ij}^k,$$

and we write

$$P(K_{ij} = \infty) = P(x_k \neq j, k = 1, 2, \ldots | x_0 = i) = 1 - \sum_{k=1}^{\infty} q_{ij}^k.$$

Of course, it is possible that $\Sigma_{k=1}^{\infty} q_{ij}^k < 1$. This will occur, for example, if j cannot be reached from i in which case $q_{ij}^k = 0$ for all $k = 1, 2, \ldots$. The *mean first passage time* from i to j is the expected value of K_{ij}:

$$E\{K_{ij}\} = \begin{cases} \sum_{k=1}^{\infty} kq_{ij}^k, & \text{if } \sum_{k=1}^{\infty} q_{ij}^k = 1, \\ \infty, & \text{if } \sum_{k=1}^{\infty} q_{ij}^k < 1. \end{cases}$$

It may be proved that if i and j belong to the same ergodic class then

$$E\{K_{ij}\} < \infty.$$

If i and j belong to two different ergodic classes, then $E\{K_{ij}\} = E\{K_{ji}\} = \infty$. If i belongs to an ergodic class and j is transient, we have $E\{K_{ij}\} = \infty$. For detailed presentations, see [A9], [C2], [K6], and [R8].

References

[A1] Anderson, B. D. O., and Moore, J. B., *Optimal Filtering*. Prentice-Hall, Englewood Cliffs, N.J., 1979.

[A2] Aoki, M., *Optimization of Stochastic Systems—Topics in Discrete-Time Systems*. Academic Press, New York, 1967.

[A3] Aoki, M., *Introduction to Optimization Techniques*. Macmillan, New York, 1971.

[A4] Aoki, M., and Li, M. T., Optimal discrete-time control systems with cost for observation, *IEEE Trans. Automatic Control* **AC-14** (1969), 165–175.

[A5] Arrow, K. J., *Aspects of the Theory of Risk Bearing*. Yrjo Jahnsson Lecture Series, Helsinki, Finland, 1965.

[A6] Arrow, K. M., Blackwell, D., and Girshick, M. A., Bayes and minimax solutions of sequential design problems, *Econometrica* **17** (1949), 213–244.

[A7] Arrow, K. J., Harris, T., and Marschack, J., Optimal inventory policy, *Econometrica* **19** (1951), 250–272.

[A8] Arrow, K. H., Karlin, S., and Scarf, H., *Studies in the Mathematical Theory of Inventory and Production*. Stanford University Press, Stanford, California, 1958.

[A9] Ash, R. B., *Basic Probability Theory*. Wiley, New York, 1970.

[A10] Ash, R. B., and Gardner, M. F., *Topics in Stochastic Processes*. Academic Press, New York, 1975.

[A11] Aström, K. J., *Introduction to Stochastic Control Theory*. Academic Press, New York, 1970.

[A12] Aström, K. J., Theory and applications of adaptive control—a survey, *Automatica,* **19** (1983), 471–486.

[A13] Aström, K. J., and Wittenmark, B. *Computer Controlled Systems*. Prentice-Hall, Englewood Cliffs, N.J., 1984.

[A14] Aström, K. J., and Wittenmark, B., On self-tuning regulators, *Automatica* **9** (1973), 185–199.

[A15] Atkinson, R. C., Bower, G. H., and Crothers, E. J., *An Introduction to Mathematical Learning Theory*. Wiley, New York, 1965.

[B1] Bar-Shalom, Y., and Tse, E., Dual effect, certainty equivalence, and separation in stochastic control, *IEEE Trans. Automatic Control* **AC-19** (1974), 494–500.

[B2] Baras, J. S., Dorsey, A. J., and Makowski, A. M., Two competing queues with linear costs: The μc-rule is often optimal, Report SRR 83-1, Department of Electrical Engineering, University of Maryland, 1983.

[B3] Baras, J. S., and Dorsey, A. J., Stochastic control of two partially observed competing queues, *IEEE Trans. Aut. Control* **AC-26** (1981), 1106–1117.

[B4] Bather, J., Optimal decision procedures for finite Markov chains, *Advances in Appl. Probability* **5** (1973), 328–339, 521–540, 541–553.

[B5] Bellman, R., *Dynamic Programming*. Princeton University Press, Princeton, N.J., 1957.

[B6] Bellman, R., and Dreyfus, S., *Applied Dynamic Programming*. Princeton University Press, Princeton, N.J., 1962.

[B7] Bensoussan, A., and Lions, J. L., *Applications des Inequations Variationnelles en Controle Stochastique*. Dunod, Paris, 1978.

[B8] Bertsekas, D. P., On the separation theorem for linear systems, quadratic criteria, and correlated noise, unpubl. rep., Electronic Systems Lab., MIT, Cambridge, Mass., September 1970.

[B9] Bertsekas, D. P., Control of uncertain systems with a set-membership description of the uncertainty.'' Ph.D. Dissertation, MIT, Cambridge, Mass., 1971.

[B10] Bertsekas, D. P., Stochastic optimization problems with nondifferentiable cost functionals with an application in stochastic programming, *Proc. IEEE Decision and Control Conf.,* New Orleans, La., December 1972.

[B11] Bertsekas, D. P., On the solution of some minimax problems, *Proc. IEEE Decision and Control Conf.,* New Orleans, La., December 1972.

[B12] Bertsekas, D. P., Infinite time reachability of state space regions by using feedback control, *IEEE Trans. Automatic Control* **AC-17** (1972), 604–613.

[B13] Bertsekas, D. P., Stochastic optimization problems with nondifferentiable cost functionals, *J. Optimization Theory Appl.* **12** (1973), 218–231.

[B14] Bertsekas, D. P., Linear convex stochastic control problems over an infinite time horizon, *IEEE Trans. Automatic Control* **AC-18** (1973), 314–315.

[B15] Bertsekas, D. P., Necessary and sufficient conditions for existence of an optimal portfolio, *J. Econom. Theory* **8** (1974), 235–247.

[B16] Bertsekas, D. P., Monotone mappings with application in dynamic programming, *SIAM J. Control and Optimization* **15** (1977), 438–464.

[B17] Bertsekas, D. P., On error bounds for successive approximation methods, *IEEE Trans. Automatic Control* **AC-21** (1976), 394–396.

[B18] Bertsekas, D. P., Convergence of discretization procedures in dynamic programming, *IEEE Trans. Automatic Control* **AC-20** (1975), 415–419.

[B19] Bertsekas, D. P., Distributed dynamic programming, *IEEE Trans. Automatic Control* **AC-27** (1982), 610–616.

[B20] Bertsekas, D. P., and Castanon, D., Dynamic Aggregation Methods for Discounted Markovian Decision Problems, Proc. of 25th IEEE Conference on Decision and Control, Athens, Greece, Dec. 1986; *IEEE Trans. on Aut. Control* (to appear).

[B21] Bertsekas, D. P., and Rhodes, I. B., On the minimax reachability of target sets and target tubes, *Automatica* **7** (1971), 233–247.

[B22] Bertsekas, D. P., and Rhodes, I. B., Sufficiently informative functions and the minimax feedback control of uncertain dynamic systems, *IEEE Trans. Automatic Control* **AC-18** (1973), 117–124.

[B23] Bertsekas, D. P., and Shreve, S. E., *Stochastic Optimal Control: The Discrete Time Case*. Academic Press, New York, 1978.

[B24] Bertsekas, D. P., and Shreve, S. E., Existence of optimal stationary policies in deterministic optimal control, *J. Math. Anal. and Appl.* **69** (1979), 607–620.

[B25] Billinsgley, P., The singular function of bold play, *American Scientist* **71** (1983), 392–397.

[B26] Blackwell, D., Discrete dynamic programming, *Ann. Math. Statist.* **33** (1962), 719–726.

[B27] Blackwell, D., Discounted dynamic programming, *Ann. Math. Statist.* **36** (1965), 226–235.

[B28] Blackwell, D., Positive dynamic programming, *Proc. 5th Berkeley Symp. Math., Statist., and Probability* **1** (1965), 415–418.

[B29] Blackwell, D., On stationary policies, *J. Roy. Statist. Soc. Ser. A,* **133** (1970), 33–38.

[B30] Blackwell, D., and Girshick, M. A., *Theory of Games and Statistical Decisions*. Wiley, New York, 1954.

[B31] Blake, I. F., and Thomas, J. B., On a class of processes arising in linear estimation theory, *IEEE Trans. Information Theory* **IT-14** (1968), 12–16.

[B32] Borkar, V., and Varaiya, P. P., Identification and adaptive control of Markov chains, *SIAM J. on Control and Optimization* **20** (1982), 470–489.

[B33] Borkar, V., and Varaiya, P. P., Adaptive control of Markov chains, I: Finite parameter set, *IEEE Trans. Aut. Control* **AC-24** (1979), 953–958.

[B34] Brown, B. W., On the iterative method of dynamic programming on a finite space discrete Markov process, *Ann. Math. Statist.* **36** (1965), 1279–1286.

[C1] Chernoff, H., *Sequential Analysis and Optimal Design*. Regional Conference Series in Applied Mathematics, SIAM, Philadelphia, Pa., 1972.

[C2] Chung, K. L., *Markov Chains with Stationary Transition Probabilities*. Springer-Verlag, Berlin and New York, 1960.

[C3] Cooper, C. A., and Nahi, N. E., An optimal stochastic control problem with observation cost, *Proc. Joint Automatic Control Conf.*, Atlanta, Ga., June 1970.

[C4] Courcoubetis, C., and Varaiya, P. P., The service process with least thinking time maximizes resource utilization, *IEEE Trans. Aut. Control* **AC-29** (1984), 1005–1008.

[C5] Crabill, T. B., Gross, D., and Magazine, M. J., A classified bibliography of research on optimal design and control of queues, *Operations Res.* **25** (1977), 219–232.

[D1] DeGroot, M. H., *Optimal Statistical Decisions*. McGraw-Hill, New York, 1970.

[D2] Denardo, E. V., Contraction mappings in the theory underlying dynamic programming, *SIAM Rev.* **9** (1967), 165–177.

[D3] D'Epenoux, F., Sur un probleme de production et de stockage dans l'aleatoire, *Rev. Francaise Automat. Informat. Recherche Operationnelle* **14** (1960) (English Transl.: *Management Sci.* **10** (1963), 98–108).

[D4] Derman, C., *Finite State Markovian Decision Processes*. Academic Press, New York, 1970.

[D5] Deshpande, J. G., Upadhyay, T. N., and Lainiotis, D. G., Adaptive control of linear control systems, *Automatica* **9** (1973), 107–115.

[D6] Dial, R., and others, A computational analysis of alternative algorithms and labeling techniques for finding shortest path trees, *Networks* **9** (1979), 215–248.

[D7] Doshi, B., and Shreve, S., Strong consistency of a modified maximum likelihood estimator for controlled Markov chains, *J. of Applied Probability* **17** (1980), 726–734.

[D8] Dreyfus, S. E., *Dynamic Programming and the Calculus of Variations*. Academic Press, New York, 1965.

[D9] Dubins, L., and Savage, L. M., *How to Gamble If You Must*. McGraw-Hill, New York, 1965.

[D10] Dynkin, E. B., Controlled random sequences, *Theor. Probability Appl.* **10** (1965), 1–14.

[D11] Dynkin, E. B., and Juskevic, A. A., *Controlled Markov Processes*. Springer-Verlag, New York, 1979.

[E1] Eaton, J. H., and Zadeh, L. A., Optimal pursuit strategies in discrete state probabilistic systems, *Trans. ASME Ser. D. J. Basic Eng.* **84** (1962), 23–29.

[E2] Eckles, J. E., Optimum maintenance with incomplete information, *Operations Res.* **16** (1968), 1058–1067.

[E3] Ephremides, A., Varaiya, P. P., and Walrand, J. C., A simple dynamic routing problem, *IEEE Trans. Aut. Control* **AC-25** (1980), 690–693.

[F1] Federgruen, A., Schweitzer, P. J., and Tijms, H. C., Denumerable undiscounted semi-Markov decision processes with unbounded rewards, *Math. of Operations Res.* **8** (1983), 298–313.

[F2] Feller, W., *An Introduction to Probability Theory and Its Applications,* 3rd ed. Wiley, New York, 1968.

[F3] Fleming, W., and Rishel, R., *Optimal Deterministic and Stochastic Control.* Springer-Verlag, New York, 1975.

[F4] Forney, G. D., The Viterbi algorithm, *Proc. IEEE* **61** (1973), 268–278.

[F5] Fox, B. L., Finite state approximations to denumerable state dynamic programs, *J. Math. Anal. Appl.* **34** (1971), 665–670.

[G1] Gittins, J. C., Bandit processes and dynamic allocation indices, *J. Roy. Statist. Soc., B,* **41** (1979), 148–164.

[G2] Gittins, J. C., and Jones, D. M., A dynamic allocation index for the sequential design of experiments, in *Progress in Statistics* (J. Gani, ed.). North-Holland, Amsterdam, 1974, pp. 241–266.

[G3] Goodwin, G. C., and Sin, K. S. S., *Adaptive Filtering, Prediction, and Control.* Prentice-Hall, Englewood Cliffs, N.J., 1984.

[G4] Groen, G. J., and Atkinson, R. C., Models for optimizing the learning process, *Psychol. Bull.* **66** (1966), 309–320.

[G5] Gunckel, T. L., and Franklin, G. R., A general solution for linear sampled-data control, *Trans. ASME Ser. D. J. Basic Engrg.* **85** (1963), 197–201.

[H1] Hajek, B., Optimal control of two interacting service stations, *IEEE Trans. Aut. Control* **29** (1984), 491–499.

[H2] Hajek, B., and van Loon, T., Decentralized dynamic control of a multiaccess broadcast channel, *IEEE Trans. Aut. Control* **AC-27** (1982), 559–569.

[H3] Harrison, J. M., A priority queue with discounted linear costs, *Operations Res.* **23** (1975), 260–269.

[H4] Harrison, J. M., Dynamic scheduling of a multiclass queue: Discount optimality, *Operations Res.* **23** (1975), 270–282.

[H5] Hastings, N. A. J., Some notes on dynamic programming and replacement, *Operational Res. Quart.* **19** (1968), 453–464.

[H6] Haurie, A., and L'Ecuyer, P., Approximation and bounds in discrete event dynamic programming, *IEEE Trans. Aut. Control* **AC-31** (1986), 227–235.

[H7] Hendrikx, M., Van Nunen, J., and Wessels, J., On iterative optimization of structured Markov decision-processes, *Math. Oper. u. Statist.* **15** (1984), 439–459.

[H8] Heyman, D. P., and Sobel, M. J., *Stochastic Models in Operations Research,* McGraw-Hill, New York, Vol. I, 1982, Vol. II, 1984.

[H9] Hinderer, K., *Foundations of Non-Stationary Dynamic Programming with Discrete Time Parameter.* Springer-Verlag, New York, 1970.

[H10] Hoffman, K., and Kunze, R., *Linear Algebra.* Prentice-Hall, Englewood Cliffs, N.J., 1961.

[H11] Holt, C. C., Modigliani, F., and Simon, H. A., A linear decision rule for production and employment scheduling, *Management Sci.* **2** (1955), 1–30.

[H12] Hordijk, A., and Tijms, H., The method of successive approximations and Markovian decision problems, *Operations Res.* **22** (1974), 519–521.

[H13] Hordijk, A., and Tijms, H. C., Convergence results and approximations for optimal (s, S) policies, *Management Sci.* **20** (1974), 1432–1438.

[H14] Hordijk, A., and Tijms, H. C., On a conjecture of Iglehart, *Management Sci.* **21** (1975), 1342–1345.

[H15] Howard, R., *Dynamic Programming and Markov Processes.* MIT Press, Cambridge, Mass., 1960.

[H16] Howard, R., *Dynamic Probabilistic Systems,* Vols. I and II. Wiley, New York, 1971.

[I1] *IEEE Trans. Aut. Control,* special issue on Linear–Quadratic Gaussian Problem, **AC-16** (1971).

[I2] Iglehart, D. L., Optimality of (S, s) policies in the infinite horizon dynamic inventory problem, *Management Sci.* **9** (1963), 259–267.

[I3] Iglehart, D. L., Dynamic programming and stationary analysis of inventory problems, *in* Scarf, H., Gilford, D., and Shelly, M. (eds.), *Multistage Inventory Models and Techniques.* Stanford University Press, Stanford, Calif., 1963.

[J1] Jacobson, D. H., Optimal stochastic linear systems with exponential performance criteria and their relation to deterministic differential games, *IEEE Trans. Aut. Control* **AC-18** (1973), 124–131.

[J2] Jacobson, D. H., A general result in stochastic optimal control of nonlinear discrete-time systems with quadratic performance criteria, *J. Math. Anal. Appl.* **47** (1974), 153–161.

[J3] Jazwinski, A. H., *Stochastic Processes and Filtering Theory.* Academic Press, New York, 1970.

[J4] Jewell, W., Markov renewal programming I and II, *Operations Res.* **11** (1963), 938–971.

[J5] Joseph, P. D., and Tou, J. T., On linear control theory, *AIEE Trans.* **80** (II) (1961), 193–196.

[K1] Kalman, R. E., A new approach to linear filtering and prediction problems, *Trans. ASME Ser. D. J. Basic Engrg.* **82** (1960), 35–45.

[K2] Kalman, R. E., and Koepcke, R. W., Optimal synthesis of linear sampling control systems using generalized performance indexes, *Trans. ASME* **80** (1958), 1820–1826.

[K3] Karush, W., and Dear, E. E., Optimal stimulus presentation strategy for a stimulus sampling model of learning, *J. Mathematical Psychology* **3** (1966), 15–47.

[K4] Katehakis, M., and Veinott, A. F., *The Multi-Armed Bandit Problem: Decomposition and Computation,* T.R. 41, Department of Operations Research, Stanford University, Stanford, Calif., July 1985.

[K5] Kaufmann, A., and Cruon, R., *Dynamic Programming*. Academic Press, New York, 1967.

[K6] Kemeny, J. G., and Snell, J. L., *Finite Markov Chains*. Van Nostrand-Reinhold, New York, 1960.

[K7] Kimemia, J., Gershwin, S. B., and Bertsekas, D. P., Computation of production control policies by a dynamic programming technique, in *Analysis and Optimization of Systems* (A. Bensoussan and J. L. Lions, eds.), Springer-Verlag, New York, 1982, pp. 243–269.

[K8] Kimemia, J., Hierarchical control of production in flexible manufacturing systems, Ph.D. thesis, MIT, Department of Electrical Engineering and Computer Science, April 1982.

[K9] Kleinman, D. L., On an iterative technique for Riccati equation computations, *IEEE Trans. Aut. Control,* **AC-13** (1968), 114–115.

[K10] Kumar, P. R., A survey of some results in stochastic adaptive control, *SIAM J. Control Optimization* **23** (1985), 329–380.

[K11] Kumar, P. R., Optimal adaptive control of linear–quadratic–Gaussian systems, *SIAM J. Control Optimization* **21** (1983), 163–178.

[K12] Kumar, P. R., and Lin, W., Optimal adaptive controllers for unknown Markov chains, *IEEE Trans. Aut. Control* **AC-27** (1982), 765–774.

[K13] Kumar, P. R., and Varaiya, P. P., *Stochastic Systems: Estimation, Identification, and Adaptive Control*. Prentice-Hall, Englewood Cliffs, N.J., 1986.

[K14] Kushner, H. J., *Introduction to Stochastic Control*. Holt, Rinehart and Winston, New York, 1971.

[K15] Kushner, H. J., Optimality conditions for the average cost per unit time problem with a diffusion model, *SIAM J. Control Optimization* **16** (1978), 330–346.

[L1] Lasserre, J. B., A mixed forward–backward dynamic programming method using parallel computation, *J. Optimization Theory Appl.* **45** (1985), 165–168.

[L2] Levy, D., *The Chess Computer Handbook*. B. T. Batsford Ltd., London, 1984.

[L3] Lin, W., and Kumar, P. R., Optimal control of a queueing system with two heterogeneous servers, *IEEE Trans. Aut. Control* **AC-29** (1984), 696–703.

[L4] Lippman, S., Applying a new device in the optimization of exponential queuing systems, *Operations Res.* **23** (1975), 687–710.

[L5] Liusternik, L., and Sobolev, V., *Elements of Functional Analysis*. Ungar, New York, 1961.

[L6] Ljung, L., On positive real transfer functions and the convergence of some recursions, *IEEE Trans. Aut. Control* **AC-22** (1977), 539–551.

[L7] Ljung, L., *System Identification: Theory for the User*. Prentice-Hall, Englewood Cliffs, N.J., 1986.

[L8] Ljung, L., and Soderstrom, T., *Theory and Practice of Recursive Identification*. MIT Press, Cambridge, Mass., 1983.

[L9] Luenberger, D. G., *Optimization by Vector Space Methods*. Wiley, New York, 1969.

[L10] Luenberger, D. G., *Linear and Nonlinear Programming*. Addison-Wesley, Reading, Mass., 1984.

[M1] Malinvaud, E., First order certainty equivalence, *Econometrica* **37** (1969), 706–718.

[M2] Mandl, P., Estimation and control in Markov chains, *Advances in Applied Probability* **6** (1974), 40–60.

[M3] Manne, A., Linear programming and sequential decisions, *Management Sci.* **6** (1960), 259–267.

[M4] Markovitz, H., *Portfolio Selection*. Wiley, New York, 1959.

[M5] McQueen, J., A modified dynamic programming method for Markovian decision problems, *J. Math. Anal. Appl.* **14** (1966), 38–43.

[M6] Meditch, J. S. *Stochastic Optimal Linear Estimation and Control*. McGraw-Hill, New York, 1969.

[M7] Mendel, J. M., *Discrete Techniques of Parameter Estimation—The Equation Error Formulation*. Dekker, New York, 1973.

[M8] Morton, T. E., On the asymptotic convergence rate of cost differences for Markovian decision processes, *Operations Res.* **19** (1971), 244–248.

[M9] Morton, T. E., and Wecker, W., Discounting, ergodicity and convergence for Markov decision processes, *Management Sci.* **23** (1977), 890–900.

[M10] Mossin, J., Optimal multi-period portfolio policies, *J. Business* **41** (1968), 215–229.

[N1] Nahi, N., *Estimation Theory and Applications*. Wiley, New York, 1969.

[N2] Nemhauser, G. L., *Introduction to Dynamic Programming*. Wiley, New York, 1966.

[N3] Newborn, M., *Computer Chess*. Academic Press, New York, 1975.

[N4] Norman, J. M., Dynamic programming in tennis—When to use a fast serve, *J. Opl. Res. Soc.* **36** (1985), 75–77.

[O1] Odoni, A. R., On finding the maximal gain for Markov decision processes, *Operations Res.* **17** (1969), 857–860.

[O2] Omura, J. K., On the Viterbi decoding algorithm, *IEEE Trans. Information Theory* **IT-15** (1969), 177–179.

[O3] Ornstein, D., On the existence of stationary optimal strategies, *Proc. Amer. Math. Soc.* **20** (1969), 563–569.

[O4] Ortega, J. M., and Rheinboldt, W. C., *Iterative Solution of Nonlinear Equations in Several Variables*. Academic Press, New York, 1970.

[P1] Pallu de la Barriere, R., *Optimal Control Theory*. Saunders, Philadelphia, 1967.

[P2] Papadimitriou, C. H., and Steiglitz, K., *Combinatorial Optimization: Algorithms and Complexity*. Prentice-Hall, Englewood Cliffs, N.J., 1982.

[P3] Papadimitriou, C. H., and Tsitsiklis, J. N., The complexity of Markov decision processes, *Math. of Operations Research* (to appear).

[P4] Pape, V., Implementation and efficiency of Moore algorithms for the shortest path problem, *Math. Progr.* **7** (1974), 212–222.

[P5] Papoulis, A., *Signal Analysis*. McGraw-Hill, New York, 1977.

[P6] Papoulis, A., *Probability, Random Variables and Stochastic Processes*. McGraw-Hill, New York, 1965.

[P7] Parzen, E., *Modern Probability Theory and Its Applications*. Wiley, New York, 1960.

[P8] Pattipati, K. R., and Kleinman, D. L., Priority assignment using dynamic programming for a class of queueing systems, *IEEE Trans. Aut. Control* **AC-26** (1981), 1095–1106.

[P9] Pearl, J., *Heuristics*. Addison-Wesley, Reading, Mass., 1984.

[P10] Platzman, L., Comments on "Optimal and suboptimal stationary controls for Markov chains," *IEEE Trans. Aut. Control* **AC-24** (1979), 375.

[P11] Platzman, L., Improved conditions for convergence in undiscounted Markov renewal programming, *Operations Res.* **25** (1977), 529–533.

[P12] Popyak, J. L., Brown, R. L., and White, C. C., Discrete versions of an algorithm due to Varaiya, *IEEE Trans. Aut. Control* **AC-24** (1979), 503–504.

[P13] Porteus, E., Bounds and transformations for finite Markov decision chains, *Operations Res.* **23** (1975), 761–784.

[P14] Porteus, E., Some bounds for discounted sequential decision processes, *Management Sci.* **18** (1971), 7–11.

[P15] Porteus, E., Overview of iterative methods for discounted finite Markov and semi-Markov decision chains, in *Rec. Developments in Markov Decision Processes,* R. Hartley, L. C. Thomas, and D. J. White (eds.), Academic Press, London, 1980.

[P16] Puterman, M. L. (ed.), *Dynamic Programming and Its Applications,* Academic Press, New York, 1978.

[P17] Puterman, M. L., and Brumelle, S. L., The analytic theory of policy iteration, in *Dynamic Programming and Its Applications,* M. L. Puterman (ed.), Academic Press, New York, 1978.

[P18] Puterman, M. L., and Shin, M. C., Action elimination procedures for modified policy iteration algorithms, *Operations Res.* **30** (1982), 301–318.

[P19] Puterman, M. L., and Shin, M. C., Modified policy iteration algorithms for discounted Markov decision problems, *Management Sci.* **24** (1978), 1127–1137.

[R1] Rivest, R. L., Network control by Bayesian broadcast, MIT, LCS Report, August 1985.

[R2] Rockafellar, R. T., *Convex Analysis*. Princeton University Press, Princeton, N.J., 1970.

[R3] Rockafellar, R. T., and Wets, R., Stochastic convex programming: Basic duality, *Pacific J. Math.* **62** (1976), 173–195.

[R4] Rosberg, Z., Varaiya, P. P., and Walrand, J. C., Optimal control of service in tandem queues, *IEEE Trans. Aut. Control* **AC–27** (1982), 600–609.

[R5] Ross, S. M., Arbitrary state Markovian decision processes, *Ann. Math. Statist.* **39** (1968), 2118–2122.

[R6] Ross, S. M., *Applied Probability Models with Optimization Applications.* Holden-Day, San Francisco, 1970.

[R7] Ross, S. M., *Introduction to Stochastic Dynamic Programming.* Academic Press, New York, 1983.

[R8] Ross, S. M., *Stochastic Processes.* Wiley, New York, 1983.

[R9] Royden, H. L., *Real Analysis.* Macmillan, New York, 1968.

[R10] Rudin, E., *Principles of Mathematical Analysis.* McGraw-Hill, New York, 1964.

[S1] Saridis, G. N., *Self-Organizing Control of Stochastic Systems.* Dekker, New York, 1977.

[S2] Saridis, G. N., and Dao, T. K., A learning approach to the parameter-adaptive self-organizing control problem, *Automatica* **8** (1972), 589–597.

[S3] Sawaragi, Y., and Yoshikawa, T., Discrete-time Markovian decision processes with incomplete state observation, *Ann. Math. Statist.* **41** (1970), 78–86.

[S4] Scarf, H., The optimality of (s, S) policies for the dynamic inventory problem, *Proceedings of the 1st Stanford Symposium on Mathematical Methods in the Social Sciences.* Stanford University Press, Stanford, Calif., 1960.

[S5] Schal, M., On the optimality of (s, S) policies in dynamic inventory models with finite horizon, *SIAM J. Appl. Math.* **30** (1976), 528–537.

[S6] Schal, M., Conditions for optimality in dynamic programming and for the limit of n-stage optimal policies to be optimal, *Z. Wahrscheinlichkeitstheorie und Verw. Gebiete* **32** (1975), 179–196.

[S7] Schweitzer, P. J., Perturbation theory and finite Markov chains, *J. Appl. Prob.* **5** (1968), 401–413.

[S8] Schweitzer, P. J., Bottleneck determination in networks of queues, Graduate School of Management Working Paper No. 8107, University of Rochester, Rochester, N.Y., February 1981.

[S9] Schweitzer, P. J., Data transformations for Markov renewal programming, talk at National ORSA Meeting, Atlantic City, N.Y., November 1972.

[S10] Schweitzer, P. J., Iterative solution of the functional equations of undiscounted Markov renewal programming, *J. Math. Anal. Appl.* **34** (1971), 495–501.

[S11] Schweitzer, P. J., Puterman, M. L., and Kindle, K. W., Iterative aggregation–disaggregation procedures for solving discounted semi-Markovian reward processes, *Operations Research* **33** (1985), 589–605.

[S12] Schweitzer, P. J., and Federgruen, A., The asymptotic behavior of value iteration in Markov decision problems, *Math. Operations Res.* **2** (1977), 360–381.

[S13] Schweitzer, P. J., and Federgruen, A., The functional equations of undiscounted Markov renewal programming, *Math. Operations Res.* **3** (1978), 308–321.

[S14] Serfozo, R., An equivalence between discrete and continuous time Markov decision processes, *Operations Res.* **27** (1979), 616–620.

[S15] Serfozo, R., Optimal control of random walks, birth and death processes, and queues, *Adv. Appl. Prob.* **13** (1981), 61–83.

[S16] Shannon, C., Programming a digital computer for playing chess, *Phil. Mag.* **41** (1950), 356–375.

[S17] Shapley, L. S., Stochastic games, *Proc. Nat. Acad. Sci. U.S.A.* **39** (1953).

[S18] Sharpe, W., *Portfolio Theory and Capital Markets.* McGraw-Hill, New York, 1970.

[S19] Simon, H. A., Dynamic programming under uncertainty with a quadratic criterion function, *Econometrica* **24** (1956), 74–81.

[S20] Smallwood, R. D., The analysis of economic teaching strategies for a simple learning model, *J. Math. Psychology* **8** (1971), 285–301.

[S21] Smallwood, R. D., and Sondik, E. J., The optimal control of partially observable Markov processes over a finite horizon, *Operations Res.* **11** (1973), 1071–1088.

[S22] Sobel, M. J., The optimality of full-service policies, *Operations Res.* **30** (1982), 636–649.

[S23] Sondik, E. J., The optimal control of partially observable Markov processes. Ph.D. Dissertation, Department of Engineering–Economic Systems, Stanford University, Stanford, Calif., June 1971.

[S24] Stein, G., and Saridis, G. N., A parameter adaptive control technique, *Automatica* **5** (1969), 731–739.

[S25] Stidham, S., and Prabhu, N. U., Optimal control of queuing systems, in *Mathematical Methods in Queuing Theory* (Lecture Notes in Economics and Math. Syst., Vol. 98), A. B. Clarke (Ed.), Springer-Verlag, New York, 1974, pp. 263–294.

[S26] Stidham, S. S., Optimal control of admission to a queueing system, *IEEE Trans. Aut. Control* **AC-30** (1985), 705–713.

[S27] Strang, G., *Linear Algebra and Its Applications.* Academic Press, New York, 1976.

[S28] Strauch, R., Negative dynamic programming, *Ann. Math. Statist.* **37** (1966), 871–890.

[S29] Striebel, C. T., Sufficient statistics in the optimal control of stochastic systems, *J. Math. Anal. Appl.* **12** (1965), 576–592.

[S30] Striebel, C. T., *Optimal Control of Discrete Time Stochastic Systems.* Springer-Verlag, New York, 1975.

[S31] Sussman, R., Optimal control of systems with stochastic disturbances, Electronics Research Lab., University of California, Berkeley, Rep. No. 63-20, November 1963.

[S32] Sworder, D. D., Bayes' controllers with memory for a linear system with jump parameters. *IEEE Trans. Auto. Control* **AC-17** (1972), 119–121.

[T1] Thau, F. E., and Witsenhausen, H. S., A comparison of closed-loop and open-loop optimum systems, *IEEE Trans. Auto. Control* **AC-11** (1966), 619–621.

[T2] Theil, H., Econometric models and welfare maximization, *Weltwirtsch. Arch.* **72** (1954), 60–83.

[T3] Tse, E., and Athans, M., Adaptive stochastic control for a class of linear systems, *IEEE Trans. Auto. Control* **AC-17** (1972), 38–52.

[T4] Tse, E., and Bar-Shalom, Y., An actively adaptive control for linear systems with random parameters via the dual control approach, *IEEE Trans. Auto. Control* **AC-18** (1973), 109–117.

[T5] Tse, E., Bar-shalom, Y., and Meier, L., III, Wide-sense adaptive dual control for nonlinear stochastic systems, *IEEE Trans. Auto. Control* **AC-18** (1973), 98–108.

[T6] Tsitsiklis, J. N., Convexity and characterization of optimal policies in a dynamic routing problem, *J. Optimization Theory Appl.* **44** (1984), 105–136.

[T7] Tsitsiklis, J. N., Periodic review inventory systems with continuous demand and discrete order sizes, *Management Sci.* **30** (1984), 1250–1254.

[T8] Tsitsiklis, J. N., *Analysis of a Multiaccess Control Scheme,* Lab. for Info. and Decision Systems Report LIDS-P-1534, MIT, Feb. 1986.

[T9] Tsitsiklis, J. N., A lemma on the multiarmed bandit problem, *IEEE Trans. Aut. Control* **AC-31** (1986), 576–577.

[V1] Vajda, S., Stochastic programming, Chapter 14 *in* Abadie, J. (ed.), *Integer and Nonlinear Programming,* North-Holland, Amsterdam, 1970.

[V2] Varaiya, P. P., Optimal and suboptimal stationary controls of Markov chains, *IEEE Trans. Aut. Control* **AC-23** (1978), 388–394.

[V3] Varaiya, P. P., Walrand, J. C., and Buyukkoc, C., Extensions of the multiarmed bandit problem: The discounted case, *IEEE Trans. Auto. Control* **AC-30** (1985), 426–439.

[V4] Veinott, A. F., Jr., On finding optimal policies in discrete dynamic programming with no discounting, *Ann. Math. Statist.* **37** (1966), 1284–1294.

[V5] Veinott, A. F., Jr., The status of mathematical inventory theory, *Management Sci.* **12** (1966), 745–777.

[V6] Veinott, A. F., Jr., Discrete dynamic programming with sensitive discount optimality criteria, *Ann. Math. Statist.* **40** (1969), 1635–1660.

[V7] Veinnot, A. F., Jr., The optimal inventory policy for batch ordering, *Operations Res.* **13** (1965), 424–432.

[V8] Veinott, A. F., Jr., and Wagner, H. M., Computing optimal (s, S) policies, *Management Sci.* **11** (1965), 525–552.

[V9] Vershik, A. M., Some characteristic properties of Gaussian stochastic processes, *Theory Probability Appl.* **9** (1964), 353–356.

[W1] Wald, A., *Sequential Analysis.* Wiley, New York, 1947.

[W2] Walkup, D., and Wets, R., Stochastic programs with recourse, *SIAM J. Appl. Math.* **15** (1967), 1299–1314.

[W3] Weiss, G., and Pinedo, M., Scheduling tasks with exponential service times on nonidentical processors to minimize various cost functions, *J. Appl. Prob.* **17** (1980), 187–202.

[W4] White, C. C., and Harrington, D. P., Application of Jensen's inequality to adaptive suboptimal design, *J. Optimization Theory Appl.* **32** (1980), 89–99.

[W5] White, C. C., and Schlussel, K., Suboptimal design for large scale, multimodule systems, *Operations Res.* **29** (1981), 865–875.

[W6] White, D. J., Dynamic programming, Markov chains, and the method of successive approximations, *J. Math. Anal. Appl.* **6** (1963), 373–376.

[W7] White, D. J., *Dynamic Programming.* Holden-Day, San Francisco, 1969.

[W8] White, D. J., Finite state approximations for denumerable state infinite horizon discounted Markov decision processes: The method of successive approximations, in *Recent Developments in Markov Decision Processes,* Hartley, R., Thomas, L. C., and White, D. J. (eds.), Academic Press, New York, 1980, pp. 57–72.

[W9] Whitt, W., Approximations of dynamic programs I, *Math. Oper. Res.* **3** (1978), 231–243.

[W10] Whitt, W., Approximations of dynamic programs II, *Math. Oper. Res.* **4** (1979), 179–185.

[W11] Whittle, P., *Optimization over Time.* Wiley, New York, Vol. 1, 1982, Vol. 2, 1983.

[W12] Whittle, P., *Prediction and Regulation by Linear Least-Square Methods.* English Universities Press, London, 1963.

[W13] Witsenhausen, H. S., Minimax control of uncertain systems, Ph.D. Dissertation, Department of Electrical Engineering, MIT, Cambridge, Mass., May 1966.

[W14] Witsenhausen, H. S., Inequalities for the performance of suboptimal uncertain systems, *Automatica* **5** (1969), 507–512.

[W15] Witsenhausen, H. S., On performance bounds for uncertain systems, *SIAM J. Control* **8** (1970), 55–89.

[W16] Witsenhausen, H. S., Separation of estimation and control for discrete-time systems, *Proc. IEEE* **59** (1971), 1557–1566.

[Z1] Zangwill, W. I., *Nonlinear Programming: A Unified Approach.* Prentice-Hall, Englewood Cliffs, N.J., 1969.

Index

D

E

F

G

H

I

K

L

M